Learning C++

Learning C++

Tom Swan

SAMS

A Division of Macmillan Computer Publishing
11711 North College, Carmel, Indiana 46032 USA

International Standard Book Number: 0-672-22785-1
Library of Congress Catalog Card Number: 91-60330

Product Line Developer: *Gregory Croy*
Technical Editor: *Alan C. Plantz*
Production Editor: *Katherine Stuart Ewing*
Art Director: *Glenn Santner*
Book Designer: *Scott Cook*
Production Assistance: *Sandy Grieshop, Denny Hager, Betty Kish, Bob LaRoche, Sarah Leatherman, Howard Peirce, Dennis Sheehan, Suzanne Tully, Christine Young*
Indexer: *Sharon Hilgenberg*

Printed in the United States of America

To my lifelong friend Jere Eshelman, who had the good sense to install a hot tub where I often recovered from many long hours at the computer terminal.

Acknowledgments

Most books are the result of a team effort, and this book is no exception. Special thanks are due all members of the team that worked long and hard on Learning C++, especially Gregory Croy, Kathy Ewing, Sharon Hilgenberg, Alan Plantz, Richard Swadley, Joe Wikert, and others in the editing, art, production, and sales departments at SAMS. Thanks also to Walter Bright and Paul Leathers at Zortech for agreeing to supply the C++ compiler included with this book and to Eric Meyer for allowing me to distribute on disk the VDE shareware text editor. I'm also indebted to my brother David Swan, who read the manuscript and made many useful suggestions, as did my wife and assistant Anne Swan. Many thanks to all of you for your valuable contributions.

Trademarks

In this book, terms suspected of being trademarks or service marks have been appropriately capitalized. SAMS cannot attest to the accuracy of this information. Use of a term in this book should not be regarded as affecting the validity of any trademark or service mark.

Overview

1 Discovering C++   1

2 Making Statements and Building Structures   53

3 Functions: Programming in Pieces   127

4 Pointers about Pointers   181

5 Class Objectives   253

6 Building a Class Library—Part 1   335

7 Building a Class Library—Part 2   379

8 Files and Directories   451

9 Advancing Your C++ Knowledge   505

10 The C++ Function Library   573

A Reserved Key Words   679

B Operator Precedence   681

Bibliography   683

Answers to Questions and Exercises   685

Index   731

Contents

Introduction   **xxix**

Requirements   xxx
  Required Hardware   xxx
  Optional Hardware   xxx
  Required Software   xxx
  Optional Software   xxx
Installing the Zortech C++ Compiler   xxxi
  Hard Drive Installations   xxxi
  Large-Capacity Floppy Disk Installations   xxxii
  360K Floppy Disk Installations   xxxiii
  Testing Your Installation   xxxiv
Using the VDE Shareware Editor   xxxv
Compiling Programs   xxxvi

1 Discovering C++   **1**

A C++ Anatomy Lesson   1
  Streams   3
  A Note about Semicolons   5
  Comments about Comments   6
  Identifiers   9
  Case: A Sensitive Issue   9
  Key Words   10
  Punctuators   10
  Separators   11
  Header Files   11
Variables   12

Initializing Variables with Definitions   14

Initializing Variables with Assignments   16

Scoop on Scope   17

Initializing Global and Local Variables   19

Input and Output   20

Output Streams   21

Old-Style Output   22

Formatted Output   23

Stream Input   27

Old-Style Input   28

Formatted Input   28

A Simple Decimal-to-Hex-and-Octal Converter   31

Constants   31

Types of Constants   32

Literal Constants   33

Character Constants   33

String Constants   35

Whole Number Constants   36

Floating Point Constants   37

Defined Constants   37

Declared Constants   39

Enumerated Constants   40

Assigning Enumerated Element Values   43

Operators   45

Operators and Precedence   45

Increment and Decrement Operators   46

Expressions   49

Questions and Exercises   50

2 Making Statements and Building Structures   53

Advanced Operators   54

Good Relations   54

Introducing if/else, the Decision Maker   56

Making Sense Out of Logical Operators   59

Forget Me NOT   62

Bitwise Operators—Programming One Bit at a Time   62

Shifty Operations   68

Combined Assignments—Expressive Shorthand   70

So It Flows   71

A Proper Exit   71

Reducing Complexity   73

Filters and while Statements   74

Making Decisions with `if/else`   77
The Ol' `switch`-aroo   80
Using `switch` Statements   83
Upside Down `do/while` Statements   85
C++'s Most Popular Statement—The `for` Loop   87
Multiple `for`-Loop Elements   89
`do-forever` Loops   90
Taking a `break`   91
The Plot `continues`   92
Avoiding `goto`   93
Data Structures—Sand Castles in RAM   95
Structures for Safe Keeping   96
Nested Structures   102
Preserving the `union`   103
Vectoring in on Arrays   105
Making the Grade   108
Initializing Arrays   110
Arrays and the Multiple Dimension   111
The True Character of Strings   115
Character Array Initializations   116
Arrays and Pointers   117
Fielding Bits   118
Sizing Up Your Variables   122
Questions and Exercises   124

3 Functions: Programming in Pieces   **127**

Keeping It Simple   127
Writing Your Own Functions   128
Designing from the Top Down   131
Functions and Their Variables   138
Local Variables   139
External Variables   141
Register Variables   143
Static Variables   145
Functions that Return Values   147
Parameter Passing   152
One if by Value; Two if by Reference   153
Default Arguments   161
Recursion: It's All Done with Mirrors   166
Inline Functions   171
Turning Point   174
Questions and Exercises   179

4 Pointers about Pointers   181

Declaring Pointers   181
  Pointer Dereferencing   182
  Pointers and Type Checking   185
  NULL and Void Pointers   185
  Casting Roles for Pointers to Play   187
  Near and Far Pointers   190
  Pointers to System Locations   191
  Far Pointers and the Keyboard   193
Managing Your Memory   198
  Pointers to Structures   201
  Out of Memory   203
  Why Use Dynamic Variables?   203
  Creating Dynamic Lists   205
  Dynamic Arrays   213
  Reserving Memory with `malloc`   214
Pointers as Function Arguments   220
Pointers to Functions   225
Pointers and Arrays   229
  Pointer Arithmetic   232
  Arrays of Pointers   232
Functions that Return String Pointers   234
String Functions   236
  Common String Functions   237
  Joining Strings   239
  Comparing Strings   240
  Searching Strings   240
Command-Line Arguments   242
  Character Arguments   245
  Numeric Arguments   247
Questions and Exercises   249

5 Class Objectives   253

Go to the Head of the Class   255
  Creating Classes   257
  Inline Member Functions   261
  Classes Are Data Types   264
  Introducing Constructors   267
  Class Tactics   269
  Modules and Classes   273
Compiling The Elevator Simulation   276

Using Header Files   278
The person Class   282
  Person Data Fields   284
  The Person Collection Class   284
  person and perscollection Member Functions   285
The floor Class   296
  Implementing the floor Class   297
The elevator Class   305
  Implementing the elevator Class   307
Introducing Inheritance   316
  Using Inheritance   316
The building Class   323
  Replacement Member Functions   324
  Implementing the building Class   325
Completing the Elevator Simulation   329
Questions and Exercises   333

6 Building a Class Library—Part 1   **335**

Last Things First—WinTool   336
  Compiling WINTOOL   336
  The WINTOOL.H Header   338
  Pointers to Class Variables   342
  Pointers to Derived Classes   346
  Virtual Functions and Polymorphism   347
  Polymorphism in Action   350
  Early and Late Binding   353
  The WINTOOL.CPP Main Program   354
  Static Member Functions   355
Mixing OOP and NonOOP Code   364
  The KEY Module   364
  Defining KEY Values   369
  Testing the KEY Module   369
  Error Handling   370
  Testing the ERROR Module   375
Questions and Exercises   377

7 Building a Class Library—Part 2   **379**

First Things Last—The Class Library   379
  Class Hierarchies   380
  At the Root of the Library   381
  The ITEM.H Header   381

Protected Members   382
Choosing Among `private`, `public`, and `protected`   384
`Destructors`   385
Using the `item` Class   385
The ITEM.CPP Module   388
`this` Is Where It's At   389
A Class for `Lists`   392
  The LIST.H Header   392
  Using the `list` Class   394
  The LIST.CPP Module   397
A Class for Strings   400
  The STRITEM.H Header   401
  Multiple Constructors   402
  Using the `strItem` Class   403
  The STRITEM.CPP Module   404
  Making Lists of Strings   407
A Class for `windows`   409
  The WINDOW.H Header   409
  Static Member Functions   412
  Static Member Fields   414
  Overloaded Constructors   414
  Reference Functions   415
  Designing Displays with Windows   416
  The WINDOW.CPP Module   421
A Class for Selections   431
  The SELECTOR.H Header   432
  Multiple Inheritance   432
  Using the `selector` Class   433
  The SELECTOR.CPP Module   436
A Class for Commands   440
  The COMMAND.H Header   441
  Using the `command` Class   443
Recap   448
Exercises   448

8 Files and Directories   451

File and DOS Functions   452
Text Files   452
  Basic Text-File Techniques   452
  Creating Text Files   453
  Formatted Output   456
  Errors from File Functions   457

Reading Text Files   458
Reading Text One Character at a Time   458
Reading Text One Line at a Time   460
Sorting Text Files   462
Data Files   467
Basic Data-File Techniques   467
Readin' and Writin' Data Files   468
Writing Binary Values to Disk   468
Reading Binary Values from Disk   471
Creating Database Files   473
Reading Database Files   476
Working with Directories   479
Determining Free Space on Disk   479
Changing the Current Directory   480
Displaying a Directory   482
Decoding Directory Information   483
Modifying Directory Entries   487
A Class for Directories   488
The DIR.H Header   488
Using the Directory Classes   490
The DIR.CPP Module   493
Directory Navigator   497
READ: An OOP Text-File Reader   499
Compiling and Using READ   499
The READ.CPP Program   500
Questions and Exercises   504

9 Advancing Your C++ Knowledge   505

Good Friends and Neighbors   506
Friend Classes   506
Mutual Friend Classes   510
Friend Functions Part 1   511
Friend Functions Part 2   512
Function Overloading   515
Name Mangling Revisited   516
The overload Key Word   517
Overloading Conventional Functions   518
Overloading Class Member Functions   518
Operator Overloading   520
Overloading Operator Member Functions   524
Overloading Unary Operators   526
Tips for Successful Operator Overloading   528

Overloading Array Indexing   529
Overloading and User-Defined Type Conversions   533
Overloading the Assignment Operator   536
  Copying Class Instances   538
  Memberwise Initialization   539
  Copying Pointer Fields   541
  The Copy Constructor   543
  Memberwise Assignment   545
  Calling operator= from a Copy Constructor   547
  Copying Derived Class Instances   548
Overloading and Memory Management   549
  Assignments to this   549
  Overloading new   551
  Overloading delete   553
Overloading Streams   554
  Overloading Output Streams   554
  Overloading Input Streams   556
Miscellany   558
  Other I/O Streams   558
  Conditional Expressions   559
  Resolving Global Function Conflicts   561
  Default Status of Inherited Classes   562
  Pointers to Member Functions   563
  Virtual Base Classes   566
Now That You've Learned C++...   568
  Differences Between C and C++   568
  Using Other C++ Compilers   569
Questions and Exercises   570

10 The C++ Function Library   **573**

How to Use the Reference   573
Function Reference   575

A Reserved Key Words   **679**

B Operator Precedence   **681**

Bibliography   **683**

Answers to Questions and Exercises   **685**

Chapter 1   686
Chapter 2   690
Chapter 3   698
Chapter 4   702
Chapter 5   706
Chapter 6   709
Chapter 7   713
Chapter 8   722
Chapter 9   728

Index   **731**

Introduction

Question: Is this a book, or is it software? Answer: It's both! Inside this book's back cover, you'll find two diskettes with a full-featured C++ compiler, linker, library, and related files. You'll also find all of the book's sample listings, a class library for creating pop-up windows and menus, an editor for modifying and browsing listings, plus dozens of example programs.

On the book side of the equation, chapters 1 through 9 present a complete tutorial to the C++ language. You'll learn conventional and object-oriented techniques for writing C++ programs. You'll learn about classes, single and multiple inheritance, disk files, friends, operator overloading, streams, and other features that have prompted thousands of experienced and beginning programmers to learn C++. In chapter 10, you'll find a reference to more than 150 functions in the C++ library—all of which are included on disk. After you've finished the tutorial, you can use this reference as a guide for writing your own C++ programs.

Every ounce of source code to every program listed in the book is also included on disk. The compiler, written by Walter Bright and supplied by Zortech—one of the first software companies to market a C++ compiler for MS-DOS systems—is fully operational and conforms to AT&T's specifications for C++ version 2.1. There's nothing else to buy. *Learning C++* and the included companion disks contain everything you need to get started learning and using C++.

Read this introduction for a list of minimum requirements, for instructions about how to install your C++ compiler, and for suggestions about getting the most from the information in this book. After that, you'll be ready to turn to chapter 1 and compile your first C++ program.

> **Note:** The files on the accompanying diskettes are compressed. Before you can compile any programs, you must run the INSTALL program on Disk #1 to install the files on your hard drive or a 1.2-megabyte or larger-capacity floppy disk. For best results, install the software on a hard disk drive. If you are in a hurry to begin, skip to "Installing the Zortech C++ Compiler" in this introduction for installation instructions.

Requirements

The following sections list required and optional hardware and software. If you are having trouble installing or using the disks packed with this book, check here to be sure your computer meets these minimum specifications.

Required Hardware

- IBM PC, XT, AT, PS/2, or 100% compatible system
- 384K to 512K RAM available after booting
- Hard disk drive (recommended)
- 5 1/4-inch floppy disk drive required for installation only (3 1/2-inch disks available on request)

Optional Hardware

- Printer
- Color monitor
- For systems without a hard drive, at least one 1.2- or 1.44-megabyte floppy disk drive. A hard drive is recommended for best results.

Required Software

- MS- or PC DOS 2.0 or a later version. (A few programs may require DOS 3.0 or a later version.)
- All other required software is included with this book.

Optional Software

- Your favorite text editor for modifying listing files. If you don't have an editor, you can use the shareware VDE editor supplied with this book.

- Zortech C++ 2.1. If you already own the full development system, you can, of course, use it to compile programs. However, you do *not* have to purchase the development system to compile and run the listings included in this book and stored on disk. (Note: Later versions of Zortech C++ may require changes to be made to some listings before they will compile. See chapter 9.)

Installing the Zortech C++ Compiler

Make sure you have about 3 megabytes of hard disk space available. Or if you are installing to a high-capacity floppy disk, format a blank diskette now. Then insert the diskette labeled Disk #1 into drive A: and enter the following two commands, pressing **<Enter>** after each line:

```
a:
install
```

That runs the automated INSTALL program. Read and follow the instructions on-screen. To stop INSTALL, you may press **<Esc>** at any time. To reinstall the software, just repeat these commands.

During installation, you'll be asked to select a drive letter. For best results, choose a hard disk drive. You'll also be asked to supply a directory name. The default name is \LCPP. You may change this name to any legal path. However, you should not install the software to your hard drive's root directory. For best results, press **<Enter>** to keep the suggested \LCPP path name.

For floppy disk drive installation only, you may specify a path name with a single backslash, (\). That will save a little room on disk and will transfer the compiler, editor, and linker files to the diskette's root directory. Do this *only* on a high-density floppy disk, never when installing to a hard drive.

When installation is finished, INSTALL will run the READ.EXE program, which displays a text file named README.TXT. You can also run READ from DOS. Locate the file (it's on Disk #1 in uncompressed form). Then with READ.EXE in the current directory, enter **read**. Select README.TXT or another text file to view. Use the **<Cursor>** and **<Page>** keys to browse and press **<Esc>** to return to the directory display or to DOS. (If you type **read readme.txt** at the DOS prompt to read a specific file, READ does not list a directory.)

By the way, the source code for READ.EXE is listed in chapter 8. READ is just one of many programs you'll learn how to write with C++.

Hard Drive Installations

After installing to a hard drive and reading the README.TXT file, the C:\LCPP directory should be current. If not, press **<Esc>** if necessary to get back to DOS. Then enter **c:** and **cd \lcpp** or similar commands to switch to the newly created directory. (If you selected a different drive letter or path name, use them in place of C:\LCPP in these instructions and elsewhere in this book.)

Use DIR to inspect the directory's contents. Among other items, you should see three files, LCPP.EXE, LIB.EXE, and VDE.EXE. Next, you'll extract several files contained in the three self-extracting programs. To perform these steps, enter the commands

```
lcpp
lib
vde
```

If you have a text editor and don't want to use the shareware VDE editor, you may skip the VDE command. However, you may want to copy VDE.EXE to another disk to preserve it. VDE is a very capable text editor and word processor. (The VDE.EXE file contains complete documentation about how to use the editor.)

During decompression, you'll see several rows of periods and lowercase o letters while the self-extracting programs deposit their contents in the current directory. After these steps are completed, you may delete the original files; you won't need them again. To delete the files, enter

```
del lcpp.exe
del lib.exe
del vde.exe
```

If you delete a file by accident before extracting its contents, you'll have to restart INSTALL and reinstall all files. You may repeat the installation as many times as necessary.

Note: Skip the next two sections and continue reading under "Testing Your Installation."

Large-Capacity Floppy Disk Installations

After installing the files to a 1.2- or 1.44-megabyte floppy diskette, you'll need to use a special command to extract the files compressed into three self-extracting programs, LCPP.EXE, LIB.EXE, and VDE.EXE. Insert the installed diskette into drive A:.

Insert a second blank formatted diskette into B:. Then enter the following commands, pressing **<Enter>** after each line:

```
a:
lcpp /eb:\
lib /eb:\
vde /eb:\
```

Those commands will extract the contents of the three .EXE files to the diskette in B:. You can then copy those files to other diskettes for compiling and editing programs. Erase the LCPP.EXE, LIB.EXE, and VDE.EXE files from the installed disk to make room.

> **Note:** Skip the next section and continue reading under "Testing Your Installation."

360K Floppy Disk Installations

First, let me discourage you from trying to run the C++ compiler on systems with only two 360K floppy disk drives and no hard drive. If you're determined to try this setup, here are a few suggestions that *might* work.

After installing the files to a friend's hard drive, or to a large-capacity floppy, format and label three disks: LINKER, COMPILER, and EDITOR. Copy these files to the LINKER disk:

```
blink.exe
pls.lib
zls.lib
```

Copy these files to the COMPILER disk:

```
*.h     (minus page.h and emm.h)
*.hpp
ztc.com
ztc2.exe
ztcpp1.exe
```

Copy these files to the EDITOR disk:

```
examples.vdk
vde.com
vde.doc
vde154.upd
```

```
vinst.com
vinst.doc
wp.vdf
ws4.vdf
```

You'll also need a couple of disks to hold source code listings. To those disks, copy all files and subdirectories from the SOURCE, ANSWERS, and LIB directories.

You should now be able to compile programs by inserting the appropriate disk for compiling and linking. You might have to create special diskettes to compile some of the programs. Obviously, this setup is going to be a lot of trouble to use, and I urge you to get a hard drive if possible. Without a hard drive, it may not be possible to compile some of the larger programs.

Testing Your Installation

After installing and extracting all files, you're almost ready to begin using the C++ compiler. First, you need to change your PATH statement and to set up two environment variables. These steps will let you compile programs stored in any subdirectory, and they will let the compiler and linker find various files needed during compilation and linking.

Edit or create a plain text file AUTOEXEC.BAT in your disk's root directory. Change or insert a PATH statement so it reads something like this:

```
path c:\dos;c:\lcpp
```

The PATH statement may list other path names separated with semicolons. Also add the following two lines to AUTOEXEC.BAT:

```
set include=c:\lcpp\include;c:\lcpp\lib
set lib=c:\lcpp
```

Those commands prepare two environment variables, INCLUDE and LIB, which tell the compiler and linker where to find various files. Notice that the \LIB directory goes with the INCLUDE variable. Stored in \LIB are the files for the class library explained in chapters 6 and 7. Adding this path name to INCLUDE's setting is necessary to allow programs in other chapters to find the class declarations stored on disk.

Save the modified AUTOEXEC.BAT file and reboot your computer. If you receive an Out of environment space error, you'll also have to modify or create a plain text CONFIG.SYS file in your disk's root directory. Add this command to CONFIG.SYS:

```
shell=command.com /E:512 /P
```

When you reboot, the 512 in this SHELL command will reserve additional space in the environment for the expanded PATH, INCLUDE, and LIB variables. For more or less space, change 512 to the number of bytes needed.

Using the VDE Shareware Editor

The VDE shareware editor is included on disk for readers who do not have text editors. You may use VDE to modify or browse the source code listings and to create new programs.

Before using the editor, change to the C:\LCPP directory and enter the command **vinst**. Follow instructions on-screen for installing the software for your computer. Press S to save the configuration to disk even if you did not change any settings. After this step, get back to the DOS prompt. Then, change to a directory that contains listing files (C:\LCPP\SOURCE\C01 for example) and enter a command such as

```
vde welcome.cpp /n
```

The file name WELCOME.CPP can be an existing file or a new one you want to create. The /n option tells VDE to read and write the file in plain ASCII form. If you save a file edited without the /n option, you may not be able to compile the result. If you will use VDE to edit only program files, you can use the VINST.COM utility to change the default file type to nondocument. For more information about how to make that and other changes to VDE, read the instructions in the text files VDE.DOC and VINST.DOC. To print copies of these instructions, make sure your printer is powered on and has plenty of paper. Then, enter the commands

```
type vinst.doc >prn
type vde.doc >prn
```

Note: Don't use the READ program to examine VDE's DOC files. Those files are too large for READ to handle. You may want to consider modifying READ to be able to use the program with large text files. See chapter 8.

If you know WordStar or if you've used Turbo Pascal, Turbo C, or SideKick from Borland International, you'll be right at home with VDE. The program's commands mirror those in the WordStar and Borland editors.

To quit VDE, type **<Ctrl>-KQ**. If you changed the current file, press **Y** to save your changes or **N** to throw them away. To save changes and not return to DOS, enter **<Ctrl>-KS**. To quit the editor, save the current file, and return to DOS, enter **<Ctrl>-KX**.

Compiling Programs

A good way to test your installation is to compile a few programs. This will also show you how to compile listings in the coming chapters. These notes will get you started:

- From DOS, make sure your PATH, INCLUDE, and LIB variables are set properly. Enter **set** at the DOS prompt and inspect the list of variables. You should find the C:\LCPP directory in PATH, plus the directories in the other two variables as explained earlier.

- Enter **cd \lcpp\source\c01** to switch to the directory that contains chapter 1's listings. Except for chapters 6 and 7, use a similar command to switch to the appropriate directories for other chapters. (The files for chapters 6 and 7 are stored in C:\LCPP\LIB.)

- Enter **ztc welcome** to compile and link the WELCOME.CPP program, Listing 1.1 in chapter 1. You should see lines like the following on your screen.

```
ztcpp1 -oztc_APC.tmp welcome
Zortech C++ Demo Compiler
ztc2 ztc_APC.tmp -owelcome.obj
BLINK welcome/noi;
```

- You should now have the finished code file WELCOME.EXE in the current directory. Enter **welcome** to run the program.

- Enter similar **ztc** commands to compile most programs in this book. Some of the more complex programs require special instructions to compile. I'll list these as needed.

- If you receive an error, especially `Error: 'ztc1' not found`, make sure the correct .CPP file is in the current directory. (ZTC1 is Zortech's C compiler—it's not included on disk or needed. However, ZTC tries to run the C compiler at some times, leading to the error message. No harm done. Just correct your typing and try again.)

After compiling the simple WELCOME program, you may want to try some of the more sophisticated examples such as the elevator simulation. To compile and run that program, follow these steps:

- Enter **cd \lcpp\source\c05** to change to the directory for chapter 5.

- From DOS, type **zz** to run the ZZ.BAT file. The batch file contains all the instructions required to compile and link the program. This may take a few seconds or minutes depending on your computer's speed.

- When the DOS prompt returns, enter **elevsim** to run the program. Press **<Esc>** to quit.

Another program you can compile and run is POPUP.CPP in C:\LCPP\SOURCE\C04. Compile with the command **ztc popup**. Then run POPUP and press the **<Spacebar>** several times to erase the pop-up windows. You may also run the ZZ.BAT file in C:\LCPP\LIB to compile the WINTOOL program. As you'll learn in chapter 6, you can use WINTOOL to design your own pop-up windows. After running WINTOOL, press **<Esc>** to return to DOS.

Note: As you read each chapter, use the CD command to change to C:\LCPP\SOURCE\C0n where *n* is the chapter number. Listings for chapters 6 and 7 are stored in C:\LCPP\LIB. You'll find many additional listings in C:\LCPP\ANSWERS. Use VDE, your editor, or READ to view program listings in a directory. To just view a listing, type **read** and select a file to view. Select a directory name to change to that directory. You can then follow the discussion in the book while you examine the program's source code on-screen.

Chapter 1

Discovering C++

This chapter will help you discover what C++ is and how easy it is to use. If you know Pascal or C, so much the better. You can skim this chapter as a guide to how C++ differs from those popular, and in many ways similar, languages. I'll assume that you know only a few basics, such as what bits and bytes are, how to give DOS commands, and how to run programs.

I'll begin at the beginning (a good place to start) with an introduction to the parts of a C++ program—items shared by all programs in this book. After that, I'll cover a lot of ground quickly, exploring streams, constants, variables, input and output, and operators. Nearly all C++ programs use one or more of these fundamentals, so take the time to go through the examples and run the sample listings. The discoveries you make now will be invaluable later.

A C++ Anatomy Lesson

All C++ programs are related—that is, their skeletons share some of the same bones. A good way to learn how those bones are connected is to dissect a small sample program like WELCOME.CPP (Listing 1.1). Locate that file on disk (or type the lines into your editor). Then, at the DOS prompt, or using an appropriate instruction in your editor to give DOS commands, enter **ztc welcome** to create WELCOME.EXE. Run that program by typing its name, or use your normal method for running programs.

> **Note:** From now on, compile and run sample listings this same way, but substitute the appropriate file names for WELCOME.CPP. Unless a program requires special compilation instructions, I won't repeat the steps for every listing.

Listing 1.1. WELCOME.CPP

```
1:    #include <stream.hpp>
2:
3:    main()
4:    {
5:        cout << "Welcome to C++ programming!\n";
6:    }
```

Skip line 1 for now and train your sights on lines 3-6, which form the substance of this small program. Taking out line 5 leaves the shell

```
main()
{
}
```

This is called a *function*—one of C++'s most important features. In this case, there's only one function named main. In other C++ programs, there might be dozens, hundreds, or more functions of unique names written in this same form. But no matter how many functions a program has, it *must* have one and only one function called main. When a C++ program runs, it always begins at main.

Note: Don't confuse the term function with mathematical functions. Functions in C++ may perform mathematical chores, but they don't have to. In C++, functions are named groups of instructions that perform one or more actions. As you'll learn, a function's actions are completely up to you to describe.

The empty parentheses after the function name tell the compiler that the function receives no information from the outside world. Later, you'll learn how to list *parameters* inside the parentheses, allowing functions to process incoming information. For example, you might pass to main a command-line option letter or a file name that you want the program to use.

The left and right braces that follow the function name and its parentheses bracket the function's body. Returning to Listing 1.1, you can see that main's body contains a single line of programming:

```
{
    cout << "Welcome to C++ programming!\n";
}
```

Because of the surrounding braces, the compiler knows that the enclosed programming line—called a *statement*—belongs to function main. Generally speaking, a statement is anything in a program that performs an action when that program runs. Everything else is either a *declaration*, a *definition*, an *expression*, or an instruction for the compiler to do something during compilation. Typically, declarations give the compiler some information, such as the format of a new data type. Definitions create space for storing values in memory, perhaps a variable of a previously declared data type. Expressions like 1 + m are evaluated to a single value. Other instructions may alter the way the compiler works, or they may select among different sections of the program's text to compile based on various conditions.

Don't be concerned about memorizing all these terms. Authors and even experienced programmers frequently mix up the words *declaration* and *definition* anyway, and you can't rely on all texts to use the phrases consistently. At this early stage, it's more important for you to understand the purpose of C++ braces—to group one or more statements, expressions, declarations, or definitions as a unit that attaches to something immediately above. Together, the braces and the programming inside are called a *block*—a collection of items that you want the compiler to treat as one.

Streams

When you run the sample program, you'll see that it displays the message We l come to C++ programming! There are different ways to accomplish this, but the most convenient method in C++ is to use an *output stream*. Take a close look at Listing 1.1's sample output-stream statement:

```
cout << "Welcome to C++ programming!\n";
```

First comes the name of the output-stream object, cout, short for "character output." (By the way, I like to pronounce cout and similar words as "see out," not "kout." This makes cryptic phrases in programs sound better to my inner ear, but if you want to say "kout," I won't argue.) The object cout is the output's destination—a place where you can send information that you want the program to display or print in character form.

The double-character symbol << represents the stream's output symbol. It's *one* symbol even though it's composed of two characters. The symbol appears to point to cout, implying that the items to the right *flow* in that direction toward the destination object at the left, like water flowing down a stream to the sea. At the source of the program's stream is this *string*:

```
"Welcome to C++ programming!\n"
```

The double quotes tell the compiler to take the enclosed text literally—that is, not to process the quoted characters as programming statements or other instructions. The \n symbol—another single symbol composed of two characters—is called the *new-line character*. Inserting \n inside a string (it doesn't have to be at the end) causes the program to start a new line on the terminal or printer.

A good way to learn how output streams work is to try several on your own. Load a copy of Listing 1.1 into your editor. (I usually name my temporary test programs X.CPP, but you can use any name you like.) Then add these lines inside `main`'s body, between the opening and closing braces:

```
cout << "Welcome ";
cout << "to ";
cout << "C++ programming!\n";
```

Notice that these three lines produce the same results as the original program. Because the first two lines do not end with \n, the program displays them on the same line. Try adding \n inside the closing quotes near the end of the first two lines. What happens when you run the program?

Another way to produce similar results is to use a single output-stream statement with multiple parts. For example, you can write

```
cout << "Welcome " << "to\n"
     << "C++ programming!\n";
```

Examine this and the preceding example carefully. Run them in sample programs and observe the results. In the first example, there are three statements, each ending with a semicolon—C++'s *statement terminator*. All statements in C++ programs must be terminated with semicolons. (That's "terminated" as in "ended," not "terminated" as in the movies.) In the second example, there are three strings, but only one statement divided into two lines. C++ ignores line endings in the text, and it doesn't matter if you write statements on one line or several.

In general, you can write output-stream statements in this form:

```
cout << a << b << ... << c;
```

Items a, b, and c flow to the output-stream object cout. You can string together as many items this way as necessary, typing them on one line or separate lines:

```
cout << a
     << b
     << ...
     << c;
```

In each case, a semicolon terminates the statement, not the line. You can also split long strings over several lines to make typing easier. For example, insert this statement into Listing 1.1:

```
cout << "There was a young lady named Bright, \
Whose speed was far faster than light; \
She set out one day, \
In a relative way, \
And returned home the previous night.\n";
```

That's one output-stream statement, and a *single* string. The backslashes at the end of each line tell the compiler to join the previous characters with those on the next line. No spaces should appear after the backslashes, which the compiler throws away. When you run the program, you'll see that the limerick is displayed as one string (probably on two lines if your terminal automatically wraps around at the right border). To display the verses on separate lines, you need to insert \n symbols at their ends. Notice that there are only two quote marks—one at the beginning of the string and one at the end. There is no limit to the length of a string you can create with this trick.

> **Note:** The phrase "no limit" may rub some people the wrong way. Of course, there has to be a limit—you can't store a 100-megabyte-long string on a 20-megabyte hard disk. You also can't type more characters than there are hydrogen atoms in the universe. But there's no reason to be so technically finicky. Generally, "no limit" simply means the compiler imposes no *specific* limit on a construction.

We'll return to streams, strings, and characters later. Until then, try writing your own programs, using Listing 1.1 as a guide. Display various strings. Insert one or more \n new-line characters inside your test strings at different places to see the effect this symbol has.

A Note about Semicolons

One of the most difficult lessons to learn about C++ is where to use semicolons. Look one last time at Listing 1.1. As you can see, line 5 ends with a semicolon, but the other line endings are bare. The reason for this is that line 5 is a statement, and all statements *must* end with semicolons. As I mentioned earlier, a semicolon terminates a statement. This tells the C++ compiler that it has reached the end of a statement, which means you can write single statements like this on multiple lines:

```
cout << "This is "
    << "one statement "
    << "on three lines\n";
```

Because there is only one semicolon at the end of the last line, C++ reads that text as if you had written

```
cout << "This is one statement...\n";
```

Don't try to memorize a lot of semicolon rules. At first, you'll probably insert semicolons where they don't belong and leave them out where they do. The trick to learning where semicolons go is to learn the elements of C++. Observe which of those elements require terminating characters. Eventually, semicolon placement will seem natural and obvious.

> **Note:** If you happen to use a semicolon in the wrong spot, the compiler will display an error message that tells you what's wrong. Even experienced C++ programmers misuse a semicolon or two, so don't be concerned if you receive a lot of these errors at first.

Comments about Comments

While writing this book, I made many notes on the side, reminding me to expand a thought, research a fact, or insert a program listing in the text. Editors also insert notes to ask me to clarify a badly worded sentence. (With luck, and their skill, none will remain by the time you read this.)

Comments in programs are exactly like those notes—private messages for your eyes only or for another programmer's. To insert a comment into a program, surround it with the double-character symbols /* and */. Here are a few sample comments that might appear at the beginning of a program:

```
/* Title: MYPROGRAM by Mr. Software */
/* Revision 1.00B -- all bugs fixed (I hope) */
/* Original author skipped town */
```

Comments in this style may extend over one or more lines, and many programmers like to preface their files with a descriptive section like this:

```
/*    welcome.cpp by Tom Swan
 *    Date: 1/1/1991
 *    Revision: 1.0
 */
```

The vertical asterisks are merely an illusion—they have no practical significance. If you look carefully, you'll see that this text is a single comment starting with /* and reading left to right until reaching the */ symbol on the fourth line. The compiler completely ignores everything else in between, including the two extra asterisks that align with those in the two comment brackets.

You also can insert comments inside statements, although this often leads to confusing programs. Try adding this statement to Listing 1.1:

```
cout << "No comment " /* Oh, yeah? */ << "here!\n";
```

Running this statement displays the string No comment here! The compiler ignores the comment /* Oh, yeah? */ in the middle of the line.

Comments bracketed with / * and * / are called *C-style comments*. You can use them in C or C++ programs. In addition to this basic comment style, C++ also adds a second kind of comment, which is not available in C. A C++ *comment* must appear at the end of a line or on a line by itself. A C++ comment begins with a double slash. Here are the same comments used earlier but converted to C++ style:

```
// welcome.cpp by Tom Swan
// Date: 1/1/1991
// Revision: 1.0
```

When the compiler encounters a // symbol, it ignores all text from that point to the start of the next line (which might be another comment). This means that you can't use // inside statements, only at their ends. You also can't write multiline C++ comments. Typically, you'll use C++ comments to notate individual statements:

```
cout << "Your name? ";   // Prompt for user's name
```

The statement displays Your name? The comment at the end is a private note that describes the purpose of the statement to the left.

C++ and C comments can also be nested—that is, inserted inside each other. Nesting is useful for temporarily removing a section of a program while hunting for bugs (it's often helpful to delete programming to see what effect that has on a problem):

```
/*
cout << "Doesn't display";    // Output one string
cout << "Neither does this";  // Output another string
*/
```

Because of the C-style comment brackets on the first and last lines, the compiler ignores everything else in between—including the two C++ comments at the ends of the middle two lines.

To delete an entire line temporarily, just add // at the beginning. For example,

```
// cout << "Your age? "; // Prompt for user's age
```

Even though the line already ends in a C++ comment, the slashes at the front of the line cause C++ to ignore everything to the right—including that original comment at the end of the line.

Listing 1.2, COMMENT.CPP, demonstrates C and C++ comment styles, showing how to use // to create a distinctive "box" at the beginning of a listing and how to use C-style comments to insert multiline comments in programs.

Listing 1.2. COMMENT.CPP

```
1:  // comment.cpp -- Demonstrates C and C++ comment styles
2:
3:  #include <stream.hpp>
4:
```

```
 5:   /////////////////////////////////////////////
 6:   // Author    : Tom Swan
 7:   // Revision  : 1.0  07/13/1990    Time: 03:50 pm
 8:   // Purpose   : Demonstrates C++ comment styles
 9:   /////////////////////////////////////////////
10:
11:   main()
12:   {
13:      cout << "A Brief C++ Commentary\n";   // Display title
14:      cout << "\n";   // Display blank line under title
15:
16:   /* This paragraph demonstrates that
17:   C-style comments can occupy more
18:   than one line. */
19:
20:   cout << "// This is not a comment.\n\n";
21:
22:   cout << "/* This also is not a comment.*/ \n\n";
23:
24:   cout /* This is a comment. */ << "This text is displayed.\n";
25:   }
```

When you run COMMENT, you'll see that the compiler ignores any comment brackets inside strings. This happens because a string's double quotes tell the compiler to stop processing text as programming, but to take that text literally. That goes for comment brackets too. Inside a string's quotes, comment brackets are treated just like any other character.

From now on, listings in this book will begin with a C++ comment similar to the one at line 1 in the preceding example. This line identifies the program by file name and describes what it does. As you probably know by now, the accompanying disk files that contain this book's listings also end with a copyright notice and *revision history,* which look something like this:

```
// Copyright (c) 1990 by Tom Swan. All rights reserved
// Revision 1.00    Date: 07/14/1990    Time: 11:33 am
```

I inserted these lines at the end so that I could remove them for printing here and still have the line numbers in the printed listings match those in your text editor. Most programmers put their copyright notices and other details at the beginning of their files where they pop into view when you load a file for editing.

> **Note:** Always check the revision history number and date. I may update the files on disk from time to time to correct any errors discovered after the listings were printed in the book.

A second comment sample in Listing 1.3, NOTHING.CPP, uses a C comment and a C++ comment for no other reason than to explain that this program does nothing.

Listing 1.3. NOTHING.CPP

```
1:   // nothing.cpp -- A mere shell of a program
2:
3:   main()
4:   {
5:      /* This program does nothing! */
6:   }
```

The NOTHING program is the smallest C++ program you can write (ignoring the comments, that is). From the DOS prompt, list a directory to find out NOTHING.EXE's file size. On my system, the file occupies 3,650 bytes. This represents the compiler's minimum overhead—the various items that it adds to *all* C++ programs. As compilers go, 3,650 bytes is very efficient. Some compilers add 8K, 10K, or more to all EXE files.

Identifiers

Identifiers are unique symbols that you type into programs. The function name m a i n is an identifier—it identifies the function by name. Well-chosen identifiers are your primary tool for writing programs that make sense.

C++ recognizes many native identifiers such as m a i n. Others are up to you to invent and use. Identifiers may contain only upper- or lowercase letters, digits, and underlines, and may be up to 127 characters long. In addition, identifiers must begin with an upper- or lowercase letter from A to Z, as in f n 1 or C a t c h 2 2. The identifier 1 2 3 a b c is not legal; a b c 1 2 3 is.

You can also use underlines to separate words in long identifiers such as h e a d _ c o u n t and b o t t o m _ o f _ t h e _ b a r r e l. However, don't put underlines at the beginning of identifiers, a common practice in C. C++ will accept identifiers such as _ v a l u e and __ o v e r a n d u n d e r, but you risk causing a conflict with system identifiers that often begin similarly. If you never preface your own identifiers with underlines, you'll never accidentally invent an identifier that conflicts with a native symbol.

Case: A Sensitive Issue

C++ is *case sensitive*, and all symbols count. This means that k e y P r e s s, k e y p r e s s, and k e y _ p r e s s are *different* identifiers, even though they seem similar to our eyes.

For this reason, it pays to adopt a typing style and stick to it. If you mix styles in your programs—using uppercase at some times, and lowercase at others—you'll just make life with programming more difficult than necessary.

Most C and C++ programmers prefer to type identifiers in lowercase. Words such as `XYCOORD` and `PAYMENT` appear to shout from the screen, and a display-full of uppercase text can seem to compete with the program's logic. In lowercase, `xycoord` and `payment` don't crowd the screen and are easier on the eyes. Many people also prefer to write multiword identifiers as `arrayOfNames` instead of `array_of_names` or `arrayofnames`. Any of these styles is okay as long as you use it consistently. (I use upper- and lowercase, and I rarely capitalize the initial letter. Alternatively, you could write `ArrayOfNames`.)

Key Words

Key words are identifiers that C++ reserves for its own use. Sample key words include `auto`, `float`, `signed`, `void`, and `while`. These are symbols that you may not use for your own purposes—they have special meanings to the compiler, and those meanings can't be changed.

Appendix A lists all reserved C++ key words, but don't try to memorize that list—just consult it when you suspect that you have accidentally used a reserved key word for another purpose. You'll learn C++'s key words as you read about each one. Before finishing this book, you'll meet them all.

Punctuators

You already know that a semicolon terminates C++ statements. Technically, a semicolon is a *punctuator*. The left and right braces you learned about earlier are also punctuators.

A punctuator is a kind of abbreviated key word. It's a symbol (which might be composed of one, two, or three characters) with special meaning to the compiler. The full set of C++ punctuators includes these symbols:

```
#   ()   []   {}   ,   :   ;   ...
```

As with other key words and symbols, it's best to learn about punctuators as you meet them. Their uses are mostly intuitive, and you don't have to memorize this list now.

Separators

Separators differ from punctuators in one important way—they're invisible! Because separators are nowhere to be seen, the term *white space* describes them. C++ separators include blanks, tabs, carriage returns, and line feeds embedded in text.

Usually, C++ ignores white space, as long as you don't use spaces to *separate* identifiers, numbers, and other constructions that belong together. All white space is the same to C++, which explains why statements can be written on multiple lines. To C++, it's all the same if two statements are divided by a carriage return or a blank. In fact, in place of the common indented style demonstrated in Listing 1.1, you can even write programs like this:

```
#include <stream.hpp>
main() {cout << "Hello!\n";}
```

The compiler cares only that the parts and symbols in function `main` are properly separated and punctuated. C++ doesn't care if those separations are line endings or blanks. Obviously, though, this style makes programs more difficult to read and to debug.

Header Files

Most of the preceding sample programs and listings include a line like this near the beginning:

```
#include <stream.hpp>
```

When the compiler processes this line, it reads the contents of the file STREAM.HPP—one of the *header files* supplied with your compiler. The result of including a header file is the same as if that file's text appeared at this location. Obviously, this strategy saves space because you don't have to copy the lines from STREAM.HPP into every program you write. It also means that changes to STREAM.HPP automatically affect all programs that include that file.

Header files typically contain declarations, definitions, and other instructions that many programs need to use. For an experiment, delete the `#include` directive from a copy of Listing 1.1 and compile the program. When you try this, you'll receive several error messages from the compiler. It reacts in this way because `cout` and related programming are stored in the STREAM.HPP file. If you don't include that file in your programs, the compiler won't know what `cout` is or how to use output streams.

The keyword #include (actually, it's a two-part symbol: the punctuator # plus the keyword include), is an instruction to the compiler, followed by the name of the disk file to include at this spot. Most C++ listings begin with one or more similar *include directives.* The angle brackets < and > surrounding the file name tell the compiler to look for the file in the standard *include directory* where other .HPP and .H files are stored, usually located on the path specified by the INCLUDE environment variable. You can also write include directives like these:

```
#include <stdio.h>
#include "newmath.h"
#include "program.h"
```

The first sample line includes a file named STDIO.H stored in the include directory. The second and third samples include files named NEWMATH.H and PROGRAM.H. Because these names are surrounded with double quotes instead of angle brackets, the compiler looks for the files in the current directory—not in the include-directory path.

Always use angle brackets to include standard header files supplied with your compiler. Use double quotes around include files of your own making. You'll see many examples of both types of include files in future listings.

> **Note:** Header files usually end with the extension .H (plain C headers) or .HPP (C++ headers). The extension is not too important; you could include files ending with any name up to three characters long, but it's probably best to stick with convention and name your header files .H or .HPP. That way, a quick look at a disk directory will tell you which files are headers. I'll use .H for all header files listed in this book.

Variables

In C++, a *variable* is a named location in memory (see Figure 1.1). Variables can store all sorts of data—strings, numbers, and multipart structures. A variable typically has a name that describes its purpose, and in general, you're free to use any names you like for your program's variables. As the figure illustrates, the name points to the location where the value is stored, though you can ignore that fact and just use the name in a program as though it *is* the value.

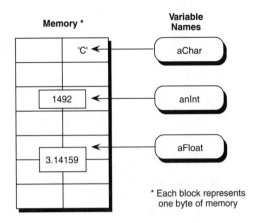

Figure 1.1. A variable is a named location in memory where a value is stored.

All variables have one common characteristic: an associated data type. This means that, in addition to choosing an appropriate name for a variable, you also have to tell the compiler what kind of information you want it to store. Table 1.1 lists C++'s common data types, showing examples of each, a type's size in bytes, and the range of values that variables of a type can hold.

Table 1.1. Common C++ Data Types

Data Type	Example	Size	Minimum	Maximum
char	'c'	1	0 ...	255 (or ASCII)
short	-7	2	-128 ...	127
int	1024	2	-32,768 ...	32,767
long	262144	4	-2,147,483,648 ...	2,147,483,637
float	10.5	4	1.5E-45 ...	3.4E38 (approx)
double	0.00045	8	5.0E-324 ...	1.7E308 (approx)
long double	1e-8	8	same as	double

> **Note:** All versions of C++ do not necessarily store variables of certain data types in the same number of bytes. The information in Table 1.1 is for the compiler included with this book. Other compilers may list different storage details for these same data types. However, a char variable always occupies one byte.

To create a variable in a program, start with the data type and finish with an identifier and semicolon. For example, to create a c h a r variable named y e s n o, you can type:

```
char yesno;
```

This is called a *definition* because it *defines* space for storing a variable in memory—in this case, a character in a single byte of space. You can insert this and other variable definitions just about anywhere—inside a function, outside a function, between other statements, in a block, and so on. However, as you'll learn, the location of definitions affects the way the compiler creates space for storing variables and may affect the way a program runs. For now, I'll define all variables either above the function m a i n or just after m a i n's opening brace.

Initializing Variables with Definitions

There are two ways to initialize variables—that is, to give them starting values. The first way is probably the best in most cases, because it combines the definition of a variable with the assignment of its initial value:

```
char yesno = 'Y';
```

This creates a variable y e s n o of type c h a r and assigns to that variable the character ' Y '. By *assigns,* I mean "stores in memory at the location represented by the variable's name." This definition is similar to the preceding one, but ends with an equal sign and the value to store in the variable. Here are two more samples:

```
int counter = 1;
float weight = 155.5;
```

Variable c o u n t e r is of type i n t and is assigned the initial value of 1. Variable w e i g h t is of type f l o a t and is assigned the initial value of 155.5. If you insert these definitions into a test program, you can display their values with statements such as these:

```
cout << "yesno = " << yesno << '\n';
cout << "counter = " << counter << '\n';
cout << "weight = " << weight << '\n';
```

When you compile these statements, the compiler replaces the variable names y e s n o, c o u n t e r, and w e i g h t with instructions that retrieve the associated values from memory. The compiler then converts the values to text form, which the output-stream statements display. Because each variable is bound to a specific data type, C++ knows that it should display y e s n o as a character, c o u n t e r as an integer, and w e i g h t as a floating-point number.

Listing 1.4, VARIABLE.CPP, demonstrates how to initialize variables of all data types from Table 1.1. Each variable definition assigns a starting value in a form that's appropriate for each data type. Output-stream statements then display those values.

Listing 1.4. VARIABLE.CPP

```
1:   // variable.cpp -- Common variables
2:
3:   #include <stream.hpp>
4:
5:   main()
6:   {
7:       char slash = '/';
8:       short month = 3;
9:       int year = 1991;
10:      long population = 308700000;
11:      float pi = 3.14159;
12:      double velocity = 186281.7;
13:      long double lightYear = 5.88e12;
14:
15:      cout << "Date = " << month << slash << year << '\n';
16:      cout << "Population of the U.S.A. = " << population << '\n';
17:      cout << "Pi = " << pi << '\n';
18:      cout << "Velocity of light = " << velocity
19:           << " mi./sec." << '\n';
20:      cout << "One light year = " << lightYear << " mi." << '\n';
21:  }
```

When you run VARIABLE, it displays each of the variables defined at lines 7-13. The output-stream statements at lines 15-20 display these values, using forms that are appropriate for the variables' data types:

```
Date = 3/1991
Population of the U.S.A. = 308700000
Pi = 3.14159
Velocity of light = 186281.7 mi./sec.
One light year = 5.88e+012 mi.
```

Initializing Variables with Assignments

Another way to initialize variables is to use separate assignment statements after defining the variables. For example, instead of line 7 in Listing 1.4, you can create the variable with the following definition:

```
char slash;
```

Then, later in the program, you can use an *assignment statement* to store a value in slash:

```
slash = '/';
```

The compiler interprets the equal sign as an instruction to assign the value on the right to the variable on the left. Technically speaking, the compiler generates code to store a value representing an ASCII slash character in a memory location reserved for the variable named slash (see Figure 1.2).

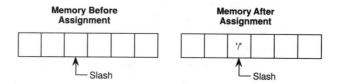

Figure 1.2.   The assignment statement slash = '/'; stores an ASCII slash character at the location reserved for the slash variable.

You can also assign values to the other variables in Listing 1.4. For example, add this statement after line 14:

```
population = -500;
```

When you run the modified program, it displays the population of the U.S.A. as –500. Obviously, that value is incorrect, but it shows how an assignment can *replace* a variable's initial value. This is an important characteristic of variables. A program can change a variable's value as often as necessary, and every time the program assigns a value to a variable, the new value replaces the old. A variable can hold only one value at a time.

No matter which of the two methods you decide to use for assigning values to variables, initializing variables in programs is important. If you forget to assign starting values to variables, they will use whatever values exist in memory at the variables' reserved locations. Uninitialized variables are responsible for all sorts of programming bugs—from incorrect bank balances to faulty satellite orbits. To avoid such problems in your own code, be sure to give all variables starting values.

Scoop on Scope

Statements can refer to variables, but only if the variables are within the same *scope,* or level. The scope of a variable extends to the boundaries of its defining block.

Figure 1.3 shows a sample program (not included on disk) that contains nested blocks inside the m a i n function. The sample program is artificial, and you wouldn't write programs this way in practice. However, it is a correct C++ program (it will compile), and it demonstrates how scope limits the visibility of variables.

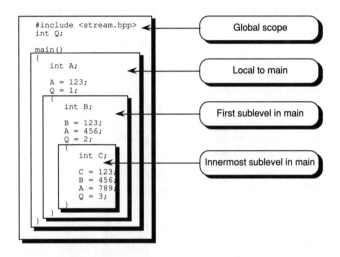

Figure 1.3. The scope of a variable extends only to the boundaries of the block that defines it.

The figure illustrates several important facts about scope. First, the *global scope* includes the entire program. This means that the integer Q is accessible to all statements, no matter where they are located. Q is a *global variable*—its scope extends to the four corners of the program's world.

Definitions inside m a i n's braces, such as the integer A, are *local* to m a i n. Thus, only statements inside m a i n—that is, within the same scope as m a i n's block delimited with braces—may use A. Any statements outside this block may not use A. (In this sample program, there are no such statements.) In fact, outside its defining block, A doesn't even exist in memory!

Farther inside m a i n is a *nested block,* labeled in the figure "First sublevel in m a i n." Because the block is nested inside m a i n's primary block, the nested block can use its own definition of B plus the integer A defined on the outer layer. The nested block also can use the global variable Q. Nested blocks can always "see" the definitions in their surrounding blocks. However, those outer layers can't "see" into the inner nest. This means that if you insert a statement immediately after A = 123, the program would no longer compile:

```
B = 456;
```

That won't work inside the block that's "Local to main" because B exists only within its defining block. Main's primary block can't access B because B's scope is nested inside that outer level. Similarly, the statements inside the first sublevel in main can't use the definitions inside the next and innermost level labeled "Innermost sublevel in main" in the figure. On this level, a fourth integer, C, is defined. As the figure illustrates, statements inside this innermost block can use all the variables defined in the program, but *only* this block can use C. Statements outside the innermost block can't see into this inner sanctum nested deeply in main.

A good way to think about nested blocks and scope is to imagine a house with rooms built inside each other. Windows in each room are made of one-way glass through which a room's occupant can look to the outside. Because the glass is one-way only, anyone outside can't see into inner rooms. The contents of a room are private except to the room's occupants (the block's statements) and to the occupants of other rooms nested inside this one.

For another example of how scope limits access to variables, compile and run Listing 1.5, SCOPE.CPP.

Listing 1.5. SCOPE.CPP

```
 1:   // scope.cpp -- Demonstrate nested scopes
 2:
 3:   #include <stream.hpp>
 4:
 5:   int outer = 100;     // Global variable
 6:
 7:   main()
 8:   {
 9:      int inner = 200;  // Local variable
10:
11:      cout << "outer = " << outer << '\n';
12:      cout << "inner = " << inner << '\n';
13:      {
14:         int noseeum = 300;
15:         cout << "noseeum = " << noseeum << '\n';
16:      }
17:  //   cout << "noseeum = " << noseeum << '\n';
18:   }
```

The SCOPE demonstration defines three variables: outer, inner, and noseeum. The first definition at line 5 is global to the program. All statements in all scopes, no matter how deeply nested, can read and write this global variable. Line 9 is different—it's defined inside main's block (between the braces at lines 8 and 18). This is an example of a *local variable,* a variable defined inside a block. The third variable definition at line 14 is also local, but it's nested inside a small block delimited by the braces at lines 13 and 16. Only statements inside this block's scope can read and write noseeum.

Prove this to yourself by removing the // comment symbol from the beginning of line 17 and activating the cout statement there. When you compile the modified program, the compiler reports an error even though this statement is identical to the one at line 15. The reason for the error is that noseeum is available only to statements within its scope. The statement at line 17 is outside that scope and therefore can't look in to "see" noseeum inside the inner level.

Initializing Global and Local Variables

Even though they appear similarly in programs, global and local variables are stored differently in memory. The compiler allocates fixed space in a memory area called the *data segment* for all global variables. This memory stays put during the program's execution, and any variables in that memory keep their values while the program runs. If a statement assigns 100 to the global variable x, that variable equals 100 until another statement changes its value, no matter what else the program does.

Local variables don't work that way. Instead of storing them in the program's data segment, the compiler creates temporary space for all local variables defined inside a block. This space is part of another segment called the *stack,* which grows and shrinks as needed to accommodate information *pushed* onto it. That same information can then be *popped* from the stack, which shrinks when data is removed from its top. Using this device, C++ allocates space for variables when they are in scope. When a variable is not in scope, no stack space is assigned to the variable. Not only is that variable out of scope; it doesn't even exist in memory.

Another sample program demonstrates some of the important differences between global and local variables. Compile and run Listing 1.6, GLOBAL.CPP.

Listing 1.6. GLOBAL.CPP

```
1:   // global.cpp -- Demonstrate global and local variables
2:
3:   #include <stream.hpp>
4:
5:   int global = 100;
6:   int globalDefault;
7:
```

```
 8:    main()
 9:    {
10:        int local = 200;
11:        int localDefault;
12:
13:      cout << "global = " << global << '\n';
14:      cout << "local   = " << local  << '\n';
15:
16:      cout << "globalDefault = " << globalDefault<< '\n';
17:      cout << "localDefault   = " << localDefault << '\n';
18:    }
```

Lines 5 and 6 define two global variables. The first, global, is similar to other global definitions you've examined. Because it's a global variable, it's accessible by any statement and is stored in a fixed location in the program's data segment. Line 6 defines another global variable, but does not assign a starting value to the variable.

By definition, all uninitialized global variables like globalDefault at line 6 are assigned the starting value 0 when the program runs. You can rely on this—globalDefault will equal 0 unless another statement changes its value. However, because line 5 specifies an initial value for global, that variable will equal 100, not 0, when the program runs.

The two local variables at lines 10-11 use the same forms as the global definitions. Line 10 assigns a starting value to local, which the program displays. Line 11 does not assign a starting value. Even so, when the sample program runs, it still displays *some* value for localDefault.

That value illustrates one of the most important differences between global and local variables. Uninitialized globals are guaranteed to equal 0 when the program runs. Uninitialized locals come with no similar warranty. Because local variables are stored temporarily on the stack, they will have whatever values were left in that space from a previous operation. Those values *may* be 0, but they also may be something else. In no case can you rely on local variables having any specific starting values.

Input and Output

Loading information into memory and transferring it from there to somewhere else are two jobs that probably occupy the lion's share in the jungle of statements that make up most programs. A program's *Input and Output* (I/O) statements are responsible for all comings and goings—for example, displaying text on terminals, printing reports, prompting for responses from users, and communicating with remote systems over telephone lines.

Output Streams

Previous sample programs used output-stream statements to display strings and the values of variables. Listing 1.7, DT.CPP, shows a more practical example of this, displaying the date and time.

Listing 1.7. DT.CPP

```
1:   // dt.cpp -- Display the date and time
2:
3:   #include <stream.hpp>
4:   #include <dos.h>
5:
6:   main()
7:   {
8:       struct dos_date_t today;
9:       struct dos_time_t theTime;
10:
11:      dos_getdate( &today );
12:
13:      cout << "The date is " << (int)today.month
14:           << "/" << (int)today.day << "/" << today.year << "\n";
15:
16:      dos_gettime( &theTime );
17:      cout << "The time is " << (int)theTime.hour << ":";
18:
19:      if (theTime.minute < 10)
20:         cout << '0';
21:      cout << (int)theTime.minute << ":";
22:
23:      if (theTime.second < 10)
24:         cout << '0';
25:      cout << (int)theTime.second << "\n";
26:   }
```

There are a few items in DT.CPP that you haven't learned about yet. For example, lines 8-9 define two struct variables named today and theTime. Lines 11 and 16 use functions to read the date and time into these variables—two examples of statements responsible for this program's input. Two other unfamiliar statements at lines 19 and 23 use if control statements to perform actions based on conditions the statements determine. Notice also that lines 3 and 4 include two header files— STREAM.HPP and DOS.H.

Don't be concerned with fully understanding the formats of DT.CPP's unfamiliar items. Instead, concentrate on how the program uses output-stream statements to display text, characters, and the values that represent dates and times. These statements are similar to the samples you've seen in earlier listings, except for one difference. For example, at line 25 is this statement:

```
cout << (int)theTime.second << "\n";
```

The construction (int)theTime.second is called a *type cast*. Like a director casting a play, a type cast in C++ assigns new roles for variables to perform. In this case, the variable is theTime.second, which is defined in DOS.H as a single-byte char which usually stores small values or ASCII characters. In this case, the program uses a char variable to store small integer values, not characters. However, because I don't want to display seconds as ASCII characters, I had to tell the compiler to show the value as an integer. Prefacing the variable with (int) does this by casting the char to type int.

A good way to see the effect of type casting is to remove all the (int)s from a copy of DT.CPP. Then compile and run the result. As you'll see from this experiment, it's important to format output statements correctly to get the results you want.

Note: Don't be too surprised if the output from the modified DT program displays unreadable garbage characters, beeps, or even clears the screen. Displaying arbitrary values as ASCII characters can produce some interesting (but harmless) effects when output-stream statements write control codes to the terminal.

Old-Style Output

When reading C programs, you'll often run into statements such as these:

```
printf("Enter your name: ");
printf("Your balance is $%d\n", balance);
```

These are roughly equivalent to C++'s output-stream statements. The function printf transfers arguments in parentheses to the standard output, usually the display. The first sample statement here displays a simple string. The second displays a string also, but uses a special notation (%d) to add items to the characters between the quote marks. In this case, that item is a variable named balance, which printf converts to characters and inserts at the marked location in the string for output. Running the program displays this result:

```
Your balance is $75.68
```

> **Note:** To use p r i n t f in C++ programs, insert the directive # i n c l u d e < s t d i o . h > at the beginning of your program. However, because output streams can accomplish everything that p r i n t f can and more, they're usually a better choice than p r i n t f. Also, in some cases, the compiler can generate more efficient code for output streams than for p r i n t f function calls.

Formatted Output

Plain output streams don't always produce the needed effects. For example, writing an integer value named c o u n t displays the variable's value in decimal:

```
cout << "The count is " << count;
```

To display c o u n t and other values in hexadecimal or octal, you can pass any i n t or l o n g variable to one of three *output-formatting functions:* o c t, d e c, and h e x. These examples show how to use the functions:

```
cout << "The octal count is " << oct(count);
cout << "The decimal count is " << dec(count);
cout << "The hexadecimal count is " << hex(count);
```

The functions at the end of each line convert the value of the item inside parentheses to a string, which the output-stream statement then displays.

Another reason to use formatting functions is to align or *justify* columns of numbers. To do this, add the minimum number of character positions after the value:

```
cout << "The count is " << dec(count, 10);
```

This statement displays the value of c o u n t, adding spaces to the left to fill at least 10 character columns. If the number of columns is less than needed to display the value, it will be displayed correctly, but it won't be aligned as expected.

Listing 1.8, JUSTIFY.CPP, demonstrates how to use the three output-formatting functions for integers (o c t, h e x, and d e c) plus two others—c h r and s t r—for variables of type c h a r and for strings.

Listing 1.8. JUSTIFY.CPP

```
1:  // justify.cpp -- Justifying characters and strings
2:
3:  #include <stream.hpp>
4:
5:  char *cutline = "\n-------------------------------\n";
6:
7:  main()
```

```
 8:   {
 9:       int value = 249;
10:       char c = 'X';
11:       char *s = "I Brake for Butterflies";
12:
13:       cout << cutline << "Left justified:" << cutline;
14:       cout << value        << '\n';
15:       cout << hex(value) << '\n';
16:       cout << oct(value) << '\n';
17:       cout << c            << '\n';
18:       cout << s            << '\n';
19:
20:       cout << cutline << "Right justified:" << cutline;
21:       cout << dec(value, 30) << '\n';
22:       cout << hex(value, 30) << '\n';
23:       cout << oct(value, 30) << '\n';
24:       cout << chr(c, 30)     << '\n';
25:       cout << str(s, 30)     << '\n';
26:   }
```

Three variables at lines 9-11 create integer, character, and string values for the demonstration. Line 11 creates a *pointer* named s, which points to the first character of the string delimited by double quotes. (Pointers are an advanced topic explained in chapter 4.) The output-stream statements at lines 13-18 show the default appearances of each variable, using h e x and o c t to convert v a l u e to hexadecimal and octal. It's not necessary to use the other formatting functions for d e c, c h r, and s t r because these are the default formats for integer, character, and string values.

Lines 20-25 show the same variables displayed within 30 columns. The only differences between these statements and the previous ones are the column-width arguments (30) and the use of the d e c, c h r, and s t r functions.

Even fancier formatting is possible in output streams with another function named f o r m. However, it would take pages of text to describe all that f o r m can do—it's one of the most complex functions available in C++'s library. For now, we'll look at only a few of f o r m's capabilities. See chapter 10 for complete details about how to use this output-formatting tool.

Listing 1.9 demonstrates how f o r m can display values in a variety of formats. A good way to learn how to use f o r m is to run the sample program and then read the descriptions after the listing.

Listing 1.9. FORMAT.CPP

```
1:   // format.cpp -- Demonstrate formatted output
2:
3:   #include <stream.hpp>
4:
```

```
 5:   main()
 6:   {
 7:      int value = 0x79AF;
 8:      long longValue = 123456789;
 9:      double pi = 3.14159;
10:      double balance = 572.63;
11:      char *name = "Judy";
12:
13:      cout << form("Plain decimal    = %d\n", value);
14:      cout << form("Signed decimal   = %+d\n", value);
15:      cout << form("Right justified = %10d\n", value);
16:
17:      cout << form("\nPlain hexadecimal      = %x\n", value);
18:      cout << form("Prefaced hexadecimal   = %#x\n", value);
19:      cout << form("Uppercase hexadecimal = %#X\n", value);
20:
21:      cout << form("\nBinary = %b\n", value);
22:
23:      cout << form("\nUnsigned long decimal = %ld\n", longValue);
24:      cout << form("Signed long decimal   = %Ld\n", longValue);
25:
26:      cout << form("\nFloating point       = %f\n", pi);
27:      cout << form("Scientific notation = %e\n", pi);
28:      cout << form("Default notation    = %g\n", pi);
29:      cout << form("FP precision 10     = %.10f\n", pi);
30:
31:      cout << form("\n%s's balance = $%8.2f", name, balance);
32:   }
```

As in other sample programs in this chapter, FORMAT begins by defining several test variables at lines 7-11. The first three output statements (lines 13-15) then display the int variable value, using output-stream statements and form. These statements display the following lines:

```
Plain decimal   = 31151
Signed decimal  = +31151
Right justified =      31151
```

Take a good look at line 13. The percent sign inside the string tells the form function to insert a value at this spot. The percent sign (%) is called an *escape character* because it temporarily causes C++ to "escape" from normal processing and treat the *next* characters specially. In this case, the d after the percent sign indicates that you want to display an integer value in decimal format at this location in the string. That integer—in this case, value—must then follow the formatting string after a separating comma.

The second statement (line 14) expands the formatting instruction to %+d. The plus sign tells form to display a signed value, adding a + or – sign as needed. Without the plus sign in the formatting instruction, form adds a minus sign to negative values, but does not add a plus sign to positive ones.

The third statement (line 15) uses the formatting instruction %10d. This is similar to the dec function you examined earlier. The 10 tells form to display the value (a decimal integer in this sample) in a minimum of 10 character columns. As you can see on your display, this shoves the value toward the right to occupy at least 10 column positions.

Lines 17-19 display the same value variable but use formatting instructions %x, %#x, and %#X. The first of these lines displays values in unornamented hexadecimal. The second prefaces values with 0x, C++'s standard hexadecimal indicator. The third is nearly the same as the second, but displays the output in uppercase. On screen, the three statements produce these lines:

```
Plain hexadecimal      = 79af
Prefaced hexadecimal   = 0x79af
Uppercase hexadecimal  = 0X79AF
```

In addition to displaying decimal and hexadecimal formats, form can also display values in binary. The formatting instruction for this is %b. Using that instruction, line 21 displays this value:

```
Binary = 111100110101111
```

To display long decimal values (in this book's version of C++, whole numbers represented by 32-bit variables), use the instructions %ld or %Ld. The first of these (lowercase l) displays unsigned long integers. The second (uppercase L) displays signed values. Lines 23-24 demonstrate the output from these instructions:

```
Unsigned long decimal = 123456789
Signed long decimal   = -13035
```

The form function also handles a variety of display formats for floating-point values. As lines 26-29 show, you can display values in standard decimal notation (%f), in scientific notation (%e), or in decimal or scientific notations depending on the quantity of the value (%g). To display values using a different precision from normal, follow the percent sign with a decimal point and the number of significant digits to use. For example, the instruction %.10f outputs floating-point values in decimal format, using 10 significant digits after the decimal place. Here are samples of the floating-point instructions displayed by the statements at lines 26-29:

```
Floating point       = 3.141590
Scientific notation  = 3.141590e+000
Default notation     = 3.14159
FP precision 10      = 3.1415900000
```

The final statement at line 31 shows a typical use for the f o r m function in output-stream statements—displaying multiple values inserted into one string. Examine the statement carefully:

```
form("\n%s's balance = $%8.2f", name, balance);
```

Inside the opening double quote, a \ n symbol starts a new display line. Then the instruction % s tells f o r m to insert a string here. After a few other characters, the second instruction % 8 . 2 f tells f o r m to display a floating point value using a total of 8 character positions with 2 significant digits after the decimal place. Running this statement displays the line:

```
Judy's balance = $   572.63
```

Notice that line 31 in the sample listing specifies three arguments inside f o r m's parentheses: the formatting string and the two values n a m e and b a l a n c e. Those two values are needed to account for the two formatting instructions % s and % 8 . 2 f inside the formatting string. When using f o r m, you must specify exactly as many values after the formatting string as there are formatting instructions inside that string. There is no limit to the number of instructions and values you can insert in f o r m strings. (Or perhaps I should say there's no *practical* limit.)

Note: The f o r m function uses the same notations as p r i n t f, supplied with all C and C++ compilers, including the one accompanying this book. The only difference is that you can include f o r m, but not p r i n t f, in an output-stream statement.

Stream Input

Up to now, sample programs have done little more than send information to the outside world—that is, the display. It's time to consider the other side of the coin: how to get information from "out there" into a program. For the moment, I'll limit "out there" to the keyboard, but eventually, I explain ways to get information from other sources into programs.

The simplest way to get responses entered at the keyboard is to use an *input-stream statement*. For example, these two statements prompt for and read an integer value into a variable defined as i n t c o u n t D o w n:

```
cout << "Start countdown from? ";
cin >> countdown;
```

The first line uses an output-stream statement to display a prompt. The second uses an input-stream statement to read a response into the c o u n t d o w n variable. In that statement, c i n represents the source of the input—here the standard character input, meaning the keyboard (unless input has been redirected by a DOS command). The symbol >> represents the stream's action, indicating that the information flow is from left to right—from the source (c i n) to its destination (countdown).

As you can see, input and output streams are similar. They just use different stream objects (c i n instead of c o u t), and they direct the information flow from left to right (>>) instead of from right to left (<<).

Although it's probably more common to read one variable at a time with an input-stream statement, you can read multiple values by stringing them together, similar to the way you can display multiple values in output streams. For example, to prompt for the values v 1 and v 2, you can write statements such as these:

```
cout << "Enter v1 v2: ";
cin >> v1 >> v2;
cout << form("v1=%d  v2=%d\n", v1, v2);
```

The first line prompts for the two values. The next line reads those values from c i n into v 1 and v 2. After that, a second output-stream statement uses f o r m to display the entered values. Because the input-stream statement lists both values together, when the program runs, you must enter your responses by typing a blank character between them or by pressing **<Enter>**. If you prefer to have people enter values one at a time, use statements like these instead:

```
cout << "Enter v1: ";
cin >> v1;
cout << "Enter v2: ";
cin >> v2;
cout << form("v1=%d  v2=%d\n", v1, v2);
```

Old-Style Input

C programs typically use another function, s c a n f, for input. C++ recognizes this function, just as it does p r i n t f. However, because s c a n f is rarely needed in C++, which can accomplish with streams everything that s c a n f can do, there's no reason to waste time covering the function here. (Chapter 10 explains how to use the function.)

Formatted Input

When you use input streams to read numeric values, it's important to consider what happens if people enter characters other than digits and numeric punctuation characters. To see how this can cause headaches, compile and run Listing 1.10, NUMIN.CPP.

Listing 1.10. NUMIN.CPP

```
1:   // numin.cpp -- Simple way to input numbers
2:
3:   #include <stream.hpp>
4:
5:   main()
6:   {
7:     double fp;       // A floating point value
8:     long k;          // A long int value
9:
10:    cout << "Enter a floating point value: ";
11:    cin >> fp;
12:    cout << "Value entered is: " << fp << '\n';
13:
14:    cout << "Enter an integer value: ";
15:    cin >> k;
16:    cout << "Value entered is: " << k << '\n';
17:  }
```

When you run NUMIN, enter a floating point value such as 3.14159 and press **<Enter>**. Then enter an integer value such as 100 and press **<Enter>** again. The program seems to run smoothly enough, pausing for input and displaying the values you type.

Run NUMIN again, but this time, enter a nonsense value such as ABCDEFG or XQ45 for the first prompt. As you can see, when you press **<Enter>**, instead of pausing for the next input, the program displays apparently random output values and ends.

This odd behavior occurs because input streams expect their information to be in the correct formats. Although input streams reject badly formatted input, they consider even simple typing mistakes to be serious errors. Worse, the slightest problem causes *subsequent* input statements to fail. Obviously, a finished program has to deal with these kinds of problems—it can't just display random values and halt as NUMIN does.

A good way to deal with errors is to read input into character strings and then convert those strings to integers, floating-point values, and other binary forms. Because you can type anything into a string variable, you can use this technique to perform your own error checking, or you can simply ignore any errors. If you type ABC rather than 123, the program may use an incorrect value, but at least the code won't "crash and burn" just because you pressed the wrong keys. Listing 1.11, ATONUMS.CPP, demonstrates how to read input values into strings and convert those values to other data types.

Listing 1.11. ATONUMS.CPP

```
1:  // atonums.cpp -- Demonstrate safe way to input numbers
2:
3:  #include <stream.hpp>
4:  #include <stdlib.h>
5:
6:  main()
7:  {
8:     double fp;      // A floating point value
9:     long k;         // A long int value
10:    char s[80];     // 80-character string for input
11:
12:    cout << "Enter a floating point value: ";
13:    cin >> s;
14:    cout << "Original entry: " << s << '\n';
15:    fp = atof(s);
16:    cout << "After converting to double: " << fp << '\n';
17:
18:    cout << "Enter an integer value: ";
19:    cin >> s;
20:    cout << "Original entry: " << s << '\n';
21:    k = atol(s);
22:    cout << "After converting to long: " << k << '\n';
23: }
```

ATONUMS runs like NUMIN, prompting and pausing for a floating point number and an integer value. This time, however, when you enter nonsense values like ABCDEFG, instead of causing problems, the program simply assigns the value 0 to variables. A more sophisticated program might go even further to detect typing mistakes and repeat the input statements, letting people correct their errors.

The program has a few features you haven't seen before. Because some of them are declared in the header file STDLIB.H, the program includes that file along with STREAM.HPP. What's also new are the assignment statements at lines 15 and 21. These statements use two functions declared in STDLIB.H, atof (ASCII to floating point) and atol (ASCII to long). As their names suggest, these functions translate strings of ASCII characters to floating point and long integer values.

Earlier, I explained how to use functions like form and hex in output-stream statements. Those and other functions operate on an *argument* in parentheses and return a character string that represents the argument's value. Functions atof and atol work similarly but have the opposite effect. The functions process string arguments in parentheses, and they return equivalent floating point and long-integer values, respectively. Usually, you'll assign those values to variables as in this statement:

```
fp = atof(s);
```

This calls the function a t o f, which processes the string argument s and then passes back the result of that operation. In this case, that result is a floating point value, which the assignment statement (=) stores at the location in memory reserved for the floating point variable f p.

A Simple Decimal-to-Hex-and-Octal Converter

Combining input and output streams with the formatting functions you learned about earlier leads to useful C++ programs. For example, Listing 1.12, CONVERT.CPP, prompts for numbers and then displays your entries in decimal, hexadecimal, and octal. Use the program to convert values in decimal to these other number bases (or *radixes*).

Listing 1.12. CONVERT.CPP

```
 1:    // convert.cpp -- Convert integers to hex and octal
 2:
 3:    #include <stream.hpp>
 4:    #include <stdlib.h>
 5:
 6:    main()
 7:    {
 8:        long value;
 9:        char s[80];      // 80-character string for input
10:
11:        cout << "Value? ";
12:        cin >> s;
13:        value = atol(s);
14:        cout << "Decimal="        << dec(value)
15:             << "  Hexadecimal=" << hex(value)
16:             << "  Octal="       << oct(value) << '\n';
17:    }
```

Constants

Constants are values that don't change when a program runs. You'll see many examples of constants throughout this book's sample programs, and you should get into the habit of using constants correctly in your own code.

Because constants can't change values, they provide programs with a reliable bedrock on which you can build other foundations. The unchanging constants give you confidence that your structures won't fall because of unexpected changes in critical values. For example, it would be senseless to make P I a variable. If people could change P I's value of 3.14159 to something else, any formulas that depend on P I would no longer give correct results.

Note: Constants in C and C++ are typically written in all uppercase, although that's not required. Uppercase letters make a constant's name stand out clearly in a long listing, which often helps make the code more readable.

Good use of constants also helps make a program's logic clear by associating recognizable names with values. Again, P I is a good example—the letters P I are probably recognized even by people who don't know P I's value by heart.

In other cases, constants are useful for representing values that change only rarely. For instance, in a program that stores test scores, you might create a constant named MAX_SCORES and associate that identifier with a value, perhaps 10. If the maximum number of scores changes to 15 later, all you have to do is revise the one constant and recompile. There's no need to hunt through the program to change every instance of 10 to 15.

Types of Constants

In C++ programs, there are four kinds of constants:

- Literal constants
- Defined constants
- Declared constants
- Enumerated constants

Literal constants are the most common variety. They are the values such as 123, 3.14159, or "Enter your name" that you type directly into the program's text. *Defined constants* are identifiers that you associate with literal constant values. Defined constants are the same as literal constants; they just have names. *Declared constants* are like variables: Their values are stored in memory, but the compiler refuses to let you change them. *Enumerated constants* let you associate an identifier such as Color with a sequence of other names like Red, Blue, and Green.

Literal Constants

When encountering a literal constant like 100, the compiler determines the value's data type from its form. In a sense, C++ "knows" that 100 is an integer value. It also knows that 5.5 is a floating point value and that "Bees make honey" is a string. The form of a literal constant determines its data type, which can be any of the types listed earlier in Table 1.1 for variables. In fact, the *Example* column of that table lists examples of literal constants for each of C++'s fundamental data types.

Because the compiler determines a constant's type from its form, it is important to enter constant values in the correct formats. A few sample constants for each of C++'s fundamental data types will help you learn those forms.

Character Constants

Like a double-edged sword, a char constant can cut two ways. Usually, chars represent symbols in the ASCII character set and are enclosed in single quotes. Examples of char constants are '$', 'U', 'z', and '?'. Because these symbols are represented internally as values from 0 to 255, chars can also be used for numbers in that same range. This makes char convenient for storing small values in exactly one byte of space.

That brings up a sore subject in programming—whether a data type holds *signed* or *unsigned* values. Signed values represent negative and positive quantities; unsigned values represent only positive numbers. The four integer types—char, short, int, and long—are signed by default. To make these types represent unsigned values, preface the type name with the key word unsigned. A few samples will make the idea clear:

```
char sc = 10;
unsigned char uc = 255;
 short ss = -12345;
unsigned short us = 65535;
int si = -12345;
unsigned int ui = 65535;
long sl = -999999;
unsigned long ul = 999999;
```

In place of char sc, you could write signed char sc. The same is true of the other integer types—values are signed by default. Notice also that short and int values represent the identical ranges of values (see Table 1.1). This isn't necessarily true in all C++ implementations, but it is for the Zortech compiler included with this book.

Although unsigned char constants can represent values from 0 to 255, signed char constants (the default for type char) can represent values from -128 to +127. The same is true for unsigned int constants, which can range from

0 to 65535; `signed int` constants can range from –32768 to +32767. If you have trouble visualizing why these ranges differ, examine Figure 1.4, a familiar number line with 0 in the center. Imagine that the range of values for an integer data type, which is stored in a fixed number of bits, is a box of a fixed "length." Mentally position that box so that its left end is at zero, representing the range of unsigned values in that `unsigned` data type. Now shift the box halfway toward the left. After that, the left half of the box represents negative values, but the highest positive value has been lowered. Visualizing signed and unsigned values with a number line explains why `signed` data types can represent fewer positive values than their `unsigned` counterparts.

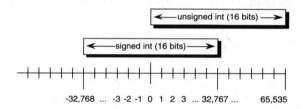

Figure 1.4. A familiar number line shows that signed and unsigned ranges are the same "lengths," but represent different ranges of value. Only signed data types can represent negative values.

As explained earlier, to enter `char`s that you can't type directly on the keyboard, you can use a form like `'\n'` to represent a new-line character (actually two characters on PCs, a carriage return and line feed). Table 1.2 lists other escape codes that C++ understands as control codes. You can use these symbols as individual `char` constants (surrounded by single quotes) or in strings (surrounded by double quotes). Because the backslash precedes these symbols, you must enter a backslash by typing that character twice like this: `'\\'`. Also because quote characters have special meaning, you must type them as `char` constants by preceding them with a backslash. The prefaced question mark in the table is required only when using *trigraphs* (three-character symbols that begin with ?) to form certain symbols on some terminals. For example, the trigraph `??<` represents an opening brace, `{`. On PCs, you don't have to use trigraphs, and therefore, you can type question marks directly in strings.

Table 1.2. Character Escape Codes

Escape Code	Meaning	ASCII value(s)		
		Dec	Hex	Symbol(s)
`'\a'`	Bell	7	07	BEL
`'\b'`	Backspace	8	08	BS
`'\f'`	Form feed	12	0C	FF

Escape Code	Meaning	ASCII value(s)		
		Dec	**Hex**	**Symbol(s)**
`'\n'`	New line	13 10	0D 0A	CR LF
`'\r'`	Carriage return	13	0D	CR
`'\t'`	Horizontal tab	9	09	HT
`'\v'`	Vertical tab	11	0B	VT
`'\\'`	Backslash	92	5C	\
`'\''`	Single quote	39	27	'
`'\"'`	Double quote	34	22	"
`'\?'`	Question mark	63	3F	?
`'\000'`	ASCII octal	all	all	all
`'\x00'`	ASCII hexadecimal	all	all	all

At the bottom of Table 1.2 are two special escape sequences, \000 and \x00. The zeros in these symbols represent digits, which can stand for any ASCII character value. For example, to insert the ß symbol into a string, which some programmers use to represent "Beta" test versions for their programs, you can write

```
"Version v7.54\xE1"
```

In place of the symbol \xE1, the compiler inserts the ASCII value E1 hexadeci-mal. To represent values in octal, replace x with a digit from 0 to 7, such as \341. Either way, the result is this string:

```
"Version v7.54ß"
```

String Constants

Strings should be no strangers to you by now. In C++, strings can be any length, and they can contain any characters that you can type between two double quotes. Strings can also contain any of the escape codes listed in Table 1.2.

In memory, strings are represented by a series of ASCII character values plus 0, or NULL. The NULL "character" marks the end of the string and is inserted automati-cally by C++ at the end of string constants. NULL is a constant defined in four header files: STDDEF.H, STDIO.H, STDLIB.H, and STRING.H. To use the symbol NULL in a program, it's usually better to include one or more of these files than to define NULL with the following line:

```
#define NULL 0
```

Although that works, header files for other C++ compilers (or for the professional version of the compiler included with this book, which can compile programs to use different memory models on PCs) may define NULL differently based on various conditions. For that reason, it's better to include the header files than to define NULL explicitly, which doesn't take those conditions into account.

Because strings end with NULL, don't use double quotes to represent single characters. If you do, you may waste space. For example, "J" is a string that takes two characters—one to represent the J and another for the invisible NULL at the end of the string. 'J' is a single character. It takes only one byte of space, and it does not require a terminating value.

> **Note:** Chapter 4 explains how to use NULL with pointers. Whether it terminates a string or represents a pointer value, it's the same NULL. Think of NULL as 0 with special status, but *don't* use 0 in place of NULL.

Whole Number Constants

When typing short, int, and long values, you normally can enter the number you need and not be concerned with its type. If you enter 1024 into a program, C++ will treat the value as type int. If you type 999999, C++ will assume the value is long. However, there are a few less obvious details associated with whole number constants in programs. Remember these points:

- Never use commas or other punctuation in numbers. Enter 123456, not 123,456.

- To force a value to be long, end it with a capital L. For example, 1024 is type int, but 1024L is type long. Usually this is necessary only when mixing values of different types in expressions, and when you must force the result of that expression to be a certain type.

- To force a value to be unsigned, end it with a capital U. You can combine U and L to create unsigned long constants, as in 3452UL.

In the Zortech C++ compiler supplied with this book, short and int represent the same ranges in two bytes (16 bits), and for that reason, I'll use only int, not short, in programs from now on. Constants of type long are stored in four bytes (32 bits) and are very useful for representing large integer values.

> **Note:** Try not to write programs that rely on the sizes of certain data types. Otherwise, your programs may not work correctly when compiled by other C++ compilers.

Floating Point Constants

Like whole numbers, floating point constants represent values within a fixed number of bits (see Table 1.1). However, floating point values are always signed, and they are best used for representing measurements rather than exact counts.

As I mentioned before, you can enter floating point constants in the usual way—for example, 1.2 and –555.99. Or you can use scientific notation, following a whole number with E and a positive or negative *exponent.* A positive exponent means to move the decimal place that many times to the right. A negative exponent means to move it to the left. The value 2.5E4 is equivalent to 25000; 4.257E–3 is the same as 0.004257.

Defined Constants

Literal constants are common and useful, but they also lack clarity. For instance, what is 53? Is it somebody's age? The number of potatoes in a stock bin? The payoff at the track? "53" could be any of those values, or an infinite number more. Because literal constants like 53 and 9823 may confuse readers of your programs (including *you* months after you construct the code), it's a good idea to give names to values that help jog your memory about what the values represent.

One way to give a constant a name is to use a #define macro. Here are some samples:

```
#define PAYOFF 53
#define NEWLINE '\n'
```

These are not statements, and for that reason, they do not end with semicolons. They're *control lines,* or *macros,* and they do not take up any space in the compiled code. In the body of a program, the compiler replaces a #defined symbol with the associated text. For example, consider this statement:

```
cout << "Payoff was $" << PAYOFF << NEWLINE;
```

C++ replaces PAYOFF and NEWLINE with the text associated with those symbols, 53 and '\n', respectively.

In complex settings, named constants can lend a great deal of clarity to programs. In fact, some programmers *never* use literal whole number constants other than 0 and 1 (and sometimes –1). They assign names to all other values such as FACTOR, RATE, and TAX. Names such as those make programs read like stories that explain what the program is doing.

Most of the time, you'll use #define as illustrated in Listing 1.13, DEFINE.CPP. The program associates several literal constants of various C++ data types, giving the values recognizable names. The main function then uses those names in output-stream statements. DEFINE uses all uppercase for the constant identifiers—a typical style that makes the names pop out on the page.

> **Note:** Macros in C++ are far less common than they are in C. A macro uses a kind of minilanguage built into C and C++ that lets #define create complex commands. For reasons that will not be clear until much later in this book, other C++ features can do anything macros can, and more. That's why I use only simple #defines in my own programs, and I suggest that you do the same.

Listing 1.13. DEFINE.CPP

```
 1:   // define.cpp -- Demonstrate #defined constants
 2:
 3:   #include <stream.hpp>
 4:
 5:   #define CHARACTER        'a'
 6:   #define STRING           "Learning C++"
 7:   #define OCTAL            0233
 8:   #define HEXADECIMAL      0x9b
 9:   #define BINARY           0b10011011
10:   #define DECIMAL          155
11:   #define FLOATING_POINT   3.14159
12:
13:   main()
14:   {
15:       cout << CHARACTER        << '\n';
16:       cout << STRING           << '\n';
17:       cout << OCTAL            << '\n';
18:       cout << HEXADECIMAL      << '\n';
19:       cout << BINARY           << '\n';
20:       cout << DECIMAL          << '\n';
21:       cout << FLOATING_POINT << '\n';
22:   }
```

Each of the seven constants at lines 5-11 is associated with the text to the right of the identifier in uppercase. These values are aligned vertically to make them easier to read. However, a single space is all that's required to separate an identifier from its value. C++ ignores the extra spaces used here.

You can also add a comment after a #define control line. To do this, insert at least one space and a double slash after the constant's value:

```
#define FLOATING_POINT  3.14159    // Value for Pi
```

Or you can use C-style comments:

```
#define FLOATING_POINT  3.14159    /* Value for Pi */
```

Declared Constants

A second, and often preferred, way to create constants in programs is to preface a normal variable definition with the key word const. The compiler rejects any statements that attempt to change values defined this way.

Listing 1.14 demonstrates how to create constants with const. Compare this program with DEFINE.CPP. Notice that the const definitions specify data types, end with semicolons, and are initialized like variables. The earlier #defined symbols do not specify data types, do not use the assign symbol (=), and do not end with semicolons.

Listing 1.14. CONST.CPP

```
 1:   // const.cpp -- Demonstrate declared constants
 2:
 3:   #include <stream.hpp>
 4:
 5:   const char  CHARACTER       = '@';
 6:   const char  STRING[]        = "Learning C++";
 7:   const int   OCTAL           = 0233;
 8:   const int   HEXADECIMAL     = 0x9b;
 9:   const int   BINARY          = 0b10011011;
10:   const int   DECIMAL         = 155;
11:   const float FLOATING_POINT  = 3.14159;
12:
13:   main()
14:   {
15:       cout << CHARACTER       << '\n';
16:       cout << STRING          << '\n';
17:       cout << OCTAL           << '\n';
18:       cout << HEXADECIMAL     << '\n';
19:       cout << BINARY          << '\n';
20:       cout << DECIMAL         << '\n';
21:       cout << FLOATING_POINT  << '\n';
22:   }
```

Except for the STRING constant at line 6, the constant identifiers are declared the same way in the DEFINE and CONST programs. In CONST.CPP at line 6, STRING ends with square brackets ([ ]). You'll understand the purpose of this better after you learn about arrays in C++, which are symbolized by brackets. The brackets after STRING tell C++ to create an *array* of characters—in other words, a string of multiple char variables. Without the brackets, the compiler would consider line 6 to define a *single* char, not an array of them. The brackets aren't needed in the DEFINE program because #defined constants simply associate text with symbols; the compiler doesn't care what that text is composed of until the symbol is used.

Another significant difference between #defined constants and those created with const is *when* the compiler evaluates a value. For instance, suppose that you write

```
#define X 5
#define Y X + 10
```

As you might expect, X is associated with the value 5. Y is associated with X + 10. Be careful with such definitions, however. They can introduce bugs! Only the *text* X + 10 is associated with Y, not the result of that expression. This may cause surprising consequences in statements like this:

```
cout << "X = " << X << " Y = " << Y;
```

When C++ compiles that statement, it inserts the *text* 5 and the *text* X + 10 in place of X and Y. The expression X + 10 is then evaluated when this statement is compiled, *not* earlier when the Y constant was defined. Because of this, if the program executes the following lines before the output-stream statement:

```
#undef   X
#define X 10
```

X will have a different value when the statement is compiled; and, therefore, so will the expression X + 10. The #undef control command *undefines* a symbol previously created with #define. Undefining a symbol throws that symbol away—necessary to avoid an error if you later redefine the same symbol with another #define.

If you try these lines in a test program, you'll see that redefining X causes Y to change because the expression associated with Y is evaluated only later when Y is used, not when Y is defined. In some cases, this might be useful, but it does reduce the "constant-ness" of #defined symbols, which as this experiment proves, are easily changed to new values. Constants defined with const can *never* be changed like this, and, therefore, they are safer. (Or, at least, they are "more constant.")

There are two other advantages to using const to create constants in programs instead of #define. One, the compiler can often generate more efficient code with const constants. Two, because the definitions specify data types, the compiler can immediately check whether the literal constants in the const definitions are in the correct forms. With #define, the compiler can't do that until a statement uses the constant identifier, making any errors in the constant more difficult to recognize.

Enumerated Constants

Some things just naturally go together: paper and pens, gears and motors, ice and snow. To categorize such lists, you might give them names like implements, gizmos, and badWeather. In programs, to represent these kinds of lists, you might begin by defining a few constants:

```
#define PAPER 0
#define PEN 1
```

Then you could use the constant names PAPER and PEN to make programs more readable, letting the compiler replace the descriptive names with the underlying values 0 and 1. The values have no special meanings; they serve only to give the identifiers substance so that they can be used in statements.

You'll see this idea applied often in programs, and there's nothing wrong with the technique. But instead of defining individual constants this way and giving them underlying values, you can use *enumerated constants* to create categorized lists that accomplish the same goal and let the compiler do more of the work. The classic example of an enumerated constant is a list of colors, which you might declare this way:

```
enum colors {RED, ORANGE, YELLOW, GREEN, BLUE, INDIGO, VIOLET};
```

This associates the constant elements listed between the braces—RED, ORANGE, ..., VIOLET—with the identifier colors, the name assigned to this new data type. The key word enum tells the compiler that these items should be *enumerated*—that is, associated with sequential numbers. When processing this directive, the compiler assigns a value starting with 0 to each enumerated element so that RED is equivalent to 0, ORANGE is 1, and so on. The compiler *enumerates* the identifiers, so you don't have to.

After declaring a new enumerated data type, you can create variables of that type just as you do for other data types. For example, to define a variable of type colors, you can write:

```
colors favoriteColor = INDIGO;
```

This creates a variable named favoriteColor of type colors and assigns to that variable the initial value INDIGO. Because favoriteColor is a variable, an assignment statement can also give it a new value like this:

```
favoriteColor = ORANGE;
```

By using const, you can define a constant color that other statements can't change:

```
const colors lastingColor = RED;
```

However you use enumerated constants, as these samples show, they greatly enhance a program's readability. In a program, if you come across an uncommented statement like color = 4, you'll have to track down the meaning of 4 in a reference to find out what color the program is assigning to color. The assignment color = BLUE is perfectly clear on its own.

Listing 1.15, ENUM.CPP, shows a few more examples of enumerated constants, and illustrates some of the ways programs can use them.

Listing 1.15. ENUM.CPP

```
1:    // enum.cpp -- Demonstrate enumerated types
2:
3:    #include <stream.hpp>
4:
5:    enum LANGUAGE {ASSEMBLY, BASIC, C, CPP, FORTRAN, PASCAL} language;
6:    enum scale {DO, RE, MI, FA, SOL, LA, TI};
7:    enum {FALSE, TRUE};
8:
9:    main()
10:   {
11:       scale tone = LA;
12:       int timeFlies = TRUE;
13:
14:       language = CPP;
15:       cout << "language = " << (int)language << '\n';
16:       cout << "tone = " << (int)tone << '\n';
17:       cout << "timeFlies = " << timeFlies << '\n';
18:   }
```

Line 5 declares the enumerated type LANGUAGE, using all uppercase letters for the data type name. At the end of this same line, the declaration also defines a variable named language, using all lowercase letters. As you can see, line 14 then assigns one of the listed LANGUAGE elements to the variable.

> **Note:** This typical style is used by many C and C++ programmers—create a new data type with uppercase letters and a variable of the same name but in lowercase. Programmers use this style when they want to create the data type and a variable of that type with a single declaration, but I included this sample only because it's so common. In my own code, I prefer to avoid using case to distinguish between data types and variables.

Line 6 declares only a new type, no variable—my preferred style. The declaration associates the data type name scale with music's sol-fa symbols, DO, RE, ME, FA, SOL, LA, and TI. (Because they are constants, I spell these elements in uppercase. In music, the symbols are usually written in lowercase.) After creating the scale data type, line 11 defines a variable tone of type scale and also assigns to tone the initial value LA.

Line 7 demonstrates how to create unnamed enumerated data types, which are occasionally useful. C++ allows this to simplify the job of creating enumerated lists of names that you can use in place of int values. In this sample, the elements FALSE and TRUE add these *Boolean* values to C++ (which Pascal fans will recognize).

FALSE equals 0, and TRUE equals 1. As with other enumerated types, using these names in statements that deal with the truth or falsity of various conditions makes programs more readable than if those same statements used the literal constant values 0 and 1.

Notice that line 12 makes use of the new Boolean names to define the variable timeFlies, to which it assigns the value of TRUE. It's possible to assign TRUE or FALSE to int variables this way because those symbols were listed in an unnamed enumerated type at line 7. If that link had declared the type in the usual way with a name

```
enum Boolean {FALSE, TRUE};
```

then the definition at line 12 would no longer compile. C++ is strict about assigning values to variables—in all cases, the data types must agree. Even though the underlying elements TRUE and FALSE are associated with integer values 0 and 1, because they are declared in the named Boolean type, C++ will allow assigning the symbols only to variables of that same type. Because of C++'s strict typing rules, int and Boolean types are incompatible.

But there's nothing wrong with using a data type name in an enum declaration like Boolean. To create a variable of that type, change line 12 to this:

```
enum Boolean timeFlies   = TRUE;
```

If you make this change, line 17 also needs changing. An output stream doesn't know what a Boolean data type is (without modification, it recognizes only standard C++ data types). To display the value of timeFlies requires a type cast:

```
cout << "timeFlies = " << (int)timeFlies << '\n';
```

When you run Listing 1.15, you'll have this same problem with displaying the other two enumerated data types. Even though it seems as though the output-stream statements in lines 15-17 should display the enumerated constant elements CPP, LA, and TRUE, the program instead displays these values:

```
language = 3
tone = 5
timeFlies = 1
```

Because output streams don't know what scale and LANGUAGE are, the output statements must cast the values to type int. Furthermore, names associated with these enumerated data types exist solely in the program text. When the program runs, the elements are converted to the numbers that this sample code displays.

Assigning Enumerated Element Values

Usually, it's best to let the compiler assign sequential values to enumerated data type elements. But when the need arises, you can change the values that the compiler associates with each element. For example, suppose that you are writing a program to play chess. You might begin by creating an enumerated data type that lists the piece names:

```
enum piece {PAWN, KNIGHT, BISHOP, ROOK, QUEEN, KING};
```

By design, the compiler assigns the values 0 to PAWN, 1 to KNIGHT, 2 to BISHOP, and so on, up to 5 for the KING. However, it would be more useful if the enumerated values reflected the relative importance of each piece—information that the program could use to calculate the computer's next move. To assign specific values to the enumerated elements, follow one or more elements with an equal sign and the value you want:

```
enum piece {PAWN= 2, KNIGHT= 6, BISHOP= 7, ROOK= 10,
   QUEEN = 18, KING = 10000};
```

These values correspond with standard chess-piece values; a knight is worth three pawns, a rook is worth five pawns, and so on. I doubled these values because a bishop is typically worth 3.5 pawns (just a little more valuable than a knight). It's not possible to assign floating point values like 3.5 to enumerated elements—only integer values are allowed. Doubling the standard rates keeps the ratios the same ($2 \times 3.5 = 7$).

You don't have to assign values to every element as in this sample. After the last explicit assignment, the compiler starts the next element with the next value in sequence. For example, consider this declaration:

```
enum trafficLight {GREEN, YELLOW = 10, RED};
```

In this case, GREEN equals 0, YELLOW equals 10, and RED equals 11. If any elements came after RED, they would have increasing values starting with 12. You can also assign more than one explicit value, giving those between increasing values in sequence:

```
enum error {NO_ERROR, ERR_MEMORY, ERR_INPUT, ERR_OUTPUT,
   ERR_DISK = 100, ERR_READ, ERR_WRITE, ERR_NOTFOUND,
   ERR_KEYBOARD = 200, ERR_BADKEY, ERR_DIGIT_EXPECTED,
   ERR_PRINTER = 300, ERR_NOPAPER, ERR_JAMMED};
```

In the error enumerated type, NO_ERROR equals 0—the default starting value for all enumerated types. Because successive symbols increase by one automatically unless the type specifies another value, ERR_MEMORY, ERR_INPUT, and ERR_OUTPUT equal 1, 2, and 3, respectively. ERR_DISK begins a new sequence starting at 100. After that, symbols begin increasing by one again, so ERR_READ equals 101, ERR_WRITE is 102, and ERR_NOTFOUND is 103. Similarly, ERR_KEYBOARD and ERR_PRINTER begin new sequences at 200 and 300. The symbols following these two equal 201, 202, 301, 302, and so on.

As a result of this design, you can add new error names—for example, inserting ERR_EOF (end of file) at the end of the second line without changing the underlying values of the other symbols. When you need to create enumerated data types of elements with values that match other constants (such as operating system error numbers, I/O-port values, and other fixed quantities), the capability to start new sequences inside an enum type declaration is extremely useful. Most of the time, however, you can let C++ choose the element values for you.

Operators

C++ is loaded with operators—symbols that perform various operations on their arguments. The lowly plus sign (+) is an operator. In an expression, as you might expect, it adds two values:

```
a = b + c;
```

The symbols a, b, and c could be of any numeric data types, and the effect is obvious: b is added to c, and the result is assigned to a.

The equal sign in that expression is itself an operator, with the unique capability of copying a value to its right to the memory location represented by the symbol to its left. Two terms represent this action: *rvalue* and *lvalue*. (These are not programming symbols, but you'll find them in other C and C++ references, so you should understand what they mean.) An *rvalue* is something that can appear on the right side of an equal sign, and *lvalue* is something that can appear on the left. With minor exceptions, rvalues are temporary items, usually the results of expressions like b + c, and lvalues are the names of variables or other constructions that refer to places in memory where values can be stored.

Technical terms like rvalue and lvalue are not as important to memorize as compiler instruction manuals and some references would have you believe. The purpose of a = b + c is pretty darn obvious whether or not you can identify which part is the rvalue and which is the lvalue. Just be aware of these terms in case you encounter them elsewhere.

Operators and Precedence

Of course, C++ has a few more operators in addition to the plus sign. Besides the usual + (plus), – (minus), / (divide), and * (times), there are operators that create functions, operators for arrays, operators that increment and decrement values, and complex operators that perform more than one job at a time. As you read this book, you'll see all these operators in action.

Appendix B lists C++'s operators and also shows their *precedence* levels. In normal use, operators of higher precedence perform their operations in expressions before operators of lower precedence. For example, the expression to the right of the equal sign in this statement

```
a = b + c * d;
```

multiplies c and d and then adds that product to b before assigning the total to a. The expression works this way because the times operator (*) has a higher precedence than +. To force a different evaluation order, use parentheses:

```
a = (b + c) * d;
```

There's no need to enclose the entire expression in parentheses, although you can write ((b + c) * d) if you want. The = operator in C++ has a lower precedence than *; therefore, the entire expression is evaluated before the result is assigned to a.

Regardless of precedence level, operations inside parentheses are always completed before operators outside get their chance to act. In this sample, the parentheses force the addition to occur before the multiplication, which may give different results depending on the initial values of b, c, and d.

Increment and Decrement Operators

Two of C++'s most intriguing operators, which are also available in C, are ++ (increment) and −− (decrement). The ++ operator (pronounced "plus plus") adds one to its argument. The −− operator ("minus minus") subtracts one.

> **Note:** C++ ("C Plus Plus") takes its name from the ++ operator. It's one step beyond C.

A few examples show how useful the increment and decrement operators can be:

```
i = i + 1;   // Add 1 to i
i++;         // Same as above
j = j - 1;   // Subtract 1 from j
j--          // Same as above
```

The first line adds 1 to an int variable i, assigning the result of that addition back to i and replacing i's original value. The effect, of course, is to increment i by 1—an operation neatly performed by the second line. The expression i++ has the identical result of i = i + 1, but requires you to type the variable name only once. Similarly, the third line subtracts 1 from another int variable j. The fourth line is shorter and is functionally identical to the line above.

A concept that strikes some people as strange at first is that expressions such as i++ have actions (increasing i by 1) and values (the value of i *before* the increase). The concept will be clearer if you consider that (b + c) (an expression) also has a value—the value of the two elements added together.

Normally, if you do nothing else with an expression's value—usually storing it in memory—it just floats away. But the expressions i++ and j-- are special; they perform an action on their arguments (incrementing i and decrementing j), and they have values. However, because the operator follows its argument, the value of the expression i++ equals the o r i g i n a l value before the increment takes effect. In other words, if i equals 100, i++ has the value 100 *and* increases i to 101—an action with significance in expressions like this:

```
j = i++;
```

Again, if i equals 100, this expression sets j to 100 *before* ++ increments i. The expression does *not* assign i + 1 to j as many people assume on first glance. In fact, the preceding expression is just a convenient way to write these statements:

```
j = i;
i = i + 1;
```

If you remember this expanded version, you'll never forget that the value of i++ equals i. This is always true when the ++ operator follows its argument. But if the ++ or -- operators appear in front of their arguments, they take effect *before* the expression's value is formed. Once again, assuming that i equals 100, this statement, like the previous ones, increments i:

```
j = ++i;
```

However, because ++ appears before i, the operator increments i *before* the result is assigned to j; therefore, after the assignment, if i was originally 100, both i and j now equal 101. Expressions like j = ++i are simply shorthand for these two statements:

```
i = i + 1;
j = i;
```

The only difference between i++ and ++i is the value of the expression. The effect on the target variable is the same—both forms increment i. Similarly, both i-- and --i subtract 1 from i, but the expression *values* of i++ and i-- equal i. The expression values of ++i and --i equal the original value of i plus or minus 1.

When you don't assign the result of ++ and -- to a variable, it doesn't matter whether the operator precedes or follows its argument. Assuming that the following identifiers are int variables, these statements increment each of those variables by one:

```
weight++;     // weight = weight + 1
balance++;    // balance = balance + 1
score++;      // score = score + 1
```

Placing the operators first gives the identical results:

```
++weight;     // weight = weight + 1
++balance;    // balance = balance + 1
++score;      // score = score + 1
```

Most programmers follow arguments with ++, but the choice is yours to make. However, you don't have this same option when using ++ and -- in complex expressions or in assignment statements. For example, this statement

```
n = (x++) * (y--);
```

does not give the same results as the following expression for all values of x and y:

```
n = (++x) * (--y);
```

In the first case, the ++ and -- operators follow their arguments; therefore, n is assigned the product of x * y. In the second case, the operators precede their arguments, thus giving those expressions the results *after* the increments take place. In this second example, n is assigned the product of (x + 1) * (y - 1). In both examples, the effects on the final values of x and y are identical.

Using ++ and -- takes practice and careful thought at first, but eventually, you'll find these special operators among the most useful in C++. A sample program will help make the concepts clear. Compile and run Listing 1.16, INCDEC.CPP. Enter test integer values to see the effects of applying ++ and -- on variables equal to the values you supply.

Listing 1.16. INCDEC.CPP

```
 1:   //incdec.cpp -- Demonstrate increment(++) and decrement(--) operators
 2:
 3:   #include <stream.hpp>
 4:
 5:   main()
 6:   {
 7:       int v;
 8:
 9:       cout << "Enter an integer value: ";
10:       cin >> v;
11:       cout << "\n         Before   During   After\n";
12:       cout << "v++    " << v << "         " << v++ << "         " << v << '\n';
13:       cout << "v--    " << v << "         " << v-- << "         " << v << '\n';
14:       cout << "++v    " << v << "         " << ++v << "         " << v << '\n';
15:       cout << "--v    " << v << "         " << --v << "         " << v << '\n';
16:   }
```

Run INCDEC and enter a value such as 100, which the program assigns to an i n t variable v. Four output-stream statements in lines 12-15 then display the value of v before, during, and after applying the operators ++ and -- in front of and after v. When examining the displayed values, remember that you are seeing the results of the *expressions,* not necessarily the final value of v after an operator is applied to it.

Expressions

Computers are great at crunching numbers. Who hasn't used one to chew up a formula and spit out the results? *Expressions* are a computer language's number crunchers—a way for you to give instructions to a program about what it should do with various values.

In this chapter, you learned about input and output, variables and constants, and expressions and operators. Combining these elements—by no means the whole C++ story—lets you write useful programs that can quickly give answers to complex problems.

As an example, Listing 1.17, TAX.CPP, implements the answer to a simple problem in algebra. Given a dollar amount such as $155.76, and a tax rate of 0.06, what is the retail price of the item, and how much tax was charged? Before running the listing, you might want to try writing your own program to give the correct answer for any value and tax rate.

Listing 1.17. TAX.CPP

```
1:   // tax.cpp -- Calculate list price knowing tax rate and price paid
2:
3:   #include <stream.hpp>
4:   #include <stdlib.h>
5:
6:   main()
7:   {
8:       float list, paid, rate, tax;
9:       char s[80];  // Input string
10:
11:      cout << "Price paid? ";
12:      cin >> s;
13:      paid = atof(s);
14:      cout << "Tax rate (ex: .06)? ";
15:      cin >> s;
16:      rate = atof(s);
17:
18:      list = paid / ( 1 + rate );
```

```
19:        tax = paid - list;
20:        cout << form("List price = $%8.2f\n", list );
21:        cout << form("Tax paid   = $%8.2f\n", tax );
22:    }
```

You should have little trouble understanding how TAX.CPP works. The program contains nothing you haven't seen before. After defining a few local variables at lines 8-9, input- and output-stream statements prompt for prices and tax rates. To prevent errors, responses are stored in a string (s) and converted to floating point values. Then two assignment statements at lines 18-19 use expressions to calculate the list price and tax paid, displayed by two more output statements at lines 20-21.

This completes your introduction to C++. As TAX.CPP illustrates, you have learned enough of the language to write simple programs. Before continuing with the next chapter, try to complete some of the exercises that follow. You can finish them all by using only the fundamental elements of C++ introduced in this chapter. (If you get stuck, you'll find the answers to the exercises in the back of this book.)

As you use the features covered in this chapter to write your own C++ programs, you'll soon realize that something is missing. Programs often need to make decisions—to change course based on various conditions and to execute the same statements more than once. You'll notice also that simple variables can't store more complex items such as database records and arrays of multiple values. To accomplish these and other goals, you need to learn about C++'s advanced operators, and you'll need ways to alter the flow of a program, bending its normal straightforward course to follow new paths. As you'll learn in the next chapter, these features alone can add an amazing level of power to C++ programs.

Questions and Exercises

1.1. Write a program that prompts for your first name and then prints a message that includes the name you enter.

1.2. Explain the significance of the symbols //, /*, and */ in these lines:

```
/* prompt for input */
cout << "Enter value: ";    // Prompt for a value
cin >> value;               // Get value from user
```

1.3. Write the smallest possible C++ program that compiles and runs.

1.4. Which of these identifier(s) are legal: myMoney, 2for1, _max, max_Value, $Balance, A_L_P_H_A_B_E_T_? How can you prove your answer?

1.5. Write a program that displays C++'s punctuators.

1.6. Explain what white space is and what it's used for.

1.7. Enter the following program into a file named OUT.CPP. The program demonstrates two ways to write text to the standard output (usually the display). Unfortunately, when you compile OUT, you receive an error from the compiler. Why? Fix the program so that it runs.

```
main()
{
    cout << "\nSample C++ output-stream statement";
    printf("\nSample C and C++ prntf() statement");
}
```

1.8. What data type or types can store the values 145540, 145.543, and 10? What is the *smallest* type that can store those values?

1.9. With a single line of code, define a variable named alpha of type char and assign the character 'A' to the variable.

1.10. What are the two main differences between a local and a global variable?

1.11. Write a statement to display the value 134 justified to the right of a 12-character column.

1.12. Write a program to display the following line where the values 64, 10, 11, 27, and 1300.76 are stored in integer variables named age, month, day, year, and a floating point variable balance:

```
Age = 64, Birth Date = 10/11/27, Balance = $1300.76
```

1.13. Write two programs that prompt for a floating-point value named rainFall (the exact name doesn't matter). Use an input-stream statement in the first program to store your response directly in the variable. Use a string in the second program and convert that string to a floating-point value. Why is the second method safer?

1.14. Write a program that displays the sentence "It's raining "dogs and cats" in here!" *including* the four double quotes and apostrophe.

1.15. Write a program that assigns the single quote character (') to a character variable and then displays that variable.

1.16. Write a program that declares two constants named MIN equal to 1 and MAX equal to 999. Display the constants in output-stream statements.

1.17. Create an enumerated data type named flowers with the elements ROSE, CARNATION, ORCHID, and GARDENIA.

1.18. If count equals 98, what do the expressions count++, ++count, count--, and --count equal if executed in that order? What is the final value of count? Predict the results and then insert the statements into a program to prove your answers.

1.19. The circumference of a circle equals its diameter times π. Write a program that prompts for the diameter of a circle and displays the circle's circumference.

Chapter 2

Making Statements and Building Structures

Computer programs operate a lot like engines. They burn fuel (use data) and perform work (execute statements). Without fuel, the engine won't go, and, without an engine, the fuel may as well stay in the ground.

Most programs need both fuel and a working engine—that is, data and statements—to perform useful jobs. As you may expect, C++ has a variety of data structure types for storing information in memory. It also has a number of statement forms that, among other tasks, can make decisions, repeat actions, and select matching elements from a set of values.

Learning C++'s fundamental data structures and statement types isn't difficult. In fact, when you first meet them, these elementary programming tools may seem to be almost too simple to be of much practical use. This is natural, and it illustrates one of the reasons that many people never advance beyond a simple knowledge of programming with a general-purpose language like C++ (or C or Pascal). They memorize the basics—the way they might commit to memory a list of parts in a machine shop—but they fail to learn how to combine those parts to create programs that can shift computers into high gear.

For that reason, instead of documenting each data structure and statement form one by one as a compiler manual might do, in this chapter, I'll introduce C++ data and statement fundamentals in (mostly) practical settings. You'll learn not only *what* a structure is, but *how* you can apply it to solve problems. Later chapters will expand this "learn by doing" theme.

The doings in this chapter begin with C++'s advanced operators, which among other things, let you write programs that can make decisions and manipulate bits in memory—two seemingly unrelated topics that, like religion and politics, have more in common than many people suppose. You'll also learn how to alter the flow of a program, making certain statements execute based on various conditions—a simple concept that gives most programs their true power.

> **Note:** Compile and run the listings in this chapter as you did the examples in chapter 1. Try also to modify the statements to add personal touches—to display a title when the program starts, to modify a constant value, or to perform I/O with a custom twist. Making changes to existing programs and then seeing the effects of those changes is a great way to learn C++ and to gain more experience with programming in general.

Advanced Operators

In chapter 1, you learned about some of C++'s operators—symbols that perform actions on their arguments. For example, the plus sign (+) is an operator with an obvious purpose in life and programming—to add two values.

In this section, you'll meet some of C++'s less obvious operators, which can compare values, evaluate expressions, and manipulate bits in memory. You'll also learn how to use handy shorthand notations for writing expressions.

Good Relations

C++'s *relational operators* let you write program statements to compare values. Suppose that you need to determine whether a count variable is less than 10. To do that, you can use the less-than relational operator (<) to compare count and a target value in an expression such as count < 10.

When a program executes a relational expression like that, it *evaluates* its arguments to produce a true or false result, which a program can then use to decide what to do next. Obviously, count is either less than 10 or it's not; there's no middle ground to consider. The expression count < 10 therefore will either be true or false. The same is true of all relational expressions that use one or more of the operators listed in Table 2.1. In every case, expressions that use these operators evaluate to a single true or false result.

Table 2.1. Relational Operators

Operator	Description	Example
<	Less than	(a < b)
<=	Less than or equal	(a <= b)
>	Greater than	(a > b)
>=	Greater than or equal	(a >= b)
==	Equal	(a == b)
!=	Not equal	(a != b)

Note: Internally, C++ reduces a relational expression to an integer value 0 for false or 1 for true. Store this fact in the back of your mind. You'll need it later.

You can use any of the operators in Table 2.1 in expressions to compare two integer, character, or floating-point values. (Comparing strings requires more work—more on that in chapter 4.) Notice especially that the symbol for equality is *two* equal signs (==), not one. The expression (a == b) evaluates to true only if a and b represent the same value. The expression (a = b) *assigns* the value of b to a. Confusing these two nearly identical expressions is one of the most common mistakes that C++ (and C) programmers make. Worse, the compiler frequently allows you to interchange the relational expression and assignment statements, so it's up to you to use the correct forms.

The first sample program in this chapter, Listing 2.1, MILES.CPP, uses relational operators in a typical way—to let people choose various options from a menu displayed on screen. In this case, the problem is to convert miles and kilometers or to quit without making a calculation. Depending on which choice people make, the program performs different actions. When you run MILES, enter 1 and then a number of miles to convert to kilometers. Enter 2 and a number of kilometers for the equivalent in miles. Or enter 3 to quit. Also try entering other values to see how the program deals with illegal menu choices.

Listing 2.1. MILES.CPP

```
1:  // miles.cpp -- Miles to Kilometers converter
2:
3:  #include <stream.hpp>
4:
5:  #define MILES_PER_KM 0.6214
6:  #define KMS_PER_MILE 1.6093
7:
8:  main()
```

```
 9:    {
10:        int choice;
11:        float km, miles;
12:
13:        cout << "\nMiles and Kilometers Converter\n";
14:        cout << "-----------------------------\n";
15:        cout << "1 : Miles to kilometers\n";
16:        cout << "2 : Kilometers to miles\n";
17:        cout << "3 : Quit\n\n";
18:        cout << "Enter 1, 2, or 3: ";
19:        cin >> choice;
20:
21:        if (choice == 1) {
22:          cout << "Miles? ";
23:          cin >> miles;
24:          km = miles * KMS_PER_MILE;
25:          cout << miles << " miles = " << km << " kilometers\n";
26:        }
27:        else if (choice == 2) {
28:          cout << "Kilometers? ";
29:          cin >> km;
30:          miles = km * MILES_PER_KM;
31:          cout << km << " kilometers = " << miles << " miles\n"
32:        }
33:        else if (choice != 3)
34:            cout << "Illegal choice!";
35:    }
```

Introducing if/else, *the Decision Maker*

MILES.CPP uses a statement form that I'll dissect for you later in more detail. This statement, called i f / e l s e, is C++'s main decision maker. It's simple to use—just add a relational expression after the key word i f and then type the statements you want the program to perform *if* that expression evaluates to true. For example, to display the value of a variable c o u n t only if that value is greater than 100, you could use the statement

```
if (count > 100) cout << "Count = " << count << '\n';
```

Only if c o u n t is greater than 100 does the output-stream statement execute. If c o u n t is less than or equal to 100, the program completely skips the statement. The expression (c o u n t > 100) *must* be enclosed in parentheses.

Small if statements like this one are typically written on a single line. Usually I prefer to use two lines, indenting the target statement one tab stop like this:

```
if (count > 100)
    cout << "Count = " << count << '\n';
```

Either way is correct; C++ cares nothing about how a program looks, only that its parts and pieces are in place. Putting the output statement on its own indented line just makes the program easier to read. It doesn't change the way it compiles or runs.

To make an if statement "decide" whether to perform more than one statement, surround those statements with braces. This is called a *compound statement* or a *block*. In chapter 1, you learned that blocks can nest inside other blocks, creating levels or scopes in a program. A more practical use for blocks is to create compound statements that combine one or more statements into a *single* statement. For example, using a block, you can revise the previous sample to execute two statements if count is less than or equal to 10:

```
if (count <= 10) {
    cout << "Count is less than or equal to 10\n";
    cout << "Count = " << count << '\n';
}
```

This if statement is composed of two output stream statements, but syntactically, it's a single statement, and it can go wherever single statements are allowed in a program. This is a powerful tool. Anywhere you can write a single statement, you can *always* insert a compound statement delimited with braces. In this way, you can make programs execute multiple statements even though the language specifications may tell you that only a single statement is allowed at such and such a place.

The positions of the braces aren't critical. They could go anywhere as long as they mark or *delimit* the compound statement that should execute only if the relational expression is true. As in the sample before this one, the indentations are purely stylistic; they have no effect on the program's outcome. Every programmer, it seems, has a unique brace and indentation style, and you're free to pick one that suits you. The style shown here is one of the most popular, and it isolates the fragment nicely in the program text, making it stand out clearly. However, some programmers insist on placing all braces on separate lines like this:

```
if (count <= 10)
{
    ...
}
```

> **Note:** Although most compound-statement blocks consist of at least two statements, surrounding a single statement with braces does no harm.

Getting back to Listing 2.1, MILES.CPP, examine lines 21-26 to see another sample compound i f statement. In this case, if the menu selection variable choice equals 1 (note the double equal sign), the four statements surrounded by braces execute. If choice is not 1, the program skips these statements and continues at line 27.

At that line, you see an example of the if statement's alter ego, else. An else clause, which is always optional, executes a statement or block if the if's relational expression is false. In other words, if displays the value of count if it's greater than 100, but if not, you can display an error message by writing

```
if (count > 100)
    cout << "Count = " << count << '\n';
else
    cout << "ERROR: Count is not greater than 100\n";
```

Either or both of the target statements after if and else may be surrounded by braces to allow multiple statements in those locations:

```
if (count > 100) {
    // statements to execute if expression is true
} else {
    // statements to execute if expression is false
}
```

The else clause can also begin a new if statement, as in line 27 of MILES.CPP. This is handy for selecting one of a number of possibilities:

```
if (choice == 1) {
    // statements to execute for choice == 1
} else if (choice == 2) {
    // statements to execute for choice == 2
} else if (choice == 3) {
    // statements to execute for choice == 3
} else {
    // statements to execute for all other choice values
}
```

The final else clause in this construction executes if all other relational expressions in the preceding if statements evaluate to false. Lines 33-34 of MILES.CPP use this same idea a little differently:

```
else if (choice != 3)
    cout << "Illegal choice!";
```

If choice is 3, the program simply quits. If choice is not 3, it must be a value not listed in the menu, and the program displays an error message. Considerations like these—what to do when a value falls outside a specified range or when it doesn't match known possibilities—are important to ponder. Always do your best to write if/else and other statements that take all potential events into account.

Making Sense Out of Logical Operators

As you learned in the previous section, relational operators enable you to write expressions that perform actions based on the truth or falsehood of various conditions. Logical operators expand on this idea, giving you the means to evaluate multiple relational expressions to a single true or false result. For example, suppose that you want to display the value of count only if it's *between* 1 and 100. One way to do that is for a program statement to combine the results of two relational expressions using C++'s *logical AND* operator, &&:

```
if ((count >= 1) && (count <= 100))
    cout << "Count = " << count << '\n';
```

You could also write the statement in a form that resembles the one used by mathematicians to express a value within range of high and low limits, as in *1 <= count <= 100:*

```
if ((1 <= count) && (count <= 100))
    cout << "Count = " << count << '\n';
```

Either way, in both of these samples, the if statement's relational expression ((1 <= count) && (count <= 100)) is true only if count represents a value from 1 to 100. To reach that conclusion, C++ evaluates the two inner relational expressions, and then it combines the results using the rules for logical AND, which gives a true result only if one argument *and* another are both true.

Note: Actually, C++ employs a concept known as *short-circuit expression evaluation.* This means that as soon as the result of a complex relational expression is known beyond a doubt, C++ stops evaluating other parts of that expression. For example, if count equals 0, the program "knows" that the full expression ((1 <= count) && (count <= 100)) is false as soon as it evaluates the first inner expression (1 <= count), and there's no reason to evaluate the second half of the complete expression. This helps keep programs running fast by eliminating wasteful execution of purposeless code.

Another logical operator is the *logical OR,* represented in C++ by the symbol
||. As with &&, you can use || to create complex relational expressions, for
example, to execute statements if one condition *or* another is true:

```
if ((count == 1) || (count == 100))
   cout << "Count is 1 or 100\n";
```

The effect of this sample is to execute the output stream statement only if c o u n t
equals 1 or 100. Any other values cause the full relational expression to be false,
skipping the output statement. You can also create even more complex expressions
by using parentheses judiciously to combine && and ||:

```
if (((1 <= count) && (count <= 100)) || (count == -1))
   cout << "Count is -1 or is between 1 and 100\n";
```

Here the output-stream statement executes only if c o u n t is a value between 1
and 100, or if it equals –1. Try to work through the logic until it's clear. As you can
see, even simple expressions like this one are difficult to decipher. For that reason,
it's often just as well to use multiple i f statements to improve the program's clarity:

```
if ((1 <= count) && (count <= 100))
   // Statement if count is a value from 1 to 100
else if (count == -1)
   // Statement if count is -1
```

Listing 2.2 demonstrates how to use the && logical operator to calculate a
vehicle's gas consumption and report whether the fuel use is poor, good, or
excellent. Run the program, enter your starting and ending odometer reading, and
then the number of gallons of fuel purchased. The program will use these figures to
report the average miles per gallon traveled. (The units are arbitrary, and you can just
as well enter kilometer readings and liters purchased, but in that case, you'll probably
want to change the prompts and other messages.)

Listing 2.2. GAS.CPP

```
 1:   // gas.cpp -- Gas consumption calculator
 2:
 3:   #include <stream.hpp>
 4:   #include <stdlib.h>
 5:
 6:   main()
 7:   {
 8:       float start, end, gallons, miles, consumption;
 9:
10:       cout << "Enter starting odometer reading: ";
11:       cin >> start;
12:       cout << "Enter ending odometer reading: ";
13:       cin >> end;
```

```
14:   if (start > end) {
15:       cout << "Odometer readings are reversed\n";
16:       exit(1);
17:   }
18:   cout << "Enter gallons purchased: ";
19:   cin >> gallons;
20:   miles = 1 + (end - start);
21:   consumption = miles / gallons;
22:   cout << "Consumption = " << consumption << " miles per gallon\n";
23:
24:   cout << "Your vehicle's fuel use is ";
25:       if (consumption < 20.0)
26:           cout << "poor\n";
27:       else if ((consumption >= 20.0) && (consumption < 25.0))
28:           cout << "good\n";
29:       else
30:           cout << "excellent\n";
31:}
```

After prompting for starting and ending odometer readings, GAS.CPP uses an i f statement and relational expression to detect whether s t a r t is greater than e n d (see lines 14-17). If so, the program displays an error message and halts by executing e x i t (1)—a standard function that you haven't seen before. Using e x i t to halt a program causes it to pass back to DOS the value inside parentheses, in this case 1. A batch file can retrieve this value by examining the DOS variable e r r o r l e v e l and taking an appropriate action if that value is not 0. You'll see other examples of this in later programs.

Note: Before you can use e x i t, you must include the header file STDLIB.H as GAS.CPP does at line 4. The e x i t function is declared in that file—it's not native to C++.

A second and more complex i f statement at lines 25-30 displays a message that tells you if your vehicle's gas consumption is poor, good, or excellent. Line 25 uses a simple relational expression to detect c o n s u m p t i o n values less than 20. Line 27 uses a logical AND operator and two relational expressions to handle values above 20 and less than 25. A final e l s e clause takes care of any values greater than or equal to 25. (You'll have to adjust the literal constants in these statements if you are converting GAS.CPP to report on kilometers per liter or other units.)

The important lesson to learn from GAS.CPP is how relational expressions and logical operators are used to change the way the program operates. GAS.CPP "decides" which of several statements to execute based on relational expressions, all of which evaluate to true or false results. Using relational expressions and i f / e l s e statements lets the program change course based on its input data—a simple but complete example of how data and action cooperate in programs to create meaningful results.

Forget Me NOT

In addition to the relational operators that take two arguments, C++ also has one unary relational operator called *NOT* and represented by an exclamation point (!). The *NOT* operator reverses the result of a relational expression, changing true to false or false to true. To execute a statement if a condition is *not* true, you can write something like this:

```
if (!(count < 100))
    cout << "Count is >= 100" << '\n';
```

The expression (! (count < 100)) is actually two. First, the inner expression (count < 100) evaluates to true or false. Then the *not* operator is applied to that result, flipping its value. The final effect is to execute the output statement only if count is *not* less than 100. Of course, the expression (count >= 100) gives the same result and is simpler.

Bitwise Operators—Programming One Bit at a Time

A little bit goes a long way in programming. In many computer languages, it's difficult to manipulate lone bits in memory, but not in C++. As in C, programmers can write high-level C++ statements that operate on low-level details—for example, to control hardware registers by setting and resetting specific bits at certain addresses in the computer's memory space where those registers are logically located. C++ is a high-level language, but it doesn't prevent you from writing code that operates at the system level.

Another reason for accessing bits in memory is to store information in the smallest possible space. For example, a certain bit in a database record could represent a fact's current status: 1 for yes and 0 for no, or 0 for male and 1 for female. A series of bits could also represent a set of values: If bit 1 is set, value A is considered to be in the set; if bit 2 is set, value B is in the set; and so on.

Many programmers prefer to use assembly language for low-level programming that manipulates memory and hardware on a bit-by-bit level. But it's probably easier to use C++'s *bitwise operators* listed in Table 2.2. With these operators, you can manipulate single bits in integer values, with results that are comparable in speed and efficiency to assembly language.

Table 2.2. Bitwise Operators

Operator	Description
&	Bitwise AND
|	Bitwise inclusive OR
^	Bitwise exclusive OR
<<	Shift bits left
>>	Shift bits right
~	Form one's complement

> **Note:** When using bitwise operators, be careful not to confuse the first two, &
> and |, with the logical operators && and ||. As with the relational == and
> assignment = operators, C++ allows you to use the wrong operator in many
> cases without a whimper. It's up to you to use these operators correctly.

In expressions, the first three bitwise operators in Table 2.2 combine two values
according to the rules for logical AND (&), OR (|), and exclusive OR (^). Three
sample programs, TAND.CPP, TOR.CPP, and TXOR.CPP, demonstrate the effects of
these operators and also make useful tools for previewing the effects of logical
expression values you plan to use in other projects. (The *T* in these program names
stands for *Test; XOR* is a common abbreviation for *exclusive OR.*) The three programs
are nearly identical except for the operators they demonstrate. Run each one and
enter two values separated by a blank, for example **1234** 7. If you press **<Enter>** by
accident after the first value, just enter the second alone and press **<Enter>** again.

Listing 2.3 shows the first of the three test programs, TAND.CPP.

Listing 2.3. TAND.CPP

```
1:   // tand.cpp -- Test program for bitwise AND
2:
3:   #include <stream.hpp>
4:
5:   main()
6:   {
7:      unsigned int v1, v2, v3;
8:
9:      cout << "Enter values to AND: (ex: 1234 15) ";
10:     cin >> v1 >> v2;
11:
12:     v3 = v1 & v2;
```

```
13:
14:        cout << form("        %5u   %#06x   %016b\n", v1, v1, v1);
15:        cout << form("AND     %5u   %#06x   %016b\n", v2, v2, v2);
16:        cout << "======================================\n";
17:        cout << form("        %5u   %#06x   %016b\n", v3, v3, v3);
18:   }
```

Line 12 in TAND.CPP uses the rules for *bitwise AND* (see Table 2.3) to combine two unsigned int values v1 and v2. This statement also assigns the result of that combination to a third variable, v3. Lines 14-17 display the three values, using form to show the unsigned, hexadecimal, and binary forms of each value and the result of the bitwise combination.

Table 2.3. Rules for bitwise AND

A & B == C
0 & 0 == 0
0 & 1 == 0
1 & 0 == 0
1 & 1 == 1

As Table 2.3 shows, the result of combining two values *A* and *B* with the *bitwise AND* operator is 1 only if the two original bits are also 1. In all other cases, the result is 0. Run TAND.CPP and enter various test values to illustrate these rules.

A typical use for the bitwise AND operator is to mask a portion of a value, allowing only part of that value to *pass through* to the result. For example, run TAND and enter **1021 15**. The 1021 represents the original value. The 15 is called a *mask*. Here's what you see on screen:

```
        1021   0x03fd   0000001111111101
AND       15   0x000f   0000000000001111
======================================
          13   0x000d   0000000000001101
```

The mask allows bits in the original value to pass through to the result. Any place a 1 appears in the mask, the result contains the same bit as in the original value. Any place a 0 bit appears, a 0 appears in the result. The 0 in the mask *blocks* the bit in the original from passing through.

The next program, Listing 2.4, TOR.CPP, demonstrates the *bitwise inclusive OR* operator.

Listing 2.4. TOR.CPP

```
1: // tor.cpp -- Test program for bitwise inclusive OR
2:
```

```
 3:   #include <stream.hpp>
 4:
 5:   main()
 6:   {
 7:     unsigned int v1, v2, v3;
 8:
 9:     cout << "Enter values to OR inclusively: (ex: 1234 15) ";
10:     cin >> v1 >> v2;
11:
12:     v3 = v1 | v2;
13:
14:     cout << form("        %5u   %#06x   %016b\n", v1, v1, v1);
15:     cout << form("OR      %5u   %#06x   %016b\n", v2, v2, v2);
16:     cout << "====================================\n";
17:     cout << form("        %5u   %#06x   %016b\n", v3, v3, v3);
18:   }
```

TOR.CPP combines the two unsigned int values v1 and v2 using the rules for bitwise inclusive OR (see Table 2.4) or just *bitwise OR*. In this case, the result of using the | operator is 1 if either or both bits in the two arguments are 1. The result is 0 only if both bits are also 0.

Table 2.4. Rules for bitwise OR

A	B == C
0	0 == 0
0	1 == 1
1	0 == 1
1	1 == 1

The bitwise OR operator is often used to insert bits into values. Suppose that a variable contains the value 152, or 10011000 in binary. To change the 6th and 8th bits to 1, use a mask value of 5. Try this by running TOR and enter **152 5**. On screen, you'll see

```
        152   0x0098   0000000010011000
OR        5   0x0005   0000000000000101
====================================
        157   0x009d   0000000010011101
```

The result contains all of the bits from the original with the bits of the mask inserted where 0s appeared before. This technique is useful for setting bits in registers and other variables without disturbing other bits already there.

Listing 2.5, TXOR.CPP, illustrates how to use the bitwise exclusive OR operator.

Listing 2.5. TXOR.CPP

```
 1:    // txor.cpp -- Test program for bitwise exclusive OR
 2:
 3:    #include <stream.hpp>
 4:
 5:    main()
 6:    {
 7:        unsigned int v1, v2, v3;
 8:
 9:        cout << "Enter values to OR exclusively: (ex: 1234 15) ";
10:        cin >> v1 >> v2;
11:
12:        v3 = v1 ^ v2;
13:
14:        cout << form("      %5u   %#06x   %016b\n", v1, v1, v1);
15:        cout << form("XOR   %5u   %#06x   %016b\n", v2, v2, v2);
16:        cout << "=====================================\n";
17:        cout << form("      %5u   %#06x   %016b\n", v3, v3, v3);
18:    }
```

TXOR demonstrates how the *bitwise exclusive OR* operator (^) works. Line 12 combines v1 and v2 according to the rules listed in Table 2.5, which shows that only if the two argument bits are *different* is the result 1. If the arguments are both 0 or both 1, the result is 0.

Table 2.5. Rules for bitwise exclusive OR

A ^ B == C
0 ^ 0 == 0
0 ^ 1 == 1
1 ^ 0 == 1
1 ^ 1 == 0

Knowing how, when, and why to apply the &, |, and ^ operators takes practice. As I mentioned before, & is frequently used to mask bits in values, usually to force some bits to zero while allowing other bits to remain unchanged. For another example, run TAND and enter **45001 15**. This displays

```
        45001   0xafc9   1010111111001001
AND        15   0x000f   0000000000001111
        =====================================
            9   0x0009   0000000000001001
```

Notice how the value 15 decimal, or 1111 in binary, serves as a mask, allowing the four rightmost bits in 45001 to pass through to the result on the bottom. All other bits, whether they are 0 or 1 are forced to 0 by the zeros in the mask. This property is characteristic of a bitwise AND—bits equal to 1 in the mask allow bits in the other argument to pass through. Bits equal to 0 block bits, no matter what their values.

You can also use bitwise AND to reset individual bits to 0. For example, run TAND and enter **45001 65534**. All bits except the rightmost in 65534 equal 1, and combining that value with another therefore forces the rightmost bit in the original value (45001) to 0.

The | (bitwise OR) operator is typically used for the opposite purpose—to set bits to 1 without disturbing other bits in an integer. To see the difference between & and |, run TOR and enter the same values you entered for TAND, **45001 15**.

```
        45001   0xafc9   1010111111001001
OR         15   0x000f   0000000000001111
====================================
        45007   0xafcf   1010111111001111
```

This time, instead of serving as a mask, the value 15 (1111 in binary) forces the lower 4 bits to ones. Bits on the top pass through the zeros in the mask. This property is useful for setting individual bits. For instance, run TOR again and enter **45000 1**. As you can see, this sets the rightmost bit to 1, leaving the other bits undisturbed.

The ^ (bitwise exclusive OR) operator's properties are almost enough to make one believe in magic. The rules for XOR state that a 1 bit appears in the result only if the original two bits are different. Because of this, the XOR operator can serve as a toggle to turn 1 bits to 0 and 0 bits to 1. To see how to use XOR for this purpose, run TXOR and enter the same values, **45001 15**, that you've been using for other bitwise operators. Compare the result with the TAND and TOR tests you ran earlier:

```
        45001   0xafc9   1010111111001001
XOR        15   0x000f   0000000000001111
====================================
        44998   0xafc6   1010111111000110
```

Unlike the other two tests, the XOR operator toggled the four rightmost bits in the top value from 1 to 0 and from 0 to 1, effectively converting 1001 to 0110. Bits on top of 0 bits in the mask (the second value), are undisturbed. This becomes even more interesting when you run TXOR again and enter the result from the previous experiment along with the *same* mask, **44998 15**.

```
        44998   0xafc6   1010111111000110
XOR        15   0x000f   0000000000001111
====================================
        45001   0xafc9   1010111111001001
```

The result is the original value from the previous test, a strange but true characteristic of XOR. Applying the same operator twice with the same mask restores the original value!

Graphics programs often make use of this property to allow shapes to move on-screen without disturbing images in the background. Displaying an image by XORing its bits with other bits that represent shapes already on display, and then using the identical mask to XOR those same bits again, displays an image on top of another, then wipes the background clean without disturbing the original picture.

Another use for XOR is encryption, where a mask is XORed with all bytes in a file, thus scrambling their contents. To restore the original file contents, that same operation is simply repeated. Although this simple scheme is easily broken, more sophisticated algorithms still make use of XOR's special capability to restore original values just by applying the same mask twice.

Shifty Operations

So far, you've examined only three of C++'s six bitwise operators (see Table 2.2). The other three allow expressions to shift bits left and right and to complement all bits in integers, changing zeros to ones and ones to zeros.

If you've done any assembly language programming, you'll recognize the left shift (<<) and right shift (>>) operators as corresponding with similar processor instructions s h r and s h l. In addition to their ability to move bits around in values—which imaginative programmers put to all sorts of uses—shifting bits left and right are useful operations for performing fast integer multiplications and divisions by powers of 2.

Use C++'s bitwise shift operators in expressions such as (v 1 << 2) (shift the value in v 1 left by two bits) and (v 1 >> 1) (shift the value in v 1 right by two bits). Remember that like other expressions, the operators do not change the argument values, but instead evaluate to a result, which you will probably want to assign to another variable or use as part of a complex expression.

> **Note:** You may have noticed an unfortunate resemblance between the shift operators and I/O streams. However, even though these statements use the same symbols, because they are used so differently, it's unlikely you'll confuse them in practice. C++ *never* confuses them and can easily determine whether >> and << are shift operators or I/O stream symbols from the context of the program.

On disk are two programs TSHL.CPP and TSHR.CPP, which demonstrate the left and right shift operators. Because these programs are nearly identical to TAND.CPP, TOR.CPP, and TXOR.CPP, they aren't listed here.

Compile and run TSHL first, and enter the values **4 1**. Notice that the result is 8, or 4 * 2. Run TSHL again and enter **10 4**. This time the result is 160, or 10 * 2 ^ 4. As this shows, shifting values left a bit at a time gives the same results as multiplying those same values by successive powers of 2. Because computers typically can shift bits faster than they can multiply—which is true even with a math coprocessor—when you need to multiply by powers of 2, it's usually wise to employ bit shifts rather than multiplications.

Similarly, shifting integers right effectively divides values by successive powers of 2. Compile and run TSHR and enter test values such as **160 4** and **32767 8**. Prove to yourself that shifting values right divides those values by powers of 2.

The final bitwise operator in C++ is represented by the symbol ˜, but it works a little differently from the other bitwise operators. Instead of taking two arguments, ˜ is a unary operator that is applied to a value at right (similar to the way the NOT operator (!) works). For example, the expression ˜count complements the value of count, toggling all 1 bits to 0 and 0 bits to 1. Like other operators (except for ++ and --), this does not change count directly, and you'll need to use the result in an expression or assign it to another variable, as Listing 2.6, TCOMP.CPP, demonstrates. Run the program and enter values like **15** or **12345** to experiment with ˜.

Listing 2.6. TCOMP.CPP

```
 1:   // tcomp.cpp -- Test program for bitwise complement
 2:
 3:   #include <stream.hpp>
 4:
 5:   main()
 6:   {
 7:      unsigned int v1, v2;
 8:
 9:      cout << "Enter value to complement: ";
10:      cin >> v1;
11:
12:      v2 = ˜v1;
13:
14:      cout << form("      %5u  %#06x  %016b\n", v1, v1, v1);
15:      cout << "=====================================\n";
16:      cout << form("COMP  %5u  %#06x  %016b\n", v2, v2, v2);
17:   }
```

Combining the complement operator with other operators, often &, can sometimes be useful. For example, to set the second bit in a value count to 1, you can write

```
count = count & ˜1;
```

This is the same as executing count = count & 65534. Although the purpose of an expression like count & ˜1 is anything but crystal clear, you'll see it often in C++ and C programs. In your own code, be sure to document exactly what you are attempting to achieve with expressions like this, and use the test programs in this and previous sections to verify the results.

Combined Assignments—Expressive Shorthand

Look again at that last sample statement in the previous section, `count = count & ˜1`. It takes the value of `count`, applies the & operator to the one's complement of 1, and then assigns the result back to `count`. In this and similar cases where an operation is to be performed on a variable and then assigned right back, C++ allows a special operator shorthand known as a *combined assignment*.

To create a combined assignment operator, add an equal sign to any of the symbols +, −, *, /, %, <<, >>, &, ^, or |. For example, instead of `count = count & ˜1`, you can write

```
count &= ˜1;
```

C++ interprets the combined operator as an instruction to perform an operation on the initial value (`count` in this case) and then assign the result back to that same variable. Here are a few more samples with comments that show the equivalent longhand expressions:

```
count += 10;        // count = count + 10;
count *= 2;         // count = count * 2;
count *= count;     // count = count * count;
count %= 16;        // count = count % 16;
```

Try to use these shorthand forms whenever possible. In many cases, the results will be no different, but sometimes, the compiler will be able to generate more efficient code for a combined assignment operator than for the equivalent longhand expressions. It's difficult to predict reliably when the shorthand forms will produce such benefits, so it's best to use them when you can. In any case, the results are *never* less efficient than the longhand, although some people find the short forms a bit harder to read. If you find them confusing, add a comment, as shown in the previous samples, to explain what's going on.

That wraps up C++'s fundamental operators. With what you've learned so far, you can write some very sophisticated expressions, manipulate bits in integer values, and use the results of expressions to make decisions. By now, however, you may also have noticed a deficiency in all of the sample listings you've compiled so far. In every case, the programs begin at the top and race like mad to the finish. Of course, most computer programs don't work that way. Instead, they loop around, jump from one section to another, and don't quit until you tell them to. The next section explains how to add these capabilities and others to your code.

So It Flows

C++ programs start with the first statement inside main's block and continue to execute one statement after the other until reaching the block's closing parenthesis. At least that's true unless a statement does something to change the normal top-to-bottom flow of a program. I like to call statements in this category *program flow statements,* although that's not an official term. They're also known as *control structures.*

A program flow statement controls the order in which other statements execute. Those other statements can be of any kind—assignments, expressions, and other program flow statements. Program flow statements can halt programs dead in their tracks, make decisions, choose matching elements from sets, and repeat one or more statements. All of these actions are what give programs personality. Without program flow statements, programs simply start at the top and keep going until they run out of steam. With program flow statements, you can write programs that run until a planned event occurs or until *you* tell them to stop.

A Proper Exit

Left to their own devices, programs stop after executing the final statement in main. After that, DOS usually regains control so that you can give commands and run other programs.

Another way to halt a program is to execute an exit statement, which you saw earlier in GAS.CPP. This passes an unsigned integer value back to DOS, which a batch file can retrieve by examining errorlevel. Before using exit, a program must include the STDLIB.H header file.

Listing 2.7, YESNO.CPP, puts this idea to practical use and also demonstrates how exit affects the normal top-to-bottom flow of a program. YESNO solves a problem with DOS batch files—the lack of a batch file command to prompt a user for a yes or no answer and then change course based on the response. Compile YESNO.CPP now, but don't run the program just yet. I'll let you know when to do that.

Listing 2.7. YESNO.CPP

```
1:  // yesno.cpp -- Return errorlevel == 0 (No), 1 (Yes)
2:
3:  #include <stream.hpp>
4:  #include <stdlib.h>
5:  #include <ctype.h>
6:
```

```
 7:   main()
 8:   {
 9:       char answer;
10:
11:       cout << "Type Y for yes, N for no: ";
12:       cin >> answer;
13:       answer = toupper(answer);
14:       if (answer == 'Y')
15:           exit(1);
16:       else
17:           exit(0);
18:       cout << "This statement never executes!\n";
19:   }
```

Line 13 in YESNO.CPP assigns the value of toupper(answer) to answer, a variable of type char that holds the response to the prompt at line 11. In other words, if answer currently equals 'y', line 13 changes answer to 'Y'. This makes the if statement in line 14 easier to write because it doesn't have to test whether a response is in upper- or lowercase.

The result is that either line 15 or 17 executes depending on the answer. Any answer other than yes—for example, pressing the X key—is considered a no response. Consequently, line 18 never executes—the if/else statement at lines 14-17 guarantees that the program's normal flow will be interrupted by one of the two marked exits. I added line 18 only to demonstrate the finality of exit. You can remove this statement if you want.

Technically, toupper is a *macro*, which C++ expands to the necessary commands to convert letters to uppercase. Other symbols passed to toupper—digits and punctuation, for example—are unchanged. To use toupper, a program must include the CTYPE.H header as YESNO.CPP does at line 5.

A similar macro, tolower, also declared in CTYPE.H, converts characters to lowercase. Here are a few samples of toupper and tolower with the results listed in comments to the right:

```
toupper('a');    // == 'A'
toupper('#');    // == '#'
tolower('Q');    // == 'q'
toupper('3');    // == '3'
```

Note: Macros like toupper in C++ and in C can be very complex, and some programmers use them extensively. Strictly speaking, however, macros are not part of the C++ language, and you don't need to master them in order to write C++ programs.

Listing 2.8, TESTYN.BAT, demonstrates how to use YESNO.CPP. With YESNO.EXE and TESTYN.BAT in the current directory, enter **TESTYN** to run the batch file from the DOS prompt. When you see the message, Type Y for yes, N for no:, type **Y** or **N** and press **<Enter>**. You'll then receive a message telling you whether you answered yes or no and proving that the batch file was able to determine that answer by examining errorlevel at line 7.

Listing 2.8. TESTYN.BAT

```
 1:    echo off
 2:    rem
 3:    rem * Test YESNO.CPP
 4:    rem
 5:    echo Continue program?
 6:    yesno
 7:    if errorlevel == 1 goto YES
 8:    echo You answered no!
 9:    goto end
10:    :YES
11:    echo You answered yes!
12:    :END
```

> **Note:** The errorlevel test at line 7 in Listing 2.8 is deceiving. Although written if errorlevel == 1, the effect is the same as the C++ statement if (errorlevel >= 1). In DOS batch files, == performs the same job as >= in C++.

Reducing Complexity

There's another way to write YESNO.CPP that doesn't require an if statement and that reduces the size of the program text. As I said before, exit ends a program and passes an unsigned integer value back to DOS. Instead of writing expressions like exit(0) and exit(1), which specify literal constants inside the parentheses, you can replace those values with any expression that evaluates to an unsigned integer.

For example, consider the expression (toupper(answer) == 'Y'). This compares the result of toupper(answer) with 'Y', leaving in its wake the value 0 if the expression is false or 1 if it's true. Because the expression's value is passed to DOS via exit, there's no reason to go to all the trouble in Listing 2.7 at lines 14-17 to test whether answer equals 'Y' and execute either exit(0) or exit(1).

Instead, it's possible to eliminate that entire section by passing the expression result directly to exit:

```
exit((toupper(answer) == 'Y'));
```

Be sure that you understand how and why this works. If expressions like this throw you, take them apart, starting with the innermost items. First, toupper operates on answer, converting that character to uppercase. Then, == compares the result with 'Y'. The result of *that* expression is false (0) or true (1), and this is the value that the program passes to exit.

Using expression results this way—and taking advantage of the fact that C++ represents false as 0 and true as 1—is a common trick. Make yourself familiar with it, because you'll see it used time after time. However, because such expressions are difficult to understand without carefully examining the code, they can obscure the program's purpose. For that reason, adding a comment to explain what's happening is probably a good idea.

Listing 2.9, YESNO2.CPP shows how to pass a relational expression directly to exit to shorten the original YESNO program. After compiling YESNO2.CPP, delete YESNO.EXE and rename YESNO2.EXE to YESNO.EXE. Then run the TESTYN.BAT batch file to verify that both versions of the program operate identically.

Listing 2.9. YESNO2.CPP

```
 1:   // yesno2.cpp -- Shortened version
 2:
 3:   #include <stream.hpp>
 4:   #include <stdlib.h>
 5:   #include <ctype.h>
 6:
 7:   main()
 8:   {
 9:      char answer;
10:
11:      cout << "Type Y for yes, N for no: ";
12:      cin >> answer;
13:      exit((toupper(answer) == 'Y'));
14:   }
```

Filters and while Statements

A *filter* is a useful kind of program that takes every character you can throw at it, performs some operation on that input, and writes the result to the standard output. By using filters along with DOS's redirection symbols < (*take input from*) and > (*send output to*), you can process text files stored on disk without having to do a lot of fancy programming: opening, reading, and writing files—subjects covered later.

You can also connect multiple filters using a pipe, represented by a vertical bar |. A pipe lets one filter pump its output to the input of another filter, which can direct the information flow to yet another filter and so on. Connecting filter programs this way enables you to construct sophisticated DOS commands out of relatively simple building blocks. For example, using the DOS SORT and FIND filters, you can type a command such as the following to list a sorted directory of files and subdirectories created or updated on July 20, 1990:

```
dir | find "7-20-90" | sort
```

Using the redirection symbols, you can send the contents of a text file to a filter and then write the processed result to a new file. To sort a file named MYNAMES.TXT, you can type

```
sort < mynames.txt > sorted.txt
```

This directs the contents of MYNAMES.TXT to SORT and then writes the sorted text lines to a new file named SORTED.TXT.

Writing your own filters with C++ is easy and takes only a few lines of programming. Typically, a filter program uses a statement form called a `while` statement, also called a `while` *loop*. A `while` loop repeats another statement or block *while* a condition remains true. For example, if `count` is an `int` variable, the following `while` loop displays 1 through 10:

```
count = 1;
while (count <= 10)
   cout << count++ << '\n';
```

Try writing your own test program to execute this loop. Remember to define the variable `int count;` and insert the preceding lines inside `main`. Notice how the output stream statement both displays the current value of `count` and increments that variable using the `++` operator. This ensures that the relational expression (`count <= 10`) eventually becomes true. If it didn't, the `while` loop would never end, that is, until you reboot or pull the computer's plug.

You can also execute a compound block of statements in a `while` loop by enclosing the block with braces in the usual way. In general, a multistatement `while` loop has the form

```
while (expression) {
 // statements to execute while expression is true }
```

The (`expression`) can be any expression that evaluates to a true or false result. To use a `while` loop in a filter, the program needs some way to *get* input characters and *put* those characters to the standard output. For this, C++ has two functions `getchar` and `putchar`, declared in STDIO.H (which a program must include before using the functions).

Listing 2.10, FILTER.CPP, shows how to combine these elements with a `while` loop that copies the standard input to the standard output. The program will serve as a shell for more elaborate filters to come, but it can be used to copy text files. Of course, DOS already has COPY and XCOPY commands that work more rapidly and can copy other kinds of files as well. The purpose of FILTER.CPP is to demonstrate the mechanics of writing filter programs, not to replace those DOS commands.

Note: If you try to run a filter program like FILTER by simply typing its name—as you do to run other programs—DOS expects you to supply input manually for the program. This can seem to make the computer "hang." If you do this by accident, or after you're done typing input for a filter, press **<Ctrl>-Z**, DOS's end-of-file character, to return to the DOS prompt.

Listing 2.10. FILTER.CPP

```
 1:   // filter.cpp -- Filter shell (copies input to output)
 2:
 3:   #include <stdio.h>
 4:
 5:   main()
 6:   {
 7:      char c;
 8:
 9:      while ((c = getchar()) != EOF)
10:          putchar(c);
11:   }
```

Carefully examine lines 9-10 in FILTER.CPP. The `while` loop continually executes `putchar(c)` while the expression `((c = getchar()) != EOF)` is true. To understand what that expression accomplishes, take it apart, starting with the innermost parentheses enclosing the assignment `c = getchar()`.

That assignment uses `getchar` to get one character from the standard input. It then assigns that character to a `char` variable named `c`, declared at line 7. The empty parentheses at the end of `getchar()` are necessary because this function requires no arguments--a rule that will make more sense when you learn more about functions in chapter 3. Because the equal sign in C++ is an operator, the expression `(c = getchar())` has a value--the same value that is assigned here to `c`. In other words, the value of `(c = getchar())` *equals* the value assigned to `c`—a handy fact that applies to all similar assignment expressions. In FILTER, after assigning the input character to `c`, that same value is then compared with a symbol called `EOF`, meaning *end of file*, also declared in STDIO.H. `EOF` represents the value that `getchar` returns when it has reached the end of the standard input.

> **Note:** In other languages such as Pascal and BASIC, the assignment symbol is a statement, not an operator. This means that constructions such as a := b in Pascal and a = b in BASIC perform actions, but they do not have values. In C++ (and in C), the expression (a = b) does both—it performs the action of assigning b to a, *and* as an evaluated expression, it has the value of that assignment, the same as the original value of b.

The effect of the while loop at line 9 in FILTER is to get characters until there aren't any more left to get. And because any other condition causes the while loop's expression to remain true, putchar(c) sends every character that precedes EOF to the standard output.

To run FILTER, compile the program and then from DOS, type the command **filter < filter.cpp**. As you'll see, this copies the contents of FILTER.CPP to the default output, usually the display. To copy FILTER.CPP to a temporary file named TEMP.TXT, type the command **filter < filter.cpp > temp.txt**. To print a file, type **filter < filter.cpp > prn**.

> **Note:** Be careful when specifying an output filename after the > redirection symbol. If you type the name of an existing file, the filter will erase that file's contents permanently and without warning. This is true for all filter programs, not just those written in C++.

Making Decisions with if/else

Earlier, you learned how to write decision-making statements with if/else. Combining that concept with a while loop filter makes it possible to write a program like Listing 2.11, LINENUM.CPP, which attaches line numbers to the lines in a text file.

Listing 2.11. LINENUM.CPP

```
1:   // linenum.cpp -- Counts number of lines in a text file
2:
3:   #include <stream.hpp>
4:   #include <stdio.h>
5:
6:   #define NEWLINE '\n'
7:
```

```
 8:    main()
 9:    {
10:        char c;
11:        int linenum = 1;
12:
13:        cout << dec(linenum, 4) << ": ";
14:        while ((c = getchar()) != EOF) {
15:            if (c == NEWLINE) {
16:                linenum++;
17:            cout << NEWLINE << dec(linenum, 4) << ": ";
18:            } else
19:                putchar(c);
20:        }
21:    }
```

After compiling LINENUM.CPP, type a command such as **linenum < linenum.cpp** to preface every line in LINENUM.CPP with a line number and colon, similar to the line numbers printed with the listings in this book. Or enter the command **linenum < linenum.cpp > temp.txt** to add line numbers to LINENUM.CPP and write the results to TEMP.TXT, which you can then examine with the DOS TYPE command, or with your text editor.

LINENUM works by first writing the initial line number with an output-stream statement at line 13. The while loop beginning at the next line (14) is identical to the one in FILTER. But this time, instead of sending every input character to the standard output, an if/else statement at lines 15-19 examines the value of each character returned by getchar and assigned to c. If a character equals the symbol NEWLINE, defined at line 6, the if statement increments linenum, starts a new output line, and writes the *next* line number. If c is any character other than NEWLINE, the else clause uses putchar to write that character to the standard output. The effect is to attach a line number in front of every new line.

> **Note:** There are other ways to write LINENUM, which has two tiny flaws. As listed here, the program numbers the first nonexistent line in a zero-length file, and it appends an extra line number if the last line in the file ends with NEWLINE. These are minor annoyances, and the program is still useable, but after you know more about C++, you may want to refine LINENUM to take care of these problems.

Another example, Listing 2.12, WORDS.CPP, uses a similar while loop to count the number of words, characters, and lines in a text file. The program also demonstrates some new C++ techniques you haven't seen before.

Listing 2.12. WORDS.CPP

```cpp
 1:  // words.cpp -- Count words in standard input
 2:
 3:  #include <stream.hpp>
 4:  #include <ctype.h>
 5:
 6:  main()
 7:  {
 8:      char c;
 9:      int words, chars, lines, insideWord;
10:
11:      words = chars = lines = insideWord = 0;
12:
13:      while ((c = getchar()) != EOF) {
14:        chars++;
15:        if (c == '\n') {
16:            lines++;
17:            chars++;
18:        }
19:        if (insideWord)
20:            insideWord = !isspace(c);
21:        else {
22:            insideWord = !isspace(c);
23:            if (insideWord)
24:                words++;
25:        }
26:      }
27:
28:      cout << chars << " total character(s)\n";
29:      cout << words << " word(s)\n";
30:      cout << lines << " line(s)\n";
31:  }
```

To use WORDS, compile the program and give a DOS command such as **words < words.cpp**. In a moment, you'll see a report of the total number of characters, words, and lines in WORDS.CPP. Substitute the name of any plain ASCII text file for WORDS.CPP to see a report on that file's contents.

Of course, WORD.CPP can't read; therefore, it defines a "word" to be any series of characters separated by *white space*—that is, any tab, line feed, vertical tab, form feed, new-line, or blank. Lines 20 and 22 detect these characters by using the `isspace` function declared in CTYPE.H. Other similar functions are `isalpha`, `isdigit`, `islower`, and `isupper` (see chapter 10).

Line 11 in WORDS.CPP demonstrates a shorthand technique for assigning the same value to a series of variables. In general, for int variables a, b, and c, instead of writing

```
a = 0;
b = 0;
c = 0;
```

you can accomplish the same tasks on one line:

```
a = b = c = 0;
```

This also works for other types of variables, as long as all are the same type, and all should be initialized to the same value.

WORDS.CPP employs another technique that you'll find useful in many situations. Variable insideWord of type int is known as a *flag*. Its sole purpose is to store a true (1) or false (0) value that the program can inspect to determine whether a certain condition exists at that time.

In this program, that condition is whether or not the while loop is currently reading the characters in a word (insideWord is true). If so, line 20 assigns the result of !isspace(c) to insideWord. This changes insideWord to false when the loop finds the *next* space character, which marks the end of the current word. (Remember, ! means *NOT.*) If insideWord is false, lines 22-24 set insideWord according to the current character. If that indicates that the loop has reached the beginning of a word, the if statement at lines 23-24 increments the words counter.

Note: There are many ways to write WORDS.CPP. For example, see exercise 2.8, which eliminates the duplicated statement at lines 20 and 22.

The Ol' switch-*aroo*

When a program "needs" to select one of several actions, it can use a series of if / else statements. For example, suppose that you want the program to change gears depending on whether a char variable c equals 'A', 'B', or 'C'. To do that, you can write

```
if (c == 'A')
    // statement for 'A';
else if (c == 'B')
    // statement for 'B';
else if (c == 'C')
    // statement for 'C';
```

```
else
   // statement for all other characters;
```

Any or all of the single statements represented by comments here could also be compound blocks surrounded with braces. There's nothing wrong with this type of lengthy if/else construction, but another C++ statement called a switch lets you accomplish the same goals with a much clearer form that resembles a table. In this statement, the *cases* ('A', 'B', and 'C' in this example) mark the sections that should execute if the *selector* (c here) matches those values. Here's the switch statement version of the previous if/else:

```
switch (c) {
   case 'A':
      // statement(s) for 'A';
      break;
   case 'B':
      // statement(s) for 'B';
      break;
   case 'C':
      // statement(s) for 'C';
      break;
   default:
      // statement(s) for all other characters;
}
```

The statement begins with the key word switch and an expression in parentheses. This expression must reduce to an integer or character, and the case selectors must be character or integer constants or constant expressions (in other words, expressions with all constant arguments, no variables). The result of the switch expression—here, simply the value of c—is compared with every subsequent case selector constant, each of which must end with a colon. Only the statements below the first matching case are then executed. The case values must be unique, but they do not have to be in any particular order. The multiple break statements mark the end of each case's statements. Without break, the program would simply start executing statements with the first matching case value and continuing to the end of the switch statement. If none of the case values matches the switch statement's expression, the statements following the optional default: case at the end are executed.

Unlike other C++ flow statements, multiple statements for cases inside a switch statement do not need to be surrounded by braces. In other words, it is not necessary to write

```
switch (c) {
   case 'A': {
      statement;
      statement;
      break;
```

```
    }
    case 'B': {
        statement;
        break;
    }
    default: {
        statement;
    }
}
```

The extra braces are unnecessary and confusing. Instead, write such code like this:

```
switch (c) {
    case 'A':
        statement;
        statement;
        break;
    case 'B':
        statement;
        break;
    default:
        statement;
}
```

Once again, pay close attention to the break key words, which mark the end of each case section. This holdover from the C language, which has the identical switch statement, is one of C and C++'s weakest foundations. Misuse break and your code may crumble. For example, if you forget the break after the last statement at the end of a case, the statements in the *next* case will begin to execute! Suppose that by accident you write

```
switch (c) {
    case 'A':
        statement1;
        statement2;    // ???
    case 'B':
        statement3;
        break;
    default:
        statement4;
}
```

If c equals 'A', statement1 and statement2 will execute as expected. But, because the case 'A' section fails to include a break after statement2, statement3 will also execute when c is 'A'. Usually, this is not intentional. However, there are rare times when this switch-statement quirk is advantageous.

Selectively leaving out b r e a ks allows one c a s e section to *fall through* to the next, thus executing multiple c a s es for a single matching selector. Experience teaches that the risks of bugs far outweigh the benefits of such designs, and in most cases, you're probably wise to end every c a s e section with a b r e a k.

To match more than one c a s e for a given value, list them after each other this way:

```
switch (c) {
    case 'A':
    case 'B':
    case 'C':
        statement1;
        statement2;
        statement3;
        break;
    case 'D':
        statement4;
}
```

This code executes statements 1 through 3 if c equals 'A', 'B', or 'C'. Usually, it's much clearer to use multiple c a s e selectors this way than to write the equivalent i f statement:

```
if ((c == 'A') || (c == 'B') || (c == 'C')) {
    statement1;
    statement2;
    statement3;
} else if (c == 'D')
    statement4;
```

Both forms give identical results, and you can use whichever is appropriate.

Because the d e f a u l t : selector in a s w i t c h statement always comes last, it doesn't need to have a b r e a k. Also, the d e f a u l t : is optional—if you are absolutely sure that the s w i t c h statement's c a s es cover *every* possible expression value or if you don't need a default action for unmatched c a s es, you can safely leave out the d e f a u l t : section.

Using switch *Statements*

A s w i t c h statement comes in handy any time a program needs to select among several possible actions based on the result of an expression or variable that evaluates to a character or integer value. A typical example where a s w i t c h statement works well is a program that displays a menu of choices. To select a choice, you type its first letter. Inside the program, a s w i t c h statement examines the characters you type and executes various statements for each selection.

To demonstrate how this works, Listing 2.13, MENU.CPP, displays a simple menu of four choices, A(dd, D(elete, S(ort, and Q(uit. The parentheses in these names remind you that typing the first letter of each choice selects that operation. Although this example doesn't actually add, delete, or sort any real information, you can use MENU as a shell for your own designs that need a simple program menu.

Listing 2.13. MENU.CPP

```
1:  // menu.cpp -- Using switch to create a simple program menu
2:
3:  #include <stream.hpp>
4:  #include <stdlib.h>
5:  #include <ctype.h>
6:
7:  #define INUSE 1
8:
9:  main()
10: {
11:    char choice;
12:
13:    while (INUSE) {
14:       cout << "\nMenu: A(dd D(elete S(ort Q(uit: ";
15:       cin >> choice;
16:       switch (toupper(choice)) {
17:          case 'A':
18:             cout << "You selected Add\n";
19:             break;
20:          case 'D':
21:             cout << "You selected Delete\n";
22:             break;
23:          case 'S':
24:             cout << "You selected Sort\n";
25:             break;
26:          case 'Q':
27:             exit(0);
28:          default:
29:             cout << "\nIllegal choice. Try again!\n";
30:       }
31:    }
32: }
```

In line 7, a #define control line associates the value 1 with the identifier INUSE. Because 1 represents true, the while expression (INUSE) in line 13 will always evaluate to true. In other words, this while loop will run "forever," meaning that another statement must provide a way to end the program. Here, the `case` for `'Q'` executes `exit(0)`, halting the program when you select the Q(uit command.

Carefully study the `cases` in the `switch` statement at lines 16-30. In another program, you would insert statements at these locations to handle each menu choice. Notice how `break` marks the end of each `case`. To prove that `break` is needed, make a copy of MENU.CPP, delete line 22 from that copy, and then compile and run the modified test. When you enter D to select the D(elete option, the program reports that you selected D(elete and S(ort, which is obviously wrong. The missing `break` causes the `case` for `'D'` to fall through to the `case` for `'S'`.

Upside Down `do/while` *Statements*

A kind of upside-down `while` statement performs one or more actions *until* an expression is true. This statement form is called the `do/while`. To use it to count to 10, you could write

```
int count = 1;

do {
    cout << count << '\n';
    count++;
} while (count <= 10);
```

This is similar to the way a plain `while` loop works, except that the expression that controls whether the loop repeats or ends comes at the bottom of the construction, not at the top. Also, a `do/while` loop requires both key words—`do` at the beginning and `while` at the end. Statements to execute come between `do` and `while`. Because of this special design—two key words separated by statements to execute--most programmers type the braces even when there's only one statement inside. For example, the previous loop can be rewritten like this:

```
do {
    cout << count << '\n';
} while (++count <= 10);
```

Technically, you can remove the braces and just write

```
do
    cout << count << '\n';
while (++count <= 10);
```

However, you'll almost never see that form of `do/while`, and you probably should include the braces to make the loop stand out clearly on the page.

The key difference between a `while` and a `do/while` loop is that `while` loops may never execute if the controlling expression is false at the start. But a `do/while` loop *always* executes its statements at least once because the program doesn't evaluate the controlling expression until it runs through those statements one time. For example, if `count` equals 10, the following `while` loop effectively does nothing:

```
while (count < 10) {
    cout << "This never executes\n";
    count++;
}
```

But using a `do/while` loop causes the statements inside to execute at least once. Again, if `count` equals 10, consider what happens if you write

```
do {
    cout << "This executes one time\n";
    count++;
} while (count <= 10);
```

Even though `count` already equals 10 at the start of the loop, the two statements inside execute once because the program doesn't evaluate the terminating condition (`count <= 10`) until running through the loop the first time.

In practice, `while` loops tend to be more common than `do/while`, although both have uses. A good way to decide which to use is to ask the question, "Is there a condition when this loop should not execute, not even once?" If the answer is yes, a `while` loop is appropriate. If the answer is no—in other words, if the statements in the loop *must* execute at least once—use a `do/while`.

Listing 2.14, HEAD.CPP, shows `do/while` in action. The program is a filter that writes the first 10 lines of input to the standard output. This can be useful for examining the contents of text files when you don't want to list the entire file with the DOS TYPE command, a file lister, or your text editor.

Listing 2.14. HEAD.CPP

```
 1:  // head.cpp -- Write first 10 lines of input to output
 2:
 3:  #include <stream.hpp>
 4:  #include <stdlib.h>
 5:
 6:  #define MAXLINE 10
 7:  #define NEWLINE '\n'
 8:
 9:  main()
10:  {
11:      char c;
12:      int linenum = 1;
13:
```

```
14:     do {
15:         if ((c = getchar()) == EOF) exit(0);
16:         if (c == NEWLINE) {
17:             linenum++;
18:             cout << NEWLINE;
19:         } else
20:             putchar(c);
21:     } while (linenum <= MAXLINE);
22: }
```

To use HEAD, enter a DOS command such as **head < head.cpp** or specify any other text file after the < redirection symbol. The program will display the first 10 lines from the file. If you want to change this number, change the value in line 6 to the maximum number of lines you want HEAD to display.

The program repeats the statements at lines 15-20 until linenum exceeds the constant MAXLINE. Two if statements inside this loop examine characters returned by getchar, ending the program early at line 15 if EOF appears before at least 10 lines are written. The second if statement watches for a NEWLINE character to come along, in which case line 17 increments linenum, and line 18 starts a new line. Line 20 sends other characters on their way to the standard output as in previous filters.

You might want to try your hand with while and do/while loops by rewriting HEAD.CPP using while. In this example, there's no compelling reason to use either statement type, and they both can do the job equally well.

C++'s Most Popular Statement—The for *Loop*

When you know, or when a program can calculate in advance, the number of times a statement block should execute, a for statement is usually the best choice for writing a loop. All for statements have these elements:

- The key word for

- A three-part expression in parentheses

- A statement or block to execute

A for loop combines these elements, using this general layout:

```
for (statement; expression1; expression2) {
    // statement(s) to execute
}
```

Inside the parentheses after the for key word are three elements that control the loop's action. First comes a *statement,* which is executed a single time before the loop begins. Usually, this initializes a variable used by the next two elements. The first of these, *expression1,* is a relational expression that the for statement tests at the beginning of the loop. The second, *expression2,* is executed at the bottom of the loop after the statements to execute are done.

The preceding description will make much more sense when you compare it to an equivalent w h i l e loop that executes the identical steps:

```
statement;
while (expression1) {
   // statement(s) to execute
   expression2;
}
```

The statement, expression1, and expression2 may be any statements and expressions that could appear in other places. For example, using f o r to display the digits 1 through 10, you could first define an i n t variable c o u n t and then write

```
for (count = 1; count <= 10; count++)
   cout << count << '\n';
```

This is *exactly* equivalent to the w h i l e loop

```
count = 1;
while (count <= 10) {
   cout << count << '\n';
   count++;
}
```

Although the effects of the two loops are identical, the f o r loop is more concise and, after you learn how to put f o r loops together, you'll find them to be easier to read and understand than equivalent w h i l e statements. Also, a f o r's "business" is neatly stowed inside parentheses at the top of the loop, but a w h i l e's mechanisms are strewn throughout the loop. This makes f o r a little better at documenting what it does without requiring you to add comments to explain the statement's intentions.

A sample program shows a f o r loop in action. Listing 2.15, ASCII.CPP, displays a chart of the ASCII characters for the values 32 to 127.

Listing 2.15. ASCII.CPP

```
 1:   // ascii.cpp -- Display ASCII chart
 2:
 3:   #include <stream.hpp>
 4:
 5:   main()
 6:   {
 7:      unsigned char c;
 8:
 9:      cout << '\n';
10:      for (c = 32; (c < 128); c++) {
```

```
11:            if ((c % 32) == 0) cout << '\n';
12:            cout << c;
13:        }
14:        cout << '\n';
15:    }
```

The `for` loop in ASCII.CPP (lines 10-13) initializes the `unsigned char` variable c to the value 32. (As you learned in chapter 1, `chars` can hold ASCII characters or small integer values in the range –128 to 127. Unsigned `chars` can store values from 0 to 255.) After setting c to 32, the `for` loop tests whether the first expression is true. If so, it executes the statements inside the `for`'s block, in this case, the two statements at lines 11 and 12. After that, the `for` loop executes its final expression, in this program, `c++`. This increments the `for` loop's *control variable*.

Usually, a control variable will be an `int` or `char` variable, but it doesn't have to be. Anything that you can test in a relational expression will do. Also, you can define the variable separately as in this fragment:

```
int i;

for (i = 1; i <= 10; i++)
    cout << dec(i, 8);
```

Or you can define and initialize the variable directly in the `for` statement:

```
for (int i = 1; i <= 10; i++)
    cout << dec(i, 8);
```

When a variable like i in these samples is needed only inside the loop, this is the best plan. When C++ runs this loop, it allocates stack space for i only within the scope of the block that contains the `for` statement. Outside of that block, i does not exist in memory; therefore, that memory is available for another variable. In small examples like these, the benefits are minor, and either method works equally well. But in a complex program, defining control variables directly inside nested statement blocks can save a significant amount of memory.

Multiple `for`-Loop Elements

You can separate multiple `for`-loop elements with commas to perform more than one initialization and expression in the same loop. For instance, to count an `int` variable i from 0 to 9 and at the same time count another `int` j from 9 down to 0, you can write

```
int i, j;
for (i = 0, j = 9; ((i <= 9) && (0 <= j)); i++, j--)
    cout << "\ni=" << i << "   j=" << j;
```

As with other less-complex `for` loops, this one is easier to understand when compared to the equivalent `while` statement:

```
int i, j;
i = 0;
j = 9;
while ((i <= 9) && (0 <= j)) {
    cout << "\ni=" << i << "  j=" << j;
    i++;
    j--;
}
```

In the `for`-loop version, each element separated by commas becomes a separate statement in the `while` construction. Despite the extra business in the `for` loop, however, there are still only three sections: the initialization and the two expressions. The sections are separated by semicolons; the multiple elements in each section are separated by commas. Technically, there's no limit to the number of elements you can string together with commas in a `for` loop, but it's rare to use more than a couple at a time. As the preceding examples show, even two additional elements make the statement difficult to read.

do-forever *Loops*

Make sure that your `for` loops contain an expression such as `c++` that advances the condition expressed in the first expression towards a false result. In other words, if the first expression is `(c < 128)` as it is here, the second expression should do something to `c` to make that expression evaluate to false some time later. If you don't do this, the `for` loop may get "stuck." The simplest example of a stuck `for` loop is

```
for (;;) ;        // Loop "forever"
```

This loop initializes nothing, tests no condition, and advances no control variable. The two semicolons inside parentheses are required as place holders for the missing elements. The space before the final semicolon is optional, but avoids a warning from the compiler that it may be extraneous. This is an example of a *null statement*—empty except for its terminating semicolon. The space in front of the semicolon makes it clear that the invisible statement is intentional and is not a typing error.

Although this *do-nothing* or *do-forever* loop may seem silly, it can be useful. You might use it to make a program appear to stop running, thus forcing people to switch off power or to reboot, or you can use it in an interrupt-driven environment, where an external signal from a device such as a modem or a timer causes another action to occur. In that case, the do-forever loop pauses the program until the awaited event wakes up another portion of the code.

Taking a break

It's sometimes useful to interrupt a while, do/while, or for loop in progress. To do that, insert a break statement, as Listing 2.16, BREAKER.CPP, demonstrates.

Listing 2.16. BREAKER.CPP

```
1:  // breaker.cpp -- Demonstrate break statement
2:
3:  #include <stream.hpp>
4:
5:  main()
6:  {
7:      int count;
8:
9:      cout << "\n\nfor loop:\n";
10:     for (count = 1; count <= 10; count++) {
11:         if (count > 5) break;
12:         cout << count << '\n';
13:     }
14:
15:     cout << "\n\nwhile loop:\n";
16:     count = 1;
17:     while (count <= 10) {
18:         if (count > 5) break;
19:         cout << count << '\n';
20:         count++;
21:     }
22:
23:     cout << "\n\ndo/while loop:\n";
24:     count = 1;
25:     do {
26:         if (count > 5) break;
27:         cout << count << '\n';
28:         count++;
29:     } while (count <= 10);
30:
31:  }
```

BREAKER contains a for loop (lines 10-13), a while (17-21), and a do/while (lines 25-29), all of which count from 1 to 10 using an int variable, count. However, in each case, a break statement interrupts the loop before count reaches the loop's target value. Because of the statements at lines 11, 18, and 26, the three loops count only to 5 before stopping.

A b r e a k statement is useful for error handling inside complex f o r and other loops. It can also provide a means to exit a do-forever loop as the following fragment illustrates:

```
for (;;) {
   cout << "\nMenu: A(dd D(elete Q(uit: ";
   cin >> choice;
   choice = toupper(choice);
   if (choice == 'A')
      cout << "You selected Add\n";
   else if (choice == 'D')
      cout << "You selected Delete\n";
   else if (choice == 'Q')
      break;
}
```

This is similar to the w h i l e loop in Listing 2.13, MENU.CPP, but uses a do-forever f o r loop to execute menu choices. After displaying the menu and reading a character into a c h a r variable c h o i c e, a series of i f / e l s e statements select various actions for ' A ' and ' D '. If c h o i c e equals ' Q ', the b r e a k statement ends the do-forever loop, continuing the program after the f o r block's closing brace.

The Plot cont i nues

While b r e a k immediately exits a loop, a similar statement c o n t i n u e forces a loop to start its next iteration from the top. Listing 2.17, CONTINUE.CPP, demonstrates the difference between the two statement forms.

Listing 2.17. CONTINUE.CPP

```
1:  // continue.cpp -- Demonstrate continue
2:
3:  #include <stream.hpp>
4:
5:  main()
6:  {
7:     int count;
8:
9:     cout << "\nStarting for loop with continue...\n";
10:    for (count = 1; count <= 10; count++) {
11:       if (count > 5) continue;
12:       cout << count << '\n';
13:    }
14:    cout << "After for loop, count = " << count;
```

```
15:
16:        cout << "\n\nStarting for loop with break...\n";
17:        for (count = 1; count <= 10; count++) {
18:           if (count > 5) break;
19:           cout << count << '\n';
20:        }
21:        cout << "After for loop, count = " << count;
22:   }
```

CONTINUE uses two `for` loops (lines 10-13 and 17-20) to count up to 10, similar to the way Listing 2.16 works. In this case, however, line 11 inside the first `for` loop executes a `continue` statement if `count` is greater than 5. Line 18 inside the second `for` executes `break`. Except for this difference, the loops are identical.

When you run the program, you'll see that both `for` loops count up to 5 and stop. After the first loop, however, the value of `count` is 11. After the second, it's 6. This is because the `continue` statement in the first loop causes the expression `count++` to execute while the `break` in the second causes the loop to end immediately.

A `continue` statement in any `for` loop jumps immediately to the control expression in parentheses. In other words, given this loop,

```
for (statement; expression1; expression2) {
   if (expression3) continue;
   // statement(s) to execute
}
```

if `expression3` is true, the `continue` statement immediately causes `expression2` to be evaluated, and any following statements (those marked by the comment here) are skipped during this iteration. Similarly, a `continue` in a `while` or `do/while` statement causes the loop's relational expression to be evaluated immediately.

Avoiding `goto`

I hesitate to tell you about this one—some people are convinced that `goto` statements hatch more bugs than a bayou. That may not be true, but in practice, I find that `goto`s, which let code jump from place to place, are rarely of much use. If I discover a need for a `goto`, it usually means my program needs redesigning. In fact, I've probably used more `goto`s in this paragraph than I ever have in my programs.

On the other hand, you shouldn't avoid a `goto` if one solves a problem for you. At the very least, you should be familiar with how `goto` works in case you come across one in somebody else's code. The `goto` statement is easy to use. First, insert a label—any unique identifier ending with a colon—before any statement. Then use a `goto` statement to continue the program at the marked location. For example, to use goto s to count from 1 to 10, you can write

```
int count = 1;

TOP:
cout << count << '\n';
count++;
if (count <= 10) goto TOP;
```

I completely agree with goto's detractors that such a "loop" is a disgrace: It doesn't even look like a loop. The equivalent for and while loops listed earlier are much easier to read and have obvious effects. The goto version requires hand work to trace through each line in order to figure out what the statements do. Still, it works, which is about all you can say in its favor.

The place where a goto is sometimes useful is inside a deeply nested series of if statements when some condition occurs and the program needs to fly the nest— that is, to start execution with the statement following the nested ifs.

```
for (;;) {
   for (...) {
      // various statements in the for loop;
      while (...) {
         // more statements in the while loop;
         if (done == TRUE)
            goto FASTEXIT;
      }
   }
}
FASTEXIT:
// statements to execute following the goto
```

Here, a goto exits the three nested if statements inside a do-forever for loop. This is similar to the way a break statement works, except that in this case, because the ifs are nested inside each other, replacing the goto with a break would exit only the innermost if.

Sometimes, a goto is also useful in a complex switch statement where a case needs to jump to another case. There's no other way to do this without goto, although there are probably other ways to design the code so that it doesn't require so much jumping around. In general, you can write

```
switch (c) {
   CASEA:
   case 'A':
      // statement(s) for 'A';
      goto CASEC;
   case 'B':
```

```
      // statement(s) for 'B';
      goto CASEA;
   CASEC:
   case 'C':
      // statement(s) for 'C';
      break;
}
```

If c equals `'A'`, the statements for the first `case` execute, followed by the statements for `case 'C'`. If c equals `'B'`, those statements execute, followed by those in `case 'A'`, followed in turn by those in `'C'`. If c equals `'C'`, only those statements execute.

Notice that the labels—`CASEA:` and `CASEC:`—are *not* `case` selectors, as are `case 'A':` and `case 'B':`. They are labels that mark locations inside a `switch` statement. However, the labels don't belong to that statement, and they could be named anything: `BANANA:`, `AQ120x:`, or `L99:`. The `gotos` simply cause the program to begin running from somewhere in the middle of the `switch` statement at the labeled locations.

Note: Please don't get the idea that I'm recommending you write programs this way. You should be aware of this special use for `gotos` embedded inside `switch` statements, but you should hunt for alternatives until you turn blue before resorting to such nonsense in your own work.

Data Structures—Sand Castles in RAM

Computer memory chips are made with silicon, literally from plain ol' sand. Like sand particles, memory is just a pile of bits without form. To give form to memory, C++ has several features that impose structures on memory the way sand castles impose structure on sand. Data structures are still composed of memory's bits, and sand castles are still composed of sand particles. Both are simply fresh ways to view the same raw material.

In this section, you'll meet C++'s data structures, which let you collect fields of variables, store information in arrays, and manipulate bits using techniques that are usually more convenient than the bitwise operators described at the beginning of this chapter. I'll also explain more about strings here. Up to now, you've been using strings without paying close attention to some important details about their structures. It's time to dig deeper into what strings really are.

Structures for Safe Keeping

You can collect variables—even those of different types—in a structure with the struct key word to create a new data type that reserves enough memory to hold many related variables in one place.

A typical example where struct is useful is a database program set up to store records that contain a variety of fields. For example, suppose that you are the president of a weight reduction club and you need to store the names, weights, and phone numbers of the club's members. You might use a series of variables such as

```
char   name1[]  = "Marta";
float  weight1  = 142.5;
char   phone1[] = "803-555-1212";
char   name2[]  = "Mel";
float  weight2  = 165.0;
char   phone2[] = "209-555-1212";
char   name3[]  = "Bobbi";
float  weight3  = 135.0;
char   phone3[] = "none";
```

Separately typing each name, weight, and phone number gets tedious fast and clutters the program with confusing variables. Worse, if you need to insert or delete a name, you'll have to write new statements that work with each variable. This is too messy to be practical.

A better method is to create a new data type that can store names, weights, and phone numbers together. You can then write statements that operate on that kind of structure and, therefore, on any club member's information. To do this, start by declaring the data type with struct:

```
struct member {
   char name[30];
   float weight;
   char phone[12];
};
```

That declares a new data type named member, with the capacity to store three fields: name (a 30-character string), weight (of type float), and phone (a 12-character string). Don't forget the required semicolon at the end of the declaration after the closing brace. (This is easy to forget because statement blocks, which look similar to struct declarations, do not end with a semicolon.) Always remember also that a struct data type does not reserve any memory for storing information; it merely creates a template that tells the compiler the nature of the structure. The fields look like they define variables, but because the declarations appear inside a struct, they don't.

After creating a struct type, you can create variables of that type just as you do for other data types:

```
member oneMember;
```

The preceding creates a variable named `oneMember` of type `member`. It reserves space for all of the fields declared inside the `struct`, in this case, a 30-character string, a floating point value, and another 12-character string. Here's another sample:

```
struct sampleStruct {
    float aFloat;
    int anInt;
    char aString[8];
    char aChar;
    long aLong;
};
```

This `sampleStruct` contains five fields, all of different sizes. After declaring the `struct`, you can define variables of the new data type:

```
sampleStruct sampleVar;
```

This reserves space for variables of each of the five fields declared in type `sampleStruct` and points `sampleVar` to the first of those fields. In memory, the bytes for these fields are packed tightly together (see Figure 2.1).

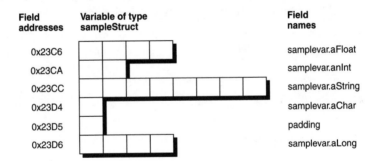

Figure 2.1. The bytes for each field in a `struct` variable are stored consecutively in memory.

Note: In some cases, a `struct` variable's size might be greater than the sum of the sizes of the declared fields. This is because C++ pads fields containing an odd number of bytes so that every field begins at an even-numbered address. (See the single byte labeled `padding` in Figure 2.1.) The reason for this is to keep the program running fast on systems powered by 16-bit 80x86 processors, which can read data more quickly from even addresses than from odd ones. See the `sizeof` operator later in this chapter for a method of determining the exact sizes of `struct`s.

You can also declare a `struct` data type such as `member` and create a variable `m1` of that type in one statement:

```
struct member {
   ...
} m1;
```

Written this way, `m1` is a variable of type `member`; you don't have to define the variable separately. If you don't want to create a named data type, however—for example, when you only need a single `struct` variable of a certain type—use a nameless `struct` like this:

```
struct {
   int a;
   float f;
} onemember;
```

Declared that way, `onemember` is a variable that contains all the fields listed between braces, in this sample, an `int` and a `float`.

These forms are perfectly acceptable, but it's more common to declare a `struct` data type separately and then to define one or more variables of that type. Using the `member` declaration again, to create a variable `m1` and assign values to each of the `struct`'s fields, you can write

```
member m1;          // Define variable m1 of type member
m1.name = "Tom";            // Assign string to name
m1.weight = 155;            // Assign value to weight
m1.phone = "812-555-1212";  // Assign string to phone
```

Variable `m1` is a structure of type `member`. It has the three fields declared in `member`, each of which is accessible by following the variable name with a period and the field name. This is sometimes known as *dot notation*. The period, or "dot," relates the variable with the fields that it contains. The expressions `m1.name`, `m1.weight`, and `m1.phone` are *fully qualified*, meaning that they contain enough information to let the compiler treat them as simple types. The expression `m1.weight` is an integer variable and is treated exactly the same as variable `count` defined as `int count`. You can't write `m1 = "Tom"` because `m1` is of type `member`. It's not a string. The qualified expression `m1.name` is a string, and you can assign a character string to it.

As you can with other variables, you can define and initialize a `struct` with a single statement. To do this, insert field values in braces after the variable's definition:

```
member m1 = { "Anne", 110, "676-555-1212" };
```

Each field must be separated from the next by a comma. (Note the semicolon at the end.) Also, you can't skip any fields, but you can stop before assigning values to every one. For example, to assign only a `name` and `weight` to a `member`, leaving the `phone` field uninitialized, you could write

```
member m2 = { "Kathy", 112 };
```

After declaring a s t r u c t data type and defining one or more variables of that type, you can assign values to those variables, write their values to the display, use them in expressions, and so on. To demonstrate some of these possibilities, suppose that you need to track the models, speeds, capacities, and other facts about the computer systems in your company. You decide to store this information in a s t r u c t named computer. Listings 2.18, COMPDB.H, and 2.19, COMP1.CPP, show some of the required statements to write the database program. Compile the second listing, which includes the first, in the usual way (enter **ztc comp1**).

Listing 2.18. COMPDB.H

```
 1:   // compdb.h -- Computer database header file
 2:
 3:   #define NEWLINE '\n'
 4:
 5:   enum Boolean {FALSE, TRUE};
 6:
 7:   struct computer {
 8:       char *model;              // Computer's model name
 9:       char *cpu;                // Type of CPU
10:       char *display;            // Type of installed display
11:       float speed;              // Speed in MHz
12:       int numflop;              // Number of floppy drives
13:       int hdcapacity;           // Hard drive capacity in megabytes
14:       float memcapacity;        // Memory capacity in megabytes
15:       enum Boolean modem;       // Whether a modem is installed
16:   };
```

Listing 2.19. COMP1.CPP

```
 1:   // comp1.cpp -- Computer database demonstration #1 using struct
 2:
 3:   #include <stream.hpp>
 4:   #include "compdb.h"
 5:
 6:   main()
 7:   {
 8:       computer mysystem;
 9:
10:       mysystem.model       = "ALR 386/2";
11:   mysystem.cpu         = "80386";
12:   mysystem.display     = "MDA";
13:   mysystem.speed       = 16.0;
14:   mysystem.numflop     = 1;
```

```
15:   mysystem.hdcapacity  = 40;
16:   mysystem.memcapacity = 2.0;
17:   mysystem.modem       = FALSE;
18:
19:   cout << "\nMy old system:\n\n";
20:   cout << "Model ...... " << (mysystem.model)      << NEWLINE;
21:   cout << "CPU ........ " << (mysystem.cpu)        << NEWLINE;
22:   cout << "Display .... " << (mysystem.display)    << NEWLINE;
23:   cout << "Speed Mhz .. " << (mysystem.speed)      << NEWLINE;
24:   cout << "No. floppies " << (mysystem.numflop)    << NEWLINE;
25:   cout << "HD Capacity  " << (mysystem.hdcapacity) << " mb" << NEWLINE;
26:   cout << "Memory ..... " << (mysystem.memcapacity) << " mb" << NEWLINE;
27:   cout << "Modem ...... ";
28:
29:      if (mysystem.modem)
30:          cout << "True\n";
31:      else
32:          cout << "False\n";
33:   }
```

These two listings are the first of many sample programs stored in multiple files. Listing 2.18 is a header file that declares a few common items, including the s t r u c t that will store the facts about your company's computers. Other programs that need to create variables of type c o m p u t e r can simply # i n c l u d e this file—they don't have to redeclare the data type. This saves typing and keeps the common declarations in a single location so that if it becomes necessary to modify the fields in a c o m p u t e r, only one file needs editing.

> **Note:** COMPDB.H uses the construction c h a r * m o d e l and similar declarations. These are examples of *pointers,* a topic covered in chapter 4. For now, just think of this as another way to create string variables, for example, one named m o d e l. I'll explain more about this data type format later in this chapter.

Notice that the i n c l u d e " c o m p d b . h" statement at line 4 in COMP1.CPP surrounds the header filename with quotes rather than the angle bracket used to include STREAM.HPP. The brackets tell the compiler to look for a system header—one that's supplied with the compiler. The quotes tell the compiler that the file is not part of the system, but contains declarations belonging only to this program. These differences merely affect where on disk the compiler looks for its header files, not the way the file contents are processed.

> **Note:** Pay attention to the listing file names. If they end in .H or .HPP, they are header files. Compile only the files that end in .CPP. If you receive error messages during compilation, be sure that any included header files are in the current directory or listed in the INCLUDE environment variable (see Introduction to this book).

Line 8 in COMP1 defines a variable named `mysystem` of type `computer`. It can do this because it included the declaration for the `computer struct` back at line 4. Lines 10-17 assign values to each field in `mysystem`, using dot notation. Then lines 19-27 display these same values, again using dot notation to "get to" the separate fields in the structure.

In every case, the only difference between the statements in COMP1 and those you've seen before is the presence of the structure name and its qualifying dot. Structures are simply collections of variables that behave like others defined as loners. The key difference in a `struct` is that you can safely assume that all of the variable's fields are stored one after the other in memory. With individual variables, even those defined next to each other in the source text, you can make no such assumption.

> **Hint:** Individual variables may be, and often are, stored consecutively in memory. C++, however, has no rule that guarantees this order, and you should never write programs that assume one variable's position is relative to another. When variables must be adjacent, put them into a `struct`.

Listing 2.20, COMP2.CPP, is similar to COMP1.CPP but uses a single statement at lines 8-17 to define and initialize `mysystem`. This is a convenient method for initializing structures, and you should become familiar with the format. The rest of the listing is identical to COMP1.CPP. Because line 4 includes COMPDB.H (see Listing 2.18), there's also no need to repeat the declaration for a `computer` structure in this new program—a space-saving technique especially valuable in large programs containing dozens of `struct` declarations.

Listing 2.20. COMP2.CPP

```
1:   // comp2.cpp -- Computer database demonstration #2 using struct
2:
3:   #include <stream.hpp>
4:   #include "compdb.h"
5:
6:   main()
7:   {
```

```
 8:      computer mysystem = {
 9:          "Everex 386/25",           // model
10:          "80386",                   // cpu
11:          "VGA",                     // display
12:          25.0,                      // speed
13:          2,                         // numflop
14:          150,                       // hdcapacity
15:          8.0,                       // memcapacity
16:          TRUE                       // modem
17:      };
18:
19:      cout << "\nMy new system:\n\n";
20:      cout << "Model ...... " << (mysystem.model)      << NEWLINE;
21:      cout << "CPU ........ " << (mysystem.cpu)        << NEWLINE;
22:      cout << "Display .... " << (mysystem.display)    << NEWLINE;
23:      cout << "Speed Mhz .. " << (mysystem.speed)      << NEWLINE;
24:      cout << "No. floppies " << (mysystem.numflop)    << NEWLINE;
25:      cout << "HD Capacity  " << (mysystem.hdcapacity)  << " mb" << NEWLINE;
26:      cout << "Memory ..... " << (mysystem.memcapacity) << " mb" << NEWLINE;
27:      cout << "Modem ...... ";
28:
29:      if (mysystem.modem)
30:          cout << "True\n";
31:      else
32:          cout << "False\n";
33:  }
```

Nested Structures

One s t r u c t can nest inside another to create a complex data type with a world of possibilities for storing all sorts of information. For instance, in a name and address database, you may want to include information about the personal computer that your correspondents own. Instead of redeclaring all the fields you just designed in the previous listings, you can *nest* a c o m p u t e r structure inside the new s t r u c t:

```
struct person {
    char *name;
    char *address;
    int age;
    computer comp;
};
```

Declared this way, a person is a struct with four fields: the person's name, address, age, and comp. The first three fields are identical in form to those you've seen before. The last is of type computer, the struct declared in COMPDB.H. To create a variable oneperson and assign a name, address, and age, you can write

```
person oneperson;

oneperson.name = "George";
oneperson.address = "543 West End Ave.";
oneperson.age = 32;
```

However, to assign values to the comp field requires a bit more effort. Because this field is a structure of type computer nested inside another structure of type oneperson, use dot notation along with *both* data type names in order to qualify the expression to reach the computer data type's fields:

```
oneperson.comp.model    = "AT Clone";
oneperson.comp.cpu      = "80286";
oneperson.comp.display  = "Hercules";
```

In a way, this resembles the way subdirectories on your computer's disk nest inside each other. For example, you've probably used directory pathnames such as C:\ZDEMO\EXAMPLES to refer to a location where a set of files are stored. In a similar way, a fully qualified struct expression uses dots rather than backslashes to refer to a location in memory where data is stored along with other related fields. The expressions give the compiler the information it needs to pinpoint exactly where in memory the individual fields in structures are stored.

Preserving the union

Unions are nearly identical to structures, and in fact, if you're not careful, you can easily confuse the two with disastrous results. Although structures and unions have near twin-like forms, they are related more like cousins than identical twins.

As you learned in the previous section, structures collect various fields into one convenient package. A struct lets you store related variables together, as you might need to do for keeping database records. Unions, declared with the union keyword, also store multiple fields in one package. But instead of placing those fields one after the other, in a union, all fields overlay each other at the *same* location.

This may seem odd at first, but there are many times when a union comes in handy. The most common use is to design a data type that can be used as two or more different other types. For example, you can create a union with a float field, but also treat that field as a char or a long. That doesn't mean C++ unions convert fields from one type to another. They don't. The bytes in memory that store the information for each field are just interpreted as one data type for some statements and as another for other statements. Consider a union declared as

```
union sampleUnion {
    float aFloat;
    long aLong;
}
```

In a variable of type sampleUnion, fields aFloat and aLong are stored at the same address (see Figure 2.2). This means that if a program assigns a value to aFloat, it will also change aLong. It doesn't mean that there are two variables in the union. There's only one value represented two ways. The size of the union equals the size of the largest element.

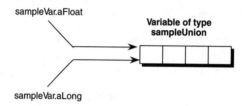

Figure 2.2. A union stores its data fields at the same location.

An example will help make unions clear. Compile Listing 2.21, UNION.CPP, and run the program. Are you surprised at the result? Before reading on, try to figure out how the program works.

Listing 2.21. UNION.CPP

```
 1:  // union.cpp -- Description
 2:
 3:  #include <stream.hpp>
 4:
 5:  main()
 6:  {
 7:      union charint {
 8:          char c;
 9:          int i;
10:      } ci;
11:
12:      int i;
13:
14:      for (i = 65; i < 91; i++) {
15:          ci.i = i;       // Assign i to ci.i
16:          cout << ci.c;   // Display c field in ci
```

```
17:        }
18:    }
```

To understand how UNION displays the alphabet, look closely at lines 7-10. These declare a union named `charint` with two fields, a `char` `c` and an `int` `i`. Except for the `union` key word, this is the identical form used by `struct` declarations. In fact, any fields that can go in a `struct` (which includes any of C++'s data types) can also go in a union. To keep the program simple, line 10 defines a variable `ci` of type `charint`. But you could also create union variables in the usual way:

```
charint anothervar;
```

Any of the methods discussed earlier for declaring `struct` types and variables also apply to unions. Lines 14-17 in UNION.CPP execute a `for` loop that cycles an `int` variable `i` from 65 to 90. On each pass through the loop, line 15 assigns the value of `i` to `ci.i`, using the same dot notation that `struct` expressions employ to "get to" the `i` field in `ci`. Line 16 then displays the *other* field in the union, the `char` variable `c`. Even though no statements assign any values to `c`, the program still displays the alphabet. Obviously, something is changing `c`.

That something is the assignment at line 15. Because all fields in a union overlay each other, assigning a value to one field affects others in the variable. In this example, assigning the values 65 to 90—the ASCII codes for the letters A through Z—to `i` also assigns those same values to `c`, which the program displays.

Vectoring in on Arrays

Like structures and unions, arrays also collect multiple pieces of information. Unlike those other data types, however, arrays always store one or more variables of the *same* type. A simple analogy is a stack of dishes, all of the same size and shape, but not necessarily the same color. Each dish (array element) sits next to its neighbors on the stack (the array). To retrieve a certain dish from the stack in order to inspect its color, you might count from the top down to the dish you want. You could then say that dish number 5 is red or dish number 12 is purple. In arrays, those numbers are called *indexes*.

All arrays have two main characteristics. First, they are declared to hold one or more variables of a certain data type. For example, an array might hold variables of type `float`. Another might hold variables of type `int` or a `struct` that you declared earlier in the program.

The second telling characteristic of arrays is their size. When defining arrays, you must choose in advance how many elements of the array's type you plan to store in the array. This is important because the compiler can only reserve enough memory for the array if you tell it how many items you will store there. Simply stated, the compiler multiplies the number of items by the size of each one and reserves that many bytes for the array.

> **Note:** Using pointers, it's possible to write programs that calculate array sizes at runtime and allocate space for an array. With this technique, you can design programs that create arrays of varying sizes on demand. I'll return to this subject in chapter 4.

A demonstration of arrays shows how to create and use them. Listing 2.22 declares, fills, and displays an array (appropriately named `array`).

Listing 2.22. ARRAY.CPP

```
 1:   // array.cpp -- Demonstrate arrays
 2:
 3:   #include <stream.hpp>
 4:
 5:   main()
 6:   {
 7:      int array[100];     // Define array of 100 integers
 8:      int index;          // Index for accessing array elements
 9:
10:   // Fill array with values from 0 to 99:
11:
12:      for (index = 0; index <= 99; index++)
13:         array[index] = index;
14:
15:   // Display array contents forwards and back:
16:
17:      cout << "\nArray values from [0] to [99]:\n";
18:      for (index = 0; index <= 99; index++)
19:         cout << dec(array[index], 8);
20:
21:      cout << "\nArray values from [99] down to [0]:\n";
22:      for (index = 99; index >= 0; index--)
23:         cout << dec(array[index], 8);
24:   }
```

Line 7 shows how to define arrays in C++. The definition is similar to others you've seen before, but adds square brackets around a literal constant after the variable name. The two brackets are C++'s array symbol:

```
int array[100];
```

That creates an array of 100 integers stored consecutively in memory. Each of the integers in the array is a distinct variable with its own space (see Figure 2.3).

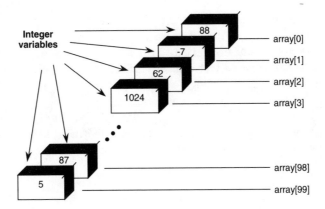

Figure 2.3. An array of 100 integers.

To get to one of the elements in the array—for example, to display its value—specify the element you want by its index number inside brackets after the array name. For example, to display the value of the integer at index location 3, write

```
cout << array[3];
```

Because the array is declared to contain int values, the effect of this statement is equivalent to passing any other int variable to cout. In this case, the statement displays the value of the fourth element.

Why does array[3] refer to the fourth element and not the third? The answer is that the first element in all C++ arrays have the index number 0, not 1. In other words, to display the first five int values in array, you could write

```
cout << array[0] << '\n';
cout << array[1] << '\n';
cout << array[2] << '\n';
cout << array[3] << '\n';
cout << array[4] << '\n';
```

Of course, doing this is much easier (and more efficient) with a for loop:

```
for (i = 0; i <= 4; i++);
   cout << array[i] << '\n';
```

The idea is the same in both cases. To display the first five array elements, use index values 0, 1, 2, 3, and 4. In the first sample, literal values (0, 1, ..., 4) were used for the index values. In the second, an int variable i specifies the index. Both methods are equally useful. You can also index arrays with expressions:

```
cout << array[i + k];
```

Any expression, variable, or constant that represents or evaluates to an integer value makes a legal array index.

Turning back to the ARRAY.CPP demonstration, take a look at lines 12-13. Here, a for loop cycles the int variable index through the values 0 to 99. Line 13 then assigns the value of the index to each array element. It can do this because the array is declared to hold int variables (see line 7). After that, lines 17-19 display the values in the array, again cycling index from 0 to 99 in a for loop. Lines 21-23 do the same, but display the values in reverse order.

A good use for arrays is to store multiple struct variables. For example, to create an array of 50 computer records (using the declarations in COMPDB.H, Listing 2.18), you could write

```
computer systems[50];
```

That defines an array named systems with enough space to hold 50 computer struct variables—a more convenient structure than 50 individual computer variables. To change the name of the sixth computer record, you can write

```
systems[5].name = "PS/2";
```

As with the simple arrays of int variables, the array name (systems) is followed by square brackets and an index value ([5]). C++ recognizes that part of the expression as referring to one array element—in this case, one computer record. Because that record is a struct, in order to get to its fields, the statement qualifies the reference by using dot notation and the field name (name).

Combining data types this way—arrays of struct that contain other fields, maybe even other arrays of some other type—is a powerful concept. In general, you are free to combine simple data types such as int and float with structs, unions, and arrays to build all sorts of sand castles in your programs.

Making the Grade

Another sample program shows how arrays can be used to store information that a program can use later. Listing 2.23, GRADE.CPP, lets you enter up to 18 test scores into an array. It then uses that information to compute the average grade. (The 18-score limit simplifies the program's output. You can change this value in line 6 if you need to enter more than 18 grades.)

Listing 2.23. GRADE.CPP

```
1:  // grade.cpp -- Grade average calculator
2:
3:  #include <stream.hpp>
4:  #include <stdlib.h>
5:
6:  #define MAXGRADES 18
7:
```

```
 8:   double grades[MAXGRADES];   // Array of grade values
 9:
10:   main()
11:   {
12:       int i, numgrades;
13:       double total, average;
14:
15:   // Prompt user for grades, and store values in array:
16:
17:       for (numgrades = 0; numgrades < MAXGRADES; numgrades++) {
18:           cout << "Enter grade #" << (numgrades + 1) << "(-1 to quit): ";
19:           cin >> grades[numgrades];
20:           if (grades[numgrades] < 0) break;
21:       }
22:       if (numgrades <= 0) exit(0);   // No grades entered
23:
24:   // Display the values stored in the array:
25:
26:       cout << "\n\nGrades:\n\n";
27:       for (i = 0; i < numgrades; i++)
28:           cout << dec(i + 1, 2) << ':'
29:                << form("%8.2f", grades[i]) << '\n';
30:
31:   // Total the scores:
32:
33:       total = 0.0;
34:       for (i = 0; i < numgrades; i++)
35:           total += grades[i];
36:
37:   // Compute and display the average:
38:
39:       average = total / numgrades;
40:       cout << "\nTotal scores     = " << form("%8.2f", total);
41:       cout << "\nNumber of grades = " << dec(numgrades, 5);
42:       cout << "\nAverage grade    = " << form("%8.2f", average);
43:   }
```

Line 8 defines the grades array and specifies its elements to be of type double. Notice how the constant MAXGRADES is used in place of a literal value in the brackets. That same constant is then used in line 17 to limit the number of for loops that are performed. Because of this design, to change the array size, just modify the value in line 6 and recompile. Both the array size (line 8) and statement (line 17) are then automatically adjusted.

Line 19 shows an input stream statement that stores a new value directly in an array element, grades[numgrades]. That expression is treated exactly as a variable of type double—the array's element type. The expression grades[numgrades] *is* a double variable. If d is a variable of type double, the statement cin >> d performs identically to cin >> grades[numgrades]. The first reads a value into a lone double variable; the second reads a value into a double stored in an array.

Other statements in GRADE display the values entered in the array, calculate the average score, and display the results. Run the program several times and examine the statements as you enter values. Be sure that you understand how the values in grades are used, especially at lines 8, 19-20, 29, and 35.

Note: If you have trouble with line 35, remember from earlier how combined operators work. Here, the statement adds the current total and a grade value and is equivalent to the more wordy assignment total = total + grades[i].

Initializing Arrays

When you define an array of any type, like other variables, its values may or may not be initialized. If an array is global, all the bytes that belong to the array's elements are set to 0. You can prove this by compiling and running a test program containing these lines:

```
int array[10];
main()
{
    int i;

    for (i = 0; i <= 9; i++)
        cout << "\narray[" << i << "] == " << array[i];
}
```

As you can see, the for loop displays 0 for all 10 array values. Try a second test, but this time move the int array[10]; definition to between the opening brace and the for statement. Now when you run the program, it displays values seemingly chosen at random.

This happens because arrays behave like all variables in C++. Global variables are initialized to 0 by default, but variables that are local to a function (main in this case) are not initialized to any specific values. You must perform all initializations with statements.

One way to initialize an array is to assign values to all array elements. To do this, you can use a `for` loop such as

```
for (i = 0; i <= 9; i++)
   array[i] = 0;
```

This sets every array value to 0. Of course, if your program is going to assign other values to array positions anyway, it doesn't have to pre-assign other values to the arrays. Still, it's a good idea to initialize arrays (and other variables) to prevent bugs caused by using variables that have unpredictable values.

Another way to initialize arrays is to list constant values in braces after the array definition. C++ reads each listed value and assigns it to successive array positions. For example, to initialize a 10-integer array to the values 10 down to 1 and then display those values in reverse order, you can write

```
int countdown[10] = {10, 9, 8, 7, 6, 5, 4, 3, 2, 1};

for (i = 9; i >= 1; i--)
   cout <<"\ncountdown[" << i << "] == " <<
countdown[i];
```

Arrays and the Multiple Dimension

Arrays such as `int array[100]` and `computer systems[50]` are *flat*—they have only one dimension. These and similar arrays are like boxes that you can stack in no other way but straight up. Sometimes, however, arrays need to be two dimensional, like a honeycomb in a beehive or like mail boxes in a post office.

On your desk is another example of an array that needs more than one dimension—your computer's display. The rows and columns on screen are easily represented by a two-dimensional data structure containing 25 rows and 80 columns. In C++, you could define this as an array using the definition

```
char display[25][80];
```

Defined with two sets of brackets and sizes, `display` is technically an *array of arrays* capable of storing 25 80-character arrays of type `char`. However, it's often easier to visualize such an array as having rows and columns, like a computer screen. Here's another sample:

```
int multi[6][8];
```

The array `multi` is an array of 6 8-integer arrays, but most people simply view this as a structure having six rows and eight columns with integer values stored at the intersections (see Figure 2.4).

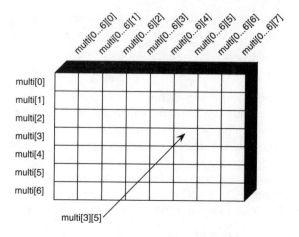

Figure 2.4. A two-dimensional a r r a y is an array of arrays, but you can also view it as a single structure that has rows and columns.

Because multidimensional arrays are stored as arrays of arrays, there are two ways to refer to the array's elements. The expression multi[4] or multi[2] refers to one 8-integer array or row. To read or write an individual integer stored in that row, add a second index expression. For example, to display the value of the integer stored in the fourth row at the sixth column, you can write

```
cout << multi[3][5];
```

As I mentioned before, all arrays are indexed from 0 in C++, a rule that includes those with multiple dimensions. For that reason, the fourth row is indexed by [3]; the sixth column by [5]. To display all integers in multi, you could use a nested for loop:

```
for (int row = 0; row <= 6; row++) {
   for (int col = 0; col <= 7; col++)
      cout << dec(multi[row][col], 8);
   cout << '\n';
}
```

> **Note:** Some languages allow combined array indexes using a single set of brackets, as in the expression array[row, col]. In C++, this must be converted to array[row][col]. However, the results are the same.

Multidimensional arrays are tailor-made for storing a series of facts covering a series of categories. A made-up example demonstrates the idea nicely. (With a little work, the program I'm going to discuss could make a useful utility.) Suppose that you are the manager in an office of busy people, and you want to find out what times everyone has free for group meetings. One way to do this is to stick your head out your office door and ask everyone when they want to get together. If that doesn't work, you might consider writing a computer program to search an array of meeting times, looking for slots that everyone has free.

Listing 2.24 shows how to solve this problem with a multidimensional array. Run the program and enter an employee number from 0 to 3. Then enter the hours from 8 to 17 (5 pm) for which this person has scheduled an appointment. Enter –1 when you're done typing the hours. Then type another employee number and enter scheduled hours for that person. Repeat these steps for up to 4 employees and then enter a final –1 to end. The program will display a chart of the current schedule and list possible meeting times when all employees are free.

Listing 2.24. MEETING.CPP

```
1:   // meeting.cpp -- Multidimension array demonstration
2:
3:   #include <stream.hpp>
4:
5:   #define NUMEMPLOYEES 4
6:   #define NUMHOURS 10
7:   #define STARTHOUR 8
8:
9:   #define JOE 0
10:  #define SAM 1
11:  #define PAULA 2
12:  #define MARY 3
13:
14:  int schedule[NUMHOURS][NUMEMPLOYEES];
15:
16:  main()
17:  {
18:      int empnum, hour;
19:
20:  // Enter employee appointments:
21:
22:      for (;;) {
23:          cout << "Employee number? (-1 to quit): ";
24:          cin >> empnum;
25:          if (empnum < 0) break;
26:          if (empnum > NUMEMPLOYEES) {
27:              cout << "Employee number is out of range\n";
28:              continue;
29:          }
30:          for (;;) {
31:              cout << "Hour of appointment? (8-17, -1 to quit): ";
```

```
32:                 cin >> hour;
33:                 if (hour < 0) break;
34:                 if ((STARTHOUR <= hour) && (hour < STARTHOUR + NUMHOURS))
35:                     schedule[hour - STARTHOUR][empnum] = 1;
36:                 else
37:                     cout << "Hour is out of range\n";
38:             }
39:         }
40:
41:     // Display schedule:
42:
43:         cout << "\nSchedule:\n";
44:         cout << "          Joe     Sam     Paula   Mary\n";
45:         for (hour = 0; hour < NUMHOURS; hour++) {
46:             cout << dec(hour + STARTHOUR, 2) << ":00";
47:             for (empnum = JOE; empnum < NUMEMPLOYEES; empnum++) {
48:                 cout << '\t';
49:                 if (schedule[hour][empnum] != 0)
50:                     cout << 'X';
51:             }
52:             cout << '\n';
53:         }
54:
55:     // Calculate hours when all employees can meet:
56:
57:         cout << "\nPossible meeting times:\n";
58:         for (hour = 0; hour < NUMHOURS; hour++) {
59:             int k = 0;
60:             for (empnum = 0; empnum < NUMEMPLOYEES; empnum++) {
61:                 k += schedule[hour][empnum];
62:             }
63:             if (k == 0)
64:                 cout << dec(hour + STARTHOUR, 2) << ":00\n";
65:         }
66: }
```

After preparing several constants, MEETING declares a two-dimensional array schedule at line 14. As programmed here, the schedule array has room for 10 hourly appointments for four employees. Imagine this structure as having rows for hours and columns for the employees.

Two do-forever for loops at lines 22 and 30 control the entry portion of the program. Two break statements and one continue provide an exit path from the otherwise endless loops. The statement at line 35 stores 1 in an appointment slot for the employee and hour that you enter. The program considers 1 to mean this hour is filled. Any slots containing 0 are free.

Lines 43-53 use the information stored in the `schedule` array to display the appointments for all employees. Study line 49 carefully. It checks the values at `schedule[hour][empnum]`. If this value is not 0, the program displays an X for this hour and employee. If the value is 0, the program skips this position, leaving it blank on screen.

After displaying the full schedule, lines 57-65 search for rows (hours) that contain all 0s, indicating a free period for every employee. To do this, the values in each array position are summed in a variable `k`. If the sum is 0, this hour is free, and line 64 displays the hour as a candidate for a group meeting.

When examining MEETING.CPP, pay close attention to the way constants such as `STARTHOUR` and `NUMHOURS` are used to calculate array indexes. Because all arrays in C++ use indexes that start at 0, having arrays of hours indexed by values from 8 to 17 requires careful programming. Of course, you could just declare an array of 24 hours and waste the unused slots, but I wanted to show examples of typical index calculations because you'll probably have to deal with similar problems.

Note: To be truly useful, MEETING.CPP should be able to read a file that lists employee schedules. After reading about C++ file handling techniques in chapter 8, you might want to modify this program to make it easier to use.

The True Character of Strings

Now that you have a clear picture of arrays, you're ready to consider the true nature of strings. What is a string? If you answered "an array of characters," you're right on the button. As you've seen in other sample listings, to declare an 80-character string, you simply write

```
char string[80];
```

That, of course, is just an array definition that creates a variable named `string` with room for 80 `char` elements. In C++, a string is an array of characters; there is no "string" data type as there is in other programming languages, such as Pascal and BASIC.

Despite the lack of an explicit string data type, however, C++ does give special status to arrays of `char`. As you know, you can create and initialize a string this way:

```
char firstPresident[] = "George Washington";
```

This is still an array of `char`, but instead of requiring you to fill in a literal size in the brackets, C++ simply counts the number of characters between the double quotes and uses that number to reserve space for the array, here named `firstPresident`.

But think carefully about this assignment of a series of characters to an array. Where are the characters stored and how does `firstPresident` "know" where to find them? Other assignments copy values to locations in memory. For example, this statement stores the value 52 in a location reserved for an `int` variable:

```
int numstates = 52;
```

The same is not true of string assignments, even though they appear to be similar:

```
char firstvp[] = "John Adams";
```

Unlike the previous assignment, this does *not* copy the characters in the string `"John Adams"` to the memory locations reserved for the `char` array `firstvp`. That would be a waste of time and effort; in order to make the assignment in the first place, the characters are *already* in memory. Copying those characters from there to somewhere else just to stuff them into an array would be silly.

Recognizing this, C++ doesn't copy *characters* in a statement or definition that assigns a literal string to an array of `char`. Instead, it assigns the *address* of the first character in the string to the array variable.

Consider how this works. The literal string "John Adams" has to be stored somewhere in the compiled program, so instead of copying its characters from that location to another, C++ simply stores the string in one place. Statements that assign that literal string to a `char` array simply make that variable *point* to the first character where the string is stored. The variable is a *pointer*—a subject that I'll return to in chapter 4. The variable—`firstvp` or `firstPresident`—points to the string stored in memory. C++ uses this fact to keep programs running quickly. It takes a lot less energy to cause a variable to point to a string already stored in memory than it would to copy the characters in long strings from location to location.

Note: As you learned in chapter 1, string constants in C++ are terminated with a `NULL` byte equal to 0. Because assignments of string constants don't actually copy characters, you don't have to be concerned about whether an assignment also transfers the `NULL` terminator.

Character Array Initializations

Like other arrays, you can initialize arrays of `char` by listing individual elements in braces after the array's definition. Usually, however, it's easiest just to assign a string as in the previous samples. If you prefer, however, you can initialize a character array like this:

```
char kbtype[6] = {'Q', 'W', 'E', 'R', 'T', 'Y'};
```

This appears to assign the individual characters to successive array positions, but as with all character arrays, what actually occurs is that C++ stores the characters plus a NULL terminator in memory and assigns the address of 'Q' to kbtype. The result is identical to

```
char kbtype[6] = "QWERTY";
```

Usually, that form of string assignment is easier than listing individual characters in braces.

Arrays and Pointers

You've also seen another kind of string declaration in previous programs. For instance, char *model in COMPDB.H declares a variable named model that *points* to a string. The asterisk tells C++ that model is a pointer to one or more char variables stored at a location in memory. Despite the lack of brackets in the defnition, C++ allows model to be used as an array. For instance, you can assign a literal string to model with

```
system.model = "XT Clone";
```

This is similar to the earlier assignments to arrays that use brackets. And in fact, the effect is identical. C++ does not copy any characters or shuffle any bytes to carry out such assignments. It simply assigns to the model pointer the address of the string "XT Clone", which is already stored somewhere in memory. After that, the variable model points to the first character of the string.

The similarity between pointers like char *model and arrays such as char model[18] is more than just superficial. *All* arrays in C++ are implemented as pointers. Suppose that you define an array like this:

```
int array[10];
```

When the compiler processes this definition, it allocates space for 10 integers and assigns the address of the first integer to the variable array. It may appear as though array stores the integers inside itself, but in the program's compiled code, array is implemented as a pointer to the array's first element. As you learned earlier, to display the third item for an array defined like this, you can write

```
cout << array[2];
```

Now consider the same declaration using a pointer:

```
int *arrayPtr;
```

Because arrays in C++ are implemented as pointers, even though `array` is defined differently, you can still write a statement like this to display the second element:

```
cout << arrayPtr[1];
```

Watch out, however. The bracketed definition `int array[10]` reserves space in memory for an array of 10 integers. The equivalent definition `int *arrayPtr` reserves space *only for a pointer named* `arrayPtr`. It does *not* reserve any space for integers. When an array is defined as a pointer, you'll have to take additional steps to reserve memory in which to store the array's elements. It's too early to list those steps here; I'll get back to them in chapter 4.

> **Note:** That's enough about pointers for the moment. Don't be concerned if the details seem a bit fuzzy; most people have trouble understanding the relationship between arrays and pointers on a first reading. For now, you need to know only that variables defined as `char x[10]` and `char *x` are functionally equivalent, meaning you can use `x` in many of the same ways in program statements. Both definitions create pointers to memory where characters are stored, but only the one with brackets reserves memory for those characters. For that reason, until you learn how to use pointers in chapter 4, in your own programs, use the bracketed type of definition to create arrays. Inside `struct` declarations, though, you must use the pointer form to create variable-length string fields as COMPDB.H illustrates.

Fielding Bits

It often happens that fields in a structure will never exceed a certain small value. For example, in a database of facts on parents, a field that represents the number of children is unlikely to be higher than 15 and will usually be 2 or 3. A field that represents a person's sex will need only a single bit if 0 is taken to mean male and 1 female. Such a structure might look like this:

```
struct person {
    unsigned age;           // 0 ... 99
    unsigned sex;           // 0=male, 1=female
    unsigned children;      // 0 ... 15
};
```

That takes six bytes, two per `int` field. Unfortunately, there's lots of wasted space in this structure. For example, `sex` requires only a single bit to hold its value, and the other 15 bits in that `int` are never used. If the structure could *pack* the information into a smaller space that takes only as many bits as needed to represent each field, it could squeeze out most of those wasted bits.

The way to do this is to use a *bit field.* This resembles a structure—it uses the same `struct` keyword—but specifies the number of bits that each field occupies within the size of an `int` (16 bits on PCs). Here's how the previous structure looks when converted to a bit-field:

```
struct person {
   unsigned age : 7;        // 0 ... 127
   unsigned sex : 1;        // 0=male, 1=female
   unsigned children : 4;   // 0 ... 15
   unsigned : 4;            // Not used
};
```

Following each field name with a colon and unsigned literal value packs that field into the specified number of bits in the structure, which can total up to 16 bits for all such fields. In this sample, 7 bits are allotted for the `age` field. Because an unsigned integer can range from 0 to 127 when represented in binary by 7 bits, the age of a person in this record is similarly limited. The other two fields `sex` and `children` are also packed into 1- and 4-bit spaces, limiting the ranges of values these fields can hold.

> **Note:** The compiler supplied with this book allows bit fields structures to be larger than 16 bits. However, the official size limit is the same as an `int`. There's no set rule about whether a bit field structure may be larger than the size of an `int`, and each compiler is likely to construct bit fields differently.

The last field in the `person` bit field is unnamed. This is a place holder and is used to keep the total number of bits at 16. A place holder is optional but is usually included to account for every bit in a structure. You may also use more than one place holder to force fields to begin at certain bits. For example, here's a fictitious sample with three place holders marked `Not used`:

```
struct hardware {
   unsigned reset : 1;       // 0 ... 1
   unsigned level : 4;       // 0 ... 15
   unsigned : 1;             // Not used
   unsigned selector : 2;    // 0 ... 3
   unsigned : 3;             // Not used
   unsigned active : 1;      // 0 ... 1
   unsigned : 4;             // Not used
};
```

Structures with multiple place holders are often necessary to match the fixed bits stored in a register. For example, an input port might define certain bits to mean various things: Whether a byte is available, what the status of the port is, whether it's ready to send another byte, and so forth. You could use a bit field structure to read that information into a program, but you might have to use place holders to force some fields to match the positions of specific values.

Use bit fields as you do fields in other structures. For example, to display the age and number of children in a person bit field, you could write

```
person p;
...
cout << "\nAge      = " << p.age;
cout << "\nChildren = " << p.children;
```

Unlike many other computer languages, in C++, you don't have to extract the bits from the structure, and you don't have to use logical operators to isolate field values from their neighbors. Instead, just use the fields as though they were integers. C++ takes care of the messy details of extracting and inserting the packed bit fields in the structure without disturbing other bits there. Of course, you must be careful not to assign values greater than a field can represent. Except for this detail, you can use bit fields as though they were separate unsigned integer variables.

> **Note:** Bit fields must be declared in struct structures. They are not allowed in unions.

Listing 2.25, EQUIP.CPP, shows how to use bit fields to extract information packed inside computer hardware. The program uses a bit field structure to interpret the information returned by a function named _bios_equiplist, which is declared in the header file BIOS.H. Run the program to detect how many disk drives, serial ports, and printers are installed, whether a game adaptor is available, and the startup video mode of your PC.

Listing 2.25. EQUIP.CPP

```
1:  // equip.cpp -- Display list of computer's equipment
2:
3:  #include <stream.hpp>
4:  #include <bios.h>
5:
6:  struct equipment {
7:      unsigned hasdiskette : 1;
8:      unsigned : 1;                  // Not used
9:      unsigned planar : 2;
```

```
10:        unsigned videomode : 2;
11:        unsigned numfloppy : 2;
12:        unsigned : 1;                 // Not used
13:        unsigned numserial : 3;
14:        unsigned gameadaptor : 1;
15:        unsigned : 1;                 // Not used
16:        unsigned numprinters : 2;
17:    };
18:
19:    union twotypes {
20:        equipment eq;      // The bit field structure
21:        int k;             // Same bytes as an integer
22:    };
23:
24:    main()
25:    {
26:        twotypes t;
27:
28:        t.k = _bios_equiplist();    // Get list as integer
29:
30:        cout << "\nNumber of printers         " << t.eq.numprinters;
31:        cout << "\nGame adaptor installed (1) " << t.eq.gameadaptor;
32:        cout << "\nNumber of serial ports     " << t.eq.numserial;
33:        cout << "\nNumber of diskette drives  ";
34:        if (t.eq.hasdiskette)
35:            cout << t.eq.numfloppy + 1;
36:        else
37:            cout << 0;
38:        cout << "\nInitial video mode (2)     " << t.eq.videomode;
39:        cout << "\nPlanar RAM size (3)        " << t.eq.planar;
40:
41:        cout << "\n\n(1): 0=FALSE, 1=TRUE";
42:        cout << "\n(2): 1=40x25 color, 2=80x25 color, 3=monochrome";
43:        cout << "\n(3): 3=64K on XTs\n";
44:    }
```

EQUIP.CPP declares a bit field named equipment at lines 6-17. Inside this structure are a number of fields and place holders (marked with the comment Not used). These fields are positioned to match the values stored in your system's toggle switches (or perhaps in a small amount of battery-powered RAM). Using a bit-field structure to extract these values makes it easy to display them, as shown at lines 30-39.

The program also shows good use of a union. Lines 19-22 declare twotypes as a union with two overlayed fields, eq of type equipment and k of type int. Because

equipment is a 16-bit bit field and because an **int** also occupies 16 bits, the two fields in this union exactly overlay each other.

The program then defines a variable of type **twotypes** (line 26) and assigns the result of the **_bios_equiplist** function to **t.k**—in other words, to the **int k** field in the **t** union. The compiler would reject a direct assignment to the **eq** field because, even though the **int** and **equipment** fields are the same size, they are different data types.

After assigning the function value to **t.k**, the statements at lines 30-39 use the other field (**t.eq**) in the union to extract the bit-field values from this same value. As this shows, the union makes it easy for the program to manipulate the values as an integer (**t.k**) and as a bit field structure (**t.eq**).

Note: Bit fields typically restrict programs to running on specific hardware. Running EQUIP on anything but a true-blue PC, AT, PS/2, or clone may cause the program to fail. Also, because the code relies on the declarations in BIOS.H, it probably won't make it through other C++ compilers. That's not to discourage you from using bit fields, only to point out that doing so usually makes a program totally dependent on a specific computer system. Because the **int** data type may be a different size on other systems, if you want your code to be portable, it's probably best to use plain **struct**s rather than bit fields. However, if you write your program carefully and *never* assume that a bit field is in a specific location, it *may* be possible for your bit fields to work correctly on more than one type of system.

Sizing Up Your Variables

Now that we are talking about system-dependent items, this is a good place to introduce one last C++ operator, **sizeof**. Use **sizeof** to determine the number of 8-bit bytes occupied by a variable or a data type. For example, to display how many bytes **float** occupies, you can write

```
cout << "Size of float = " << sizeof(float);
```

C++ replaces the expression **sizeof(float)** with the number of bytes that a **float** variable takes in memory. Similarly, you can use **sizeof** to determine the size of an array, union, bit field, or other structure. Just put the name of the variable or data type in parentheses after **sizeof** and use the expression where you might use an **unsigned int**.

Listing 2.26, SIZEOF.CPP, demonstrates how to use **sizeof**. Run the program to determine the sizes of all basic C++ data types. The program makes a useful test that you can compile and run with other compilers or even on other computer systems. Do this to compare one compiler's assumed sizes for fundamental data types. (You may have to change `stream.hpp` in line 3 to `stream.h` for some C++ compilers.)

Listing 2.26. SIZEOF.CPP

```
 1:  // sizeof.cpp -- Determining the sizes of variables
 2:
 3:  #include <stream.hpp>
 4:
 5:  main()
 6:  {
 7:      char c;
 8:      short s;
 9:      int i;
10:      long l;
11:      float f;
12:      double d;
13:      long double ld;
14:
15:      cout << "Size of char ...... = " << sizeof(c)<< " byte(s)\n";
16:      cout << "Size of short ..... = " << sizeof(s)<< " byte(s)\n";
17:      cout << "Size of int ....... = " << sizeof(i)<< " byte(s)\n";
18:      cout << "Size of long ...... = " << sizeof(l)<< " byte(s)\n";
19:      cout << "Size of float ..... = " << sizeof(f)<< " byte(s)\n";
20:      cout << "Size of double .... = " << sizeof(d)<< " byte(s)\n";
21:      cout << "Size of long double = " << sizeof(ld)<<" byte(s)\n";
22:  }
```

Careful programmers use `sizeof` as in the SIZEOF demonstration to write system-independent programs. Instead of assuming an `int` variable takes two bytes, a statement can use the expression `sizeof(int)`. Compiling this expression on a different system gives the program a way of determining how many bytes an `int` occupies on the new machine.

You can also use `sizeof` to determine the sizes of structures and arrays. Specify either a data type identifier or the name of a variable in parentheses after `sizeof`. For example, using the declaration of a `computer struct` in COMPDB.H (Listing 2.18), include that file and use a statement like this to display the `struct`'s size in bytes:

```
#include "compdb.h"
cout << "Size of a computer struct = " << sizeof(computer);
```

Or replace `computer` with the name of any array, or an array variable, to determine its size:

```
int array[100];
cout << "Size of array = " << sizeof(array);
```

Using sizeof this way is preferable to assuming that an array or structure takes a certain number of bytes. Also, because C++ inserts padding bytes to keep fields in structs aligned to even addresses, sizeof is the *only* reliable way to determine a struct's true size. Applying sizeof to a union returns the size of the largest element.

You've now seen most of C++'s operators and data structures in action. With these elements, and with the help of program-flow statements like for and while, you can write sophisticated programs that repeat actions and make decisions. Unfortunately, as your programs grow larger, you'll begin to notice that main() tends to expand like a hot-air balloon with its valve stuck open. Unless you do something to relieve the pressure, sooner or later, the balloon will burst.

And, unless you do something to prevent overstuffing main() with statement after statement, your programs may also "crash and burn" as they become more difficult to create and maintain. A main() function that extends for page after page in a listing is awkward, bug-prone, and just plain bad form. Good programmers avoid writing code that way. Instead, they divide their programs into small, manageable chunks. Like main(), those chunks are called functions, and it's time to explain exactly what functions are and how you can use them to write even highly complex C++ programs while never working on more than small, easy-to-understand pieces of the code at a time.

Questions and Exercises

2.1. In relational expressions, what values does C++ use internally to represent true and false?

2.2. Explain the difference between == and =.

2.3. Write a program using a loop that prompts for a value between 1 and 100. If someone types a value outside of that range, the program should display an error message and redisplay the prompt.

2.4. Write the equivalent while statement for the following for loop (assume counter is type int):

```
for (counter = 0; counter > -8; counter--) {
   cout << "\nValue of counter = " << counter;
   cout << "\n--";
}
```

2.5. Using bitwise operators, write a program that limits the range of an `int` variable to 0 through 31.

2.6. Write a program that encrypts a string after you enter a password and then recovers that same string. Use the bitwise XOR operator in your answer.

2.7. Write a program that passes an integer value to DOS for a batch file to receive through the `errorlevel` variable.

2.8. Write a version of WORDS.CPP (Listing 2.12) that eliminates the duplicate statements at lines 20 and 22.

2.9. Rewrite HEAD.CPP (Listing 2.14) to use a `while` statement rather than `do/while`.

2.10. Write a filter program that converts input strings to uppercase.

2.11. Write a program that determines whether an integer value is odd or even.

2.12. Write `for`, `while`, and `do/while` loops that display the alphabet. Insert your loops into a `switch` statement that lets people select which loop variety to run.

2.13. Why do programmers frown on using `goto` statements?

2.14. Create a structure that can store the date and time.

2.15. Define an array of 50 date and time structures from exercise 2.13.

2.16. Write a program to display a string's characters separated by blanks. If you type ABCDEFG, the program should display A B C D E F G.

2.17. Pack your data and time structure into one or more bit fields. How many bytes does the bit field save? Use `sizeof` to prove your answer.

Chapter 3

Functions: Programming in Pieces

A *function* is a kind of miniprogram inside a program. Functions collect various statements under a single name that a program can then use one or more times to execute those statements. Functions save space by reducing repetition, and they make programming easier by giving you a way to divide a large project into small, easy-to-handle modules.

If you've programmed in BASIC or assembly language, you'll recognize functions as being similar to subroutines. If you know Pascal, you'll notice that functions are equivalent to Pascal procedures *and* functions. If you have a background in C, you should still read this chapter. Functions look much the same in C and C++, but looks can be deceiving, and there are many differences between C and C++ functions that you'll want to learn.

Keeping It Simple

Beginners often think that learning about functions is where C++ programming starts to "get hard." Not so. *The main reason for using functions is to keep programs simple.* Functions modularize a program by dividing it into manageable pieces. With functions, you can write major programs while working on only a few relatively small, simple chunks of code at a time.

You've already seen one function in every program listed so far—`main`. As you know, when a C++ program runs, it begins by executing the first statement inside `main`. You've also used *library functions*—those that are provided with C++ and declared in header files. When you called `dos_gettime` in DT.CPP (Listing 1.7) or `_bios_equiplist` in EQUIP.CPP (Listing 2.25), you saved the effort that you would have had to spend writing those same instructions yourself.

As those sample programs show, library functions can serve as specialized tools for constructing new programs. Instead of reinventing a tool, if the right one exists in the C++ library, you can just use it as is. In this way, functions extend the C++ language by providing custom commands that you can pull in and use as needed to solve problems.

Writing Your Own Functions

The key to writing good functions is to choose good tasks for functions to perform. A "good" task is one with a narrow, clear purpose. For example, a function clearDisplay might clear the display. Or a function factorial might compute the factorial of a number, but it's probably not a good idea to write a function named clearDisplayAndComputeTheFactorial. That's way too much for one function to bite off and chew.

It's also important to choose good function names such as clearDisplay, factorial, promptForInput, or showErrorMessage. Even without seeing those functions in use, you already have some idea what they do. Good function names can make C++ statements read more like stories than computer programs. You can use any unique identifiers for function names, but your programs will be easier to read and maintain if you create names that describe what functions accomplish. If you name your functions fn64, axp9b, or other equally cryptic names, you'll need to add comments to the code to explain what's going on. With good function names, programs can serve as their own documentation, and comments are often unnecessary.

Listing 3.1 demonstrates how to create functions in C++ programs. Although not useful for any other purpose, FNCOUNT.CPP includes the basic elements that all programs with custom functions require.

Listing 3.1. FNCOUNT.CPP

```
 1:  // fncount.cpp -- Function demonstration
 2:
 3:  #include <stream.hpp>
 4:
 5:  void countup(int value);
 6:  void countdown(int value);
 7:
 8:  main()
 9:  {
10:      countup(20);
11:      countdown(10);
12:  }
13:
```

```
14:    void countup(int value)
15:    {
16:        int i;
17:
18:        cout << "\n\nCounting up\n";
19:        for (i = 1; i <= value; i++)
20:            cout << dec(i, 8);
21:    }
22:
23:    void countdown(int value)
24:    {
25:        int i;
26:
27:        cout << "\n\nCounting down\n";
28:        for (i = value; i >= 1; i--)
29:            cout << dec(i, 8);
30:    }
```

When writing your own functions, type them into the program text just as you do function ma i n. Most programmers insert functions after ma i n as done here in lines 14-30, but that's not a requirement, and functions can precede ma i n if you prefer. In general, for all of a program's functions *except* ma i n, you need to carry out these three steps (in no particular order):

- Declare a prototype that describes the function

- Use the function in at least one statement

- Write the function's body

FNCOUNT implements these goals. First, it declares two *function prototypes* at lines 5-6. A function prototype describes the name of the function (c o u n t u p and c o u n t d o w n), sets down what kind of value the function returns (v o i d, meaning no return value), and lists any parameters in parentheses that the function needs (i n t   v a l u e). Each prototype declaration ends with a semicolon.

Function prototypes tell the compiler the name and nature of the custom functions the program uses. You must declare a prototype for every function in your program *before* the program uses that function. For that reason, function prototypes are usually placed above ma i n. This also lists the prototypes in a convenient spot where you can examine and modify them.

Lines 10-11 *call* the two functions c o u n t u p and c o u n t d o w n. "Calling a function" simply means that you type the function's name in a statement or expression. When C++ compiles the program, it replaces those names with code that executes the statements collected inside the functions. Usually, it does this by inserting a machine language subroutine call instruction to the address where the function is stored, though you don't need to bother with this fact in order to use functions.

In addition to declaring a function's prototype and to calling the function from another statement, you also have to write the statements that perform the function's action. The implementation describes what the function does. When you implement the function's body, usually by typing it after the end of `main`, begin with the function's prototype minus the semicolon at its end. This first line in the function's implementation is called the *function declaration.* Then, inside a pair of opening and closing braces insert the variables and statements belonging to the function. For example, here's the implementation of function `countup` from FNCOUNT:

```
void countup(int value)
{
    int i;

    cout << "\n\nCounting up\n";
    for (i = 1; i <= value; i++)
        cout << dec(i, 8);
}
```

You'll recognize this format as nearly identical to the one used by `main`. A function may define variables such as `int i` for its own use, and it may include statements, control structures, and any other items that you've come across in other sample listings inside the `main` function.

You must be sure to implement every function prototype (see 23-30 in FNCOUNT.CPP for another example). To put that into a rule: For every prototype, there must be a corresponding implementation of that function. The prototype and function declaration—for example, lines 6 and 23—also must agree exactly. In this way, the compiler helps you write reliable programs by insisting that the function designs in the prototypes are identical to the function implementations. Of course, it wouldn't make any sense to design and use a function prototype as returning a `float` value but then to implement that function to return type `int`. In a large program with hundreds of functions, it's all too easy to make that kind of mistake. C++'s strict rules about prototyping functions guard against using functions improperly—a common mistake that C programmers know all too well. (ANSI C allows, but does not require, function prototypes.)

Note: When designing functions, try to keep them short. A good rule of thumb is to limit your function lengths to one printout page, about 55 or 60 lines. Even that's fairly long, and you should try to keep most functions below about half that size. At first, you may have trouble meeting this goal, but it's a good one to strive for. Experience teaches that simple functions are easier to write and maintain, especially months or years after you write them. Do yourself a favor now, and keep your functions as small as you can.

Designing from the Top Down

You may have heard the phrase "top-down programming." This isn't some obscure scientific term. It's a description of an approach to the craft of programming. When practicing top-down programming, the general idea is to begin with a broad concept—the goal you are trying to achieve. You then chisel that concept into smaller and smaller chunks, carving out the details of a complex project until you reach rock bottom. At that point, you have an assortment of easy-to-implement definitions suitable for converting to C++ functions. By implementing these small, purposeful functions, you can write major applications while never working on more than a few simple lines of code at a time.

For example, suppose that you are writing a program to play checkers. That's the main goal—to play the game of checkers—and starting the ball in motion might be all that function `main` does:

```
main()
{
    playCheckers();
}
```

Then in function `playCheckers`, you'd call other functions to initialize a new game board, make moves, check if a player has won or lost, and so on. A diagram of all the modules and submodules that make up the finished program resembles an organizational "tree"—like those managers use to chart a company's departments. (See Figure 3.1.)

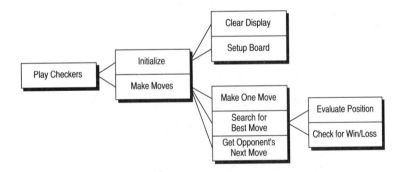

Figure 3.1. Top-down programming divides a complex job into modules. Diagramming those modules shows their relationship to the program, here a fictitious (and incomplete) game of checkers.

Unfortunately, like most theories, top-down programming in practice is a bit more difficult than these descriptions make it sound. There are several reasons for this. Projects may be poorly defined at the start, project managers may misunderstand key goals, and while implementing the details, programmers may discover a need to refashion code that was already finished and tested. Still, top-down programming has an important role to play, and you should learn how to apply the concept when designing your own code. I'll get back to this idea in chapter 5 when I introduce C++ object-oriented features. As you'll learn then, object-oriented programming patches many of the flaws in top-down programming's shell.

To understand more about functions and to explore how you can use them in top-down fashion, in this section you'll complete a small program that checks for mismatched braces and parentheses in C++ source-code files. It's a common error to leave out a closing brace in a statement block or to forget to match every opening and closing parenthesis in a complex expression. If you receive errors during compilation that you don't understand, you can use the program to eliminate a mismatched brace or parenthesis as the cause.

The first step is to sketch what the program should do. It will have to read characters from a text file, keep track of encountered braces and parentheses, and display the results. To give it a professional appearance, the program should also display a brief welcoming message. Instead of writing the instructions right off the bat in C++, I'll use *pseudo code* to describe the program's design. Pseudo code is a free-form approximation of real statements that look like programming but can't be compiled. Designing programs with pseudo code is like penciling in the figures for a painting you'll finish with oils when you get back to the studio. Here's the "main loop" in pseudo code:

```
welcome user to program
open the input file
while (nextcharacter != EOF) {
    count braces and parens
}
display results
close the file
```

This is a complete program, although it isn't yet in a form that C++ can compile. The pseudo code describes the program, but doesn't include every tiny detail. This completes the forest. Next, it's time to plant a few trees.

At this stage, after settling on the outer design, I like to rewrite the pseudo code in a form that's as close as possible to the final program. I do this by replacing the pseudo-code descriptions with function names. The functions don't yet exist, and the program will not yet compile, but this lets me see whether my design is on track before going further:

```
main()
{
    char c;

    welcome();
    openfile();
    while ((c = fgetc(fp)) != EOF)
```

```
        countchars(c);
    showresults();
    fclose(fp);
}
```

I replaced "welcome user to program" with we l come( ), a call to a function of that name. The empty parentheses are required because this function does not require any values to be passed to it for processing. Similarly, I converted "open the input file" to openfile( ), another parameterless function call.

As you become more experienced with the top-down method, you'll discover that you can invent your function names directly. Instead of writing "welcome user to program" in the pseudo code design, you'll just write we l come( ). That's fine, but don't make the mistake of adding too many details too early. Concentrate on one level at a time. When you're satisfied with that level, then go below decks to polish the trim.

There are two items in this example you haven't seen before. The while loop calls fgetc for a character from a file, represented here as fp. This is a file-handling function declared in STDIO.H, which the program will have to include. That and other header files contain function prototypes for the C++ library. You might want to use your editor to examine STDIO.H and study the prototypes. You can also print copies of the various header files on your compiler disk. This will give you a handy reference to the requirements of the many functions included with the compiler.

If you look back at the filter programs in chapter 2, you'll see that this new while loop is nearly identical to the ones used there. The only difference in this case is that the program prompts for a file name and uses a variable to read that file's contents. This lets you run the program by typing its name, supplying a file name, and seeing the results—a design that's more appropriate to the job at hand than a filter, which is better suited to processing a stream of text, often the output of another filter.

> **Note:** Chapter 8 covers file handling in more detail. In this chapter, I'll introduce only the file concepts required to understand how the sample programs work.

Another file-handling function from STDIO.H f close closes the file opened by openfile. DOS limits the total number of files available to programs; therefore, your program's functions should always close files when they're done using them. This recovers the space used by DOS and releases a file *handle* for the program to use for other purposes. Handles are just identifying numbers that DOS assigns to open files. (When a program ends, it automatically closes any open files.)

So far so good. The program's outer layer is coming together and calls several functions, even though those functions don't exist yet. The next step is to create the function prototypes, which describe each function more completely:

```
void welcome(void);
void openfile(void);
void countchars(char c);
void showresults(void);
```

The program's main function calls four functions, none of which returns any values. For that reason, the prototypes all begin with the key word void. (Think of the word *void* as meaning *nothing*, not as *invalid*. A void function is not like a *void* check.) Next come the function names—welcome, openfile, countchars, and showresults. After each of those names are any parameters that the function requires. Three functions have none, represented by another void in parentheses. However, countchars needs a character to count, so the prototype tells the compiler about that character by listing (char c) after the function's name.

Notice how the parameter declaration (char c) resembles a variable definition. In fact, that's what a parameter is—a variable that the function receives from its caller. However, parameters are special in the sense that they don't exist until the caller passes a value, called an *argument*, to the function. The declaration (char c) simply tells the compiler what to expect. It doesn't create a character named c until the program runs. For this reason, you don't even need to name the variable, and you could write the prototype this way:

```
void countchars(char);
```

This gives the compiler everything it needs to know about the function: its return value (void meaning none), its name (countchars) and the data type of any parameters (char). Even though this style of nameless parameters is permitted in C++, I prefer to include parameter names in my prototypes. A function that requires more than one parameter helps document the code. For example, the prototype

```
void proto(int, int, int);
```

is permissible. But I prefer to write something like this:

```
void proto(int count, int min, int max);
```

Implementing the countchars function demonstrates the final stage in the top-down design method. Here's how I wrote that function:

```
void countchars(char c)
{
    if (c == '(') openparen++;
    else if (c == ')') closeparen++;
    else if (c == '{') openbrace++;
    else if (c == '}') closebrace++;
}
```

Because this is the real McCoy, the function declaration now requires a full accounting of its parameters—data types *and* names. It's not enough to write (char) for the single parameter used by countchars. In the function implementation, all parameters must have names. Statements inside the function (but nowhere else) can then use the parameter names to "get to" the values passed as arguments to the function.

The body of the function consists of a four-part i f / e l s e statement that inspects the value of the character passed to the function. Inside the function, the statements refer to the c h a r parameter by its name c. You could use any name you want here, even the same names used elsewhere. Function parameters are scoped to the function. Outside of that scope, they don't exist.

Examine how this sample function compares the parameter c with literal braces and parentheses. Matches increment one of four variables, o p e n p a r e n, c l o s e p a r e n, o p e n b r a c e, and c l o s e b r a c e. Next, it's time to define those variables:

```
int openparen, closeparen, openbrace, closebrace;
```

By making the four variables global (defined outside of m a i n), they are automatically initialized to 0. For that reason, there's no need to include statements to assign starting values to them.

The program is shaping up. All that remains is to complete the other three functions. As you can see from this small demonstration, top-down programming lets you focus on one small section of the program at a time. Instead of worrying about how to open files, read characters, and perform other necessary jobs, I concentrated on completing the outer design and then spent time on one function, c o u n t c h a r s. I completed that function *out of context,* leaving the rest of the program for another time.

The final result is Listing 3.2, BP.CPP. You should be able to understand most of the program, except that is, for the file handling details. (I'll explain those items in a moment.) Try to pick out the function prototypes, and study the implementations for each function.

Listing 3.2. BP.CPP

```
 1:   // bp.cpp -- Count braces and parentheses in C++ programs
 2:
 3:   #include <stream.hpp>
 4:   #include <stdio.h>
 5:   #include <stdlib.h>
 6:
 7:   void welcome(void);
 8:   void openfile(void);
 9:   void countchars(char c);
10:   void showresults(void);
11:
12:   int openparen, closeparen, openbrace, closebrace;
13:   char filename[128];
```

```
14:   FILE *fp;
15:
16:   main()
17:   {
18:     char c;
19:
20:     welcome();
21:     openfile();
22:     while ((c = fgetc(fp)) != EOF)
23:       countchars(c);
24:     showresults();
25:     fclose(fp);
26:   }
27:
28:   void welcome(void)
29:   {
30:     cout << "\n\nBraces and Parentheses Counter";
31:     cout << "\nby Tom Swan.\n";
32:   }
33:
34:   void openfile(void)
35:   {
36:     cout << "\nFilename? ";
37:     gets(filename);
38:     fp = fopen(filename, "r");  // Open file for reading
39:     if (!fp) {
40:       cout <<"\nError opening file\n";
41:       exit(1);
42:     }
43:   }
44:
45:   void countchars(char c)
46:   {
47:     if (c == '(') openparen++;
48:     else if (c == ')') closeparen++;
49:     else if (c == '{') openbrace++;
50:     else if (c == '}') closebrace++;
51:   }
52:
53:   void showresults(void)
54:   {
55:     if (openparen < closeparen)
56:       cout << "\nMissing " << (closeparen - openparen)
57:            << " ( character(s)";
```

```
58:      else if (openparen > closeparen)
59:         cout << "\nMissing " << (openparen - closeparen)
60:             << " ) character(s)";
61:      else
62:         cout << "\nParentheses match";
63:
64:      if (openbrace < closebrace)
65:         cout << "\nMissing " << (closebrace - openbrace)
66:             << " { character(s)";
67:      else if (openbrace > closebrace)
68:         cout << "\nMissing " << (openbrace - closebrace)
69:             << " } character(s)";
70:      else
71:         cout << "\nBraces match";
72:
73:      cout << "\n\n";
74:   }
```

Function `openfile` (lines 34-43) uses a few C++ features you haven't seen before. After displaying a message that prompts you to enter a filename, line 37 calls `gets`, a function declared in STDIO.H. You can use this function to let people type characters into string variables, such as the `filename` string defined in BP.CPP at line 13. There are other ways to read strings into programs, but `gets` works well enough. (It doesn't prevent you from typing too many characters, so it's best to define strings of at least 128 characters, the maximum that `gets` can handle. This prevents bugs caused by people entering characters beyond the memory allocated to a string.) After getting the file's name, the program executes:

```
fp = fopen(filename, "r");
```

Variable `fp` is declared at line 14 as type `FILE`, which STDIO.H declares. (The asterisk in this definition creates a pointer to a `FILE`, a concept you'll meet again in chapter 4. A `FILE` variable is a `struct` that contains the fields C++ needs to keep track of open files. Normally, you don't need to use these fields directly, although you can study them in STDIO.H if you want. Instead, most programs only need to create a `FILE` variable such as `fp` and assign to it the result of a function such as `fopen`.

That function's job is to instruct DOS to find a file by name on disk, to prepare various internal variables to let other statements read the file's contents, and to return the address of a `FILE` structure, which this program saves in `fp`. The `"r"` in the function call specifies "read only access," meaning that statements will be allowed to read the file's contents, but not write new data to the file. I'll show you other ways to open files in chapter 8.

After opening the file, an `if` statement tests `fp` to see whether it contains a valid address. If `fopen` failed for some reason, usually because it couldn't find a file of the specified name, it returns `NULL`, which as you know, is represented by the value 0.

If f open succeeds, it returns a nonzero value that the program can then use to refer to the opened file. Because NULL and 0 represent false in C++, and 1 and other nonzero values represent true, the if statement can test fp as though it were an int variable:

```
if (!fp) {
    cout <<"\nError opening file\n";
    exit(1);
}
```

The expression (!fp) is exactly equivalent to (fp == 0) or (fp == NULL), and it's a typical C++ (and C) trick that you'll see time and again. Some people prefer the longer forms, but both styles are acceptable and there's no reason to avoid using the shorthand. To make the shorthand easier to remember, I like to pronounce (!fp) mentally as "if fp is not valid."

To see the effect of these statements, run BP and enter a filename that you know doesn't exist. The program will display the error message and exit. Always deal with similar possibilities in your own programs. Many C++ functions are designed to return the results of their operations, and it's your responsibility to check those results to see whether the functions encountered any errors. Forgetting or ignoring errors returned by functions is sure to lead to bugs.

Functions and Their Variables

Just about the only task you can't perform inside a function is to declare another function. Aside from that, you can insert statements and variables of all types inside functions.

Defining variables in a function limits those variables for the function's private use. A variable inside a function can be "seen" only by statements that are also in that same block. Statements in other functions can *never* peer over another function's shoulders in order to read or write variables defined there. A function's boundaries are like impenetrable stone walls.

This is not a limitation but a main advantage of the way functions work. Because the scope of a function's *local variables* is limited to the statements inside that function, you can be certain of a few helpful facts:

- Inside a function, unless you explicitly change a variable's value, that variable can't be changed by any statements outside of the function.

- The names of local variables do not have to be unique. Two, three, or more functions can all define variables named count. Each such variable is distinct, and each belongs only to its declaring function.

- Local variables in functions do not exist in memory until the function runs. This conserves memory by letting multiple functions share the same memory for their local variables (but not at the same time). This is an important concept—more on it in the next section.

Local Variables

In addition to having a restricted scope, local variables are special for another reason. They exist in memory only when the function is active—that is, only while the function's statements are executing. When the function is not running, its local variables do not occupy even one bit of memory. They simply do not exist at all.

This apparent magic is accomplished by storing variables on the computer's stack, an area of memory that grows and shrinks as needed. When a function begins running, it expands the stack by enough space to hold local variables declared in the function. When the function ends, the stack shrinks by the same amount. Then the next time that same function runs, the process repeats, again expanding the stack to hold variables and shrinking it when the function is done.

Between the time a function runs and the next time it is called to action, other functions may also run. If they also declare local variables, their values might be stored in the *same* locations on the stack used by other local variables declared in now inactive functions. In this way, functions share the same memory for their local variables, and it's possible for the total number of bytes of all local variables in a program to exceed the amount of available RAM without running out of memory!

However, as a consequence of this design, you can't store values in local variables and then expect those variables to have the same values the next time the function runs. In the meantime, another function may have stored its own variables in the same locations on the stack, overwriting those values. While the function runs, its variables are protected, but when the function is inactive, its variables do not exist.

A short program demonstrates these ideas. Listing 3.3, LOCAL.CPP, declares three functions at lines 6-8. One function, p a u s e, displays a message and waits for you to press the **<Spacebar>**. The other two functions define and display local string variables.

Listing 3.3. LOCAL.CPP

```
1:   // local.cpp -- Local variables demonstration
2:
3:   #include <stream.hpp>
4:   #include <conio.h>
5:
6:   void pause(void);
```

```
 7:    void function1(void);
 8:    void function2(void);
 9:
10:    main()
11:    {
12:        function1();
13:    }
14:
15:    void pause(void)
16:    {
17:        cout << "Press <Spacebar> to continue...";
18:        while (getche() != ' ') ;
19:    }
20:
21:    void function1(void)
22:    {
23:        char s[15] = "Philadelphia\n";
24:
25:        cout << "\nBegin function #1.   s = " << s;
26:        pause();
27:
28:        function2();  // Call function2 from function1
29:
30:        cout << "\nBack in function #1. s = " << s;
31:    }
32:
33:    void function2(void)
34:    {
35:        char s[15] = "San Francisco\n";
36:
37:        cout << "\nBegin function #2.   s = " << s;
38:        pause();
39:    }
```

The first thing to notice about LOCAL is that both of the two local variables at lines 23 and 35 have the same name (s). Because local variables are visible only inside the function that declares them, there is no conflict. Each variable is distinct even though it has the same name as the other.

The second important observation to make is at line 28, where function1 calls function2 (lines 33-39). During this time, while function2 runs, function1 is in suspended animation. Function1 is still active, but it has transferred control *temporarily* to function2. Because function1 remains active during this time, its local variables retain their values. Line 30 proves this by displaying the value of s after function2 returns control to its caller. This also shows that the two local variables are distinct even though they share the same name. Running LOCAL displays

```
Begin function #1.   s = Philadelphia
Press <Spacebar> to continue...
Begin function #2.   s = San Francisco
Press <Spacebar> to continue...
Back in function #1. s = Philadelphia
```

As you can see, after calling `function2`, the local s string in `function1` retains its value (`"Philadelphia"`). Though they share the same name, the two local variables do not occupy the same space.

External Variables

Most of the time, you declare a local variable in a function by just inserting its data type and name inside the function's block. Local variables use the same forms as global variables declared outside of `main` or as variables local to `main`. There are no differences in form between local and global variables—only differences between where and how those values are stored in memory.

But sometimes the standard ways don't cut it, and you need other means to declare variables. For example, suppose that a function needs to use a value that *another* function initializes. Because local variables exist only temporarily while their declaring function is running, a plain local variable won't solve this problem.

Listings 3.4, EXTERN1.CPP, and 3.5, EXTERN2.CPP, demonstrate one way to write functions that can share variables. To simulate a situation that occurs in many larger programs, the demonstration program is stored in two files. To compile it, use the command **ztc extern1 extern2**. This will compile both source-code files and link them together to create a single program, EXTERN1.EXE. Run this program to execute the test.

Listing 3.4. EXTERN1.CPP (1 of 2)

```
1:   // extern1.cpp -- Extern variable demonstration part 1
2:
3:   #include <stream.hpp>
4:
5:   void getfloat(void);
6:
7:   float f;
8:
9:   main()
10:  {
11:     getfloat();
```

```
12:         cout << "Value of float = " << f;
13:    }
```

Listing 3.5. EXTERN2.CPP (2 of 2)

```
 1:    // extern2.cpp -- Extern variable demonstration part 2
 2:
 3:    #include <stream.hpp>
 4:
 5:    getfloat(void)
 6:    {
 7:        extern float f;
 8:
 9:        cout << "Enter floating-point value: ";
10:        cin >> f;
11:    }
```

The problem to solve is this: How can a function in a separate source-code file use a variable defined in another file? One solution is to declare the local variable with the extern key word, as I did here at line 7 in EXTERN2.CPP. By prefacing the declaration with extern, you are telling the compiler that this variable's space is defined elsewhere. You are saying, "Don't create space on the stack for this one. Another part of the program will take care of allocating some memory for this variable."

That happens in EXTERN1.CPP at line 7, which declares the variable with the same name (f) and data type (float) as in the other file. The extern key word in the getfloat function tells the compiler to assume that f is defined elsewhere. Later, when the separate files are linked, the declarations are combined so that they all refer to the same location in memory.

Variable f in getfloat is a local variable in the sense that its scope is limited *in this source-code file* to that function. No other function can "see" f unless it also declares it to be extern. This is a safety measure that prevents any old function from changing the value of f.

There's no limit on the number of times you can declare the same variable extern, but you can define space for it only once. This makes extern suitable for header files that are included in multiple modules. You can declare a program's variables extern in the header file and include that file in all modules that need to use the variables. In the main module, you then define each global variable.

> **Note:** Try not to use extern too frequently. There are superior ways to pass information between functions. In general, only use extern to refer to global variables that are defined elsewhere. Because this creates permanent space for the variables, most local variables should *not* be extern.

Register Variables

A *register variable* looks the same as any other local variable, but instead of being stored on the stack, it's placed directly in a processor register such as SI or BX. Because there are a limited number of registers, and because those registers are limited in size, the number of register variables that a program can create at once is severely restricted.

To declare a register variable, preface it with the `register` key word. For example, to create an integer variable k and place it in a register, use this local-variable declaration:

```
register int k;
```

A register variable must be local to a function; it can never be global to the entire program. You also can't make register variables external to a function by using the `extern` key word. Only pure local variables can be placed in registers.

Using the `register` key word does not guarantee that a value will be stored in a register. That will happen only if a register is available. If there aren't enough processor registers to go around, C++ ignores the `register` keyword and creates the variable locally as normal. Declaring `register` variables is only a suggestion to the compiler that it should try to place this value in a register if it can.

Why do that? Because operations on values in registers are usually faster than those same operations when performed on values stored in memory. Used in critical code, register variables can boost performance by reducing the number of times the program has to access the computer's slower and less accessible memory circuits. Register variables can help optimize a program's performance by giving the CPU direct access to a program's key values.

Note: The Zortech C++ compiler included with this book, and the professional version, use register variables by default for the first one or more local variables declared in a function. Other C++ (and many C) compilers do the same; therefore, a local variable might be placed in a register even if you *don't* use the `register` keyword. The Zortech compiler also is particularly good at using all available registers to hold local variables. By *not* using the `register` keyword, you let the compiler decide which values to place in registers, and the code may actually run faster. This suggests that using `register` variables is a tricky business. The only reliable way to decide whether one is appropriate is to test the code extensively.

Listing 3.6 demonstrates register variables and shows how to use `register`'s opposite, `volatile`, when you *don't* want C++ to store a value in a processor register. The program counts from 1 to 100 twice, first using a register variable k (line 16) and then using a `volatile` (nonregister) variable at line 25.

Listing 3.6. REG.CPP

```
 1:   // reg.cpp -- Register variable demonstration
 2:
 3:   #include <stream.hpp>
 4:
 5:   void useregister(void);
 6:   void usevolatile(void);
 7:
 8:   main()
 9:   {
10:       useregister();
11:       usevolatile();
12:   }
13:
14:   void useregister(void)
15:   {
16:       register int k;
17:
18:     cout << "\nCounting with a register variable\n";
19:       for (k = 1; k <= 100; k++)
20:           cout << dec(k, 8);
21:   }
22:
23:   void usevolatile(void)
24:   {
25:       volatile int k;
26:
27:     cout << "\nCounting with a volatile variable\n";
28:       for (k = 1; k <= 100; k++)
29:           cout << dec(k, 8);
30:   }
```

When you run REG.CPP, you'll probably notice no difference in speed between the two functions useregister and usevolatile. This goes to show that register variables are beneficial only in critical places. Most of the time, it won't make much difference if a value is stored in memory or in a register.

Be aware also that register variables can have other consequences. In chapter 4, for instance, you'll learn how to find a variable's address in memory. Because a register variable isn't stored in memory, it doesn't have an address and it won't be possible for statements to refer to the variable in that way.

Use volatile for values that must be stored in memory, either because you need to find the addresses of those values or because other statements may change a local variable in ways that C++ will not know about. For example, if an external event such as a subroutine activated by an interrupt stores values in memory, those values must not be stored in registers.

Use register variables for a for-loop's control variable or in the conditional expression for a while statement that must run at top speed. But don't expect too much from register—it's no cure-all for a poor design, and using it does not guarantee a boost in performance.

Note: The register key word is available in all modern C++ (and C) compilers. Obviously, however, different computer systems have different registers, and a program that relies on values being placed in a processor register may not run correctly if ported to another system. Remember that using register does not guarantee that a value will be stored in a register.

Static Variables

Earlier, I stressed that local variables are temporary—they exist only while their declaring function is active, and they do not retain their values between calls to that function.

Rules are made to be broken, and you can break this one by declaring a local variable static. A static variable is local to its function, but like a global variable, it is stored in a fixed memory location. For this reason, a static variable retains its values between calls to a function. Unlike normal local variables, a static variable is initialized only one time (provided that initialization is included in the variable's definition).

An example helps to show the difference between a static and a plain local variable. Run Listing 3.7, STATIC.CPP, to execute two for loops that call two functions, next1 and next2. As you can see, although the loops and functions are nearly identical, their output is different.

Listing 3.7. STATIC.CPP

```
 1:   // static.cpp -- Demonstrate static variables
 2:
 3:   #include <stream.hpp>
 4:
 5:   int next1(void);
 6:   int next2(void);
 7:
 8:   main()
 9:   {
10:       int i;
```

```
11:
12:        cout << "\nCalling next1():\n";
13:        for (i = 1; i <= 10; i++)
14:            cout << " " << next1();
15:        cout << "\nCalling next2():\n";
16:        for (i = 1; i <= 10; i++)
17:            cout << " " << next2();
18:    }
19:
20:    int next1(void)
21:    {
22:        static int value = 1;          // Static variable
23:
24:        return value++;
25:    }
26:
27:    int next2(void)
28:    {
29:        int value = 1;                 // Normal local variable
30:
31:        return value++;
32:    }
```

The first for loop (lines 13-14) calls next1, which declares an int variable value as static (line 22). It also initializes this variable to 1, an action that occurs only the first time this function runs. The function *returns* value++ at line 24, which passes the value of value back to the calling statement and increments value. (The next section describes the return statement in detail.) Because the static variable retains its value between calls to next1, the for loop displays 1 2 3 4 5 6 7 8 9 10.

The second for loop (lines 16-17) calls next2, which also declares an int variable value, but leaves out the static key word. Because of this, value in next2 exists only temporarily and does not retain its value between function calls. The result of value++ at line 31 is thrown out when the function ends and when the for loop calls next2 again, it recreates space for value and again initializes it to 1. This second loop displays 1 1 1 1 1 1 1 1 1 1, proving that the pure local value does not retain its value between function calls.

Note: Like extern, a static variable is stored in a fixed location in memory. For this reason, you should use static sparingly. Unlike plain local variables, which exist temporarily and can share the same memory on the stack, all static variables in a program take up permanent storage which is not available for any other purpose while the program runs.

Functions that Return Values

The previous sample program (Listing 3.7, STATIC.CPP), used a `return` statement to pass a value back to the caller of a function. Until now, most functions in this book were declared as `void`, meaning they return no value:

```
void centerText(int x, int y);
```

Declaring function `centerText` as type `void` tells the compiler that this function does not pass any value back to its caller. To use a function declared with a `void` return value, simply type its name in a statement, supplying values for any arguments in parentheses:

```
centerText(10, 15);
```

Other kinds of functions perform calculations and *return* the results for use by other statements. For example, let's say you need a function that sums three integers. You could declare the function's prototype like this:

```
int threesum(int a, int b, int c);
```

The `int` data type replaces the `void` you've seen in other prototypes. Typing `int` in front of the function name tells the compiler that `threesum` *returns* an `int` value. Because the function returns a value, its name can appear inside an expression such as

```
int sum;
sum = threesum(10, 18, 25);
```

The effect of this is to call `threesum` with the three arguments 10, 18, and 25. After the function finishes, it passes the result (10 + 18 + 25) back to the caller. That value is then assigned to `sum`, another `int` variable.

In order for all of this to work, `threesum` has to perform its job correctly. It has to add the three arguments and return the result, using a `return` statement this way:

```
int threesum(int a, int b, int c)
{
    return (a + b + c);
}
```

When the function runs, it adds `a + b + c` and uses `return` to pass that sum back to the caller. Many statements can call `threesum` with any three values to add, and the function will faithfully sum those values and pass back the result.

Functions that return values are useful to solve all sorts of problems. Many times, functions that return values perform mathematical operations, but there are exceptions. A function might return a pointer to a variable (see chapter 4), or it might return an error code. For example, it's typical to declare a function like this:

```
int openFiles(void);    // Returns true if successful
```

This function executes `return (1)` if it's successful. If the function encounters an error, it executes `return (0)`, passing back C++'s value for false. Without filling in every detail, the function's body might be coded along these lines:

```
int openFiles(void)
{
    unsigned errorCode;    // > 0 = error
    ...    // Statements that "open files"
    return (errorCode == 0);
}
```

The function declares a local variable `errorCode`, in which other statements (not shown) store a value representing any errors that occur, for example, if a file isn't found on disk. The final statement in `openFiles` evaluates the expression `(errorCode == 0)`, which is true only if no errors were detected earlier. The result of this expression is passed back to the function's caller by `return`. Another statement can then call `openFiles` in an `if` statement:

```
if (!openFiles()) {
    cout << "\nERROR opening files!";
    exit(1);
}
```

Reading the expression `if (!openFiles())` as "if *not* `openFiles`" or as "if `openFiles` does *not* succeed" makes the sense of this fragment perfectly clear. By using `return` to pass a true (1) or false (0) value back to its caller, the function tells the `if` statement whether the function's actions were successful. The `if` statement detects any errors, and halts the program if the function fails, giving the program the capability of detecting and dealing with problems.

Commonly, functions return mathematical values. Using a function to perform a calculation and `return` the result saves space by storing the formula's statements in one place. Other statements that need to use the same formula can then call the function. By building a library of math functions, you can concentrate on writing new code instead of reinventing your formulas every time you begin a new project. If you make a mistake in a function's calculations, you need only fix the problem in one place.

C++ already has many mathematical functions, such as `pow` (power) and `sin` (sine). These are common enough to warrant a place in the C++ library. Other functions you can create yourself. For example, programs often need to find the *factorial* of a number, which equals the product of all integer values in sequence from 1 to that number. The factorial of 3 is 6 (1 * 2 * 3). The factorial of 8 is 40,320 (8 * 7 * ... * 1), and so on.

Listing 3.8 shows how to write a factorial function and puts that function to good use. For small input values, the program calculates what's known as a *combinatorial coefficient*—a mouthful of a phrase that describes a method of calculating the number of ways to arrange a certain number of items. For example, if you are the manager of an ice cream parlor and you want to know the number of triple-dipper ice cream cones you can make from 28 flavors, you can use the formula for a combinatorial coefficient to calculate the answer.

> **Note:** I got the idea for this section from *Innumeracy,* by John Allen Paulos, a superb book on "mathematical illiteracy and its consequences." If you like numbers, don't miss this intriguing book.

Listing 3.8. COCO.CPP

```
1:    // coco.cpp -- Combinatorial coefficients
2:
3:    #include <stream.hpp>
4:
5:    long factorial(int number);
6:
7:    main()
8:    {
9:       int i, selections, elements;
10:
11:       cout << "Number of selections? ";
12:       cin >> selections;
13:       cout << "Out of how many elements? ";
14:       cin >> elements;
15:
16:       double answer = elements;
17:
18:       for (i = 1; i < selections; i++)
19:          answer *= --elements;
20:       cout << "Nonunique combinations = " << answer << '\n';
21:
22:       answer /= factorial(selections);
23:       cout << "Unique combinations= "<< answer << '\n';
24:    }
25:
26:    long factorial(int number)
27:    {
28:       long value = 1;
29:
30:       while (number > 1)
31:          value *= number--;
32:       return value;
33:    }
```

Run COCO and enter two values: the number of selections (3 for the triple-dipper example) and the number of elements from which to make those selections (in this case, the 28 flavors). The program then displays the number of nonunique combinations, or 19,656. This represents the total number of ice cream cones you can make if you consider chocolate-peach-banana to be a *different* flavor than peach-chocolate-banana. This value equals 28 * 27 * 26—the total number of ways to arrange 28 items in groups of three.

However, if you advertise your parlor as having 19,656 flavors, your customers might question whether you have crossed the line that divides truth in advertising from fraud. You probably should promise to supply only the total number of *unique* flavor combinations that can be made from 28 flavors. This value equals the total number of nonunique combinations divided by the factorial of the number of selections (3), or in this case, 3276 (19,656/6). This makes sense if you consider that, for any three flavors, there are exactly 6 ways to arrange the scoops. In other words, if you give each flavor a number from 1 to 3, the list of possible combinations of those three flavors is 1-2-3, 1-3-2, 2-1-3, 2-3-1, 3-1-2, and 3-2-1. That's six ways to make three. Because this holds for all sets of flavors, dividing the total number of nonunique combinations by 6 equals the number of *unique* sets of three flavors that are possible to make from all *nonunique* combinations.

Getting back to C++, this formula is easy to implement by first calculating the number of nonunique combinations (lines 18-19) and then dividing that answer by the factorial of the number of selections (line 22). The f a c t o r i a l function at lines 26-33 is a good example of a mathematical function that returns a value to its caller:

```
long factorial(int number)
{
    long value = 1;

    while (number > 1)
        value *= number--;
    return value;
}
```

Examine the function closely and be sure you understand how it operates. The function receives a value (n u m b e r) from its caller. It declares one local variable (v a l u e) initialized to 1. A w h i l e loop cycles while n u m b e r > 1 and during each of those cycles, it multiplies v a l u e * n u m b e r, assigning the result of that expression back to v a l u e and reducing n u m b e r on each pass. You should recognize the shorthand used in this statement, but in case you're struggling with this, here is the equivalent of v a l u e *= n u m b e r-- written "the hard way:"

```
value = value * number;
number = number - 1;
```

The final statement in `factorial` executes `return value`, which passes the result in `value` back to the function's caller. Because `value` is a local variable inside `factorial`, it doesn't exist outside the function, and you may wonder how it's possible for a function to pass such a value back. The answer is that a function makes a *copy* of the value that it passes back via `return`. It's not the actual *variable* `value` that gets passed, but only a copy of that value. As a result, another statement can use `factorial` in an expression:

```
answer /= factorial(selections);
```

When C++ executes that line, it calls `factorial` with the current value of `selections`. The function takes that value, calculates its factorial, and returns the result. C++ then finishes the statement by dividing `answer` by the value returned by the function. The statement then assigns the final result of the calculation to `answer`.

As you can see here, functions are great for hiding messy implementation details. Instead of having to write yet another `while` loop, store the result of that calculation in a temporary variable, and then use that value to compute the `answer`, the statement simply calls `factorial` as though the function was a native C++ command. Using the function lets you forget about how that function is implemented. The details are hidden, and you don't have to think about them. You can assume that `factorial` gives the correct answer and use the function directly in statements.

When coding complex expressions, using functions this way can reduce a program's complexity and also help ensure that the code works correctly. Of course, if your functions are buggy, any expressions that use them might give wrong results. Most of the time, however, if you take the time to test your functions thoroughly, you'll find that using numerous functions is a good way to write programs that run correctly the first time through.

Note: Function-return values might be stored temporarily on the stack, in some other memory, or in one or more CPU registers. C++ doesn't guarantee anything about the locations of `return` values. However, a compiler manual will usually explain how it implements values returned by functions. Normally, you can ignore these details. After all, one of the reasons for using a high-level language like C++ is to let the compiler do the dirty work like deciding where to store temporary function-return values.

Parameter Passing

In previous sections, you examined functions that received *arguments* from callers. For example, the `factorial` function uses a single argument, a `number` that the function is to process:

```
long factorial(int number);
```

Inside the function prototype's parentheses is a variable declaration `int number`. This declaration has the same form as a local variable, except that it doesn't end with a semicolon. As I mentioned earlier, in the prototype, it's not necessary to give the variable a name and you could also write the line this way:

```
long factorial(int);
```

But I prefer to include the name; it helps me remember the purpose of the values I plan to pass to the function. For example, suppose that you need to write a graphics routine to draw a circle. (This is just a hypothetical example—don't bother to compile it.) You might declare the function prototype like this:

```
void circle(int x, int y, int diameter);
```

The three values `x`, `y`, and `diameter` obviously establish the location and size of the circle. Without the names, the prototype is still technically correct, but it's anything but clear:

```
void circle(int, int, int);
```

I'll use named parameters in (almost) all functions from now on. To use the fictitious `circle` function, you must pass as many arguments as declared in `circle`'s prototype. For example, to draw a circle, you might use the statement:

```
circle(5, 10, 100);
```

When the function runs, it *receives* the three arguments. At this time, variable `x` equals 5, `y` is 10, and `diameter` is 100. The parameters receive their *actual values* from the arguments passed to the function. Keep these key points in mind:

- A function prototype declares the *parameters* that it expects to receive from a caller.

- To call the function, a statement passes *arguments* to the function's parameters, one argument of the correct data type for each declared parameter.

- Inside the function, statements use the named parameters the same way as they use other local variables in the function. When the program runs, the parameters receive copies of the actual values passed to them by callers.

This last point is one of the most important concepts to learn about function parameters. Normally, a function receives a *copy* of any arguments passed to the function's parameters. Returning to the `factorial` function again, consider what happens when you write:

```
answer /= factorial(selections);
```

This statement passes a copy of the value `selections` to `factorial` for processing. When the function runs, it retrieves this value from its parameter `number`. In effect, C++ performs an assignment `number = selections` and then calls `factorial`. Inside the function, because `number` now holds a copy of `selections`' value, `factorial` can change `number` (it doesn't) without affecting `selections`.

One if by Value; Two if by Reference

Normally, parameters in C++ functions receive copies of values passed as arguments to those functions. As explained in the previous section, if a program calls `factorial` with an expression such as `q = factorial(n)`, and assuming that `q` is a `long` and `n` is an `int` variable, you can be 100% certain that `factorial` does not change the value of `n`. The function receives a *copy* of `n`, and it can't reach back and change the original variable's value.

Because function parameters receive copies of argument values, those arguments are said to be "passed by value." The actual variables aren't passed to the function. Only copies of those values are passed. (See Figure 3.2.)

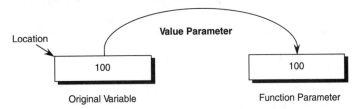

Figure 3.2. A value parameter receives a copy of an argument value passed to a function.

But there are times when you need exactly the opposite capability. For example, suppose you need a function that prompts a user to enter a number. You begin by writing:

```
void prompt(int n)
{
    cout << "Enter a value: ";
    cin >> n;  // ???
}
```

Next, you write a statement to call the function, passing it the value of a local variable, perhaps named `newvalue`:

```
main()
{
   int newvalue;

   prompt(newvalue);   // ???
   cout << "newvalue = " << newvalue;
}
```

The trouble is, `prompt` receives a copy of `newvalue` in its parameter n. And, even though the function executes `cin >> n` to let you enter a value for n, that value is thrown away when the function ends. Remember, like local variables, parameters exist only as long as the function is active. Assigning new values to parameters doesn't change the value of a variable passed to a function as an argument.

> **Time out:** By now, you should be able to collect fragments from this text into a file, shape them into the correct forms, and compile them to experiment with the concepts discussed here. If you're not already doing this, start now. Learn to be your own teacher. If you find this hard, start by loading a copy of a program from the diskette that comes with this book. Cut the meat from that program and replace it with the fragments printed here. Remember to add prototypes for all functions before calling them in `main` or elsewhere.

There are a couple of ways to solve this sticky problem: How can a function pass values back to arguments passed to a function parameter? One solution is to redesign a function like `prompt` to return a value, using a prototype such as

```
int prompt(void);
```

And then, back in `main`, you could write

```
newvalue = prompt();
```

There's nothing wrong with this approach, except that now, the function has to declare a local variable, read a value into that variable, and use a `return` statement to pass it back to the caller:

```
int prompt(void)
{
   int temp;    // temporary variable

   cout << "Enter a value: ";
   cin >> temp;
   return (temp);
}
```

That will work, but it seems to require more work than necessary. I also liked that original statement:

```
prompt(newvalue);
```

To my eye, the purpose of this is clear—to prompt somebody to enter a new value. In general, programs that are understandable are easier to fix and maintain, but, the problem remains: How can prompt change newvalue directly? The answer is to pass the parameter by *reference*.

Reference parameters look similar to others you've seen, but they begin with the character &. This character tells the compiler that you want it to allow the function direct access to a variable passed to the function as an argument. Instead of passing a copy of the argument's value, the program will pass a *reference* that tells the function where in memory that variable exists. (See Figure 3.3.)

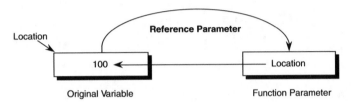

Figure 3.3. A reference parameter receives a reference to a variable passed as an argument to a function.

The reference that a function receives is the variable's address. Passing an argument by reference is just another way of saying "passing the address of the argument." With a reference parameter, the new function prototype is

```
void prompt(int &n);
```

And the function's implementation is now

```
void prompt(int &n)
{
    cout << "Enter a value: ";
    cin >> n;
}
```

That's much simpler than the previous version, which declared and passed a local variable back in a return statement. The new function simply declares n to be a reference parameter. Because of that, when cin >> n executes, the value you type is assigned directly to the argument passed to prompt. In other words, when main executes

```
void prompt(newvalue);
```

the input stream statement operates as though it were written:

```
cin >> newvalue;
```

Another sample program, Listing 3.9, REF.CPP, shows the difference between value and reference parameters. The program prompts twice for you to enter a "new value." Enter 100 each time. Only the second time does the program correctly report the value you enter. As you'll see, a reference parameter makes the difference between code that runs correctly and code that's broken (but not beyond repair).

Listing 3.9. REF.CPP

```
 1:   // ref.cpp -- Description
 2:
 3:   #include <stream.hpp>
 4:
 5:   void prompt1(int n);
 6:   void prompt2(int &n);
 7:
 8:   main()
 9:   {
10:       int newvalue = 0;
11:
12:       prompt1(newvalue);
13:       cout << "After prompt1, newvalue = " << newvalue;
14:
15:       prompt2(newvalue);
16:       cout << "After prompt2, newvalue = " << newvalue;
17:   }
18:
19:   void prompt1(int n)
20:   {
21:       cout << "\n\nEnter new value: ";
22:       cin >> n;
23:   }
24:
25:   void prompt2(int &n)
26:   {
27:       cout << "\n\nEnter new value: ";
28:       cin >> n;
29:   }
```

REF has two functions, prompt1 and prompt2, implemented at lines 19-29 and prototyped at lines 5-6. The functions are identical except for their names and the presence of an & character in front of their single int parameters. In prompt1, parameter int n is a *value parameter*. When a statement calls the function, it passes a copy of an argument value to the function parameter. In prompt2, parameter int &n is a *reference parameter*. When a statement calls this function, it passes a reference to the original argument.

Running the program shows what a difference a single character (&) can make. Line 12 calls prompt1(newvalue), passing the value of newvalue to prompt1. When line 22 reads a new value into n, the program simply throws that value away without changing the original newvalue. But when line 15 makes a similar call to prompt2(newvalue), line 28 also reads a new value into n. Because that's a reference parameter, line 28 stores the value you enter directly back to newvalue.

When you use value and reference parameters, keep these important facts in mind:

- Value parameters (declared *without* &) receive copies of argument values passed to them.

- Assignments to value parameters in a function *never* change the original argument's values passed to the parameters.

- Reference parameters (declared *with* &) receive the address of argument values passed to them.

- In a function, assignments to reference parameters *always* change the original arguments' values.

Usually, you can use value and reference parameters in exactly the same ways. However, there is one other difference to be aware of. When passing arguments to parameters, you'll sometimes use the names of variables. At other times, you'll pass literal values. For example, suppose that you have a function that positions the cursor at an X and Y coordinate on a display. The prototype might look like this:

```
void gotoxy(int x, int y);
```

Because x and y are declared as value parameters, it's possible to pass a mix of variables and literal values to them:

```
int x, y;

x = 5;
y = 10;
gotoxy(x, y);
gotoxy(0, 24);
gotoxy(0, y);
gotoxy(x, 1);
```

The same is not possible with reference parameters, which require an argument to be a variable—in other words, to be stored in a location that has an address. Obviously, this must be so for reference parameters to receive the addresses of arguments passed to them. For that reason, you can pass to reference parameters only arguments that have addresses:

```
void gotoxy(int &x, int &y);
```

Declared that way, only the first of the previous calls to gotoxy would be accepted by the compiler. The calls that specify literal values, such as 0, 24, and 1, are rejected because those values aren't stored in memory. Literal constants do not have addresses; therefore, programs can't pass them to a function's reference parameters.

This leads to a good rule of thumb for deciding whether to use value or reference parameters. If a function needs only the value of arguments to perform a job, value parameters are appropriate. If a function needs to pass values back to a caller, and if doing that with a return statement isn't convenient—for example, to pass back two or more values—reference parameters are probably the best choice.

> **Note:** All function parameters in C are passed by value. C has no equivalent to the reference parameters in C++.

Let's look at a practical use for value and reference parameters. Listing 3.10, BOX.CPP, prompts you to enter four display coordinate values (two pairs of two values). It then draws a box on screen using the values you enter as the positions of the box's upper left and bottom right corners. You can use similar functions in your own programs to create good-looking displays where text is divided on screen into neatly outlined boxes.

Listing 3.10. BOX.CPP

```
 1:  // box.cpp -- Display text boxes
 2:
 3:  #include <stream.hpp>
 4:  #include <disp.h>
 5:
 6:  void getcoords(int &toprow, int &topcol, int &botrow, int &botcol);
 7:  void drawbox(int toprow, int topcol, int botrow, int botcol);
 8:
 9:  main()
10:  {
11:      int toprow, topcol, botrow, botcol;
12:
13:      disp_open();
14:      getcoords(toprow, topcol, botrow, botcol);
15:      disp_move(0, 0);
16:      disp_eeop();
17:      drawbox(toprow, topcol, botrow, botcol);
18:      disp_move(24, 0);
19:      disp_close();
20:  }
```

```
21:
22:    void getcoords(int &toprow, int &topcol, int &botrow, int &botcol)
23:    {
24:        cout << "\nEnter top row and column (ex: 3 7): ";
25:        cin >> toprow >> topcol;
26:        cout << "Enter bottom row and column (ex: 20 64): ";
27:        cin >> botrow >> botcol;
28:    }
29:
30:    void drawbox(int toprow, int topcol, int botrow, int botcol)
31:    {
32:        disp_box(0, DISP_NORMAL, toprow, topcol, botrow, botcol);
33:    }
```

In addition to showing off value and reference parameters, BOX demonstrates another way to display text on screen. The method, which I'll use in other listings, employs Zortech C++'s display package. To make the package's commands available, you must include the DISP.H header file as BOX does at line 4.

After that, you're ready to use display commands to write text to the screen. Unlike other methods you've examined for this purpose, the display package lets you display all 256 characters available on PCs, including the normal ASCII set plus various Greek letters, line-drawing shapes, and other symbols that are useful for creating good-looking screens. (Another program in this chapter, ASC.CPP, Listing 3.15, uses the display package to show the full set of extended ASCII symbols available on most PCs.)

To use the display package, you first have to initialize it. This detects the type of display on your computer, and prepares other internal variables to let your programs run under a variety of conditions. You don't need to select among various display types. Just call disp_open before using most other display commands. For example, to initialize the display package, clear the display, move the cursor to midscreen, display a message, and quit with the cursor on the bottom line, you can write

```
#include <disp.h>                        // Include DISP.H header
main()
{
    disp_open();                         // Initialize display package
    disp_move(0, 0);                     // Send cursor to row 0, col 0
    disp_eeop();                         // Erase to end of page
    disp_move(12, 32);                   // Send cursor to row 12, col 32
    disp_printf("Display package");      // Display some text
    disp_move(24, 0);                    // Send cursor to last row
    disp_close();                        // Close display package
}
```

This is a complete program. You can type it into your editor, save it, compile, and run. The comments explain what each line does. For help with other display commands, look up functions that begin with disp_ in chapter 10. I'll explain other display-package functions as needed for future listings.

Note: The display-package commands are not part of the C++ language. They are part of the Zortech C++ library. Using display-package commands in your programs may prohibit you from compiling your unmodified programs with other C++ compilers.

Back to BOX.CPP, examine the function prototypes at lines 6-7. Notice that the functions getcoords and drawbox declare the same four parameters. However, in getcoords, the parameters are passed by reference (declared with &). In drawbox, the parameters are passed by value (no &). The reason for this should be obvious: The purpose of getcoords is to *return* (get) new values for each of its four parameters; the purpose of drawbox is only to use those values, not to change them.

Lines 22-28 demonstrate how getcoords directly enters new values into the argument variables passed to the function from line 17. Because getcoords' parameters are passed by reference, the input statements at lines 25 and 27 directly change the original argument variables passed to the function.

Lines 30-33 use copies of those values to draw a box on screen. Function drawbox doesn't need to pass any values back to its caller, so value parameters are appropriate here. To display a box on screen, line 32 calls disp_box, another function in the display package. The first argument to disp_box selects the box's type; try values from 0 to 4 to see the different styles available. The second argument to disp_box selects the kind of display mode. Replace DISP_NORMAL with DISP_REVERSEVIDEO to change the box's display attribute (or color on a color monitor). The last four arguments represent the box's coordinates.

Because drawbox declares value parameters, you can also pass literal values to the function. For example, load BOX.CPP into your editor and insert this line just after the drawbox statement at line 17:

```
drawbox(0, 0, 24, 79);
```

If drawbox declared its parameters to be passed by reference, the compiler would not accept that statement. However, because the parameters are passed by value, literal values are okay. The effect is to draw another box around the display's borders and around (or on top of) the box you defined by entering coordinate values to the prompts.

Default Arguments

In everyday terms, a default argument might be one that you have regularly with your boss or a "friend" at work, but in C++, a *default argument* is a parameter that a caller to a function doesn't have to supply. Default arguments might also be named optional parameters. If you pass a value to one, it uses that value. If you don't pass a value to an optional parameter, it uses a default value as the argument.

This is a very useful device, especially when designing functions that perform one way in the absence of certain input, but do something else on demand. For example, here's a function named `dashes` that displays a certain number of dash characters at any screen location:

```
void dashes(int row, int col, int num, int c = '-');
```

The function's prototype specifies four `int` values. The first two, `row` and `col`, let you choose where the first dash is to appear. Next, `num` holds the number of dashes to display at this location. And the final parameter is the character to use. In addition to the usual data type (`int`) and variable name (`c`), the parameter declaration includes an assignment and a default literal value (= `'-'`). C++ interprets this construction to mean "if the caller supplies an argument for this parameter, use that argument's value; otherwise, use the default value specified in the declaration."

You can now call `dashes` in one of two ways. First, to display 40 dashes at row 4, you can write

```
dashes(4, 0, 40);
```

Even though the function prototype specifies four parameters, because the last parameter includes a default argument value, you don't have to supply that value when calling the function. In this case, C++ compiles the program as though you wrote

```
dashes(4, 0, 40, '-');
```

However, if you want to change the character used by the function, you can write

```
dashes(4, 0, 40, '+');
```

The explicit argument overrides the default specified in the prototype. Now, the function will display plus signs instead of dashes.

When implementing a function prototype that declares default arguments, don't repeat the assignments. Just write the function as you normally would if none of the parameters had default argument values. For example, here's one way to implement the `dashes` function:

```
void dashes(int row, int col, int num, int c)
{
    disp_move(row, col);
    while (--num >= 0)
        disp_putc(c);
}
```

The default assignment to c appears only in the prototype, not in the implementation's function declaration. A few other rules to memorize when using default arguments are:

- Default arguments must be passed by value. A default argument's name can't be passed by reference (prefaced with an & character).

- Default argument values (the n in the declaration int x = n) may be literal values or const definitions. They may *not* be variables. In other words, if n were declared int n, int x = n would be rejected as a default parameter. If n is declared as const int n = 1, the declaration will be accepted.

- All default arguments must come last in the function prototype. After the first default argument, all subsequent arguments must also include default values.

This last point is important and also has implications that affect how programs can call functions with default arguments. A small example helps to explain the rule:

```
void f(int width, float v = 3.14159, char q = '$');
```

Although it's just for demonstration, function f shows a typical case that uses default parameters. The first parameter, width, could not be declared anywhere else. Placing it between v and q, or at the end of the parameter list, is not allowed. Both of f's default parameters come last in the parameter list, as they must.

When calling f, a program must specify a width. You always have to supply argument values for a function's normal parameters. But a program has the option of including v and q. These are legal calls:

```
f(10);
f(10, 5.5);
f(10, 5.5, '@');
```

The first call specifies no overriding values for the default arguments. The second specifies a value for v, overriding the default assignment of 3.14159. The third overrides both defaults, also specifying a character '@' for q in place of its default '$'. However, the following sort of call is not allowed:

```
f(10, , '#');    // ???
```

The compiler rejects this statement because it attempts to skip one of the default parameters. In all cases, C++ requires you to supply overriding values for all default arguments starting with any one of those declared by the function. You can't skip others in between. If a function prototype is declared like this:

```
void g(int a = 1, int b = 2, int c = 3, int d = 4);
```

then you have the option to use any of these function calls:

```
g();
(9);
g(9, 8);
g(9, 8, 7);
g(9, 8, 7, 6);
```

However, there is no way to supply override values, say, to parameters a and d while skipping b and c. Unfortunately, this does not compile:

```
(9, , , 6);   // ???
```

> **Note:** I surely wish that C++ default parameters allowed skipping arguments by accepting place-holding commas as in that dysfunctional sample. If they worked this way, default function arguments would be much more useful.

Some of C++'s library functions use default arguments. For example, in earlier programs, we used the d e c and h e x functions to display decimal and hex values in output stream statements like these:

```
cout << dec(value);
cout << hex(value);
```

The prototypes for these two functions are

```
extern char *dec(long, int = 0);
extern char *hex(long, int = 0);
```

Ignoring the e x t e r n   c h a r   * part of the declarations (I'll explain this in the next chapter), you can see that these prototypes specify default arguments i n t   =   0 as their second parameters. (Notice also that these prototypes do not specify names for their parameters, which is legal but differs from the style that I prefer.) To display a value in a 10-column space, you can write

```
cout << dec(value, 10);
```

If you don't supply the 10 (or another override argument), the default of 0 is used. If C++ didn't allow default arguments, when you didn't want to specify a column width, you would be forced to write

```
cout << dec(value, 0);
```

That takes more typing (a little in this case, but probably a lot in large programs with many functions that use default arguments). Worse, because the 0 serves no practical purpose, it makes the program more difficult to understand. To clarify the statement, you'll probably want to insert a comment that "0 is ignored."

Another good use for default parameters is to add new parameters to existing function declarations without having to modify programming that calls those functions. For example, suppose that you are writing a simulation of an audio circuit, and you write this function and declaration:

```
#define MAXVOLUME 100
void setVolume(int level);
```

You call this function from a dozen or more statements strewn throughout various modules. The function sets the simulation's volume level, limiting it to the MAXVOLUME constant. Later, you discover that you need to add a *variable* maximum; therefore, the constant is no longer useful. One solution is to make MAXVOLUME a global variable, but that's not usually wise because it makes the variable too accessible to other statements, and might cause a bug to creep into the code. Another is to add a parameter to setVolume:

```
void setVolume(int level, int maxLevel);
```

Now, you also have to hunt through the source text and change every use of setVolume to include an argument for the new parameter. A better plan is to give maxLevel a default value:

```
void setVolume(int level, int maxLevel = MAXVOLUME);
```

After making this alteration, you can write new statements like setVolume(n, 50) to change a volume and limit it to 50. Previous statements such as setVolume(quiet) work as they did before, giving maxLevel the default value specified by the constant MAXVOLUME.

Note: There are other ways to deal with modifications to programs that help keep existing code intact—a good idea for preventing bugs. (You know: "if it isn't broke, don't fix it.") I'll explain more about the subject in chapters 5 and 9, which cover object-oriented programming techniques and a feature in C++ called *overloading*.

As a final example of default arguments, Listing 3.11, CENTER.CPP, demonstrates a useful function that centers text on the display. You can copy this function into your own programs to display titles, prompts, for help screens, and so forth.

Listing 3.11. CENTER.CPP

```
1:  // center.cpp -- Center text on screen
2:
3:  #include <stream.hpp>
4:  #include <stdio.h>
5:  #include <disp.h>
6:  #include <string.h>
```

```
 7:
 8:    void center(int row, int col, char *s, int width= 0, int fill= '-');
 9:
10:    char s[128];        // String to center
11:
12:    main()
13:    {
14:       int length;      // Length of string
15:
16:    // Prompt for a string to center
17:       cout << "Enter a string: ";
18:       gets(s);
19:       length = strlen(s);        // Get length of string
20:
21:    // Prepare display
22:       disp_open();
23:       disp_move(0, 0);
24:       disp_eeop();
25:
26:    // Display string using all defaults
27:       center(10, 40, s);
28:
29:    // Display string with only fill default
30:       center(12, 40, s, length + 8);
31:
32:    // Display string with no defaults
33:       center(14, 40, s, length + 16, '*');
34:
35:       disp_move(24, 0);
36:       disp_close();
37:    }
38:
39:    void center(int row, int col, char *s, int width, int fill)
40:    {
41:       int wd2;        // Width divided by 2
42:       int c;          // for-loop control variable
43:
44:       if (width > 0) {
45:          wd2 = width / 2;
46:          for (c = col - wd2; c <= col + wd2; c++)
47:             disp_pokew(row, c, (DISP_NORMAL * 256) + fill);
48:       }
49:       disp_move(row, col - (strlen(s) / 2));
50:       disp_printf(s);
51:    }
```

Function `center` in CENTER.CPP (lines 39-51) makes good use of default parameters. As the prototype at line 8 shows, the `width` and `fill` arguments are optional. Unless you supply override values for these items, the `width` will default to 0 and the `fill` character will be a dash `'-'`. To use the function to center text on screen, execute a statement such as

```
center(10, 40, "Learning C++");
```

That will display the string in quotes at row 10. The center of the string will be at column 40. To surround the quote with dashes, use a statement like this:

```
center(10, 40, " Learning C++ ", 24);
```

Supplying the width argument 24 displays dashes around the string. The two extra blanks inside quotes make a nicer title line:

```
----- Learning C++ ------
```

By overriding both of the default argument values, you can control the width of the string and the character used at each end. For example, to display asterisks rather than dashes, you can write

```
center(10, 40, " Learning C++ ", 24, '*');
```

Study how the `center` function works (lines 39-51 in CENTER.CPP). The function first checks whether `width` is greater than 0; it will be only if a statement overrides that default value. If `width` is greater than 0, a `for` loop at lines 46-47 calls `disp_pokew` to insert a character into the display. (I'll explain more about this function later.) Lines 49-50 then display the string passed to the function on top of any characters drawn with the previous `for` loop.

You won't use default arguments all the time, but as these samples show, the arguments are useful for designing functions that operate in different ways depending on the values you pass to them. If a parameter isn't always needed, consider making it optional by giving it a default value in the function's prototype. This can go a long way toward making functions easier to use.

Recursion: It's All Done with Mirrors

Computers owe their existence, in part, to the need for putting things in order. Today, modern computers of all kinds spend a good bit of their time sorting data. Most database programs include instructions to sort records alphabetically on a text field or numerically on a field such as a ZIP code or a customer balance.

C++ has a sorting function that I'll explain how to use in chapter 9. (Also see chapter 10.) It's instructive to write your own sorting function, and it's useful to have one in your personal library for the times when you don't want to use the standard code in the library.

One of the most famous sorting *algorithms* is called *Quicksort,* and it was invented by C. A. R. Hoare. (For those who are getting started with programming, an *algorithm* is a method for solving a problem and is often described in step-by-step terms that are suitable for converting to computer language statements.) Basically, the Quicksort algorithm divides a set of data over and over, matches items in pairs, and swaps items repeatedly until all items are in order.

There are many ways to implement a Quicksort algorithm in a computer program, but one of the simplest uses a concept known as *recursion.* Recursion is what happens when a function calls itself during the course of its own actions. At first, the idea of a function calling itself may strike you as strange, but there's nothing magical about it, and it's a useful technique to know.

Note: For a complete description of the Quicksort and other sorting algorithms, see Donald E. Knuth's The Art of Computer Programming, Vol. 3, *Sorting and Searching,* Addison Wesley.

A simple program demonstrates how to use recursion to count from 1 to 10—nothing exciting, but a good way to learn what recursion is. Compile and run Listing 3.12, RECOUNT.CPP. See whether you can figure out how it works before reading the descriptions that follow the listing.

Listing 3.12. RECOUNT.CPP

```
 1:   // recount.cpp -- Count from 1 to 10 using recursion
 2:
 3:   #include <stream.hpp>
 4:
 5:   void recount(int top);
 6:
 7:   main()
 8:   {
 9:       recount(10);
10:   }
11:
12:   void recount(int top)
13:   {
14:       if (top > 1) recount(top - 1);
15:       cout << dec(top, 4);
16:   }
```

Look closely at function `recount` at lines 12-16. Line 14 tests the value of parameter `top`. If that value is greater than 1, the statement calls `recount`—the same function that is now executing. For this call, the program passes to the function the result of the expression `top - 1`.

When a function calls itself this way, it starts over from the top. The same physical code in memory runs again, but because local variables and parameters are created on the stack when a function runs, a completely new set of those variables and parameters is reserved for each recursive call.

When the recursively called function ends, it picks up where it left off at the place where the function called itself. This action resembles what you see when you look into a mirror when there's another mirror behind you. The endless series of reflections are caused by mirror A reflecting mirror B, which reflects mirror A's reflection, which reflects B's, and so on.

Unlike light's capacity to shine, a computer's stack can grow only so large, and too many recursive calls can quickly lead to a stack overflow by reserving too many fresh sets of variables and parameters for each recursion. When using recursion, you must be certain to provide a well-lighted exit, in this case, the if statement at line 14.

Think this through. Suppose that you call the function with recount(3). When recount calls itself, it passes the value of top - 1. When the function begins again, the freshly allocated top argument will equal 2. Because 2 is larger than 1, the if statement again calls recount. Again it passes top - 1 as the argument. On this third restart of recount, top will equal 1. This time, however, the if statement fails, causing the program to *fall through* to the output stream statement at line 15. That statement displays the value of top, which now equals 1. Then the function ends, causing the previous call to the function to pick up where it left off, executing the output statement and displaying the value of top as it was on that level, or 2. This repeats again and again until reaching the bottom level of function calls, displaying the initial value for top, or 3. The result is to display 1 2 3.

When you run RECOUNT, you'll see that it displays the numbers 1 through 10. To count up to higher values, change the starting value in line 9. (If you use a value that's too high, you may run out of stack space, which in extreme cases could force you to reboot your computer, although that probably won't happen.)

Now that you have an idea of how recursion works, let's see it in action in a more useful setting. Listing 3.13, SORTER.CPP, demonstrates one way to sort an array of values. You can use similar methods in programs to sort other kinds of data.

Listing 3.13. SORTER.CPP

```
1:  // sorter.cpp -- Array sorter
2:
3:  #include <stream.hpp>
4:  #include <stdlib.h>
5:  #include <time.h>
6:
7:  #define ARRAYSIZE 100
8:
9:  void fillArray(void);
```

```
10:    void displayArray(char *s);
11:    void quicksort(int left, int right);
12:    void sortArray(int n);
13:
14:    int array[ARRAYSIZE];         // Array of integers
15:
16:    main()
17:    {
18:        fillArray();
19:        displayArray("Before");
20:        sortArray(ARRAYSIZE);
21:        displayArray("After");
22:    }
23:
24:    // Fill global array with values taken at random
25:    void fillArray(void)
26:    {
27:        int i;
28:
29:        srand(time(NULL));           // Randomize generator
30:        for (i = 0; i < ARRAYSIZE; i++)    // Fill array
31:            array[i] = rand();
32:    }
33:
34:    // Display contents of array before and after sorting
35:    void displayArray(char *s)
36:    {
37:        int i;
38:
39:        cout << '\n' << s << " sorting:\n";
40:        for (i = 0; i < ARRAYSIZE; i++)
41:            cout << dec(array[i], 8);
42:    }
43:
44:    // Quicksort algorithm by C. A. R. Hoare
45:    void quicksort(int left, int right)
46:    {
47:        int i = left;
48:        int j = right;
49:        int test = array[(left + right) / 2];
50:        int swap;
51:
52:        do {
53:            while (array[i] < test) i++;
54:            while (test < array[j]) j--;
```

```
55:          if (i <= j) {
56:              swap = array[i];
57:              array[i] = array[j];
58:              array[j] = swap;
59:              i++;
60:              j--;
61:          }
62:      } while (i <= j);
63:      if (left < j) quicksort(left, j);
64:      if (i < right) quicksort(i, right);
65:  }
66:
67:  // Sort n elements in global array
68:  void sortArray(int n)
69:  {
70:      if (n > 1) quicksort(0, n - 1);
71:  }
```

The key feature to understand about SORTER is the way lines 63 and 64 call the quicksort function recursively. These two statements are *inside* quicksort; therefore, calling quicksort from these locations causes the function to start over from the top with a brand new set of local variables and parameters. The if statements in the recursive calls provide the well-lighted exits that prevent the function from calling itself "forever," that is, until running out of stack space.

SORTER defines a global array at line 14, which it fills with values selected at random in function fillArray (lines 25-32). In that function, line 29 calls srand to "seed" a random-number generator. This scrambles the generator's starting value so that rand produces a different sequence each time the program runs. If the program didn't perform this step, the values from rand at line 31 would be the same for each new run.

Note: It may strike you as odd that random sequences may be repeated each time you run a program. Doesn't that mean they aren't random? The answer is no. A random sequence is "random" if values in that sequence can't be predicted from previous values. Numeric sequences are "random" simply because they follow no ordained pattern.

Line 31 assigns a value selected at random to the global array variable, one value for each space in the array. Function rand returns an integer value. Calling it returns the next number from the current random sequence.

After filling the array and displaying its initial values (see function displayArray at lines 35-42), the program calls quicksort to rearrange the values in the array. By comparing values and exchanging those that are out of order—

and by dividing the array into sections to avoid examining the same pairs of values too many times, which would slow the action considerably—the function puts the array of values into numeric order. Finally, the program displays the same array, showing its contents after sorting.

Inline Functions

Calling functions takes time—not much time, but enough to make a difference in performance when a program calls a function many thousands of times. To call a function, the compiled program has to save the address of the current location on the stack. It also has to "push" onto the stack any argument values needed by the function. Finally, the code executes a `call` assembly language instruction to start the function's ball rolling.

You don't need to know all those underlying details about function calls to write most C++ programs. Just be aware that, when all those details are taken together, they waste time. In critical applications, you may be able to eliminate some of the overhead associated with function calls by declaring them `inline`.

An `inline` function may contain any statements and perform any actions that normal functions can. Unlike a normal function, however, the `inline` variety does not have a prototype, and it's usually declared before `main`. That's not a requirement; `inline` functions need to be declared only before they are used, not necessarily before `main`. But they are usually stored in header files, and because those files are usually included into a program before `main`, this is the most common place to insert `inline` functions.

To create an `inline` function, insert the `inline` keyword in front of a normal function declaration and body. For example, here is an `inline` function that adds 10 to a parameter `n`:

```
inline int add10(int n) { return (n + 10); }
```

Let's take that one element at a time. First, comes the `inline` keyword. Next, comes the function declaration (`int add10(int n)`), which is no different than other declarations you've seen. The function returns an `int` value, and it specifies one parameter, `int n`.

The major difference is the body of the function, which appears immediately after the declaration. The statement inside braces returns the result of the expression (`n + 10`). In a larger `inline` function, there could be more than one statement, with each statement terminated by a semicolon. Notice the semicolon at the end of the single statement in this sample. Some people are confused by this because there is no semicolon after the brace. If you examine the same code written in the usual one-line-per-element style, you'll see that it's no different from the single-line version:

```
inline int add10(int n)
{
    return (n + 10);
}
```

I wrote the inline sample on one line because that's the style most C++ programmers prefer. But there's no technical reason for writing the code that way, and you can type inline functions on multiple lines if you want.

When the compiler encounters a statement that uses an inline function, as in this sample,

```
int x;
x = add10(5);
```

instead of calling add10 as it would for a normal function, the compiler inserts the function's body *directly into the program*. In other words, the compiler *expands* the inline function as though you had written

```
x = 5 + 10;
```

This is a silly example, of course, but you can see that processing the expression 5 + 10 in line with the rest of the program takes less time than calling a function with all its associated overhead.

Most of the time, you'll use inline functions inside a for or other loop that executes many times and that must run as fast as possible. For another example, compile and run Listing 3.14, CONE.CPP.

Listing 3.14. CONE.CPP

```
 1:  // cone.cpp -- Use an inline function to find the volume of a cone
 2:
 3:  #include <stream.hpp>
 4:
 5:  #define Pi 3.14159265
 6:
 7:  inline float cone(float radius, float height)
 8:      { return ((Pi * (radius * radius) * height) / 3.0); }
 9:
10:  main()
11:  {
12:      float radius, height, volume;
13:
14:      cout << "Enter cone's radius at base: ";
15:      cin >> radius;
```

```
16:        cout << "Enter cone's height: ";
17:        cin >> height;
18:
19:        volume = cone(radius, height);
20:
21:        cout << "Cone's volume = " << cone(radius, height);
22:    }
```

Lines 7-8 declare an inline function that calculates the volume of a cone. After prompting you for the cone's radius and height (lines 14-17), the statement at line 19 assigns the result of the cone function to a variable volume, which the program displays in an output statement at line 21.

Instead of calling cone at 19, however, C++ expands the inline function by replacing the expression to the right of the equal sign with the instructions declared in the function back at line 8. As in the previous examples, this use of inline functions isn't required here; a few milliseconds (or however much time it takes) difference between calling a function and expanding its statements in line will hardly matter, and cone may as well be a regular function.

Don't hesitate, however, to use inline functions if you need to give a loop the sharpest possible edge in performance. When doing so, be aware of these restrictions and suggestions:

- The compiler will ignore the inline key word on occasion. Usually, it will do this if you try to create an inline function that is too large. The exact limit is difficult to predict, but if your inline functions exceed a few statements, C++ may or may not convert them to regular functions.

- Numerous inline functions can greatly expand the final size of a compiled program. If you call a large inline function 100 times, the compiler will faithfully expand that function in 100 places! Use inline functions judiciously and only where their benefits outweigh this and other potential drawbacks.

- If you are familiar with C, you have probably used macros to create instructions that are roughly similar to C++ inline functions. In most cases, inline functions are easier to write than macros, and the type checking of parameters—which, for example, ensures that you don't use a floating-point value where only an integer is allowed—gives the program an added measure of safety.

- Remember that the benefits from inline functions are likely to be small except in the most critical of applications. Don't make the mistake of converting all functions to the inline kind. This is *not* a good way to optimize most programs for better performance.

Turning Point

You'll be pleased (any maybe a tad surprised) to learn that you've now passed the halfway mark in your quest for learning C++. In fact, you're farther than halfway. You've already seen most all there is to know about C++ fundamentals, and you've seen most of the tools in action that you'll use to write your own C++ programs.

Don't be *too* surprised, though. C++ is a terse language with only the minimum number of native features required to write programs. That doesn't mean that C++ is simple-minded. C++'s relatively simple set of fundamental commands can be combined in unlimited ways, and you haven't learned about two of C++'s more advanced features—pointers and classes—which I'll cover in the next two chapters.

Before doing that, however, this is a good place for you to review what you know about C++ so far. Be sure that all of the previous material in chapters 1, 2, and 3 is clear. Run and study the sample listings again, and be sure you understand how they work. Write a few test programs and complete the exercises at the ends of this and the previous two chapters if you haven't done that already. The better you learn the fundamentals in these three chapters, the easier you'll be able to pick up the more advanced material to come.

Listing 3.15, ASC.CPP, is a useful program for marking this turning point in your goal to learn C++. It's the longest program listed so far, and it's a useful utility to boot. Instead of chapter 2's simple ASCII chart displayed by ASCII.CPP (Listing 2.15), the all new ASC shows all 256 characters available on PC screens. After compiling and running the program, use the cursor keys to highlight any character and see its ASCII value in decimal and hex in the upper right corner. Press **<Esc>** to quit.

Listing 3.15. ASC.CPP

```
 1:   // asc.cpp -- Interactive ASCII chart
 2:
 3:   #include <stdio.h>
 4:   #include <disp.h>
 5:
 6:   #define ESC 27
 7:   #define TOPROW   3
 8:   #define TOPCOL   7
 9:   #define BOTROW 21
10:   #define BOTCOL 73
11:
12:   void showChart(void);
13:   void showASCII(unsigned c, int attrib);
14:   void movecursor(unsigned c);
15:   void showvalues(unsigned c);
16:   int rowasc(unsigned c);
17:   int colasc(unsigned c);
```

```
18:
19:    int oldc;          // Previously displayed character
20:
21:    main()
22:    {
23:      unsigned c = 1;            // Currently highlighted character
24:      unsigned key;              // Command from keyboard
25:
26:      disp_open();                            // Initialize display package
27:      showChart();                            // Display ASCII chart
28:      movecursor(c);                          // Initialize cursor position
29:      while ((key = getch()) != ESC) {        // Get user command
30:          switch (key) {
31:              case 'H': c -= 32; break;    // Move up
32:              case 'P': c += 32; break;    // Move down
33:              case 'K': c--; break;        // Move left
34:              case 'M': c++; break;        // Move right
35:          }
36:          c %= 256;             // Make sure c is in range 0 ... 255
37:          movecursor(c);        // Highlight and report on character c
38:      }
39:      disp_move(24, 0);     // Move cursor to last line before ending
40:      disp_close();         // Close the display package
41:    }
42:
43:    void showChart(void)
44:    {
45:        unsigned c = 0;        // for-loop control variable
46:
47:    // Clear display
48:
49:        disp_move(0, 0);
50:        disp_eeop();
51:
52:    // Display box and ASCII characters inside
53:
54:        disp_box(3, DISP_NORMAL, TOPROW, TOPCOL, BOTROW, BOTCOL);
55:        for (c = 0; c <= 255; c++)
56:            showASCII(c, DISP_NORMAL);
57:
58:    // Display other text on screen
59:
60:        disp_move(TOPROW - 1, TOPCOL);
61:        disp_printf("Cursor keys move; <Esc> quits");
```

```
 62:        disp_move(BOTROW + 1, TOPCOL);
 63:        disp_printf("Learning C++");
 64:        disp_move(BOTROW + 1, BOTCOL - 22);
 65:        disp_printf("ASCII Chart by Tom Swan");
 66:    }
 67:
 68:    // Display one ASCII character using a display attribute
 69:    void showASCII(unsigned c, int attrib)
 70:    {
 71:        disp_pokew(rowasc(c), colasc(c), (attrib * 256) + c);
 72:    }
 73:
 74:    // Return row number for character c
 75:    int rowasc(unsigned c)
 76:    {
 77:        return(2 + TOPROW + ((c / 32) * 2));
 78:    }
 79:
 80:    // Return column number for character c
 81:    int colasc(unsigned c)
 82:    {
 83:        return(2 + TOPCOL + ((c % 32) * 2));
 84:    }
 85:
 86:    // Unhighlight old character and highlight a new one
 87:    void movecursor(unsigned c)
 88:    {
 89:        showASCII(oldc, DISP_NORMAL);
 90:        showASCII(c, DISP_REVERSEVIDEO);
 91:        oldc = c;
 92:        showvalues(c);
 93:    }
 94:
 95:    // Display character and its ASCII value in decimal and hex
 96:    void showvalues(unsigned c)
 97:    {
 98:        disp_move(TOPROW - 1, TOPCOL + 35);
 99:        disp_printf("Character =    ASCII = %d  %#x", c, c);
100:        disp_eeol();
101:        disp_pokew(TOPROW - 1, TOPCOL + 47, (DISP_NORMAL * 256) + c);
102:    }
```

After you read ASC's text, you'll discover that this program is different from earlier examples that simply print a few numbers or display some text and quit. ASC carefully formats the screen. It clears the display of old text. It centers its lines, and it draws a stylish box around the "main action." These items aren't just fluff. Many programs succeed or fail based on how well their interfaces let people interact with the program's operation. Later chapters will show other ways to design good looking screens with a "class library" of objects for displaying text in pop up windows—but more on that later.

ASC also takes advantage of C++'s rich function library, including the display-package functions introduced earlier. Statements in ASC are collected into well-named functions, which are short and to the point. This makes the text clear, and you should be able to understand it by reading the statements a couple of times. Also read the comments as a guide through ASC's operation. If you find any of the statements in ASC unintelligible, you need to go back over this and the previous two chapters. There isn't anything in the program that you haven't met before.

But there are a few areas that might give you a little trouble. One is at line 36, which assigns to c the result of c *modulo* 256. This is just the remainder left after dividing c by 256. Because that remainder has to be a value from 0 to 255, the effect is to limit c's value to that same range. This is a useful trick to remember, and the most frequent reason for using the C++ modulo operator %.

A second element of ASC that needs explanation occurs twice. (Earlier, I promised to explain this.) In function showASCII at line 71, you'll find the statement

```
disp_pokew(rowasc(c), colasc(c), (attrib * 256) + c);
```

The first two arguments call the two functions rowasc and colasc, which together return the row and column coordinate where character c is displayed. The calls to these functions occur *before* the program calls disp_pokew. It passes the values from those functions to the value parameters declared by disp_pokew. This is a common use for functions and avoids code like this:

```
int row, col;

row = rowasc(c);
col = colasc(c);
disp_pokew(row, col, ...);
```

Instead of calling the functions and saving their results in variables such as row and col, you can just call the functions and pass their values as arguments directly. However, you can do this only for value parameters. You can't pass a function result (which you should consider to be constant) to a reference parameter. Reference parameters, you'll recall, must refer to an address of a variable somewhere in memory. Function return values don't have defined addresses.

The call to disp_pokew (the w stands for a 16-bit *word*) ends with the expression (attrib * 256) + c. It's a little out of place in this chapter on functions to describe what this expression does, but because it's in the final program and similar expressions are so common, this is as good a time as any. Here, attrib represents an attribute to use for displaying a character. Various attribute values control the color of characters, or on monochrome screens, whether a character is displayed in bold, is underlined, blinks, and so forth. (See the d i s p_ functions in chapter 10 for more details about display attributes.)

Multiplying a t t r i b by 256 has the opposite effect as the modulo expression described earlier. Because the value 256 is a power of 2, multiplying any value by 256 effectively shifts that value into the upper 8 bits of a 16-bit integer. In other words, if a t t r i b equals 7, multiplying that value by 256 equals 1792. In binary, the shifting action is easier to see:

```
      7     0000 0000 0000 0111
  x 256     0000 0001 0000 0000
  -----
   1792     0000 0111 0000 0000
```

As this shows, the multiplication by 256 shifts the bits that represent 7 in binary to the left eight places, in a sense opening up a hole of eight 0s at the end of the value. Adding the value of a character in the ASCII range 0 to 255 to this intermediate result drops that value into the hole. For example, if c is 65 (the ASCII value for the character 'A'), adding c to 7 x 256 equals 1857, or in binary:

```
0000 0111 0100 0001
```

The addition affects only the lower 8 bits. It doesn't change the upper 8 bits in any way. Using this trick, the expression (a t t r i b * 256) + c *combines* the value of a t t r i b and the value of c into a single 16-bit word, provided, of course, that the two uncombined parts are no larger than can be represented in 8 bits. This packed format—two 8-bit quantities squeezed into a 16-bit word—is inserted directly in the PC's video display buffer by calling d i s p_p o k e w to display a character in its selected colors (or other attributes).

That may be a long-winded explanation of a relatively simple process, but the method for combining two 8-bit bytes into a 16-bit word is a good one to know and comes in handy all the time. In general, given two 8-bit values A and B in the range 0 to 255, you can combine those values into one 16-bit word C by using the expression

```
C = (A * 256) + B;
```

To extract the original two values from C, use these expressions:

```
B = C % 256;
A = (C - B) / 256;
```

Even better, use logical operators (shifts, ANDs, and ORs) rather than mathematical ones to perform these same tasks. Because the logical operators relate directly to similar assembly language instructions, the equivalent expressions may run more efficiently. You also may find the results of using logical operators easier to visualize, if you have a good understanding of the binary number system (see chapter 2's sample programs TAND, TOR, TSHR, TSRL, and others).

To combine the two values A and B into C, using a logical shift left (<<) and a logical OR (|), use the expression

```
C = (A << 8) | B;
```

That shifts A left 8 bits and "ORs in" the value of B. To extract the original two values from C, use these expressions:

```
A = (C >> 8);
B = (C & 0x0ff);
```

Questions and Exercises

3.1. Describe some of the reasons for using functions.

3.2. What's the difference between a function prototype and a function implementation? Where are the prototype and implementation usually stored in relation to function ma i n?

3.3. How do you call a function?

3.4. What key word represents "no return type?"

3.5. What is the one item that a function can't declare?

3.6. Write a function that uses one or more register variables, and an identical function that uses common variables. Compare the disk sizes of the two functions inserted into a sample program. Are the sizes the same? If not, why not?

3.7. Write a function that knows how many times it was called. You may *not* use any global variables in the program.

3.8. Listing 3.8, COCO.CPP, calculates a combinatorial coefficient. Extract the necessary statements from this program and create a function named c o c o that returns the correct answer for this formula. What parameters does the function need? What data type should it return?

3.9. Write one or more functions that prompt for and return two i n t values within a specified range. The function(s) should require one value to be less than or greater than the other.

3.10. Design a single function a r e a that can calculate the area of a square *and* a cube. (Hint: use default parameters.)

3.11. Write a recursive version of the factorial function from Listing 3.8, COCO.CPP.

3.12. Convert your factorial function from exercise 3.11 into an in-line function. What effect will this have on the size of a program?

3.13. How many times can you declare a variable to be extern? Where is a good place to store extern declarations, and what are they good for?

3.14. Write a function that accepts two char parameters and returns those values packed into an unsigned 16-bit integer.

3.15. Write a function similar to the one in exercise 3.14 that can extract the two 8-bit int values packed into an unsigned integer passed to the function as an argument.

Chapter 4

Pointers about Pointers

The point I'm trying to make is . . .
I'd like to point out that . . .
Didn't I tell you it's not nice to point?!
Could you point me to the nearest exit?
Only point a weapon at something you are sure you want to hit.
Why don't you just get to the point?

Our world is filled with pointers. The ideas of an arrow pointing out a one-way street and a finger pointing to a destination are natural and intuitive. Why then, do many programmers think of pointers in programming as though they were poison spears with the programmers' names written on them?

I don't know the answer, but there's no reason for you to have any reservations about using pointers. Forget what you may have heard about pointers causing bugs in code. That's rubbish. Pointers don't cause bugs. People do. You can learn how to use pointers successfully. Many programmers have done so, and you can be one of them.

This chapter describes C++ pointer fundamentals. Along the way, I'll "point out" tips and tricks that will help you to use pointers effectively in your programs. You can write programs without pointers, but as you'll learn, pointers offer practically unlimited control over memory storage in ways that put other techniques to shame.

Declaring Pointers

To create a pointer, add a space and an asterisk after any data type identifier. For example, `int p` creates a plain integer, but `int *p` creates a pointer *to* an integer. (Some programmers place the asterisk after the data type, writing `int* p` rather than `int *p`. It's all the same to the compiler, but I prefer to use the form `int *p`.) Regardless of how you create pointers, remember these key facts:

- A pointer is a *variable* just like any other.

- A pointer variable contains an *address* that points to another location in memory.

- Stored at that location is the *data* that the pointer addresses.

A pointer points to a variable stored in memory. If you declare a variable like this:

```
int *ptr;
```

you are telling the compiler that the variable p t r is a pointer to an integer stored somewhere else in RAM. (See Figure 4.1.)

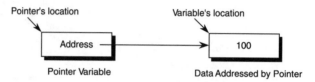

Figure 4.1.   A pointer is a variable that contains an address.

Like all variables, p t r requires initializing before use. If you fail to initialize a pointer, its address may equal a leftover value from another operation. When you initialize a pointer, you give it an address that you know points to a valid location in memory. Uninitialized pointers are like arrows spilled from a quiver—a bunch of dangerous pick-up sticks that may point every which way.

There are several ways to initialize pointers—most of which are covered in this chapter—but the results are identical. Initializing a pointer gives that pointer the address of its target data. After initialization, you can then use the pointer to reference the addressed data.

There is a significant difference, however, between normal variables and those addressed by pointers. Programs can manipulate pointers in ways that can't be applied to normal variables. By altering, reassigning, and tweaking the address held by a pointer, it's possible to create many interesting data structures such as lists, trees, and stacks that use pointers as links to items in memory. In this way, pointers operate as chains connecting variables that may be stored anywhere and making it possible to design structures that grow and shrink to accommodate whatever you want to store in them. Pointers also let you peek into memory to extract and even change values that belong to DOS, to the ROM BIOS, or to the CRT's display buffer. With pointers, all bytes in memory are at your disposal.

Pointer Dereferencing

After defining a pointer variable, the next step is to initialize the pointer and to use it to address some target data in memory. Using a pointer to "get to" its target is called *dereferencing the pointer.* When you dereference a pointer, you tell the compiler to use the data addressed by the pointer rather than the address value that the pointer contains. In all expressions involving a pointer, you must specify whether you intend an operation to use a pointer's address or to use the data stored at that location.

Listing 4.1, ALIAS.CPP, demonstrates the concepts of creating, initializing, and dereferencing a pointer variable. These are the most important details to learn about pointers, and you should run the sample program several times until the statements and their effects are perfectly clear.

Listing 4.1. ALIAS.CPP

```
 1:   // alias.cpp -- Demonstrate alias pointers
 2:
 3:   #include <stream.hpp>
 4:
 5:   char c;                // A character variable
 6:
 7:   main()
 8:   {
 9:       char *pc;          // A pointer to a character variable
10:
11:       pc = &c;
12:       for (c = 'A'; c <= 'Z'; c++)
13:           cout << *pc;
14:   }
```

Are you surprised at ALIAS's output? Running the program displays the alphabet—nothing to shake the earth, but consider *how* the program accomplishes this simple task. The only output statement is at line 13. That statement does not refer to the character variable c, to which the for loop at line 12 assigns the characters 'A' through 'Z'. If the output statement doesn't use the character variable directly, how can it display the letters that c contains?

To understand the answer to this riddle, first examine line 9, which creates a pointer variable named pc. The pointer is *bound to* a variable of type char by the definition char *pc. If this line read char pc, pc would be a simple character variable. Written as char *pc with the asterisk, pc is a *pointer* to a character variable stored somewhere in memory. However, at this early stage in the program, pc doesn't yet address any valid location. Like all variables, the pointer requires initializing before use.

Line 11 accomplishes that job by assigning to pc the address of variable c. The expression &c means "the address of c." In general, you can use the & character in a similar way to obtain the address of any variable. The expression &value is the address where value is stored.

Because p c is a pointer, C++ allows programs to assign addresses to it. By executing the statement p c = & c, the program assigns the address of the variable c to p c. After this, p c points to c. Both p c and c then refer to the *same* location in memory. (See Figure 4.2.)

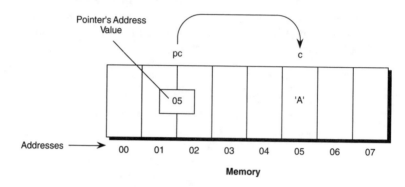

Figure 4.2.   *pc* and *c* address the same memory location.

Now if the variable c, which is stored somewhere in memory, and p c, which points to that same location, refer to the same data, changing one must affect the other. This is how ALIAS works. The f o r loop at lines 12-13 cycles c through the letters ' A ' through ' Z '. Because p c addresses the same location where c is stored, using the pointer in the output statement at line 13 displays the value of c. Technically speaking, p c is called an *alias* because it serves as another name for c.

Note: All pointers are not aliases, only those that point to the location where another program variable is stored.

Look closely at the output statement c o u t << *p c at line 13 in ALIAS.CPP. Notice the asterisk in front of the pointer's name. This symbol tells C++ to dereference the pointer—in other words, to use the data that the pointer addresses. In this case, the data is a character, and therefore, the statement displays that character's value. C++ knows that p c addresses a character because the program declared it to be bound to a c h a r data type back at line 9.

Load ALIAS.CPP into your editor and change the output statement to c o u t << c ; . Running the modified program produces the same results as the original. This proves that both c and p c refer to the same location in memory. To use a plain variable like c, you need to type only its name. To use the data addressed by a pointer, you must dereference that pointer by prefacing its name with an asterisk as in *p c. The expression p c refers to the pointer itself as a variable. The expression *p c refers to the data that the pointer addresses. In fact, to C++, the expression *p c *is* a c h a r variable no different from c.

When you dereference other pointers, think of them as variables of their bound data types. For a pointer declared as `float *fp`, the expression `*fp` in a statement is treated identically to a common `float` variable. For a pointer declared as `myStructType *mstp`, the expression `*mstp` is identical to a plain variable of type `myStructType`. The expressions `fp` and `mstp` are pointers; in other words, they are address values. The expressions `*fp` and `*mstp` refer to variables of the data types bound to the pointers when the program declared them.

Pointers and Type Checking

Because pointers are bound to specific data types, C++ can verify that you don't accidentally assign the address of one sort of data to the wrong kind of pointer. If you declare a pointer to `float`, you can't assign to it the address of a character or an integer. For example, this will never work:

```
float *fp;
char c;
fp = &c;   // ???
```

Because `c` is a `char` variable and `fp` is bound to a variable of the `float` data type, C++ does not allow assigning `c`'s address to `fp`. All similar assignments are checked for data-type consistency—one of the ways that C++ helps you to write programs that run correctly.

When you receive a `type mismatch` compiler error for a statement that assigns an address to a pointer variable, check that the pointer's bound data type is the same as the addressed item's. There is a way to get past this rule, as the next section explains, but in general, C++ demands that pointer variables actually address variables of the same data types bound to the pointers in their declarations.

NULL and Void Pointers

You now know how to declare a pointer (add a space and asterisk to a data type), initialize it (assign an address to the pointer), and dereference it to use the addressed data (preface the pointer's name with an asterisk). Two other important and related concepts are `NULL` and `void` pointers.

A `NULL` pointer points nowhere in particular. It's like an arrow without a tip or a sign that's fallen onto the ground. A `NULL` pointer is C++'s way of saying that, at least for the moment, "this pointer does *not* address any valid data in memory."

The purpose of a `NULL` pointer is to give programs a way of knowing when a pointer addresses valid information. `NULL` is a macro equivalent to 0 and defined in the header files STDDEF.H, STDIO.H, STDLIB.H, and STRING.H. You must `#include` one or more of these headers—or another header that includes one or more of them such as STREAM.HPP—before you can use the NULL identifier. Or, you can define NULL at the top of your program (or in a custom header file) with the line:

```
#define NULL 0
```

> **Note:** Usually, it's best to include a system header file than to define NULL yourself. Professional versions of C++ from Zortech, Borland, and other manufacturers may alter NULL's definition to accommodate different memory models. (The C++ compiler included with this book uses only the small memory model.) Other C++ compilers on other computers may define NULL to suit that hardware. By including standard header files, your programs are more likely to run with fewer modifications on those systems.

Like all global variables, global pointers are initialized to 0. Because NULL and 0 are equivalent, if you declare a global pointer fp this way:

```
float *fp;      // fp == NULL
main()
{
   ...
}
```

you can be 100 percent certain that fp equals NULL when the program begins. However, if you declare fp or any other pointer as a local variable in a function, like all local variables, the pointer has no particular value when the function runs:

```
void f(void)
{
   float *fp;  // fp == ???
   ...
}
```

Declared as a local variable, a pointer is uninitialized; its contents are unpredictable, and therefore, the pointer may point just about anywhere. Before using such a pointer, it's vital that you give it a valid address. Usually, the compiler will warn you if you use a variable or pointer before initializing it. Ignoring this warning for common variables may cause trouble, but if you ignore such warnings for pointers, the program may store information at a random location in memory—a sure road to disaster. Using an uninitialized pointer may overwrite other data, DOS, or even the program itself, and it's a nasty bug to find and fix. Luckily, you can avoid this problem easily by *always* initializing your pointer variables.

Throughout this book, listings have used the void key word to stand for "nothing in particular." Like a void function that does not return any value, a void pointer points to no specific type of data. Create a void pointer like this:

```
void *noWhereLand;
```

The `void` pointer `noWhereLand` may address any location in memory, but the pointer is not bound to a specific data type. Similar `void` pointers may address a `float` variable, a `char`, or an arbitrary location, perhaps one belonging to DOS or to the ROM BIOS. Think of `void` pointers as generic vehicles for addressing data without having to specify the type of that data in advance.

Note: Don't confuse `NULL` and `void` pointers. A `NULL` pointer does not address any valid data. A `void` pointer addresses data of an unspecified type. A `void` pointer may equal `NULL` if it doesn't currently address any valid data. `NULL` is a value; `void` is a data type—one without any specific form.

Casting Roles for Pointers to Play

A typical use for `void` pointers is to address buffers—large blocks of RAM used to store data, often coming in from a file or on its way out to another file or device such as the printer. One way (not necessarily the best) to create buffers is to first define some memory and then create one or more pointers to address that location in RAM:

```
char buffer[1024];    // A 1,024-byte buffer
void *bp;             // A pointer to nothing in particular
...
bp = &buffer;         // Address buffer with bp
```

This fragment defines `buffer` as an array of 1,204 `char` elements. Pointer `bp` is then declared to address `void`, meaning that C++ allows the program to assign to `bp` the address of a variable of any data type. The last line assigns `buffer`'s address (`&buffer`) to `bp`. At this point, `bp` addresses `buffer`, but there's a problem here that needs fixing. Because `bp` is a pointer to `void`, a statement can't dereference the pointer to get to the data it addresses. This won't work:

```
cout << *bp;    // ???
```

As you learned before, the expression `*bp` should dereference `bp`, but because that pointer addresses nothing in particular, C++ is unable to know what to do with this statement. Does `*bp` address a `char`, a `float`, a `struct`, or an `int`? There's no way for C++ to know, and for that reason, the compiler rejects the statement.

To get out of this dilemma, you must tell C++ what data type a `void` pointer addresses. This requires a *pointer type cast* expression, which temporarily binds the pointer to a data type that C++ knows about. A pointer type cast is your way of telling the compiler to "treat this pointer as though it addresses a variable of type X." You can use a type cast to change the bound type of any pointer temporarily, but you *must* use a type cast before you can refer to data addressed by a typeless void pointer.

Listing 4.2, VOID.CPP, demonstrates pointer type casts and also contains a useful function that you can extract for your own programs. When you run the program, you'll see that it displays the values and addresses of variables and pointers. To perform those actions, the program makes good use of void pointers.

Listing 4.2. VOID.CPP

```
 1:  // void.cpp -- Type-cast demonstration
 2:
 3:  #include <stream.hpp>
 4:  #include <dos.h>
 5:
 6:  void disp_pointer(void *p);
 7:
 8:  main()
 9:  {
10:      char buffer[1024];
11:      void *bp;
12:
13:      bp = &buffer;          // Assign buffer address to bp
14:      *(char *)bp = 'A';     // Store character via pointer
15:      buffer[1] = 'B';       // Store character directly
16:      buffer[2] = 0;         // Insert null after "AB"
17:
18:      cout << "address of buffer = ";
19:      disp_pointer(&buffer);
20:
21:      cout << "data in buffer = ";
22:      cout << (char *)bp;
23:  }
24:
25:  void disp_pointer(void *p)
26:  {
27:      cout << hex(FP_SEG(p)) << ":" << hex(FP_OFF(p)) << '\n';
28:  }
```

Line 10 declares a 1,024-character array named buffer. Line 11 declares a void pointer bp to which the program assigns the address of buffer (see line 13). Though bp addresses buffer, line 14 must use a type-cast expression *(char *)bp to assign a character to the array. In effect, the expression says, "Assume that the void pointer bp addresses a char array." You can't write a statement such as *bp = 'A'; because the compiler has no idea what kind of data bp addresses. You must use a type-cast expression to supply specific data-type information before the compiler will allow using a `void` pointer such as `bp` to address data of that type.

Lines 15 and 16 also store data inside the array. No type-cast expressions are needed here because the compiler knows from the declaration at line 10 that you intend to store `char` values in the array.

Line 19 shows how to pass the address of a variable to `disp_pointer`, which displays that address. The expression `&buffer` equals the address where `buffer` is stored in memory. Similarly, you could display that same address this way:

```
disp_pointer(bp);
```

That passes the address *value* of `bp` to the function. To display the address of the pointer variable, you would have to write

```
disp_pointer(&bp);
```

In each of these expressions, the value passed to `disp_pointer` is an address. Because the function's parameter is declared at line 6 as `void *`, arguments can be pointers to any kind of data. Think of `void *` as a "generic pointer," one that can specify any address in memory.

Inside `disp_pointer`, a seemingly complex statement actually performs a simple job—displaying the value of a pointer passed to the function:

```
cout << hex(FP_SEG(p))<< ":" << hex(FP_OFF(p))<< '\n';
```

If you find such statements difficult to understand, you are not alone. Take the pieces one at a time, and you'll see that the line is not as complicated as it appears. First the statement displays `hex (FP_SEG(p))`, next a colon, then `hex (FP_OFF(p))`, and finally a new-line symbol.

The statement takes advantage of the fact that the value of a pointer—in other words, the address that the pointer holds—is composed of two parts, a segment and an offset. Ignoring the complexities of expanded and extended memory found in most PCs today, all addresses in memory can be expressed with these two values. The address space is *segmented*—divided into 16-byte chunks called paragraphs. To find a value in RAM, the processor starts at a chunk address represented by a segment register, usually DS or ES. It combines that address with the value of another register representing the offset from that segment boundary. Together, the two values pinpoint a variable's location in memory.

Two functions, which C++ might supply as macros, `FP_SEG` and `FP_OFF` return an `unsigned int` value representing any pointer's segment and offset values. Although it appears lengthy, the output statement at line 27 passes the `void` pointer p to these two functions and displays those values with the help of `hex`. (It's common to express addresses in hexadecimal, but you could show them in decimal, too.)

The key point to learn about VOID.CPP is the way function `disp_pointer` accepts a `void` pointer parameter, which could represent the address of a variable of *any* data type. For example, insert these definitions and statements between lines 12 and 13:

```
float f = 3.14159;
float *fp = &f;
cout << "*fp = " << *fp << '\n';
cout << "address held by fp = ";
disp_pointer(fp);
```

The first line defines a `float` variable named f and initializes its value to 3.14159. The second line defines a pointer to `float` named `fp` and assigns the address of f to that pointer. The `fp` pointer now addresses the same location where the value of f is stored. After these lines, an output stream statement displays the value of f using the dereferenced pointer `*fp`, proving that `fp` does address the same location where f is stored in memory. The last two lines then display the address of `fp`. As this shows, `disp_pointer`'s `void` pointer parameter accepts `fp` even though it addresses a specific data type (`float`). You can always assign the value of *any* pointer to a `void` pointer variable or function parameter.

> **Note:** Obviously, programs that rely on a PC's segmented memory are highly dependent on the hardware. Other computer systems may or may not use a segmented address architecture, and programs written to recognize a PC's addressing peculiarities won't run on those systems without modification. Because this book's compiler runs only on PCs, this is not something to worry about. But, if your programs need to run on different computers, it's wise to avoid coding them to expect pointer address values to have a specific format.

Near and Far Pointers

Whether a pointer is *near* or *far* is another highly system-dependent aspect of C++ pointers. These terms do not refer to the relative locations of pointers. Despite their names, they don't even have much to do with how far away an addressed variable is in memory.

Instead, the words near and far refer to the internal format used to represent the addresses stored in pointers. A *near pointer* takes 2 bytes one 16-bit word. (A *far pointer* takes 4 bytes two 16-bit words). Listing 4.3, NEARFAR.CPP, demonstrates this difference.

Listing 4.3. NEARFAR.CPP

```
1:   // nearfar.cpp -- Description
2:
3:   #include <stream.hpp>
4:
5:   main()
6:   {
```

```
 7:        float *fp1;            // A "near" pointer
 8:        float far *fp2;        // A "far" pointer
 9:
10:        cout << "\nSize of fp1 = " << sizeof(fp1) << " bytes";
11:        cout << "\nSize of fp2 = " << sizeof(fp2) << " bytes";
12:  }
```

NEARFAR defines two pointers to float, fp1 and fp2. The two pointers are identical except for their names and the presence of the key word far in the second definition at line 8. Using the expression far * tells the compiler that you want to represent this pointer with a full 4 bytes rather than the usual 2. When you run the program, it displays

```
Size of fp1 = 2 bytes
Size of fp2 = 4 bytes
```

The difference between the two pointers is that fp1 can hold addresses restricted to the range 0 to 65,535. On PCs, this value represents an offset from a fixed location (the segment value), which the program and operating system select at runtime. The far pointer represents an address using a full four bytes—two for the segment value and two for the offset. Because of this, a far pointer can point to any location in a PC's memory, not just addresses offset from a fixed segment boundary. (Again, I am purposely ignoring the complexities of expanded and extended RAM plus the 32-bit addressing capabilities of newer 80x86 processors.)

Before going any farther out on this highly system-dependent limb, you need to understand that far pointers are not part of the "pure" C++ definition. They were added to the C++ compiler supplied with this book precisely to allow programs to deal with a PC's segmented memory architecture. It's possible to write useful C++ programs without using a single far key word, and for most purposes, that's probably a good idea. Also, when using C++ compilers that can create programs to run in different memory models (but not the C++ compiler packaged with this book), plain pointers might be far in nature even though you didn't declare them that way.

However, there are times when only a far pointer will do. For example, when you need to address external variables that belong to the operating system, there's no reason not to use system-dependent far pointers. You know the program will run only on PCs anyway, and the code may as well include system-dependent features. Let's examine a couple of cases that put these ideas into practice.

Pointers to System Locations

Listing 4.4, CRTSTAT.CPP, demonstrates a useful trick for programs that will run on PCs, and it shows how to use far pointers to access system information.

Listing 4.4. CRTSTAT.CPP

```
 1:  // crtstat.cpp -- Get CRT's mode and number of columns
 2:
 3:  #include <stream.hpp>
 4:  #include <dos.h>
 5:
 6:  main()
 7:  {
 8:    char far *mode = MK_FP(0x0040, 0x0049);
 9:    int far *cols = MK_FP(0x0040, 0x004a);
10:
11:    cout << "CRT startup mode = " << dec(*mode) << '\n';
12:    cout << "CRT columns      = " << *cols << '\n';
13:  }
```

Lines 8 and 9 in CRTSTAT define and initialize two far pointers, mode and cols. The first pointer addresses a char variable (in other words, a single 8-bit byte value). The second pointer addresses an int. Each of these pointers is initialized using a macro MK_FP (make far pointer), defined in the DOS.H header file. (Even though it's a macro, you use MK_FP as a function. Examine the DOS.H header file if you want to know how MK_FP is constructed.)

The result of MK_FP is a far pointer containing a 16-bit segment value and a 16-bit offset. Both mode and cols use the same segment value—0x0040, the base address in hexadecimal where DOS and the PC's ROM BIOS routines store various system variables. The offsets (0x0049 and 0x004a) in the two initialization assignments represent the offset addresses from the fixed base. These addresses locate values specifying the system's startup video mode and the number of columns available for text displays.

After these setup chores, mode and cols address the appropriate system values inside the segment at 0x0040. You can use similar techniques to assign other known addresses to pointer variables in order to read and even change system-dependent variables. Obviously, changing system variables requires a thorough knowledge of how PC's operate. Even a simple modification could have disastrous results, so be careful when using these methods.

Notice how the two output stream statements at lines 11-12 display the system variables by dereferencing the pointers. The expression dec(*mode) evaluates to the decimal value of the byte addressed by the mode pointer. The program has to use dec here because mode addresses a char. If it didn't convert that char to a decimal value, the statement would display an ASCII character rather than the mode number. Some early versions of C++ did not work this way, but most newer releases do. The expression *cols evaluates to the int value stored at the location addressed by cols, representing the number of columns available on the terminal.

If CRTSTAT did not specify the two pointers as far, C++ would consider them to address variables belonging to the program. To address information outside of that realm, it's necessary to declare the pointers to be far and to assign full 32-bit addresses to them.

Note: To reduce the system dependency of your programs, isolate statements that refer to specific memory locations. A good way to do that is to insert system-dependent statements in functions. When porting your code to another computer, you can replace the functions and reduce the amount of work required to modify the code for a different environment.

Far Pointers and the Keyboard

Another example shows how to use far pointers to sense whether someone is pressing the **<Alt>**, **<Ctrl>**, **<Shift Left>**, or **<Shift Right>** keys. The program also detects the current state (on or off) of the **<Insert>**, **<Caps Lock>**, **<Num Lock>**, and **<Scroll Lock>** keys. This can be a useful technique in programs that need to check for keypresses that combine a letter key and one or more of these other keys.

The program is printed in Listing 4.5, KEYSTAT.CPP. Compile the program and run it. Then press any of the keys mentioned before. (These key names are also displayed on screen for reference.) Notice that some of the keys turn on (1) and off (0) as soon as you press and release them and that the program distinguishes between the **<Shift Left>** and **<Shift Right>** keys. Other keys such as **<Caps Lock>** and **<Num Lock>** serve as toggles and may be on or off when you start the program. When you're done experimenting with KEYSTAT, to quit the program, press and hold the three keys **<Ctrl>-<Alt>-<Shift Left>** simultaneously.

Listing 4.5. KEYSTAT.CPP

```
 1:  // keystat.cpp -- Keyboard status and bit field demonstration
 2:
 3:  #include <stream.hpp>
 4:  #include <dos.h>
 5:  #include <string.h>
 6:  #include <disp.h>
 7:
 8:  struct keyboard {
 9:      unsigned shiftRight   : 1;        // Keyboard flags
10:      unsigned shiftLeft    : 1;
11:      unsigned ctrl         : 1;
12:      unsigned alt          : 1;
```

```
13:        unsigned scrollLock   : 1;
14:        unsigned numLock      : 1;
15:        unsigned capsLock     : 1;
16:        unsigned insert       : 1;
17:        unsigned              : 8;        // Not used
18:    };
19:
20:    int cmpkeys(void far* p1, void far* p2);
21:
22:    main()
23:    {
24:    keyboard far *keys = MK_FP(0x0040, 0x0017);  // Make pointer
25:    keyboard oldkeys;        // Holds copy of last known key state
26:        int done = 0;        // True (1) when user quits program
27:
28:        disp_open();         // Initialize display package
29:
30:        while (!done) {
31:          disp_move(0, 0);   // Move cursor to upper left corner
32:          disp_eeop();       // Clear to end of page (clears screen)
33:
34:    // Display states of various keys
35:
36:        disp_printf("Keyboard State\n");
37:        disp_printf("\nState bits (press and release):");
38:        disp_printf("\n <Insert> ....... %d", keys->insert);
39:        disp_printf("\n <Caps lock> .... %d", keys->capsLock);
40:        disp_printf("\n <Num lock> ..... %d", keys->numLock);
41:        disp_printf("\n <Scroll lock> .. %d", keys->scrollLock);
42:        disp_printf("\n\nShift bits. (press, hold, and release):");
43:        disp_printf("\n <Alt> .......... %d", keys->alt);
44:        disp_printf("\n <Ctrl> ......... %d", keys->ctrl);
45:        disp_printf("\n <Shift left> ... %d", keys->shiftLeft);
46:        disp_printf("\n <Shift right> .. %d", keys->shiftRight);
47:        disp_printf("\n\nPress above keys to change state");
48:        disp_printf("\nPress <Ctrl>-<Alt>-<shiftLeft> to quit");
49:
50:    // Press <Ctrl>-<Alt>-<Shift Left> to quit
51:
52:        done = (    keys->alt
53:                 && keys->ctrl
54:                 && keys->shiftLeft);
55:
56:        oldkeys = *keys;     // Save key state in oldkeys
```

```
57:            while (cmpkeys(&oldkeys, keys)) ; // Pause until change
58:        }
59:        disp_move(25, 0);      // Move cursor to bottom line
60:        disp_close();          // Close the display package
61: }
62:
63: // Return true (1) if bytes at p1 and p2 are the same
64: int cmpkeys(void far* p1, void far* p2)
65: {
66:        return *(char far *)p1 == *(char far *)p2;
67: }
```

In addition to showing a good use for far pointers, KEYSTAT also demonstrates how to address struct variables with pointers. Lines 8-18 declare a bit-field structure data type named keyboard. Each field in this structure matches the bits that are stored in memory by the ROM BIOS when you press certain keys. Inspecting this value, called the *keyboard flag byte,* and extracting its various bits gives programs the capability to detect whether specially named keys are toggled or being pressed.

Line 20 declares a prototype for the function cmpkeys, which returns true (1) if the bytes addressed by the void far pointers p1 and p2 are equal. If those bytes differ, the function returns false (0). Comparing before and after values of the keyboard flag byte gives the program a way to detect a change in a key's status.

To cause the program to address the keyboard flag byte, line 24 uses MK_FP as in the previous listing to create a far pointer named keys. The address assigned to keys is 0x0040:0x0017, the location of the keyboard flag byte. (A good PC reference lists the addresses of this and other system variables.) Notice that keys is a far pointer to a keyboard structure. Declaring the structure and then defining a pointer bound to that same type makes it easy to extract formatted information stored in memory.

Most of KEYSTAT's action occurs inside a long while loop (lines 30-58). Lines 36-48 display text using the display package's disp_printf routine, which operates like C and C++'s printf function and also like C++'s form (see chapter 1). Here, the %d escape codes inside most of the statement formatting strings are replaced with the value of a bit field in the keyboard structure.

Let's examine one of those statements closely. It contains a symbol you haven't seen before. Line 45 is as good as any:

```
disp_printf("\n <Shift left> ... %d", keys->shiftLeft);
```

When I wrote this, I included the %d escape code inside the formatting string to be replaced by the value of the **<Shift Left>** key, or rather the value of the shiftLeft bit field in the keyboard structure addressed by the keys pointer. Because keys is a pointer, to locate a field in the structure requires using the -> symbol. This picks out an individual field in the structure that keys addresses.

Recall from chapter 2 that a period is the usual way of qualifying a structure's name and one of its fields. If `keysvar` is a variable of type `keyboard`, you could access the `shiftLeft` field and others like this:

```
keyboard keysvar;
cout << keysvar.shiftLeft;
```

But, since `keys` is a pointer and not a `keyboard` variable, you must use another symbol to get to the fields in the addressed structure. The reason for this is obvious if you consider that the illegal expression `keys.shiftLeft` would mean "the `shiftLeft` field in the pointer `keys`." That's senseless—there aren't any structure fields in a pointer. Pointers hold addresses, not structures. For this reason, in place of the usual period, you must use `keys->shiftleft`, which stands for "the `shiftLeft` field in the `keyboard` structure addressed by the `keys` pointer."

Hint: The `->` symbol resembles an arrow, which is a good way to remember that you can use it only with a pointer that points like an arrow to a variable in memory. Also, when you use `->` to refer to an addressed structure field, you do not also have to dereference the pointer name with an asterisk.

You can see other uses of `->` at lines 52-54 in KEYSTAT, which set a variable `done` to true or false. This continues or ends the `while` loop that checks `done` at line 30. The assignment to `done` uses two logical ANDs (`&&`) to combine the bits that represent the **<Alt>**, **<Ctrl>**, and **<Shift Left>** keys. Only when all three of these bit fields equal 1 is the result of this expression 1, which sets `done` to true and causes the `while` loop to end.

While running KEYSTAT, you probably noticed that the program somehow manages to detect each change in the keyboard flag byte. To make this happen, line 56 assigns the flag's value to a variable named `oldkeys`. Because `oldkeys` is a `keyboard` structure, the assignment dereferences `keys` to obtain the flag's current value:

```
oldkeys = *keys;
```

Remember that when C++ dereferences a pointer prefaced with an asterisk, it considers that expression to be a variable of the pointer's declared data type. In the case of `keys`, that data type is a `keyboard` structure. Thus, `*keys` *is* a `keyboard` variable and so is `oldkeys`. C++ allows assignments between variables of the same data types (except for arrays, which I'll get to momentarily), and the assignment simply transfers the value addressed by `keys` to the memory reserved for the `oldkeys` variable.

Also take a look at the way line 57 calls `cmpkeys` with two `void` pointers to pause until the keyboard flag byte changes state:

```
while (cmpkeys(&oldkeys, keys)) ;
```

Because `oldkeys` is a variable, it's necessary to use the & operator to find that variable's address. However, `keys` is a pointer; it already *is* an address, and for that reason, the program can pass it directly to `cmpkeys`. The space before the semicolon is not accidental, but technically, it is optional. The space lets the compiler know that this `while` loop is supposed to wait until an external condition changes the conditional expression inside parentheses. Some compilers, including the one supplied with this book, display a warning message if you forget to add the space. They do this because such constructions are rarely needed, and you may have accidentally inserted a semicolon incorrectly at the end of a `while` or other loop's starting line.

Line 66 inside `cmpkeys` shows how to cast the function's two `void` pointers to new types. At the same time, it dereferences the recast pointers to access the addressed data. Unless you have some experience with C pointers, this single line in the function may appear unreadable at first:

```
return *(char far *)p1 == *(char far *)p2;
```

Constructions like `*(char far *)p1` throw most people for a loop on a first meeting. Taking this line apart shows that it's really not that complex. First, you know that `p1` is a `void far` pointer. The `far` keyword indicates that the pointer is 32 bits long, but like all `void` pointers, it doesn't address any data type in particular. For that reason, the statement must use a type cast expression to tell C++ what kind of data `p1` addresses. In this case, the data type is a single byte, represented in C++ by `char`.

In other words, `p1` is *declared* a `void far` pointer. To have C++ treat that pointer as `char far`, the statement uses the type cast expression `(char far *)`. This much of the statement,

```
(char far *)p1
```

tells C++ to consider `p1` the same as if the program had declared it to be a `char far *`.

So far so good, but there's more to cover in this statement. The asterisk in front of the expression `*(char far *)p1` dereferences the pointer, just as the asterisks in simpler constructions like `*pint` and `*pfloat` dereference those typed pointers. The final dereference tells the compiler to use the data addressed by `p1`, which is temporarily recast to a `far` pointer to `char`.

Returning to line 66 in KEYSTAT, you'll see a similar expression that recasts and dereferences the `void` pointer `p2`. It then returns the result of the comparison of the two bytes addressed by `p1` and `p2`. Study this construction well—you'll see (and use) it time and again.

Managing Your Memory

As you've seen many times so far, programs can create variables that are global or local. Global variables are stored at fixed locations in the program's data segment, and all functions can use those variables. Local variables are stored on the stack and exist only while their declaring functions are active. It's also possible to create variations of global variables that are static, meaning they are stored in a fixed location but are available only to the module (that is, the text file) or function that declares them.

All of those kinds of variables share one common characteristic: They are defined when you compile the program. When you compile definitions like `int x` or `float *fp` the compiler reserves (defines) space for storing values of the declared data types.

But there's another way to create variables that delays their definition until the program runs. Such variables are *dynamic*—they are stored in a block of memory known as the *heap*, but their locations aren't known until runtime. Dynamic variables are also called *pointer-addressable variables* because they are always addressed by a pointer. As Figure 4.3 shows, a pointer defined as int *p can address a variable allocated space on the heap. Using that pointer, a program can store values at locations determined at runtime.

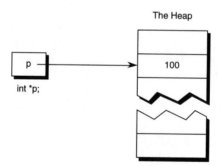

Figure 4.3. Pointer variables can address dynamic variables.

There are several ways to reserve space on the heap for dynamic variables. The first is the easiest; use the C++ `new` operator. For example, suppose that you want to create a string, but you don't know how much space to reserve for the string variable until the program runs. You can begin by defining a string pointer:

```
char *string;   // A string pointer
```

Variable `string` is a pointer to type `char`. At that location (which doesn't yet exist) will be a string of zero or more characters, ending in a null (ASCII 0) byte. Suppose there also is an `int` variable named `size` that specifies how big the string should be. To reserve that much space at runtime and to assign to `string` the address of the reserved memory, the program executes:

```
string = new char[size + 1];
```

The `new` operator returns the address of newly reserved memory. After `new` is the data type of the item you plan to store in that memory. C++ uses this data type to determine how much space to allocate. In this case, the type is an array of `char` equal to the value of `size` plus 1. The expression adds 1 to `size` to reserve space for the string's null byte at the end. (The program also assumes that `size` is not negative.)

After reserving memory with `new` and assigning its address to `string`, the program can use that pointer to "get to" the assigned memory space. For example, to read characters from the keyboard into the string (`size` should be at least 128 in this case), you can execute:

```
gets(string);
```

You can display the current value of `string`—that is, the ASCII characters addressed by the `string` pointer—in an output stream statement:

```
cout << string;
```

Later, when you are done using the memory allocated to `string`, you can dispose of it. This makes that memory available for future variables created with `new`. To dispose of memory addressed by a pointer, use the `delete` operator followed by the name of the pointer that addresses the memory to be reclaimed:

```
delete s;
```

Because you reserved space with `new`, you can use `delete` to dispose exactly that same space. C++ saves the size of a reserved memory block with that block—which, by the way, also implies that the actual amount of reserved memory will be a few bytes more (probably 2 more) than you request. Also, there may be additional overhead that C++ stores along with allocated memory to keep track of it.

Note: Only `delete` memory that you allocate with `new`. Never pass any other pointers to `delete`; the results of disposing memory not allocated by `new` could be catastrophic.

In general, you can use `new` to reserve space for any data type or an array of elements of any type. Here are a few more samples that show how to use `new` in programs. First, create a few pointers of various types:

```
int *ip;      // ip is a pointer to int
float *fp;    // fp is a pointer to float
long *lp;     // lp is a pointer to long
```

Remember that, when you define pointers, like all variables they are not initialized (unless they are global variables, in which case they are initialized to

NULL). To reserve some memory and assign that memory's address to each pointer, use statements like these along with the new operator:

```
ip = new int;      // Reserve space for an int
fp = new float;    // Reserve space for a float
lp = new long;     // Reserve space for a long
```

After these statements execute, ip, fp, and lp address reserved space on the heap. That space is guaranteed to be at least large enough to hold values of the declared data types (int, float, and long). The values stored in the heap are not yet initialized; however, they may be set to any value previously stored in the newly reserved locations.

You should also test each pointer to see whether new failed. If new can't allocate the requested space, it returns NULL. Usually, instead of putting all your faith in the computer, you should follow each use of new with a statement like this:

```
ip = new int;
if (ip == NULL)
   error("Out of memory");
```

After defining pointers and reserving heap space with new, you can use the newly created dynamic variables stored on the heap by dereferencing the pointers in the usual way. Examine these statements, which assign values to each of the three variables defined and initialized earlier:

```
*ip = -1234;    // Assign value to int addressed by ip
*fp = 3.14159;  // Assign value to float addressed by fp
*lp = 99999;    // Assign value to long addressed by lp
```

Prefacing each pointer with an asterisk tells the compiler to refer to the addressed location, in other words, the space reserved on the heap for values of the declared types. The assignments store values at those heap locations. Similarly, to use the data stored on the heap, you must dereference the pointers as in these statements:

```
cout << *ip << '\n';   // Display value at ip
cout << *fp << '\n';   // Display value at fp
cout << *lp << '\n';   // Display value at lp
```

These uses of pointers to memory reserved on the heap by new are no different from the uses you saw in earlier examples. Regardless of where a pointer points, you dereference that pointer in exactly the same way. Dynamic variables are called that because they are created at runtime on the heap by new and disposed by delete. However, they are used just like other variables created by other means.

Pointers to Structures

Creating simple variables dynamically as in the previous samples may strike you as being silly. If so, you're right—it is. Pointers to integers or floating-point values take up about the same amount of space as the data the pointers address. For that reason, simple variables are best created as you've seen in other listings—as global or local variables directly in the program's text.

Pointers come into their own when they address larger or more complex variables, for example, a struct, an I/O buffer, or an array of values. To create pointers to structures, first declare the struct data type and then allocate space for one or more structures by using new as you did in Listing 4.5, KEYSTAT.CPP. Finally, assign the address of the dynamic structure variable to a pointer and use that pointer to refer to the variable in memory. As an example of this technique, Listing 4.6, DSTRUCT.CPP, declares a structure named xyrec, creates space for a variable of that type, and then uses a pointer to store and display data held in the reserved memory.

Listing 4.6. DSTRUCT.CPP

```
 1:  // dstruct.cpp -- Dynamic structure demonstration
 2:
 3:  #include <stream.hpp>
 4:  #include <stdlib.h>
 5:
 6:  struct xyrec {
 7:     int x;
 8:     int y;
 9:  };
10:
11:  main()
12:  {
13:     xyrec *xyp;    // xyp is a pointer to an xyrec structure
14:
15:     xyp = new xyrec;    // Reserve space for an xyrec variable
16:     if (xyp == NULL) {  // Make sure that new worked
17:        cout << "\nOut of memory!";
18:        exit(1);
19:     }
20:
21:     xyp->x = 10;  // Assign 10 to x field in structure at xyp
```

```
22:        xyp->y = 11;   // Assign 11 to y field in structure at xyp
23:
24:        cout << "x = " << xyp->x << "; y = " << xyp->y;
25:    }
```

Lines 6-9 declare a structure of two i n t fields, x and y. This structure might be useful in a program that plots points on a graphics display. Instead of storing the locations of various points separately in variables like x 1 and y 1, with the x y r e c s t r u c t, a program can define a variable as x y r e c x y and then use statements like x y . x = 5 and x y . y = 1 0 0 to store coordinate values in the x and y fields.

To do the same with a pointer requires using the -> operator introduced earlier. First, line 13 defines a pointer named x y p which is bound to the s t r u c t data type, x y r e c. Remember that this and similar definitions only create space for the pointer. No space is yet reserved for storing information in memory.

That happens at line 15, which uses n e w to reserve enough space (and possibly a few bytes of overhead) to hold one x y r e c variable. The statement assigns the address of the allocated memory to the pointer variable x y p. After this, x y p addresses a dynamic variable of type x y r e c ready to use. Before doing that, however, lines 16-19 perform the ever-important task of checking that n e w worked. (In this small example, it's unlikely there won't be enough space for one teensy structure, but it's still a good idea to check.)

Now that space is reserved for an x y r e c and the address of that space is assigned to x y p, the program can use the newly created variable. Lines 21-24 demonstrate this by first assigning the values 10 and 11 to the x and y fields and then displaying those same values in an output stream statement. Figure 4.4 illustrates how the heap and the program's variables are organized in memory.

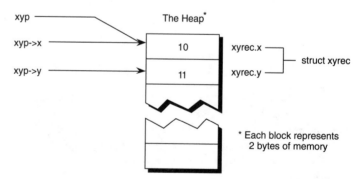

Figure 4.4.   After creating a dynamic *struct* variable on the heap, a pointer *xyp* can be used with the -> operator to address the structure's fields.

Notice that in each of the assignments at lines 21-22 and 24, the program uses the -> operator along with the pointer's name to refer to a field in the dynamic s t r u c t variable. The pointer x y p addresses the full structure stored on the heap.

The expressions x y p -> x and x y p -> y address individual fields in that structure. As I mentioned before, you do not need to dereference the pointer in these cases with an asterisk—C++ knows from -> that you mean to use the addressed information.

Out of Memory

For small to medium programs, there's usually plenty of memory available on PCs. The pool of available RAM is more of a lake than an ocean, however, and large programs can easily run out of room. If you allocate too many dynamic variables or load resident programs into memory, n e w may not be able to satisfy your request to reserve heap space.

Although I hinted at this subject before, it's worth repeating. Every time you call n e w, test whether the space you requested was actually reserved. If not, n e w returns NULL and does not reserve *any* space. Even if the amount you request is only one byte too large for the amount of space available, n e w refuses to allocate any memory unless it can reserve it all. For this reason, after every use of n e w, you should check the results, amending the earlier statement to

```
string = new char[size + 1];
if (string == NULL) {
   cout << "\nOut of memory!";
   exit(1);
}
```

Note: Because NULL and C++'s value meaning false both equal zero, some people shorten expressions like (s t r i n g == NULL) to (s t r i n g), which has the same result, but is a whole lot less clear. On the other hand, the short form may also be less likely to cause a bug if you are prone to writing (s t r i n g = NULL) which mistakenly *assigns* NULL to s t r i n g. It's your choice, but I prefer the long version. The compiler will warn you about bad assignments like (s t r i n g = NULL) in i f statements.

Why Use Dynamic Variables?

There are many advantages (and some drawbacks) that dynamic variables bring to C++. Among their strong points are the capabilities for dynamic variables to

- Determine a variable's size at runtime. This is useful for creating arrays and buffers that grow and shrink to accommodate whatever you need to store in them.

- Form lists that link multiple dynamic variables using pointers to form a chain of data in memory. Such chains have many uses, for example, storing information related to a variable number of disk files or storing lists of strings in a text editor.

- Use all memory available to a program without knowing or having to calculate in advance how much memory is free until the program runs.

The main disadvantage of dynamic variables occurs after creating and disposing many of them during a program run. When C++ creates a dynamic variable, it reserves a block of memory from an area called the heap. After a program is done using a dynamic variable, it can dispose of it to reclaim the previously reserved space. This returns that space to the heap's available pool of memory for use by other dynamic variables.

The fly in the ointment is that a disposed variable might be surrounded by other dynamic variables that are still in use. This creates a "hole" in memory equal to the size of the disposed item. Unless the next variable the program creates dynamically is no bigger than that hole, this area of memory may remain unusable.

One or two such holes won't make much difference, as long as there's plenty of other free memory available. But when a program creates and disposes hundreds of variables, a condition known as *fragmentation* can occur. Figure 4.5 shows what can happen after a program has disposed numerous variables, leaving tiny holes in memory between other dynamic items. Those items are strewn through memory, chopping it up into pieces that are too small to be used for new variables. The result is plenty of free memory in total, but all of it fragmented uselessly into small chunks.

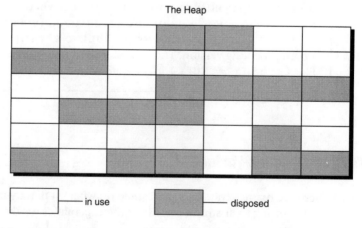

The Heap

in use   disposed

Figure 4.5. After disposing numerous variables, available memory (shaded boxes) may be divided, or fragmented, into unconnected regions.

A badly fragmented heap can make life with pointers extremely unattractive. Unfortunately, C++ doesn't have the capability to collect disposed fragments into one large space that the program could use for new variables. Such a feature is known as a *garbage collector* because it collects all the disposed garbage bytes discarded in the heap. (Maybe we should call it a dump?) C++ has a lot of features, but it lacks a garbage collector.

One answer to this problem is to reserve only large structures, preferably of the same sizes or of sizes that are multiples of some fixed value. For example, you could add dummy fields to pad structs to 32, 64, 128, and 256 bytes, all of which are powers of 2 and multiples of 16. Because C++ will combine adjacent disposed areas, this may help to reduce the number of small unusable fragments.

Another answer is to allocate a large space for arrays of structs. Then write your own functions to use these spaces as needed. Instead of disposing individual structs, you would keep track of which structs in the array are in use. This method may be wasteful because it reserves a large amount of memory at once, but it lets the program rely on space being available as needed.

One other possible answer is to tap into the heap manager and change the way new and delete work. This is a highly advanced subject that I'll touch on later in chapter 9. Writing your own memory management routines is an ambitious project, and most programers will not have to follow that route, but it's good to know that C++ offers the capability to let you provide a custom heap manager if that becomes necessary.

Creating Dynamic Lists

The old saw that the data should structure the program is as true today as it was when Brian W. Kernighan and P. J. Plauger coined the phrase in their 1974 book, *The Elements of Programming Style*. Always keep this advice in mind. The more planning you do on the layout of the data your programs will process, the easier it will be to write the code. This concept will be even more important when you start to use C++'s object-oriented features introduced in the next chapter.

Many programs need to store multiples of some data type, often a struct. When the exact number of those items is impossible to predict until the program runs, and if an array is inappropriate, you should consider storing the items as a list. This takes a bit more work than creating an array (see chapter 2), but the results are often worth the effort. Lists can grow and shrink as needed to store zero, one, or more items in memory. They also tend to use available heap space efficiently by letting the list structure weave in and out of other items (even other lists) stored in the heap at the same time.

For example, a series of file names in the current directory is a good use for a list. You might also store a list of strings to sort into alphabetic order. We'll see these and other uses for lists in this and in future chapters.

Stacks are a good place to begin learning about lists. If you've done any assembly language programming, you undoubtedly know about the system stack that stores return addresses for subroutine calls plus other items such as register values saved on the stack for restoring later. There's a system stack for all programs, including those written in C++. But it's also possible to create your own stacks as dynamic data structures. You can then *push* (insert) and *pop* (retrieve) variables of any kinds from your program's custom stacks.

All stacks share some of the same properties: they grow to accommodate new items pushed onto the stack, and they shrink as items are popped from the stack for the program's use. Like cards in a deck (not a *stacked* deck, that is), a stack's top item is the only one available; to get to the items below, you must remove those above. This means that, as you push items onto the stack (place new cards onto the deck), you can pop those items off (deal out the cards) in last-in, first-out order. There's an acronym for this, LIFO. A stack is a LIFO data structure. There are also FILO (first-in, last-out) and FIFO (first-in, first-out) variations on this basic scheme, but I'll stick to the more common LIFO variety here.

Figure 4.6 shows the evolution of a stack as values (represented by the numbered boxes) are pushed onto the top of the stack. A pointer (sp) always addresses the top item. To retrieve items, they must be popped from the top of the stack in the reverse order they were pushed there before.

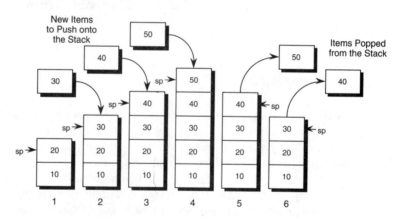

Figure 4.6.   To retrieve items, they must be popped from the top of the stack in the reverse order they were pushed.

Listing 4.7, STACK.CPP, creates two stacks. The program also demonstrates how to manage a linked list of items created dynamically at runtime with the `new` operator. When you run STACK, press A to add new items to the *Item list*. Press D to delete items from that list and push them onto a second stack named the *Avail list*. If you delete more items than available on the Item list, the program creates new items automatically. For demonstration purposes, only integer values are stored on the stacks. The program can handle other kinds of data, however, with only minor changes.

Listing 4.7. STACK.CPP

```
1:   // stack.cpp -- Implement a linked list stack
2:
3:   #include <stream.hpp>
4:   #include <stdlib.h>
5:   #include <disp.h>
6:   #include <ctype.h>
7:
8:   #define FALSE 0
9:   #define TRUE 1
10:
11:  struct item {
12:      int data;               // Could be any data
13:      item *next;             // Points to next item in list
14:  };
15:  typedef item *itemptr;   // Create itemptr data type
16:
17:  // Function prototypes
18:  void push(itemptr newitem, itemptr &list);
19:  void pop(itemptr &newitem, itemptr &list);
20:  void showlist(itemptr p);
21:  void display(void);
22:  void additem(void);
23:  void delitem(void);
24:  void clearscreen(void);
25:
26:  itemptr avail = NULL;            // The "avail" stack
27:  itemptr itemlist = NULL;         // The "item" stack
28:
29:  main()
30:  {
31:      int done = FALSE;       // When TRUE, program ends
32:      int c;                  // User command character
33:
34:      disp_open();
35:      while (!done) {
36:         display();
37:         disp_move(24, 0);
38:         disp_printf("A-dd, D-elete, Q-uit");
39:         c = getch();
40:         switch (toupper(c)) {
41:            case 'A': additem(); break;
42:            case 'D': delitem(); break;
43:            case 'Q': done = TRUE;
```

```
44:              }
45:          }
46:      }
47:
48:     // Push newitem onto list. Modifies list pointer.
49:     void push(itemptr newitem, itemptr &list)
50:     {
51:         newitem->next = list;    // Item's next now points to list
52:         list = newitem;          // List now points to new item
53:     }
54:
55:     // Pop newitem from list, or create a new item if list is empty
56:     void pop(itemptr &newitem, itemptr &list)
57:     {
58:         if (list == NULL) {      // If list is empty...
59:             newitem = new item;  //   Create new item
60:             newitem->data = -1;  //   Initialize data to -1
61:         } else {                 // Else...
62:             newitem = list;      //   Pass back item at top of list
63:             list = list->next;   //   Adjust list to next item
64:         }
65:     }
66:
67:     // Display contents of list addressed by p
68:     void showlist(itemptr p)
69:     {
70:         while (p != NULL) {
71:             disp_printf("\n%d", p->data);
72:             disp_eeol();
73:             p = p->next;         // Address next item in the list
74:         }
75:     }
76:
77:     // Display the avail and item stacks
78:     void display(void)
79:     {
80:         clearscreen();
81:         disp_printf("\n\nAvail list:");
82:         showlist(avail);
83:         disp_printf("\n\nItem list:");
84:         showlist(itemlist);
85:     }
86:
```

```
87:   // Add item with random data to item stack
88:   void additem(void)
89:   {
90:       itemptr newitem;
91:
92:       pop(newitem, avail);        // Get or create new item
93:       if (newitem->data < 0)      // If this is a new item
94:           newitem->data = rand(); // Assign random data to it
95:       push(newitem, itemlist);    // Put new item onto item stack
96:   }
97:
98:   // Delete item from item stack. Save same item on avail stack
99:   void delitem(void)
100:  {
101:      itemptr newitem;
102:
103:      pop(newitem, itemlist);     // Get new item from item stack
104:      push(newitem, avail);       // Save item on avail stack
105:  }
106:
107:  // Clear the display
108:  void clearscreen(void)
109:  {
110:      disp_move(0, 0);
111:      disp_eeop();
112:  }
```

To understand how STACK operates, start with the data structures. (This is also a good plan of attack for investigating other programs you've never seen before.) The key data structure in STACK is item, a struct declared at lines 11-14:

```
struct item {
    int data;
    item *next;
};
```

The int data field in item could store any kind of data, or perhaps, one or more pointers to other items created dynamically at runtime. To modify the program for other uses, you'll want to replace or add to this field. Field item *next looks like the pointers you've declared before, but this line uses a technique that's new. Notice that the field's type (item *) refers to the *same* structure in which the field is declared. In other words, next is a pointer to an item variable, which contains another field named next, which points to another item variable, and so on. Each item is linked to the next by the next pointer. Together, the linked items form a list. (See Figure 4.7.)

Figure 4.7.   Store pointers in structure fields to link multiple variables
of the *struct* type together, forming a list.

Usually, C++ prevents you from referring to undeclared items, but in this special case—creating a pointer to a structure inside that same structure—the compiler breaks its own rule. It does this to allow creating *recursive data structures,* those that refer to other variables of the same types. Like recursive functions that can call themselves, recursive data structures can point to other items that are exactly like themselves.

To refer to items stored on a linked list of item structures, line 15 uses typedef (type define) to create a new data type named itemptr:

```
typedef item *itemptr;   // Create itemptr data type
```

The declaration tells the compiler that itemptr and item * mean the same thing. Both can be used to create a pointer to an item structure. Using typedef to create a pointer data type this way is merely a convenience—it allows statements and other declarations to use the identifier itemptr rather than item *. This can reduce the number of confusing asterisks in the program text.

After taking care of these details and declaring several function prototypes, the program is ready to create two lists. This is done at lines 26 and 27, which define two itemptr variables named avail and itemlist. Because these are global variables, they are automatically initialized to NULL at runtime.

These two pointers are usually known as *list heads,* or *root pointers.* They point to the first item on a list, which points to the next item, which points to the next, and so on until reaching the end of the list. As Figure 4.7 shows at far right, a list's end is often drawn using an electrical grounding symbol. A program can know when it has reached the end of a list by examining the next field in an item. If that field equals NULL, it's the last in the list; otherwise, it points to another item.

Two functions, push and pop, use these careful definitions to create stacks of item structures in memory. Push at lines 49-53 is the simpler of the two, so let's take it apart first:

```
void push(itemptr newitem, itemptr &list)
{
    newitem->next = list;
    list = newitem;
}
```

Pay close attention to the two parameters, newitem and list. The first is an itemptr—a pointer to an item. The second is the same, but is passed by reference (&) rather than by value. As you learned in chapter 3, this means that any changes made to list inside the function will affect the pointer variable passed to the function by another statement. Any change to newitem, however, will not be passed back.

The first line inside push assigns the value of list (in other words, the address that this pointer holds) to the next field in the structure addressed by newitem. The item addressed by newitem now points to the same item that list addresses; newitem is linked (pushed) onto the list.

The second line inside push then assigns the value of newitem to list. Because list is passed to the function by reference, this assignment directly changes the argument passed to push. Suppose that someitem addresses an item in memory. To push that item onto the avail stack, the program could execute

```
push(someitem, avail); // Push someitem onto avail stack
```

When this statement calls push, the function first sets someitem->next to where avail points (or to NULL if avail equals NULL.) Then it changes avail to point to someitem. Verify these actions on paper, a blackboard, or by tracing Figure 4.8. The process of linking items onto lists is much easier to visualize by working through a few examples on your own than it is to read a description of how the linking works.

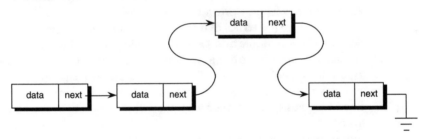

Figure 4.8. Pushing items onto a list links those items to others previously joined by similar operations.

The second key function in STACK is pop (lines 56-65), which reverses push's accomplishments. The function's declaration is similar to push's, but this time, both parameters newitem and list are passed by reference. This means that if the function changes either of these two pointers, it directly affects the arguments passed to the function by a calling statement:

```
void pop(itemptr &newitem, itemptr &list)
{
    if (list == NULL) {
        newitem = new item;
        newitem->data = -1;
    } else {
        newitem = list;
```

```
        list = list->next;
    }
}
```

It's a grievous error to pop more data than is available on a stack—sort of like digging into your pockets too deeply and poking a hole in the fabric. For this reason, pop first checks whether list is NULL. If so, the stack is empty, and list addresses no valid item structure in memory.

In that event, the function uses new to create a new item, assigning the address of this structure to the newitem argument passed to the function. At the same time, pop initializes the data field in the item to –1. I did this just so you could see on screen the items created by this section when you try to delete more items than are available. (To see the effect, run the program and press D a few times.) You can remove this statement when using the programming in your own code.

If list is not NULL, the function assumes the pointer addresses at least one item variable. To return that item to the caller—the reason that a statement is called pop in the first place—the function assigns the address of list to newitem. Now newitem addresses the current top of the stack. So that the next call to pop returns the next item from the list, the last statement in pop assigns the value of the next field to list. After this, list either addresses the next listed item or it equals NULL if there was only one item on the list.

That covers the basics of how STACK pushes and pops items to and from a list. Next, turn to function additem at lines 88-96. First, this function calls pop, which may seem strange; if pop removes an item from the stack, why call it when we want to add a new one? The reason for this is because, as I explained a moment ago, pop executes new to create a new item when the stack is empty, or in this case, when avail equals NULL. Either way, the effect is to return the address of an item structure addressed by newitem. In additem, an if statement examines this address to see whether it equals –1. If so, the program assigns a value at random to the item's data field and calls push to store it on the itemlist. In short, additem calls pop to get an item variable from the avail stack (or to create a new item), possibly assigns new data to it, and then calls push to save the item on the other stack.

> **Note:** The data field is set to –1 here only for demonstration purposes. You can remove data and the associated tests for its value if you want to incorporate STACK into your own programs.

The opposite function, delitem at lines 99-105, is even simpler than additem. First, the function calls pop to delete the topmost item from itemlist. Then push transfers this item to the avail stack. The effect is to transfer one item from the stack addressed by itemlist to the stack addressed by avail. (If itemlist is NULL when calling pop, new item with its data field initialized to –1 is created and transferred to avail.)

One other function in STACK contains a few techniques that you haven't seen before. Function s h o w l i s t (lines 68-75) is responsible for displaying the lists of values that you see on screen when you run the program. It does this with a w h i l e loop that cycles until an i t e m p t r pointer p passed as an argument to the function equals NULL:

```
while (p != NULL) {
   disp_printf("\n%d", p->data);
   disp_eeol();
   p = p->next;
}
```

The intention is for p to address the first i t e m in a linked list. After displaying the value of the data addressed by p with the d i s p _ p r i n t f function, the loop executes d i s p _ e e o l to clear the display to the end of the line. This removes any leftover values displayed previously on this same screen row.

The final statement in the w h i l e loop assigns the value of the n e x t field in the i t e m addressed by p to p. Think about what this does. If n e x t contains the address of the next item in the list, the assignment of p - > n e x t to p causes p to point to that i t e m. On the next pass through the loop, p will then point to the next i t e m and so on until n e x t equals NULL—the value that marks the last i t e m in the list. This also ends the w h i l e loop.

As a result of these actions, the w h i l e loop causes p to point to each i t e m in a list, no matter where those items are stored. They might be stored one after the other physically, but, more likely, they will be scattered in various locations. Because of this, following the n e x t pointers is the *only* way to locate a list's items. The pointers form a kind of chain, with each link attaching two i t e m s. The w h i l e loop pulls in the string of items like a winch winding up a chain until reaching the last link.

Dynamic Arrays

One good use for n e w is to create dynamic arrays. Instead of having to declare an array's size in the program's text, with n e w, you can allocate space on the heap for an array at runtime. This lets the program itself decide how big to make an array.

The usual method for creating arrays is to add brackets and a value after the array's name. For example, this creates an array of 100 floating-point numbers:

```
float af[100];
```

When you don't know how many items to allow for, create a pointer to the data type you need to store in the array. Then, use n e w to reserve space at runtime for as many items as you need:

```
float *afp;
```

```
int n;
...
n = 100;
afp = new float[n];
if (afp == NULL)
   error("Out of memory");
```

The value of n might come from a calculation, or it might be entered by an operator. The call to new allocates space for 100 floating-point variables and assigns the address of that space to the a f p pointer. You can then use that pointer as an array of float:

```
cout << "Fifth element = " << afp[4];
```

Later, I'll return to the subject of using pointers as arrays. First, let's examine other ways to allocate memory on the heap.

Reserving Memory with malloc

The new and delete operators belong to the C++ language, not to C, which has other ways for reserving memory for dynamic variables. These same methods are also available in C++, and it's a good idea to understand how they work.

The most common technique is to call a library function named malloc for "memory allocation." You can call malloc to reserve a number of bytes and to assign the address of the first of those bytes to a pointer:

```
char *sp;          // sp is a pointer to char
sp = malloc(129);  // Reserve 129 bytes
if (sp == NULL)    // Call error function
   error();        //  if malloc fails
```

After defining a pointer named s p to type c h a r, the second line calls malloc with the value 129 in parentheses. This reserves a space of 129 bytes and assigns the address of the first byte of that space to s p. However, if malloc returns NULL, there isn't enough room in memory to satisfy the request for new storage, and the program needs to take evasive action. In this fragment, the i f statement calls function error (not shown).

A similar function, calloc, also reserves memory, but requires a different set of arguments. Pass the number of items to reserve and the size of a single item to calloc and assign the resulting address to a pointer:

```
int *bp;
bp = calloc(1024, sizeof(int));
```

The first line defines a pointer bp to type int. The call to calloc attempts to reserve 1,024 int-sized chunks of memory and then assigns the address of the first byte of the first chunk to bp. Unlike malloc, which sets aside the requested memory but doesn't change its current values, calloc sets all reserved bytes to 0. As usual, if the function can't reserve as much space as you request, it returns NULL, and you should follow each call to calloc with a test for this condition. In this sample, because an int takes 2 bytes, the statement reserves 2,048 bytes of memory. On another system, an int may take more or less room, which would change the outcome. Even so, the statement ensures that, no matter what int's size, unless calloc returns NULL, bp will address an area of reserved memory that can hold 1,204 integer values.

Used this way, calloc can help you to write system-independent programs. Generally, calling calloc to reserve space for a certain number of variables is better than statements such as malloc(2048), which assumes an int's size will always be 2 bytes—a dangerous assumption to make. However, it is possible to use malloc to write system-independent code, too. For example, malloc(1024 * sizeof(int)) would also work for different sizes of int.

> **Note:** The function name calloc may stand for *clear and allocate*. No doubt some reader will know, but despite searching a dozen references, I could not find the origin of this word. It might also mean *core allocation*, a reference to earlier "core" memory made from magnets.

Although it's probably best to use new and delete, malloc comes in handy for allocating buffers—large spaces into which you can stuff bytes for various purposes. Listings 4.8 and 4.9, POPUP.H and POPUP.CPP, show a good example of this. (Be sure to have both files in the current directory when compiling.) The program uses malloc to create buffers for storing text behind a series of "windows." When you run the program, you'll see these windows—in color, if you have a color display—pop up on top of each other at random locations. After the tenth window appears, press the **<Spacebar>** ten times to remove each window, exposing the ones below. Actually, though, there aren't any windows "below" the ones on top. It's just an illusion brought to you by malloc and a few pointers.

Listing 4.8. POPUP.H (1 of 2)

```
1:  // popup.h -- Header file for popup.cpp
2:
3:  #include <stream.hpp>
4:  #include <stdlib.h>
5:  #include <time.h>
6:  #include <disp.h>
7:
8:  #define MAXWINDOW 10   // Maximum number of windows
```

```
 9:   #define MAXCOLOR 7        // Maximum background color (min = 0)
10:   #define MAXROW 22         // Maximum row number (min = 0)
11:   #define MAXCOL 79         // Maximum column number (min = 0)
12:   #define WHITE 15          // Color number for whiter than white
13:   #define MONOCHROME 7      // Monochrome display mode number
14:
15:   struct winrec {           // Window record
16:      void * bufptr;         // Saved text. NULL if window is closed
17:      unsigned trow;         // Top row number
18:      unsigned lcol;         // Left column number
19:      unsigned brow;         // Bottom row number
20:      unsigned rcol;         // Right column number
21:      int attribute;         // Background & foreground color
22:   };
23:
24:   typedef winrec *winrecptr;      // Define winrecptr data type
25:
26:   /* -- Function prototypes */
27:
28:   void error(char *errmsg);
29:   void pause(void);
30:   int randrange(int low, int high);
31:   void openWindow(winrecptr wrp, int backcolor, unsigned trow,
32:      unsigned lcol, unsigned brow, unsigned rcol);
33:   void displayText(winrecptr wrp, char *message);
34:   void closeTopWindow(winrecptr wrp);
```

Listing 4.9. POPUP.CPP (2 of 2)

```
 1:   // popup.cpp -- Display overlapping "pop-up" windows
 2:
 3:   #include "popup.h"
 4:
 5:   main()
 6:   {
 7:      int wnum;
 8:      unsigned trow, lcol, brow, rcol; // Window coordinates
 9:      winrec buffer[MAXWINDOW];         // Array of winrecs
10:
11:      srand(time(NULL));    // Randomize
12:      disp_open();          // Initialize display package
13:
14:   /* -- Display MAXWINDOW windows at random locations and colors */
15:
```

```
16:        for (wnum = 0; wnum < MAXWINDOW; wnum++) {
17:          trow = randrange(0, MAXROW / 2);        // Set top row
18:          lcol = randrange(0, MAXCOL / 2);        // Set left column
19:          brow = randrange(trow + 4, MAXROW);     // Set bottom row
20:          rcol = randrange(lcol + 12, MAXCOL);    // Set right column
21:          openWindow(
22:            &buffer[wnum],                  // Pass winrec pointer
23:             randrange(1, MAXCOLOR),        // Background color
24:             trow, lcol, brow, rcol);       // Location
25:          displayText(&buffer[wnum], form("Window #%d", wnum + 1));
26:        }
27:
28:    /* -- Close windows one by one */
29:
30:      disp_move(24, 0);
31:      disp_printf("Press <Spacebar> to erase top window...");
32:      for (wnum = MAXWINDOW - 1; wnum >= 0; wnum--)
33:         closeTopWindow(&buffer[wnum]);
34:      disp_move(24, 0);      // Move cursor to last row
35:      disp_close();          // Close display package
36:    }
37:
38:    /* -- Display error message and quit */
39:
40:    void error(char *errmsg) {
41:       disp_move(24, 0);                 // Move cursor to last row
42:       disp_close();                     // Close the display package
43:       cout << "ERROR: " << errmsg;      // Display error message
44:       exit(1);                          // Return to DOS
45:    }
46:
47:    /* -- Pause for a keypress (no message displayed) */
48:
49:    void pause(void)
50:    {
51:       int c = getch();      // Wait for any keypress
52:    }
53:
54:    /* -- Return random number from low ... high */
55:
56:    int randrange(int low, int high)
57:    {
58:       return low + (rand() % ((high - low) + 1));
59:    }
```

```
60:
61:    /* -- Open a new window at these coordinates and fill with color.
62:    Background color is ignored on monochrome displays. */
63:
64:    void openWindow(winrecptr wrp, int backcolor, unsigned trow,
65:       unsigned lcol, unsigned brow, unsigned rcol)
66:    {
67:       int bcolor, tcolor;   // Border color, text color
68:       unsigned bufsize;      // Saved-text buffer size
69:
70:    /* -- Determine color to use for background and foreground */
71:
72:       if (disp_getmode() == MONOCHROME) {
73:          bcolor = DISP_REVERSEVIDEO;            // Monochrome display
74:          tcolor = bcolor;
75:       } else {
76:          bcolor = (backcolor << 4) + WHITE;  // Color display
77:          tcolor = bcolor - WHITE;
78:       }
79:
80:    /* -- Calculate number of bytes needed to save text behind window */
81:
82:       bufsize =
83:        ((brow - trow + 1) * (rcol - lcol + 1)) * sizeof(unsigned);
84:
85:       wrp->bufptr = malloc(bufsize);   // Reserve space for buffer
86:       if (wrp->bufptr == NULL)         // If that fails, return
87:          return;                       //   leaving bufptr == NULL
88:
89:    /* -- Save text behind window in buffer just created */
90:
91:       disp_peekbox(wrp->bufptr, trow, lcol, brow, rcol);
92:       wrp->trow = trow;    // Save coordinates and color, too
93:       wrp->lcol = lcol;
94:       wrp->brow = brow;
95:       wrp->rcol = rcol;
96:       wrp->attribute = tcolor;     // Text color
97:
98:    /* -- Pause and then display the window */
99:
100:       msleep(250);    // Pause for 1/4 second
101:       disp_fillbox(((bcolor * 256) + ' '), trow, lcol, brow, rcol);
102:       disp_box(0, bcolor, trow, lcol, brow, rcol);
103:    }
```

```
104:!
105:    /* -- Display some text inside this window (assumes that window is
106:    frontmost on display) */
107:
108:    void displayText(winrecptr wrp, char *message)
109:    {
110:        if (wrp->bufptr == NULL) return;   // Exit if window not open
111:        disp_move(wrp->trow + 2, wrp->lcol + 2);
112:        disp_setattr(wrp->attribute);
113:        disp_printf(message);
114:        disp_setattr(DISP_NORMAL);
115:    }
116:
117:    /* -- Close window using winrec struct addressed by wrp. Assumes that
118:    this window is frontmost on display. */
119:
120:    void closeTopWindow(winrecptr wrp)
121:    {
122:        if (wrp->bufptr == NULL) return;   // Exit if window not open
123:        pause();
124:        disp_pokebox(
125:            wrp->bufptr, wrp->trow, wrp->lcol, wrp->brow, wrp->rcol);
126:        free(wrp->bufptr);   // Dispose buffer
127:        wrp->bufptr = NULL;   // Prevent further use of buffer
128:    }
```

Despite the program's size, POPUP.CPP (Listing 4.9) contains very little that you haven't seen before. To understand how the program works, it's probably best to start with the header file in Listing 4.8. Most important is the winrec structure at lines 15-22 and the winrecptr (pointer to a winrec structure) type at line 24. The structure collects various details about a window's location and color, and also has a field bufptr declared as void *. This untyped pointer will address a block of memory that saves a copy of the text "behind" a window. Redisplaying that text on top of where the window appears is how POPUP causes pop-up windows to pop *off*. Also, if this pointer is NULL, POPUP considers the window closed.

The main program in Listing 4.9 stores an array of winrec records in buffer (line 9). A for loop (lines 16-26) creates several variables to open a window at a random location on screen and then calls openWindow. Then a for loop passes the address of one of the winrec variables in the buffer array (line 22) along with other items that tell this function where to place the window and what color to use for its background. After this, the program displays the window's number (line 25) and then calls closeTopWindow (line 33), letting you press **<Spacebar>** to close all windows one by one.

Line 85 inside function openWindow calls malloc to reserve space for the buffer that will store the text behind a new window, which is not yet visible. Notice how the next line tests whether the result is NULL. If so, the function immediately returns (line 87). This prevents an accidental (and disastrous) use of the NULL pointer. Because NULL equals 0, writing data to the location addressed by a NULL pointer (if you can get away with doing that) would overwrite the system's interrupt vectors—pointers to various system routines—stored in low memory. To say the least, this is a serious mistake!

If all proceeds normally, line 91 calls disp_peekbox to save the text now on display where the window will appear in the buffer space reserved a moment earlier. The rest of the function saves other details about the window in the winrec variable passed to openWindow and then displays the window with calls to disp_fillbox and disp_box (lines 101-102). Line 100 delays each window's appearance by about 1/4 second so that you can see the windows one by one as they are drawn. Remove this line to open windows at full speed.

The other new area in POPUP is in function closeTopWindow (lines 120-128). There disp_pokebox "closes" a window by redisplaying the text saved earlier by disp_peekbox. After this, free deletes the memory where that text is stored. Even though this program doesn't reuse that space, deleting the memory would be necessary in a more active setting that opens and closes many windows. Also notice how line 127 sets the bufptr pointer to NULL, a safety measure that helps prevent using a disposed pointer.

Hint: Never use the memory addressed by a pointer passed to free or delete. That memory has been returned to the general pool from which new, malloc, and calloc obtain fresh memory space to reserve. To help prevent accidents, it's a good idea to set disposed pointers to NULL. That way, before using a pointer, a simple check like if (p != NULL) tells whether a pointer has been disposed or addresses a valid memory space.

Pointers as Function Arguments

Pointer function parameters are more common in C than in C++. The reason for this is simple (and no doubt aggravatingly clear to C experts in the audience). C lacks C++'s reference parameters (those declared with &); therefore, to pass an argument to a function for direct use, a statement must pass the *address* of that argument to a pointer parameter. In C therefore, it's your responsibility to crank out the mechanics that make reference parameters work automatically in C++.

Still, it's a good idea to know how to pass arguments by address to function pointer parameters. Sometimes it is more convenient to design functions that way, and many library functions are designed to take pointer parameters. Learning the technique will also make it easier for you to read published C listings, which frequently declare function pointer parameters.

Because you already know how to use C++ reference parameters, compare that method with C's pointer parameters. Suppose that you create a structure to keep track of high and low temperatures:

```
struct temperature {
    float high;
    float low;
}
```

You plan to use temperature in a program that keeps track of high and low readings from a thermometer somehow attached to the computer. A key function in that program reads the current temperature and modifies the appropriate field, high or low, in a temperature structure passed by reference to the function. In C++, this is easy to write:

```
void recordtemp(temperature &t)
{
    float current;
    getcurrenttemp(current);
    if (current > t.high)
        t.high = current;
    else if (current < t.low)
        t.low = current;
}
```

The temperature parameter &t is passed by reference. This means that a statement can call recordtemp with a temperature variable passed as an argument, and the function will deposit the correct values (if necessary) directly in that variable:

```
temperature thetemp;
recordtemp(thetemp);
```

Because recordtemp's parameter is passed by reference, the function directly operates on thetemp variable. If the parameter were not declared with &, the function would operate only on a *copy* of that argument's value. Except for the & character, however, the function statements are identical regardless of whether a parameter is passed by value or by reference. Even though technically the parameter &t is a pointer that addresses the actual variable passed as an argument (thetemp in this case), this detail is conveniently hidden by the compiler, making the function easier to write and maintain.

The same is not true in C, which does not have reference parameters. In C, *all* parameters are passed by value. For that reason, to refer back to an actual argument requires passing that argument's address to a parameter pointer. Here's the same `recordtemp` function written in C (the code also works in C++):

```
void recordtemp(temperature *t)
{
    float current;

    getcurrenttemp(current);
    if (current > t->high)
        t->high = current;
    else if (current < t->low)
        t->low = current;
}
```

Now the statements in the function must be aware that `t` is a pointer and not a variable. Instead of using expressions like `t.high` and `t.low` to refer to fields in the structure, statements must use the symbol `->`. Also, although not shown here, it's necessary to dereference the pointer `t` using `*t` in expressions that need to refer to the addressed information. To call the function, you must use the form `recordtemp(&t)`, passing the address of `t` to the pointer parameter.

> **Note:** Don't confuse the & (address of) operator in statements with C++'s unique & (reference parameter) symbol. Although both use the same character, their contexts are different. Both C and C++ can use & as an operator in expressions that evaluate to the addresses of identifiers, for example, `&var`. However, only C++ can use & in a function declaration to create reference parameters that are passed by address to a function. In C, a declaration like `int f(int &var)` is not allowed.

Although less common than in C, pointer arguments are still useful in C++ programming, especially when a function needs to operate on arguments of more than one data type. Listing 4.10, SWAP.CPP, shows an example.

Listing 4.10. SWAP.CPP

```
1:  // swap.cpp -- Use pointers to swap any two same-size variables
2:
3:  #include <stream.hpp>
4:  #include <stdlib.h>
5:  #include <string.h>
6:
```

```
 7:   struct rec {            // Sample structure to swap
 8:      char *title;
 9:      char *author;
10:      int pages;
11:   };
12:
13:   /* -- Function prototypes */
14:
15:   void swapbytes(void *p1, void *p2, unsigned size);
16:   void showrecs(char *s);
17:
18:   rec r1, r2;             // Two rec global variables
19:
20:   main()
21:   {
22:
23:   /* -- Assign test values to the global variables */
24:
25:      r1.title = "The C++ Programming Language";
26:      r1.author= "Bjarne Stroustrup";
27:      r1.pages = 328;
28:      r2.title = "Mastering Turbo Pascal 5.5";
29:      r2.author= "Tom Swan";
30:      r2.pages  = 877;
31:
32:   /* -- Display variables before and after swapping */
33:
34:      showrecs("Before");
35:      swapbytes(&r1, &r2, sizeof(r1));
36:      showrecs("After");
37:   }
38:
39:   /* -- Swap size bytes addressed by p1 and p2 */
40:
41:   void swapbytes(void *p1, void *p2, unsigned size)
42:   {
43:      unsigned char t;       // Temporary place to hold each byte
44:
45:      while (size-- > 0) {
46:         t = *(char *)p1;
47:         *(char *)p1++ = *(char *)p2;
48:         *(char *)p2++ = t;
49:      }
50:   }
```

```
51:
52:  /* -- Display values of r1 and r2 */
53:
54:  void showrecs(char *s)
55:  {
56:  cout << "\n\n" << s << "\n=============";
57:  cout << "\nr1.title  = "   << (r1.title);
58:  cout << "\nr1.author = "   << (r1.author);
59:  cout << "\nr1.pages  = "   << (r1.pages);
60:  cout << "\n\nr2.title  = " << (r2.title);
61:  cout << "\nr2.author = "   << (r2.author);
62:  cout << "\nr2.pages  = "   << (r2.pages) << '\n';
63:  }
```

Although just a demonstration, the SWAP program contains a function that you'll want to keep around for your own programs. The function, swapbytes, can swap the values of two variables, no matter what their data types and sizes. Line 15 declares the function's prototype:

```
void swapbytes(void *p1, void *p2, unsigned size);
```

The first two parameters p1 and p2 are pointers to void. Whenever you need general purpose pointers that can address variables of any types, declare them like this. The third parameter equals the size in bytes of the variables to be swapped. The function assumes that the pointers address two variables of at least this size. Usually, the two variables will be of the same types, although they don't have to be.

Because void pointers can hold the addresses of any variables, using swapbytes is easy. Just insert the address-of operator & in front of each argument to swap, as at line 35:

```
swapbytes(&r1, &r2, sizeof(r1));
```

This swaps r1 and r2, two global variables defined at line 18 of type rec, a structure declared earlier at lines 7-11. Notice how the sizeof operator lets the program calculate how many bytes to swap. Using sizeof this way instead of specifying a literal value is usually the best course.

SWAP displays the before and after values of r1 and r2, proving that swapbytes is doing its job. Take a look at the while loop inside that function (lines 45-49):

```
while (size-- > 0) {
    t = *(char *)p1;
    *(char *)p1++ = *(char *)p2;
    *(char *)p2++ = t;
}
```

While size is greater than 0 (and decrementing size at the same time with the -- operator), the loop executes three statements. The first statement assigns the byte addressed by p1 to a temporary char variable t, using a type cast expression (char *) to force the compiler to consider p2 as it would an explicitly declared char pointer. The second statement assigns the byte at p2 to the address where p1 points. The third statement assigns t to where p2 points. The last two statements also apply the increment operator ++ to each pointer. This advances the pointers to address the next bytes in line to be swapped on the next pass through the loop.

Note: Be sure to understand that operations such as p1++ and p2++ in swapbytes increment *copies* of addresses passed to these function parameters. Even though the parameters are pointers, they are passed by value to the function. Changing those values inside the function never directly affects the actual arguments passed.

Pointers to Functions

So far in this chapter, you've spent a lot of time examining pointers to data. As you've seen, a program can declare pointers to any type of variable, structure, or array. Also, functions can declare pointer parameters to allow statements to pass the addresses of arguments to those functions.

It's also possible to create pointers to functions. Instead of addressing data, function pointers point to executable code. Dereferencing a pointer to data lets statements read and write values stored in memory. Dereferencing a pointer to a function causes that function to run.

The trick to learning how to create pointers to functions is to investigate why the obvious approach doesn't work. As you know, to create a pointer to a variable, you preface the variable's name with an asterisk. For example, this creates a pointer named myptr to a variable of type float:

```
float *myptr;
```

Without the asterisk, myptr would be a plain float variable. With the asterisk, it's a pointer *to* a float variable. However, this same rule doesn't work for function pointers. Suppose that you want to create a pointer to a function that returns a float value. You might try to do this by declaring the function's prototype prefaced with an asterisk, the way you create other pointers:

```
float *myfnptr(void);   // ???
```

That appears to create a function pointer named myfnptr that addresses a function with no parameters that returns float. The declaration is faulty, however, because the asterisk binds with float, not with myfnptr. Despite appearances, what the previous command line creates is a function that returns a pointer to a float value! It is as though you wrote

```
(float *)myfnptr(void);
```

This might be useful in other circumstances, but it's not what was intended. To create a pointer to a f u n c t i o n that returns a f l o a t value, you must surround the asterisk and function name with parentheses:

```
float (*myfnptr)(void);
```

The parentheses tell the compiler that the asterisk binds to the function name, not its data type. This is the correct way to create all function pointers. Some programmers also add a space between the asterisk and function name to make their intentions perfectly clear:

```
float (* myfnptr)(void);
```

Either method is correct, but adding the space can make function pointer declarations easier to spot in a lengthy text file. If the function requires parameters, add them as usual inside parentheses in the function's parameter list:

```
float (* myfnptr)(int x, int y);
```

That sets up a pointer to a function that returns a f l o a t value and requires two integer arguments. To call such a function from a statement, first initialize the pointer to address a real function written in the usual way. Like all pointers, before using one that addresses a function, you must initialize the pointer to address executable code. Suppose that the function you want to call via a pointer is named t h e f u n c t i o n. You can assign its address to m y f n p t r like this:

```
myfnptr = &thefunction;
```

This is no different from the way you assign addresses of variables to common pointers. Here, t h e f u n c t i o n is the name of a function (not shown). After this statement executes, m y f n p t r addresses that function. The & sign is not strictly required, but I include the symbol to make it clear that an address is assigned to m y f n p t r. To call the function, use this expression:

```
float answer;
answer = (* myfnptr)(5, 10);
```

If the function requires no arguments, leave the final parentheses blank:

```
answer = (* myfnptr)();
```

This calls the function addressed by m y f n p t r. Of course, you could always call the function directly without using a pointer:

```
answer = thefunction();
```

When using the pointer, for clarity, you should add the parentheses and asterisk to the function pointer's name. As in the declaration, the extra space between the asterisk and function name is optional, and you could write

```
answer = (*myfnptr)();
```

Now that you've seen the basic forms, look at a program that puts a function pointer to good use. Listing 4.11, PLOT.CPP, plots a graph of a mathematical function. As you'll see when you examine the statements, using a pointer to that function makes it easy to replace it with another mathematical function to plot.

Listing 4.11. PLOT.CPP

```
1:   // plot.cpp -- Plot a function
2:
3:   #include <stream.hpp>
4:   #include <math.h>
5:   #include <disp.h>
6:   #include <time.h>
7:
8:   #define XSCALE 20        // X display adjustment
9:   #define YSCALE 10        // Y display adjustment
10:  #define XMIN 0           // Display coordinate ranges
11:  #define XMAX 78
12:  #define YMIN 0
13:  #define YMAX 24
14:
15:  /* -- Define pointer to float function with an int parameter */
16:
17:  typedef float (* pfptr)(int x);
18:
19:  /* -- Function prototypes */
20:
21:  void pause(void);
22:  void yplot(int x, float f);
23:  float afunction(int x);
24:
25:  main()
26:  {
27:      int x;
28:      pfptr pf = &afunction;
29:
30:      disp_open();            // Initialize display package
31:      disp_move(0, 0);        // Move cursor to upper left corner
32:      disp_eeop();            // Clear screen
33:
34:      for (x = XMIN; x <= XMAX; x++)        // Cycle for range of x
35:          yplot(x, (* pf)(x * XSCALE));     // Plot function result
36:      pause();                              // Wait for keypress to end
37:  }
```

```
38:
39:    /* -- Wait for a keypress, then continue */
40:
41:    void pause(void)
42:    {
43:        int c = getch();
44:    }
45:
46:    /* -- Plot value of f on y axis at x */
47:
48:    void yplot(int x, float f)
49:    {
50:        disp_move(YSCALE + (f * YSCALE), x);
51:        msleep(50);          // Optional. Remove to plot at full speed
52:        disp_putc('*');      // Display asterisk on graph
53:    }
54:
55:    /* -- The function to plot */
56:
57:    float afunction(int x)
58:    {
59:        return sin((x * PI) / 180.0);
60:    }
```

This small example doesn't show the full value of using a function pointer. In a larger program where this program might be only one of many related modules, it would be tedious to change the function name or to have to recompile the entire module just to plug in a new plot function. Function pointers make that easy.

A pointer to a function can simplify the job of replacing one function with another. So that other places in the program can create function pointer variables of the same type, a `typedef` declaration at line 17 declares the design for a pointer to the plot function:

```
typedef float (* pfptr)(int x);
```

Except for `typedef`, this construction is similar to the one used before. Instead of creating a pointer *variable,* this line creates a new *data type* named `pfptr` (plot-function pointer). Other places in the program can then use that new data-type identifier to create function-pointer variables. For example, line 28 creates a pointer named `pf` of type `pfptr` and initializes it at the same time to address a function named `afunction`:

```
pfptr pf = &afunction;
```

At this point, `pf` addresses a `function`, which is written elsewhere. (In a larger program, the function would probably go into a separate module, and a statement would pass `pf` to the plot module so that it would call the new function.) Look carefully at a f u n c t i o n's prototype at line 23 and at its implementation at lines 57-60. The function's declaration matches that of the function pointer's:

```
float afunction(int x);
```

After assigning the address of this function to p f, PLOT calls the function at line 35 inside a f o r loop. The call to the function appears as an argument to another function, y p l o t:

```
yplot(x, (* pf)(x * XSCALE));
```

This calls y p l o t to plot one value on screen. The first parameter is simply the x coordinate value—the column where this value should be plotted. The second argument uses the form (* p f) to call the function addressed by p f. To this function, the expression passes the argument (x * X S C A L E), representing the y coordinate value for the plot. Dereferencing p f with the expression (* p f) causes the program to call the function addressed by p f, or in this case, a f u n c t i o n. This calculates a formula (here, the sine of a value representing an angle). The function returns a f l o a t value, which is then passed to y p l o t for plotting.

As you can see from this section, function pointers can be tricky to use and to set up. (Use the samples here as guides the next time you need to create a function pointer.) A good place for function pointers is in precompiled library routines to which you can pass function pointers to force a routine to call a new function in your own program. (Chapter 8 lists a program, SORTTXT.CPP, that demonstrates how to call functions via pointers this way with the q s o r t library function.)

Now, back to a subject I promised to complete earlier—one that confuses even expert C programmers from time to time—pointers and arrays. As you are about to learn, in C and C++, these are just birds of the same feather.

Pointers and Arrays

Most people who are learning C++ or C are surprised to discover that arrays and pointers are one and the same. All array names are actually pointers, and all pointers actually address arrays.

Sound strange? If so, consider the nature of an array. As you learned in chapter 2, an array stores one or more variables of the same data type in memory. Those variables are stacked up like jets over O'Hare. The array name locates the start of the array. In that sense, the array identifier in a C++ program (and in C) acts like a *pointer* to the first element in the array.

A simple example proves this important concept. Run Listing 4.12, ARRAYPTR.CPP. As you can see, the program assigns integer values to an array and then uses indexing (the normal technique) to display that value. It also uses the array name as a pointer to do the same, proving that the array name *is* a pointer.

Listing 4.12. ARRAYPTR.CPP

```
 1:   // arrayptr.cpp -- Show relationship between arrays and pointers
 2:
 3:   #include <stream.hpp>
 4:
 5:   #define MAX 10          // Size of array
 6:
 7:   void showFirst(void);
 8:
 9:   int array[MAX];         // Global array of MAX integers
10:
11:   main()
12:   {
13:       array[0] = 123;     // Assign value using indexing
14:       showFirst();        // Display value both ways
15:       *array = 321;       // Assign value using pointer
16:       showFirst();        // Display value both ways
17:   }
18:
19:   void showFirst(void)
20:   {
21:       cout << "array[0] = " << array[0] << '\n';   // Via index
22:       cout << "*array   = " << *array   << '\n';   // Via pointer
23:   }
```

Line 9 declares a global a r r a y of i n t values. Line 13 then assigns the value 123 to the first element in the array using the index value [0]. After this, s h o w F i r s t displays that value. First, at line 21, an output stream statement uses the expression a r r a y [0]—the normal way of selecting an array element with an index value.

The next line (22) displays the same value, but instead of the brackets and an index value, the statement treats a r r a y as though the program had declared it as a pointer. In fact, that's exactly what a r r a y is—a pointer to its arrayed elements. The expression * a r r a y in line 22 dereferences the pointer to "get to" the addressed data and is exactly equivalent to the expression a r r a y [0].

This idea may be easier to visualize if you think about what the compiler must do in order to process an indexed array expression such as a r r a y [4]. To "find" the fifth element in the array (remember, the first element is at index 0, so the fifth is at index 4, not 5), the compiler has to

- Locate the start of the array. Let's call it s t a r t.

- Calculate the distance from s t a r t to the indexed element. In this case, the array contains 2-byte integers, so the fifth element is 4 * 2, or 8 bytes beyond the first. Let's call this value the o f f s e t.

- Add o f f s e t to s t a r t, creating a pointer to the fifth element.

It's this pointer that the program actually uses when the program executes an expression such as i = array[4]. To make that assignment work, the compiler creates instructions to form a pointer (let's call it p) to the fifth element in array. It then executes i = *p to complete the assignment. You don't see any of this happening, of course, but it's useful to know what's going on underfoot.

Although it's usually best to let C++ handle the details of array addressing, it's sometimes useful to take that job away from the compiler and use pointers to address array elements directly. For example, run Listing 4.13, PTRARRAY.CPP.

Listing 4.13. PTRARRAY.CPP

```
1:   // ptrarray.cpp -- More about arrays and pointers
2:
3:   #include <stream.hpp>
4:
5:   #define MAX 10        // Size of array
6:
7:   void showFirst(void);
8:
9:   int array[MAX];        // Global array of MAX integers
10:
11:  main()
12:  {
13:      int *p = array;    // p is an int pointer to array
14:      int i;             // i is a plain int variable
15:
16:  /* -- Fill array with values from 0 to MAX - 1 */
17:
18:      for (i = 0; i < MAX; i++)
19:          array[i] = i;
20:
21:  /* -- Use pointer p to display the array's values */
22:
23:      for (i = 0; i < MAX; i++)
24:          cout << *p++ << '\n';
25:
26:  /* -- Use pointer p to display one array value */
27:
28:      p = &array[5];
29:      cout << "\narray[5] = " << array[5];
30:      cout << "\n*p ..... = " << *p;
31:  }
```

This program is similar to the previous one, but it shows how to use pointers to access any element in an array, not only the first. Line 13 defines a pointer variable p as a pointer to type `int`, the same type as the `array`'s elements (see line 9). Line 13 also assigns the address of `array` to p. Using the address-of operator here as in `&array` would not be correct and will not compile. Remember, `array` *is* a pointer; therefore, you can assign it directly to another pointer that's bound to the same type (`int` in this case).

Lines 18-19 use normal indexing to fill `array` with a few values from 0 to MAX − 1. After that, a second `for` loop at lines 23-24 displays the contents of the array. This time, however, the program uses the pointer p rather than array indexing to refer to each value in `array`.

Carefully study the expression `*p++` in this statement. There are two actions occurring here. The first dereferences `*p`, returning the value of the `int` variable that p addresses. After this, the increment operator `++` advances p to the next `int` in `array`. As a result, the loop displays all array elements just as though you had written `array[i]` rather than `*p++`.

Pointer Arithmetic

You might wonder how it's possible for an expression like `*p++` to advance p to the address of the next item in memory. In this case, those items are integers, which on PCs take two bytes each. For this reason, so that p++ advances p to the next integer value—not to the next byte—C++ has to add 2, not 1, to p.

That's exactly what happens. The compiler uses p's data type to calculate how many bytes to advance p in an expression such as `*p++`. Likewise, `*p--` subtracts 2 from the address held in p. When adding and subtracting pointers and values, C++ considers the values to represent *units* of the data types that the pointers address. If a pointer `ap` addresses a 10-byte structure, `ap++` advances the address in `ap` by 10 bytes. You never have to calculate these details, but you should be aware that C++ multiplies values added and subtracted to and from pointers by the size of the addressed data.

You can also use pointer arithmetic expressions such as `p += 10` to advance p 10 units from its present position. And you can compare pointers, using expressions like `(p1 < p2)`. But these are turbulent waters. Although the compiler accepts such statements, they may not work correctly with far pointers. You may compare pointers this way only if they are not declared to be `far`.

Arrays of Pointers

A useful construction is an array of pointers. Each element in such an array points to the "real" data located elsewhere. This is a good way to keep track of many items of different sizes, for example, a series of strings loaded from a text file. If those strings were stored in fixed string variables, perhaps declared as `char c[128]`, each 80-character string would waste 48 bytes. Multiplied by a few hundred lines, that much waste can add up quickly.

> **Note:** Because PCs use segment and offset values to represent far pointers, it's possible for two different combinations of those values to address the identical location in memory. Pointer comparison expressions do not take this fact into account, and for that reason, they may fail unless the pointers are *normalized* before the comparison. To normalize a far pointer, which ensures that its offset address value is in the range 0 ... 15, and that its combined segment and offset values are unique, include the DOS.H header file in your program. Then execute a statement such as `p = _farptr_norm(p)`. This function is intended to be used only on PCs and with the compiler supplied with this book, and the same function may not exist on other systems.

Listing 4.14, READSTR.CPP, shows how to avoid such waste. The idea is to create an array of pointers, allocate just enough storage to hold each string, and save a pointer to that string in the array. Despite the fact that the array itself takes some memory, this plan tends to save space because most strings will not be of the same lengths.

Listing 4.14. READSTR.CPP

```
 1:  // readstr.cpp -- Read strings into dynamic variables
 2:
 3:  #include <stream.hpp>
 4:  #include <string.h>
 5:
 6:  #define MAX 3        // Maximum number of strings
 7:
 8:  char *readstring(void);
 9:
10:  main()
11:  {
12:     int i;               // i is an index into the following
13:     char *array[MAX]; // an array of MAX char pointers
14:
15:     cout << "Enter " << MAX << " strings:\n";
16:     for (i = 0; i < MAX; i++)
17:        array[i] = readstring();   // Save pointer to each string
18:
19:     cout << "\n\nYour strings are:\n";
```

```
20:        for (i = 0; i < MAX; i++)
21:            cout << array[i] << '\n';  // Display strings via pointers
22:    }
23:
24:    char *readstring(void)
25:    {
26:        char *p;             // p is a pointer to a char
27:        char buffer[128]; // buffer for reading each string
28:
29:        gets(buffer);           // Read string from user or stdin
30:        p = new char[1 + strlen(buffer)]; // Create dynamic string
31:        strcpy(p, buffer);    // Copy buffer into dynamic string
32:        return p;             // Return the new string's address
33:    }
```

Although READSTR is just a demonstration, the principles are the same no matter how many strings you need to hold in memory. Line 13 defines an array of pointers to type char. Each element in the array is a pointer. By storing the strings in memory, and saving the address of each string's first character in the array, the program demonstrates a convenient way to find its strings, no matter where they are stored.

Function readstring (lines 24-33) lets you enter one string (or type a DOS command such as **readstr < file.txt** to pass strings from a file to the program). Line 29 calls gets to read a string into a local buffer. After this, line 30 uses new to allocate just enough space to hold the string's characters. This is equal to one plus the result of function strlen, a library function that returns the length of a string (minus its terminating ASCII NULL.) Finally, strcpy copies the bytes from the local buffer to the newly allocated memory addressed by pointer p. The function then passes p back to the caller (see line 32).

This means that line 17 receives from readstring the address of a newly allocated string in memory. By saving these addresses in the array of char pointers, the program can easily display or perform other operations on the strings, as lines 20-21 demonstrate. Notice that there is no need to dereference the pointers in the array at line 21. This is because C++ understands that strings (arrays of char) are represented by char pointers. Remember, arrays and pointers are equivalent, and for that reason, pointers to char do not require special treatment to let C++ know that it should treat the pointer as the address of a string.

Functions that Return String Pointers

Chapter 1 lists a program DT.CPP that displays the date and time. By calling string functions in the C++ library, it's possible to write that same program with fewer statements.

> **Note:** This brings up an interesting point. If C++ treats a pointer to char as addressing a string—that is, an *array* of characters—how do you declare a pointer to a *single* character? The answer is, you don't. A single character takes one byte of memory. Declaring a pointer, which takes two or more bytes, to address a single char would be silly. However, if you need only one character addressed by a pointer declared as char *p, the expression p[0] does the trick. Because p, a pointer, is equivalent to an array, indexing p with [0] returns a single element at the address specified by p.

Most string functions actually return a pointer to type char. Because C++ considers such pointers to address strings, you can pass any string function directly to a function parameter declared as char *or as const char * (including const tells the compiler not to permit assignments to the addressed data). For example, Listing 4.15, THEDATE.CPP, calls the string function asctime to convert the date and time into an ASCII string. This function's prototype is in the header file TIME.H, which the program includes at line 4.

Listing 4.15. THEDATE.CPP

```
1:   // thedate.cpp -- Improved date and time display
2:
3:   #include <stream.hpp>
4:   #include <time.h>
5:
6:   main()
7:   {
8:       time_t t;
9:
10:      time(&t);
11:      cout << asctime(localtime(&t));
12:   }
```

THEDATE defines a variable t of type time_t—also declared in TIME.H. Line 10 passes the address of t to time, which expects to receive a pointer to a variable of this type. In TIME.H, you'll find that time is declared as time(time_t *);. Its single parameter is a pointer to type time_t.

The time function copies the date and time in binary format to the structure addressed by the pointer you pass to the function. Then line 11 passes t's address to function localtime, which converts the raw date and time information into a structure that asctime requires. That function converts this information to a string displayed here in an output-stream statement. The result is a line like this:

```
Sat Sep  1 12:59:17 1990
```

Cascading functions inside functions as at line 11 is a common practice. When dealing with string functions, however, be aware that when a function returns type char *, that pointer (unless equal to NULL) addresses space that's best treated as temporary. String functions do not return strings. They return pointers to strings. The characters that belong to that string are stored somewhere in memory, of course, but the next time you call the same function, it will probably use that same memory for the next string.

For this reason, you'll almost certainly introduce bugs into your programs if you write code like this:

```
char *sp;  // sp is a pointer to a string
sp = asctime(localtime(&t));  // ???

cout << sp;
```

This dangerous practice saves the result of asctime in a string pointer, sp. It then displays the string by passing the pointer to cout. Although this will probably work, the program may fail later if it again executes asctime or another string function, which may change the string that sp addresses.

To guard against this, if you need to save the results of a string function, first create new storage to hold a string of the same length as the string at the address returned by asctime or another function. Then use the strdup function declared in STRING.H. This function calls malloc to allocate memory to hold a string passed to the function as a char pointer. It then copies the characters addressed by that pointer into the newly allocated memory. Finally, it returns the address of that memory, which you can save in a pointer so that you can find the copy of the string later. Here's one way to accomplish all of this:

```
char *sp;  // sp is a pointer to a string
sp = strdup(asctime(localtime(&t)));

cout << sp;
```

This inserts the call to asctime inside a call to strdup. Now, the program can be certain that sp addresses a string that won't change unexpectedly.

String Functions

Supplied with C++ are a rich set of functions that operate on strings. Most of these functions return pointers to strings, and most take one or more string pointers as parameters. You've seen a few of these functions such as strdup and strlen in action in previous sections. With what you have learned about arrays and pointers—and especially about pointers to arrays of characters—you're ready to begin using C++'s string functions in your own programs.

I'll cover a few of the more common string functions here. For descriptions of others, look up function names that begin with s t r in chapter 10.

Note: To use the string functions described in this section, insert the directive `#include <string.h>` at the beginning of your program.

Common String Functions

Copying one string to another doesn't work as you might expect it to, especially if you have some experience with BASIC or Pascal. If s1 and s2 are both c h a r * pointers, this assignment does *not* make a copy of the string addressed by s2:

```
s1 = s2;
```

That copies the *pointer* s2 to s1, not the characters addressed by s2; therefore, after the assignment, s1 and s2 address the *same* string in memory. Sometimes this can be useful, and there's nothing technically wrong with the statement. Just be sure that it accomplishes what you expect.

Dereferencing the pointers is also no help:

```
*s1 = *s2;
```

That only copies *one* character addressed by s2 to the memory addressed by s1 (to which you were careful to allocate at least one byte beforehand).

Note: When two or more pointers address the same memory space allocated on the heap, you *must* be careful never to d e l e t e or f r e e more than one of those pointers. Deleting the same allocated memory space more than once will corrupt the heap and cause your program to fail. There are no exceptions to this rule!

To copy the characters addressed by one string pointer to space addressed by another, call s t r c p y. For example, this copies the string addressed by a character pointer s o u r c e to the memory addressed by a similarly declared character pointer destination:

```
char *source;
char *destination;
...
strcpy(destination, source);
```

Two observations are important here. One, the "direction" is right to left (from source to destination), which is easy to mix up. Second, the memory addressed by destination must be large enough to hold the characters in the string addressed by source. If there's not enough room to hold the string, the statement may overwrite other variables or code in memory, causing a serious problem.

To make sure that destination addresses enough space, use statements like these:

```
destination = new char[strlen(source) + 1];
if (destination == NULL)
   error("Out of memory");

strcpy(destination, source);
```

Using strlen to find the length of the source string, and allocating that much space plus one byte, ensures that destination addresses enough space to hold the string copy.

You'll find strlen useful in many other situations. The function returns an integer value equal to the number of characters in a string, but *not* including the string's NULL terminator. Even a zero-length string has a terminating byte, and therefore, occupies at least one byte of memory.

To make it easier to copy strings of different sizes, you can also use strncpy. This is similar to strcpy, but takes a third argument specifying how many characters to copy from the source to the destination:

```
strncpy(destination, source, 10);
```

That copies 10 characters addressed by source to the memory addressed by destination. If the source string is longer than the space allocated to destination, the function does *not* terminate the new string with a NULL. For that reason, it's usually a good idea to fill the destination string with NULLs before calling strncpy. Assuming that n represents the number of bytes, one way to do this is to follow strncpy with

```
int n = 11;
destination = new char[11];

strncpy(destination, source, 10);

destination[n - 1] = NULL;
```

The statements allocate 11 bytes to destination (enough room for 10 characters plus a NULL terminator). Then strncpy copies up to 10 characters from source to destination. To make sure that the copied string is terminated correctly, the final statement assigns NULL to the last byte allocated to destination. If strncpy copied less than 10 characters, no harm is done.

Another way to copy strings is to use strdup. Like strcpy and strncpy, strdup copies a string. Unlike those other functions though, strdup also allocates space to hold the new copy. The function returns char *, and you will usually assign it to a character pointer like this:

```
destination = strdup(source);
```

This is one of my favorite string functions. Assuming that source addresses a character string, the statement allocates just enough space to hold those characters. It assigns the address of the space to destination and copies the characters addressed by source (including the NULL terminator) to the newly allocated space. If enough free memory is not available to hold the string copy, strdup returns NULL. For that reason, you should follow each use of strdup with a check of the results:

```
destination = strdup(source);
if (destination == NULL)
    error("Out of memory");
```

Joining Strings

When you need to join two or more strings, call strcat or strncat. (The *cat* stands for *concatenate*, meaning "to join.") Suppose that you have these three string pointers:

```
char *lastName = " Lincoln";
char *firstName = "Abraham";
char *name;
```

You can join Abe's first and last names by first allocating some space to name and then calling strcat:

```
name = new char[strlen(lastName) + strlen(firstName) + 1];
strcpy(name, firstName);

strcat(name, lastName);

cout << name;
```

The call to strcat attaches a copy of the string addressed by lastName onto the end of the string addressed by name. The function returns a pointer to the result, letting you use it directly. For example, the last two lines could be written

```
cout << strcat(name, lastName);
```

A similar function, strncat, adds a third parameter that specifies the number of characters to copy:

```
strncat(name, lastName, 5);
```

The statement copies up to 5 characters or `strlen(lastName)`, whichever value is smaller, from `lastName` to the end of `name`.

Comparing Strings

Comparing two strings is another operation that may not work as you expect it to. As with copying strings, if a program has two string pointers `s1` and `s2`, this expression does *not* compare the strings addressed by the pointers:

```
if (s1 == s2)
   cout << "The strings are equal!\n";    // ???
```

The expression `(s1 == s2)` compares the two *pointers,* not the characters they address. Dereferencing the pointers doesn't help:

```
if (*s1 == *s2)
   cout << "The strings are equal!\n";    // ???
```

Looks good, but it compares only the first character addressed by each pointer, not the full strings at those locations. To do that, call the `strcmp` function:

```
if (strcmp(s1, s2) == 0)
   cout << "The strings are equal!\n";
```

This is the correct way to compare two strings. The `strcmp` function returns an `int` value less than 0 if the string at `s1` is alphabetically less than the string at `s2`. It returns 0 if the two strings are equal. It returns a positive value if the string at `s1` is alphabetically greater than the string at `s2`. To test whether `s1` is greater than `s2`, you can write

```
if (strcmp(s1, s2) > 0)
   cout << "The first string is greater!\n";
```

A similar function, `strcmpl`, takes upper- and lowercase into consideration when comparing the two strings. Replace `strcmp` with `strcmpl` when you *don't* want case to matter. In other words, `strcmp("A", "a")` is less than 0; `strcmpl("A", "a")` equals 0.

Searching Strings

Programs that break down strings into their components, an action called *parsing,* can use several string functions for searching one string for occurrences of characters and other strings.

One such function is strchr, which locates the first character in a string that matches a given argument. For example, to find a period in a string addressed by a pointer named file name, you can write

```
char *file name = "TEST.DAT";
cout << strchr(filename, '.');
```

If the character in the second argument to strchr isn't found in the string addressed by the char * in the first argument, strchr returns NULL. If it can find the specified character, it returns a pointer to it of type char *.

It's important to realize that strchr returns a character pointer, which can be treated as another string that starts somewhere in the middle of the original. However, strchr does *not* copy the string, so you must be aware that you now have two pointers addressing the same characters. To copy the tail of a string after searching it for a specific character, use statements like these:

```
char *filename = "TEST.DAT";
char extension[4] = "none";
char *p;

if ((p = strchr(filename, '.')) != NULL)
    strcpy(extension, p);
cout << extension;
```

Try running this sample and then change "TEST.DAT" to "TEST". The function call strchr(filename, '.') returns a character pointer to the first period in the string addressed by filename, or it returns NULL, a condition the if statement carefully checks before using the data addressed by p.

To find the last occurrence of a character, use strrchr. For example, strrchr(filename, 'X') returns a pointer to the last X in the string addressed by filename. If there are no Xs in the string, strrchr returns NULL.

You can also search for the occurrences of one string inside another. To do this, call strstr:

```
char *source = "ABCDEFGHIJKLMNOPQRSTUVWXYZ";
char *pattern = "MNOP";
char *p;

if ((p = strstr(source, pattern)) != NULL)
    cout << p;
```

This searches for the string addressed by pattern inside the string addressed by source, setting p to the address of the first matching character or to NULL if no match was found. The output stream statement displays the string starting with the matching character.

To ignore differences between upper- and lowercase arguments passed to strstr, call strlwr for both strings before the search:

```
char *source = "ABCDEFGHIJKLMNOPQRSTUVWXYZ";
char *pattern = "mnop";
char *p;
strlwr(source);
strlwr(pattern);
if ((p = strstr(source, pattern)) != NULL)
    cout << p;
```

This converts all characters in both source and pattern strings to lowercase before calling strstr. (If you don't want to alter the original strings, use strcpy or strdup to make copies of them and pass those copies to strlwr). You can also call strupr to convert strings to uppercase rather than lowercase if you prefer.

Because strlwr and strupr return pointers to their string arguments, you can use them directly in a statement:

```
if ((strstr(strlwr(source), strlwr(pattern))) != NULL)
    cout << "\nFound " << pattern << " in " << source;
```

Command-Line Arguments

You've undoubtedly used programs that accept command-line arguments. In fact, the compiler packed with this book is such a program. When you enter a command like **ztc thedate** to compile THEDATE.CPP, the argument *thedate* is passed to ZTC.COM for processing.

Other programs often let you select various options, for example, by entering –s or /m to change the way a program operates. Passing instructions to programs this way is convenient, and it eliminates the need for a program to prompt users for required and optional details.

Writing programs that can pick up arguments passed on the command line is not difficult. The first step is to change the way you declare function main. In place of the usual empty parentheses, add two parameters this way:

```
main(int argc, char *argv[])
{
    // ...
}
```

The first parameter, argc (argument count), is a plain integer. It represents the number of arguments passed to main. This kind of argument is defined as any unbroken sequence of characters.

The second parameter is an array of char pointers. The empty brackets indicate that the array's size is not fixed but is determined at runtime. C++ guarantees that argv (argument vectors, or pointers) will hold as many char pointers as specified by argc. Together, the two variables make it easy to pick up arguments passed to a program on the command line.

Note: Remember always that char *argv[] creates an array of char pointers, *not* an array of strings. Each element in argv is a pointer that addresses a string stored somewhere in memory. Forgetting this fact is a common source of bugs. Figure 4.9 illustrates the relationship between argv and its collection of argument strings.

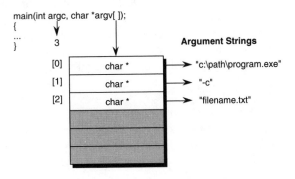

Figure 4.9. How argument strings are organized in memory after calling a fictitious program with the command line *c:\path\program -c filename.txt*.

A simple program demonstrates how to access arguments passed to a C++ program. Listing 4.16, CMDLINE.CPP, also makes a useful test for investigating the forms of arguments that another program will receive. When designing new code to pick up command-line arguments, run CMDLINE and type test arguments, for example **cmdline arg1 myname.txt -s -p/x**. The program simply displays all of the arguments you pass to it. It doesn't take any action on them, so feel free to experiment.

Listing 4.16. CMDLINE.CPP

```
1:  // cmdline.cpp -- Demonstrate command-line arguments
2:
3:  #include <stream.hpp>
4:
5:  main(int argc, char *argv[])
6:  {
7:      while (--argc > 0)
8:          cout << *++argv << '\n';
9:  }
```

Though it's only a shorty, CMDLINE shows the three essential elements that most command-line processing programs need. First, line 5 declares ma i n as described earlier, adding the a r g c and a r g v parameters to ma i n. When the program runs, it passes to ma i n the number of command-line arguments in a r g c. It also passes an array of c h a r pointers in a r g v. These pointers address each argument string.

The wh i l e loop at line 7 decrements a r g c before testing whether it's greater than 0. This means that if a r g c equals 1 at the start of the program—indicating that there is one argument to process—the statement at line 8 will never execute. The reason for this is that a r g v always addresses at least one argument: the path name of the currently running program. If you need this path name string, you can retrieve it by using the expression a r g v [0] or just * a r g v. Either of these expressions selects a single c h a r pointer from the start of the a r g v array.

Line 8 in CMDLINE demonstrates a typical trick with command-line arguments. The expression displays one string addressed by a r g v:

```
cout << *++argv << '\n';
```

Think this through. Because a r g v is an array, you can treat it as a pointer. Applying the ++ operator to a r g v advances that pointer to the next element in the array—in other words, to the next string pointer. Applying the dereference symbol * to the result retrieves one c h a r pointer from the array, which C++ treats as the address of a string.

Another way to access the string pointers in the a r g v array is to index that variable as an array. For example, a r g v [2] locates the third command-line string pointer. Either method—indexing or using a r g v as a pointer—is acceptable, and you should be familiar with both of these common techniques. To demonstrate this, replace lines 7 and 8 in CMDLINE.CPP with this f o r loop:

```
for (int i = 0; i < argc; i++)
   cout << argv[i] << '\n';
```

This shows that you can index a r g v as an array of c h a r pointers or use it as a pointer to an array of type c h a r * elements as in the original program. When you run the modified CMDLINE, enter **cmdline aaa bbb ccc**. You'll see those three arguments along with the program's path name.

Note: Versions of MS-DOS and PC DOS earlier than 3.0 are not capable of passing the current program's path name to programs. When running under those DOS versions, a r g v [0] may address a zero-length string, and the previous changes will not work as expected. If your own programs require path names to their own files, run that program only on DOS versions 3.0 or later or include programming that lets people enter a path name manually when s t r l e n (a r g v [0]) equals 0.

Character Arguments

A common use for command-line arguments is to pass *switches* to a program to select one or more options. For example, a sorting program might accept commands like `sort -d myfile` to sort the contents of MYFILE in descending (`-d`) order.

By tradition, option letters are preceded by dashes (`-d`) or slashes (`/d`). This distinguishes the letters from file names, which normally don't begin with those same characters. (However, DOS permits file names to begin with a dash, but not a slash, which can play havoc with this scheme.)

There are many ways to retrieve command-line options, and most programmers develop their favorite methods. Listing 4.17, OPTIONS.CPP, demonstrates one way to accomplish this. Run the program and type commands such as **options -a, options -b -c,** or **options /a -c** to test the results of applying the option letters a, b, and c. The program detects these options and displays them for confirmation. You might want to convert the program into a function that you can add to any program needing options from the command line.

Listing 4.17. OPTIONS.CPP

```
1:   // options.cpp -- Command-line options demonstration
2:
3:   #include <stream.hpp>
4:   #include <stdlib.h>
5:   #include <ctype.h>
6:
7:   enum {FALSE, TRUE};
8:
9:   int aoption = FALSE;
10:  int boption = FALSE;
11:  int coption = FALSE;
12:
13:  main(int argc, char *argv[])
14:  {
15:     char ch;
16:
17:     while (--argc > 0) {
18:   ch = (*++argv)[0];   // ch = first char of next argument
19:       if ((ch == '-') || (ch == '/')) {
20:     ch = toupper((*argv)[1]);   // ch = second char of argument
21:         switch (ch) {
22:           case 'A':
23:               aoption = TRUE;
24:               break;
25:           case 'B':
```

```
26:                        boption = TRUE;
27:                        break;
28:                    case 'C':
29:                        coption = TRUE;
30:                        break;
31:                    default:
32:                        cout << "Unknown option letter " << ch << '\n';
33:                        exit(1);
34:                }
35:            }
36:            else {
37:                cout << "Unknown option switch " << ch << '\n';
38:                exit(2);
39:            }
40:        }
41:        cout << "Results (0=FALSE, 1=TRUE):\n";
42:        cout << "aoption = " << aoption << '\n';
43:        cout << "boption = " << boption << '\n';
44:        cout << "coption = " << coption << '\n';
45:    }
```

Lines 9-11 declare three options, `aoption`, `boption`, and `coption`. These global variables are declared as type `int` and are intended to be `TRUE` (1) or `FALSE` (0). Even though C++ initializes global variables to 0, I assigned default `FALSE` values here for clarity. You don't have to do this in your own programs.

Line 17 begins a `while` loop similar to the one in CMDLINE.CPP. The loop cycles while `--argc` is greater than 0—once for each command-line argument passed to the program but skipping the program's path name.

Line 18 sets local variable `ch` to the first character of the next argument. Examine this line carefully. You can use this technique to extract characters from command-line strings:

```
ch = (*++argv)[0];
```

The expression in parentheses should look familiar; it's identical to the similar one in CMDLINE.CPP. As there, `*++argv` advances and dereferences the `argv` pointer to the next `char` pointer in the array. C++ evaluates this much of the expression as a `char` pointer—a pointer to a string. Because a string is an array of `char` variables, applying the index `[0]` to the `char` pointer retrieves the first character from that string.

In general, to extract a single character from a string, use brackets and an index value such as `s[5]` or `mystring[23]` as you do for any other array. The parentheses in the expression `(*++argv)[0]` are required because `argv` is *not* a pointer to a string. The expression `argv[0]` is a `char` pointer. The expression `(*argv)[0]` is a `char` variable in the string addressed by `argv[0]`. (Remember, expressions like `argv[0]` and `*argv` are equivalent because of the relationship between arrays and pointers.)

Lines 19-20 in OPTIONS test whether `ch` is a dash or a slash, indicating that the next character should be an option letter. Line 20 picks up that character with the assignment expression

```
ch = toupper((*argv)[1]);
```

Spend a moment examining the expression `(*argv)[1]`. First, `(*argv)` dereferences the `argv` pointer to *another* pointer, which addresses a string. Second, the index expression `[1]` selects the second character of that string. This should be the option letter, which a call to the `toupper` function converts to uppercase. (The "function" `toupper` might be implemented as a macro, but even so, it's used like any function.)

Note: Shouldn't line 20 test the length of the argument before indexing the string's second character? What if the string is only one character long? Think about this. If the first character in the string is a dash or a slash, and if that's the only character in the string, the next "character" will be the string's `NULL` terminator, which the program will ignore. In many cases, however, it is a good idea to make sure that strings (and other arrays) have valid information in them before applying index expressions to reference that data.

A large `switch` statement at lines 21-34 completes the job of detecting command-line options by setting the three global variables to `TRUE` for their letters. OPTIONS then displays the results at lines 41-44.

Numeric Arguments

In addition to passing strings as command-line arguments, it's frequently useful to pass numeric values to programs. For example, Listing 4.18, COLUMN.CPP, accepts commands such as `column 1 12`. This specifies the starting column number (1) and width of the column (12) that you want to extract from the standard input. One way to use COLUMN is to enter the command `dir | column 1 12`, which lists a disk directory, passes each full line of that directory listing to COLUMN, and extracts 12 columns of text starting with column 1 12. The result is a list of file names minus the other information, such as the date and time, normally listed with directory entries. (The result also contains a few lines of extraneous information that you can ignore.)

Listing 4.18. COLUMN.CPP

```
 1:    // column.cpp -- Extract a column from input lines
 2:
 3:    #include <stream.hpp>
 4:    #include <stdlib.h>
 5:
 6:    #define NEWLINE '\n'
 7:
 8:    main(int argc, char *argv[])
 9:    {
10:       char c;                 // I/O character
11:       int cstart, cend;       // Start and end column numbers
12:       int cpos = 0;           // Column position on current line
13:
14:    /* -- Display instructions if 1 or 0 arguments entered */
15:
16:       if (argc < 3) {
17:          cerr << "COLUMN   v1.00   (c) 1991 by Tom Swan\n";
18:          cerr << "To use: Enter column number and width\n";
19:          cerr << "Example: dir | column 1 12\n";
20:          exit(1);
21:       }
22:
23:    /* -- Calculate starting and ending columns */
24:
25:       cstart = atoi(argv[1]);
26:       cend = cstart + atoi(argv[2]) - 1;
27:       if (cstart < 1) cstart = 1;
28:       if (cend < cstart) cend = cstart;
29:
30:    /* -- Copy selected column from input lines to output */
31:
32:       while ((c = getchar()) != EOF) {
33:          cpos++;
34:          if (c == NEWLINE) {
35:             cout << NEWLINE;
36:             cpos = 0;
37:          } else if ((cstart <= cpos) && (cpos <= cend))
38:             putchar(c);
39:       }
40:    }
```

Because COLUMN requires two arguments, lines 16-21 test whether a r g c is less than 3. If so, the program displays a reminder about how to use it—a good idea in most programs that need specific numbers of arguments. Remember that argc is always at least 1 because the first argument string is the program's path name. To test whether there are at least n arguments available, argc should be greater or equal to n + 1.

After checking that there are at least two arguments available, COLUMN extracts each string and converts it into an integer value. It does this at lines 25-26 with the assignment statements:

```
cstart = atoi(argv[1]);
cend = cstart + atoi(argv[2]) - 1;
```

The expressions argv[1] and argv[2] retrieve the second and third command-line arguments. (The program's path name is in argv[0], the first argument.) This is another illustration of the way that argv can be treated as an array of character pointers. Indexing argv as an array is probably the easiest method when you simply need to access arguments in full, as in this program.

Each of the two argument strings is then passed to atoi (ASCII to integer). This converts the arguments to integer values that are used to calculate cstart and cend, representing the starting and ending columns to cut from the input. The while loop at lines 32-39 uses these values to write text from these columns; text in other columns is ignored.

Note: Lines 27-28 check the values of cstart and cend, altering them so that cstart is never less than 1 and that cend is greater or equal to cstart. This shows another way to deal with data entry errors. Instead of stopping the program with an error message, if someone enters the wrong values—for example, typing **column –5 –12**—the program simply adjusts the arguments to a reasonable range.

Questions and Exercises

4.1. Show the definitions for creating a pointer named pfloat to a variable of type float, a pointer named string to type char, and a pointer prec to a struct named customer.

4.2. What does a pointer variable contain?

4.3. Given a pointer named fp to type float, write an output-stream statement that displays the value addressed by fp.

4.4. What does the phrase *dereferencing a pointer* mean?

4.5. Suppose that a program defines a variable named b i g V a l u e of type d o u b l e. Using a pointer, define an alias named a l i a s P t r for b i g V a l u e. Write a statment that uses a l i a s P t r to display b i g V a l u e's value.

4.6. What is the main difference between NULL and void.

4.7. Suppose that a program defines a void pointer p that addresses an i n t value in memory. Write an output-stream statement that uses p to display that value.

4.8. A program defines a pointer counter to a variable of type d o u b l e. Write two statements that show the size of the pointer and the size of the data addressed by the pointer.

4.9. In most models of PCs, address 0x0040:0x006C contains a 4-byte integer that stores the current number of clock ticks since startup. (One clock tick equals about 0.055 seconds.) Write a program to display this value.

4.10. Write a program to allocate space for a string on the heap and then prompt for and store in that space characters entered at the keyboard. Display the results to prove that they are inserted into your string.

4.11. Write a program that creates an array of 100 floating point values on the heap. Include statements that fill the array with values and then display those values in a table.

4.12. Given the following s t r u c t, write a program to create space for a record variable on the heap, assign the address of that space to a pointer r p (record pointer), and use the pointer to assign test values to each of the struct's fields:

```
struct record {
    int count;
    double balance;
    char *title;
};
```

4.13. Using the s t r u c t from exercise 4.12, allocate fresh space on the heap for an 80-character string. Assign the address of this space to the title field in a record variable that's addressed by a pointer r p.

4.14. After assigning heap space to a variable of type r e c o r d in exercise 4.12, and assigning heap space to the title field in the s t r u c t, what statement or statements are required to delete these spaces from the heap?

4.15. What value does n e w return if that function can't fulfill a request to reserve heap space?

4.16. What is *fragmentation*?

4.17. Create a s t r u c t that keeps a string's length in a field along with a pointer to the string's characters. Write a function that assigns a string and length to a variable of your new data type. What advantage does your function offer over using common string functions and the s t r l e n function?

4.18. Show three equivalent statements using n e w, m a l l o c, and c a l l o c that reserve space for an array of 100 integer values on the heap. Show the statements required to delete the reserved space in each case.

4.19. Write a function that removes extra blanks from the end of a string. The function does not have to alter the physical size of the string. (Hint: Remember that a byte equal to 0 marks the end of a string of characters.)

4.20. Declare a pointer f p to a function that returns type d o u b l e and takes two parameters, one of type i n t and one of type f l o a t. Write a statement that calls the function. (If you want to complete the program, you can implement the function to multiply an i n t and f l o a t arguments and return the result.)

4.21. Write a program named m u l t that accepts two floating-point arguments from the DOS command line and displays the product of those values.

Chapter 5

Class Objectives

So far, you've learned most of C++'s fundamentals, you've studied many sample programs, and you may even have written a few of your own. If so, how did you begin? Like most programmers, you probably started with an idea, maybe scratched a few notes, and then started typing. Perhaps you copied one of the sample programs in the previous four chapters as a template for your new design. At the very least, you probably referred to some of the programming in this book for guidance.

Building on other programmers' code (or on your own past efforts) is a natural way to work. But suppose that you need to tackle a heftier project. How would you proceed? One way would be to apply the top-down design principles outlined in chapter 3. With this concept, or *paradigm,* you begin with the larger goals—for example, to play chess, to compute a spreadsheet, or to sort a database file—and work toward finishing the details—to move pieces, to evaluate expressions, and to compare records. Eventually, you write low-level code to carry out small, well-defined functions that perform easily understood tasks. In this way, the job of writing even the most complex software reduces to the relatively simple steps of creating small functions that even novice programmers should be able to handle. With luck, you'll be able to refashion existing functions from your personal library to fit the new code.

Unfortunately, as experienced programmers will tell you, this solid theory frequently develops serious flaws in practice. A strict top-down approach fails to recognize that software specifications often change after projects are well under way. During coding, programmers typically discover fundamental errors in the design, requiring retooling from the top and recoding of functions that were already tested. This wastes time and effort, and it increases the likelihood that new bugs will be introduced into code that was already in the can.

To "solve" these problems, software companies and programmers have traditionally started new projects by writing detailed specifications about what a program is supposed to accomplish. Today's software houses and consultants typically require customers to approve detailed specifications before any work begins. Worse, customers are often discouraged from changing their minds later, even when a change might be justified. ("Sorry, but you signed off on that spec weeks ago. We can't change the size of the database fields now. It's too late!")

Such rigidity is the death of software. As its name suggests, *software* needs to be malleable so that it can mold to fit changing needs. It's unreasonable to expect people to choose perfect goals from the outset of a complex project. Software should be able to grow, not strictly from the top down, but from the inside out to meet new demands without requiring a complete rewrite just to incorporate minor changes. Programmers should be able to reuse their well-tested functions and build on the foundations laid down by others.

Few people would disagree with that statement, but why then is such an obvious concept so poorly realized in so much existing code? Just think of the mountain of wasteful programming that probably exists on your computer's disk drive. It's a good bet that most of the programs in your collection have dozens of similar display functions, input routines, and expression parsers that the programmers rewrote from scratch only because the subroutines they composed for their previous programs didn't exactly fit the score for the new ones. Wouldn't it be great if there was an alternative—a way to build flexibility into software while making the code more reusable for future projects?

There is. Like top-down design, *object-oriented programming*, or OOP, is a paradigm that can help you to create programs that are easy to modify and that contain functions and other declarations that are simple to reuse. Among C++'s strong points are its many features that let programmers use object-oriented programming techniques. Unlike "pure" OOP languages, which require you to use OOP for everything a program does, C++ is a *hybrid* language that mixes OOP and non-OOP methods. With C++, you can use OOP where it does the most good, but you don't have to abandon what you've learned about conventional programming as described in the previous four chapters. You can mix and match as you please.

While introducing C++'s OOP capabilities in this chapter, I'll also explain some of the reasons that OOP is gaining in popularity among programmers. Understanding how and why others are turning to OOP is a good way to learn the fundamentals of this new wave in software design. By studying certain problems with conventional programming, and seeing how OOP solves those problems, you'll be able to put OOP into practice in your own work without having to wade through a lot of theory that, unfortunately, seems to flood many current OOP texts.

We'll begin with a general problem that OOP is particularly good at solving—making computers simulate actions in the real world, for example, the movement of shoppers passing through a mall or the flow of traffic in a busy city. As you'll see, OOP simplifies the job of writing programmed simulations by letting you focus on the properties of the system instead of making you fuss with time-consuming details about how a program ties its many pieces together. Instead of working towards the far-off goal of a finished program, to write the simulation in C++, you'll spend most of your efforts designing objects that model the system's elements—its buttons, switches, vehicles, people, or whatever items contribute to the events you are trying to simulate. In C++, these objects are called *classes*.

Go to the Head of the Class

A *class* is to OOP what a s t r u c t is to conventional C++ (and C). Classes combine, or *encapsulate,* functions and the data on which those functions operate. This is the heart of OOP—the binding of action and data into new data types that "know" what they are supposed to do. As Figure 5.1 illustrates, in conventional programming, data is passed to functions, which may pass modified (or new) data back. In OOP, a class encapsulates data and functions, making their relationship part of the program's structure.

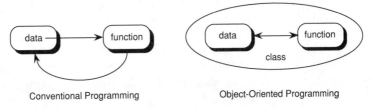

Conventional Programming   Object-Oriented Programming

Figure 5.1. In conventional programming, data is passed to and from functions; in object-oriented programming, classes encapsulate data and functions.

A simple example shows the value of C++ classes. Suppose that you've been assigned the job of writing a program to simulate the ups and downs of a bank of elevators in an office building. Your goal is to make it easy to test various schemes and to see how many people can be moved through the system in a given amount of time. Just for fun—and to prove to your boss that you are indeed working hard on the problem—you decide to include a visual display of the elevators in action.

At this stage in the program's development, only a few rough goals exist. You know that the code will simulate the movements of people and elevators. You know that it will have to update the display to show the simulation in progress. There are numerous other details to consider, but for now, that much will serve as a starting place. At least it's possible to sketch out the main program's design. Listing 5.1, SIMULATE.CPP, shows my first crack at the problem. Don't compile the program yet. I'll let you know when to do that.

Listing 5.1. SIMULATE.CPP

```
1:   // simulate.cpp -- Sample C++ simulation
2:
3:   #include <stream.hpp>
4:   #include "action.h"
5:
6:   action theAction;
```

```
 7:
 8:    main()
 9:    {
10:        theAction.display();
11:        while (theAction.continues()) {
12:            theAction.perform();
13:            theAction.display();
14:        }
15:        theAction.results();
16:    }
```

As the simulation develops, I'll list the files in the order I created them originally. This will give you a better sense about how to think in OOP's terms—a hurdle that most people have some difficulty with at first. Following the top-down philosophy, I started by writing the program's outer module and main function. Lines 3 and 4 include the usual STREAM.HPP header file plus another called ACTION.H, which doesn't exist yet. I'm assuming that ACTION.H will contain various declarations needed for the simulation.

One of those declarations will be a new data type named action (see line 6). An action will be a C++ class. It will contain everything there is to know about this simulation. The action class stores data associated with the events being simulated, and it performs various calculations and operations on that data. The action class is a black box, a magic module, a completely self-contained unit that, folks, requires absolutely no maintenance. In no cases will statements outside of the class be permitted access to action's data; the class itself will handle every detail needed to step through the simulation.

Four of those steps are perform, display, results, and continues. Lines 10-15 call these functions in a while loop to run the simulation, update the display, and so forth. I probably wouldn't have to explain all this. A glance at SIMULATE's source code should give you a rough idea of what the program is doing. But don't be concerned about how the program accomplishes these tasks. Just accept for now that the action class can hold (encapsulate) the fuel (data) and the engine (functions) that will power the simulation.

As you examine SIMULAT.CCP, you may notice that its statements differ in one significant way from those in conventional C++ programs. Instead of calling perform and other functions directly, the program uses statements such as theAction.perform() and theAction.continues(). Similar to the way expressions access data fields in structures, these statements use dot notation to call functions associated with theAction, which the program defines at line 6 as a variable of the action class. In fact, except for a few exceptions I'll get to later, referring to a variable of a class data type is the *only* way a program can call a class's functions.

> **Note:** If you have any experience with other OOP languages, you're probably familiar with the concept of *message passing*. In a "pure" OOP language, the statement `theAction.perform()` is said to pass a message named `perform()` to an object named `theAction`. The object receives the message and acts on it. With C++ and other hybrid OOP programming languages, the distinction between passing messages and calling functions is unimportant—they are only different models of the same machinery.

Creating Classes

That a variable like `theAction` can contain functions is one of the backbones of OOP. Because `theAction` specifies the functions that operate on itself, it's completely self contained. The *only* way to call `theAction`'s functions is to refer to them through that object.

Unless you're familiar with another OOP language, you may not appreciate the value of encapsulating data and variables this way. If so, a short program will show some of the benefits of the OOP way. Listing 5.2, BUTTON.CPP, creates a class named `button` that a program can "push."

Listing 5.2. BUTTON.CPP

```
 1:   // button.cpp -- Creating a class
 2:
 3:   #include <stream.hpp>
 4:
 5:   class button {
 6:      private:
 7:          int isUp;
 8:      public:
 9:          void push(int upDown);
10:          int state(void);
11:   };
12:
13:   main()
14:   {
15:      button myButton;
16:
17:      myButton.push(1);
18:      cout << "\nButton state = " << myButton.state();
19:      myButton.push(0);
```

```
20:          cout << "\nButton state = " << myButton.state();
21:     }
22:
23:    void button::push(int upDown)
24:    {
25:          isUp = upDown;
26:    }
27:
28:    int button::state(void)
29:    {
30:          return isUp;
31:    }
```

When you run BUTTON, it displays the state of a variable named myButton of type button (see line 15). In this demonstration, a button is considered to be "pushed" if its state equals 1. It is not "pushed" if its state is 0.

The button class at lines 5-11 describes everything needed to simulate a button. Notice how the declaration resembles a struct. First comes the class key word, followed by the class name (button). A pair of parentheses delimit the items inside the class, which are divided into two sections marked private: and public:

```
class button {
   private:
       int isUp;
   public:
       void push(int upDown);
       int state(void);
};
```

Items, or *members,* in a class's private section are strictly to be used by the class's functions. Except from inside those functions, no statement may refer to a class's private members. Only items declared in the class's public section are visible from outside of the class. Any statement anywhere in a program may refer to a class's public members. Statements outside the class may *never* refer to the class's private declarations. (See Figure 5.2.)

If you don't specify either the private: or public: key words, all members of a class default to private status. Usually, data fields are placed in a class's private section, and member functions are stored publicly; therefore, most classes will have a public: section or there would be no way for a program to access any of the class's members. But that's only a guideline, not a rule. Fields and functions may be declared either privately or publicly. There's also a third section header called protected:, which I'll describe in chapter 7.

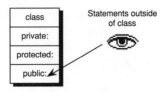

Figure 5.2. Statements outside a class can "see" only the class's public members. Private members are strictly for the class's own use. (Protected members are described later in this book.)

In the sample button class, there is one private data member, an int field named isUp. There are also two public member functions, push and state. These functions carry out whatever the class is supposed to do—in this case, push a button and return a button's current state. The member functions are just prototypes, similar in form to the prototype functions you've seen in earlier listings. The prototypes describe the functional details of these class members.

As with all prototype functions, you must implement class member functions somewhere in the program. BUTTON does this at lines 23-31. For example, the completed push function is

```
void button::push(int upDown)
{
    isUp = upDown;
}
```

This resembles a typical function definition but includes the name of the class plus a double-colon symbol (::) in front of the function name. Adding button:: to the function name this way uniquely identifies the function to the compiler as a member of the class and not just an ordinary function named push. Because of this notation, other classes may declare functions named push, and the program may include a common C++ push function that is not a member of a class. Because the implementations of those functions will all begin with unique declarations, such as button::push, anotherclass::push, or simply push, there's no possibility of a conflict between these identically named functions.

Note: Consider how important it is to be able to invent new classes and never have to worry about using names that conflict with others in a large program. This is a real boon to software development, especially in projects maintained by several people. You are free to use any names you want for class member functions. It is simply *not possible* to create a conflict with another function of the same name that may exist elsewhere.

Except for the class name and double-colon symbol, the push member function looks the same as a common function. In fact, it is the same! The implementations of class member functions and classic C++ functions are identical except for their declaration lines. Anything a common function can do, a member function can do as well.

There are a few differences in the way a class member function can access other class members, however. For example, in push, there's a single statement that assigns the value of parameter upDown to the private data field isUp. Because push belongs to the same class as isUp, it can refer to that data field directly. Other fields outside of the class can't do that.

The second member function in button returns the current value of isUp. Again, the function implementation is similar to a common C++ function, but it includes the class name and a double-colon symbol in the declaration line:

```
int button::state(void)
{
    return isUp;
}
```

Classes typically need functions to return the values of private data fields. Because isUp is private to the class, only member functions in the class can "see" this variable. Statements outside of the class must call functions like state to obtain a private data member's value. This rule, which may seem arbitrarily restrictive to you now, lets you change the way a class stores its data without having to modify any code outside of the class. In a large program, this can greatly simplify modifications by limiting the amount of required work to a small section of the code.

Now have a look at BUTTON's main function. After defining a variable myButton of type button, the program executes these four statements:

```
myButton.push(1);
cout << "\nButton state = " << myButton.state();
myButton.push(0);
cout << "\nButton state = " << myButton.state();
```

First, myButton.push(1) calls the push member function, which sets the private isUp field to 1. The second line then displays the current state of the button by calling myButton.state(). The next two lines are similar, but pass 0 to the push function, resetting the button's state.

Programming this same example in a conventional way reveals some of the benefits of the OOP method, which small examples like BUTTON tend to obscure. OOP shines in large projects, and it's difficult to demonstrate OOP's value in small samples that could easily be written using non-OOP techniques. Instead of creating a button class, a programmer might solve this problem without OOP by

- Creating a button data type

- Writing functions that accept button parameters

After creating a structure or another data type, perhaps named buttonType, you might then write a function named push(buttonType &b) to operate on a variable of the new type. This will work, of course, but can also lead to bugs if you accidentally pass the wrong data type to the function (a situation that modern C and C++ compilers are better at catching than in the past) or if you pass an uninitialized pointer to the function, causing it to "push" heaven knows what value in memory.

The OOP approach neatly avoids these and other problems associated with passing data to functions. With OOP, data and function are one, which more closely mirrors the way the world works. To push a real button, you don't unscrew it, pass it to a button-pushing machine, and then plug it back into its socket. You just press it, and the button, which can be pushed, responds to the pressure of your finger.

This is what OOP does—lets you create data types that have associated properties: buttons that can be pushed, wheels that can turn, and elevators that can travel up and down. Because of this encapsulation of data and code, programs are easier to maintain, and bugs are easier to find. If something goes wrong with a button object, you need to examine only the data and functions associated with a single class. You don't have to hunt around looking for errant statements that affect your data. *No statements outside a class can access that class's private data.*

Inline Member Functions

After examining one or two OOP programs, you may object to calling functions for simple jobs like assigning values to integer variables. For example, to push a button, you have to write

```
myButton.push(1);
```

Obviously, a simple assignment such as int aButton = 1 would be more efficient. Calling functions requires the program to push values and a return address onto the stack, transfer control to the function's compiled code, and then clean up the stack when the function returns. Multiplied by thousands of functions in even a medium-size program, this amount of overhead can quickly add up to gross inefficiencies.

The solution is to use *inline member functions* where speed matters. Although inline member functions resemble the normal variety in their declarations and use, the compiled result is often as good as what you can achieve by "unrolling" your functions manually. In other words, although you write a statement like myButton.push(1), the compiler generates inline code that directly assigns the value 1 to the data field in a button. With inline functions, there's no function call and therefore no overhead.

Performing this neat trick is simple—just include the function's inline statements in the class declaration. Listing 5.3, BUTTON2.CPP, shows how. It's the same program as BUTTON.CPP but defines all of a button's member functions in line.

Listing 5.3. BUTTON2.CPP

```
1:   // button2.cpp -- Inline member functions
2:
3:   #include <stream.hpp>
4:
5:   class button {
6:      private:
7:         int isUp;
8:      public:
9:         void push(int upDown) { isUp = upDown; }
10:        int state(void) { return isUp; }
11:   };
12:
13:   main()
14:   {
15:      button myButton;
16:
17:      myButton.push(1);
18:      cout << "\nButton state = " << myButton.state();
19:      myButton.push(0);
20:      cout << "\nButton state = " << myButton.state();
21:   }
```

The main function is identical in BUTTON and BUTTON2, proving an important point about inline member functions: Only their definitions are special. When used, inline functions appear and operate identically to normal member functions.

Lines 9 and 10 show how to define inline functions. Unlike the earlier example, this time there are no function implementations in the listing—the inline functions are complete. Until you get used to the format, however, inline functions may appear a little odd:

```
void push(int upDown) { isUp = upDown; }
```

Two rules to remember: There is no semicolon after the function declaration nor is there one after the closing brace. If you view this the way most functions are usually written, you'll see that the single-line style is no different from a usual multiline function implementation:

```
void push(int upDown)
{
    isUp = upDown;
}
```

Compare that character for character with the inline definition. The functions differ only in style; their contents are identical. In fact, you could write inline functions this way, though the one-line style is more common.

Don't forget to end the statement inside braces with a semicolon, as you must end all statements in C++. Again, this is identical to normal function forms—but the single-line style typically used for inline member functions may make the semicolon's position seem out of place.

There's no need to limit member functions to one statement. You can include multiple statements inside the braces. For example, a better push function might force upDown to be 1 or 0:

```
void push(int upDown)
   { if (upDown == 0) isUp = 0; else isUp = 1; }
```

Notice where the semicolons go—at the end of the two statements, not after the end of the definition's closing brace. The common one-line style makes this hard to see, and you can write the statements on separate lines if you want:

```
void push(int upDown)
{
    if (upDown == 0)
       isUp = 0;
    else
       isUp = 1;
}
```

When C++ compiles a program that uses inline member functions, it inserts code to perform that function's actions for a specified class variable. In place of myButton.push(1) the compiler inserts the statements defined inside the inline definition's braces. This eliminates all the usual overhead associated with function calls while letting you keep the program's text looking sharp.

But don't define every member function in line. There are several reasons why that would be a mistake. In general, inline member functions

- Increase the compiled code size. If you overuse inline functions, your program will take more room in memory.

- Are easily modified by programmers who have access to your class declarations but not to the implementations of your other function prototypes and classes.

- Are limited by the compiler to a small size. Although this limit is not exactly defined, if the compiler decides an inline function is too large, it will convert the code to a normal member function implementation.

- Cause the compiler to run out of memory sooner because it has to store all inline statements for inserting into the program.

- May not be supported by all C++ compilers or may be supported in different ways. Never write code that relies on member functions being defined in line.

- Complicate debugging. If you are using a debugger, it may not be possible to trace calls to inline member functions.

The second of these is easy to deal with. Instead of coding inline member functions inside the class declaration, you can change the function implementations in BUTTON.CPP (Listing 5.2) to these:

```
inline void button::push(int upDown)
{
    isUp = upDown;
}

inline int button::state(void)
{
    return isUp;
}
```

Adding the key word `inline` in front of the function declarations has the same effect as defining the inline member functions directly in the class. But there is one drawback to this approach: In addition to the `inline` keyword, you must insert the function implementations before they are used in a module. In BUTTON.CPP, this means you would also have to move the functions to above `main`, or the compiler will treat them as common functions, and it will not insert the inline statements directly into the compiled code.

For debugging, or if inline functions cause the compiler to run out of memory, use the `-C` option (it must be a capital C) to turn off inline expansion:

```
ztc -C mycode
```

Executed this way, the compiler will convert all inline functions to normal ones, and it will not expand inline calls to functions.

Note: Classes with inline member functions may be declared in header files. Even if two or more modules in a large program include the same header, the redefinition of the inline members does not cause a conflict.

Classes Are Data Types

Now that you've seen a few examples of C++ classes, let's get back to the elevator simulation. Listing 5.1, SIMULATE.CPP, used a class named `action`, and it called the class's member functions associated with a variable `theAction`.

This is a key concept. A class is a data type, and like other data types, it can be used to define variables in memory. This is no different from the way other data types are used. For example, an `int` is a data type, but you can't use `int`s to store values. To do that, you first have to define `int` *variables*. Then, you can store values in those variables:

```
int myValue;    // Define variable myValue of type int
myValue = 123;  // Store value 123 in myValue
```

Classes behave in exactly the same way; they are data types just like others built into the language. To use a class's members, you first have to create a variable of the class. Then you can call its functions:

```
action theAction;   // Define variable theAction of type action
action.display();   // Call display member function in theAction
```

Before using any members of a class, you must create a variable of that class. Then you can call the class's public functions and use other public declarations belonging to that variable.

> **Note:** Although it seems as though class variables *contain* their member functions, the actual code for those functions is *not* stored inside the class variable. If you define six variables of class `action`, there is only one copy of `display` and other class member functions in memory. However, distinct space for data fields in a class is set aside for each class variable. This mirrors the way other data types work. For example, you can create multiple `int` variables, but there's only one "plus" routine somewhere that can add two integers. In this sense, the plus operator behaves as though it were a member function named + in a class named `int`. You certainly wouldn't expect the compiler to create a new "plus" subroutine for each integer variable in a program!

Classes give you the means to create new data types that add to those supplied with C++ such as `int` and `float`. But unlike C++'s built-in types, the nature of a new class is completely up to you.

As BUTTON and BUTTON2 demonstrated, creating a new class is similar to creating a `struct` that you can then use to define variables. Listing 5.4, ACTION.H, shows the declaration for the `action` class that Listing 5.1 uses and that other modules in this chapter will use in the final elevator simulation. Don't try to compile the program yet. There are a few more details to cover first.

Listing 5.4. ACTION.H

```
1:  // action.h -- Action header file
2:
3:  #ifndef __ACTION_H
4:  #define __ACTION_H        1      // Prevent multiple #includes
```

```
 5:
 6:    class action {
 7:       private:
 8:          long timeAtStart;        // Seconds for simulation
 9:          long timeRemaining;      // Seconds remaining to end
10:       public:
11:          action();               // The "constructor"
12:          int continues(void);
13:          void setTime(int secs);
14:          int getTime(void);
15:          void reduceTime(int secs);
16:          void perform(void);
17:          void display(void);
18:          void results(void);
19:    };
20:
21:    #endif   // __ACTION_H
```

ACTION.H shows a typical class declaration in C++. It also demonstrates how to organize a large program into headers and modules. In my programs, I prefer to use many small files, each with a distinct purpose. Rarely do my source code files contain more than a few hundred lines.

Because many other .H and .CPP files may include ACTION.H in order to use the action class, it's possible that ACTION.H will be included more than once during compilation. This is never allowed and produces an error when the class action identifier is redeclared. To avoid this tricky situation, which is very common in large programs, ACTION.H begins with two *conditional directives:*

```
#ifndef __ACTION_H
#define __ACTION_H      1
```

The #ifndef directive evaluates the following argument (here __ACTION_H) as true (1) if that identifier was *not* previously defined in a #define directive. A similar directive #ifdef (not shown) evaluates as true if an identifier *was* previously defined. Each of these directives must be followed at some point by #endif (see line 21). The #define directive is the same as the one you've used to create constants in other program. But in this case, it's used for a different purpose—to define a symbol named __ACTION_H.

Both #ifndef and #ifdef cause the compiler to compile whatever follows on subsequent lines only if the directives are true. As a result, the sequence

```
#ifndef __ACTION_H
#define __ACTION_H      1
...
#endif
```

tells the compiler to skip everything between #ifndef and #endif if __ACTION_H was previously defined. But if that symbol was not yet defined, the #ifndef directive will be true, and the compiler will compile every line between #ifndef and #endif. The first time this occurs, #define defines the __ACTION_H symbol; therefore, the *next* time this same file is read, that symbol will be defined and the compiler will skip every significant line in the file! This means that, if ACTION.H is included a dozen times, the action class declaration is compiled only the first time, neatly avoiding the redeclaration conflict that would otherwise occur.

Other files can also test whether __ACTION_H is already defined and if so, avoid including that file:

```
#ifndef __ACTION_H
#include "action.h"
#endif
```

For better clarity, the listings in this chapter do not use this trick, but in a monstrous program, it may shave a few seconds from long compilations.

Note: The notation used for symbols like __ACTION_H is just a convention. You can name any identifier for this purpose as long as it's unique. But the two underscores plus the file name with its usual period replaced by a third underscore pretty much ensures that the same symbol will not be defined elsewhere.

Introducing Constructors

As in the button class, action declares a private section, this time containing two long integer fields, timeAtStart and timeRemaining. Because these fields are private to the class, only the class member functions may use them. There are eight such functions in action, none of which is defined inline (see lines 11-18). The first of these needs some explaining:

```
action();
```

As you can see from this function prototype, it has the same name as the action class. All such functions are called *constructors* and have the sole purpose of initializing variables of the class type. Unlike other function prototypes, constructors do not specify a void return type. In fact, they may *never* return values. They may specify a void parameter list (action(void);), although the form action() without void is more widely used and serves the same purpose. (It's possible for constructors to accept arguments, but in this example, action() requires none.) These small differences in form make it easy to pick out the constructors in a class declaration.

> **Note:** A constructor's counterpart is called a destructor, which is covered in chapter 7.

Most programmers insert constructor prototypes immediately after the `public:` header in a class declaration. This is not a requirement, and the constructor may go anywhere in the public section.

A class constructor runs automatically when you define storage for a class variable. This mean that, when SIMULATE (Listing 5.1) defines `theAction` with the line

```
action theAction;
```

the program automatically calls the class constructor function `action()` to initialize `theAction`. This is completely optional. If you don't include a constructor in a class, no code runs automatically when a variable of the class comes into existence. But because it's so handy to be able to rely on this automatic initialization feature, most classes should have constructors.

> **Note:** The implementation for a constructor function is no different from any other member function. The only difference between a constructor and another member function is that the constructor runs automatically when storage is defined for a class variable.

I'll explain more about constructors later. For the moment, just remember that a constructor

- Has the same name as the class

- May not declare a return data type

- May declare a parameter list

- Runs automatically when space for a class variable is defined

> **Note:** Because `theAction` is a global variable, the program defines its space before `main` starts to run. This means that the constructor in the `action` class runs before `main`'s first statement. At that time, the constructor initializes `theAction` variable, preparing that variable for use. If `theAction` was defined local to another function, the constructor would run when that function was called. If `theAction` is created on the heap, the constructor would run when that space was reserved. In all cases, constructors run automatically when space for the class variable is defined.

You should have no trouble understanding the prototypes for the other member functions in the action class (see lines 12-18). Function continues returns true as long as the class "wants" the simulation to continue. That will be so as long as timeRemaining is greater than zero. Functions setTime and getTime set and return the simulation time, but reduceTime reduces the amount of time remaining. Function perform activates the simulation, and display shows what's happening. The last function, results, displays a final report after the simulation is finished.

Take a moment to study ACTION.H in Listing 5.4, and before continuing, be sure that you understand what each line does. You don't need to know how the action class performs its duties—just be comfortable with the format of the class's declaration. This is another benefit that OOP brings to programming. To learn how to use a new class, you need only study its declaration (assuming, that is, there's some documentation to go along with the source code as there is in this book). Rarely will you have to pick through the implementation of a class to understand how to use it. A well-designed class fully describes what it can do. Though you can't tell much about a book from its cover, the same isn't true of a C++ class. You *can* tell most of what you need to know about a class simply by reading its declaration.

Also examine how SIMULATE.CPP in Listing 5.1 calls the class functions through variable theAction to run the simulation. The next step is to fill in those class member functions so that you can compile and run the SIMULATE test program and begin writing the elevator modules.

Class Tactics

Even without looking at more than a few simple programs and class declarations, you've already met many of the class tactics that you'll employ in other C++ programs. So far, the elevator simulation has a main module SIMULATE.CPP that uses a class named action declared in ACTION.H. Before SIMULATE is ready to be compiled and run, however, the program needs a few essential ingredients—the implementations for the functions that carry out the action class's duties. Creating a new class like action is like drawing the plans for a cabinet. After getting the design just as you want it, you've got to do some sawing and hammering before you can place books on the shelves.

Listing 5.5, ACTION.CPP, bangs out the function definitions for the action class members declared in ACTION.H. You can now compile the full program by entering the command **ztc simulate action**. This compiles and links SIMULATE.CPP and ACTION.CPP into the final program file, SIMULATE.EXE. When you run the program, press **<Spacebar>** to activate each pass through the simulation. At this early stage, the simulation merely counts the number of times through the main loop. The program displays this value plus the time at start and the time remaining. This doesn't look much like an elevator simulation, does it? But don't be concerned: You need to excavate more of OOP and C++'s grounds before you'll be ready to add elevator shafts to the program.

Listing 5.5. ACTION.CPP

```
 1:   // action.cpp -- Action class module
 2:
 3:   #include <stream.hpp>
 4:   #include <conio.h>
 5:   #include "action.h"
 6:
 7:   /* -- The action's "constructor." Runs when an action object (in
 8:   other words, a variable of type action) comes into being. */
 9:
10:   action::action()
11:   {
12:      timeAtStart = 3600;            // Seconds to run simulation
13:      timeRemaining = timeAtStart;  // Time remaining to end
14:   }
15:
16:   /* -- Return TRUE if time remaining is greater than 0. The
17:   program's main loop continues the action until this function
18:   returns FALSE. */
19:
20:   int action::continues(void)
21:   {
22:      return timeRemaining > 0;
23:   }
24:
25:   /* -- Set time counters to this many seconds. */
26:
27:   void action::setTime(int secs)
28:   {
29:      timeAtStart = secs;
30:      timeRemaining = timeAtStart;
31:   }
32:
33:   /* -- Return time remaining for simulation. */
34:
35:   int action::getTime(void)
36:   {
37:      return timeRemaining;
38:   }
39:
40:   /* -- Reduce time remaining for simulation. Minimum resolution,
41:   or "granularity," is one second. Can't reduce time to < 0. */
42:
43:   void action::reduceTime(int secs)
```

```
44:    {
45:        if (secs > timeRemaining)
46:            timeRemaining = 0;
47:        else
48:            timeRemaining -= secs;
49:    }
50:
51:    /* -- Perform the action. In this case, the function is just a shell.
52:    Later, we'll add programming to simulate a real action. */
53:
54:    void action::perform(void)
55:    {
56:        cout << "\n\nAction! (Press <Spacebar> to continue...";
57:        while (getch() != ' ') ;     // Pause for <Spacebar> keypress
58:        reduceTime(900);             // Decrease time remaining 900 secs
59:    }
60:
61:    /* -- Display the current action status. Calling display() is the
62:    only way a statement outside of the action object can access the
63:    timeRemaining value. */
64:
65:    void action::display(void)
66:    {
67:        cout << "\n\nTime remaining: " << timeRemaining << " sec.";
68:    }
69:
70:    /* -- Display final results. As in action::display(), calling
71:    results() is the only way a statement outside of the action object
72:    can access the private data fields in the action class. */
73:
74:    void action::results(void)
75:    {
76:     cout << "\n\nSimulation results";
77:     cout << "\n==================";
78:     cout << "\nTime at start .. : " << timeAtStart << " sec.";
79:     cout << "\nTime at end .... : " << timeRemaining << " sec.\n";
80:    }
```

ACTION.CPP contains full function definitions for each of the member functions declared in ACTION.H. One reason for storing these items separately is to let many other files such as SIMULATE.CPP include the ACTION.H header file. That way, the main program (or another module) can use the elements in ACTION without forcing you to compile the entire program over and over for each change you make. Instead, you can compile each .CPP module individually. In a program with dozens or more such modules, this can save a lot of time that would otherwise be wasted by needlessly recompiling source code that didn't change.

The division of classes into header and module files also lets software companies distribute compiled class libraries along with the associated headers. For example, if I were to distribute ACTION as a developer's tool, I could compile ACTION.CPP to create ACTION.OBJ. Then I could sell that *object-code* file plus ACTION.H. You could include the header file in your own programs and link your code to my object code. But you would not be able to modify or learn my trade secrets. You may accuse a company that takes this approach of being overly protective of their sources, but later, you'll learn that OOP lets you build on commercial class libraries even if they don't come with full source code—often impossible to do with common subroutine libraries.

> **Note:** All source code is included with this book for *all* functions, modules, headers, classes, and other listings. Just wanted to make that clear.

The first function in ACTION is the `action` constructor (lines 10-14). As I explained earlier, the constructor runs automatically when a variable of type `action` comes into being.

```
action::action()
{
    timeAtStart = 3600;           // Seconds to run simulation
    timeRemaining = timeAtStart;  // Time remaining to end
}
```

On a first meeting, the form of a constructor's implementation may seem confusing. But you are not seeing double. Remember, all member function implementations are uniquely identified by the class name plus a double-colon *scope-resolution* operator (`action::`) in front of the member function name and parameter list (`action()`). (In this case, the parameter list is empty.) Although the double whammy looks redundant, `action::action()` simply tells the compiler that this constructor belongs to the `action` class. This format allows you to declare other nonOOP functions named `action` without causing a conflict.

The two statements inside the `action` constructor assign 3600 to the `timeAtStart` and `timeRemaining` private fields in the class. This means that all variables of type `action` will be initialized for a simulation lasting 3600 seconds, or 1 hour, without the program having to "lift a finger." (The "seconds" are not necessarily in real time, however.)

But what if somebody later wants to change the simulation startup time to another value? Shouldn't you spend time now allowing for this possibility? That's always a difficult question, but in general with OOP, the answer can be "no" without causing problems down the road. As you'll see, it's not difficult to alter the fundamental nature of a class to accommodate situations like changing the startup time. OOP allows you to forge ahead and get the program working rather than waste time dealing with countless details about initializations, interfaces, and other items that may very well change tomorrow anyway.

This doesn't mean you don't have to do *some* planning, but it does mean that you won't be locked into a corner next week just because of the decisions you make today. In this example, you may as well let the a c t i o n class initialize itself to 3600 seconds. You can always change this minor detail later without affecting any other parts of the program.

Note: This is another benefit of encapsulating code and data. Because the two time fields are private to the a c t i o n class, you can be certain that no other statements outside the class depend on those values or change them directly. All references to the class's private data are in the class itself. If you need to modify the class, you can do so without causing a conflict with another module.

The other function implementations in ACTION.CPP have obvious purposes and use simple statements. Read the comments in the program to understand what each function does. Notice how the function declarations include the a c t i o n : : symbol that uniquely identifies each function as a member of the a c t i o n class. Except for those declaration lines, the function forms and statements are no different from others you've seen. They use common C++ features, send text to output streams, get characters from the keyboard, and so on. As this demonstrates, anything you can do in normal C++ functions you can do in class member functions. It's the declaration of classes as new data types and the use of variables of those types that separate C++ OOP from conventional C and C++ programming. You are free to use any and all OOP and non-OOP techniques *inside* class functions to specify the actions those functions are to perform.

Modules and Classes

Except for simple examples, I usually write programs using many individual files. This helps me to organize the program's pieces, and it makes it easier for me to keep track of changes that I make. Instead of reprinting long listings for every minor change, I need only print the modules that I modify in order to keep an up-to-date listing for an entire program. I can also compile modules separately instead of wasting time recompiling a single monster file that contains every function in a large project.

Before continuing to develop this chapter's elevator simulation, this is a good time to pause for some technical details about organizing large programs. Especially when using C++ classes, you'll find that spreading your program over many modules, each with a specific purpose, will pay big dividends when it comes time to modify the code.

Listings 5.1, 5.2, and 5.3 show one way to do this by dividing a program into separate text files. As you can see, ACTION.CPP is not a full program. It's only a module—a unit that contains the implementations for class member functions declared in the ACTION.H header file. Because ACTION.CPP lacks a `main` function, you can't compile this file into a finished program. Instead, you have to compile and link this and other modules to a main program module like SIMULATE.CPP to create the final product.

You can insert whatever functions you want into a module, and you can declare classes and define their implementations in the same file. But it's usually best to insert only one or two (or maybe three) classes in each header file. Then insert the implementations for the class member functions into a corresponding .CPP file with the same name as I did with ACTION.CPP, which contains the implementation details described in ACTION.H. You can then compile the separate module with a command such as

```
ztc -c action
```

The `-c` option tells the compiler to "compile only," and not to link the result into an executable .EXE code file. After compiling all your separate modules using similar commands, you can then compile and link the final program by typing

```
ztc simulate action.obj
```

This compiles SIMULATE.CPP and links the result to ACTION.OBJ—the *object-code* file that the previous instruction created. The result is SIMULATE.EXE with all the necessary elements linked. If you have more than one module, just specify them on the same line. For example, to compile and link a main program stored in MAIN.CPP to three submodules compiled separately with the `-c` option, enter

```
ztc main sub1.obj sub2.obj sub3.obj
```

As your programs grow more complex, long compilation commands like that one will take too much time to enter. A better plan is to store the command text in a DOS batch file, perhaps named ZZ.BAT. (I use ZZ because it vaguely resembles the Unix CC command that typically runs a C++ compiler. You can name the batch file anything you like.) In the batch file, you'll insert commands to compile individual modules, for example, `ztc -c sub1` and `ztc -c sub3`. You can then enter **zz** to compile the main program and link it to its various object-code files.

This approach works well for medium-sized programs, but when linking many object-code files, you may bump into DOS's 128-character command-line limit. In that case, you'll need to create a *linker response file.* This is a plain-text file that contains the commands needed to link multiple object-code files. There's no limit to the number of such commands you can specify.

A linker response file also lets you enter linker commands on separate lines. The linker on your compiler disk or directory is named BLINK.EXE, and it requires a command line in the form

```
blink objfiles, exefile, mapfile, libfiles [switches];
```

The `objfiles` (object files) must be separated by plus signs as in `main.obj+sub1.obj+sub2.obj+sub3.obj`. The first object-code file should contain a `main` function. BLINK creates an .EXE file of that object-code file's name unless you supply a different file as the second argument (`exefile`). For example, to name the output NEWNAME.EXE rather than the default MAIN.EXE, assuming file MAIN contains a `main()` function, enter

```
blink main.obj+sub1.obj+sub2.obj+sub3.obj,newname.exe/noi
```

The option `/noi` selects case sensitive linking. The `mapfile` and `libfiles` arguments are optional. Supply these file names if you want to create a .MAP file listing a program's public symbols and entry-point address, and if you need to link the code to various libraries of object-code modules. (You don't need to specify any library files to use the compiler and listings in this book.)

Instead of typing all of that at the DOS command line, you can enter the commands into a linker response file. For example, to link MAIN.EXE, create a file named MAIN.LNK with the lines

```
main.obj+sub1.obj+sub2.obj+
sub3.obj
main.exe
main.map
/noi
```

The first one or more lines may specify any number of object-code file names, either separated by plus signs or listed individually. Make sure all object code files, even if they're on separate lines, have a plus sign between them. For example, the plus sign at the end of the first sample line here connects to SUB3.OBJ on the second line. After the last object-code file, you can list an optional output file name (MAIN.EXE here) and a map file (MAIN.MAP), or you can leave these lines blank. Specify any linker options such as `/noi` at the end.

To use the linker response file, first compile the separate modules with the `-c` option to create .OBJ files. Then enter **blink @main.lnk** to pass the commands in MAIN.LNK to the linker. For example, to compile and link the fictitious MAIN program using the MAIN.LNK linker response file, you would enter these commands:

```
ztc -c main
ztc -c sub1
ztc -c sub2
ztc -c sub3
blink @main.lnk
```

Along with some of the listings in this book, I'll include batch and linker response files that you can use to compile and link programs. You can also use these files as templates for your own multifile projects.

> **Note:** Most professional development systems come with a program called MAKE that can help automate compiling and linking large programs. The listings in this book do not require using MAKE, which can selectively compile only the minimum number of files needed to keep an entire program up to date. However, there are public domain and commercial versions of MAKE available, and if you have one, you can certainly use it along with the compiler and linker supplied with this book.

Compiling The Elevator Simulation

The listings in the rest of this chapter complete the elevator simulation. Many of the elements in the coming listings will find their way into your own work, and examining a program of a non-trivial size will demonstrate many of the benefits of using C++ OOP techniques. As I mentioned earlier, I'll list the files in the order that I created them, though, of course, I didn't just sit down and write each file from start to finish. Like most programs, ELEVSIM grew in stages, and I made many changes to the files along the way.

Before I explain the first of the simulation's modules, it will be helpful for you to compile the program and run it. To do this, you'll need to have in the current directory the files listed in Table 5.1.

Table 5.1. Elevator Simulation Files

File name	Description
ACTION.CPP	Action class module
ACTION.H	Header file for ACTION.CPP
BUILDING.CPP	Building class module
BUILDING.H	Header file for BUILDING.CPP
ELEVATOR.CPP	Elevator class module
ELEVATOR.H	Header file for ELEVATOR.CPP
ELEVSIM.CPP	Main elevator simulation program
ELEVSIM.H	General simulation header file
ELEVSIM.LNK	Linker response file
FLOOR.CPP	Floor class module
FLOOR.H	Header file for FLOOR.CPP
PERSON.CPP	Person class module
PERSON.H	Header file for PERSON.CPP
ZZ.BAT	Batch file to compile simulation

Next, to compile and link the program, type **zz** at the DOS prompt. This runs the ZZ.BAT file (Listing 5.6), which contains all the commands needed to compile the modules and link them into the final executable file, ELEVSIM.EXE. Notice how ZZ.BAT checks the DOS `errorlevel` variable after compiling each module. This halts the batch file if any errors are detected, so the error messages won't scroll away before you can read them.

Listing 5.6. ZZ.BAT (compiles elevator simulation)

```
 1:   echo off
 2:   ztc -c action
 3:   if errorlevel==1 goto END
 4:   ztc -c person
 5:   if errorlevel==1 goto END
 6:   ztc -c floor
 7:   if errorlevel==1 goto END
 8:   ztc -c elevator
 9:   if errorlevel==1 goto END
10:   ztc -c building
11:   if errorlevel==1 goto END
12:   ztc -c elevsim
13:   if errorlevel==1 goto END
14:   echo on
15:   blink @elevsim.lnk
16:   :END
```

If no errors are detected, ZZ.BAT calls BLINK (line 15), which reads the commands in the linker response file ELEVSIM.LNK (Listing 5.7). These commands tell the linker which object-code files to join in order to create the final ELEVSIM.EXE file. The final command in this file (`/noi`) selects case sensitive linking so that two identifiers such as `myClass` and `MyClass` are considered different. Always include this option. C++ (and C) programs may depend on case to distinguish between symbols that are otherwise spelled the same.

Listing 5.7. ELEVSIM.LNK (linker response file)

```
1:   elevsim.obj+
2:   action.obj+
3:   building.obj+
4:   elevator.obj+
5:   floor.obj+
6:   person.obj
7:   /noi
```

After compiling, run ELEVSIM to start the simulation. Your display will appear as illustrated in Figure 5.3. Along the left of the screen are the floor numbers 0 through 9, followed by indicators that tell whether the up (U) or down (D) buttons are pressed on these floors. The numbers to the right of those characters represent the number of people waiting for elevators.

The elevators are represented by small reverse-video boxes dangling from elevator cables—shown on screen by vertical columns of colons. Each elevator shows its direction: Up, Dn, or none (--). At the top of the elevator's cable is the current floor number—what people normally see while waiting for a lift in front of closed elevator doors.

Along the bottom of the display are several statistics that the program constantly updates as it runs. The first value shows the total number of people who have passed through the system. The next value represents the number of people now in the building. Until people begin to leave (the third statistic), this will be the same as the total number of people passing through the simulation. The fourth and fifth values show the running average number of people currently waiting for and riding in elevators. One of the goals of the simulation is to keep the number of riders high compared to the number waiting.

Sometimes, people will get tired of waiting for elevators and will decide to take the stairs (the fifth value at the bottom of the display). As a rule, these people will also live longer due to the increased activity of their heart muscles. (Just kidding.)

The other statistics show the number of elevators, the number of floors, the number of seconds remaining in this simulation run, and the total elapsed time in hours, minutes, and seconds. You can easily change the number of elevators, the number of floors, and the decision logic to change the character of the simulation. As I explain the files, I'll suggest many such changes you may want to make.

Using Header Files

Most large programs need one main header file to describe various global facts about a program. Also, it may be necessary to declare a few global variables for other modules to share. In general, it's not a good idea to use too many global variables. Local variables and dynamic structures on the heap tend to use memory more efficiently. Because any statement can modify a global variable's value, they also make debugging difficult. If something goes wrong with a global value, there's no telling where to begin searching for the fault.

But that doesn't mean you should *never* use globals. For example, the statistics displayed at the bottom of the elevator simulation may as well be global. The modules in the program need to update these values, and passing them around as function parameters is probably more trouble than it's worth.

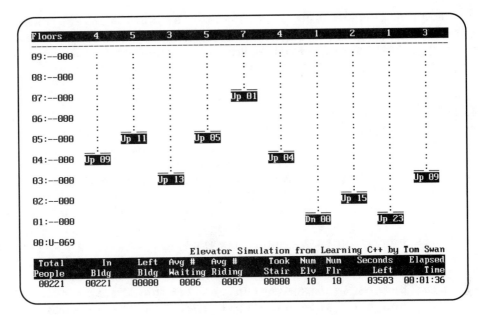

Figure 5.3. The elevator simulation's display.

Other global items in the simulation include several #defines, which set various parameters—for example, how long it takes for an elevator to travel between floors, how long an elevator waits at a floor before closing its doors, how many people can fit into an elevator at one time, and so on. Listing 5.8. ELEVSIM.H, stores all these items and more in one handy package.

Listing 5.8. ELEVSIM.H

```
1:  // elevsim.h -- General header file for elevator simulation
2:
3:  #ifndef __ELEVSIM_H
4:  #define __ELEVSIM_H        1        // Prevent multiple #includes
5:
6:  /* -- Various constants. Don't change these. */
7:
8:  #define FALSE 0          // Value meaning false
9:  #define TRUE 1           // Value meaning true
10: #define UP 1             // Value for direction == up
11: #define DOWN -1          // Value for direction == down
12: #define NODIRECTION 0    // Value for direction == none
13: #define ESCKEY 27        // ASCII value for <Esc> key
14:
15: /* -- Other constants. Okay to change with care. MAXPERSONS is
16: limited by available memory--you may not be able to increase this
```

```
17:    value much beyond 1000 or so. Also, be sure to keep MAXELEVS and
18:    MAXFLOORS within the ranges stated in the comments below. Values
19:    outside of these ranges may work, but too many floors or elevators
20:    will turn the simulation's display to mush. */
21:
22:    #define MAXELEVS 10      // Number of elevators (1 to 10 only)
23:    #define MAXFLOORS 10     // Number of floors (2 to 10 only)
24:    #define MAXPERSONS 500   // Maximum people in building
25:    #define ELEVWAIT 15      // Min. seconds to wait at floors
26:    #define CAPACITY 24      // Maximum people in an elevator
27:    #define TRAVELTIME 5     // Seconds to travel between floors
28:
29:    /* -- Formulas using rand() function to make various decisions.  Feel
30:    free adjust these values to alter the simulation. WANTS_TO_ENTER
31:    controls how frequently people enter the building. ENTER_DEST selects
32:    the destination floor which must be within 1 to MAXFLOORS - 1.
33:    MAX_WAIT determines how many seconds a person will wait for an
34:    elevator before getting fed up and taking the stairs. BUSINESS
35:    controls how many seconds people spend at their destination floors
36:    before going elsewhere or leaving the building. LEAVING controls
37:    whether a person will leave or go to another floor; it's currently
38:    set to force people to decide to leave about 2/3 of the time. */
39:
40:    #define WANTS_TO_ENTER   rand() < 200
41:    #define ENTER_DEST       1 + (rand() % (MAXFLOORS - 1))
42:    #define MAX_WAIT         180 + (rand() % 180)
43:    #define BUSINESS         400 + (rand() % 6200)
44:    #define LEAVING          rand() < 22000
45:
46:    /* -- Global variable declarations. These variables are defined in
47:    elevsim.cpp and are the only global variables in the program except
48:    for the building object (see elevsim.cpp). The program uses these
49:    values to display the simulation statistics on the bottom line. All
50:    other program variables are class variables or are local to class
51:    functions. */
52:
53:    extern unsigned totalPeople;    // Number of people handled
54:    extern unsigned inBuilding;     // People in building now
55:    extern unsigned leftBuilding;   // People who left building
56:    extern unsigned avgWait;        // Average no. people waiting
57:    extern unsigned avgRide;        // Average no. people in elevators
58:    extern unsigned tookStair;      // Number people who walked
59:    extern unsigned totalTime;      // Seconds simulation has run
60:
61:    #endif   // __ELEVSIM_H
```

Several files include ELEVSIM.H during compilation to access its declarations. Lines 8-13 list a few miscellaneous items that you should not change. Lines 22-27 define several parameters that can affect the simulation; these you can change, but only within the limits described in the comments. For example, try setting MAXELEVS to 2, or lower MAXFLOORS to 4 or 5 and set the number of elevators to 1. Having these values in one file is important because it lets you quickly modify the program without having to hunt through other source files. Also, you can make copies of ELEVSIM.H, recopy one of the copies back to that file, and compile to create a simulation with a specific set of parameters.

The definitions at lines 40-44 in ELEVSIM.H control the program's decision logic. All these definitions call the rand() function for a number selected from a randomized sequence. Two of these expressions (WANTS_TO_ENTER and LEAVING) evaluate to true or false values that can be used in an if statement such as

```
if (WANTS_TO_ENTER) {
    // programming to have a person enter the building
}
```

The compiler replaces WANTS_TO_ENTER with the expression rand() < 200 listed in the #define at line 40. You could always type such expressions directly into if statements, of course, but using identifiers like WANTS_TO_ENTER makes the code more readable while keeping that and other logic expressions together in the header file where they are easily modified.

The other three symbols (ENTER_DEST, MAX_WAIT, and BUSINESS) choose the floor numbers to which people travel, select the maximum time that people will wait for elevators before deciding to take the stairs, and designate the amount of time that people will spend on floors attending to business before deciding to take an elevator to another floor or to leave the building. Feel free to alter any of these to modify the simulation's characteristics.

Finally in ELEVSIM.H are several global variables, declared at lines 53-59 with the extern keyword. This allows other modules to refer to these variables, but it does not define storage space for them. A good place to do that is in the program's main module, in this case ELEVSIM.CPP, listed near the end of this chapter. As I mentioned earlier, these variables hold the values displayed along the bottom of the screen. With one exception, which you'll see later, these are the *only* global variables in the program.

Note: If ELEVSIM.H declared global variables directly, the compiler and linker would still be able to sort out the mess and create only one copy of each variable in memory. However, using extern in header files clearly indicates that the variables are defined elsewhere—a good source-code management practice.

The person Class

In many simulations, the goal is to let people pose "what if" questions, run the model, and observe the results. For example, you might want to answer the question, "If we have only 3 elevators, what happens when the volume of people increases to 350 at lunch time?"

Another good reason to run simulated computer models is to investigate potentially harmful situations without injuring the test subjects. Flight simulators fall into this category.

The elevator simulation in this chapter is of the "what if" variety. In a nutshell, the goal is to determine how many people a certain number of elevators can handle in a given amount of time. By varying the parameters to set up the test bed, the simulation quickly shows the effects of changes in the algorithms used to move elevators.

Before designing the elevators, however, we need some people to enter a building, travel to a destination, and then leave the system. For the purposes of writing this program, "people" are objects with properties—the property to exist on a certain floor or to be inside an elevator. The program creates the people it needs from a C++ class named person. Listing 5.9, PERSON.H, declares this and one other class, persCollection (person collection).

Listing 5.9. PERSON.H

```
1:   // person.h -- Header file for person.cpp
2:
3:   #ifndef __PERSON_H
4:   #define __PERSON_H        1        // Prevent multiple #includes
5:
6:   #include "elevsim.h"
7:
8:   class person {
9:      private:
10:         int floorNowOn;         // Floor (-1 if outside)
11:         int destination;        // Destination floor number
12:         int maxWaitTime;        // Aggravation level
13:         int waitingForElev;     // True (1) if waiting
14:         int takingStairs;       // True (1) if walking
15:         int elevNowIn;          // Elevator number (-1 if none)
16:      public:
17:         person();
18:         void action(void);
19:         int upwaiting(int floorNumber);
```

```
20:           int dnwaiting(int floorNumber);
21:           int loadIfWaiting(int elevNumber,
22:              int floorNumber, int &pdest);
23:           int loadIfGoing(int elevNumber,
24:              int floorNumber, int direction, int &pdest);
25:           int discharge(int elevNumber, int floorNumber);
26:    };
27:
28:    class persCollection {
29:       private:
30:           person pa[MAXPERSONS];    // Array of person objects
31:       public:
32:          void action(void);
33:          void numWaiting(int floorNumber, int &nup, int &ndn);
34:          int loadAny(int elevNumber,
35:             int floorNumber, int &pdest);
36:          int loadOne(int elevNumber,
37:             int floorNumber, int direction, int &pdest);
38:          int discharge(int elevNumber, int floorNumber);
39:    };
40:
41:    #endif    // __PERSON_H
```

Reading through PERSON.H, you may wonder how I knew what to include in the person class. At this stage, I hadn't designed the other modules, and later on, I would make changes to person. However, the PERSON.H listing is almost identical to the one I wrote originally. But I don't mean to pat myself on the back. I just want to point out a subtle benefit of OOP. When creating new classes, you'll be forced to carefully consider your program's goals. If you *don't* know what a class should contain, it's a sure sign that you need to think more about what you're trying to accomplish. In this program, I knew where I was headed, and therefore, I had a good idea what a person class needed to do. My planning paid off by making this class relatively easy to write.

Hint: When designing new classes, be careful not to fall into the common trap of throwing every old thing that comes to mind into the class declaration. If you don't have a good reason for adding a member to a class, leave it out; you can always add it later. When class declarations grow to page after page of fields and functions, it may be a sign that you need to rethink your program's goals. Short and sweet is far preferable to big and juicy when it comes to C++ classes.

Person Data Fields

Lines 10-15 declare six private data fields, all of type i n t. These values record certain facts about a p e r s o n object—what floor that person is on, the person's destination, and other information. The comments in the listing describe each variable. Most have obvious purposes. (The aggravation level represents the amount of time a person will wait for an elevator before taking the stairs.)

Remember, when a class variable is created, C++ allocates new space for all of a class's fields. This means that each person in the simulation will have its own set of the six fields in the class's private section. ELEVSIM.H defines MAXPERSONS to be 500; therefore, when this version of the program runs, there will be 500 sets of the six fields in a p e r s o n class, one set per person. (At 2 bytes per integer, this takes 6,000 bytes of space.)

Remember also that only the class's functions may access these private fields. No other statement anywhere in the program has any access to a person's inner secrets. If it becomes necessary to change how p e r s o n works—packing w a i t i n g F o r E l e v and t a k i n g S t a i r s into a bit-field structure to conserve space, for example—the only affected functions are those that belong to this class. No statements outside this module have access to these variables; therefore, changing them requires no modification to other parts of the program.

The Person Collection Class

PERSON.H also declares a second class, p e r s c o l l e c t o n (see lines 28-39). The purpose of this class is to give the simulation a simple way to work with a large number of p e r s o n objects. Instead of defining an array, a list, or another kind of data structure to hold the people that will pass through the simulation, the simulation simply creates one variable of type p e r s c o l l e c t i o n.

In general, when a program needs a large number of objects, it's a good idea to provide a new class with functions to manipulate the population of the collected class objects, whatever they are. Because classes hide their inner details in the private section, collecting other objects into a class limits the program's access to those details. This can be important if you later need to modify the way the program stores its object collections. For example, in PERSON.H, all people in the simulation are stored in an array pa of p e r s o n objects (see line 30). Because *only* the p e r s c o l l e c t i o n functions at lines 32-38 may access that array, these are the *only* functions that will need modifying if you later decide to change the array into a list or, perhaps, to store "people" on disk and read them in as needed.

Another benefit of using a class to store collections of objects concerns efficiency. Instead of wasting time now trying to choose the best storage methods, you can use whatever works and go on to the next task. Later, after the program is up and running, you can return to each class and modify the data structures to improve performance.

Imagine how difficult this would be if the program itself defined an array of `person` objects for the simulation. To change that array to a list would require hunting through the program for every use of the array. The `perscollection` class neatly eliminates that tedious job. It hides the details of its implementation—not from you, but from other modules. This tends to keep modules autonomous, which in turn, makes them easier to maintain.

`person` *and* `perscollection` *Member Functions*

Like most classes, `person` contains a number of public functions that perform the actions of the class. A `person` variable is initialized by the `person()` constructor (line 17 in PERSON.H), which along with other `person` member functions, are the only parts of the program permitted to access the class's private data fields. The value of this encapsulation of code and data is invaluable during debugging; if people start acting strangely, you can limit your diagnosis to the `person` class.

The class's member functions at lines 17-25 specify the actions that a variable of type `person` may perform. Because the implementations of those functions (and those for the `perscollection` class) are lengthy, I'll list the PERSON.CPP module (Listing 5.10) in a slightly different way from previous programs. The lines are numbered as usual, but the descriptions for various functions are scattered throughout the listing; therefore, don't turn the pages to find where the text continues; just keep reading to learn how a `person` class operates. Of course, on disk, despite being broken up here, PERSON.CPP is stored in one file.

Listing 5.10. PERSON.CPP

```
1:   // person.cpp -- Person class module
2:
3:   #include <stdlib.h>
4:   #include "person.h"
5:
6:   /* -- The person class constructor. Runs when a person object comes
7:   into being. Assigns defaults values to person data fields. */
8:
9:   person::person()
10:  {
11:      floorNowOn = -1;        // Not in the building
12:      waitingForElev = 0;     // Not waiting for an elevator
13:      destination = -1;       // No destination assigned
14:      maxWaitTime = 0;        // Not waiting until next action
15:      takingStairs = 0;       // Not walking the stairs
16:      elevNowIn = -1;         // Not in any elevator
17:  }
18:
```

As is typical for C++ classes, the `person()` constructor (lines 9-17) initializes a variable of this class type. In this case, the initialization steps are simple—merely assigning default values for each of the six member fields in a `person`. Because constructors run automatically when a variable of the class comes into being, you can be certain that *all* people start in life with equal potential, at least in this simulation.

Try to design your own classes along these same lines. Instead of inserting initialization details into other member functions that you'll have to remember to call, place those statements into the class constructor. You can then forget about them and let C++ initialize your class variables automatically.

The next fragment from PERSON.CPP fills in the `action` member function, which controls what a person does during each tick of the simulation's clock. To get a feel for the programming, scan the comments of this section before reading on. As I mentioned earlier, this and future fragments belong to the same PERSON.CPP file, but are divided here among the descriptions to reduce the number of pages you have to flip while reading the code:

Listing 5.10. PERSON.CPP (continued)

```
19:   /* -- Perform an action for this person. Called once for every tick
20:   of the simulation's clock. */
21:
22:   void person::action(void)
23:   {
24:
25:   /* -- Decide whether a person outside should enter building. */
26:
27:       if (floorNowOn < 0) {              // If not in bldg
28:           if (WANTS_TO_ENTER) {          // Decide to enter
29:               destination = ENTER_DEST;  // Select destination
30:               floorNowOn = 0;            // Enter on ground floor
31:               maxWaitTime = MAX_WAIT;    // Set aggravation level
32:               waitingForElev = 1;        // Person is waiting
33:               takingStairs = 0;          // Not taking stairs
34:               elevNowIn = -1;            // Not inside an elevator
35:               totalPeople++;             // Count people handled
36:               inBuilding++;              // Count people in bldg
37:           }
38:
39:   /* -- If person is inside and waiting for an elevator, depending on
40:   the person's aggravation level, decide whether to take the stairs and
41:   walk to the destination floor. */
42:
43:       } else {                           // If in bldg
44:           if (waitingForElev) {          // If inside and waiting
45:               if ((maxWaitTime--) <= 0) { // Mark time waiting
```

```
46:                    waitingForElev = 0;            // Tired of waiting
47:                    takingStairs = 1;             // Take stairs instead
48:                    maxWaitTime =                 // 30 secs per floor
49:                        30 * abs(destination - floorNowOn);
50:                    tookStair++;                  // Count people who walk
51:                }
52:            }
53:
54: /* -- If person is inside and is walking up or down the stairs, check
55: whether that person has arrived.  If so, set the amount of time the person
56: will spend on this floor. */
57:
58:            else if (takingStairs) {
59:                if ((maxWaitTime--) <= 0) {     // Mark time walking
60:                    floorNowOn = destination;   // Reached destination
61:                    takingStairs = 0;           // Not walking on stairs
62:                    maxWaitTime = BUSINESS;     // Time on this floor
63:                }
64:            }
65:
66: /* -- If a person is not inside an elevator, that person must be on a
67: floor taking care of business. Check whether the person is done and
68: select another destination. Most people will decide to leave the
69: building, but some will travel to another floor. */
70:
71:            else if (elevNowIn < 0) {           // If not inside an elevator
72:                if ((maxWaitTime--) <= 0) {     // Mark time on floor
73:                    if (LEAVING)                // Most people will want
74:                      destination = 0;          //   to leave on floor 0
75:                    else                        // Some will travel to
76:                      destination = ENTER_DEST; //   another floor
77:                    if (destination == floorNowOn) // Don't let people
78:                       destination = 0;            // travel to same floor
79:                    maxWaitTime = MAX_WAIT;     // Set aggravation level
80:                    waitingForElev = 1;         // Person is waiting
81:                }
82:            }
83:
84: /* -- Check for any person who is in the building, has arrived at the
85: ground floor, and is ready to leave the building. */
86:
87:            if ((floorNowOn == 0) && (destination == 0)) {
88:                floorNowOn = -1;                         // Send person outside
```

```
89:            leftBuilding++;          // Count people leaving
90:            inBuilding--;            //   and no longer in bldg
91:          }
92:        }
93:    }
94:
```

The action member function serves as a person's heartbeat. Several if statements examine the current state of a person object to determine whether that person is out of the building (floorNowOn < 0), riding in an elevator, or is taking the stairs.

The simulation calls the action function for each clock tick (a non-real time second) for each person in the system. To have people behave differently, the program uses a timing value maxWaitTime. When that value counts down to 0, depending on what a person is now doing, the variable *changes states* and begins doing something else. In other words, when a person's time on a floor is up, that person will decide on the next destination, which is usually the ground floor. (All people enter and leave on the ground floor.)

Because it changes states this way, the programming in the action function is often called a *state machine.* Unlike many functions that operate the same way or nearly so each time a program calls them, a state machine may perform widely different operations each time it runs. A state machine like action is a good way to model objects that assume different modes or states.

Although action seems long, because of its state-machine nature, it's composed of relatively short parts. For example, lines 58-64 describe what happens if people are taking the stairs. First, the program subtracts one from maxWaitTime. If this causes the timing value to be less or equal to 0, the three statements at lines 60-62 run. These statements alter the values of the floorNowOn, takingStairs, and maxWaitTime data fields in this variable. The effect is to change a person's state from walking up or down the stairs to performing business on the destination floor. The next time the action function runs for this same person, lines 71-82 will perform the steps required to operate people taking care of business on floors.

Also notice how action uses the logical definitions from ELEVSIM.H to make decisions. For example, line 73 executes if (LEAVING) to decide whether a person should leave the building. By the way, those people who do leave are free to reenter the building later in a new incarnation.

The rest of the person member functions are short and simple. For instance, two functions, upwaiting and dnwaiting return true or false to let the program know whether this person is waiting for an elevator:

Listing 5.10. PERSON.CPP (continued)

```
95:  /* -- Return true if this person is now waiting for an up elevator at
96:  the specified floor number. */
97:
98:  int person::upwaiting(int floorNumber)
```

```
 99:   {
100:       return ((waitingForElev              ) &&
101:               (floorNowOn == floorNumber) &&
102:               (destination > floorNowOn ));
103:   }
104:
105:   /* -- Return true if this person is now waiting for a down elevator
106:   at the specified floor number. */
107:
108:   int person::dnwaiting(int floorNumber)
109:   {
110:       return ((waitingForElev              ) &&
111:               (floorNowOn == floorNumber) &&
112:               (destination < floorNowOn ));
113:   }
114:
```

Each of these two functions (lines 98-103 and 108-113) contains a single
return statement. The expressions in each of those statements are similar, differing
only in the test for whether a person's destination variable is less or greater than
floorNowOn, which specifies a person's present location. The floorNumber
parameter indicates on which floor the simulation is checking for people waiting for
elevators.

As you learn more about OOP and C++, you'll discover opportunities to create
many such small functions with distinct purposes. This is always a good sign, because
it means you have identified some of the atomic properties of a class. Lots of small
functions are desirable—if you're concerned about efficiency, you can always
convert them to inline code later.

Most functions, of course, will have more than only one statement. For example,
loadIfWaiting is a bit more complex than the previous two:

Listing 5.10. PERSON.CPP (continued)

```
115:   /* -- Have person enter elevator if waiting for an elevator on this
116:   floor regardless of direction. (Elevator is empty and the person will
117:   determine its direction.) Return the person's destination in pdest to
118:   simulate that person pressing one of the elevator's floor buttons. */
119:
120:   int person::loadIfWaiting(int elevNumber,
121:       int floorNumber, int &pdest)
122:   {
123:       if (waitingForElev && (floorNowOn == floorNumber)) {
124:           waitingForElev = 0;      // Not waiting any longer
125:           elevNowIn = elevNumber; // Save elevator number
```

```
126:            pdest = destination;      // Pass person's destination back
127:            return TRUE;              // Person got on board
128:        }
129:    return FALSE;                     // Person did not get on board
130: }
131:
```

Function loadIfWaiting is one of the additions I made to person after creating the elevator class, which I haven't explained yet. Because the function's purpose has not been discussed and is out of context, it may be difficult to understand. When empty and directionless, an elevator calls loadIfWaiting to allow one person to enter and choose the direction. This mirrors a real person getting into an idle elevator and pressing a floor button. In such cases, the first person in decides whether the elevator travels up or down. To simulate the action of pressing a floor button, function loadIfWaiting returns the person's destination in the reference parameter &pdest.

> **Note:** By the way, this is a typical situation. You write one class and discover the need for various functions in other classes. That's fine, and it helps to keep classes stripped of unnecessary functions. Don't insert every member function under the sun that *might* be needed. Stick to the necessities.

Another similar function, loadIfGoing, lets others enter an elevator that is traveling in a known direction. If the elevator is going up, it will call loadIfGoing to load as many people as possible going in that same direction. No doubt you've seen a group of people charge an elevator about to leave. Here's the function that simulates that mob scene:

Listing 5.10. PERSON.CPP (continued)

```
132: /* -- Load person if waiting for an elevator going in the specified
133: direction. Return the person's destination in pdest to simulate that
134: person pressing one of the elevator's floor buttons. Similar to
135: loadIfWaiting(), but loads only people going up or down. */
136:
137: int person::loadIfGoing(int elevNumber,
138:     int floorNumber, int direction, int &pdest)
139: {
140:     int pdir;        // Person's direction, up or down
141:
142:     if (destination > floorNumber)
143:         pdir = UP;
144:     else
145:         pdir = DOWN;
```

```
146:        if (waitingForElev && (floorNowOn == floorNumber) &&
147:        (direction == pdir)) {
148:        waitingForElev = 0;
149:        elevNowIn = elevNumber;
150:        pdest = destination;
151:        return TRUE;
152:    }
153:    return FALSE;
154: }
155:
```

Only a little more complicated than `loadIfWaiting`, `loadIfGoing` places a person inside an elevator if that person is waiting for a lift in the specified direction. Most of the programming in the function simply adjusts various data fields in the variable to represent a person's new state. This will cause the `action` function to select a different section when the simulation calls on it to advance the people through the building.

Of course, after having people enter an elevator, they also need to be able to leave. This is handled by function `discharge`, which completes the `person` class:

Listing 5.10. PERSON.CPP (continued)

```
156:    /* -- If this person is in the specified elevator and is headed for
157:    the designated floor number, make that person get off the elevator.
158:    Return true if the person gets off; otherwise, return false. Set the
159:    person's wait time to the number of seconds this person will remain
160:    on the floor unless that floor is 0, in which case the person will
161:    exit the building immediately. */
162:
163:    int person::discharge(int elevNumber, int floorNumber)
164:    {
165:        if ((elevNowIn == elevNumber) && (destination == floorNumber)) {
166:            elevNowIn = -1;             // Get out of elevator
167:            floorNowOn = destination;   // Set floor person is on
168:            if (floorNowOn != 0)
169:                maxWaitTime = BUSINESS; // Set time to spend on floor
170:            return TRUE;                // Person got off elevator
171:        } else
172:            return FALSE;               // Person did not exit
173:    }
174:
```

As with most of the other member functions, this one simply adjusts data fields in the class variable to represent the new state of a person. In this case, when a person object leaves an elevator, it sets its `maxWaitTime` to a random number of seconds (specified by the `BUSINESS` symbol from ELEVSIM.H). This causes that person to spend a certain amount of time on this floor. However, most people will leave the building on reaching floor 0. For the purposes of this simulation, the program assumes that a person is out of the building as soon as the person leaves the elevator. (You might say that the building's doors are next to the elevator shaft.)

That's all there is to a person class. If you scan back through the previous 174 lines of code, you may be surprised to discover only simple statements that assign a few values and make a few decisions. One of the myths of object-oriented programming is that it tends to be more complex than conventional techniques. Not so. The design of a class may involve much planning, but its implementation is typically easier than in conventional programming. There's a good reason for this. By concentrating on what an object *does* instead of fretting about how that object is *used,* you limit your sights to the task at hand. If you can describe what an object is supposed to do, you can program it. And you can do that out of context from the rest of the program.

For another good example of how OOP helps to reduce a program's complexity, let's examine the perscollection class, which is stored along with person in the same PERSON.CPP module. Some programmers prefer to store only one class per module, but when the classes are intimately related as are these two, they're probably best stored together. Here's the first member function:

Listing 5.10. PERSON.CPP (continued)

```
175:   /* -- Call action() function for every person. Runs once for every
176:   tick of the simulation's clock. */
177:
178:   void persCollection::action(void)
179:   {
180:       for (int i = 0; i < MAXPERSONS; i++)
181:           pa[i].action();
182:   }
183:
```

There is no constructor in the perscollection object. Always remember that constructors are optional: If you include one in a class, it runs automatically when a variable of the class comes into being. If you don't include a constructor, the class variable is uninitialized and you may need to call a member function to perform various startup duties.

But you may wonder, if a perscollection object stores an array of person class variables, how do *those* individual variables become initialized? And when does this occur?

The answer is the same as for all class variables: The constructors run when the variables of the class come into being. In this case, when the program defines space for a variable of type perCollection, that space consists of an array of person variables (line 30 in PERSON.H):

```
person pa[MAXPERSONS];
```

Array pa is a collection of person objects. MAXPERSONS specifies the number of those objects in the array. When C++ allocates space for the array, it calls the person constructor for *each* object in the array. Every object, then, is initialized by the person() constructor at lines 9-17 in PERSON.CPP. This happens automatically; you don't need to insert function calls into your program to make it happen.

The automatic initialization of objects in programs has enormous benefits. It simplifies the program and helps reduce bugs caused by using uninitialized values—one of the most common errors programmers make. It also means you can use class variables without thumbing around in your code to make sure that variables have been properly initialized.

For example, the action function in persCollection (lines 178-182) calls the action function for every person object in the pa array. To put all the people through their paces, the program needs only call the collection's action function.

Notice that there are two action functions in this module, one belonging to the person class and the other to persCollection. Because each function implementation is preceded by the class name and the double-colon symbol, there is no conflict between these identical names (see lines 22 and 178). C++ classes let you use the same names for member functions even when those functions are declared in the same module.

One of the jobs that perCollection needs to perform is to call member functions for every person variable stored in the pa array. For instance, the numWaiting function counts the number of people waiting for an elevator on a specified floor:

Listing 5.10. PERSON.CPP (continued)

```
184:   /* -- Count number of persons waiting on a floor. Returns nup (number
185:   of persons going up) and ndn (number of persons going down) on the
186:   specified floor. */
187:
188:   void persCollection::numWaiting(int floorNumber,
189:       int &nup, int &ndn)
190:   {
191:       nup = ndn = 0;
192:       for (int i = 0; i < MAXPERSONS; i++) {
193:           nup += pa[i].upwaiting(floorNumber);
194:           ndn += pa[i].dnwaiting(floorNumber);
195:       }
196:   }
197:
```

Here again, the persCollection simplifies the main program by providing a high-level operation that accesses the individual person objects stored in the pa array. The function returns two int values, nup and ndn, representing the number of people waiting to travel up or down.

To determine these numbers, a for loop at lines 192-195 calls two functions for every person object, upwaiting and dnwaiting. As you recall from earlier, these functions return true (1) if a person is waiting for an elevator or false (0) if not. The program simply adds these function results to nup and ndn. This quickly counts the number of people traveling in both directions.

Be sure to understand the form of the expression pa[i].upwaiting(floorNumber). First, the array is indexed with pa[i], which selects an individual person variable. The dot notation specifies a class member function for that person. The floorNumber is passed to that function, using the same notation for passing arguments to common C++ functions.

A persCollection object can call person member functions this way because those functions are declared in the person's public section (see PERSON.H, lines 16-25). Items in a class's public section are visible to statements outside of the class (including statements inside other classes, as in persCollection here.) But items in a class's private section are strictly hidden from view. Only members of that same class can access such items.

This applies equally to other classes, even those in the same module. For example, although persCollection is declared in the same file as person, it has no access to person's private data. For that reason, statements like this one won't compile:

```
pa[i].destination = 5;  // ???
```

It's not possible for persCollection to refer directly to the destination field in a person variable. That field is strictly for the use of the member functions in person. No other statements may use those fields directly.

Note: Like most rules, it's possible to break the one in C++ that limits access to a class's private data fields. However, because this chapter introduces OOP concepts, I'll take the "pure" approach here and postpone discussing the exceptions until later. As the program in this chapter demonstrates, it's possible (and desirable) to write complete programs that obey the fundamental rules about data hiding in class objects. Yes, you can break the rules. But you'll get more from C++ and OOP if you learn to play by those rules before breaking them.

The three remaining functions in persCollection load people into elevators (loadAny and loadOne) and discharge an elevator's passengers traveling to a specified floor (discharge). These functions operate much like the others, and you should be able to understand them by reading the comments in the listing:

Listing 5.10. PERSON.CPP (continued)

```
198:    /* -- Load any person waiting for an elevator at this floor number.
199:    Return the person's destination in pdest so that the elevator can begin
200:    traveling in the necessary direction. Return true if a person is
201:    loaded, else return false. If false, pdest is undefined. */
202:
203:    int persCollection::loadAny(int elevNumber,
204:        int floorNumber, int &pdest)
205:    {
206:        for (int i = 0; i < MAXPERSONS; i++)
207:            if (pa[i].loadIfWaiting(elevNumber, floorNumber, pdest))
208:                return TRUE;    // Person got on board
209:        return FALSE;           // No person got into an elevator
210:    }
211:
212:    /* -- Load one person waiting for an elevator at this floor number,
213:    and headed in the specified direction.  Return true if a person is
214:    loaded, else return false. Similar to loadAny, but loads only persons
215:    traveling in a specified direction. */
216:
217:    int persCollection::loadOne(int elevNumber,
218:        int floorNumber, int direction, int &pdest)
219:    {
220:        for (int i = 0; i < MAXPERSONS; i++)
221:            if (pa[i].loadIfGoing(elevNumber,
222:                floorNumber, direction, pdest))
223:                return TRUE;    // Person got on board
224:        return FALSE;           // No person got into an elevator
225:    }
226:
227:    /* -- Discharge all persons in this elevator who are traveling to
228:    the specified floor. Return number of people who got off elevator. */
229:
230:    int persCollection::discharge(int elevNumber, int floorNumber)
231:    {
232:        int n = 0;      // Number of people who get off elevator
233:
234:        for (int i = 0; i < MAXPERSONS; i++)
235:            n += pa[i].discharge(elevNumber, floorNumber);
236:        return n;
237:    }
```

The `floor` Class

The simulation is moving along. Finished so far are some of the mechanical details needed to compile the program and to specify global definitions and variables. You've also examined two full classes: `person` and `persCollection`.

It's time to begin constructing the building. For this simulation, a "building" will be a collection of floors. It's not important what's on those floors—only that people have somewhere to travel. Also, the program will need programming to model the up and down elevator buttons that people will press to call for an elevator. All these details go into the next two classes, `floor` and `floorCollection` in Listing 5.11, FLOOR.H.

Listing 5.11. FLOOR.H

```
1:   // floor.h -- Header file for floor.cpp
2:
3:   #ifndef __FLOOR_H
4:   #define __FLOOR_H         1        // Prevent multiple #includes
5:
6:   #include "person.h"
7:
8:   class floor {
9:      private:
10:         int floorNumber;   // Lobby is floor 0
11:         int up, down;      // 1 = up or down buttons pressed
12:         int np;            // Number of people waiting for elev
13:      public:
14:         floor();
15:         void setFloorNumber(int n) { floorNumber = n; }
16:         int downButton(void) { return down; }
17:         int upButton(void) { return up; }
18:         void resetUpButton(void) { up = 0; }
19:         void resetDownButton(void) { down = 0; }
20:         int getNumWaiting(void) { return np; }
21:         void setUpButton(void);
22:         void setDownButton(void);
23:         void showFloor(persCollection &thePersons);
24:   };
25:
26:   class floorCollection {
27:      private:
28:         floor fa[MAXFLOORS];       // Array of floor objects
29:      public:
```

```
30:          floorCollection();
31:          void showFloors(persCollection &thePersons);
32:          void resetButton(int direction, int floorNumber);
33:          int signalUp(int floorNumber);
34:          int signalDown(int floorNumber);
35:          int signalSameDir(int direction, int floorNumber);
36:          int avgWaiting(void);
37:   };
38:
39:   #endif    // __FLOOR_H
```

The floor class (lines 8-24) has the same general organization as a person. It declares a few variables in its private section and a few member functions in the public area. A floor has a number (floorNumber), two buttons (up and down), and keeps track of the number of people waiting for an elevator on this floor (np).

Also like the PERSON.H header, FLOOR.H declares a second class, floorCollection. This class holds all the floors in a building and performs several important functions that elevators will need. As with persCollection, an array fa at line 28 declares a data structure for holding a collection of floor objects. Notice how the MAXFLOORS constant from ELEVSIM specifies the number of floors in the collection.

Implementing the floor *Class*

One area where FLOOR.H differs from PERSON.H is its reliance on inline member functions. For example, see lines 15-20. The inline functions greatly reduce the size of the FLOOR.CPP module in Listing 5.12 while adhering to good OOP practices of using class members to access data inside a floor variable. Because the functions are declared and defined inline directly in the class, there's no overhead to worry about as there would be with common functions that simply read or change a variable. Functions not inline are implemented in the usual way in the FLOOR.CPP module.

Listing 5.12. FLOOR.CPP

```
1:   // floor.cpp -- Floor class module
2:
3:   #include <disp.h>
4:   #include "floor.h"
5:
6:   /* -- The floor class constructor. This function initializes an
7:   object (variable) of the floor class. Note: The collection of floors
8:   is expected to assign a floor number to each floor in a building.
```

```
 9:   Until that happens, the floorNumber field is uninitialized. */
10:
11:   floor::floor()
12:   {
13:       up = down = np = 0;      // Reset up and down buttons
14:   }
15:
```

First comes the floor constructor: The function that automatically initializes a variable of type floor as soon as that variable comes into being. In this case, the constructor simply sets the up and down buttons and the np variable to 0, using the classic C++ trick of stringing multiple assignments together. The statement up = down = np = 0 is equivalent to

```
up = 0;
down = 0;
np = 0;
```

Looking back at the declaration for the floor class, you'll notice that the constructor fails to initialize the floorNumber field. The reason for this omission points out a flaw in C++ that makes it difficult to initialize collections of objects requiring function arguments. In other words, to give each floor a different number, the constructor would have to be declared with a floor-number parameter, perhaps like this:

```
floor(int fn);
```

That's perfectly legal, and it's often useful for constructors to accept arguments this way. But the addition of the integer fn parameter poses a problem for C++ when another class such as floorCollection declares an array of floor variables. Earlier, you learned that the person constructor runs automatically for every variable in the pa array. The same happens here for the fa array of floors. But this would *not* occur if the constructor declared one or more parameters.

In general, for an array of class variables like pa and fa, the constructor in the class is called automatically only if the constructor declares no arguments. Given this class,

```
class firstClass {
    private:
        // private data fields
    public:
        firstClass();
}
```

if you then define an array of five `firstClass` objects,

```
firstClass fca[5];
```

C++ will call the `firstClass` constructor for each of the variables stored in the `fca` array. But if the class is declared like this,

```
class firstClass {
   private:
      // private data fields
   public:
      firstClass(int aValue);
}
```

C++ can't call the constructor. In fact, it can't even compile the definition:

```
firstClass fca[5];
```

This simply doesn't give the compiler the information it needs to know how to initialize the constructors. To do that, you must complete the definition this way:

```
firstClass fca[5] = { 5, 200, 19, 64, -12 };
```

Defined with initializing values inside braces, the array passes each value in turn (5, 200, ..., –12) to the class constructor, initializing the array's variables with those arguments. Unfortunately, this cements the definition in place, and the code now requires two changes to modify the number of variables stored in `fca`—the number in brackets, plus the initializing values. This complicates maintenance because this and similar definitions are likely to be buried inside one or more source modules.

Probably a better solution is to declare another member function to complete the initialization of class variables. This is the approach I took in FLOOR, where the inline `setFloorNumber` function assigns a value to the private `floorNumber` data field (see line 15 in FLOOR.H). This allows the `floorCollection` object to initialize its array of `floor` objects automatically, but it also means I'll have to remember to call `setFloorNumber` for each object to complete its initialization.

Note: Another way to deal with the construction of class variables in arrays is to declare more than one constructor. In that case, C++ will call the constructor that has no parameters by default unless you specify one or more values in the array definition to pass to the constructors that have parameters. (I'll return to the advanced topic of multiple constructors in chapter 7.)

After implementing the `floor` constructor, FLOOR.CPP fills in a medium-size function, `showFloor` that handles the display details for each floor object:

Listing 5.12. FLOOR.CPP (continued)

```
16:   /* -- Display a representation of this floor, showing its number and
17:   the state of its up and down buttons. */
18:
19:   void floor::showFloor(persCollection &thePersons)
20:   {
21:       int col = 0;
22:       int row = 20 - (floorNumber * 2);
23:       char uc = '-';
24:       char dc = '-';
25:       int nup, ndn;       // Number of persons going up and down
26:
27:   /* -- Get number of persons waiting on floor going up or down. */
28:
29:       thePersons.numWaiting(floorNumber, nup, ndn);
30:       np = nup + ndn;
31:       if (nup > 0) setUpButton();       // Sense up button push
32:       if (ndn > 0) setDownButton();     // Sense down button push
33:       if (up) uc = 'U';                 // Init up and down symbols
34:       if (down) dc = 'D';               //  for the display
35:
36:   /* -- Display information for this floor. */
37:
38:       disp_move(row, col);
39:       disp_printf("%02d:%c%c%03d", floorNumber, uc, dc, np );
40:   }
41:
```

The showFloor member function differs in one significant way from others you've examined. Look closely at the function's declaration:

```
void floor::showFloor(persCollection &thePersons)
```

The function declares a single reference parameter &thePersons of type persCollection, the class from the PERSON.H described earlier. Floor objects need to call functions in the collection of people entering the simulation, and it's through this parameter that the collection of floors gains access to the person objects. For example, line 29 calls the numWaiting member function to retrieve how many people in thePersons are currently waiting for an elevator at this floor.

It's perfectly legal to pass objects as function parameters this way. Just as you can pass int and float arguments to common C++ functions, you can pass arguments of class data types. However, when a class is large, it's probably best to pass it by address, as done here with the & symbol, or as a pointer.

> **Note:** Because most classes protect their data fields in private sections, passing objects by reference or as pointers to functions doesn't open the same dangerous doors that can lead to bugs in conventional programming. Even though the class variable is passed by address to a function, that function can *still* only access the private data by calling member functions. This increases the program's efficiency by passing small pointers rather than large objects on the stack while preventing functions from accidentally modifying data that should remain untouched.

Because the program calls showFloor for every tick of the simulation's clock, I decided to include calls to setUpButton and setDownButton at lines 31-32, which set the floor's up or down buttons if there are any people waiting for an elevator at this floor. (In retrospect, it probably wasn't the best plan to perform these actions in the display function. If you modify the program, perhaps to display the elevators on a graphics screen instead of using only text, you'll have to remember to include these two calls.)

As with the person object, other functions in the floor class are simple and contain only single statements. Again, in your own code, don't be concerned if you find that you are writing dozens of small functions like these. Small, tightly written functions lead to programs that are easy to maintain, and you can always convert them to inline definitions if you're concerned about speed. Here are the remaining two member functions in the floor class:

Listing 5.12. FLOOR.CPP (continued)

```
42:  /* -- Turn on the floor's up button, signaling that someone is
43:  waiting for an elevator to travel to a higher floor. The up button on
44:  the top floor is permanently off. */
45:
46:  void floor::setUpButton(void)
47:  {
48:      if (floorNumber < MAXFLOORS - 1)
49:          up = 1;
50:  }
51:
52:  /* -- Turn on the floor's down button, signaling that someone is
53:  waiting for an elevator to travel to a lower floor. The down button
54:  on the ground floor is permanently off. */
55:
56:  void floor::setDownButton(void)
57:  {
58:      if (floorNumber > 0)
```

```
59:            down = 1;
60:    }
61:
```

A floor's setUpButton and setDownButton functions do what you probably expect—set the floor's up and down buttons that call for elevators to pick up waiting passengers. The functions also test whether this floor is on the ground or at the top of the building and prevent people from pressing the down button in the lobby or the up button in the penthouse.

That completes the floor class. As with the person class, a floor is a fairly simple object. Of course, one floor does not make a building, just as one person does not make a crowd. Like the people in the simulation, another class, floorCollection, stores a collection of floors in an array of floor objects. Like most classes, the collection includes a constructor to initialize all of the floors in the simulated building:

Listing 5.12. FLOOR.CPP (continued)

```
62:    /* -- The constructor for a floorCollection object. This function
63:    initializes all floor objects in a collection--in other words, all of
64:    the floors in the building. */
65:
66:    floorCollection::floorCollection()
67:    {
68:        for (int i = 0; i < MAXFLOORS; i++)
69:            fa[i].setFloorNumber(i);    // Assign floor numbers
70:    }
71:
```

You may recall that the persCollection class had no constructor. As I've said before, constructors are completely optional; include one only if you want C++ to initialize variables of a class type automatically when those variables come into being.

The reason floorCollection needs a constructor is to take care of the uninitialized floorNumber field in the floor objects. Remember, because the floor constructor has no parameters, that field is left uninitialized. Rather than use the solution described before of inserting floor numbers in braces directly in the fa array definition (see line 28 in FLOOR.H), the floorCollection calls setFloorNumber for every floor object to complete the initialization of those objects.

To make updating the display quick and easy, the floorCollection class also includes a function that calls showFloor for every floor in the collection:

Listing 5.12. FLOOR.CPP (continued)

```
72:   /* -- Call showFloor() function for every floor. This function
73:   updates the display for all floors in the building. */
74:
75:   void floorCollection::showFloors(persCollection &thePersons)
76:   {
77:       for (int i = 0; i < MAXFLOORS; i++)
78:           fa[i].showFloor(thePersons);
79:   }
80:
```

Notice how the call to showFloor at line 78 passes thePersons to that member function. Somewhere, the program declares a variable of type persCollection and passes that variable to showFloors in floorCollection. The collection object then passes that same variable to showFloor, which takes care of the display details for that floor. All of this gives floor objects access to the people objects in the building while neatly hiding the mechanics about how people objects are stored in memory. Instead of passing variables of rigid data structures from function to function, the program passes objects, which are easily modified if necessary to change how data is represented. These function calls, declarations, and parameters will need no modifications to accommodate changes in the storage details of a persCollection class.

Aim for this same degree of information hiding or *data encapsulation* in your own programs. Use classes to hide the details of their implementations from functions that use variables of the class types. By doing this now, you can reduce the amount of work you'll have to struggle through to make changes later.

The last several functions in the floorCollection class contain no new features. Read the comments in the listing to understand what these functions do:

Listing 5.12. FLOOR.CPP (continued)

```
81:   /* -- Reset the up or down button for this floor */
82:
83:   void floorCollection::resetButton(int direction, int floorNumber)
84:   {
85:       if (direction == UP)
86:           fa[floorNumber].resetUpButton();
87:       else if (direction == DOWN)
88:           fa[floorNumber].resetDownButton();
89:   }
90:
91:   /* -- Return true if there are any floors above the specified floor
92:   signaling for an elevator in any direction. */
93:
94:   int floorCollection::signalUp(int floorNumber)
```

```
 95:   {
 96:       for (int i = MAXFLOORS - 1; i > floorNumber; i--)
 97:           if (fa[i].upButton() || fa[i].downButton())
 98:               return TRUE;
 99:       return FALSE;
100:   }
101:
102:   /* -- Return true if there are any floors below the specified floor
103:   signaling for an elevator in any direction. */
104:
105:   int floorCollection::signalDown(int floorNumber)
106:   {
107:       for (int i = 0; i < floorNumber; i++)
108:           if (fa[i].upButton() || fa[i].downButton())
109:               return TRUE;
110:       return FALSE;
111:   }
112:
113:   /* -- Return true if a button in the specified direction (up or down)
114:   is pressed on this floor. Elevators use this function to help decide
115:   whether to stop at a floor. Returns false if no buttons are pressed
116:   or if direction is not set.*/
117:
118:   int floorCollection::signalSameDir(int direction, int floorNumber)
119:   {
120:       if (direction == UP)
121:           return fa[floorNumber].upButton();
122:       else if (direction == DOWN)
123:           return fa[floorNumber].downButton();
124:       else
125:           return FALSE;
126:   }
127:
128:   /* -- Return average number of people now waiting on all floors for
129:   an elevator in any direction. */
130:
131:   int floorCollection::avgWaiting(void)
132:   {
133:       int total = 0;
134:
135:       for (int i = 0; i < MAXFLOORS; i++)
136:           total += fa[i].getNumWaiting();
137:       return (total / MAXFLOORS);
138:   }
```

The elevator **Class**

Now that we have floors and people, we're ready to tackle the final object in the simulation—the elevators. As with the other classes, the declaration for the e l e v a t o r class is stored in a header file, ELEVATOR.H, Listing 5.13.

Listing 5.13. ELEVATOR.H

```
1:   // elevator.h -- Header file for elevator.cpp
2:
3:   #ifndef __ELEVATOR_H
4:   #define __ELEVATOR_H      1         // Prevent multiple #includes
5:
6:   #include "elevsim.h"
7:   #include "floor.h"
8:   #include "person.h"
9:
10:  class elevator {
11:     private:
12:        int elevNumber;          // Elevator's number
13:        int timeToAction;        // Time in secs until next action
14:        int floorNumber;         // Current floor number
15:        int stopped;             // 1 == stopped at floor
16:        int direction;           // 1 == up, -1 == down, 0 == none
17:        int buttons[MAXFLOORS];  // Flr buttons (0 == off, 1 == on)
18:        int passengers;          // Number of passengers on board
19:        int buttonUp(void);
20:        int buttonDown(void);
21:     public:
22:        elevator();
23:        int getPassengers(void) { return passengers; }
24:        void setelevNumber(int n);
25:        void showElevator(void);
26:        void setDirection(floorCollection &theFloors);
27:        int elevStopping(floorCollection &theFloors);
28:        void action(floorCollection &theFloors,
29:           persCollection &thePersons);
30:  };
31:
32:  class elevCollection {
33:     private:
34:        elevator ea[MAXELEVS];   // Array of elevator objects
35:     public:
```

```
36:          elevCollection();
37:          void showElevators(void);
38:          void action(floorCollection &theFloors,
39:              persCollection &thePersons);
40:          int avgRiding(void);
41:     };
42:
43:     #endif    // __ELEVATOR_H
```

As before, the elevator class declares several private data fields at lines 12-18. Most have obvious purposes (see the comments to the right). Line 17 declares an array named buttons that simulates the bank of floor buttons in real elevators. People will push these buttons to tell the elevator to travel to a certain floor, and the elevator uses the values in this array to decide whether to travel up, down, or to stay where it is.

Lines 19 and 20 in the elevator's private section declare two private member functions, buttonUp and buttonDown. As you'll see in the next listing, these functions let the elevator sense whether any buttons are pressed above or below the current floor. (I know little more about elevators than anyone else who's ridden in them, but I imagine there are circuits inside that perform similar jobs. These two functions at least simulate what I imagine goes on behind those locked panels inside real elevators.)

Usually, a class will store data fields privately and make all of its functions public. But as elevator illustrates, you can also make member functions private to a class. When you do, those member functions can be called *only* by other functions in this same class. No other statements outside of the elevator class can call buttonUp or buttonDown.

In this simulation, it doesn't matter whether buttonUp and buttonDown are private or public. However, this arrangement does mimic the way real elevators work; floors and people do not examine an elevator's internal circuits to determine which direction the lift is traveling. Only an elevator can do that—in real life and in the simulated environment here.

Like the PERSON.H and FLOOR.H header files, ELEVATOR.H also declares a collection class. Here, elevCollection declares an array ea of elevator objects (line 34), using the MAXELEVS constant from ELEVSIM for the array size. The collection gives the program a simple means to access all of the elevators in the building, and it simplifies the job of revising the program if you later need to change the way elevator objects are stored in memory. In that case, all you need to do is rewrite the elevCollection class. No other parts of the program will require changes.

Implementing the elevator *Class*

As you might expect, the implementations of the elevator and elevCollection member functions are the most complex in the simulation. Even so, there are almost no new elements in ELEVATOR.CPP (Listing 5.14), and you should be able to understand most of the code by reading the comments. I'll explain only the trickier parts in the listing.

Listing 5.14. ELEVATOR.CPP

```
1:  // elevator.cpp -- Elevator class module
2:
3:  #include <disp.h>
4:  #include "elevator.h"
5:
6:  /* -- The elevator class constructor. This function runs for each
7:  elevator variable as it comes into being. It initializes the
8:  elevator's location, number of people on board, etc. */
9:
10: elevator::elevator()
11: {
12:     elevNumber = -1;              // Elevator number not assigned
13:     timeToAction = ELEVWAIT;      // Time elevator waits at floor
14:     floorNumber = 0;              // Current floor number
15:     stopped = 1;                  // Elevator is stopped at floor
16:     direction = NODIRECTION;      // Elevator direction not set
17:     passengers = 0;               // No passengers on board
18:
19: /* -- Reset all floor buttons inside elevator. */
20:
21:     for (int i = 0; i < MAXFLOORS; i++)
22:         buttons[i] = 0;
23: }
24:
```

The constructor initializes an elevator variable's data fields. It also sets the buttons inside to 0 (off). As I've said before, this is typical: Most constructors do little more than initialize a few fields and quit. Keep in mind too that these actions occur when the program allocates storage space for an elevator variable.

A few other functions in the ELEVATOR module also perform simple jobs. While reading this code, imagine how elevators work, and try to picture in your mind how the program simulates a real elevator's actions. (The comments in the listing explain each function's purpose.):

Listing 5.14. ELEVATOR.CPP (continued)

```
25:    /* -- Assign number to this elevator. The first elevator must be
26:    number 0, the next 1, and so on. These numbers are not displayed. */
27:
28:    void elevator::setelevNumber(int n)
29:    {
30:        elevNumber = n;
31:    }
32:
33:    /* -- Return true if there are any buttons inside the elevator
34:    pressed for floors above the current floor. Elevators use this
35:    function to determine whether there are passengers traveling to
36:    higher floors. */
37:
38:    int elevator::buttonUp(void)
39:    {
40:        for (int i = floorNumber + 1; i < MAXFLOORS; i++)
41:            if (buttons[i]) return TRUE;
42:        return FALSE;
43:    }
44:
45:    /* -- Return true if there are any buttons inside the elevator
46:    pressed for floors below the current floor. Elevators use this
47:    function to determine whether there are passengers traveling to
48:    lower floors. */
49:
50:    int elevator::buttonDown(void)
51:    {
52:        for (int i = 0; i < floorNumber; i++)
53:            if (buttons[i]) return TRUE;
54:        return FALSE;
55:    }
56:
57:    /* -- Display this elevator, showing its direction, the number of
58:    people travelling up and down, and the elevator cable. */
59:
60:    void elevator::showElevator(void)
61:    {
62:        int row = 20 - (floorNumber * 2);    // Display row
63:        int col = 10 + (elevNumber * 7);     // Display column
64:
65:        if (floorNumber < MAXFLOORS - 2) {
66:            disp_move(row - 3, col);
67:            disp_puts("  :  ");                // Display elevator cable
```

```
68:     }
69:     if (floorNumber < MAXFLOORS - 1) {
70:         disp_move(row - 2, col);
71:         disp_puts("  :  ");                    // Display more cable
72:         disp_move(row - 1, col);
73:         disp_puts("__:__");                    // Display elevator roof
74:     }
75:     disp_startstand();                         // Start reversed video
76:     disp_move(0, col + 2);
77:     disp_printf("%d", floorNumber);            // Floor # at top of screen
78:     disp_move(row, col);
79:     if (direction == UP)                       // Display direction
80:         disp_puts("Up ");
81:     else if (direction == DOWN)
82:         disp_puts("Dn ");
83:     else
84:         disp_puts("-- ");
85:     disp_printf("%02d", passengers);           // Number of passengers
86:     disp_endstand();                           // End reversed video
87:     if (floorNumber > 0) {
88:         disp_move(row + 2, col);               // Erase old elevator so
89:         disp_puts("      ");                   //   it appears to move
90:         disp_move(row + 1, col);
91:         disp_puts("      ");
92:     }
93: }
94:
```

> **Note:** To port the program to another system, or to convert the display from text to a more realistic-looking bit-mapped graphics system, you'll need to modify showElevator to depict a single elevator, showing the direction, the number of passengers inside, and so on. OOP makes such modifications easier than conventional code because it encapsulates the programmed duties of an elevator object in the class. Even without reading the full program, you can be sure that this function handles all of the class display responsibilities.

The next three functions, setDirection, elevStopping, and action, control the movements of elevators during the simulation. Together, they implement an algorithm (see Figure 5.4) that specifies how elevators respond to various situations, what to do if buttons are pressed on other floors to signal for an elevator, whether to stop at a floor, and other tasks. I wrote the algorithm as an outline from which I coded the class functions; this is not C++, of course.

```
if elevator is stopped
  discharge any passengers
  if direction is not set
    load one passenger and set direction
  load another passenger travelling in current direction
  if ready to start moving
    if direction is not set
      decide on next direction (1)
    if direction is not set and not on ground floor
      set direction to down
    if direction is not set
      continue waiting on this floor
    else
      start moving
else if elevator is not stopped
  if elevator has reached the next floor
      change floor number
      decide on next direction (1)
      decide whether to stop at this floor (2)
      if stopping
        stop the elevator
      else
        continue moving

(1) decide on next direction
  if passengers are travelling to a higher floor
    set direction to up
  else if passengers are travelling to a lower floor
    set direction to down
  else if any floors above are signalling in any direction
    set direction to up
  else if any floors below are signalling in any direction
    set direction to down
  else
    set direction to none

(2) decide whether to stop at this floor
  stop if there are any passengers getting off here
  else stop if there are any passengers waiting for elevator in
      same direction
  else stop if this is the first floor
  else stop if this is the ground floor
  else stop if direction is none
  else don't stop
```

Figure 5.4. This algorithm, expressed in outline form, controls the movements of elevators in the simulation.

> **Note:** The elevator algorithm represents my casual observations about how elevators work, and it may not be complete. Although I've ridden in plenty of elevators, I've never built a real one. And after all, the purpose of this program is to demonstrate C++ classes in action, not to get you started with your own elevator company.

Listing 5.14. ELEVATOR.CPP (continued)

```
 95:   /* -- Decide on the direction the elevator should travel next. */
 96:
 97:   void elevator::setDirection(floorCollection &theFloors)
 98:   {
 99:       if (buttonUp()) direction = UP;
100:       else if (buttonDown()) direction = DOWN;
101:       else if (theFloors.signalUp(floorNumber)) direction = UP;
102:       else if (theFloors.signalDown(floorNumber)) direction = DOWN;
103:       else direction = NODIRECTION;
104:   }
105:
106:   /* -- Decide whether elevator should stop at the current floor. */
107:
108:   int elevator::elevStopping(floorCollection &theFloors)
109:   {
110:       if (buttons[floorNumber])
111:          return TRUE;               // Passengers getting off
112:       else if (theFloors.signalSameDir(direction, floorNumber))
113:          return TRUE;               // Persons waiting for elevator
114:       else if (floorNumber == 0)
115:          return TRUE;               // Stop at ground floor
116:       else if (floorNumber == MAXFLOORS - 1)
117:          return TRUE;               // Stop at highest floor
118:       else if (direction == NODIRECTION)
119:          return TRUE;               // No signals above or below
120:       else
121:          return FALSE;              // Keep moving
122:   }
123:
124:   /* -- Perform all required actions for this elevator. This function
125:   runs once for every tick of the simulation's clock. */
126:
127:   void elevator::action(floorCollection &theFloors,
128:       persCollection &thePersons)
129:   {
```

```
130:      int pdest;              // A person's destination
131:      int newdirection;       // New direction for elevator
132:
133:  /* -- Take care of actions for an elevator stopped at a floor. The
134:  "else" clause to this statement handles actions for elevators
135:  currently moving between floors. If elevator is stopped, the first job
136:  is to discharge any passengers travelling to this floor. */
137:
138:      if (stopped) {
139:          passengers -= thePersons.discharge(elevNumber, floorNumber);
140:
141:  /* -- If the direction is not set (nobody on board), load one person
142:  and set the direction to that person's destination. In other words
143:  if the elevator doesn't know where it's going, the first person to
144:  get on board decides the elevator's direction. */
145:
146:          if ((direction == NODIRECTION) && (passengers < CAPACITY)) {
147:              if (thePersons.loadAny(elevNumber, floorNumber, pdest)) {
148:                  passengers++;               // Count passenger
149:                  timeToAction++;             // Takes time to get in
150:                  buttons[pdest] = 1;         // Press destination button
151:                  if (pdest > floorNumber)    // First person on board
152:                      direction = UP;         //   sets elevator's direction
153:                  else
154:                      direction = DOWN;
155:              }
156:          }
157:
158:  /* -- If the direction is set (there's at least one person on board),
159:  pick up additional passengers waiting to go in that same direction.
160:  Stop doing this when elevator is full. It takes some time to load one
161:  person, so add 1 second to elapsed time.*/
162:
163:          if ((direction != NODIRECTION) && (passengers < CAPACITY)) {
164:              if (thePersons.loadOne(elevNumber,
165:              floorNumber, direction, pdest))  // Then if another person
166:              {                                //   climbs on board...
167:                  passengers++;                // Count the newcomer
168:                  timeToAction++;              // Takes time to get in
169:                  buttons[pdest] = 1;          // Press dest. button
170:                  if (passengers >= CAPACITY)  // Leave immediately if
171:                      timeToAction = 0;        //   elevator is full
172:              }
173:          }
174:
```

```
175:    /* -- If ready to start moving (elapsed time is 0 or less), perform
176:    final actions before leaving for the next floor. For instance, If the
177:    direction is still not set, there are no passengers on board. In
178:    that case, look for signals from other floors. If there are no
179:    signals, head down unless on ground floor. If a new direction is
180:    selected, reset the floor's up or down button and start moving.*/
181:
182:            if (timeToAction-- <= 0) {
183:                if (direction == NODIRECTION)
184:                    setDirection(theFloors);
185:                if ((direction == NODIRECTION) && (floorNumber > 0))
186:                    direction = DOWN;
187:                if (direction == NODIRECTION)
188:                    timeToAction = ELEVWAIT;          // Stay at floor 0
189:                else {                                // Ready to start moving
190:                    theFloors.                        // Reset floor up or
191:                        resetButton(direction,        //   down button
192:                        floorNumber);
193:                    stopped = 0;                      // Tell elevator to move
194:                    timeToAction = TRAVELTIME;        // Set time to next floor
195:                }
196:            }
197:        }
198:        else if (timeToAction-- <= 0) {               // If moved to next floor
199:            if (direction == UP)                      // Change floor number
200:                floorNumber++;                        //   to go up,
201:            else
202:                floorNumber--;                        //   or down.
203:            setDirection(theFloors);                  // Decide direction
204:            if (elevStopping(theFloors)) {            // If elevator should stop
205:                theFloors.                            // Reset floor up or
206:                    resetButton(direction,            //   down button.
207:                    floorNumber);
208:                stopped = 1;                          // Stop the elevator
209:                timeToAction = ELEVWAIT;              // Set wait time
210:                buttons[floorNumber] = 0;             // Reset button in elevator
211:            } else
212:                timeToAction = TRAVELTIME;            // Else keep moving
213:        }
214:    }
215:
```

Most of the programming in these three functions, setDirection, elevStopping, and action is simple and well explained in the comments. Notice how lines 97, 108, and 127 declare parameters of class types floorCollection and persCollection. The program passes objects of those types to the elevator::action function, which gives elevators access to the collections of floors and people in the simulation.

Passing object variables to functions in other objects is a very useful technique to know. When designing a new class, instead of referring to global variables of another class type, consider declaring a parameter of that type in the function. This will make your program more adaptable to new situations because, instead of forcing the code to use one or more fixed global variables, statements can pass many different objects to your functions. Except in unusual cases, a function parameter is almost always preferable to a global variable.

That finishes the actions of a single elevator. As I did with the person and floor classes, I also created a class that collects multiple elevator objects, elevCollection. As you'll soon see, this makes it easier for a program to work with a bank of elevators in the simulated building. And it simplifies the later job of modifying the inner storage details of that collection by encapsulating the details inside the class. Here are the function implementations:

Listing 5.14. ELEVATOR.CPP (continued)

```
216:  /* -- Elevator collection constructor. Runs when a variable of typ
217:  elevCollection comes into being. */
218:
219:  elevCollection::elevCollection()
220:  {
221:      for (int i = 0; i < MAXELEVS; i++)
222:          ea[i].setelevNumber(i);              // Assign elevator numbers
223:  }
224:
225:  /* -- Display all elevators in the building. Calls showElevator
226:  function for every elevator object. */
227:
228:  void elevCollection::showElevators(void)
229:  {
230:      for (int i = 0; i < MAXELEVS; i++)
231:          ea[i].showElevator();
232:  }
233:
234:  /* -- Call action() function for every elevator. This function run
235:  for every tick of the simulation's clock. */
236:
237:  void elevCollection::action(floorCollection &theFloors,
238:      persCollection &thePersons)
239:  {
240:      for (int i = 0; i < MAXELEVS; i++)
241:          ea[i].action(theFloors, thePersons);
```

```
242:   }
243:
244:   /* -- Return average number of passengers riding in all elevators. */
245:
246:   int elevCollection::avgRiding(void)
247:   {
248:       int total = 0;
249:
250:       for (int i = 0; i < MAXELEVS; i++)
251:           total += ea[i].getPassengers();
252:       return (total / MAXELEVS);
253:   }
```

Again, most of the code is conventional C++. The constructor (lines 219-223) calls setelevNumber for each object in the elevator array (ea) to assign unique numbers to each elevator in the collection. The showElevators function calls showElevator for every elevator, thus displaying the bank of elevators on screen. The other functions perform similarly, calling functions for each of the elevator objects collected in elevCollection.

In your own programs, when you need more than one object of a class type, consider creating a new class to contain those objects. Have the main program call functions in the new class to access every object in a collection. In general, this is easier to manage than forcing a program to create its own collections—especially when the program needs to perform jobs on groups of objects.

The alternative leads to messy code. For example, I could have designed the ELEVATOR module as only a single elevator class. But then, the main program would need to define storage for the multiple elevators needed in the simulation. This means that if I change the way elevators work, I might also have to modify the way the program stores multiple elevator variables in memory. By creating the collection class elevCollection, I contain those details inside the module where they are easily modified. No statements other than those in elevCollection functions refer to the ea array; therefore, if I want to store elevators on the heap or create separate variables for them, I can do so by modifying the class without even reading any of the other parts of the program.

Note: When creating collection classes similar to elevCollection, I find that it's helpful to use names for functions like elevCollection::showElevators (plural) that call similar functions like elevator::showElevator (singular). I also use plural names for variables of the collection type—theElevators of type elevCollection, and theFloors of type floorCollection. For individual variables of a class, I'd probably use singular names—anElevator of type elevator and onePerson of type person.

Introducing Inheritance

Before continuing with the final listings in the elevator simulation, it's time to consider one of OOP's major contributions to programming—*inheritance.* With this device, a new class can inherit all the properties of another class. In this way, classes can reuse existing programming.

Inheritance lets you mix and match data types in ways that are difficult if not downright impossible with conventional programming techniques. When writing new code, inheritance lets you select classes with features that are close to those you need and then simply add new elements that describe how the new class *differs* from the old.

For example, in a program that displays pop-up windows, you might select a `window` class from another program, or perhaps, from a class library that you purchased from a software toolkit vendor. If the existing class doesn't have all the features you need—for example, perhaps it displays only single-line titles, and you need a double-line one—you can simply create a new class that inherits the existing one. Then you can add the missing details to display double-line titles without having to rewrite any of the original class's properties.

Note: The next two chapters explain how to create and use a `window` class similar to the hypothetical one mentioned here.

After using OOP in a few projects, you'll begin to appreciate just how valuable inheritance can be. Instead of revising subroutines to accommodate new specifications, you can inherit classes and add or replace programming to remold the class to a new design. With classes, you'll rarely need to modify existing code to make it perform new tricks. With common subroutines, new demands often lead programmers to create many copies of similar routines, which are difficult to maintain and even harder to debug.

Using Inheritance

When a new class inherits the properties of another class, the new class is called a *derived class.* The original class is called the *base class.* A derived class inherits the properties of a base class—all of the data fields and functions in the base. A derived class can also be a base class—in other words, one class can inherit the properties of another class, which may inherit the properties of a third class, and so on.

> **Note:** Some OOP texts use the terms *ancestor* and *descendant* to describe the relationship between base and derived classes. I'll use the more common C++ terms derived class and base class here.

To create a derived class, insert a colon and the base class name after the new class name. For example, suppose that you are writing a program to keep track of animal statistics. You might begin with a class named `animal`, declared at lines 10-16 in Listing 5.15, ANIMAL.CPP.

Listing 5.15. ANIMAL.CPP

```
 1:  // animal.cpp -- Inheritance example
 2:
 3:  #include <stream.hpp>
 4:  #include <string.h>
 5:  #include <stdlib.h>
 6:
 7:  #define FALSE     0
 8:  #define TRUE      1
 9:
10:  class animal {
11:     private:
12:        char name[30];     // The animal's name
13:     public:
14:        animal(const char *s);
15:        const char *getName(void) { return name; }
16:  };
17:
```

The `animal` class's private section declares a 30-character string for the animal's name. A public constructor (`animal(...)`) initializes variables of class `animal`. And a single other function, `getName`, returns an animal's name.

So far, this class is similar to others you've seen. But `animal` is too general for direct use, and before the program declares any variables, it needs to declare more specific classes:

Listing 5.15. ANIMAL.CPP (continued)

```
18:  class mammal : public animal {
19:     private:
20:        int offspring;        // Number of offspring
21:     public:
```

```
22:            mammal(const char *s, int nc);
23:        int numOffspring(void) { return offspring; }
24:   };
25:
```

One of those classes is `mammal`. A mammal is an animal, and therefore, the program declares `mammal` as a derived class that inherits properties from the `animal` base class. The phrase : `public animal` after the new class name (`mammal`), tells C++ to include in `mammal` every data and function member from `animal`.

Declaring the base class to be public in a derived class tells C++ that the inherited properties should retain their original status. In other words, if the base class is public, public members from that class remain public in the derived class. Likewise, private members from the base class remain private. You could replace `public` with `private`, which makes all inherited members private, regardless of their original status:

```
18:   class mammal : private animal {
```

However, if you specify a base class as private this way, a class that derives from the newly derived class cannot use any of the base class members, even if those fields were public originally. The effect of this may be easier to understand with a simple example. Suppose that you declare one class named A and then create a derived class B that inherits the properties of A:

```
class A {
   ...
}

class B : private A {
   ...
}
```

Class B derives from A. Everything in A is also in B. However, because A is declared to be private, if you declare a third class C that derives from B,

```
class C : public B {
   ...
}
```

because A was declared private to B, C cannot use any of A's members. Only B has access to the public members in A. C can use only the public items declared in B.

Carrying this one step further, if a fourth class D derives from C, because B is public to C, D can use everything declared in B and C. But D can't reach back to the items in A; the private key word in B's class declaration prevents any future derivations from accessing A's members.

> **Note:** If you don't specify either `public` or `private` for an inherited base class, the status defaults to private. This feature is a holdover from early C++ versions and should be avoided. Always preface a base class name with `public` or `private` in a derived class declaration.

Getting back to the animal farm, because `mammal` inherits the properties of its base class, a `mammal` has a 30-character `name` data field, it has an `animal` constructor, and it has a `getName` function. To these inherited members, a `mammal` adds an `int` field (`offspring`), a new constructor (`mammal(...)`), and a member function (`numOffspring`).

In this simple example, a `mammal` class records the average number of offspring at birth for this type of animal. That statistic differentiates the new class from the base. Instead of forcing you to create a new data type for a `mammal`, C++ lets you design a new class by specifying only the items that differ from the members of another general class such as `animal`.

The program also needs to keep records on birds. A bird is an animal, of course, but it is not a mammal. So again, the demonstration creates a new class `bird` that inherits the properties of the `animal` class:

Listing 5.15. ANIMAL.CPP (continued)

```
26:  class bird : public animal {
27:      private:
28:          int eggs;          // Average number of eggs
29:          int nesting;       // True if builds nest
30:      public:
31:          bird(const char *s, int ne, int nests);
32:          int getEggs(void) { return eggs; }
33:          const char *buildsNest()
34:            { if (nesting) return "True"; else return "False"; }
35:  };
36:
```

As with `mammal`, the new `bird` class specifies its base class with a colon and the base class name in the declaration line. Because `animal` is declared to be `public` to `bird`, any further derived classes can also access the members in `animal`. For instance, suppose you write

```
class extinct : public bird {
    ...
}
```

The new extinct class inherits the properties of bird. Because bird also inherits from animal and because it did that by using the public key word (line 26), the extinct class can use all of the public members of the animal class. A variable of class extinct has a name field and a getName function for retrieving that string.

In C++, it's typical for a class to be constructed on the foundations of many such base classes. With inheritance, you can write code that builds on your previous work and on the work of others. Best of all, there's rarely any need to revise older code to meet the new specifications. The new programming simply inherits the old, updating the original design as needed to accommodate new situations as they arise.

Classes that inherit properties from other classes can use the public members of the base class, just as though those members were declared directly in the derived class. The main section of ANIMAL plus two support functions show good examples of this:

Listing 5.15. ANIMAL.CPP (continued)

```
37:    void showMammal(mammal &m);
38:    void showBird(bird &b);
39:
40:    main()
41:    {
42:        mammal homoSapiens("Homo Sapiens", 1);
43:        mammal gopher("Gopher", 9);
44:        mammal armadillo("Armadillo", 4);
45:        mammal houseMouse("House Mouse", 12);
46:
47:        bird woodDuck("Wood Duck", 15, FALSE);
48:        bird sandhillCrane("Sandhill Crane", 2, TRUE);
49:        bird loon("Loon", 3, TRUE);
50:
51:        cout << "\n\nMammals:";
52:        showMammal(homoSapiens);
53:        showMammal(gopher);
54:        showMammal(armadillo);
55:        showMammal(houseMouse);
56:
57:        cout << "\n\nBirds:";
58:        showBird(woodDuck);
59:        showBird(sandhillCrane);
60:        showBird(loon);
61:
62:        exit(0);
63:    }
```

```
64:
65:     /* -- Display functions */
66:
67:     void showMammal(mammal &m)
68:     {
69:         cout << "\nName ............... " << (m.getName());
70:         cout << "\n Avg offspring ..... " << (m.numOffspring());
71:     }
72:
73:     void showBird(bird &b)
74:     {
75:         cout << "\nName ............... " << (b.getName());
76:         cout << "\n Avg no. eggs ...... " << (b.getEggs());
77:         cout << "\n Builds a nest ..... " << (b.buildsNest());
78:     }
79:
```

Lines 42-49 show how to define variables of a class type and pass arguments to the class constructors. The first of these lines creates a variable named homoSapiens of type mammal. It passes the two arguments "Homo Sapiens" and 1 to the mammal() constructor, which saves the string and value in the class's data fields. Earlier, you learned how to create variables of class types with parameterless constructors (or with no constructors):

```
elevator anElevator;
```

To use a constructor that declares one or more parameters, just include the initializing values in parentheses after the variable name:

```
mammal gopher("Gopher", 9);
```

This *looks* like a function call, but it's not. It's a variable definition. However, the effect is to call the mammal's class constructor for the gopher variable passing a string and number to that constructor's parameters.

The other definitions are similar, but in the case of the bird variables at lines 47-49, an additional parameter is passed to the constructor.

After defining the variables used in the program, the code goes on to call two common functions, showMammal and showBird (lines 67-78). Look carefully at lines 69 and 75. These each call the getName function in the mammal and bird arguments, m and b. Looking back at the declarations of these class types, you can see there is no getName function. But there is a getName function in the animal class that each of these new classes inherits; therefore, variables of mammal and bird classes can call getName because they inherited that function along with all the other items in animal.

Finally, ANIMAL implements the class constructors. Because two of the classes (mammal and bird) inherit the properties from class animal, their constructors require special treatment:

Listing 5.15. ANIMAL.CPP (continued)

```
80:    /* -- Class constructors */
81:
82:    animal::animal(const char *s)
83:    {
84:        strncpy(name, s, 29);
85:    }
86:
87:    mammal::mammal(const char *s, int nc) : animal(s)
88:    {
89:        offspring = nc;
90:    }
91:
92:    bird::bird(const char *s, int ne, int nests) : animal(s)
93:    {
94:        eggs = ne;
95:        nesting = nests;
96:    }
```

The animal constructor is the simple case—a function that initializes a variable of the class type. In this case, the function calls the strncpy function to copy up to 29 characters of a passed argument string s to the name field in the animal variable. The constructor for the animal class is similar to those you've seen before.

The mammal and bird constructors are different. Like the animal constructor, they initialize variables of their class by assigning values to data fields. But they also include a new element at the end of their declarations: a colon, a base class name, and a parameter name in parentheses (see lines 87 and 92).

This special notation tells C++ to pass one or more arguments to the constructor of the base class. In other words, when the program creates a variable of type mammal with the line,

```
mammal dolphin("Dolphin", 1);
```

C++ calls the mammal constructor to initialize the dolphin variable. It passes a string and a value to the parameters declared by that constructor (see line 22). When that constructor runs (see line 87), it passes the first of these parameters to the base constructor for animal, which saves the animal's name in the name data field.

Chaining constructors this way is a fundamental tool in C++ programming. Each base constructor initializes the fields (and possibly, performs other duties) for its class. Derived class constructors only have to provide the additional details needed to initialize variables of the derived class and to specify which arguments or values should be passed to the base constructor.

We'll return to constructors and inheritance again—there are some other details about this subject that I'm purposely postponing. Before continuing with this chapter, be sure that you run the ANIMAL demonstration and that you understand how the derived classes mammal and bird inherit the members declared in the base animal class.

> **Note:** Constructors that have no arguments do not have to be specified in a derived class's constructor. In such cases, the base constructors will still be called automatically when variables of a derived class are allocated storage space.

The building Class

This chapter began with a simple demonstration of a simulation in its barest form (SIMULATE.CPP in Listing 5.1). The program used the declarations in ACTION.H (Listing 5.4) implemented in ACTION.CPP (Listing 5.5). The purpose of SIMULATE was to provide a starting place. It served only as a shell to demonstrate a few fundamentals.

But was that earlier effort wasted? Not at all. Try running SIMULATE again. As you can see, this program's simple output of the time remaining when you press **<Spacebar>** bears no relation to an elevator. How can the new program make use of this earlier work?

The answer is inheritance. By inheriting the properties of the action class declared in ACTION.H, the simulation can use the programming that's already completed and tested. Listing 5.16, BUILDING.H, puts this idea to the test.

Listing 5.16. BUILDING.H

```
 1:   // building.h -- Header file for building.cpp
 2:
 3:   #ifndef __BUILDING_H
 4:   #define __BUILDING_H     1       // Prevent multiple #includes
 5:
 6:   #include "action.h"
 7:   #include "person.h"
 8:   #include "floor.h"
 9:   #include "elevator.h"
10:
11:   class building : public action {
12:      private:
13:         persCollection thePersons;     // People in the system
14:         floorCollection theFloors;     // Floors in the building
15:         elevCollection theElevators;   // Elevators in the building
```

```
16:      public:
17:          int continues(void);
18:          void perform(void);
19:          void display(void);
20:  };
21:
22:  #endif   // __BUILDING_H
```

What is a building? For the purpose of writing this chapter's elevator simulation, a building is a set of people, floor, and elevator objects. The `building` class encapsulates this notion in one neat package.

Line 11 shows that `building` inherits the properties of `action`—the simulation-engine class declared in ACTION.H. This means that a `building` variable has access to all the public members in `action`. (See Listing 5.4 or examine the ACTION.H file to refresh your memory about these members.)

In addition to its inheritance from `action`, the new `building` class adds three private data members of its own. These are `thePersons`, `theFloors`, and `theElevators`—declarations of the collection classes that group `person`, `floor`, and `elevator` objects. The new class is truly a high-level object. It inherits properties of another class (`action`), and it declares data members that are themselves objects—the collections of people, floors, and elevators that make up the program's simulated building.

Replacement Member Functions

When you compare the new `building` class in BUILDING.H with the base `action` class in ACTION.H, you'll see that the three member functions in the derived `building` have the identical names, return types, and parameter lists (`void` in these cases) as in the base. As a result, the derived member functions *replace* the same functions in the base.

A `building` needs to make this modification because the original `continues`, `perform`, and `display` member functions in `action` don't perform the jobs needed for the elevator simulation. But the other base functions such as `setTime` and `getTime` will do just fine, and the derived class can use them directly. It doesn't have to replace *every* member, only those that need additional capabilities for the new class.

This is typical. A derived class inherits the properties of a base data type. Some of the base member functions perform perfectly well. Others won't do at all and need rewriting. In that event, just redeclare the original member functions in the derived class as `building` does here. The program can then call the replacement methods without losing access to the inherited methods from the base.

Replacing member functions in a derived class is your primary tool for modifying how a class behaves. When replacing inherited functions this way, the only rule is to declare the functions identically in the derived class as in the base. For example, suppose class `base` has three functions:

```
class base {
    public:
        void f1(void);
        int f2(void);
        float f3(void);
};
```

Then another class, `derived`, inherits the properties of `base`. At the same time, it replaces function `f3`:

```
class derived : public base {
    public:
        float f3(void);
};
```

If the program now defines a variable q of type `derived` and executes q.f3(), the f3 replacement function in `derived` will run, not the function inherited from the base. The statements q.f1() and q.f2() call the inherited functions in the `base` class. For this to work, however, the replacement function must have the identical return type, name, and parameter list.

Note: When a derived class replaces a base class's member function, the original function doesn't disappear. It's still available, as the implementation of the `building` class shows in the next section.

Implementing the `building` Class

Listing 5.17, BUILDING.CPP, implements the member functions declared in the `building` class. In this class, there is no constructor, and the listing begins with the first member function.

Listing 5.17. BUILDING.CPP

```
1:  // building.cpp -- Building class module
2:
3:  #include <conio.h>
4:  #include <disp.h>
5:  #include "building.h"
6:
```

```
 7:    /* -- Return true if building simulation should continue. Adds
 8:    test for <Esc> keypress to action::continues(). */
 9:
10:    int building::continues(void)
11:    {
12:        if (kbhit())                     // If there is a keypress,
13:            if (getch() == ESCKEY)       // And if it's the ESC key,
14:                setTime(0);              //  set time remaining to 0
15:        return action::continues();      // Return ancestor fn result
16:    }
17:
```

The replacement continues function in the building class takes over from the function of that same name in the base action class from which building derives. I needed to replace the original function because I wanted the program to recognize an <Esc> keypress as a signal to end the simulation. In the original continues function (see ACTION.CPP, Listing 5.5, lines 20-23), the simulation ends only when time runs out. Because ELEVSIM may be programmed to run for hours, it needs an alternate exit. At the same time however, I did not want to do away with the original function; the simulation must still end when there's no time left.

Inheritance makes it easy to solve such problems. Lines 12-14 add the new check for any keypress (line 12), and if one is sensed through the kbhit function declared in CONIO.H, line 13 checks for the <Esc> key. If it senses <Esc>, line 14 calls the setTime function inherited from action to set the remaining time to 0. This forces the simulation to run out of time and as a consequence, to end.

Examine line 15 carefully. The expression action::continues() calls the base class continues function, even though the derived building class replaces that member. Despite this, the base class function is still available from inside the replacement. To call the original code, the program specifies the base class name and a double colon (action::). This tells C++ to call the member function in the base class instead of making a recursive call to the replacement function, which it would do without the action:: preface.

The new routine shows how replacement functions can enhance a function in the base class instead of replacing the original code completely. However, it's up to you whether a replacement function should call the inherited function. If the replacement needs to do away with the old code, that's fine. There's no rule that says you must call a replaced base-class function.

The next function shows a good example of this option. As in building::continues, the function also replaces a base class function, but in this case, it completely replaces the original code:

Listing 5.17. BUILDING.CPP (continued)

```
18:    /* -- Perform the building's actions, that is, moving people in
19:    elevators between floors. Each call to this function represents the
20:    passage of one second (not necessarily in real time). */
```

```
21:
22:   void building::perform(void)
23:   {
24:       thePersons.action();
25:       theElevators.action(theFloors, thePersons);
26:       reduceTime(1);          // One second passes
27:       totalTime++;            // Count seconds for time display
28:       disp_move(24, 64);      // Display time remaining
29:       disp_printf("%05d", getTime());
30:   }
31:
```

In the original action base class, the perform member function displayed a message, waited for you to press <Spacebar>, and reduced the time remaining by 900 seconds. None of these dummy actions is appropriate for the elevator simulation; therefore, the replacement action member function in building does not call the original code.

Instead, the new perform activates the elevator simulation by calling the action functions in thePersons and theElevators—two of building's three private data fields. Line 26 calls the inherited reduceTime function to reduce the time remaining by 1 second. It also increments a global variable (totalTime) and displays the time left.

These are very different operations than those performed by the original perform function in the action base class. One of the myths of OOP is that derived classes closely resemble their base ancestors. But that's not always so. Derived classes may *radically* alter what a base class does, using only the members that perform as needed. In this example, the new building completely replaces the perform function, but it keeps the getTime and other functions from the old simulation demo that don't need modifying. The result is an entirely new use for an old class—and an efficient use of existing programming.

> **Note:** Another key point here is the way the building class reuses action's programming without requiring you to change one spec of the original code. You may have to write new code to replace an original member function, as in the new perform function. But you do not have to hack apart the rest of the ACTION module to get it to work as needed in this new situation. As a result, you can still compile the original SIMULATE program even though the new simulation radically modifies the demonstration's action class. This concept—the preservation of base class declarations—has important consequences for documenting the evolution of a program. And it aids debugging by allowing old test modules to compile and run despite radical changes made to older designs.

Finally in the BUILDING module is the replacement display function. As for perform, the display requirements of the elevator simulation are much different from the simple SIMULATE demonstration, and the new function completely replaces the old:

Listing 5.17. BUILDING.CPP (continued)

```
32:   /* -- Update the display, showing  status of floors and elevators,
33:   plus the people waiting on floors or traveling in elevators.
34:   Also show current simulation statistics and the elapsed time on
35:   the bottom row. */
36:
37:   void building::display(void)
38:   {
39:       long t;
40:       unsigned hours = 0;
41:       unsigned minutes = 0;
42:       unsigned seconds = 0;
43:
44:       theFloors.showFloors(thePersons);
45:       theElevators.showElevators();
46:       avgWait = theFloors.avgWaiting();
47:       avgRide = theElevators.avgRiding();
48:       disp_move(24, 1);
49:       disp_printf(
50:        "%05u     %05u     %05u     %04u     %04u     %05u%5d%5d",
51:        totalPeople, inBuilding, leftBuilding, avgWait,
52:        avgRide, tookStair, MAXELEVS, MAXFLOORS);
53:       disp_move(24, 71);
54:       t = totalTime;
55:       if (t >= 3600) {
56:           hours = t / 3600;
57:           t -= (hours * 3600);
58:       }
59:       if (t >= 60) {
60:           minutes = t / 60;
61:           t -= (minutes * 60);
62:       }
63:       seconds = t;
64:       disp_printf("%02d:%02d:%02d", hours, minutes, seconds);
65:   }
```

The new display function calls the appropriate member functions in theFloors and theElevators (lines 44-45). This updates most of the display by calling on these objects to represent themselves on screen.

The rest of the new function calculates and displays various statistics on the bottom line. Except for the few calls to class member functions, the code is straightforward C++. Notice how lines 46 and 47 call on the class variables for the average number of people waiting for and riding in elevators.

Completing the Elevator Simulation

At last, light at the end of the tunnel! (Or maybe it's an elevator shaft.) Listing 5.18, ELEVSIM.CPP finishes the elevator simulation.

Listing 5.18. ELEVSIM.CPP

```
1:   // elevsim.cpp -- Elevator simulation in C++
2:
3:   #include <stream.hpp>
4:   #include <stdlib.h>
5:   #include <time.h>
6:   #include <disp.h>
7:   #include "building.h"
8:
9:   /* -- Function prototype used only by main() */
10:
11:  void initDisplay(void);
12:
13:  /* -- Global variables. These are the only global variables used by
14:  the simulation. Except for the main building object (theAction), the
15:  variables hold the statistics displayed on the bottom line. */
16:
17:  unsigned totalPeople;        // Number of people handled
18:  unsigned inBuilding;         // People in building now
19:  unsigned leftBuilding;       // People who left building
20:  unsigned avgWait;            // Average no. people waiting
21:  unsigned avgRide;            // Average no. people in elevators
22:  unsigned tookStair;          // Number people who walked
23:  unsigned totalTime;          // Seconds simulation has run
24:
25:  building theAction;          // Building simulation object
26:
```

Except for system header files at lines 3-6, the main ELEVSIM program includes only a single header—BUILDING.H. With few exceptions, most of the code that drives the simulation is neatly hidden away in that file's building class declaration.

Line 11 declares one of the exceptions: a lone function, `initDisplay`, which ELEVSIM uses to initialize the Zortech display package.

Lines 17-23 define storage for the global variables declared `extern` in ELEVSIM.H. When many modules need to share the same globals, it's important that only one place in the program defines storage space for those variables. A good way to accomplish this is to declare the variables `extern` in a header file that other modules can include. Then define the global variables as done here in the main program. (You can also place the definitions into another file that the main module can include.)

Line 25 adds one additional global variable to the previous group. Variable `theAction` is of type `building`, and in this case, `theAction` is truly where the action is. This single variable collects all the people, elevators, and floors for the simulation. It also provides access to the dozens of member functions covered earlier. In a way, `theAction` *is* the program; all that remains is to set the object into motion:

Listing 5.18. ELEVSIM.CPP (continued)

```
27:  /* -- Note: Enable one of the optional sleep() or msleep() statements
28:  below to slow the simulation on a fast system. */
29:
30:  main()
31:  {
32:      srand(time(NULL));   // Randomize random-number generator
33:      initDisplay();       // Initialize the display
34:      theAction.display(); // Display the elevators and labels
35:
36:  /* -- This while-loop handles the entire simulation. It cycles
37:  while the building object (named theAction) returns true through
38:  its 'continues()' function. */
39:
40:      while (theAction.continues()) {
41:  //      sleep(1);          // 1 real second == 1 simulated second
42:  //      msleep(250);       // 1/4 real second = 1 simulated second
43:  //      msleep(125);       // 1/8 real second = 1 simulated second
44:          theAction.perform(); // Perform all simulation actions
45:          theAction.display(); // Update the display
46:      }
47:
48:  /* -- Perform an orderly exit. */
49:
50:      disp_move(24, 0);    // Position cursor on last line
51:      disp_showcursor();   // Make cursor visible
52:      disp_close();        // Close display package
```

```
53:     exit(0);                    // Exit with no errors to report
54:   }
55:
```

Most programs that are larger than a page or two benefit from a small `main` function. If you find that you are inserting low-level details into `main`, you may need to redesign the project. By the time you write the `main` function, most of the work should be done. This is certainly true in ELEVSIM, where `main` occupies only a few lines.

First, `main` scrambles the random number generator (remove line 32 to repeat the *same* simulation for each new run). It then calls `initDisplay` to prepare the screen and makes a single call to `theAction`'s `display` function to fill in the elevators and floors just before the simulation starts to roll. That happens at lines 40-46, which cycle calls to `perform` and `display` while `continues` reports that the simulation should go on. These three functions are the replacement members in `building`, and they control the entire simulation.

Because this simulation does not run in real time, lines 41-43 suggest three ways to slow the action on fast systems. Enable one of these lines by removing the comment slashes at the beginning. The `sleep` function pauses the program for about 1 second. The `msleep` function pauses for a specified number of milliseconds. With none of these lines enabled, the simulation may run at a ratio of about 10 simulated seconds to 1 second in real time or faster depending on your computer's speed.

Compare this code with the earlier SIMULATE.CPP (Listing 5.1). It's nearly in the same form. But the results, as you can see by running ELEVSIM, are not even close.

The rest of the program prepares the display, showing various static items that don't change during the simulation. There aren't any new elements in this function, and you should be able to understand how it works by reading the comments:

Listing 5.18. ELEVSIM.CPP (continued)

```
56:  /* -- Initialize the display, showing various labels that remain
57:  unchanged throughout the simulation. Also initialize the Zortech
58:  display package for fast screen writes. */
59:
60:  void initDisplay(void)
61:  {
62:      int i;
63:
64:      disp_open();                // Initialize display package
65:      disp_move(0, 0);            // Move to "home" position
66:      disp_eeop();                // Clear the display
67:      disp_hidecursor();          // Make cursor invisible
68:      disp_move(21, 30);          // Display title line
69:      disp_puts(
```

```
70:              "Elevator Simulation from Learning C++ by Tom Swan");
71:          disp_startstand();            // Begin reversed-video display
72:          disp_move(0, 0);
73:          disp_puts("Floors     ");
74:          for (i = 0; i < 10; i++)      // Show reversed video floor
75:              disp_puts("  0     ");    //   numbers at top of screen
76:          disp_move(22, 0);
77:          disp_puts(" Total        In      Left   Avg #   Avg #        ");
78:          disp_puts("Took  Num  Num   Seconds    Elapsed");
79:          disp_move(23, 0);
80:          disp_puts("People      Bldg      Bldg  Waiting Riding     ");
81:          disp_puts("Stair  Elv  Flr     Left        Time");
82:          disp_endstand();              // End reversed-video display
83:          disp_move(1, 0);
84:          for (i = 0; i < 10; i++)      // Display horizontal divider line
85:              disp_puts("--------");
86:
87:  /* -- Display elevator cables. These are redrawn by the elevator
88:  class as needed while elevators move.*/
89:
90:      for (int row = 2; row < 18; row++) {
91:          for (int col = 0; col < MAXELEVS; col++) {
92:              disp_move(row, 12 + (col * 7));
93:              disp_putc(':');
94:          }
95:      }
96:  }
```

That completes ELEVSIM and this chapter's introduction to C++ OOP features. There's more to the OOP story than I've shown you here, but you should now have a good grasp of the fundamentals and be comfortable with the concepts of

- Declaring classes

- Private and public data and function members

- Constructors

- Inline members

- Inheritance

The remaining chapters in this book cover additional OOP features in C++. But it's time to change course a little. You examined ELEVSIM in the order (more or less) that I wrote the code, wading through low-level objects until finally reaching the high level main function at the end. In the next two chapters, you'll take the opposite approach, starting at the top of an existing class library, learning how to use it, and then taking it apart to see what makes it tick. This more closely resembles the way you'll dig into a commercial class library or one that others wrote before you joined their company. As you'll discover next, one of the secrets to learning C++ is knowing how to read classes and to incorporate them into your own code.

Questions and Exercises

5.1. What does the word *encapsulate* refer to in refererence to C++ classes?

5.2. What kinds of functions may use private fields declared in a class?

5.3. What do constructors do?

5.4. Design and test a class named rectangle that outlines a rectangular area on a computer screen.

5.5. Using the rectangle class from exercise 5.4, create a derived class square that outlines a square region on a computer screen.

5.6. Convert to inline functions one or more member functions from the rectangle class in excersise 5.4. If you already used inline member functions, convert them to the normal variety.

5.7. Using the button class from Listing 5.3 (BUTTON2.CPP), design a container class that can store several buttons.

5.8. Reprogram the elevator simulation to simulate two elevators in a 5-story building.

5.9. Using your answer from exercise 5.8, reduce the frequency of new people entering the simulation.

5.10. Again using your answer from exercise 5.8, double the amount of time it takes for an elevator to travel from one floor to the next.

Chapter 6

Building a Class Library—Part 1

Learning a new language like C++ is not the end of the road. It's merely a starting place for future explorations. Sooner or later, one journey most programmers take is to purchase a library of subroutines. For example, to write a graphics program, you could spend time developing your own graphics tools, or you could pick up a library of graphics functions to link to your code. As I've said before (and, no doubt, I'll say again) building on other programmers' work saves time and helps prevent bugs.

In time, many programmers also set out on a longer trip: They build their own programming libraries. If you can't find a library that suits your needs, at least plan to store your modules in reusable form. This is especially important when several programmers need to share modules from a common code pool. Surprisingly, even in the same company, programmers often write the same kinds of routines because it's *too hard* to reuse programming from other projects.

C++ class libraries—collections of class declarations and modules—are ideal for reducing that kind of wasteful effort. Unlike standard subroutine libraries, class libraries let you use inheritance to build new software from tested classes, even if you don't have access to the original source files.

In this chapter and the next, I'll describe the workings of an extensive class library you can use to create programs with pop-up windows and menus. The library—I call it the *LC++ class library* after "Learning C++"—contains a number of classes for creating lists, strings, selection lists, text windows, and program-command menus. All the library's source text is listed here and is stored on disk. (If you ran the READ program, you already have seen an example of what the LC++ class library can do. READ uses the classes described here to control the program's display. The source code for READ is in chapter 8.)

Learning how to use a new class library takes time and patience, and one of the purposes behind these two chapters (6 and 7) is to suggest ways for cutting through the fog in a new library of programming tools. For that reason, instead of starting at the bottom of the class hierarchies as you did in the previous chapter, this time you'll start at the top, running a sample program that uses most of the LC++ class library's features. This will show you what the tools can do, rather than overwhelming you with endless details about how the code works, a common problem in the documentation of many commercial libraries.

After learning in this chapter what the LC++ class library can do, in the next chapter you'll delve into the programming behind the library's many classes. As I explain the various classes and programs in the library, I'll also point out many new C++ features you haven't met before.

> **Note:** You'll need a good bit of free memory available to compile the listings in this chapter and the next. If you have less than about 500K or so *after* booting, you may need to uninstall TSRs, remove device drivers, or take other steps to make more memory available to the compiler.

Last Things First—WinTool

The program listed in this section, WINTOOL, will help you to design pop-up windows for your own programs. It will also show you more about how to use classes and OOP techniques in C++. WINTOOL displays the effects of different attribute values for a window's border, background, and text. After designing a window with the colors or monochrome text attributes you need, you can plug WINTOOL's values into your own code to create windows with those same attributes. Figure 6.1 shows WINTOOL's main display.

Compiling WINTOOL

Make sure that the files listed in Table 6.1 are in the current directory (C:\LCPP\LIB unless you installed the files elsewhere). Then, enter **zz** at the DOS command line to run ZZ.BAT, Listing 6.1. Running the batch file compiles all the separate modules that WINTOOL uses, and links the final WINTOOL.EXE program. Go ahead and run WINTOOL now if you want. Press **<Esc>** to quit.

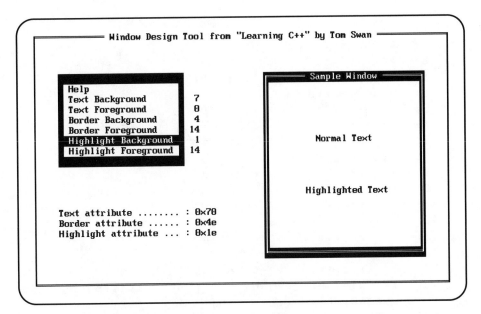

Figure 6.1. WINTOOL's main display. The program, a window-design utility, uses the LC++ class library described in this chapter and in chapter 7.

Table 6.1. Files Needed to Compile WINTOOL

File name	Description
COMMAND.H	Class command module (no corresponding .CPP file)
ERROR.CPP	Error-handling routines module
ERROR.H	Header file for ERROR.CPP
ITEM.CPP	Class item module
ITEM.H	Header file for ITEM.CPP
KEY.CPP	Keyboard-handling routines module
KEY.H	Header file for KEY.CPP
LIST.CPP	Class list module
LIST.H	Header file for LIST.CPP
SELECTOR.CPP	Class selector module
SELECTOR.H	Header file for SELECTOR.CPP
STRITEM.CPP	Class stritem (string item) module
STRITEM.H	Header file for STRITEM.CPP
WINDOW.CPP	Class window module
WINDOW.H	Header file for WINDOW.CPP
WINTOOL.CPP	The WINTOOL main program
WINTOOL.H	Header file for WINTOOL.CPP
ZZ.BAT	Batch file to compile WINTOOL

Listing 6.1. ZZ.BAT

```
 1:  @echo off
 2:  ztc -c key
 3:  if errorlevel==1 goto END
 4:  ztc -c error
 5:  if errorlevel==1 goto END
 6:  ztc -c item
 7:  if errorlevel==1 goto END
 8:  ztc -c stritem
 9:  if errorlevel==1 goto END
10:  ztc -c list
11:  if errorlevel==1 goto END
12:  ztc -c window
13:  if errorlevel==1 goto END
14:  ztc -c selector
15:  if errorlevel==1 goto END
16:  ztc wintool key.obj error.obj stritem.obj item.obj list.obj
     window.obj selector.obj
17:  :END
```

> **Note:** Line 16 in ZZ.BAT is split onto two lines for printing here. The file is stored on disk, but if you have to type it, be sure to join these two lines into one.

The WINTOOL.H Header

Like most programs, WINTOOL stores several constants and other declarations in a header file, Listing 6.2, WINTOOL.H. In addition to its miscellaneous items, the file also declares two objects that demonstrate how to use the classes in this chapter to create menu-driven programs. As in chapter 5, I'll explain this and other long listings in sections. On disk, of course, each listing is stored in a single file.

Listing 6.2. WINTOOL.H

```
1:  // wintool.h -- Header for wintool.cpp
2:
3:  #include "key.h"
4:  #include "command.h"
5:  #include "window.h"
6:  #include "selector.h"
7:
```

```
 8:   /* -- Pop-up menu position, size, and other attributes */
 9:
10:   #define MENU_ROW        4
11:   #define MENU_COL        5
12:   #define MENU_WIDTH      24
13:   #define MENU_HEIGHT     9
14:   #define MENU_TA         0x07
15:   #define MENU_BA         0x1f
16:   #define MENU_HA         0x70
17:   #define MENU_TYPE       1            // Single-line border
18:   #define MENU_TITLE      " Menu "
19:   #define MENU_POPUP      0            // Not pop-up, stationary
20:
```

WINTOOL.H begins with a few `#include` directives to bring in declarations from the LC++ class library. KEY.H describes keyboard-handling routines; COMMAND.H contains the declaration for the `command` class, which menu-driven programs use to execute commands; WINDOW.H lists the `window` class, which, as you might suppose, creates pop-up windows; and SELECTOR.H contains another class, `selector`, out of which you can create pop-up lists of items that users can select by moving a highlight bar up and down.

The `#defines` at lines 10-19 assign values to several constants used in WINTOOL's pop-up menu. These values describe the position, size, attributes, type, title, and style for the window on the left side of WINTOOL's main screen. (Run the program to see this if you haven't done so already.)

Most programs you'll create will need similar constant values. The first four constants in WINTOOL.H specify the starting row and column of a window's top-left corner plus the window's width and height in characters. The three hexadecimal values represent the text (`MENU_TA`), border (`MENU_BA`), and highlight (`MENU_HA`) attributes used to display this window. WINTOOL's main job is to let you view the results of similar values, which you can use to create your own windows in other programs.

The final three `MENU` constants select the type of window, define its title, and specify whether the menu should be the pop-up kind or stationary. The `MENU_TYPE` value can be one of the values listed in Table 6.2, which can be used to create menus and other kinds of windows. These values are the same as those used by the Zortech display package's `disp_box` function. `MENU_POPUP` can be 1 to have a menu disappear when you select a command or set to 0, as done in WINTOOL.H to have the menu window remain visible until the program ends.

Table 6.2. Menu and Window Border Type Values

Valu	Border Type
0	Double-line border
1	Single-line border
2	Solid border
3	Double-line horizontal, single-line vertical border
4	Single-line horizontal, double-line vertical border

> **Note:** Even though the classes in this chapter use Zortech's display package, they completely hide the compiler-specific details from host programs. As a result, it's possible to revise the modules to be compiled with a different C++ compiler. Because all dependent code is hidden inside classes, programs that use the revised modules *will not require modifications.* Conventional programming makes similar reusability difficult to achieve. In this chapter and the next, I'll explain how to use C++ to build this same degree of portability into your own code.

Listing 6.2. WINTOOL.H (continued)

```
21:   /* -- Sample window position, size, and other attributes */
22:
23:   #define SAMP_ROW          4
24:   #define SAMP_COL          44
25:   #define SAMP_WIDTH        31
26:   #define SAMP_HEIGHT       18
27:   #define SAMP_TYPE         3
28:   #define SAMP_TITLE        " Sample Window "
29:
30:   /* -- Unique values identifying menu commands that call
31:   the same command-object virtual function. That function uses
32:   these values to determine which command called it. */
33:
34:   #define CMD_TBG    0
35:   #define CMD_TFG    1
36:   #define CMD_BBG    2
37:   #define CMD_BFG    3
38:   #define CMD_HBG    4
39:   #define CMD_HFG    5
40:
```

WINTOOL.H continues at line 21 with a few more #defines. First are six constants that specify the position, size, type, and title for the sample window displayed on the right side of WINTOOL's main screen. Because WINTOOL lets you select attributes for this sample window, these values aren't declared as constants as they were for the program's menu window.

The six constants at lines 34-39, all of which begin with CMD_, list unique values that distinguish between some of the program's menu selections. When designing menu-driven programs using the classes in this chapter, you'll create new classes for each command. Many times, there will be one class per command in a menu. But at other times, several commands will be related and you'll want them to execute the *same* function, but to have a slightly different effect. In such cases, constants like the CMD_ values listed here let a single member function in a command determine which menu item called it.

Listing 6.2. WINTOOL.H (continued)

```
41:   /* -- Command classes for WinTool */
42:
43:   class helpCommand : public command {
44:       public:
45:           helpCommand() : command(" Help") { }
46:           virtual void performCommand(void);
47:   };
48:
49:   class attrCommand : public command {
50:       public:
51:           attrCommand(const char *s, int cn) : command(s, cn) { }
52:           virtual void performCommand(void);
53:   };
54:
55:   /* -- Function prototypes for main program */
56:
57:   void createMainWindow(void);
58:   void createSampWindow(void);
59:   void performCommands(void);
60:   void showColors(void);
61:   void showSample(void);
```

WINTOOL.H also declares two new classes, helpCommand and attrCommand. Each of these classes derives from the command class, described later. In WINTOOL, the helpCommand object displays the program's help screen. The attrCommand object takes care of all other WINTOOL commands. In your own programs, you'll declare one or more similar classes for each command.

The two classes are similar. Each has a public constructor that initializes a variable of its class. The two constructors illustrate the two basic ways you can create your own command objects. In helpCommand, the constructor is

```
helpCommand() : command(" Help") { }
```

There are no parameters listed for helpCommand, and the constructor contains no statements of its own. The constructor performs only one task: It passes a literal string " Help" to the constructor inherited from the command class. This means that any variables of type helpCommand will construct themselves with that string, the command's name as it should appear in the program's menu. (The leading blank in " Help" moves the H one space to the right of the left border in the menu's window.)

The attrCommand constructor is similar to the help command's, but its prototype lists two parameters and passes both of them to the inherited constructor

```
attrCommand(const char *s, int cn) : command(s, cn) { }
```

Because of this design, a variable of type attrCommand must specify a string for the command's name (s) plus a unique value to identify the command (cn). This will allow statements to create multiple instances of attrCommand objects, giving each of those objects unique names and integer values. As in the helpCommand class, the attrCommand constructor contains no statements of its own.

Lines 46 and 52 declare identical member functions named performCommand. Each is prefaced by the keyword virtual, making it possible for pointers to various command variables to select different performCommand functions based on the data type of each variable. (The next two sections explain how virtual functions work.) For each command object, performCommand is the function that executes when somebody selects the command from a menu. To create a menu-driven program, all you need to do is create a few objects like helpCommand and attrCommand, and to provide virtual performCommand member functions for all such objects. You then insert variables of your class types into the program's menu, and the code itself determines which performCommand function to execute when someone selects a command from the program's menu.

Finally in WINTOOLS.H at lines 57-61 are five common prototypes for functions that WINTOOL calls to execute various actions. In the next section, I'll explain what these functions do, although you can probably figure out their actions from the function names.

Pointers to Class Variables

In chapter 5 you learned how to declare new classes and how to define variables of those class types. Such variables are often called instances to distinguish them from variables of common C++ data types. (They are also less formally known as *objects.*)

I'll use the terms *class variable* and *instance* interchangeably. The term *class* always refers to the class's declaration—the template that describes the data type, not a variable or instance of that type.

In many programs, you'll define instances as local or global variables. For example, to create a variable of a class named item, you could write

```
item myItem;
```

The variable myItem is an instance (a variable) of the item class type. If item has a constructor with no parameters, the definition causes that constructor to run. If a constructor has parameters, you might declare an item instance this way:

```
item myItem(x);
```

Here, x represents an argument passed to item's constructor for initializing the new instance. It's also possible to pass more than one argument to a constructor:

```
item myItem(x, y, z);
```

This resembles a common function call, and in fact, that's exactly what it is—a call to the constructor function in item. But you can *never* call a constructor in the same way you call common functions. You *always* have to call a constructor in tandem with the definition of a variable of the class type.

When defining instances as in the preceding three examples, you must use dot notation to access the instance's public members. For example, if the item class declares a member function named showItem, you can call that function with the statement

```
myItem.showItem();
```

You can also create instances on the heap and assign the address of that allocated memory to a pointer. In chapter 4, you learned how to create pointers to common variables. To create and use a pointer to type float, you can write statements such as these:

```
float *fp;
fp = new float;
*fp = 3.14159;
cout << *fp;
delete fp;
```

The first line creates a new pointer named fp bound to the type float. The next line allocates space on the heap for a variable of that same type. The third line assigns a value to the variable's space on the heap. The fourth line displays that value, and the last line deletes the allocated space, returning it to the memory pool used by future allocations. The third and fourth lines dereference fp to obtain the data to which fp points.

You can use similar definitions and statements to allocate and use heap space for a class variable. Suppose you declare this class

```
class aClass {
   private:
      int value;
   public:
      aClass() { value = 0; }
      int getValue(void ) { return value; }
      void putValue(int n) { value = n; }
};
```

Class aClass contains a single data-field member named value. The constructor aClass() initializes the data field to 0. Member function getValue returns value. Member function putValue assigns a new value to value. (Without more substance, aClass isn't useful, but it will demonstrate fully how to address class variables with pointers.)

To create an instance of aClass, you could define a local or global variable as explained earlier, or you can call new to allocate space on the heap for the instance

```
aClass *acp;
acp = new aClass;
if (acp == NULL) error();
```

The first line defines a pointer named acp to the aClass data type. The definition is identical in form to the float *fp definition that creates a pointer to a common data type; only the names are changed. The second line calls new to allocate heap space for the instance and assign the address of that space to acp. This statement is also identical in form to the preceding one that allocated memory for a float variable stored on the heap. As always, after calling new, you should check whether the pointer equals NULL. If so, then new was unable to fulfill the request for heap space. (I'll skip this step in future samples to save space. But *don't* skip this test in your code!)

If you're thinking that creating pointers to class variables is no different from creating pointers to other data types, you're right! Classes *are* data types, and you can use them in nearly all the same ways you can use other data types built into C++.

You can also define a pointer to a class variable and call new to allocate space with a single stroke:

```
aClass *acp = new aClass;
```

Get used to this notation—you'll see it and put it to work often in C++ programs. It has the same effect as the first two lines in the previous fragment. The definition creates a pointer named acp to a variable of type aClass, and it calls new to allocate space on the heap for that variable, assigning the address of that space to acp.

When you call new either in a definition or separately to allocate space on the heap for a class variable, if that class declares a constructor, the constructor runs automatically to initialize the instance. For the hypothetical aClass, this means that the instance's v a l u e field will be set to 0 without the program having to specify this action. C++ calls the class constructor for *every* new variable of the class type that the program defines.

After allocating space for a new class variable on the heap, you can use the variable's pointer to call public member functions declared for this class (or inherited from a base class). For example, to change v a l u e to 1234, you could write

```
acp->putValue(1234);
```

This notation is identical to that used to access s t r u c t fields addressed by a pointer. The - > symbol serves a similar purpose as the dot in dot notation—it selects a member of the structure or instance. The effect of the statement is to call the p u t V a l u e function for the instance addressed by a c p, and to assign the value 1234 to the instance's private data field.

It's also possible to pass arguments to constructors to initialize instances on the heap. Suppose you change the declaration of a C l a s s to this:

```
class aClass {
    private:
        int value;
    public:
        aClass(int n) { value = n; }
        int getValue(void ) { return value; }
        void putValue(int n) { value = n; }
};
```

The only difference between that declaration and the previous one is the a C l a s s constructor. In this new version, the constructor declares an i n t parameter n and assigns it to the private v a l u e field. To create a pointer to an instance of this class and allocate heap space for that instance, you can write

```
aClass *acp = new aClass(4321);
```

That defines a pointer named a c p to type a C l a s s. The definition calls n e w to allocate space on the heap for an instance of a C l a s s, and it passes the literal value 4321 to the class constructor, which assigns that value to the instance's copy of the private v a l u e data field. You must supply arguments for each parameter a constructor declares, just as you must supply arguments for parameters in other functions.

Using the notation you learned about in chapter 3, you may declare a default parameter in a constructor. For example, to make n optional, you could change the constructor in a C l a s s to this:

```
aClass(int n = 0) { value = n; }
```

When you define a variable or pointer to type a C l a s s, you have the option of supplying an argument for n's value. All the following definitions are correct:

```
aClass v1;
aClass v2(10);
```

```
aClass *p1 = new aClass;
aClass *p2 = new aClass(20);
```

The first line defines a common variable of type aClass. Because no argument is passed to the constructor, the default value 0 is assigned to n. The second line specifies a new value for n, overriding the default. The third line defines a pointer p1 to an aClass variable, allocated heap space by new. As in the first line, the default of 0 is passed to the constructor because no argument is supplied. The fourth line also calls new to allocate heap space and assign an address to p2. This line overrides the default value, passing 20 to the constructor.

It's also possible to declare more than one constructor in a class to allow a variety of initialization formats for variables of that class. I'll explain more about this technique in chapter 7 when I introduce the strItem (string item) class.

Pointers to Derived Classes

Storing instances of class data types on the heap helps programs use memory efficiently. But there's another benefit that goes with using pointers to instances. A pointer may address an instance of a class, or it may address an instance of *any* other class that derives from that base.

The value of this concept may not be apparent now, but it's one of the most important among C++'s OOP capabilities. Suppose you have one class named A and another class B derived from A. You can declare a pointer p to a variable of type A with the definition A *p. Pointer p may then address an instance of type A. But here's the twist: p may also address an instance of type B even though you declared p to address variables of type A.

You can't perform the same sort of trick with pointers to C++'s built-in types — those types are not classes and therefore, they can't serve as base classes for derived types. If they could, you'd be able to declare a higher-order, floating-point data type, and all your pointers to type float could address the new type without your having to modify a single line of existing code.

With classes, you can do exactly that: Create a class and define a pointer to instances of that class, and then create other derived classes from that base class. All your pointers to instances of the base class can then address the new derivations. That rule even holds true for pointers in code that's already compiled! How and why this concept is important will become evident as you examine the programming in this and the next chapter. To provide some more background on the subject, the following few sections demonstrate one of the main benefits of using pointers of one class to address instances of classes derived from that class: *polymorphism.*

Virtual Functions and Polymorphism

When a pointer addresses an instance of a class, the actual type of that instance might not be known until the program runs. For example, if you declare a pointer to a class of type A, at runtime the program may assign to that pointer the address of a derived instance B.

Such assignments pose a problem, illustrated by a simple example. Here's class A's declaration:

```
class A {
   private:
      int x;
   public:
      void f(void);
};
```

Class A declares a private variable x and a single member function f. The function stores a value in x:

```
void A::f(void)
{
   x = 1234;
};
```

The exact value doesn't matter, and the assignment merely represents the effect that any member function might have on the data in a variable of a class type. Class B inherits A's properties. Here's B's declaration:

```
class B : public A {
   private:
      int y;
   public:
      void f(void);
};
```

Class B inherits all of A's properties; therefore, a variable of type B will have an x integer field and a y field declared in class B's private section. B also replaces f with its own function f, which acts on the private data stored in B:

```
void B::f(void)
{
   A::f();
   y = 4321;
};
```

B's implementation of function f calls class A's function of the same name. To tell the compiler which of the identically named functions to call, the statement uses the notation A::f(). (You saw this technique in chapter 5 when derived classes in

ELEVSIM replaced functions in their base classes. There's nothing new here so far.) In addition to calling the base class f function, the replacement function f also assigns data to B's private field y. Again, that assignment represents the effect that any member function in a derived class might have on variables of the derived type.

All these declarations and function implementations work, and there's nothing wrong with them. Replacing member functions in derived classes is a useful technique, as ELEVSIM demonstrated in the previous chapter. But when a pointer addresses an instance of the base class (A), a subtle problem arises. Suppose you define that pointer like this:

```
A *ap1 = new A;
```

Pointer ap1 addresses an instance of type A. You can then write statements to use A's public members. There's only one such member in this example, the function f. To call that function, you can use the statement

```
ap1->f();
```

As you probably expect, that calls function f in class A for the variable addressed by ap1. But here's the problem: Suppose you create another pointer and allocate space for an instance of the derived class B

```
A *ap2 = new B;
```

C++ allows ap2, declared as a pointer to the base class A, to address an instance of the derived class B. Thinking all is well, you then execute this statement

```
ap2->f();
```

and you are surprised to discover that function f in the base class A runs. Since ap2 addresses an instance of type B, you want that statement to call the replacement function in B, not the original in A. But, the code calls A's function, not B's. How can such a statement call B's function to initialize the data declared in B (in this case, the y field)?

One answer is to declare the pointer to address an instance of B

```
B *ap2 = new B;
ap2->f();
```

Now the compiler realizes that ap2 addresses an instance of type B, and it will call function f in B. However, while solving the problem, you've introduced another: You now have to declare *in advance* that ap2 addresses variables of type B. This may not be possible in all situations. Suppose, for example, that a single pointer addresses a list of class instances, many of which are of *different* derived types. That's a typical environment for object-oriented programs. Before the program runs, there's no way to tell what type of objects a pointer will address. How, then, can the program use a single pointer to call many different functions in those objects' derived classes?

The solution is to declare the functions *virtual*. A virtual member function in a class is identical to other member functions, but its prototype begins with the key word virtual. Here are the two classes, A and B, with virtual f functions:

```
class A {
   private:
      int x;
   public:
      virtual void f(void);
};
class B : public A {
   private:
      int y;
   public:
      virtual void f(void);
};
```

The only differences from the previous declarations are the two virtual key words. Notice that the key word comes *before* any return type, here void. The function implementations from before are exactly the same, and do not need corresponding virtual key words. *Any* member function, but not a constructor, can be virtual.

With virtual functions in the two related classes, an amazing transformation takes place in the program. Consider what happens when you define a pointer to an instance of type A. You call function f to act on that instance, and then delete the heap space addressed by p:

```
A *p = new A;
p->f();
delete p;
```

The statement p->f() calls function f in class A—the data type of the instance stored on the heap. In another section of the program, you reuse that *same* pointer p, but this time you assign to the pointer the address of newly allocated space for an instance of type B:

```
p = new B;
p->f();
delete p;
```

Here's where the magic comes in: The statement p->f() now calls the function declared in class B because that's the data type of the instance addressed by p. Compare that statement with the preceding one that calls f in class A. The two statements are identical, proving that *the instance itself determines which virtual function to run!* This sleight of hand is called polymorphism.

In zoology, the word polymorphism describes the growth of different forms such as sponges that share the same properties. There is a wide variety of sponges in the seas, all of different sizes, shapes, and colors. Despite their differences, they are all still sponges, and they all serve the same purposes in life (such as life must be for a sponge). In programming, polymorphism refers to the capability of multiple class instances to change form at runtime while sharing the same function names—like function f in the preceding samples.

A good example of polymorphism at work is a drawing program where shapes—circles, rectangles, and lines—are represented by classes. Each class derives from a base class, perhaps named shape. A pointer to shape might address an instance of many derived types, for example, a circle, a rectangle, or another type of graphics object. At runtime, a virtual function named draw in each class carries out the necessary instructions to draw the particular shape on-screen. The sample listing in the next section shows the basic design of this kind of program.

Polymorphism in Action

Before continuing with WINTOOL, a simple example of polymorphism in action will help you to understand the value of virtual functions and polymorphism. Compile and run Listing 6.3, POLY.CPP.

Listing 6.3. POLY.CPP

```
1:   // poly.cpp -- Demonstrate polymorphism
2:
3:   #include <stream.hpp>
4:
5:   /* -- Declare an abstract shape class */
6:
7:   class shape {
8:      public:
9:         virtual void draw(void) = 0;
10:  };
11:
12:  /* -- Declare three derived classes that inherit the properties of
13:  the shape class. */
14:
15:  class circle: public shape {
16:     public:
17:        virtual void draw(void);
18:  };
19:
20:  class square: public shape {
21:     public:
22:        virtual void draw(void);
23:  };
24:
```

```
25:   class line: public shape {
26:      public:
27:         virtual void draw(void);
28:   };
29:
```

Lines 7-10 declare a new class named s h a p e. The class contains a single virtual member function, d r a w. The special notation = 0 at the end of the prototype tells C++ that d r a w is a *pure virtual function,* and that as a consequence, s h a p e is an *abstract class.* The pure virtual function is only a prototype for a function in a derived class that you will supply later. A pure virtual function has no implementation, and you can't call it. Likewise, an abstract class is merely a schematic—you can't define a variable of an abstract class like s h a p e. Abstract classes are useful for creating base classes from which other classes will derive common properties. Abstract classes also prevent people (including yourself) from defining variables of a class that's intended only as a sketch of the common parts that other derived classes will share.

> **Note:** You do not have to supply function implementations for pure virtual functions ending with = 0 in abstract classes. However, you must supply implementations for all other member functions, except, of course, those implemented in line.

Three such derived classes appear at lines 15-28. The c i r c l e, s q u a r e, and l i n e classes derive common properties from s h a p e. Each of these classes declares a replacement function named d r a w. Because the inherited d r a w was declared to be v i r t u a l, the derivations *must* also use the v i r t u a l key word at lines 17, 22, and 27.

The three replacement functions do not end with the = 0 notation as they do in the abstract base class. The program will create instances of the c i r c l e, s q u a r e, and l i n e classes, and, therefore, these classes must not be abstract. The reason for deriving these three new classes from s h a p e is to give all the classes a common base. In a more complete program, the s h a p e class might declare other common elements such as X and Y coordinate values, a color, and a size for the shape. The derived classes could then use these items (perhaps by calling public member functions) for a variety of purposes.

> **Note:** The sample POLY program doesn't actually draw any shapes on-screen. But the principles the program illustrates are the same as they would be in a full-fledged graphics system.

Listing 6.3. POLY.CPP (continued)

```
30:    /* -- The main program */
31:
32:    main()
33:    {
34:       shape *p[3];               // Three shape pointers
35:
36:       p[0] = new circle;         // Allocate space for a circle
37:       p[1] = new square;         // Allocate space for a square
38:       p[2] = new line;           // Allocate space for a line
39:
40:    /* -- Call the virtual draw method in the instance addressed by the
41:    pointers in the p[] array. Which virtual function actually executes
42:    is determined at runtime by the instance itself. */
43:
44:       for (int i = 0; i <=2; i++)
45:           p[i]->draw();
46:    }
47:
```

POLY's main function defines an array of three pointers to the abstract shape class. Lines 36-38 then call new to allocate space for variables of the three classes that derive from shape. As I mentioned earlier, a pointer to a class may address variables of that class or of any derivation. In this example, however, the pointers would not be permitted to address an instance of type shape because that class was designated to be abstract. You can *never* create variables of an abstract type; therefore, the pointers in the p array can address *only* instances of classes that are derived from shape.

Lines 44-45 demonstrate how the relationships of derived classes to a common base can simplify certain operations. Here, a for loop cycles int i from 0 to 2, indexing the array of shape pointers, and calling the draw member function. (The "draw" functions in this small example simply display a message that confirms which function is running.)

Which draw function runs at line 45? There's a draw function in each of the three derived classes. The answer: The draw function that belongs to the addressed object is the one that runs. Even though line 45 doesn't specify which draw function to call, the program executes the correct function in the circle, square, and line instances. The instances themselves determine at runtime which draw function should run.

You can demonstrate this effect by rearranging the order of the assignments to the pointer array at lines 36-38. Or, increase the size of the array, and use new to allocate space for several more circle or other shape derivations. No matter what kinds of objects you address with the array's pointers, you never need to modify the statement at line 45. That statement always calls the correct draw function in whatever object p[i] happens to address when the loop runs.

Even more exciting: If the f o r loop at lines 44-45 was buried deeply inside a compiled module and even if you didn't have the source code to that module, the loop could still call new d r a w methods in classes you derive at a later time. You might create a new s h a p e class called s p h e r e with its own virtual d r a w function and insert a pointer to a s p h e r e variable into the p array; the f o r loop would call your new function to draw a shape that didn't even exist when the programmer wrote the original code!

Imagine the power this concept provides. In a graphics program, you can create new shapes, plug them into memory, and a precompiled program will be able to draw your designs. In a database, you can insert new data types, and the searching and sorting modules compiled earlier will be able to handle data of your new class types. In these and other cases, the original programmers would not have to know anything about your plans in order to write code that can use your custom objects.

POLY ends with the implementations of the three replacement virtual functions. These functions, which don't actually draw any shapes, are no different from common nonvirtual member functions.

Listing 6.3. POLY.CPP (continued)

```
48:    /* -- The implementations of the three classes that derive from the
49:    base class shape. Although declared to be virtual, the functions are
50:    no different in form from nonvirtual member functions. */
51:
52:    void circle::draw(void)
53:    {
54:        cout << "\nInside circle::draw()";
55:    }
56:
57:    void square::draw(void)
58:    {
59:        cout << "\nInside square::draw()";
60:    }
61:
62:    void line::draw(void)
63:    {
64:        cout << "\nInside line::draw()";
65:    }
```

Early and Late Binding

C++ calls virtual functions differently than it calls nonvirtual member functions. Normally, when a program calls a function, the compiler generates an instruction that transfers control to a fixed address in memory where the compiled code for the function is stored. Putting this in technical terms, C++ binds common function calls to static function addresses at compile time, a process known as *early binding*.

 C++ does not call virtual member functions in that same way. When a statement or expression calls a virtual function instead of generating code to call a static address, C++ creates instructions that look up the actual address of the function at runtime. That lookup action uses the instance of the class to find the correct address of a virtual function, a process called *late binding*.

 Late binding is the internal method by which C++ selects among virtual functions of the same names in related classes. To use late binding, all you have to do is declare a member function with the `virtual` key word.

> **Note:** Virtual functions require a program to perform an additional memory reference to look up a function's address. For this reason, there's a slight time penalty for using virtual functions that you don't have to pay when using nonvirtual functions. In most cases, this penalty is small compared to the benefits late binding provides.

The WINTOOL.CPP Main Program

You'll now be able to appreciate how WINTOOL uses polymorphism to call program commands. The main program, Listing 6.4, WINTOOL.CPP, begins with several declarations, a few global variables, and a simple `main` function.

Listing 6.4. WINTOOL.CPP

```
 1:   // wintool.cpp -- Select window attributes
 2:
 3:   #include <stream.hpp>
 4:   #include "wintool.h"
 5:
 6:   /* -- Global variables */
 7:
 8:   int attributes[6] = {1, 15, 7, 0, 7, 0};
 9:   unsigned wta = 0x1f;
10:   unsigned wba = 0x70;
11:   unsigned wha = 0x70;
12:   window *mainWindow;
13:   window *sampleWindow;
14:
15:   main()
```

```
16:    {
17:        window::startup();
18:        createMainWindow();
19:        createSampWindow();
20:        performCommands();
21:        delete sampleWindow;
22:        delete mainWindow;
23:        window::shutDown();
24:        exit(0);
25:    }
26:
```

WINTOOL includes the STREAM.HPP and WINTOOL.H header files. Those two files load other headers, making most of the LC++ class library available to WINTOOL. Line 8 prepares an array of byte values, one per menu selection. These are the attributes you adjust while using the program to select window colors. Lines 9-11 create variables that WINTOOL uses to display the sample window in these colors. Change the default values listed here to alter the sample's initial colors.

Lines 12-13 declare two pointers to type `window`, a class that creates pop-up windows. In your own programs, each window you plan to use must have a similar pointer, because most of the LC++ class library's objects *must* be stored dynamically on the heap. The rule may seem restrictive, but it's common in OOP, where instances are commonly created dynamically at runtime and stored on the heap. Many of the classes in the library delete instances of classes stored on the heap, and those deletions will fail for local and global variables of the `window` and other types.

Static Member Functions

In addition to calling a few internal functions and deleting the two `window` variables at lines 21-22, the `main` function initializes the `window` class with the statements at lines 17 and 23. Any program that includes the WINDOW.H header (as WINTOOL.CPP does via WINTOOL.H) *must* call the `startup` and `shutDown` functions as done here:

```
window::startup();
...
window::shutDown();
```

Until now, all calls to member functions were associated with a variable of the class. But these two statements are different. They do not call a function to act on an instance of the class. They call functions that apply to the class itself.

For most classes, you normally define a variable of the class and then use dot notation to execute a member function. For example, assume that `button` is the class type; to call a p u s h function in b u t t o n, you first need to define a variable such as button b1 and then execute a statement such as b1.push().

The startup and shutDown routines are different. These are examples of *static member functions*. To call such functions, you must precede their names with double colons and the class name. You can *never* call static member functions by referring to variables of the class type. You must call them as shown here, by referring to the class itself.

Static member functions like startup and shutDown are useful for hiding system-dependent items inside a class. In this version of the window class, startup and shutDown initialize and deactivate the Zortech display package. Hiding system-dependent items like these in a class simplifies the job of porting programs to new environments. Because the dependent statements are buried inside the class, programs that use the class should not require changes to compile with different C++ compilers for which the same class is implemented.

Note also that WINTOOL.CPP and WINTOOL.H do *not* include the DISP.H header file. The display package is totally hidden from view. In fact, to use the classes in this chapter, you do not need to be aware of the package's existence.

Listing 6.4. WINTOOL.CPP (continued)

```
27:  /* -- Create and display main program window */
28:
29:  void createMainWindow()
30:  {
31:     winStruct ws = {
32:        0, 0, 80, 25,    // row, column, width, height
33:        0x07,            // text attribute
34:        0x0f,            // border attribute
35:        0x70,            // highlight attribute
36:        3                // border type
37:     };
38:
39:     mainWindow = new window(
40:    ws, " Window Design Tool from \"Learning C++\" by Tom Swan ");
41:     mainWindow->showWindow();
42:  }
```

After main, WINTOOL continues at function createMainWindow. The function demonstrates how simple it is to create a pop-up window using the window class. First, a struct of type winStruct (declared in WINDOW.H, listed later), defines a few values that describe the window's position, size, attributes, and border type. These values have the same purposes as I described earlier for various constants in WINTOOL.H (Listing 6.2). In your own programs, each window must have a similar structure.

Next, the program calls `new` to allocate heap space for a variable of type `window`. Line 39 assigns the address of that space to a `window` pointer named `mainWindow`. The arguments in this statement pass the `winStruct` variable `ws` and the window's title.

Use similar definitions and statements in your own code to create windows. For example, it takes only one line to create a pointer named `myWP` (my window pointer), allocate space for the `window` variable, and assign the address of that variable to `myWP`.

```
window *myWP = new window(ws, " My Window ");
```

This assumes that you also prepared a `winStruct` variable `ws`. After creating the `window` variable, you can use the pointer to call various `window` member functions. For instance, to display the window, use this statement:

```
myWP->showWindow();
```

Remember to use the pointer notation `->` to access member functions in the class variable. Because you *must* allocate space for `window` variables on the heap, you *must* use pointers along with this notation to call member functions.

I'll explain other `window` functions as you see them in WINTOOL. The `window` class includes many functions that can display text, scroll lines, change attributes, and perform other actions inside pop-up windows.

Listing 6.4. WINTOOL.CPP (continued)

```
43:
44:   /* -- Create and display sample window */
45:
46:   void createSampWindow()
47:   {
48:       winStruct ws = {
49:           SAMP_ROW, SAMP_COL, SAMP_WIDTH, SAMP_HEIGHT,
50:           wta, wba, wha, SAMP_TYPE
51:       };
52:
53:       sampleWindow = new window(ws, SAMP_TITLE);
54:       sampleWindow->showWindow();
55:   }
56:
```

The next function, `createSampWindow`, is similar to `createMainWindow`. However, instead of specifying literal values for window parameters, the code uses `SAMP` constants and the three global variables `wta`, `wba`, and `wha` to prepare the `winStruct` structure. The variables control the colors that change in the sample window when you select WINTOOL's attribute commands.

Using constants keeps the source text clean and keeps the constant values together in WINTOOL.H, where they are easy to modify. Note that line 54 calls showWindow to display the window addressed by the sampleWindow pointer.

Listing 6.4. WINTOOL.CPP (continued)

```
57:    /* -- Create command menu and execute command objects */
58:
59:    void performCommands(void)
60:    {
61:       command *cp;              // Pointer to selected command
62:       winStruct ws = {
63:          MENU_ROW, MENU_COL, MENU_WIDTH, MENU_HEIGHT,
64:          MENU_TA, MENU_BA, MENU_HA, MENU_TYPE
65:       };
66:       selector *menu = new selector(ws, MENU_TITLE, MENU_POPUP);
67:
```

The performCommands function is more complex than the previous two, so I'll describe it in two stages. First, line 61 defines a pointer cp to the command class—another in the LC++ class library that I'll explain in chapter 7. This pointer gives the program a way to execute the command objects declared in WINTOOL.H.

Lines 62-65 declare a winStruct variable identical to those for the main and sample windows. *Every* window needs to have a corresponding structure that describes the window's attributes. Line 66, however, is a little different:

```
selector *menu = new selector(ws, MENU_TITLE, MENU_POPUP);
```

This creates a selector object—yet another class in the library. A selector is a window in which you can select lines of text; in this case, the commands in WINTOOL's menu. Because selector derives from window, its constructor requires a winStruct variable (ws) and a title (MENU_TITLE). But it also needs a third argument, MENU_POPUP. This constant tells the selector whether to keep the window visible after someone selects a line (0), or to hide the window at that time (1). If you don't specify this last argument, the default value is 1.

Listing 6.4. WINTOOL.CPP (continued)

```
68:    menu->insertItem(new helpCommand());
69:    menu->insertItem(new attrCommand(" Text Background",      CMD_TBG));
70:    menu->insertItem(new attrCommand(" Text Foreground",      CMD_TFG));
71:    menu->insertItem(new attrCommand(" Border Background",    CMD_BBG));
72:    menu->insertItem(new attrCommand(" Border Foreground",    CMD_BFG));
73:    menu->insertItem(new attrCommand(" Highlight Background", CMD_HBG));
74:    menu->insertItem(new attrCommand(" Highlight Foreground", CMD_HFG));
75:       showColors();
```

```
76:         while ((cp = (command *)(menu->getSelection())) != NULL) {
77:             cp->performCommand();
78:             showColors();
79:         }
80:     }
81:
```

Function `performCommands` continues at lines 68-74 with several statements that demonstrate how to create a pop-up menu of commands. The `menu` pointer, to which the function just allocated space for a variable of type `selector`, calls its `insertItem` function. Each such call adds one `command` object. For example, line 68 creates and inserts the `helpCommand` object declared in WINTOOL.H. Note how `new` is used here:

```
menu->insertItem(new helpCommand());
```

First, `menu` is dereferenced to access the `insertItem` member function. That function requires a pointer to an item to insert in the `selector`. The pointer may address any class object in the LC++ class library; therefore, instead of saving the result of `new` in a pointer variable, that result is simply passed directly to `insertItem`. What happens to the pointer? It's saved in memory on a list of commands. I'll explain later how that happens—for now, just become familiar with the use of `new` to pass an instance pointer to a member function.

Note: You may have the urge here to hunt for `insertItem`'s declaration. If so, you'll find it in LIST.H, not SELECTOR.H. The class `selector` derives from `list`, which declares `insertItem`. Class `list` in turn derives from class `item`. You'll examine the declarations of all these classes in time, and jumping ahead through the class hierarchy now may be more confusing than helpful. It's probably best to stick to the game plan—learn the high-level uses first before diving too deeply below the surface. But feel free to peek ahead if you want.

Line 69 shows a different way to insert commands into menus. Here, `new` allocates space for an instance of type `attrCommand`. Because that class's constructor declares two parameters (see Listing 6.2, line 51), the statement must supply two arguments

```
menu->insertItem(new attrCommand(" Text Background", CMD_TBG));
```

The statement calls the `insertItem` member function for the `selector` instance addressed by `menu`. The call to `new` creates an instance of `attrCommand` on the heap, initializing that instance with a string and a value `CMD_TBG`.

Use this kind of statement to insert commands for which the *same* member function will be called when people select the command from a menu. The `CMD_TBG` constant assigns a unique value to the Text Background command to distinguish this command from other attrCommand instances. Lines 70-74 insert similar commands with different titles and constant values.

The function continues at line 75 by calling showColors, which displays the attribute values you see on-screen to the right of WINTOOL's menu. A while loop shows the correct way to get and execute commands from a pop-up menu:

```
while ((cp = (command *)(menu->getSelection())) != NULL) {
    cp->performCommand();
    ...
}
```

The control expression looks more complex than it is. As with all lengthy expressions, to understand this one, it's best to take it apart from the inside out. In order of execution, the elements are as follows:

- menu->getSelection() returns a pointer to a selected command object in the menu. Or, the function returns NULL if you press <Esc>.

- (command *) recasts the result of menu->getSelection for assigning that result to cp. The menu pointer addresses a generic selection list, which in another program might select among other kinds of strings—for example, file names from a disk directory. WINTOOL knows that the selections are menu commands, but the compiler doesn't. That's why recasting is needed.

- != NULL causes the while loop to continue as long as cp is not equal to NULL. When cp is NULL (indicating that you pressed <Esc>), the loop ends.

The effect of all this is to assign the address of a single command object to cp. The statement cp->performCommand() then executes that object's virtual member function—another example of polymorphism. The type of instance cp addresses depends on which command you select from the menu. The statement at line 77 executes *every* program command, similar to the way earlier examples called different virtual functions via pointers.

Listing 6.4. WINTOOL.CPP (continued)

```
82:   /* -- Display current color attributes and sample window */
83:
84:   void showColors(void)
85:   {
86:       for (int i = 0; i < 6; i++) {
87:           mainWindow->gotorc(MENU_ROW + i + 1, MENU_COL + MENU_WIDTH);
88:           mainWindow->puts(dec(attributes[i], 2));
89:       }
90:       mainWindow->gotorc(16, 4);
91:       mainWindow->puts("Text attribute ........ : 0x");
```

```
 92:        mainWindow->puts(hex(wta,2));
 93:        mainWindow->gotorc(17, 4);
 94:        mainWindow->puts("Border attribute ...... : 0x");
 95:        mainWindow->puts(hex(wba, 2));
 96:        mainWindow->gotorc(18, 4);
 97:        mainWindow->puts("Highlight attribute ... : 0x");
 98:        mainWindow->puts(hex(wha, 2));
 99:        showSample();
100:    }
101:
```

The next WINTOOL function, showColors, demonstrates how to display text inside a window. Earlier, the program allocated space on the heap for a window instance, and assigned the address of that space to the mainWindow pointer. The showColors function calls two window class member functions for that instance: gotorc (go to row and column) and puts (put string). The function also calls hex (declared in STREAM.HPP) to convert values to hexadecimal character strings for display.

Rows and columns are relative to the window's borders. If wp is a pointer to an instance of type window, then the statement wp->gotorc(0, 0) sends the cursor to the upper left corner inside the window's boundaries. The "cursor" is only a logical position, not a visible symbol, where you want to display text.

Similarly, function puts displays a string at the current cursor location. The string's characters are colored with the window's default attributes. ("Colors" on monochrome systems appear as bold, dim, underlined, and blinking text.) I'll show you how to select different attributes in a moment. If wp is a window pointer, then wp->puts("Learning C++") displays the quoted characters inside the window at the cursor's location. After that operation, the cursor is moved to the end of the string.

> **Note:** To format integer, floating-point, and other variables for display, use the form function as you do in output-stream statements. For example, to display an int value, you could use the statement: wp->puts(form("value=%d", value));. See chapter 10 for more information about form and the related function printf.

Listing 6.4. WINTOOL.CPP (continued)

```
102:    /* -- Display sample window using selected attributes */
103:
104:    void showSample(void)
105:    {
106:        winStruct ws = {
107:            SAMP_ROW, SAMP_COL, SAMP_WIDTH, SAMP_HEIGHT,
```

```
108:            wta, wba, wha, SAMP_TYPE
109:        };
110:
111:        sampleWindow->setInfo(ws);
112:        sampleWindow->gotorc(0, 0);
113:        sampleWindow->eeow();
114:        sampleWindow->gotorc(5, 9);
115:        sampleWindow->normalVideo();
116:        sampleWindow->puts("Normal Text");
117:        sampleWindow->gotorc(10, 6);
118:        sampleWindow->reverseVideo();
119:        sampleWindow->puts(" Highlighted Text ");
120:    }
121:
```

The showSample function is similar to showColors. This function displays the sample window in the colors you select from WINTOOL's menu. Because these colors will change, the function begins by calling setInfo and passing a winStruct variable containing the global attribute values. Use this technique to change an existing window's attributes. The function also calls eeow (erase to end of window), normalVideo (unhighlighted text), and reverseVideo (highlighted text) to operate the sample window. All these functions—setInfo, eeow, and reverseVideo—are members of the window class. You can call them for any instance of type window.

Listing 6.4. WINTOOL.CPP (continued)

```
122:  /* -- Implementation of the help command */
123:
124:  void helpCommand::performCommand(void)
125:  {
126:      winStruct ws = {
127:          2, 2, 76, 21,    // row, column, width, height
128:          0x1f,            // text attribute
129:          0x70,            // border attribute
130:          0x70,            // highlight attribute
131:          0                // border type
132:      };
133:      window *helpWindow = new window(ws, " WinTool Help ");
134:
135:      helpWindow->showWindow();
136:      helpWindow->gotorc(8, 4);
137:      helpWindow->puts("No help available");
138:      helpWindow->gotorc(10, 4);
139:      helpWindow->puts("(Press <Esc> from main menu to quit program)");
```

```
140:        while (!keyWaiting()) ;
141:        getKey();
142:        delete helpWindow;
143:    }

144:
```

WINTOOL's `helpCommand` and `attrCommand` classes declare virtual `performCommand` functions. These are the functions that run when you select a command from the program's menu. Lines 124-143 show the implementation for `helpCommand`'s function, which runs when you select the Help command. (The function is unfinished. Exercise 6.8 asks you to complete this section.)

Most of the programming in the function should be familiar to you by now, except for the two statements at lines 140-141. There, a `while` loop calls `keyWaiting` from the keyboard module explained later in the chapter. The empty statement at the end of the line causes the loop to pause the program until you press a key. Then, line 141 calls another of that module's functions, `getKey`, to remove the keypress from the input buffer.

> **Note:** Be sure to call `delete` for any class instances you create with `new`, as done here at line 142. If you don't delete instances from the heap, they will remain in memory after the functions that created them end. This may cause the program to run out of room for new variables. For a graphic example of the errors that can occur by forgetting to delete instances when you're done using them, temporarily remove line 142, recompile, and run WINTOOL. Open the help window repeatedly. As you'll see, the window refuses to go away, and in time, the program halts when it runs out of memory.

Listing 6.4. WINTOOL.CPP (continued)

```
145:  /* -- Implementation of the attributes command. Increments attribute
146:  value for selected item, identified by cmdNum. Updates global window
147:  attribute values. */
148:
149:  void attrCommand::performCommand(void)
150:  {
151:      attributes[cmdNum] = ++attributes[cmdNum] % 16;
152:      wta = attributes[0] * 16 + attributes[1];
153:      wba = attributes[2] * 16 + attributes[3];
154:      wha = attributes[4] * 16 + attributes[5];

155:  }
```

The second perfomCommand implementation in WINTOOL belongs to the attrCommand class. Recall from earlier in this chapter that several variations of this object were created and inserted in the program's menu (see lines 69-74). Statements in performCommand use cmdNum to determine which variation a person selected from the menu. That variable is a member of the class, and is available to all descendents of the command class, explained in chapter 7.

In attrCommand's performCommand function, cmdNum is used as an index to the attributes array of byte values that specify the sample window's colors. (In another setting, cmdNum might select one of several subfunctions to execute.) Line 151 increments the corresponding attributes entry for each attribute command you select. The next three statements assign the final attribute values to the global wta, wba, and wha variables. These values are used in a winStruct structure to change the appearance of the sample window (see line 108 in function showSample).

That completes WINTOOL. You've now seen a full example of what the LC++ class library can do. You've learned about static functions, virtual functions, and polymorphism. And you've learned how to use some of the member functions in the window class. Chapter 7 details that class and others in the library. Before turning to those subjects, however, you need to take a short side trip back to nonOOP land.

Mixing OOP and NonOOP Code

Beginners to OOP techniques tend to forget that C++ is a hybrid language. Everything in a C++ program does *not* have to be stored in a class. You can and should mix OOP and nonOOP techniques in the same programs.

The rest of this chapter lists two modules used by some of the member functions in the LC++ class library. The modules provide keyboard and error-handling support for programs that use the library. I could have invented classes for these items, but there seemed to be several good reasons not to do so. For one, there's only one keyboard on most computers, and programs would therefore need only a single instance of a keyboard class. For another, operations such as getting keypresses and displaying error messages are global in nature. Hiding those operations inside class variables seemed pointless.

The KEY Module

The first such module is stored in two files, KEY.H and KEY.CPP. The KEY.H header file (Listing 6.5) lists the prototypes for the three functions in KEY.CPP. The KEY.CPP file (Listing 6.6) implements the three function prototypes in KEY.H.

Listing 6.5. KEY.H

```
1:  // key.h -- Header for key.cpp
2:
3:  #ifndef __KEY_H      //
4:  #define __KEY_H            1        // Prevent multiple #includes
5:
6:  /* -- Various key definitions. The values work only with the getkey
7:  function in the key module; they do not work with the getch and other
8:  standard key-input library functions. */
9:
10: int getKey(void);
11: int keyWaiting(void);
12: int ungetKey(int k);
13:
14: #endif   // __KEY_H
```

Listing 6.6. KEY.CPP

```
1:  // key.cpp -- Keyboard routines
2:
3:  #include <conio.h>
4:  #include "key.h"
5:
6:  int savedChar;     // Char saved by ungetKey()
7:
8:  /* -- Wait for and return the next keypress. Displays nothing.
9:  Returns extended PC ASCII values from 0 to 255 for alphanumeric and
10: control keys. Returns negative values for function keys such as <F1>,
11: <End>, and <Home>. Constants for these keys are defined in key.h.
12: Other similar constants (e.g. for <Alt>-key combinations) can be
13: created by taking the second character returned by getch() for that
14: key and subtracting 256 from the character's ASCII value. */
15:
16: int getKey(void)
17: {
18:    int c;
19:
20:    if (savedChar != 0) {       // If there's a saved char
21:       c = savedChar;           // Assign it to c
22:       savedChar = 0;           // Reset savedChar to none
23:    } else {
24:       c = getch();             // Else get next keypress
25:       if (c == 0)              // Check for function-key lead-in
26:          c = getch() - 256;    // Return function-key value < 0
27:    }
```

```
28:      return c;        // Return next keypress to caller
29: }
30:
31: /* -- Return true if a key was pressed and a character is waiting to
32: be read, or if the program called ungetKey and a saved character is
33: waiting to be reread. */
34:
35: int keyWaiting(void)
36: {
37:      return (kbhit() || (savedChar != 0));
38: }
39:
40: /* -- Undo the most recent call to getKey. Saves keypress value k in
41: a global variable. That key will then be returned by the next call to
42: getKey. Only one key value can be undone. If you call this routine
43: without calling getKey, it erases the previously undone key. */
44:
45: int ungetKey(int k)
46: {
47:      savedChar = k;
48: }
```

C++ has in its library several functions for getting keypresses. But I find the standard approaches lacking in two main areas: function keys and the capability to *unget* a character previously received from the keyboard. (The C++ standard ungetc function doesn't work for function keys, nor does it work with the getch function used to read keypresses without displaying them on-screen.)

KEY solves these problems by representing keys as int values, not as ASCII characters. Because of this design, the number of keys a program can recognize is practically unlimited. Using int values to represent keys also makes it easy to work with function keys such as <F1> and <F8>, as well as other named keys like <Home> and <Page Down> (<PgDn> on some keyboards).

The KEY module begins by including the C++ CONIO.H header, which declares the low-level input routines that KEY calls. The module also includes its own header, KEY.H.

Line 6 defines a variable, savedChar, used to store a key value passed to the ungetKey function described later. This variable is declared outside any function; therefore, any function in the module can use it. However, since the variable is not declared extern, and is not mentioned in the KEY.H header file, other modules have no access to savedChar. This technique for hiding data in modules isn't as effective as hiding data in a class's private section. But it's a useful device when several functions in a module need to share a few small variables. Variables like savedChar take up permanent storage in the program's data segment, however.

Function getKey at lines 16-29 reads the next keypress from the keyboard. Or, if ungetKey saved a character in savedChar, getKey returns that variable's value. An `if` statement at line 20 checks whether `savedChar` is 0. If it is not, the function returns `savedChar` and resets that variable to 0.

The `else` clause at lines 23-27 reads keypresses directly from the keyboard. The first statement in this section (line 24) shows the standard way to get a single keypress:

```
c = getch();
```

Note that c is type `int`, not `char`. For alphanumeric and punctuation keys, `getch` returns the equivalent ASCII value. But for function keys and other named keys, `getch` returns 0. In that event, the *next* call to `getch` returns a value that represents the actual key value.

This two-stage process for reading function keys and named keys overly complicates programs. For that reason, I like to convert function keys and named keys to negative values, as done here at line 26. With this technique, a program can use statements like the following to read any keypress:

```
int c;
if ((c = getKey()) < 0)
    doFunctionKey(c);
else

    doNormalKey(c);
```

The `if` statement calls `getKey` and assigns the function result to an `int` variable c. If that value is less than 0, the program calls `doFunctionKey(c)` (not shown) to process a function or other named key. If the value returned by `getKey` is greater than 0 (it can't equal 0), then `doNormalKey(c)` (also not shown) handles the keypress.

Table 6.3 lists the values that `getKey` returns for function keys and other named keys on PC keyboards. You may want to define constants of these same values to make your programs more readable. For example, you could insert the directive `#define KEY_F1 -197` into a header file, and then use statements such as `if (getKey() == KEY_F1) doSomething();`. (See also Listing 6.7 in the next section.)

Table 6.3. Function- and Named-Key Values Returned by getKey

Key	Value	Key	Value
<F1>	−197	<Home>	−185
<F2>	−196	<Cursor Up>	−184
<F3>	−195	<Page Up>	−183
<F4>	−194	<Cursor Left>	−181
<F5>	−193	<Cursor Right>	−179
<F6>	−192	<End>	−177

continued

Table 6.3. Continued

Key	Value	Key	Value
<F7>	–191	<Cursor Down>	–176
<F8>	–190	<Page Down>	–175
<F9>	–189	<Insert>	–174
<F10>	–188	<Delete>	–173
<F11>	–123*		
<F12>	–122*		

* Not available on all keyboards

Function `keyWaiting` at lines 35-38 returns false (0) if no key is waiting to be read; otherwise, the function returns true (1). Use the function to detect keypresses with `if` statements such as the following:

```
if (keyWaiting()) {
   c = getKey();
   doSomething(c);
}
```

If a keypress is waiting to be read, the statement calls `getKey` to read the key value and passes that value in an `int` variable c to `doSomething` (not shown). This fragment also demonstrates how to read keypresses without pausing the program. If no key is waiting, the program continues after the `if` statement. If the program called `getKey` without checking `keyWaiting` and no key was waiting to be read, the program would pause until you pressed a key.

The `keyWaiting` function calls the standard `kbhit` function to detect keypresses waiting in the system's type-ahead buffer, a small amount of memory set aside by the PC ROM BIOS for storing key values as you type them. The `keyWaiting` function combines the result of `kbhit` with the result of the expression (`savedChar != 0`), using the logical OR operator `||`. For this reason, calling `ungetKey` also causes `keyWaiting` to return true.

That function's implementation is at lines 45-48. Call `ungetKey` to push a key value back to the keyboard (actually, into the module's hidden `savedChar` variable). Use this function to *unget* keys, but only one at a time. For example, to have a program "press" the <Esc> key, use the statement

```
ungetKey(27);
```

The next call to `getKey` will return ASCII 27, the value for the <Esc> key. You can unget only one keypress this way. Each call to `ungetKey` overwrites a previously pushed character.

Defining KEY Values

Listing 6.7, KEY.DOC, defines several constants equal to the values from Table 6.3. (This file is also stored on disk.) Include or copy the file into your programs that use the KEY module. The constants represent function- and named-key values returned by getKey.

Listing 6.7. KEY.DOC

```
 1:  /* -- Copy any of these definitions to modules that need to call
 2:  key.cpp routines for function and special keys. These definitions
 3:  could be included in key.h, but I removed them to conserve memory
 4:  for the compiler. */
 5:
 6:  #define KEY_F1     -197       // Function keys
 7:  #define KEY_F2     -196
 8:  #define KEY_F3     -195
 9:  #define KEY_F4     -194
10:  #define KEY_F5     -193
11:  #define KEY_F6     -192
12:  #define KEY_F7     -191
13:  #define KEY_F8     -190
14:  #define KEY_F9     -189
15:  #define KEY_F10    -188
16:  #define KEY_F11    -123       // Not recognized on all systems
17:  #define KEY_F12    -122       // "      "     "     "     "
18:
19:  #define KEY_HOME   -185       // Special-purpose keys
20:  #define KEY_UP     -184
21:  #define KEY_PGUP   -183
22:  #define KEY_LEFT   -181
23:  #define KEY_RIGHT  -179
24:  #define KEY_END    -177
25:  #define KEY_DOWN   -176
26:  #define KEY_PGDN   -175
27:  #define KEY_INS    -174
28:  #define KEY_DEL    -173
```

Testing the KEY Module

Listing 6.8 demonstrates how to use the KEY module and serves as a useful utility for testing the values of various keys. Compile the program with the command **ztc tkey**

key.obj. (You compiled the KEY module when you compiled WINTOOL. If you didn't do that, enter **ztc tkey key** to compile KEY and TKEY.)

Listing 6.8. TKEY.CPP

```
 1:  // tkey.cpp -- Test KEY module
 2:
 3:  #include <stream.hpp>
 4:  #include "key.h"
 5:
 6:  #define KEY_ESC    27     // ASCII value for <Esc> key
 7:  #define KEY_SPACE  32     // ASCII value for <Spacebar>
 8:
 9:  main()
10:  {
11:      int c = 0;
12:
13:      cout << "Type any keys; <Esc> quits\n";
14:      while ((c = getKey()) != KEY_ESC) {
15:          cout << "\nc = " << c;
16:          if (c >= KEY_SPACE)
17:              cout << " ASCII-(" << char(c) << ')';
18:          else if (c < 0)
19:              cout << " (Function or other named key)";
20:          else
21:              cout << " (<Ctrl> key)";
22:      }
23:  }
```

TKEY is one of several test programs (T stands for Test) included with the modules and classes in this chapter and the next. The test programs will demonstrate how to use the LC++ class library. They also make useful tests to run if you modify the code.

Run TKEY and press some key combinations not listed in KEY.DOC. For example, press **<Ctrl>-<Cursor Left>** and **<Ctrl>-<F4>** to find the values that getKey returns for these combined keys. You might want to add to KEY.DOC the constants for heavily used combinations.

Error Handling

Every programmer, it seems, has a unique plan for handling errors in code. What are the best ways to deal with disk errors, input errors, and other misdirections a program might take?

Maybe there's no *right* answer. But here are some general guidelines I've found useful:

- Don't halt programs or display error messages at the place where errors are detected. Call a function to perform this duty. Someday you may want to modify the methods used in your code to detect and handle errors. You'll make that task easier by calling a common error routine.

- Identify each error with a unique constant value. Once an error has been assigned a value, *never* reuse that value. (A truly horrible bug to trace is one that displays the *wrong* error message for a faulty condition.)

- Give your functions the capability to halt a program if an error occurs, or to postpone error handling until later. During development, you can just let programs halt when errors happen. In the finished product, you can enhance the error handling with statements that display friendly messages rather than stopping the program.

The goal of a program's error-handling logic is to deal gracefully with goofups and foul balls. You should *always* consider the consequences of NULL pointers, bad input, and other error conditions. Never let a program follow a random course for problems that are easily trapped at the source.

The ERROR module in this section demonstrates one way to deal with errors in programs. The LC++ class library uses the functions in the module for error handling. You can also use ERROR in your own projects, even in those that don't incorporate the class library.

As usual, ERROR is divided into header and implementation files. Listing 6.9, ERROR.H, is the header.

Listing 6.9. ERROR.H

```
 1: // error.h -- Header file for error.cpp
 2:
 3: #ifndef __ERROR_H
 4: #define __ERROR_H       1       // Prevent multiple #includes
 5:
 6: #define NOERROR      0       // Value for no error
 7: #define ERRMEM       1       // Out of memory
 8: #define ERRWININIT   2       // Window class not initialized
 9:
10: void error(int errnum, const char *s = NULL);
11: int geterror(int reset = 1);
12:
13: #endif   // __ERROR_H
```

Lines 6-9 define a few error codes used by the LC++ class library. You can add additional codes to this list. Note that 0 represents "no error." Never use 0 for an error code.

Lines 10-11 declare two function prototypes. The first, error, lists an integer errnum parameter. When calling error to signal that something's amiss, pass an error code as an argument to errnum. The second parameter is optional. You can pass a string to this parameter to describe an error for which you haven't assigned a unique error code. For errors of this kind, errnum must be a value that error doesn't know about (–1 is a good choice).

The second prototype, geterror, retrieves the most recent error code. Use this function when you don't want error to halt the program.

In the following sections, I'll explain both functions in more detail. ERROR.CPP, Listing 6.10, implements the error and geterror functions. The file isn't large, but it contains a few tricky features. For that reason, I'll list and describe the programming in sections.

Listing 6.10. ERROR.CPP

```
1:   // error.cpp -- Error-handling module
2:
3:   #include <stream.hpp>
4:   #include <stdlib.h>
5:   #include "error.h"
6:
7:   int errornumber;   // Most recent error number passed to error()
8:   int errorignore;   // 0 = halt on error; 1 = don't halt on error
9:
```

The first few lines in ERROR.CPP include the STREAM.HPP, STDLIB.H, and ERROR.H header files. At lines 7-8, the module also defines two private variables, errornumber and errorignore. The first variable, errornumber, stores the error code of the most recent error passed to the error function. The second variable, errorignore, is a flag that tells the module whether to halt on detecting errors, or to continue. Both variables are stored permanently in the program's data segment, but like the savedChar variable in KEY.CPP (see Listing 6.6, line 6), the variables are not accessible to programs that use ERROR.

Or, I should say, the variables are not *normally* available. A program can gain access to private variables defined in modules such as KEY.CPP and ERROR.CPP by declaring those variables to be extern. To use the private variables in ERROR, insert these lines in your main program:

```
extern int errornumber;
extern int errorignore;
```

This tells the compiler (and linker) that the two values are defined in another module. As you can see, private variables like these two are not that private after all.

Any program can easily gain access to the values by declaring them to be extern. For that reason, when you need to hide data from other modules, it's usually best to insert that data into a class and *not* to define variables as done here. Still, the technique is useful, and you should understand it. A test program, TERROR, following this section demonstrates how to use the extern declarations.

Listing 6.10. ERROR.CPP (continued)

```
10: /* -- Call error with error number argument. If errorignore == FALSE
11: (the default), program halts with error message. If errorignore ==
12: TRUE, then program continues and the next statement should call
13: geterror() to determine whether the previous operation succeeded or
14: failed. */
15:
16: void error(int errnum, const char *s)
17: {
18:     errornumber = errnum;        // Save error number in global
19:     if (errorignore) return;     // Exit if not halting on errors
20:     if (s == NULL)               // If no string passed to function
21:        switch(errnum) {          // Assign literal string to s
22:           case ERRMEM:
23:              s = "Out of memory";
24:              break;
25:           case ERRWININIT:
26:              s = "Window class not initialized";
27:              break;
28:           default:
29:              s = "Unknown cause";
30:        }
31:     cout << "\n\nERROR: " << s << '\n'; // Display message
32:     exit(errnum);                       // Halt program
33: }
34:
```

When an error occurs in a program, call the error function listed at lines 16-33. Most of the time, you'll pass only an error code as an argument to error. For example, using the constants listed in ERROR.H, use the following statement to signal an out-of-memory error:

```
error(ERRMEM);
```

At line 18, error assigns the error-code argument to the global errornumber variable. The function then checks whether errorignore is true. If so, line 21 exits error immediately. If errorignore is false, the function continues with another if statement at line 20 that inspects the optional char * parameters. If s equals

NULL, error executes a switch statement that sets s to the address of a literal error message string based on one of the constants from ERROR.H. If s is not NULL, the function skips this step.

The effect of these statements is to allow two ways to call error. Most of the time, you'll execute statements such as

```
error(ERRWININIT);
```

If errorignore is false, the call to error displays the message string "Window class not initialized" and halts the program by calling exit at line 32.

You can also call error with an explicit string as the second argument. In this case, the error code doesn't matter; to prevent conflicts with other error constants, however, negative values are probably best:

```
#ifdef DEBUGGING
error(-154, "Internal bug. Please report at once.");
#endif
```

Surrounding such calls with #ifdef and #endif directives makes it easy to eliminate temporary error-handling statements in the final code. Execute #define DEBUGGING 1 to enable the statement; remove the #define to disable the temporary error call.

The function displays an error-message string at line 31, and then calls exit to halt the program. Line 32 also passes the current error code back to DOS. A batch file could examine errorlevel to retrieve this value.

Using the errorignore flag in error gives programs the choice of halting or continuing after encountering errors. If you choose to continue (demonstrated by TERROR.CPP later), use the next function to examine the current error code.

Listing 6.10. ERROR.CPP (continued)

```
35:   /* -- Call geterror after setting errorignore to TRUE to determine
36:   whether previous operation succeeded (geterror == 0) or failed
37:   (geterror == 1). If the optional reset parameter == 0, then the
38:   global errornumber is NOT reset. If you do not supply this argument
39:   value (or if it's not 0), then the global errornumber is reset to 0.
40:   This means that in normal use, only the first call to geterror
41:   returns useful information. */
42:
43:   int geterror(int reset)
44:   {
45:       int t = errornumber;
46:
47:       if (reset)
```

```
48:          errornumber = 0;
49:      return t;
50:  }
```

The `geterror` function returns the value of `errornumber`. Execute `geterror(0)` to call the function and *not* reset the global `errornumber` to 0. Call the function with no argument (or 1) to reset `errornumber` to 0. This action—a function modifying a global variable—is called a *side effect.* If a program isn't aware of the effect on the global value, and it calls `geterror` two or more times for the same error, it will expect the function to return the same value each time. But that's not what happens, because the first call resets `errornumber` to 0, causing the second call to return 0, the value that represents no error.

Together, `error` and `geterror` provide all the error-handling logic that most programs will need. To halt the program with an error, pass an error code to `error`. To continue the program, set `errorignore` to true (1), and use `geterror` to detect whether other statements have called `error` to signal an error condition.

The test listing in the next section demonstrates how to use the ERROR module.

Testing the ERROR Module

The name of ERROR's test program, TERROR (Test Error), was purely accidental, but I couldn't have picked a better name. Dealing with errors in programs is a terror that most programmers would rather avoid. Listing 6.11, TERROR.CPP, shows how the ERROR module can make error-busting a little less terrifying. Compile the program with the command **ztc terror error.obj**. (You compiled the ERROR module when you compiled WINTOOL. If you didn't do that, however, enter **ztc -c error** before compiling TERROR.)

> **Note:** Running TERROR displays an error message. The program is *supposed* to do that. This is not a bug!

Listing 6.11. TERROR.CPP

```
1:  // terror.cpp -- Test ERROR Module
2:
3:  #include <stream.hpp>
4:  #include "error.h"
5:
6:  extern int errorignore;      // Gain access to errorignore flag
7:
8:  void test(int n);
9:
```

```
10:    main()
11:    {
12:        errorignore = 1;          // Do not halt on errors
13:        test(1);                  // Test with reset in geterror
14:        test(0);                  // Test without reset in geterror
15:        errorignore = 0;          // Halt on errors
16:        error(-154, "Internal problem. Please report at once!");
17:        cout << "\n\nIf you are reading these lines, there is an";
18:        cout << "\nerror in the ERROR module!";
19:    }
20:
21:    void test(int n)
22:    {
23:        int err;
24:
25:        if (n == 0)
26:            cout << "\n\nTesting geterror without reset";
27:        else
28:            cout << "\n\nTesting geterror with reset";
29:        error(ERRMEM);            // Out-of-memory error
30:        if ((err = geterror(n)) != NOERROR)
31:            cout << "\nError detected. Code = " << err;
32:        else
33:            cout << "\nError in ERROR: geterror failed to return code";
34:        cout << "\nSecond call to geterror = " << geterror();
35:    }
```

Line 6 declares e r r o r i g n o r e external, gaining access to that normally private variable. Line 12 sets e r r o r i g n o r e to 1, causing the e r r o r function not to halt the program.

The next two lines call the t e s t function at lines 21-35. The test calls e r r o r, passing the constant E R R M E M to simulate an out-of-memory error. Line 30 then calls g e t e r r o r to retrieve the error code saved by e r r o r. In a real program, e r r o r would probably be called inside another function, and a statement elsewhere would call g e t e r r o r for the result of that operation.

If parameter n is 0, then g e t e r r o r does not reset the internal e r r o r n u m b e r on each call. If the parameter is 1, then g e t e r r o r resets e r r o r n u m b e r to 0. Normally, you should not pass any parameters to g e t e r r o r. Doing so will reset the internal error code to 0, and the next call to g e t e r r o r will return 0 if there have been no intervening calls to e r r o r.

That finishes your tour of the nonOOP code in the LC++ class library. In the next chapter you'll examine the class hierarchies and the programming for the class member functions. You'll also investigate a few new C++ tricks.

Questions and Exercises

6.1. Name the main reason class libraries are easier to use than conventional subroutine libraries.

6.2. Suppose canoe is the name of a class that contains a public member function declared as void row(void);. List the steps required to a) define a pointer to an instance of canoe; b) allocate space for a canoe variable on the heap; c) assign the address of that variable to your pointer; and d) call function row for the new instance.

6.3. List the declaration needed to make function row in exercise 6.2 virtual. Why might you want to do that?

6.4. What is polymorphism?

6.5. What do the terms *early binding* and *late binding* mean?

6.6. Describe a disadvantage of using virtual instead of nonvirtual member functions.

6.7. Write a short program that creates a window in the center of the screen, opens the window, and displays a message inside. (Hint: Use WINTOOL.CPP, Listing 6.4, as a guide. You'll need to include the WINDOW.H header file in your program, and you might also want to include KEY.H so you can insert a statement that waits for a keypress before ending the program. Compile and link your code to the key.obj, error.obj, stritem.obj, item.obj, list.obj, and window.obj files created when you compiled WINTOOL. Because you haven't learned how to use the full LC++ class library, finishing this exercise might be difficult. But take a stab at it before looking up the answer.)

6.8. Finish the performCommand function for WINTOOL's helpCommand class (see Listing 6.4, lines 124-143). Use puts and gotorc member functions from the window class to display strings and move the cursor. Your text should describe how to use WINTOOL.

6.9. Discuss the possible advantages and disadvantages of converting to classes the conventional functions used by the KEY and ERROR modules listed at the end of the chapter.

6.10. Design and test a function that waits for someone to press a specific key— <Esc> or <Spacebar>, for example. Use the KEY module in your answer.

6.11. What values does getkey return for keys <F7>, <Ctrl>-Q, and <Alt>-<F9>?

6.12. What steps do you need to take to prevent the error function in the ERROR module from halting a program?

6.13. Write a program that uses the ERROR module and displays the error message "Red alert!". You do *not* need to modify files ERROR.H or ERROR.CPP to solve this problem.

6.14. What's a "side effect?"

6.15. Design a class named saveCommand derived from the command class. You don't have to implement any member functions in saveCommand, just list the class declaration. (Hint: Use WINTOOL.H, Listing 6.2 as a guide.)

Chapter 7

Building a Class Library—Part 2

Some say that learning object-oriented programming requires a mental shift, a fundamental change in the way programmers conceptualize how to solve problems with computers. Programmers who are comfortable with passing data to and from functions may not appreciate the value of encapsulating data and code inside classes. What good are classes if you can't figure out how to use them?

Learning the rules of C++ and OOP is the easy part. Learning how to apply those rules to solve problems is more difficult. In a few hours, anyone can memorize how to write class declarations, how to derive new classes from others, and how to declare and use member functions. But it can take a lifetime to learn how to weave useful programs from these simple threads.

From past mistakes, I've learned that a *wrong* way to pick up a new programming language is to study the language's parts individually and then start coding a major project. I'd as soon learn to fly by strapping on wings, biting on a propeller, and jumping off a cliff with a copy of some flight jockey's *How to Fly* manual open to chapter 1.

A more sensible plan is to take a few lessons with someone who's been *up there* before. Ground your programs in the sound base of a class library, such as the LC++ library described in this chapter and in chapter 6. Choose classes that are close to those you need. Then, use inheritance to customize the classes to provide the services required to get your program off the ground. Resist the natural urge to write every scrap of code yourself, at least until you've logged a few hours in the copilot's seat.

First Things Last—The Class Library

In chapter 6, you examined a program, WINTOOL, that demonstrates some of the LC++ class library's capabilities. Now that you have an idea of what the library's classes can do, you'll be able to understand how and why the low-level code operates as it does, and you'll be able to visualize new ways to apply that code in your own projects.

In this chapter, you'll examine each class in the LC++ class library, starting at the base of the class hierarchy with a simple class named i t e m from which all other classes derive. Along with each new class, you'll also compile and run a demonstration program that illustrates how to use the class's public members. And, of course, you'll look at the source code that implements the class member functions. Study this code and read the comments carefully—the listings contain many tips and tricks that you can extract for your own work.

> **Note:** I'll list the commands necessary to compile various programs in this chapter. Alternatively, you can execute the MTESTS.BAT file on disk in the LCPP\LIB directory to compile all the programs at once. (This may take a few minutes.) Before running MTESTS, you must compile the supporting modules for the LC++ class library. If you compiled WINTOOL in chapter 6, you have already completed that step. If not, run the ZZ.BAT file now to compile the library. Then run MTESTS.

Class Hierarchies

Figure 7.1 shows the hierarchy of classes in the LC++ class library. Base classes to the left are connected to their derivations at right. For example, the diagram shows that c o m m a n d derives from the base class s t r i t e m, which in turn derives from the base class i t e m. The s e l e c t o r class is marked with an asterisk to indicate that it derives from more than one base class (l i s t and w i n d o w), and, therefore, appears more than once in the chart—a condition known as *multiple inheritance.*

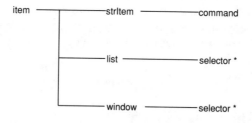

* inherits from multiple base classes

Figure 7.1.   Standard hierarchy diagram showing derived classes that inherit properties from various base classes.

Other commercial class libraries will have similar diagrams. (If you find one that doesn't, get a different library!) Because many classes in a library will inherit members from other classes, just finding all that's in a derived class can be extremely difficult. Diagrams like the one in Figure 7.1 can help by showing class relationships, and you may want to construct similar charts for your own projects.

At the Root of the Library

All classes in the LC++ class library derive from the base class item (see Figure 7.1). An item doesn't do much on its own. It simply gives other derived classes a common ancestor, and it also contains the basic mechanisms required to create lists of class instances in memory.

As you learn more about C++ and OOP, you'll discover that lists are as common in OOP as nuts in a squirrel's nest. Lists are convenient for creating *container classes* that can store a variety of items. Among other uses, a list might hold a menu of commands, file names in a directory, or the lines from a text file. More on this subject later.

The ITEM.H Header

Listing 7.1, ITEM.H, shows the header for the item class. Most of the text in this short file should be familiar to you, but there are two new elements you haven't seen before.

Listing 7.1. ITEM.H

```
 1:   // item.h -- Header file for item.cpp
 2:
 3:   #ifndef __ITEM_H
 4:   #define __ITEM_H        1        // Prevent multiple #includes
 5:
 6:   class item {
 7:      protected:
 8:         item *left;            // Address item at "left"
 9:         item *right;           // Address item at "right"
10:      public:
11:         item();
12:         virtual ~item();
13:         item *link(item *ip);
14:         item *unlink(void);
```

```
15:   };
16:
17:   #endif    // __ITEM_H
```

Before reading about item's new features, make sure that you understand the purpose of lines 8-9 and 13-14. The two item pointers left and right address instances of type item. As with structs, C++ allows fields inside a class to address variables of that same class. In this way, it's possible to declare pointers such as left and right that link variables of a class type (or any derivations) in chains, forming lists of the variables in memory.

The public member functions link and unlink carry out the instructions needed to make and break the linkage between items. To link two items, pass an item pointer to another item's link member. For example, if aItem and bItem are both pointers to item instances, you can link those instances with the statement

```
aItem->link(bItem);
```

That links the instance addressed by aItem to bItem's instance, which might be linked to another item in a list. The link function returns ip, allowing you to use it inside a nested function call such as

```
aItem->link(bItem->link(chain));
```

That links the instance at aItem to the one at bItem. The result is then linked to a third item, chain.

Call unlink to detach an item from a list. You can do this regardless of whether you previously called link. To unlink the instance that bItem addresses, use the statement

```
bItem->unlink();
```

Protected Members

The first new element in ITEM.H is the protected: key word at line 7. Like public: and private:, protected: begins a new section in the class, giving special status to all members listed below.

Members in a protected: section are both private and public. They are private to statements outside the class. But they are public to statements inside a *derived* class. Members in a protected: section are visible to the class that declares them and to any classes that derive from the class.

A simple example will help you to understand how protected members differ from those in private and public areas. Suppose you design a class named aClass with three data fields

```
class aClass {
    private:
        int A;
    protected:
        int B;
    public:
        int C;
        void f();
}
```

Integer A is visible only to member functions also in aClass. Statements in function f (the implementation is not shown here) may access A directly. Function f may also use integers B and C. All the members in the class are useable by statements in the same class. But if the program defines a variable v of type aClass, the first two of these statements outside of the class are not allowed:

```
v.A = 10;    // ???
v.B = 20;    // ???
v.C = 30;    // okay
```

A is private to the class; therefore, the statement can't access the A field directly. Likewise, B is protected—it too is invisible to statements outside the class. However, C is public, so any statement can refer to this field. (Public data items are considered to be bad form. I used one here only to demonstrate how protected members differ from private and public ones. Avoid public data fields in your own code.)

Suppose you next declare a derived class that inherits the properties of aClass. Let's call this new class bClass:

```
class bClass: public aClass {
    public:
        void g();
}
```

Because bClass inherits all of aClass's members, it can use the members declared in aClass's public and protected sections. But it can't use any of the base class's private members. For example, inside bClass's implementation of function g, the first of the following statements is not allowed:

```
A = 10;    // ???
B = 20;    // okay
C = 30;    // okay
```

Member A is private to the base class. A copy of this field exists in a variable of the derived class type, but that field is visible by name *only* to member functions inside aClass. However, since B is in a protected section, the derived class can refer to B directly. The assignment to C is always allowed. Any statement, anywhere, anytime can use a class's public members.

Remember these rules: Private members can be used only by other members of the same class. Protected members can be used by members in that class and in any derived class. Public members can be used by any statement inside or outside the class. (See Figure 7.2.)

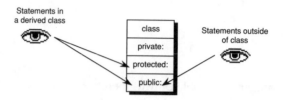

Figure 7.2.   Private members are strictly for use by their class.

Note: Chapter 9 describes *friends,* a method for allowing unrelated classes access to private and protected declarations. Friends can be useful, but are best avoided, because they bend the rules of OOP almost to breaking. The classes in the LC++ class library in this chapter and chapter 6 do not use friends.

Choosing Among `private, public,` *and* `protected`

It takes careful planning, a healthy measure of intuition, a bit of luck, and much experience to decide whether members should be private, protected, or public. Three guidelines will help you to make the right decision:

- If there's any chance you'll want to change the data type of a member field, or if you want to isolate a field to make it difficult for statements outside the class to change the field's value, then make that field *private.*

- If a derived class will benefit greatly from direct access to a data field declared in a base class, make that field *protected.*

- Make *only* member functions *public,* never data fields. Use inline member functions to provide fast access to private data fields. Don't make data fields public just to give programs quick access to those values.

If you sidestep these guidelines, your programs may compile and run, but you may not be able to modify the class declarations without also having to alter statements that use the classes. In time you'll appreciate being able to enhance your existing programs by using inheritance and virtual functions without having to rewrite statements that already work perfectly well. You can always break the rules, but if you do, you should ask yourself why you are using OOP techniques to program your project. Maybe you shouldn't!

Destructors

The second new element in ITEM.H is called a *destructor* (see Listing 7.1, line 12). A destructor is the antithesis of a constructor, which, as you know, initializes new variables of a class. Like a constructor, a destructor has the same name as its class. To distinguish the destructor, it begins with the *difference symbol* ~ from mathematics. In the item class, the ~item destructor at line 12 is declared to be virtual, though other classes may declare nonvirtual destructors. The reason for making ~item virtual is to allow pointers to base class variables to call destructors in derived classes, similar to the way other virtual member functions allow pointers to base class variables to call replacement functions in derived classes.

What does a destructor do? In a nutshell, it cleans up any leftovers in a class variable when that variable goes out of scope. As you know, constructors initialize class variables. Destructors do the opposite—they *deinitialize* variables when a program is done using them.

Programs rarely call destructors directly. Instead, C++ generates instructions that call a class's destructor automatically when

- A local or global class variable goes out of scope, or

- The program deletes a class variable stored on the heap

Other classes in this chapter declare destructors, and as you examine those classes, you'll learn more about how destructors work and why they are needed. Until then, here are a few important points about destructors to keep in mind:

- There can be only one destructor in a class.

- Destructors are often declared virtual, although they don't have to be.

- Destructors do not have parameters.

- Destructors do not have return data types (not even void).

- Destructors are optional. If a class doesn't need to clean up after itself, it doesn't need a destructor.

- Destructors are called automatically to deinitialize a class variable. Programs rarely call destructors directly.

Using the item *Class*

Listing 7.2, TITEM.CPP (test item), demonstrates how to use the item class. Because item does nothing on its own, the program derives a new class from item, to give the program something to do. While confirming that the ITEM module works correctly, the program also demonstrates a few key points about using constructors and destructors.

Listing 7.2. TITEM.CPP

```
 1:    // titem.cpp -- Test item class
 2:
 3:    #include <stream.hpp>
 4:    #include "item.h"
 5:
 6:    class derivedItem: public item {
 7:        public:
 8:            derivedItem();
 9:            virtual ~derivedItem();
10:    };
11:
12:    main()
13:    {
14:        item *ip1;
15:        item *ip2;
16:
17:        cout << "\nCreating new item on the heap";
18:        ip1 = new item;
19:        cout << "\nCreating new derivedItem on the heap";
20:        ip2 = new derivedItem;
21:        cout << "\nLinking the two items together";
22:        ip1->link(ip2);
23:        cout << "\nUnlinking derived item";
24:        ip2->unlink();
25:        cout << "\nDeleting the new item";
26:        delete ip1;
27:        cout << "\nDeleting the derived item";
28:        delete ip2;
29:    }
30:
31:    derivedItem::derivedItem()
32:    {
33:        cout << "\n Inside derivedItem's constructor";
34:    }
35:
36:    derivedItem::~derivedItem()
37:    {
38:        cout << "\n Inside derivedItem's destructor";
39:    }
```

Lines 6-10 declare a derived class named derivedItem. The class inherits all the properties of item, including item's constructor and destructor. To its inheritance, derivedItem adds its own constructor (line 8) and a new virtual destructor (line 9).

The `main` program defines two pointers, `ip1` and `ip2`, to type `item` (see lines 14-15). Then, several output-stream statements display notes about what the program is about to do at each step in the test. First, line 18 allocates space for an `item` variable, assigning the address of that space to `ip1`. Line 20 performs a similar job, but this time allocates space for a `derivedItem` variable. The constructors for `item` and `derivedItem` automatically run at this time.

The statements at lines 18 and 20 also illustrate that pointers to instances of a base class can address instances of a derived class. The reverse is not true. If you insert the following lines at line 16 in TITEM, you'll receive an error from the compiler:

```
derivedItem *ip3;   // Define pointer to derivedItem
ip3 = new item;     // ???
```

Pointers to a derived class may never address variables of a base class. However, pointers to base classes may address variables of derived classes. Figure 7.3 will help you to understand the purpose of this rule. A derived class inherits properties from a base class. In addition to those properties, a derived class usually adds new fields that do not exist in the base. For that reason, a base pointer can safely address a variable of the derived type, which, after all, has an inherited copy of the fields that exist in the base class. But the base class does *not* have any of the new items added to the derived class; therefore, a pointer to the derived class can't address a variable of the base type. If a pointer to a derived class instance addressed a base class variable, a statement might attempt to access a nonexistent field, causing a serious bug. C++ prevents this kind of error by not permitting pointers to derived classes to address variables of a base class type.

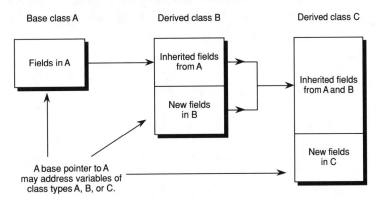

Figure 7.3. A pointer to a base class variable may address variables of derived classes but pointers to derived classes may never address variables of a base type.

Lines 22 and 24 in TITEM call the `link` and `unlink` member functions declared in the `item` class. Even though `ip2` addresses a variable of `derivedItem`, line 24 can call the `unlink` member function because `derivedItem` inherits item's members. The *same* unlink function applies to variables of type item and to variables of type derivedItem.

Lines 26 and 28 delete the variables created by new earlier. Similar to the way constructors run when the new variables come into being, destructors in a class run when the class variables are deleted. Line 38 in the derivedItem destructor displays a message that tells you when a variable of this type goes out of scope.

But there's more happening than you can tell by running TITEM. When a derivedItem variable comes into being, the constructor at lines 31-34 runs automatically. However, that happens *after* the item constructor *also* runs. Similarly, when a derivedItem variable goes out of scope, the class destructor at lines 36-39 runs, but so does the destructor in the base item class.

These effects mean that, when TITEM executes the statement ip2 = new derivedItem at line 20, C++ generates code that

- calls the base class item's constructor

- then calls derivedItem's constructor

Similarly, when the program deletes ip2, because derivedItem derives from item, C++ generates code that

- calls derivedItem's destructor

- then calls the base class item's destructor

In general, constructors in base classes run *before* the constructors in derived classes. Destructors in base classes run *after* destructors in derived classes. These rules may be easier to remember if you think of class variables as buildings that are constructed from the base up (base class constructors run first), but are torn down starting at the top (base destructors run last).

The ITEM.CPP Module

Finally in this section is the item class's implementation. At this stage, you know just about everything there is to know about item. You've examined its header file and compiled a test program. Armed with that knowledge, you should have little trouble understanding the low-level code in ITEM.CPP's text file (Listing 7.3). But there is one new element: a key word with the unusual name this.

Listing 7.3. ITEM.CPP

```
1:  // item.cpp -- Item class
2:
3:  #include <stddef.h>
4:  #include "item.h"
5:
```

```
 6:    /* -- An item object's constructor. Automatically called when space
 7:    is allocated for a new item object. */
 8:
 9:    item::item()
10:    {
11:        left = right = this;        // Point item to itself.
12:    }
13:
14:    /* -- Item's destructor. Ensures that all items are unlinked from any
15:    others before the item's memory is returned to the heap. */
16:
17:    item::~item()
18:    {
19:        if (left != this)           // If item is linked to another,
20:            unlink();               //   unlink it.
21:    }
22:
```

this *Is Where It's At*

The item constructor appears at lines 9-12. As in most constructors, the function initializes the data fields in an instance of the class. Here, line 11 carries out that duty by assigning the same value to the left and right pointer fields, which can address other item variables (and derivations) in lists.

The value assigned to left and right is a C++ key word, this. The this key word is a pointer that's available to all member functions in a class. The this pointer addresses the instance of the class that called the function. The this pointer is also available in constructors and destructors.

Assigning this to left and right causes the item object to point to its own instance in memory (see Figure 7.4). In the LC++ class library, an object that addresses itself is not a member of any list, a fact other statements can use to determine whether an object needs to be detached from other objects.

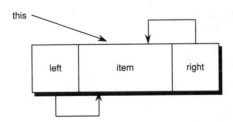

Figure 7.4. Assigning the *this* pointer to the *left* and *right* fields in an *item* instance causes the *item* to address itself in memory.

One such moment comes in i t em's destructor at lines 17-21. Again, t h i s is used to obtain the address of the instance that called the destructor. If the i t em's l e f t pointer does not equal t h i s, then that i t em must be attached to another, and line 20 calls the u n l i n k function to detach the instance. (The statement could just as well examine the r i g h t field for this purpose.) It's important to perform this step in the destructor, because the instance is about to go out of scope (a statement has deleted the object from memory). Just *before* that happens, the destructor has the opportunity to clean up any business inside the instance—in this example, detaching the i t em from another. Deleting an i t em without detaching it from another could cause other items to address an instance that has been deleted. The destructor neatly prevents that error. All the program has to do is delete the instance.

In your own classes, you should use destructors to perform similar cleanup chores. Ideally, it should be possible to delete a class instance (or end a function that defines a local class variable) without having to perform additional duties. The best classes construct themselves when they are defined, and destroy themselves completely when they are deleted or go out of scope.

> **Note:** The t h i s pointer is passed as a hidden parameter to every member function in a class. The pointer has the same type as a declared pointer to the class. In other words, in i t em's member functions, t h i s has the type i t em *; therefore, C++ allows the assignment at line 11 to the l e f t and r i g h t fields, both of which are of that same type.

Listing 7.3. ITEM.CPP (continued)

```
23:    /* -- Attach one item to another. Assuming A and B are pointers to
24:    items, to attach a new item A to an existing item B, pass B to A's
25:    link function. B may be attached to another item, or it may be
26:    solitary. The item at A will then be linked to the "left" of B. If A
27:    is already attached to another item, it will be unlinked from that
28:    item before being attached to B. */
29:
30:    item *item::link(item *ip)
31:    {
32:        if (ip ==  NULL)            // Ignore request to link to
33:            return NULL;            //  a NULL item.
34:        if (left != this)          // If item is linked to another
35:            unlink();              //  unlink it.
36:        right = ip;                // Adjust item's right and left
37:        left = ip->left;           //  pointers to link to the item
38:        ip->left->right = this;    //  addressed by ip.
39:        ip->left = this;
40:        return ip;                 // Return address of linked item.
41:    }
```

```
42:
43:    /* -- Unattach this item from another. After calling unlink for any
44:    item, you can be sure that the item is not an element of any list.
45:    It's okay to call unlink whether or not the item is currently joined
46:    to another in a list. Return address of unlinked item, allowing
47:    unlink() to be passed to another item* function parameter. */
48:
49:    item *item::unlink(void)
50:    {
51:        left->right = right;      // Unlink the item by adjusting
52:        right->left = left;       //   the attached item's pointers.
53:        left = right = this;      // Point this item to itself.
54:        return left;              // Return item's address.
55:    }
```

Lines 30-55 implement the two public member functions in the i t em class. All derived classes inherit these functions, which can link and unlink instances from others. (The next section explains how to use the functions to form lists.)

The l i nk function at lines 30-41 requires a single argument, a pointer i p to another i t em instance. An i f statement examines this argument, ending the function immediately if the pointer is NULL. This prevents a serious problem that would occur if a statement tried to link a NULL item to a list.

A second i f statement at lines 34-35 compares the l e f t pointer to t h i s, which addresses the instance of the i t em that called the l i nk function. If these two pointers are not equal, then this i t em is attached to another, and line 35 calls un l i nk to detach the item before linking. Because of this step, programs can call l i nk to move an i t em from one list to another. You don't have to detach an i t em in order to reattach it somewhere else.

Note that line 35 calls the un l i nk member function directly. The statement does not preface un l i nk in the usual way with the name of or a pointer to an instance of the class. As you know, outside the class, you normally allocate space for an instance of type i t em, and then use a statement such as p->un l i nk ( ) to call the member function for the i t em instance addressed by p. Line 35 does not require a similar instance, because it was an instance that called l i nk. Where is that instance? It's at the location addressed by t h i s. In other words, line 35 executes as though it were written

```
this->unlink();
```

Inside a member function, you can always call other member functions directly. C++ assumes that you intend to call the other function for the same class instance that called this function. Therefore, you do not have to preface such function calls with t h i s->.

The rest of l i nk at lines 36-40 adjusts the l e f t and r i ght fields in i t em to attach it to the i t em addressed by t h i s. Finally, the function returns the address of the attached item, i p.

Member function un l i nk (see lines 51-54) undoes what l i nk puts together. Again, the t h i s pointer is used to obtain the address of the instance that called un l i nk. After adjusting the l e f t and r i g h t fields to detach the i t em from another (if it's attached to one), line 53 assigns t h i s to l e f t and r i g h t. This reconfigures the i t em to its initial state, and ensures that any lists the i t em was attached to are kept sound. Finally, line 54 returns the address of the instance that called un l i nk.

A Class for Lists

The l i s t class in the LC++ class library derives from i t em (see Figure 7.1). Every l i s t is also an i t em, which means that every l i s t instance inherits a copy of all the declarations in i t em. Because l i s t derives from i t em, it may use i t em's protected and public fields and members.

Like i t em, the l i s t class doesn't do much on its own. The l i s t class is a general-purpose container—it can hold whatever kinds of objects you want a l i s t to store (up to the limits of available memory). All variables stored in a l i s t must derive from the i t em class. However, the same l i s t may store many different types of i t em derivations. Since l i s t itself derives from i t em, a l i s t can be a list of lists.

The LIST.H Header

The l i s t class is declared in LIST.H, Listing 7.4. Note that the file includes the declarations in ITEM.H (see line 7). As a result, programs that include the LIST.H header automatically receive a copy of ITEM.H.

Listing 7.4. LIST.H

```
 1:  // list.h -- Header for list.cpp
 2:
 3:  #ifndef __LIST_H
 4:  #define __LIST_H      1       // Prevent multiple #includes
 5:
 6:  #include <stdlib.h>
 7:  #include "item.h"
 8:
 9:  class list: public item {
10:      private:
11:          item *anchor;         // Anchors list head
12:          item *cip;            // "Current item pointer"
```

```
13:
14:     public:
15:
16:     // -- Constructor and destructor
17:         List();
18:         virtual ~List();
19:
20:     // -- Inline member functions
21:         int listEmpty(void)
22:             { return (anchor == NULL); }
23:         int atHeadOfList(void)
24:             { return ((anchor != NULL) && (cip == anchor)); }
25:         int atEndOfList(void)
26:             { return ((anchor != NULL) && (cip == anchor->left)); }
27:         item *currentItem(void)
28:             { return cip; }
29:         item *firstItem(void)
30:             { return (cip = anchor); }
31:         void resetList(void)
32:             { cip = anchor; }
33:         void setCurrentItem(item *ip)
34:             { cip = ip; }
35:
36:     // -- Other member functions
37:         item *insertItem(item *ip);
38:         item *removeItem(item *ip);
39:         item *prevItem(void);
40:         item *nextItem(void);
41:
42:     // Virtual member function
43:         virtual void disposeList(void);
44: };
45:
46: #endif   // __LIST_H
```

Because list inherits the properties of item, all list instances have left and right pointer fields along with the new fields, anchor and cip, declared in list at lines 11-12. Unlike the left and right fields, however, anchor and cip are private. No other classes or statements outside of list may use these two fields directly. Because of this design, it's possible to modify the way list stores items in memory without affecting programs that use the class.

The anchor pointer addresses the first item in the list. Lists are circular in this implementation, and therefore, the anchor marks a list's beginning and end. The cip pointer addresses the current item. This pointer floats from item to item, and is often used to scan all the items in a list. (Because c i p is private to the class, however, programs can't use the pointer directly.)

Lines 17-18 declare the l i s t class constructor and destructor. Because the destructor is virtual, a pointer declared as type l i s t * could address an instance of a derived class and still be deleted properly. Calling d e l e t e for such a pointer would call the proper virtual destructors in derived objects.

The functions at lines 21-34 have obvious purposes. Each of these members is declared in line, which helps keep programs running fast. Low-level classes like l i s t are good candidates for in-line member functions. Chances are, many derivations will use these functions, and it makes good sense to use in-line code to avoid the overhead required to call normal functions.

Four other regular-style member functions are prototyped at lines 37-40. The first of these, i n s e r t I t e m, inserts new items into a list. The second, r e m o v e I t e m, performs the reverse job. It deletes an item currently in the list. Functions p r e v I t e m and n e x t I t e m help you write loops that scan all the items in a list. You'll see examples of how to do this later.

The final member function is d i s p o s e L i s t, at line 43. This function is declared virtual so that statements compiled now may be redirected to a derived class's d i s p o s e L i s t function in the future. With this method, a derived class can declare its own d i s p o s e L i s t to clean up additional items added to the derivation. Any *existing* code that calls d i s p o s e L i s t will then call the new function automatically.

Using the l i s t *Class*

TLIST.CPP, Listing 7.5, demonstrates how to use the l i s t class. Compile the program with the command **ztc tlist item.obj list.obj**. You must have the ITEM.OBJ and LIST.OBJ files in the current directory. Otherwise, enter **ztc tlist item list** to compile the test program and the separate modules.

Listing 7.5. TLIST.CPP

```
 1:   // tlist.cpp -- Test list class
 2:
 3:   #include <stream.hpp>
 4:   #include "list.h"
 5:
 6:   class myItem : public item {
 7:      private:
 8:         int value;
 9:      public:
10:         myItem(int n) { value = n; }
11:         void putValue(int n) { value = n; }
```

```
12:             int getValue(void) { return value; }
13:     };
14:
15:     void showList(void);
16:
17:     list *lp = new list;
18:
19:     main()
20:     {
21:         int i;
22:         myItem *mip;
23:
24:         cout << "\nAfter allocating new list";
25:         showList();
26:
27:         cout << "\n\nInsert 10 items into the list";
28:         for (i = 1; i <= 10; i++)
29:             lp->insertItem(new myItem(i));
30:         showList();
31:
32:         cout << "\n\nAdd 100 to listed item values";
33:         lp->resetList();
34:         do {
35:             mip = (myItem *)lp->currentItem();
36:             mip->putValue(mip->getValue() + 100);
37:             lp->nextItem();
38:         } while (!lp->atHeadOfList());
39:         showList();
40:
41:         cout << "\n\nDelete first 3 items from list";
42:         lp->resetList();
43:         for (i = 1; i <= 3; i++)
44:             lp->removeItem(lp->currentItem());
45:         showList();
46:
47:         cout << "\n\nDispose of all listed items";
48:         lp->disposeList();
49:         showList();
50:     }
51:
52:     void showList(void)
53:     {
54:         cout << "\nITEMS IN LIST: ";
55:         if (lp->ListEmpty()) {
56:             cout << "List is empty";
```

```
57:          return;
58:       }
59:       lp->resetList();
60:       do {
61:          cout << ((myItem *)(lp->currentItem()))->getValue();
62:          cout << "   ";
63:          lp->nextItem();
64:       } while (!lp->atHeadOfList());
65:    }
```

To give the list something to store, lines 6-13 in the test program declare a derived class, myItem. This new class inherits the properties of item, and fulfills the requirement that all objects stored on a list are derived from item. (Such objects do not have to be *immediately* derived from item. Another class could be derived from myItem and stored in a list. As long as a class has item as a base class, no matter how distantly related, that class's instances may be stored in a list.) The derived myItem stores a single int field and has a constructor and two methods for accessing that field.

Line 17 illustrates the correct way to define list instances, using new to allocate space for the list on the heap. In this case, the lp pointer (list pointer) is declared global, but it could also be local to a function. It's important to realize that defining space for a list variable does *not* reserve any space for listed items. The definition at line 17 applies only to the lp pointer and the list instance that pointer addresses. That instance is usually called the *list head*, or the *root*.

As in the TITEM test program, the bulk of TLIST consists of a series of tests (lines 24-39) that demonstrate some of list's capabilities. Each test calls a local function, showList, to display the values of the myItem instances currently stored on the list.

Line 29 shows how to insert new items in a list instance, calling member function insertItem. Note that the argument to that function is new myItem(i). Calling new this way allocates space for an instance of myItem and passes the address of that space directly to insertItem.

After inserting a few items, lines 32-39 scan the list and add 100 to each myItem value. Lines 33-38 illustrate how to perform this scan. In general, for a list addressed by lp, these steps access every listed instance:

```
lp->resetList();
do {
   doSomething(lp->currentItem());
   lp->nextItem();
} while (!lp->atHeadOfList());
```

The first line resets the list so that the next item examined is the first in the list. A do/while loop then cycles while the expression (!lp->atHeadOfList()) remains true. Function atHeadOfList will be true when the previous statement, lp->nextItem(), advances the list back to its starting place. That will cause the negated expression to be false, thus ending the loop.

Inside the loop, the statement doSomething(lp->currentItem()) calls a function named doSomething (not shown) and passes the address of the current item as an argument. Always use the expression lp->currentItem() to obtain the address of items in a list.

Unfortunately, because currentItem returns type item *, a type cast is usually necessary to tell the compiler what kind of item derivative the function result addresses. For example, line 35 executes

```
mip = (myItem *)lp->currentItem();
```

That assigns the result of currentItem to mip, a pointer declared as type myItem *. Without the type cast (myItem *), the compiler would reject the assignment, because item * and myItem * are different types. You'll find many other situations that require similar type casts.

Instead of assigning a recast pointer to a temporary variable like mip, you can also perform and use the cast expression directly. This leads to complex expressions such as the one at line 61, repeated here:

```
((myItem *)(lp->currentItem()))->getValue();
```

Compare this with the previous sample line. The expression calls currentItem for the list addressed by lp. It casts the result (an item *) to type myItem *. Then, it uses that pointer to call the getValue member function in the myItem class. The parentheses are necessary to force the compiler to evaluate the parts in the correct order.

Writing such long expressions is tedious work. However, although the names will change, the forms in other type-cast expressions will be nearly identical. I find that it helps to #define a macro for part or all of the expression. The macro name greatly simplifies multiple uses of the same expression. For example, you might define this macro:

```
#define DP ((derived *)(bp->baseFunction()))
```

Then, you can use DP in place of the confusing type cast:

```
DP->derivedFunction();
```

Using uppercase for the macro name reminds you that DP is not a variable.

The LIST.CPP Module

The implementation for the list class is surprisingly short. LIST.CPP, Listing 7.6, weighs in at just under 100 lines.

Listing 7.6. LIST.CPP

```
 1:  // list.cpp -- List class
 2:
 3:  #include <stddef.h>
 4:  #include "list.h"
 5:
 6:  /* -- List constructor. Initializes an empty list when the list
 7:  object comes into being (i.e., is allocated storage). Note: because
 8:  a list is a descendant of an item, the item class constructor also
 9:  runs before the list constructor. */
10:
11:  List::list()
12:  {
13:      anchor = cip = NULL;     // No listed or current items
14:  }
15:
16:  /* -- List destructor. Like a snake eating itself by the tail, the
17:  destructor disposes of all items (if any) on the list, and then
18:  disposes of itself. */
19:
20:  List::~list()
21:  {
22:      if (anchor != NULL)
23:          disposeList();
24:  }
25:
```

The List class constructor sets the anchor and cip fields to NULL, indicating that the list is empty (see lines 11-14). Because List derives from item, it's important to realize that the item constructor has already finished by the time the statements at line 13 execute. This fact is easy to miss when reading the source code of a derived constructor.

The destructor at lines 20-24 runs when a program calls delete to dispose of a List instance. At this time, line 22 checks whether there are any items on a list. If so, the destructor calls disposeList, another List member function. The function deletes all listed objects, emptying the list before it too is disposed. Because of this automatic cleanup, you can delete a list without having to check whether the list holds any listed items.

The rest of List's member functions use conventional C++ techniques, and you should have no trouble understanding the statements. Comments in the listing explain the functions and point out several highlights.

Listing 7.6. LIST.CPP (continued)

```
26:  /* -- Insert a new item addressed by ip into a list object. The new
27:  item is linked in front of (to the left of) the current item. To
28:  link an item after another, find that item and call nextItem before
29:  calling insertItem. Does nothing if argument is NULL. If list is
30:  empty, then a new list is created with the single item at ip. Returns
31:  address of inserted item or NULL.*/
32:
33:  item *list::insertItem(item *ip)
34:  {
35:      if (ip == NULL)                 // Ignore request to insert
36:          return NULL;                //  a NULL item.
37:      if (anchor == NULL)             // If list is empty...
38:          return anchor = cip = ip;   //  start a new list
39:      return ip->link(cip);           // Else, link item into list
40:  }
41:
42:  /* -- Remove the item addressed by ip from the list object. Also
43:  adjust the anchor and cip pointers to make sure they do not address
44:  the unlinked item. If the addressed item is the only one in the list,
45:  then this function empties the list. Does NOT dispose the unlinked
46:  item or call its destructor. After calling removeItem, the item
47:  addressed by ip points to itself, and it can be used to begin a new
48:  list, or it can be used as a free-floating object. Returns NULL or
49:  the address of the removed item. */
50:
51:  item *list::removeItem(item *ip)
52:  {
53:      if (ip == NULL)                 // Ignore request to remove
54:          return NULL;                //  a NULL item.
55:      if (ip->right == ip)            // If list has only one item...
56:          anchor = cip = NULL;        //  then empty the list
57:      else {
58:          if (ip == anchor)           // Else adjust anchor and
59:              anchor = anchor->right; //  cip pointers to ensure that
60:          if (cip == ip)              //  they do not address the
61:              cip = cip->right;       //  unlinked item.
62:      }
63:      return ip->unlink();            // Unlink item from list
64:  }
65:
66:  /* -- Return a pointer to the previous item, the one to the "left" of
67:  the current item. Also sets the current item pointer to that item.
68:  Returns NULL if list is empty. */
```

```
69:
70:    item *list::prevItem(void)
71:    {
72:       if (cip != NULL)          // If list is not empty
73:           cip = cip->left;      //  set cip to item at left.
74:       return cip;               // Return current item pointer.
75:    }
76:
77:    /* -- Return a pointer to the next item, the one to the "right" of
78:    the current item. Also sets the current item pointer to that item.
79:    Returns NULL if list is empty. */
80:
81:    item *list::nextItem(void)
82:    {
83:       if (cip != NULL)          // If list is not empty
84:           cip = cip->right;     //  set cip to item at right.
85:       return cip;               // Return current item pointer.
86:    }
87:
88:    /* -- Remove and delete all items (if any) in the list object. If
89:    items have destructors, they are called for each item. Items are not
90:    necessarily disposed in the order they were inserted. */
91:
92:    void list::disposeList(void)
93:    {
94:       item *ip;
95:
96:       while (!listEmpty())
97:           delete removeItem(currentItem());
98:    }
```

A Class for Strings

Suppose that you need to store a bunch of strings in memory, probably one of the most common problems programmers contend with. Maybe you are writing a text editor and you need a convenient way to manage lines of text. Or maybe you need a simple way to display a set of instructions in a window. How would you attack these problems?

You could design arrays of type char. Or perhaps an array of char pointers would be suitable. Either of those solutions may work, but they come with a built-in danger: You may discover later that you picked the wrong data structure. If so, you'll have to waste time redesigning the code from scratch.

This is exactly the kind of calamity that OOP techniques help prevent. When you need a new kind of data structure, begin by examining the classes you have at your disposal. Ask whether there is a class that has at least some of the capabilities you need. Derive a new class from that class, inheriting the original class's properties, and customize the new class to perform whatever tricks you need.

To use this concept to solve the problem of storing strings in memory, review the classes you know about, item and list. A list can store any derivative of item; therefore, the logical place to begin is to create a string class that inherits the properties of item. Then it will be a simple matter to create lists of strings.

The STRITEM.H Header

The strItem class declared in STRITEM.H, Listing 7.7, adds a little meat to item's bones. Remember, since strItem inherits the properties of item, a strItem variable has a copy of all the members in item.

Listing 7.7. STRITEM.H

```
 1:  // stritem.h -- Header for stritem.cpp
 2:
 3:  #ifndef __STRITEM_H
 4:  #define __STRITEM_H  1      // Prevent multiple #includes
 5:
 6:  #include "item.h"
 7:
 8:  class strItem: public item {
 9:     private:
10:        char *sp;
11:
12:     public:
13:
14:     // -- Constructors and destructor
15:        strItem(const char *s);
16:        strItem(const char *s, int maxLen);
17:        virtual ~strItem();
18:
19:     // -- Member functions
20:        virtual char *getString(void) { return sp; }
21:        void putString(const char *s);
22:        void putString(const char *s, int maxLen);
23:  };
24:
25:  #endif   // __STRITEM_H
```

Line 10 adds to the class a new private field, s p, a c h a r pointer. This pointer will address the characters that belong in instance of the s t r I t em class. Because s p is private to the class, only member functions in s t r I t em can use s p. The private s p pointer also ensures that if you revise s t r I t em to store strings in a different manner, you won't have to change a single line of code in programs that use s t r I t em's public members.

Multiple Constructors

A new feature in s t r I t em is the use of two constructors at lines 15-16. C++ lets you *overload* constructors of the same names as long as the declarations differ in at least one parameter. (You can also overload other kinds of functions, a subject covered in chapter 9.)

The first constructor, on line 15, requires a constant string argument. The second constructor, on line 16, requires a string and a maximum length. Because there are two constructors, you can create a new string by entering the following statement:

```
strItem *sp = new strItem("A string of any length");
```

That defines a s t r I t em pointer named s p, and calls n e w to allocate heap space for a s t r I t em instance. The literal string in quotes is passed to the s t r I t em constructor to initialize the object. To limit the size of the string, add a maximum-length value

```
strItem *sp = new strItem("A string of limited length", 10);
```

That creates a new s t r I t em object limited to 10 characters. If the string argument is longer than the maximum (as it is here), the string will be truncated.

C++ is able to differentiate between the two calls to the constructors by the differences in the arguments. Not every class will need multiple constructors, but overloading is vital for creating classes that need to be initialized in different ways.

Line 17 declares the s t r I t em's virtual destructor. The function runs when a s t r I t em is deleted, giving the object the opportunity to clean up after itself.

The other member functions at lines 20-22 give you three ways to read and write characters in s t r I t em instances. Call g e t S t r i n g to obtain the address of a s t r I t em's string. Note that g e t S t r i n g is implemented in line and is declared to be v i r t u a l. C++ allows you to create inline virtual functions, but if a derived class provides a replacement function, the functions will (most likely) be converted to common function calls and will not be expanded in line.

Call p u t S t r i n g to change the characters in a s t r I t em. As with the class's double constructors, function p u t S t r i n g is overloaded. To change the string of a s t r I t em instance addressed by s p, you can write

```
sp->putString("New string of any length");
```

Or to change the string but limit its length to a maximum number of characters, you can write

```
sp->putString("New string of limited length", 10);
```

C++ figures out which of the identically named functions to call based on the different arguments passed to the functions. Of course, I could have created two functions with different names, perhaps `putString1` and `putString2`. But overloading makes it unnecessary to invent new names for nearly identical operations.

> **Note:** Declaring default parameters is another useful tool for creating constructors and functions that allow statements to pass different numbers of arguments. For example, I could have declared a single constructor as `strItem(const char *s, int maxLen = 0)`, and a single `putString` member function as `void putSTring(const char *s, int maxLen = 0)`. Then, in the implementations for these functions, if `maxLen` were 0, the program would assume that a statement called the function with no specific length value, meaning that the entire string should be used.

Using the `strItem` Class

A simple test program demonstrates how to use the `strItem` class. Compile TSTRITEM.CPP, Listing 7.8, with the command **ztc tstritem error.obj item.obj stritem.obj**. Or enter **ztc tstritem error item stritem** if you have not compiled the .OBJ files yet.

Listing 7.8. TSTRITEM.CPP

```
1:  // tstritem.cpp -- Test strItem class
2:
3:  #include <stream.hpp>
4:  #include "stritem.h"
5:
6:  main()
7:  {
8:      strItem *a = new strItem("This is item A");
9:      strItem *b = new strItem("Another item B");
10:     strItem *c = new strItem("One more item C");
11:
12:     cout << (a->getString()) << '\n';
13:     cout << (b->getString()) << '\n';
14:     cout << (c->getString()) << '\n';
```

```
15:
16:        c->putString(a->getString());
17:        cout << "After assigning a to c, c == " << c->getString() << '\n';
18:    }
```

Lines 8-10 define three strItem pointers, a, b, and c. Each of these lines calls new to create a strItem instance on the heap and store the string argument in parentheses. Lines 12-14 then display the strings by calling the getString member functions for each variable. Line 16 shows how to copy one string to another, passing the result of a string item's getString function to putString. That statement creates a distinct copy of the original string.

You normally won't use the strItem class as demonstrated in TSTRITEM, although the class is useful for storing strings in heap memory. After describing the implementation for the class in the next section, I'll return to the problem of storing lists of strings in memory. The value of strItem will then be more apparent.

The STRITEM.CPP Module

The strItem class is implemented in STRITEM.CPP, Listing 7.9. Note that the module includes ERROR.H and uses the error-handling functions described in chapter 6. To have object instances deal with error conditions directly, leave errorignore set to false. To deal with errors yourself, set errorignore to true and use geterror to retrieve a possible error code after calls to strItem member functions.

Listing 7.9. STRITEM.CPP

```
 1:   // stritem.cpp -- String item class
 2:
 3:   #include <string.h>
 4:   #include "error.h"
 5:   #include "stritem.h"
 6:
 7:   /* -- Constructor. Create copy of string addressed by s as a new
 8:   strItem object. Argument may be NULL. */
 9:
10:   strItem::strItem(const char *s)
11:   {
12:       sp = NULL;                  // Initialize private data field
13:       putString(s);               // Save argument string in object
14:   }
15:
16:   /* -- Alternate constructor. Creates copy of string containing up to
17:   the number of characters specified in maxLen. Argument may be NULL.
```

```
18:    If maxLen is 0 or less, allocate no space to string. */
19:
20:    strItem::strItem(const char *s, int maxLen)
21:    {
22:        sp = NULL;                  // Initialize private data field
23:        putString(s, maxLen);       // Save limited-length string
24:    }
25:
26:    /* -- Destructor. Deletes space occupied by string and addressed by
27:    sp, which may be NULL. Runs when a strItem object is deleted. Because
28:    object is about to be deleted anyway, sp is not set to NULL. */
29:
30:    strItem::~strItem()
31:    {
32:        if (sp) delete sp;          // i.e. delete if sp != NULL
33:    }
34:
```

The two constructors at lines 10-14 and 20-24 set sp to NULL and then call one of the overloaded putString member functions. In any constructor, you may call other member functions in the same class. Be aware, however, that the instance may not be fully constructed until after the constructor finishes; therefore, you should not call any member functions that rely on fields not yet initialized by the constructor.

If a constructor calls virtual methods declared in the same class, you should also carefully consider which methods run. Inside the constructor, C++ does *not* look up virtual function addresses from the instance being constructed. Instead, C++ generates direct calls to the function declared in the same class as the constructor.

> **Note:** In a constructor of a base class, calls to virtual member functions are fixed at compile time to the base class's declared virtual functions, even if a derived class replaces those functions and the object in construction is of the derived class. However, in the same class's destructor, calls to virtual functions operate normally, and are redirected to any replacement functions belonging to the instance being destroyed. The general rule is, "In a constructor, virtual functions behave as common member functions." Only after a constructor is finished do virtual functions among derived class instances begin to behave virtually.

The strItem destructor at lines 30-33 illustrates one of the most common uses for a destructor. An if statement checks whether char pointer sp equals NULL. If not, then the statement calls delete to dispose any heap space allocated to sp. Because of this sequence, deleting a strItem pointer will call the destructor, which will clean up the structure the instance stored on the heap. If you write all your destructors to clean up any structures created by class instances, you can simply delete those instances without worrying whether you'll inadvertently leave a variable floating on the heap.

The STRITEM module continues with the overloaded putString functions. Remember, getString is an in-line function; therefore, it's not implemented in the module.

Listing 7.9. STRITEM.CPP (continued)

```
35:  /* -- Insert string into string object, replacing any string
36:  now addressed. */
37:
38:  void strItem::putString(const char *s)
39:  {
40:     if (sp) delete sp;        // Dispose old string (if any)
41:     sp = NULL;                // Prevent accidental use of old pointer
42:     if (s == NULL) return;    // Exit if argument is NULL
43:     sp = strdup(s);           // Copy s to new string at sp
44:     if (sp == NULL)           // Test for strdup error
45:        error(ERRMEM);         // Signal error copying string
46:  }
47:
48:  /* -- Overloaded putString function. Same as putString above, but
49:  limits the new string to maxLen characters. */
50:
51:  void strItem::putString(const char *s, int maxLen)
52:  {
53:     int len;     // Length of string.
54:
55:     if (sp) delete sp;         // Dispose old string (if any)
56:     sp = NULL;                 // Prevent accidental use of old pointer
57:     if (s == NULL) return;     // Exit if argument is NULL
58:     if (maxLen <= 0) return;   // If maxLen <= 0, exit with sp==NULL
59:     len = strlen(s);           // Set len to argument string length
60:     if (len > maxLen)          // If string is longer than maxLen
61:        len = maxLen;           //   limit len to maxLen
62:     sp = new char[len + 1];    // Create space for string + NULL
63:     if (sp == NULL)            // Test whether new() found enough memory
64:        error(ERRMEM);          // If not, signal out-of-memory error
65:     else {
66:        strncpy(sp, s, len);    // Else, copy len chars to sp
67:        sp[len] = NULL;         // Make sure string ends with NULL
68:     }
69:  }
```

Both putString functions delete any current string addressed by sp before assigning a new string. The functions also watch for a NULL argument. You can use this feature to recover heap space allocated to strItem instances. Call sp->putString(NULL) to delete characters in the string but not delete the strItem instance. Zero-length, or NULL, strings are commonplace, and it's important for functions like putString to deal with them in a sensible way.

The two functions also make good use of the ERROR module from chapter 6. Lines 43 and 62 use conventional techniques to copy the string passed to a strItem instance to new space on the heap. If those operations fail, the functions call error, passing the constant ERRMEM to indicate an out-of-memory condition. Unless you set errorignore to true, as explained in chapter 6, these errors will halt the program when out of memory.

Making Lists of Strings

The strItem class neatly solves the problem of how to store a bunch of strings in memory. So far in this chapter, you've examined three classes: item, list, and strItem. A list may store any number of item instances or derivatives. Since strItem derives from item, a list can store strItem instances handily.

Test program TSTRLIST.CPP, Listing 7.10, demonstrates how to create string lists using the classes in the LC++ class library. Future programs will use similar techniques.

Listing 7.10. TSTRLIST.CPP

```
1:   // tstrlist.cpp -- Test strItem class
2:
3:   #include <stream.hpp>
4:   #include "stritem.h"
5:   #include "list.h"
6:
7:   #define CURRENT_STRING ((strItem *)(root->currentItem()))
8:
9:   main()
10:  {
11:      list *root = new list;
12:
13:      root->insertItem(new strItem("First item in list"));
14:      root->insertItem(new strItem("Second item in list"));
15:      root->insertItem(new strItem("Third and last item in list"));
16:
17:      if (root->firstItem() != NULL)
18:      do {
```

```
19:          cout << CURRENT_STRING->getString() << '\n';
20:          root->nextItem();
21:      } while (!root->atHeadOfList());
22:
23:      delete root;
24:  }
```

The test program shows all the steps required to create lists of strings. Lines 4-5 include the STRITEM.H and LIST.H headers. Line 7 associates CURRENT_STRING with the text that calls root->currentItem(), returning a pointer to the current item in a list addressed by a pointer root. The result of that expression is recast to type strItem * to allow calling member functions in the strItem class.

In function main, line 11 creates a new list pointer, root. It's not necessary to tell root about the kinds of data it will store. A list instance can store *any* other instances derived from item. Lines 13-15 put that theory to the test, calling new to allocate space for three strItem instances. The literal strings in quotes are passed to the strItem constructor to initialize each of the new instances. The result of new (a pointer to each strItem instance) is then passed to the list's insertItem member function.

Line 17 shows an alternate way to determine whether a list is empty; that is, if firstItem returns NULL. If the list at root is not empty, the program uses a do/while loop at lines 18-21 to display the listed strings. Line 19 calls the getString member function in strItem, using the CURRENT_STRING macro to obtain and recast the pointer to the current item in the list. The macro saves typing and keeps the program text clean.

Consider the series of events that takes place when TSTRLIST calls delete at line 23. Remember that class instances are destroyed from the top down. First, the list destructor runs (see lines 92-98 in LIST.CPP, Listing 7.6.), which deletes each item on the list. Those items' destructors run to clean up the items. Finally, the item destructor cleans up the list, which as you recall, is descended from item.

Think this through. When you compiled item and list, neither of those two classes knew about strItem's existence. However, the list destructor calls strItem's destructor to clean up each listed string instance. How can that be? How can code that was already compiled call a new function in a module you compiled *after* the one that's doing the calling?

Virtual functions are the answer. Look back to strItem's declaration (line 17 in STRITEM.H, Listing 7.7). The destructor is declared virtual ~strItem();. Because the destructor is virtual, when a program calls delete to dispose heap space allocated to an item pointer, the program looks up the address of the correct function to run. In this case, the instance is one of type strItem; therefore, the list destructor calls that object's destructor. Thanks to virtual functions, the code you compiled earlier in LIST can clean up a list of string instances by calling the new function you added later to STRITEM.

A Class for `windows`

WINTOOL in chapter 6 shows off the capabilities of the `window` class in this section. A window is like a small terminal in which you can display text, scroll lines up and down, select text attributes, and perform other operations. You can create as many window instances as you like, limited only by available memory. Each new instance can cover those below. Removing a window on top exposes those below—an illusion that makes the display appear to hold more information than is possible to show in the 25 rows and 80 columns of a typical PC screen.

The `window` class is the most complex in the LC++ library. The class demonstrates several key data-hiding features in C++ that you'll want to use in your own projects, especially in those that need to isolate system-dependent information inside a class. As in the previous sections, I'll explain the declarations in the header file, list a sample program, and then explain `window`'s inner workings.

The WINDOW.H Header

The WINDOW.H header file, Listing 7.11, includes STDLIB.H, STRITEM.H, and ITEM.H. A `window` class descends from `item` (as do all LC++ classes). After including WINDOW.H in your own programs, you do not have to include these other header files (although doing so does no harm).

Listing 7.11. WINDOW.H

```
1:  // window.h -- Header for window.cpp
2:
3:  #ifndef __WINDOW_H
4:  #define __WINDOW_H          1       // Prevent multiple #includes
5:
6:  #include <stdlib.h>
7:  #include "stritem.h"
8:  #include "item.h"
9:
10: /* -- Window information structure */
11:
12: struct winStruct {
13:     int row;                // Absolute row of top left corner
14:     int col;                // Absolute column of top left corner
15:     int width;              // Width of border
16:     int height;             // Height of border
17:     unsigned wtattr;        // Window normal text attribute
18:     unsigned wbattr;        // Window border attribute
19:     unsigned whattr;        // Window highlight text attribute
```

```
20:     int wtype;               // Border type (0 ... 4)
21:  };
22:
```

Lines 12-21 declare the `winStruct` structure. The fields in `winStruct` describe the upper left row and column of a window's border, its width and height, its display attributes, and the border type. You've seen several examples of `winStruct` in chapter 6. Every `window` variable needs a corresponding `winStruct`.

There are two main reasons I decided to collect `window` details in the `winStruct` structure. The first reason is clarity. When functions need more than a few arguments, it's generally easier to store the value in a `struct` and pass that entire structure as an argument than it is to pass the values one by one. Try to avoid designing functions like this fictitious one that requires `row`, `col`, `width`, `height`, and other arguments:

```
void confusingFunction(int row, int col, int width, int height,
    unsigned wtattr, unsigned wbattr, unsigned whattr, int type);
```

Reading and using hundreds of similar functions in a large class library is enough to give anybody a whopping headache. A much clearer approach is to store the details in a `struct`, and then design functions like this with a parameter or two:

```
void clearFunction(winStruct &ws);
```

But there's another good reason to pass multiple arguments in a `struct` this way (usually by reference). You can save a lot of memory. The compiler has to store all the declarations you make, and numerous function parameters can quickly eat up a lot of space. Passing structures instead of individual arguments to functions conserves memory by helping the compiler store program symbols more efficiently.

The program may also run faster. To call `confusingFunction`, the code has to push each of the declared arguments onto the stack and then call the function. To call `clearFunction`, it has to push only the address of a `winStruct` variable. On the other hand, you'll probably need to assign individual values to the structure's fields, so for a single function call, the time savings might be nil. Even so, passing structures is usually at least as fast if not faster than passing multiple variables around.

The next element of WINDOW.H is the `window` class itself. Take the time to go through each line carefully—there are several items you haven't met before.

Listing 7.11. WINDOW.H (continued)

```
23:  /* -- Window class */
24:
25:  class window: public item {
26:     private:
27:
28:     // -- Static data field (shared by all objects of class)
29:        static int dispInitialized;  // True == display initialized
```

```
30:
31:        // -- Private data fields
32:            int wbr;                // Window bottom row
33:            int wrc;                // Window right column
34:            int cr, cc;             // Logical cursor row, cursor column
35:            unsigned wca;           // Window current attribute
36:            strItem *wtitle;        // Pointer to window title strItem
37:            unsigned *save;         // If NULL, text behind not saved
38:
39:        // -- Protected data fields
40:        protected:
41:            int isOpen;             // True if window is visible
42:            winStruct ws;           // Location, size, attributes
43:
44:        // -- Private member functions
45:        private:
46:            unsigned *saveBuf(void);
47:            void commonInits(void);
48:            void showOutline(void);
49:
50:        public:
51:
52:        // -- Static member functions
53:            static void startup(void);
54:            static void shutDown(void);
55:
56:        // -- Constructors and destructors
57:            window();
58:            window(winStruct &ws, const char *title);
59:            ~window();
60:
61:        // -- Inline member functions
62:            winStruct &getInfo()
63:                { return ws; }
64:            void reverseVideo(void)
65:                { wca = ws.whattr; }
66:            void normalVideo(void)
67:                { wca = ws.wtattr; }
68:
69:        // -- Other member functions
70:            void showWindow();
71:            void hideWindow();
72:            void setTitle(const char *s);
73:            void setInfo(winStruct &ws);
74:            void gotorc(int row, int col);
```

```
75:           void puts(char *s);
76:           void scrollUp(int nrows);
77:           void scrollDown(int nrows);
78:           void eeol(void);
79:           void eeow(void);
80:    };
81:
82:    #endif    // __WINDOW_H
```

Like most class declarations, window has private and public sections. Actually, it has *two* private areas—one beginning at line 26, and another at line 45. I organized the class this way merely for convenience (and to demonstrate that multiple private and other sections are possible). In any class, you can repeat the private:, public:, and protected: key words as often as you like. This can help you to organize the declarations in a complex class by keeping related members together in the text.

Note: In a complex class like window, I like to group private member functions in separate private: areas (see lines 45-48). When creating a new class, I often need to create small functions I don't want host programs to use. For example, commonInits carries out various common initializations that the class constructors need. I want host programs to use those constructors, but not to call commonInits directly. Isolating this and similar functions in a private: section is a useful technique for preventing errors while still encapsulating the functions in the class.

In addition to its private and public sections, window also declares a protected area (lines 40-42). As you recall, members in a private section are strictly for use by member functions in the same class. Members in a public section are available to statements in the same class as well as to statements outside. Classes that derive from window may directly use protected and public members in the base class. Because of this rule, a derivative of window may use the isOpen and ws fields directly, but statements outside the class and its derivatives cannot do the same.

Static Member Functions

In chapter 6, you learned that to start up and shut down the window class, a program must call two functions, preferably in main:

```
main()
{
    window::startup();
```

```
        // other functions
        window::shutDown();
        exit(0);
}
```

The `startup` and `shutDown` functions are declared at lines 53-54 in WINDOW.H. Each prototype is prefaced by the keyword `static`, which has special meaning when applied to member functions. Unlike common member functions, such as `showWindow` at line 70, a *static member function* is never available through a variable of its class. In other words, if you create a window with

```
window *myWin = new window;
```

you can then execute statements such as `myWin->showWindow()` and `myWin->eeow()`. But you can't execute `myWin->startup()` and `myWin->shutDown()`. Those functions are static, and can therefore be called *only* by direct reference to the class name, as in the statements `window::startup()` and `window::shutDown()`.

The primary use for static member functions is to initialize a global aspect of the class that should apply equally to all variables of that class. For example, in `window`, it's necessary to initialize the Zortech display package before using any of that package's routines. That job must be done only once; therefore, it would be a mistake to perform the initialization inside a class constructor, because the constructor runs for *each* new variable of the class. Storing the global initialization steps in a static member function makes it possible for a program to initialize the class for all future variables.

Another benefit of static member functions is the isolation of low-level details inside the class. Without the `startup` and `shutDown` routines, it would be necessary for host programs to call the Zortech initialization code before using `window`. You could create other global functions for this purpose, but then the `window` class would lose its autonomy, and it would have to *know* somehow that the display package was initialized.

Avoid making your classes dependent on global variables or global functions. When a class (not just a variable of the class type) needs to be initialized in some fashion, consider storing the initialization code in a static member function. This approach will increase the portability of your programs, and will help prevent bugs by isolating low-level details inside the class.

Note: Static functions may access only static data fields in the class. A static member function does not receive a `this` pointer and therefore cannot refer to any data fields in an object of the class.

Static Member Fields

Member functions like `startup` and `shutdown` are not the only items that can be declared static. You can also declare static data fields. For example, look at line 29 in WINDOW.H. There you see the declaration

```
static int dispInitialized;
```

A *static member field* is similar in some ways to a global variable. In contrast to other member fields such as `int wbr` or `unsigned wca` at lines 32 and 35, only one copy of a static member field exists in memory, no matter how many variables of a class type a program creates. As with all global variables, a static member field takes up permanent storage, and it exists for the life of the program. When you define a variable of a class type, that variable has space for unique copies of all the data fields declared in the class. The same is not true of static fields. Only a single copy of a static field ever exists in memory. All variables of the class share that same copy.

Line 29 shows how useful static member fields can be. The static `dispInitialized` field in the `window` class indicates whether the program called the static `startup` function to initialize the class. This variable gives the class the means to know whether it has been initialized. When you define a variable of type `window`, the class constructor checks `dispInitialized`. If that variable is false, the program displays the error message `Window class not initialized` and halts. Together, the static member functions and field in `window` give the class the capability of being initialized, and allow the class to detect whether that initialization has been carried out. This is a powerful device that goes a long way toward making bug-prone global variables unnecessary.

Note: The data type of a static member field can be any common C++ type (`int` or `float`, for example), or it can be another class. That class may have a constructor with or without parameters—a feature not available in some early C++ compilers. If a static member field is declared publicly, then statements outside the class may refer to that variable with a statement such as `class::field = x`, where x is a value to assign to the public data. However, as with most data fields, and for the same reasons discussed earlier, it's usually best to declare static data in private or protected sections, and to allow only member functions of the class or its derivatives to access static fields.

Overloaded Constructors

The `window` class declares two constructors at lines 57-58. As with all constructors, these have the same name as the class. The first constructor declares no parameters.

The second declares a reference parameter &ws of type winStruct and a constant string pointer named title.

As I explained earlier for strItem, declaring two or more constructors (or other functions) of the same name is called overloading. This C++ feature is merely a convenience that lets you write functions that have the same names but perform different actions. Except for their names, the overloaded functions are not connected in any way. In all cases, overloaded constructors and functions *must* differ in at least one parameter.

The purpose of overloading constructors and functions is to make it unnecessary to invent a slew of function names that have similar purposes. There's no need in C++ to have functions named init1, init2, init3, and init4. As long as these functions have different parameters, you can name them all init and let the compiler figure out which one to call based on the function calls. For example, in a program that uses the window class, it's obvious to the compiler which constructor to call in each of the two definitions:

```
window *default = new window;
window *custom = new window(ws, " Custom Window ");
```

> **Note:** Chapter 9 covers overloading. As you'll discover then, it's also possible to overload many C++ operators such as = and +.

Reference Functions

One other new element is the member function at line 62. The function returns a reference to a winStruct data type, using the prototype declaration winStruct &getInfo(). When applied to a function's return type, the reference symbol & allows statements to assign the result of the function to a variable.

The alternative approach is to return a pointer as the function type. For example, I could have written lines 62-63 this way:

```
winStruct *getInfo()
   { return &ws; }
```

Then, to use the function, I'd need to declare a pointer variable to type winStruct and assign the function result to the pointer:

```
window *w = new window();    // Create a window
winStruct *wp;               // Define a winStruct pointer
wp = w->getInfo;             // Address private data with wp ???
```

Although this strategy will work, the effect is to set a pointer to the instance's protected data! This trick goes against the OOP grain by giving statements access to data fields that are supposed to be protected or private.

To guard against this condition, return a reference instead of a pointer to private and protected data. Statements can then assign the result of a reference function to a variable of the same data type. In the window class, the getInfo reference function illustrates the method. Using the function does not pose the same dangers as in the preceding sample code:

```
window *w = new window();    // Create a window
winStruct ws;                // Define a winStruct variable
ws = w->getInfo;             // Get copy of data from instance
```

Now, instead of using a pointer to winStruct, the program defines a winStruct variable ws. Calling the reference function getInfo *copies* the internal winStruct data from the class instance to ws. This is generally safer because it eliminates the potentially dangerous pointer that peeks into the inner sanctum of the class instance.

The rest of the member functions in window contain nothing new. You should be able to read and understand the other declarations in the listing.

Designing Displays with Windows

A short sample program will show how to use most of the window class's functions. Compile the program, TWINDOW.CPP, Listing 7.12, by executing the command **ztc twindow error.obj stritem.obj item.obj list.obj window.obj**. Or if you don't have the listed .OBJ files in the current directory, enter **ztc twindow error stritem item list window**.

Listing 7.12. TWINDOW.CPP

```
 1:  // twindow.cpp -- Test window class
 2:
 3:  #include <stdlib.h>
 4:  #include <stdio.h>
 5:  #include "window.h"
 6:
 7:  /* -- Attribute constants */
 8:
 9:  #define WA_REVERSEVIDEO   0x70
10:  #define WA_NORMAL         0x07
11:
12:  /* -- Test-function prototypes */
13:
```

```
14:    void pause(void);
15:    void runtest(void);
16:    void overlayTest(void);
17:    void scrollTest(void);
18:
19:    main()
20:    {
21:        window::startup();
22:        runtest();
23:        window::shutDown();
24:        exit(0);
25:    }
26:
```

All programs that use the window class must include the WINDOW.H header as done here at line 5. Lines 9-10 define two constants for displaying text in reversed and normal video, the default values for all windows. The listed values will work for all display types, but you can change them to 0x1e and 0xb4 if you have a color screen.

After declaring the test program's function prototypes (lines 14-17), function main shows the bare necessities required to use the window class. As in WINTOOL, line 21 initializes the class by calling the static startup function. For a useful experiment, temporarily delete this line and recompile. When you run the modified program, it displays

```
ERROR: Window class not initialized
```

The ERROR module (see chapter 6) displays this message and halts the program. You can trap the error by setting errorignore to true as explained in chapter 6, but you still must not define or use any window variables until after calling startup.

Similarly, you must call shutDown before the program ends. This deinitializes the class and returns the display to normal operation. After calling startup, you may not use input- and output-stream statements. After calling shutDown, you can use those statements again. You may call startup and shutDown as many times as necessary in a program.

TWINDOW continues after main with a small function (to pause for a keypress) and the main test function, runtest.

Listing 7.12. TWINDOW.CPP (continued)

```
27: /* -- Wait for and discard keypress */
28:
29: void pause(void)
30: {
31:     while (getch() != ' ') ;
32: }
33:
```

```
34:    /* -- Execute main test procedures */
35:
36:    void runtest(void)
37:    {
38:        int i;
39:        window *win = new window;
40:        winStruct ws;
41:
42:        int row;
43:
44:        win->setTitle(" Display String Test ");
45:        win->showWindow();
46:        ws = win->getInfo();
47:        for (row = 0; row < ws.height - 2; row++) {
48:            win->gotorc(row, row);
49:            win->puts("This line should end here: abcdefghijklmnop");
50:            win->gotorc(row, 75);
51:            win->puts("Endoftheline");
52:            if (row & 1)
53:                win->normalVideo();
54:            else
55:                win->reverseVideo();
56:            pause();
57:        }
58:
59:        win->setTitle(" Pop-Up Overlay Test ");
60:        overlayTest();
61:
62:        win->normalVideo();
63:        win->setTitle(" Erase to End of Line Test ");
64:        pause();
65:        for (row = 0; row < ws.height - 2; row++) {
66:            win->gotorc(row, row + 26 );
67:            win->eeol();
68:            pause();
69:        }
70:
71:        win->normalVideo();
72:        win->gotorc(0, 0);
73:        win->puts("Scroll down 4x test");
74:        win->eeol();
75:        win->setTitle(" Scroll DOWN 4x test ");
76:        pause();
77:        for (i = 1; i <= 4; i++) {
78:            win->scrollDown(1);
```

```
79:            pause();
80:        }
81:
82:        win->gotorc(4, 0);
83:        win->puts(" Scroll up 4x test ");
84:        win->eeol();
85:        win->setTitle(" Scroll UP 4x test ");
86:        for (i = 1; i <= 4; i++) {
87:            pause();
88:            win->scrollUp(1);
89:        }
90:
91:        win->setTitle(" Erase Window Test " );
92:        pause();
93:        win->gotorc(0, 0);
94:        win->eeow();
95:        win->setTitle(" Null Title Test ");
96:        pause();
97:        win->setTitle("");
98:        pause();
99:        win->setTitle(" Hide Window Test " );
100:       pause();
101:       win->hideWindow();
102:       delete win;
103:   }
104:
```

Run TWINDOW and press <**Space**> repeatedly while examining the runtest function's implementation. This will give you a good feel for how to use the window class's member functions. Near the beginning of runtest, the function creates a default window by executing

```
window *win = new window;
```

Variable win is a pointer to a variable of type window. The statement new window allocates space for a window on the heap and assigns the address of that variable to win. The statement calls the window's default constructor—the one with no parameters—to create a window that fills the entire display and does not save any covered text. The program can then use win to execute various functions for this window.

Among those functions are those listed in Table 7.1. Run the program, examine each statement, and use this table as a guide to learn what the various functions do. You'll learn more about how these functions operate internally when you examine the window class module later.

Table 7.1. Window Functions Used in TWINDOW

Window Function	Description
`eeol`	Erase from cursor to end of line
`eeow`	Erase from cursor to end of window
`getInfo`	Get `winStruct` details from window
`gotorc`	Position cursor to a row and column
`hideWindow`	Remove window from display
`normalVideo`	Select normal text attributes
`puts`	Display (put) a string in a window
`reverseVideo`	Select reversed text attributes
`scrollDown`	Scroll window down one or more lines
`scrollUp`	Scroll window up one or more lines
`setTitle`	Change the window's title
`showWindow`	Display the window

Listing 7.12. TWINDOW.CPP (continued)

```
105:   /* -- Display pop-up window over main window */
106:
107:   void overlayTest(void)
108:   {
109:       winStruct ws = {
110:           6, 20, 32, 12,
111:           WA_REVERSEVIDEO, WA_NORMAL, WA_NORMAL, 1
112:       };
113:       window *win = new window(ws, " Pop-Up ");
114:
115:       win->showWindow();
116:       win->gotorc(4, 2);
117:       win->puts("Pop-Up window!");
118:       win->gotorc(6, 2);
119:       win->puts("Press Space twice to erase");
120:       pause();
121:       win->gotorc(0, 0);
122:       win->eeow();
123:       pause();
124:       delete win;
125:   }
```

TWINDOW ends with a subfunction `overlayTest` that displays a small pop-up window over the main one that fills the display. Lines 109-113 illustrate an alternate way to create a window. Instead of the default method used in `runtest`, a `winStruct` named `ws` is created and assigned the position, size, attributes, and type values to use for this window. Line 113 defines a `win` pointer, using `new` to allocate

heap space for a `window` variable. The two arguments in this statement, `ws` and
`" Pop-Up "`, are passed to the `window` class's second constructor—the one that
declares parameters to match these arguments.

Line 124 calls `delete` to deallocate the heap space assigned to the `win` pointer
in the subfunction. At that time, the `window` destructor cleans up any structures
inserted on the heap by the constructor or other member functions. It's especially
important to delete objects addressed by pointers that are local to a function such
as `overlayTest`. When that function ends, its local variables no longer exist. If you
forget to `delete` space assigned to a local pointer, that pointer will be lost when
the function returns. This mistake would destroy the only means the program has to
refer to the `window` variable on the heap and would leave that space unrecoverable.
If you run out of memory while using a program, check whether you've deleted all
memory allocated to pointers defined locally in functions.

The WINDOW.CPP Module

At 314 lines (actually, there are about 200 lines, not counting comments and blank
lines), the implementation of the `window` class in WINDOW.CPP, Listing 7.13, is one
of the longest modules in this book. Even so, the functions contain mostly
conventional C++ programming, most of which you've seen in other samples.
Because `window` is the most complex class in the LC++ class library, I laced the
source with many comments, which you can read for a better understanding of how
the programming works. I'll point out only a few highlights and new items here.

Listing 7.13. WINDOW.CPP

```
 1:  // window.cpp -- Window class
 2:
 3:  #include <disp.h>
 4:  #include <stdlib.h>
 5:  #include <string.h>
 6:  #include "error.h"
 7:  #include "window.h"
 8:
 9:  #define FALSE   0
10:  #define TRUE    1
11:
12:  extern disp_numrows;      // Gain access to normally hidden
13:  extern disp_numcols;      //   display package variables.
14:
```

Like most modules, this one begins with several miscellaneous items. Lines
12-13 declare two variables, `disp_numrows` and `disp_numcols` as `extern`.
These variables are part of the Zortech display package, and they are usually hidden.

The variables represent the number of rows and columns available on the display. The display package *must* be initialized before using these variables.

Note that the data types are not listed with `disp_numrows` and `disp_numcols`, and therefore, C++ assumes the unstated data types to be `int`. I wrote these lines without types to demonstrate that it is possible to do so and because this is the format that Zortech recommends for accessing the values. However, I do *not* recommend the practice. A short test shows why the technique, although legal, is flawed:

```
#include <stream.hpp>
main()
{
    extern x;
    cout << "size of x = " << sizeof(x);
}
int x;
```

When you compile and run this small program, it reports that x's size is 2 bytes, the size of an `int` (correct, at least, for this book's version of C++). The `extern` directive tells the compiler that x is defined elsewhere. In this case, the definition (`int    x`) comes after `main`, but the definition could be in another module. Because the `extern x;` declaration does not specify x's data type, C++ assumes that x is type `int`.

Change `int x` to `long x` and you'll see the problem with the technique. When you attempt to compile the modified listing, the compiler reports an error when it discovers that it has made the wrong assumption about x. However, if the `long x;` declaration were in another module, the compiler would not report this same error. Worse, the linker would not notice that the program has used a variable that's defined as a different type in another module!

If you use typeless declarations like those at lines 12-13, make sure that the variables are actually type `int` (a fact that I am sure of here). Better still, don't use the technique. Give all variables explicit data types. If you don't, you're just asking for trouble.

Listing 7.13. WINDOW.CPP (continued)

```
15:   /* -- Define and initialize the static class member field, which
16:   indicates whether the display package has been initialized.  This
17:   variable is global--it is shared by all variables of the window
18:   class. But because it's declared private to the class, only class
19:   member functions have access to it. */
20:
21:   int window::dispInitialized = FALSE;
22:
```

Line 21 defines space for the static member field `dispInitialized`. The definition also assigns an initial value to the field, setting the flag to FALSE (0). Because the variable is global (though not globally visible outside the WINDOW module), the assignment isn't necessary. All global variables are initialized to 0 by default. However, I wrote the line in full to demonstrate how to initialize static member fields.

Static member fields like dispInitialized differ from common definitions in modules in one key way. As you recall, if a module defines a variable, another module can access that variable by declaring it to be extern. But the same trick does not work for private static member fields like dispInitialized. Because dispInitialized is private to the window class, no statements outside the class can use the variable; therefore, a future change to the module could safely eliminate dispInitialized without requiring changes to any other statements outside this one module.

Use static member fields judiciously—they occupy permanent storage during the life of a program. When you need a global value, consider creating a static member field private to the module's class, rather than using a common definition. This technique provides the good features of global variables (fast access and retention of values between function calls) and few of the negatives (accessibility to any statement and likelihood of conflict with other unrelated identifiers of the same names).

Listing 7.13. WINDOW.CPP (continued)

```
23:  /* -- Private routine (not a member of the window class). Display a
24:  string at an absolute row and column position using the specified
25:  attribute. Limit length of string to len characters. Ideally, this
26:  routine should display all possible ASCII symbols--it should not
27:  respond to control codes such as carriage returns and line feeds. */
28:
29:  void putsat(int row, int col, int len, unsigned attr, char *s)
30:  {
31:      unsigned char buffer[264];
32:      int i, j;
33:
34:      if (len == 0) return;
35:      for (i = 0, j = 0; i < len; i++, j += 2) {
36:          buffer[j] = s[i];
37:          buffer[j + 1] = attr;
38:      }
39:      disp_pokebox((unsigned *)&buffer, row, col, row, col + len - 1);
40:  }
41:
```

Function putsat displays strings at an absolute row and column on screen. The function calls the Zortech disp_pokebox routine to push the characters and attributes (prepared by the preceding for loop) directly into the PC's video-display buffer.

The function demonstrates that a module may include conventional functions. Not everything in a C++ program has to be in a class. Support functions like `putsat` are convenient and common.

But they are also a little risky. To understand why, add this line to TWINDOW.CPP (Listing 7.12) just above line 19:

```
extern void putsat(int row, int col, int len, unsigned attr, char *s);
```

Next, insert this line just above line 23 (before `window::shutDown();`):

```
putsat(3, 4, 23, WA_NORMAL, "Hello from outer space!");
```

When you run the modified program, all is well. But just before the code ends, the message `Hello from outer space!` appears on screen. This alien visitor shows how easy it is for a program to gain access to supposedly private support functions like `putsat`. All the program has to do is declare the function `extern`. A statement is then free to call the function.

At times, you may want to use this technique to gain access to functions that are normally hidden from view. But be aware that if you use this method, you will not be able to take out functions like `putsat` without also modifying all programs that use the routine. This tends to be messy; a better plan is to declare functions like `putsat` private to the class. That way, no statements outside the class will be able to peek into the module with an `extern` declaration.

Note: Another way to prevent access to private functions like `putsat` is to declare the functions `static`. To do this in the WINDOW.CPP module, add the `static` keyword to the front of the `putsat` declaration at line 29. Then it will be impossible for another module to use `extern` to gain access to the function.

Listing 7.13. WINDOW.CPP (continued)

```
42:   /* -- Program must call the class static startup function to
43:   initialize the display package (or another display library if porting
44:   the code). Because startup is a static member function, it can access
45:   only static data members of the class. It has no access whatsoever to
46:   other data fields in window class objects. */
47:
48:   void window::startup(void)
49:   {
50:       if (!dispInitialized) {        // If not initialized yet
51:           disp_open();               //   then initialize display
52:           disp_hidecursor();         // Turn off system cursor
53:           dispInitialized = TRUE;    // Set the static flag
54:       }
55:   }
```

```
56:
57:   /* -- Program must call the class static shutDown function to
58:   deinitialize the display package. Failure to call this routine could
59:   lead to display problems after the program ends. (This may or may not
60:   be the case after porting the code to a system that doesn't use the
61:   Zortech display package.) */
62:
63:   void window::shutDown(void)
64:   {
65:       if (dispInitialized) {              // If previously initialized:
66:           disp_move(disp_numrows - 1, 0 ); // Set cursor to bottom row
67:           disp_showcursor();               // Display cursor
68:           disp_close();                    // Shut down display package
69:           dispInitialized = FALSE;         // Reset the static flag
70:       }
71:   }
72:
```

The static member functions s t a r t u p and s h u t D o w n are implemented next.
Note that the s t a t i c key word does not reappear in the implementations, only in
the declarations (see WINDOW.H, Listing 7.11, lines 53-54).

The two functions perform simple jobs. Function s t a r t u p initializes the Zortech
display package. Function s h u t D o w n shuts the package down. Most important,
when porting the code to another compiler, the two functions can be gutted. All the
low-level details concerning Zortech's display package are neatly hidden in the class.

Listing 7.13. WINDOW.CPP (continued)

```
73:   /* -- Create and return pointer to a buffer for saving text behind
74:   window. Returns NULL if not enough memory is available. */
75:
76:   unsigned *window::saveBuf(void)
77:   {
78:       return malloc((ws.height * ws.width) * sizeof(unsigned));
79:   }
80:
81:   /* -- Perform various common initialization steps for all new
82:   windows. Called by all class constructors. Aborts program if window
83:   class startup function was not called, or if the class was shut down.
84:   If you add new constructors to the window class, make sure to call this
85:   routine, or failing that, at least test the dispInitialized flag and
86:   take appropriate actions if the flag is false. */
87:
88:   void window::commonInits(void)
89:   {
90:       if (!dispInitialized)                // Test if display initialized
```

```
 91:          error(ERRWININIT);              // Halt or report error if not
 92:      cr = cc = 0;                         // Home logical cursor
 93:      save = NULL;                         // Text behind not saved
 94:      isOpen = FALSE;                      // Window is not open
 95:      if (ws.row > disp_numrows - 3)       // Limit smallest window
 96:          ws.row = disp_numrows - 3;       //  to one row, one column
 97:      if (ws.col > disp_numcols - 3)
 98:          ws.col = disp_numcols - 3;
 99:      if (ws.width < 1) ws.width = 1;      // Window width must be >= 1
100:      if (ws.height < 1) ws.height = 1;   // Window height must be >= 1
101:      wbr = ws.row + ws.height - 1;        // Window's bottom row number
102:      wrc = ws.col + ws.width - 1;         // Window's right column number
103:      wca = ws.wtattr;                     // Current attr = normal text
104:      wtitle = NULL;                       // No window title (yet)
105:  }
106:
107:  /* -- Default constructor. Creates full-screen window. The save
108:  pointer is set to NULL, which causes the window not to save the text
109:  behind it. Because the default window is full screen, this saves at
110:  least 4K of memory. */
111:
112:  window::window()
113:  {
114:      ws.row = ws.col = 0;                 // Upper left corner
115:      ws.width = disp_numcols;             // Full width of display
116:      ws.height = disp_numrows;            // Full height of display
117:      ws.wtattr = DISP_NORMAL;             // Normal text attribute
118:      ws.wbattr = DISP_NORMAL;             // Normal border attribute
119:      ws.whattr = DISP_REVERSEVIDEO;       // Highlight in reverse video
120:      ws.wtype = 0;                        // Select double-line border
121:      commonInits();                       // Do other init steps
122:  }
123:
124:  /* -- Alternate constructor. Allows sizing window and selecting
125:  various attributes. Saves text behind window. */
126:
127:  window::window(winStruct &ws, const char *title)
128:  {
129:      window::ws = ws;
130:      commonInits();
131:      setTitle(title);
132:      save = saveBuf();
133:  }
134:
135:  /* -- Destructor. Deallocates save-text buffer (if allocated). Note
```

```
136:    that it is legal to pass a NULL pointer to free, but it is not okay
137:    to do the same with delete--a minor inconsistency in this version of
138:    C++ that can lead to trouble. Deleting a NULL pointer may cause the
139:    program to crash. */
140:
141:    window::~window()
142:    {
143:        if (isOpen) hideWindow();   // Close window if open
144:        free(save);                 // Dispose save buffer (if any)
145:        if (wtitle) delete wtitle;  // Dispose old title (if any)
146:    }
147:
```

The `window` destructor cleans up a deleted `window` instance. Line 145 `deletes wtitle`, a variable of type `strItem *`. Look back to WINDOW.H, Listing 7.11, line 36. There you'll see the declaration of the `wtitle` field

```
strItem *wtitle;
```

You examined the `strItem` class earlier. The `wtitle` field is a pointer to an instance of that class. There's nothing unusual about this construction, and classes will often have many data fields of other class types. Beginners to OOP sometimes neglect this technique, and assume that class data members must be only simple types like `int` and `float`. Not so. You can use any data types for fields in classes, including other classes.

Be sure to initialize any fields of class data types. Usually, the class that declares the fields will perform initializations in the constructor. For example, line 104 sets `wtitle` to `NULL`, indicating that the pointer does not address a valid `strItem` instance. Later in the module (see line 201), `new` will allocate space for a variable of type `strItem`. This action is no different from the normal allocation of space for a class instance, but in this example, the action takes place inside another class's member function.

The rest of the `window` class follows. There are no new elements here, and you should be able to read and understand the code by scanning the comments in the listing.

Listing 7.13. WINDOW.CPP (continued)

```
148:    /* -- Display window outline and title if one was assigned. Called
149:    by showWindow and if the title is changed after window is opened. */
150:
151:    void window::showOutline(void)
152:    {
153:        int len;     // String length
154:
155:        disp_box(ws.wtype, ws.wbattr, ws.row, ws.col, wbr, wrc);
156:        if (wtitle != NULL) {
```

```
157:              len = strlen(wtitle->getString());
158:              if (len > 0) {
159:                 putsat(ws.row, ws.col + ((ws.width - len) / 2), len,
160:                    ws.wbattr, wtitle->getString());
161:                 gotorc(cr, cc);
162:              }
163:        }
164: }
165:
166: /* -- Save text behind window (optional), draw window's border, erase
167: the contents. Cursor is positioned inside window at top left corner.
168: The host program is expected to display the window's contents.
169: Prevents accidentally opening an already open window, which would
170: destroy the save buffer. */
171:
172: void window::showWindow()
173: {
174:     if (isOpen) return;   // Prevent multiple openings
175:     if (save) disp_peekbox(save, ws.row, ws.col, wbr, wrc);
176:     showOutline();
177:     isOpen = TRUE;
178:     gotorc(0, 0);
179:     normalVideo();
180:     eeow();
181: }
182:
183: /* -- Restore any saved text behind window and mark window closed. If
184: there is no save buffer, the display will not change, although the
185: window will still be closed. */
186:
187: void window::hideWindow()
188: {
189:     if (!isOpen) return; // Exit if window is closed
190:     if (save) disp_pokebox(save, ws.row, ws.col, wbr, wrc);
191:     isOpen = FALSE;
192: }
193:
194: /* -- Change window title. You may call this routine whether or not
195: you specified a title when creating the window object. Window may
196: be open or closed. */
197:
198: void window::setTitle(const char *s)
199: {
200:     if (wtitle) delete wtitle;
201:     wtitle = new strItem(s, ws.width - 2);
```

```
202:        if (isOpen) showOutline();
203:    }
204:
205:    /* -- Assign new attributes to window. Use this function to move and
206:    resize windows, or just to change their colors, border types, etc.
207:    Selects normalVideo output. */
208:
209:    void window::setInfo(winStruct &ws)
210:    {
211:        int wasOpen = isOpen;
212:
213:        if (isOpen) hideWindow();
214:        if (save) delete save;
215:        window::ws = ws;
216:        save = saveBuf();
217:        if (wasOpen) {
218:            normalVideo();
219:            showWindow();
220:        }
221:    }
222:
223:    /* -- Move cursor to position inside window border. Top left position
224:    is 0, 0 (home). Row and column values are relative to window
225:    boundaries. Note: Does not make system cursor visible--instead, this
226:    function prepares the location where text will appear for the next
227:    call to puts(). Cursor is allowed to rest on the right border, but
228:    otherwise must remain within the window's boundaries.*/
229:
230:    void window::gotorc(int row, int col)
231:    {
232:        if (!isOpen) return;           // Exit if window is closed
233:        cr = row; cc = col;            // Save relative values
234:        if (cc < 0) cc = 0;            // Prevent negative
235:        if (cr < 0) cr = 0;            //   cursor positions
236:        if (cc > ws.width - 2)
237:            cc = ws.width - 2;         // Limit col to window width
238:        if (cr > ws.height - 3)
239:            cr = ws.height - 3;        // Limit row to window height
240:        disp_move(ws.row + cr + 1, ws.col + cc + 1);
241:    }
242:
243:    /* -- Display string at current cursor position. String is truncated
244:    to fit within the window boundaries. Cursor is positioned at the end
245:    of the string. (It is possible for the cursor to be on the
246:    right border, but it is not possible to display text there.) */
```

```
247:
248:    void window::puts(char *s)
249:    {
250:        int len = strlen(s);              // String length
251:        int nc = ws.width - cc - 2;       // Number chars right of cursor
252:
253:        if (!isOpen) return;      // Exit if window is closed
254:        if (nc <= 0) return;      // Exit if no space to cursor's right
255:        if (len == 0) return;     // Exit if length of string is 0
256:        if (len > nc) len = nc;   // Truncate too-long strings
257:        putsat(ws.row + cr + 1, ws.col + cc + 1, len, wca, s);
258:        gotorc(cr, cc + len);     // Position cursor to end of string
259:    }
260:
261:    /* -- Scroll up contents of current window by the number of lines
262:    specified in nrows. Blanks that many lines at bottom, using the current
263:    display attribute. */
264:
265:    void window::scrollUp(int nrows)
266:    {
267:        if (!isOpen) return; // Exit if window is closed
268:        disp_scroll(nrows, ws.row + 1, ws.col + 1, wbr - 1, wrc - 1, wca);
269:    }
270:
271:    /* -- Scroll down contents of current window by the number of lines
272:    specified in nrows. Blanks that many lines at top, using the current
273:    display attribute. */
274:
275:    void window::scrollDown(int nrows)
276:    {
277:        if (!isOpen) return; // Exit if window is closed
278:        disp_scroll(-nrows, ws.row + 1, ws.col + 1, wbr - 1, wrc - 1, wca);
279:    }
280:
281:    /* -- Erase from current cursor position to end of line; that is, to
282:    just before the window's right border. Uses the current attribute for
283:    the blanked area. */
284:
285:    void window::eeol(void)
286:    {
287:        unsigned attr = wca * 256 + ' '; // Attribute for blank line
288:        int nc = ws.width - cc - 3;        // Number of chars to erase
289:        int acr = ws.row + cr + 1;         // Absolute cursor row
290:        int acc = ws.col + cc + 1;         // Absolute cursor column
291:
```

```
292:      if (!isOpen) return;      // Exit if window is closed
293:      if (nc < 0) return;        // Exit if no space to cursor's right
294:      disp_fillbox(attr, acr, acc, acr, acc + nc);
295:   }
296:
297:   /* -- Erase from current cursor position to end of window; that is,
298:   to just before the window's bottom border. Uses the current attribute
299:   for the blanked area. */
300:
301:   void window::eeow(void)
302:   {
303:      int ocr = cr;           // Save old cr (cursor row)
304:      int occ = cc;           // Save old cc (cursor col)
305:
306:      if (!isOpen) return;                 // Exit if window is closed
307:      eeol();                              // Erase to end of current line
308:      while (++cr < ws.height - 2) {       // Erase other full lines if any
309:         gotorc(cr, 0);
310:         eeol();
311:      }
312:      cr = ocr;               // Restore saved cursor position
313:      cc = occ;
314:   }
```

A Class for Selections

Programs commonly prompt operators to choose from lists of items. A database may ask for a field's storage type, or present options for reports. A compiler may solicit options such as whether to include debugging information in the output, or whether to generate a map file of a program's symbols. Lists are tailor-made for organizing these and other data sets from which people will need to choose selections.

Because selection lists are so common, a general-purpose tool for creating and displaying them is invaluable, as several examples in this chapter and the next demonstrate. Naturally, you'll want your selectors to look good and be capable of handling any number of items.

Those requirements are easily met by marrying some of the classes you already know about. A selector will need to list strings and let people select one of those strings from a window. With that thought in mind, you may begin to create a selector based on the `window` class. Or should you use the `list` class for the base? Apparently, the selector will need to borrow elements from `list` *and* `window`. Unlike in previous examples, where derived classes inherited from only a single class, a process known as *single inheritance;* however, the selector will need to inherit from more than one base class, a feature known as *multiple inheritance*. With single inheritance, derived classes may have only one immediate ancestor. With multiple inheritance, a derived class may inherit the properties of two or more parents.

The SELECTOR.H Header

The selector class declaration in SELECTOR.H, Listing 7.14, shows how multiple inheritance allows derived classes to inherit the properties from more than one base class.

Listing 7.14. SELECTOR.H

```
1:   // selector.h -- Header for selector.cpp
2:
3:   #ifndef __SELECTOR_H
4:   #define __SELECTOR_H     1        // Prevent multiple #includes
5:
6:   #include "stritem.h"
7:   #include "list.h"
8:   #include "window.h"
9:
10:  class selector: public window, public list {
11:     private:
12:        int showHide;              // True==pop-up, false==stationary
13:        int row;                   // Current row, -1==not initialized
14:        void highlight(int row);
15:        void showItem(int row);
16:        void moveUp(int &row);
17:        void moveDown(int &row);
18:     public:
19:        selector(winStruct &ws, const char *title, int popup = 1);
20:        strItem *getSelection(void);
21:  };
22:
23:  #endif   // __SELECTOR_H
```

Multiple Inheritance

Line 10 in SELECTOR.H lists two base classes, separated by a comma. The classes are declared to be public, to retain the status of the private, protected, and public members in the base classes. The selector class lists two base classes, window and l i s t. Because these classes are in turn derived from i t e m, a s e l e c t o r is also an i t e m. Among other benefits, this means that s e l e c t o r instances inherit the properties of l i s t *and* the instances can be stored on another list. Putting that another way, a list of s e l e c t o r s is a multiway structure—in essence, a list of lists. You could use conventional techniques to code similar complex structures is possible, but rarely will they be as concise as in the s e l e c t o r class described here.

> **Note:** Chapter 9 discusses public and private inheritance in more detail. You cannot use the p r o t e c t e d : keyword in a derivation list. Usually, you'll make base classes public in a derived class, as done here.

A derived class may inherit the properties of any number of base classes, though you'll rarely need to design classes that inherit from more than two or three bases. The result of a multiply derived class is a new class that combines the properties of two or more ancestors.

Despite what you may have heard or read about multiple inheritance, the technique isn't difficult to use and understand. Detractors will tell you, however, that there are no compelling reasons to use multiple inheritance in derived classes. According to the popular argument against the technique, I could have created s e l e c t o r with two private or protected fields, one a l i s t and the other a w i n d o w. This would give the s e l e c t o r the same capabilities that multiple inheritance provides.

That argument is difficult to refute. Still, multiple inheritance can be useful for creating classes that combine the properties of two or more other classes, and those new classes may call inherited functions without having to refer to a named instance of the base classes. If I had created a field named t h e S e l e c t o r L i s t of type l i s t, then I would have to execute commands such as t h e S e l e c t o r L i s t - > c u r r e n t I t e m ( ). By inheriting from l i s t, I can simply write c u r r e n t I t e m ( ). When inheriting from several base classes, not having to refer to field names is tremendously more convenient.

The other members in s e l e c t o r are best explained by examining and running the test program in the next section.

Using the s e l e c t o r *Class*

TSELECT.CPP, Listing 7.15, shows how to use the s e l e c t o r class. Compile the program with the command **ztc tselect error.obj key.obj stritem.obj item.obj list.obj window.obj selector.obj**. If you don't have those .OBJ files in the current directory, enter the same command with ".obj" stripped from the file names. Run TSELECT and use the cursor keys to scroll up and down in the sample list. Press **<Enter>** to choose an item. Press **<Esc>** to close the test window and quit without making a selection.

Listing 7.15. TSELECT.CPP

```
 1:   // tselect.cpp -- Test selector class
 2:
 3:   #include <stream.hpp>
 4:   #include <stdlib.h>
 5:   #include <string.h>
 6:   #include "selector.h"
 7:
 8:   /* -- Test function prototypes */
 9:
10:   void pause(void);
11:   void runtest(void);
12:
13:   /* -- Pointer to a selected string */
14:
15:   char *selection;
16:
17:   main()
18:   {
19:       window::startup();
20:       runtest();
21:       window::shutDown();
22:       if (selection == NULL)
23:           cout << "\nNo item selected";
24:       else
25:           cout << "\nItem selected: " << selection;
26:       exit(0);
27:   }
28:
29:   /* -- Wait for a keypress */
30:
31:   void pause(void)
32:   {
33:       while (getch() != ' ') ;
34:   }
35:
36:   /* -- Perform the test */
37:
38:   void runtest(void)
39:   {
40:       winStruct ws = {
41:           4, 20, 18, 7,   // row, column, width, height
42:           0x07,           // text attribute
43:           0x1e,           // border attribute
```

```
44:         0x70,              // highlight attribute
45:         1                  // type
46:      };
47:      selector *sel = new selector(ws, " Items ");
48:      strItem *p;
49:
50:      sel->insertItem(new strItem("Elephants"));
51:      sel->insertItem(new strItem("Tigers"));
52:      sel->insertItem(new strItem("Lions"));
53:      sel->insertItem(new strItem("Polar Bears"));
54:      sel->insertItem(new strItem("Deer"));
55:      sel->insertItem(new strItem("Rabbits"));
56:      sel->insertItem(new strItem("Loons"));
57:      sel->insertItem(new strItem("Eagles"));
58:      sel->insertItem(new strItem("Beavers"));
59:      sel->insertItem(new strItem("Peacocks"));
60:      sel->insertItem(new strItem("Quit <Esc>"));
61:
62:      p = sel->getSelection();
63:      if (p) selection = strdup(p->getString());
64:      delete sel;
65:  }
```

Function runtest at lines 38-65 demonstrates how to create and use a
selector. The definitions and statements resemble those you used earlier to
create window instances. But that shouldn't come as a surprise. A selector *is* a
window, and you can use nearly identical winStruct structures and techniques
to create selector instances.

Line 47 defines a pointer sel to a selector instance, and calls new to allocate
space for that instance on the heap. The selector constructor (see Listing 7.14,
line 19) adds a default parameter to those declared in window's alternate constructor. Passing 0 to the new parameter causes the window to stay visible after you
select a command from it. This way, a selector allows you to make a selection,
perform some action, and then select another item without having to scroll back to
the one you selected previously. To use this feature, you can change line 47 to

```
selector *sel = new selector(ws, " Items ", 0);
```

However, you won't notice any difference when you run the test program,
because it lets you make only one selection at a time. For a better example of this
technique, see WINTOOL in chapter 6. WINTOOL's main menu uses the method to
stay visible so that you can select commands without the menu's window disappear-
ing after each new selection.

Lines 50-60 show how to insert new items into a selector. Each item in a
selection list must be a strItem instance or a derivative. In the test program, the
statements insert plain strItem instances, initializing each with the literal string

shown in quotes. Note that member function `insertItem` handles the duty of inserting the items into the list. The `selector` class inherited `insertItem` from `list`.

Line 62 calls the `getSelection` function for the `selector` instance addressed by `sel`. The result of this function is a pointer to one of the inserted `strItem` instances. If `getSelection` returns `NULL`, then the operator pressed **<Esc>** and did not choose an item. Line 63 tests for that condition by checking whether p is `NULL`. If not, a global `char *` variable `selection` (see line 15) is set to address a copy of the string inserted into the list, using the `getString` method in the instance to obtain those characters.

It's important to use `strdup` at line 63 to copy the selected string, because the next line deletes the `selector` from memory. When you use the `selector` class, be careful not to set a pointer to an item you will delete before using!

The *SELECTOR.CPP* Module

There are few new features in the `selector` implementation module, SELECTOR.CPP, Listing 7.16. Most of the programming is conventional C++ and should be easy to understand from the comments. I'll point out the more interesting sights as you tour the listing.

Listing 7.16. SELECTOR.CPP

```
 1:   // selector.cpp -- Selector class
 2:
 3:   #include "key.h"
 4:   #include "selector.h"
 5:
 6:   #define KEY_ENTER 13     // <Enter> key value
 7:   #define KEY_ESC    27     // <Esc> key value
 8:   #define KEY_UP    -184   // <Cursor Up> key value
 9:   #define KEY_DOWN  -176   // <Cursor Down> key value
10:   #define KEY_PGUP  -183   // <Page Up> key value
11:   #define KEY_PGDN  -175   // <Page Down> key value
12:
13:   /* -- Constructor. Passes arguments to the window class's alternate
14:   constructor, and initializes its own data fields. */
15:
16:   selector::selector(winStruct &ws, const char *title, int popup)
17:       : window(ws, title)
18:   {
19:       showHide = popup;        // Select pop-up or stationary style
20:       selector::row = -1;      // i.e., not initialized
```

```
21:   }
22:
```

The constructor passes the first two of its parameters, `ws` and `title`, to the `window` class constructor. This is a typical design, and you've seen the technique in other examples. A constructor in a derived class will usually pass the necessary arguments to the base-class constructor, in order to initialize fields inherited from the base.

But `selector` is not a typical class. The `selector` class inherits from *two* base classes. However, as you can see at lines 16-17, the derived constructor calls only one of the constructors in the inherited `window` base, not the constructor in `list`. The reason for this apparent discrepancy is that `list`'s constructor declares no parameters; therefore, C++ calls the constructor by default. Even though you don't name parameterless constructors, they still run before the derived constructor executes.

If a class inherits from two or more base classes that have constructors requiring parameters, then you can call those constructors in the derived class by separating the base constructor calls with commas. For example, suppose `selector` derives from a third class named `dummy` with a constructor `dummy(int popup)`. There is no such class in the LC++ class library, but if there were, the derived constructor declaration would be

```
selector::selector(winStruct &ws, const char *title, int popup)
    : window(ws, title), dummy(popup)
```

In general, in a class `derived` that inherits from multiple base classes `base1`, `base2`, and `base3`, design the constructor's implementation like this:

```
derived::derived(int x, int y, int z, int a)
    : base1(x), base2(y), base3(z)
{
    // statements in derived constructor
}
```

Parameters `x`, `y`, and `z` represent the arguments to be passed to the base-class constructors. Parameter `a` represents any data required by the derived constructor. The order in which the base class constructors are listed isn't important, though it's probably not wise to rely on C++ *calling* those functions in any specific order.

Listing 7.16. SELECTOR.CPP (continued)

```
23:   /* -- Display current item at window row, col == 0, using the current
24:   attribute. */
25:
26:   void selector::showItem(int row)
27:   {
28:       gotorc(row, 0);
```

```
29:         window::puts(((strItem *)currentItem())->getString());
30:         eeol();
31:    }
32:
```

The showItem function displays the current item in the selector at the row given by parameter row. I purposely wrote line 29 differently from lines 38 and 30, to illustrate two ways to call base class member functions. Because selector inherits from window, it can call that class's gotorc, puts, and eeol functions as though they were declared directly in selector. There is no need to preface such function calls with the class name, as I did at line 29. Specifying window:: in front of the statement is allowed but is usually unnecessary.

In the following functions, you'll see other unadorned examples of calls to member functions from the two inherited base classes, window and list.

Listing 7.16. SELECTOR.CPP (continued)

```
33:  /* -- Display current item at window row, col == 0 using the
34:  highlight attribute. This procedure displays the "selector bar." */
35:
36:  void selector::highlight(int row)
37:  {
38:      reverseVideo();
39:      showItem(row);
40:  }
41:
42:  /* -- Move selector bar up to previous item. Scrolls window contents
43:  down if necessary. */
44:
45:  void selector::moveUp(int &row)
46:  {
47:      if (!listEmpty() && !atHeadOfList()) {
48:          normalVideo();
49:          showItem(row);
50:          if (row > 0) row--; else scrollDown(1);
51:          prevItem();
52:          highlight(row);
53:      }
54:  }
55:
56:  /* -- Move selector bar down to next item. Scrolls window contents up
57:  if necessary. */
58:
59:  void selector::moveDown(int &row)
60:  {
```

```
61:      if (!listEmpty() && !atEndOfList()) {
62:         normalVideo();
63:         showItem(row);
64:         if (row < ws.height - 3) row++; else scrollUp(1);
65:         nextItem();
66:         highlight(row);
67:      }
68:   }
69:
70:   /* -- Display selector window, list items, and let operator move
71:   selector bar to any item, scrolling up and down as necessary if there
72:   are more items than can fit in the window. Returns a pointer to the
73:   selected item if operator presses <Enter>. Returns NULL if operator
74:   presses <Esc>. */
75:
76:   strItem *selector::getSelection(void)
77:   {
78:      int key;      // Keypress value
79:      int i;        // for-loop control variable
80:
81:      if (listEmpty()) return NULL;
82:      if (!isOpen) row = -1;   // Reset newly opened windows
83:      showWindow();            // Make sure window is visible
84:      normalVideo();           // Select normal text attribute
85:      if (row < 0) {           // Initialize first time
86:         row = 0;
87:         resetList();
88:         do {
89:            showItem(row);
90:            nextItem();
91:         } while (!atHeadOfList() && (++row <= ws.height - 3));
92:         row = 0;
93:         resetList();
94:      }
95:      highlight(row);
96:
97:   /* -- Get keypress and move up or down. Return NULL for <Esc>, or
98:   pointer to selected item for <Enter>. */
99:
100:      for (;;) {
101:         switch (key = getKey()) {
102:            case KEY_ESC:
103:            case KEY_ENTER:
104:               if (showHide) {
105:                  hideWindow();
```

```
106:                            row = -1;
107:                        }
108:                        if (key == KEY_ESC)
109:                            return NULL;
110:                        else
111:                            return (strItem *)currentItem();
112:                    case KEY_UP:
113:                        moveUp(row);
114:                        break;
115:                    case KEY_DOWN:
116:                        moveDown(row);
117:                        break;
118:                    case KEY_PGUP:
119:                        for (i = 0; i < (ws.height - 2) / 2; i++)
120:                            moveUp(row);
121:                        break;
122:                    case KEY_PGDN:
123:                        for (i = 0; i < (ws.height - 2) / 2; i++)
124:                            moveDown(row);
125:                        break;
126:                }
127:        }
128:    }
```

A Class for Commands

Most programs prompt for and respond to commands from operators. To have programs react to commands, programmers typically write code that reads key presses and then calls one of several functions. Usually, a switch statement controls the process, running a function after the user types a command's letter, or selects a menu item, which the program translates to a number.

The problem with that approach comes when it's time to upgrade the software. To add a new command requires tedious work: modifying switch statements, changing prompts in menu functions, and so on. Also, the conventional way makes it difficult to create dynamic menus, which insert and delete commands based on other input. For example, in a *File* menu there might be a command to *Open* a disk file. After you select *Open,* new commands to *Save* and *Close* the file appear in the menu. This design makes programs easier to use by listing only the commands that are possible to select rather than listing every command including disabled ones.

A solution to this problem jumps out of the answer to a simple question: What is a command? There may be many correct answers, but in most programs, a *command* usually has three parts:

- A name

- An action

- A selector

The name of a command is what you see in the menu. The action represents what the command does. The selector might be the letter of the key you press to select the command. Or the selector could be a unique value assigned by the program.

When faced with other problems to solve, it may help to make a similar list of observations. List the properties of the task you need to perform or the structure you need to build. Then, look for a class that comes as close to meeting your requirements as possible.

Applying that thought to the LC++ class library, the class that comes closest to meeting a command's requirements is s t r I t e m. A s t r I t e m instance can store a string, which might represent the command's name. The command's action can be a new member function in the derived class. The selector might as well be the s e l e c t o r class described in the previous section. Because s e l e c t o r derives from l i s t, this design makes it easy to create lists of commands in a window—in other words, a pop-up menu.

The COMMAND.H Header

Chapter 6 introduced the concept of an abstract class. Programs can never create variables of an abstract class, which serves only as the design for other derived classes. The c o m m a n d class, declared in COMMAND.H, Listing 7.17, is an abstract class. Instead of defining variables of c o m m a n d, you must derive new classes from c o m m a n d. Those derivatives become the commands in your program.

Listing 7.17. COMMAND.H

```
 1:  // command.h -- Header for command.cpp
 2:
 3:  #ifndef __COMMAND_H
 4:  #define __COMMAND_H   1       // Prevent multiple #includes
 5:
 6:  #include "stritem.h"
 7:
 8:  /* -- The abstract command class is a strItem with an associated
 9:  action in the form of a "pure" virtual function. Selecting a command
10:  object derived from the command class calls the derived virtual
11:  function. With this design, all commands are objects, eliminating the
12:  need for the large switch statements typically found in menu-driven
13:  programs. */
```

```
14:
15:    class command : public strItem {
16:        protected:
17:            int cmdNum;      // Unique number to identify command
18:        public:
19:            command(const char *s, int cn = 0) : strItem(s)
20:                { cmdNum = cn; }
21:            virtual void performCommand(void) = 0;
22:    };
23:    #endif    // __COMMAND_H
```

The command class has only three members. The int field cmdNum uniquely identifies multiple instances of a class derived from command. For commands that have only one instance for their class, this field isn't used. Unlike some menu systems, this one does *not* assign a value to every command in a program. The cmdNum field might be used that way, but its purpose is to distinguish between instances of the same derived type. In one program, many commands might have the same cmdNum value. (A sample program, TCOMMAND.CPP, near the end of this chapter demonstrates how to use cmdNum.)

The command constructor at line 19 is implemented as an in-line function. Because the construction of new commands isn't likely to consume much of a program's time, it may have been better to implement the constructor in the usual way. However, I wrote command as listed here to demonstrate that in some cases a class may be declared in a header but have no corresponding implementation module. Many of the classes in this book are stored in corresponding .H and .CPP files. But command is different. The entire class declaration and implementation for command are stored in the COMMAND.H header file. This trick is typical for abstract classes with pure virtual-member functions. (The technique requires constructors to be in line; otherwise, you would have to implement the class in a .CPP module.)

The pure virtual-member function performCommand at line 21 fulfills the requirement that a command perform an action. Being virtual, a derived class can replace performCommand and be confident that a pointer to type command will call the correct replacement function in an instance of any derived type. Being *purely* virtual (the function ends with the assignment = 0), it's not necessary to implement the function. In fact, the presence of the pure virtual function is what makes the class abstract (unable to be defined as a variable). If the function were not declared to be purely virtual, you would have to provide a do-nothing function implementation such as the following:

```
void performCommand(void)
{
}
```

Declaring pure virtual functions eliminates the need for these sorts of empty shells. However, in nonabstract classes, it may be necessary to declare do-nothing virtual functions that a derived class is expected to replace. In such cases, you'll need to supply a shell for the impure virtual function in the base class in order to allow variables of the base class to be defined. When doing this, you might want to create a global function named `abstract` that goes something like this:

```
void abstract(void)
{
    cout << "\n\nAbstract function called";
    exit(1);
}
```

Then, instead of the do-nothing function shell listed previously, write

```
void performCommand(void)
{
    abstract();    // Signal error in derived class
}
```

With this arrangement, if any statement accidentally calls the impure virtual `performCommand` function, the program will display an error message and halt. This debugging device can help locate derived classes that fail to provide required replacement functions inherited from a base class.

Using the command *Class*

TCOMMAND.CPP, Listing 7.18, shows how to use the `command` and `selector` classes to create pop-up menus in programs. Compile the test program with the command **ztc tcommand error.obj key.obj stritem.obj item.obj list.obj window.obj selector.obj**. As with the other test programs in this chapter, omit the ".obj" file extensions if you did not compile the separate modules before. Remember, there is no corresponding COMMAND.CPP file to accompany COMMAND.H; therefore, you do not have to link the final program to COMMAND.OBJ. In fact, there is no such file! To use the `command` class, programs need only to `#include` the COMMAND.H header file, as done here at line 6.

Listing 7.18. TCOMMAND.CPP

```
1:    // tcommand.cpp -- Test command class
2:
3:    #include <stream.hpp>
4:    #include "key.h"
5:    #include "selector.h"
6:    #include "command.h"
7:
8:    /* -- Test-function prototypes */
9:
```

```
10:    void pause(void);
11:    void runtest(void);
12:
13:    /* -- Derived command classes */
14:
15:    class openCommand : public command {
16:       public:
17:           openCommand() : command("Open") { }
18:           virtual void performCommand(void);
19:    };
20:
21:    class closeCommand : public command {
22:       public:
23:           closeCommand() : command("Close") { }
24:           virtual void performCommand(void);
25:    };
26:
27:    class saveCommands : public command {
28:       public:
29:           saveCommands(const char *s, int cn) : command(s)
30:              { cmdNum = cn; }
31:           virtual void performCommand(void);
32:    };
33:
34:    class quitCommand : public command {
35:       public:
36:           quitCommand() : command("Quit <Esc>") { }
37:           virtual void performCommand(void);
38:    };
39:
```

Lines 15-38 show how to derive command classes. Each new class derives from the abstract command. Typically, a class derived from command will contain only two items: a constructor and a replacement for the performCommand virtual function inherited from the base class. Of course, the derived class may declare other member functions and fields as needed.

The most common type of derived command will appear similar to openCommand at lines 15-19. Line 17 declares the derived class's constructor, a do-nothing shell with the sole purpose of passing the command's name to the base-class constructor. Lines 23 and 36 show two other examples of similar constructors.

Class saveCommands (lines 27-32) shows an alternate method for creating commands. As in the other three classes, the new class inherits the properties of the abstract base class command, and declares a replacement performCommand function. But the constructor at lines 29-30 is different from the others. Instead of specifying the command's name directly, the derived constructor in saveCommands lists two parameters: a constant string pointer s and an integer cn. The constructor passes the first parameter (representing the command's name) to the base class constructor and assigns the second parameter to cmdNum. The constructor can make this assignment because cmdNum is declared in a protected section in the base class; therefore, the inherited field is visible in the derived class. However, cmdNum is not visible to statements outside the class.

The purpose of this alternate construction is to give programs a way to invent classes that can handle more than one command in a menu. In the implementation of the command's replacement performCommand function, you can use the protected cmdNum as a selector to distinguish among the multiple commands.

The main function comes next. Always remember to initialize the window class, as shown here. You must do so because selector inherits from window, even though the program doesn't include the WINDOW.H header and doesn't create any window instances directly.

Listing 7.18. TCOMMAND.CPP (continued)

```
40:  main()
41:  {
42:      window::startup();
43:      runtest();
44:      window::shutDown();
45:      exit(0);
46:  }
47:
48:  /* -- Wait for a <Spacebar> */
49:
50:  void pause(void)
51:  {
52:      cout << " Press <Spacebar>...";
53:      while (getch() != ' ') ;
54:  }
55:
56:  /* -- Perform tests */
57:
58:  void runtest(void)
59:  {
60:      winStruct ws = {
61:          4, 20, 18, 7,    // Row, column, width, height
62:          0x07,            // Text attribute
63:          0x1e,            // Border attribute
64:          0x70,            // Highlight attribute
65:          1                // Type, save text (yes)
66:      };
```

```
67:        selector *sel = new selector(ws, " Items ");
68:        command *cp;
69:
70:        sel->insertItem(new openCommand());
71:        sel->insertItem(new closeCommand());
72:        sel->insertItem(new saveCommands("Save", 1));
73:        sel->insertItem(new saveCommands("Save-as", 2));
74:        sel->insertItem(new quitCommand());
75:
76:        while ((cp = (command *)(sel->getSelection())) != NULL) {
77:            cp->performCommand();
78:        }
79:
80:        delete sel;
81:    }
82:
```

Function runtest shows how to create a pop-up menu and to perform commands as you select them. The winStruct declaration at lines 60-66 should be familiar by now. The assignments specify the size, location, colors, and type of the window used to display the menu. Use WINTOOL from chapter 6 to choose values for the text, border, and highlight attributes in your own menus.

Line 67 creates a selector instance for the pop-up menu. The title can be anything you like, or it can be NULL if you don't want to give the menu a title. (For example, you might use untitled menus to create "pull-down" menus at the top of the display.) Line 18 defines a pointer cp to a command class instance. The program will use cp to execute commands in the menu.

After preparing the menu's selector, using the menu requires three basic steps:

1. Insert derived command instances into the selector.

2. Call the selector's getSelection function to prompt for a command.

3. If getSelection does not return NULL, use the pointer to call the command's replacement performCommand virtual function. This will run the selected command.

Lines 70-74 take care of the first step. The statements insert in the selector addressed by the sel pointer new instances for each derived command class. Note the difference between lines 70-71 (also 74) and 72-73. The openCommand, closeCommand, and quitCommand classes require no arguments for their constructors. But there are two instances of the saveCommands class, one for a command named "Save" and another for a command "Save-as." Multiple instances of the *same* class are inserted into the menu, using different command numbers (the arguments 1 and 2) to distinguish one command from another. In another setting, you could use this same technique to insert more than two commands of the same class into a menu.

Next come the derived class implementations. These are the functions that perform the command actions.

Listing 7.18. TCOMMAND.CPP (continued)

```
83:   /* -- The derived command-class implementations */
84:
85:   void openCommand::performCommand(void)
86:   {
87:      cout << "\nOpen command.";
88:      pause();
89:   }
90:
91:   void closeCommand::performCommand(void)
92:   {
93:      cout << "\nClose command.";
94:      pause();
95:   }
96:
97:   void saveCommands::performCommand(void)
98:   {
99:      if (cmdNum == 1)
100:        cout << "\nSave command.";
101:     else if (cmdNum == 2)
102:        cout << "\nSave-as command.";
103:
104:     pause();
105:  }
106:
107:  void quitCommand::performCommand(void)
108:  {
109:     ungetKey(27);       // "Press" the <Esc> key
110:  }
```

The derived command functions simply display a message indicating which function is running. In your own code, you'll need to write similar functions to perform your program's commands. Simple cases like openCommand's performCommand function (lines 85-89) carry out a single action. More complex cases like saveCommands's performCommand function (lines 97-105) use the value of cmdNum to detect which of the several command instances called the function. Giving each instance a unique value during construction (see lines 72-73) lets the virtual replacement function know which instance called it.

Recap

You've now examined every scrap of code in the LC++ class library. You can use the classes in the library as foundations for your own projects, or you can use the experience you've gained in this chapter and chapter 6 to help you explore a more complex commercial library. You may also want to start your own library, using the classes here as templates for your own designs.

You've also encountered nearly all of C++'s features, although a few details remain to be covered in chapter 9. With what you know so far, you can write sophisticated C++ programs that put OOP techniques to good use. However, there is one essential programming topic that I still haven't covered: file handling. It's the rare program that doesn't have to read or write at least one disk file. As you'll learn in the next chapter, C++ has an extensive array of functions designed for just that purpose.

Exercises

7.1. From Figure 7.1, what class (or classes) does strItem derive from? What class (or classes) does selector derive from?

7.2. How does multiple inheritance differ from single inheritance?

7.3. Design a new class derived from item that can hold four floating point values. What member functions are needed to allow access to the class's data?

7.4. Write a program to create and display a list of your class instances from exercise 7.3.

7.5. In the following class, which members are accessible by statements in a derived class? Which members are accessible to other members in the same class? Which members are accessible to statements outside of the class?

```
class room {
   private:
      int numChairs;
      int numTables;
   protected:
      int numBooks;
   public:
      void putInfo(int chairs, int tables, int books);
      void getInfo(int &chairs, int &tables, int &books);
};
```

7.6. Redesign the `room` class in exercise 7.5 to eliminate the multiple parameters in member functions `putInfo` and `getInfo`. (Hint: use a `struct`.) Why make this change?

7.7. Describe the main difference between a constructor and a destructor. In general terms, what should constructors and destructors do?

7.8. Suppose class B derives from class A and that each class declares a constructor and a destructor. In what order do the constructors and destructors run when instances of class B are defined?

7.9. What does the `this` pointer address? From where can you use `this`? Inside the implementation to `getInfo` in the class from exercise 7.5, what is the `this` pointer's data type?

7.10. Create a derivation of the `list` class that can report how many items are currently listed.

7.11. Create a derivation of the `strItem` class that converts its strings to uppercase.

7.12. In chapter 6, you filled in WINTOOL's Help command to display text inside a window. To accomplish this, you had to use wasteful pairs of `gotorc` and `puts` functions. Improve the `window` class by adding a new function that eliminates the need to use `gotorc` before every `puts` operation. (Hint: You may want to design your function to simulate carriage return and line feed operations.)

7.13. How does a static member field differ from a global variable?

7.14. Why is it dangerous to return pointers as member function data types? Instead of a pointer, what should these kinds of functions return?

7.15. Write a program that lets you choose a window border type (0 to 4) and shows

Chapter 8

Files and Directories

T he C++ standard library is stocked with several routines for reading and writing data stored in disk files. These routines are identical to those supplied with most C compilers; therefore, the information in this chapter applies equally to C and C++. Like identical twins, the two languages are practically indistinguishable when it comes to file handling.

Strictly speaking, however, file-handling is not an intrinsic capability of C or C++, neither of which provides native data types for accessing information in files. There are no "file" types and operators built into C and C++ as there are int and float types and operators like + and *. But the standard library's file-handling data structures and functions are so widely accepted, it's just as well to think of these elements as permanent residents.

In another sense, all file handling is the realm of the operating system—the programming language provides a mere interface to the operating system's file structures and subroutines that are responsible for storing and retrieving bytes in files. It's that interface that concerns us here. Because the compiler supplied with this book runs under MS-DOS 2.0 or later, I'll focus on MS-DOS file and directory techniques. A few programs may require later versions of DOS—if you are running version 3.3, you should be able to run all the programs without trouble.

The previous three chapters described OOP methods in C++. In the first part of this chapter, you'll learn conventional approaches for file and directory handling. Then, you'll return to OOP, using the LC++ class library from chapters 6 and 7 to create classes for listing file information in disk directories. You'll also use those classes to write two useful utilities, a directory navigator, NAV, and a text-file lister, READ.

Note: You probably ran the READ program to view the README.TXT file on disk. This chapter lists READ's source code and explains how the program works.

File and DOS Functions

The C++ library contains over 60 functions you can use to write a variety of file and directory programs. Some of these functions call low-level DOS and BIOS subroutines to perform system-dependent operations. For example, the `dos_abs_disk_read` and `dos_abs_disk_write` functions read and write disk sectors without regard to whether those sectors belong to files. With another function, `_bios_disk`, you can call even lower-level ROM BIOS disk routines.

Although these and other low-level routines are available, you will rarely need them. For most file and directory handling, higher-level library routines are safer and easier to use. The same library routines exist on other C and C++ compilers (even those that run under different operating systems). So, if you stick to the higher ground explained in this chapter, you'll be able to port your programs more easily to another system later.

Text Files

A text file is the most common file-storage format on most computer systems. By *text file,* I mean any file that contains bytes representing ASCII characters. Usually, a text file on MS-DOS systems will organize its data into lines separated by carriage-return (0x0d) and line-feed (0x0a) control codes. However, some text files may contain a stream of ASCII data that's not divided into lines.

Other computer operating systems and programs may store ASCII text in files but represent new lines differently. Still other programs modify the ASCII standard. For example, word processors usually add formatting codes to represent bold face, italics, and other special symbols. These facts complicate ASCII file processing, but in general, the techniques in this section apply to most kinds of text files.

Basic Text-File Techniques

A simple program that creates a new text file will demonstrate some of the basics of text-file handling techniques. You've already seen many examples of programs that display text on-screen. To store text in files, you can use similar methods. But instead of sending text to the console, you'll call routines that direct the text to a disk file. In most text-writing programs, there are three steps to follow:

- Open a text file by preparing a variable that other routines can use to access that file.

- Write information to the file by specifying the file variable opened previously.

- Close the file to update the file's directory information including the file's name, size, and other facts.

This final step is critical. Always close files when you're finished using them. In addition to updating the file entry in the disk directory, closing a file flushes any data held in memory. This step is necessary because DOS, various file routines, and other operating systems usually read and write data in chunks. When you write information to a file, the operating system may store that data temporarily in memory until a full chunk is available for sending to the actual file. This buffering action helps keep file I/O running fast, but it also means you must close files properly. If you end a program prematurely, you might lose any data that wasn't transferred to disk.

Creating Text Files

Listing 8.1, MAKETXT.CPP, shows how to open, write, and close text files. Compile the program in the usual way (type **ztc maketxt**.) Then, run MAKETXT by entering a command such as **maketxt test.txt**. That will create a new file, TEST.TXT, in the current directory. Next, enter several lines to store in the new file. Type a blank line to quit. After the DOS prompt returns, enter **type test.txt** to display TEST.TXT's contents and verify that MAKETXT holds the text you entered.

Listing 8.1. MAKETXT.CPP

```
 1:  // maketxt.cpp -- Create a new text file
 2:
 3:  #include <stream.hpp>
 4:  #include <stdio.h>
 5:  #include <stdlib.h>
 6:  #include <string.h>
 7:
 8:  /* -- Function prototypes */
 9:
10:  void error(const char *message);
11:  void instruct(void);
12:
13:  main(int argc, char *argv[])
14:  {
15:      FILE *fp;
16:      char s[129];
17:
```

```
18:        if (argc == 1) instruct();
19:        cout << "\nCreating file " << argv[1];
20:        cout << "\nEnter a blank line to end\n\n";
21:        fp = fopen(argv[1], "w");
22:        if (!fp) error("Creating file");
23:        while (strlen(gets(s)) > 0) {
24:            fputs(s, fp);
25:            fputc('\n', fp);
26:        }
27:        fclose(fp);
28:    }
29:
30:    /* -- Display error message and exit */
31:
32:    void error(const char *message)
33:    {
34:        cout << form("\n\nERROR: %s\n\n", message);
35:        exit(1);
36:    }
37:
38:    /* -- Display instructions and exit */
39:
40:    void instruct(void)
41:    {
42:        cout << "\nMAKETXT <file name>";
43:        cout << "\nInstructions: Enter a file name, then type";
44:        cout << "\nlines of text. End with a blank line. Note:";
45:        cout << "\nan existing <file name> will be erased!\n";
46:        exit(1);
47:    }
```

Most of C++'s file-handling routines are declared in the STDIO.H header file, included into MAKETXT at line 4. You'll almost always include this header file in any program that needs to read and write disk files. MAKETXT's main function uses a struct declaration in STDIO.H to create a file-variable pointer fp. Here's the definition:

```
FILE *fp;
```

The uppercase FILE is a struct data type that stores various details required by DOS and C++ library routines to read and write data in files. Variable fp is declared as a pointer to the FILE structure. You can safely ignore FILE's contents, although you can read the declaration in STDIO.H if you want. Most file routines in the C++ library require a pointer to a FILE variable created by a library routine; therefore, you'll rarely allocate space directly for a FILE variable.

Lines 18-20 in MAKETXT check whether you entered a file name on the DOS command line. If not, function instruct displays instructions and halts the program. This is a typical design for simple programs that operate on single files.

Line 21 shows how to open a file. The statement calls function fopen, declared in STDIO.H. That function returns a pointer to a new FILE structure, and you should always save that pointer, as done here by assigning the result of fopen to fp. The file pointer gives other routines the means to process the newly opened file.

Function fopen requires two char * arguments. The first argument represents the file's name. The second is a short command that selects one of several options listed in Table 8.1. The options affect whether and how other routines may read and write information in files. If you specify *reading only* with "r", for example, you can't write data to the file; you can only read information already stored there. If you create a new file with "w", any existing file of the same name will be erased. If you open a file with the append option, "a", new data written to the file will be attached to the end of any information currently stored in the file. Adding a plus sign to these three basic options opens the file for reading *and* writing.

Table 8.1. Text-File Options for fopen

Option	Description
"r"	Open file for reading only
"w"	Create new file for writing only
"a"	Append file for writing only
"r+"	Open file for reading and writing
"w+"	Create new file for reading and writing
"a+"	Append file for reading and writing

When you run MAKETXT two or more times, each session creates a new file on disk, erasing the old file. To have MAKETXT preserve existing text in a file, change the "w" option at line 21 to "a", which instructs fopen to append new data to information currently in the file. Compile and run the modified MAKETXT, and enter a few new lines. When you examine the appended text file, you'll see that the new text is added to the old. Simply changing the way you open the file affects how other file-handling routines operate.

After opening a file with an append or write option, you can store text in that file by calling two functions: fputs (file put string) and fputc (file put character). (See lines 24-25). Function fputs writes a string of characters. The first argument to fputs must be a pointer that addresses the string to be written. The second argument must be a pointer to a FILE struct. Function fputc is similar to fputs, but writes a single character to an open file. For both functions, the file must have been opened by fopen for writing or appending. (By the way, most file-handling functions in STDIO.H begin with the letter f to remind you that these routines require a FILE * argument.)

When you press **<Enter>** without entering text on a new line, the `while` loop in MAKETXT at lines 23-26 ends. Immediately thereafter, line 27 calls `fclose(fp)` to close the file addressed by the `fp` pointer. Closing the file updates the disk directory and flushes any buffered information to disk.

Note: When a program ends, any open files are automatically closed. For this reason, line 27 in MAKETXT is not strictly required. However, not all C++ compilers and operating systems ensure that open files will be closed when a program ends, and it's still wise to close your files explicitly. In a larger program, if another function fails to close a file, that file will remain open until the program ends. Because DOS can open only a limited number of files, not closing files may cause other functions to be unable to open new files. For these reasons, it's a good idea always to close open files, even when not absolutely necessary.

Formatted Output

Another useful function for writing text to files is `fprintf`. The function operates similarly to `printf`, supplied with most C and C++ compilers (including the one that accompanies this book). The `fprintf` function is also similar to the `form` function that's most often used to display formatted text in output-stream statements.

To use `fprintf`, supply a pointer to an open `FILE`. Next, specify a formatting string containing various escape codes prefaced with a percent sign (%). Each such code represents a value to appear at this position in the output. Finally, supply one variable or constant for each escape code in the formatting string. For example, to write a string to a file, you can use the statement

```
fprintf(fp, "%s\n", s);
```

That line is functionally equivalent to the two statements at lines 24-25 in MAKETXT. However, the file pointer `fp` comes first; in `fputs` and `fputc`, the pointer is last. This inconsistency exists because `fprintf` accepts a variable number of arguments—one for each escape code in the formatting string; therefore, fixed parameters like `fp` must come ahead of those that will vary in number.

Note: For more information about `printf` and `fprintf`, refer to the discussions of those functions (and also `form`) in chapter 10.

Errors from File Functions

With one exception, MAKETXT ignores the possibility that an error will occur during a file operation. Generally, this omission is a very bad practice, and you should *always* consider what will happen if a problem develops when a program writes data to disk. Reading data from disk files is not as critical, but programs should still include statements to recover gracefully from mishaps that occur during file reads. When it comes to working with disk drives, just about anything that can go wrong probably will sooner or later.

A typical error occurs when you tell f o p e n to read a file that doesn't exist. Or you might accidentally ask the function to create a file on a nonexistent disk drive. To simulate this kind of error, run MAKETXT and supply the name of a file on a floppy disk that has its drive door open. For example, type **maketxt a:\dummy.dat**. In a few seconds, you'll see the *critical error message*

```
Not ready error reading drive A
Abort, Retry, Fail?
```

Enter **A** to abort the critical error. This will end MAKETXT and return you directly to the DOS prompt. If you press **R**, DOS will retry the failed operation, though this won't always recover from the error, depending on what caused the problem originally. If you enter **F**, DOS returns an error code to the program that started the ball rolling. Recognizing this error, function f o p e n returns NULL, causing line 22 to call MAKETXT's e r r o r function.

> **Note:** Of all the error messages from DOS, the "Not ready error..." is one of the most confusing. To "Abort" this critical DOS error means to return control immediately to DOS (that is, to COMMAND.COM). To "Retry" means just that—to retry the same *DOS* operation that failed. Retrying does *not* cause your program to repeat the statement that led to the failure. That's what "Fail" does. Unfortunately, some programs silently repeat a failed file statement, causing Retry and Fail to give identical results. Such unfriendly error-handling in programs has led to much confusion about how to respond to critical DOS errors. You can minimize similar confusion with your programs by using good error-handling methods.

Although MAKETXT detects errors from f o p e n, the program does not test for similar errors from f p u t s and f p u t c. In this simple example, that omission probably will do no harm. Since f o p e n has to succeed before the other two functions are even called, it's unlikely that any errors will occur. Besides, the worst that can happen is a critical DOS error, forcing you to abort back to the DOS prompt.

Of course, finished commercial applications must deal sensibly with file errors. Like f o p e n, functions such as f p u t s and f p u t c also return a value that indicates whether the operation succeeded. Unlike f ope n, which returns a F I L E pointer or NULL, f put s and f putc return nonnegative int values if successful. If an error occurs, these and other int file functions in STDIO.H return a symbol called E O F (for "End of File.") E O F is also used to detect when a program has reached the last byte stored in a file.

In place of lines 24-25 in MAKETXT, use the following statements to check for any errors that occur while writing data to disk:

```
if (fputs(s, fp) == EOF) error("Writing to file");
if (fputc('\n', fp) == EOF) error("Writing to file");
```

Now, if any errors occur during either of these two function calls, the program will call the e r r o r function (see lines 32-36), display a suitable message, and end.

Unfortunately, however, the modified statements probably *won't* have the chance to detect most errors! Why? Because data is buffered somewhere in memory, and a problem such as a disk-full error may go unnoticed until the program closes the file. Therefore, line 27 also needs rewriting. This is better:

```
if (fclose(fp) == EOF) error("Closing file");
```

Reading Text Files

Writing text to files is, of course, only half the story. The other half is reading text from files stored on disk. There are two ways to proceed: read text files one *character* at a time, or read text files one *line* at a time. As you'll see, there are pluses and minuses to both approaches.

Reading Text One Character at a Time

Listing 8.2, READTXT.CPP, shows how to read text files one character at a time. Compile the program and enter a command such as **readtxt readtxt.cpp** to read and display the program's own text. Or, enter **readtxt test.txt** to read and display the file you created earlier with MAKETXT.

Listing 8.2. READTXT.CPP

```
1:  // readtxt.cpp -- Read and display a text file one character at a time
2:
3:  #include <stream.hpp>
4:  #include <stdio.h>
5:  #include <stdlib.h>
```

```
 6:
 7:    /* -- Function prototypes */
 8:
 9:    void error(const char *message);
10:    void instruct(void);
11:
12:    main(int argc, char *argv[])
13:    {
14:        FILE *fp;
15:        char c;
16:
17:        if (argc == 1) instruct();
18:        fp = fopen(argv[1], "r");
19:        if (!fp) error("Opening file");
20:        while ((c = fgetc(fp)) != EOF)
21:            cout << c;
22:        fclose(fp);
23:    }
24:
25:    /* -- Display error message and exit */
26:
27:    void error(const char *message)
28:    {
29:        cout << form("\n\nERROR: %s\n\n", message);
30:        exit(1);
31:    }
32:
33:    /* -- Display instructions and exit */
34:
35:    void instruct(void)
36:    {
37:        cout << "\nREADTXT <file name>";
38:        cout << "\nInstructions: Enter the name of a text file.";
39:        cout << "\nEnter 'READTXT <file name> | more' to display";
40:        cout << "\nlengthy files (requires DOS's MORE.COM to be";
41:        cout << "\nin the current PATH).\n";
42:        exit(1);
43:    }
```

As in MAKETXT, READTXT includes the header file STDIO.H. The program also defines a pointer fp to a FILE struct. Whether you are reading or writing files, you include the same STDIO.H header and you define FILE pointers in the same way.

Line 18 is also nearly the same as the similar `fopen` statement in MAKETXT. This time, however, the "`r`" option tells the function to open the file for reading. Because the program uses this option, any attempts to write data to the file will be rejected.

The `while` loop at lines 20-21 shows the correct way to read every character from a file. The expression (`c = fgetc(fp)`) calls function `fgetc`, which reads the next character from the file addressed by `FILE` pointer `fp`. The result of `fgetc` is assigned to `c` for displaying characters individually with an output-stream statement at line 21.

If `fgetc` attempts to read past the last byte in a file, or if an error occurs during reading, the function returns `EOF`. When this happens in READTXT, the `while` loop ends. Immediately thereafter, line 22 calls `fclose` to close the file before the program ends. Since the file was opened for reading only, there's no good reason to test whether `fclose` succeeded in closing the file as I suggested earlier.

When you run READTXT, you'll notice that the program's output is divided into lines on-screen. This happens because `fgetc` reads not only visible ASCII characters, but also any control codes embedded in the text file. As a result, carriage-return and line-feed control characters are passed to `cout` at line 21 along with visible characters. Because output-stream statements recognize those controls as commands to start new lines, the text displays normally.

Reading Text One Line at a Time

There are two main disadvantages associated with reading text files one character at a time. For one, many programs will need to process words and symbols in text files, and you'll have to write statements to build strings of single characters in memory. For another, reading files one character at a time causes the program to execute an entire loop for *every* character in a file. Processing a large file one character at a time may cause the program to run slowly.

Reading text a line at a time solves these problems. Because the program reads entire strings, you do not have to write code to construct those strings in memory. Also, the number of loops and function calls needed to process an entire file is likely to be drastically reduced, improving performance.

The primary disadvantage of the line-at-a-time approach to text-file handling is the definition of a "line." Most files have lines no longer than 80 or 132 characters, two popular column widths for many computer terminals and PCs. But there's no guarantee that a file won't have longer lines. Also, some programs mark the ends of *paragraphs* with carriage returns. Processing such files with a program designed to read lines of a fixed maximum length will either fail or chop off words in mid-sentence.

Many times, however, the line-at-time approach to text-file reading gives enough of a performance boost to make the disadvantages worth enduring. Listing 8.3, READLN.CPP, shows the result. Compile the program, then run it with a command such as **readln readln.cpp**.

Listing 8.3. READLN.CPP

```
 1:   // readln.cpp -- Read and display a text file one line at a time
 2:
 3:   #include <stream.hpp>
 4:   #include <stdio.h>
 5:   #include <stdlib.h>
 6:
 7:   /* -- Function prototypes */
 8:
 9:   void error(const char *message);
10:   void instruct(void);
11:
12:   main(int argc, char *argv[])
13:   {
14:       FILE *fp;
15:       char buffer[256];
16:
17:       if (argc == 1) instruct();
18:       fp = fopen(argv[1], "r");
19:       if (!fp) error("Opening file");
20:       while (fgets(buffer, 255, fp) != NULL)
21:           cout << buffer;
22:       fclose(fp);
23:   }
24:
25:   /* -- Display error message and exit */
26:
27:   void error(const char *message)
28:   {
29:       cout << form("\n\nERROR: %s\n\n", message);
30:       exit(1);
31:   }
32:
33:   /* -- Display instructions and exit */
34:
35:   void instruct(void)
36:   {
37:       cout << "\nREADLN <file name>";
38:       cout << "\nInstructions: Enter the name of a text file.";
39:       cout << "\nEnter 'READLN <file name> | more' to display";
40:       cout << "\nlengthy files (requires DOS's MORE.COM to be";
41:       cout << "\nin the current PATH).\n";
42:       exit(1);
43:   }
```

There are only a few differences between READTXT and the new READLN. Line 15 in the new listing defines a b u f f e r of 256 characters. That should be enough space to handle the lines in most text files.

Lines 18-19 open the file as READTXT does. You don't have to open a text file any differently in order to read its contents a line or a character at a time.

The w h i l e loop at lines 20-21 calls f g e t s to read a string of characters from the open file. (The character-by-character READTXT program called f g e t c is a similar way to read a single character.) Function f g e t s reads text from a file into a location specified by the first argument; in this example, b u f f e r. The parameter's type is c h a r * s t r, so you can use either a string buffer as defined at line 15, or you can allocate storage on the heap and pass a c h a r pointer as the argument. The second argument represents the maximum number of bytes you want f g e t s to read.

READLN's w h i l e loop ends when f g e t s returns N U L L, indicating that all text has been read from the file. After that, f c l o s e closes the file.

> **Note:** Always remember that f g e t c returns E O F to indicate that the last character from a file has been read. Function f g e t s returns N U L L to indicate the same condition. The compiler will accept expressions that compare f g e t c to N U L L, even though that will not correctly locate a file's end.

Sorting Text Files

Many text-processing programs combine the methods described in the preceding sections. A typical text-processing program reads text from a file, performs an operation on that text, and writes the result to another file.

Listing 8.4, SORTTXT.CPP, demonstrates these techniques by alphabetically sorting lines in any text file, containing up to about 500 lines. SORTTXT illustrates a useful method for storing strings efficiently on the heap. The program also fulfills a promise I made back in chapter 4—to show how a function pointer makes it possible to call custom functions from within precompiled library routines; in this case, a routine named q s o r t.

Listing 8.4. SORTTXT.CPP

```
1:   // sorttxt.cpp -- Sort lines in a text file
2:
3:   #include <stream.hpp>
4:   #include <stdio.h>
5:   #include <stdlib.h>
6:   #include <string.h>
```

```
 7:
 8:    #define MAXLINES 500
 9:
10:    /* -- Function prototypes */
11:
12:    void error(const char *message);
13:    void instruct(void);
14:    void readText(const char *fname);
15:    void sortText(void);
16:    void writeText(const char *fname);
17:
18:    /* -- Global variables */
19:
20:    char *strings[MAXLINES];    // Array of pointers to strings
21:    int index;                  // strings[] array index
22:
23:    /* -- Comparison function, called by qsort(). Zortech C++ requires
24:    the linkage directive extern "C" to allow the function to be linked
25:    and called correctly. */
26:
27:    extern "C" int compare(const char **a, const char **b)
28:    {
29:        return strcmp(*a, *b);
30:    }
31:
32:    main(int argc, char *argv[])
33:    {
34:        if (argc <= 2) instruct();
35:
36:        readText(argv[1]);
37:        sortText();
38:        writeText(argv[2]);
39:    }
40:
41:    /* -- Display error message and exit */
42:
43:    void error(const char *message)
44:    {
45:        cout << form("\n\nERROR: %s\n\n", message);
46:        exit(1);
47:    }
48:
49:    /* -- Display instructions and exit */
50:
```

```
51:   void instruct(void)
52:   {
53:       cout << "\nSORTTXT <infile> <outfile>";
54:       cout << "\nInstructions: Enter the name of a text file";
55:       cout << "\nto sort plus the name of a new file to create.";
56:       cout << "\nThe SORTTXT program will read <infile>, sort its";
57:       cout << "\nlines alphabetically, and write the results to";
58:       cout << "\n<outfile>. File size is limited by available";
59:       cout << "\nfree memory, or to " << MAXLINES << " lines.\n";
60:       cout << "\nThe original file is not changed provided you enter";
61:       cout << "\ndifferent file names for <infile> and <outfile>.\n";
62:       exit(1);
63:   }
64:
65:   /* -- Read lines from a text file, store the text on the heap, and
66:   insert the address of each line into the global strings array of char
67:   pointers. */
68:
69:   void readText(const char *fname)
70:   {
71:       FILE *fp;
72:       char buffer[256];
73:
74:       fp = fopen(fname, "r");
75:       if (!fp) error("Opening file");
76:       while ((index < MAXLINES) && (fgets(buffer, 255, fp) != NULL))
77:           if ((strings[index++] = strdup(buffer)) == NULL)
78:               error("Out of memory");
79:       fclose(fp);
80:   }
81:
82:   /* -- Using the global strings array of char pointers, sort the
83:   strings in memory. Rearranging the char pointers and not the actual
84:   strings saves time--a LOT of time. */
85:
86:   void sortText(void)
87:   {
88:       cout << "Sorting " << index << " lines\n";
89:       qsort(&strings, index, sizeof(strings[0]), compare);
90:   }
91:
92:   /* -- Create a new file and write the sorted text lines to it. */
93:
94:   void writeText(const char *fname)
95:   {
```

```
 96:        int i;
 97:        FILE *fp;
 98:
 99:        fp = fopen(fname, "w");
100:        if (!fp) error("Creating file");
101:        for (i = 0; i < index; i++)
102:            fputs(strings[i], fp);
103:        fclose(fp);
104:    }
```

Line 20 in SORTTXT defines an array of 500 char pointers. Each of these pointers will address one string in memory. This is a convenient data structure for any program that needs to sort a series of strings (see Figure 8.1). By rearranging only the pointers, the strings can be alphabetized without having to move a single character. The pointers are probably shorter than the associated strings; therefore, the program will operate more quickly, because it takes less time to shuffle small pointers than to move long character strings from location to location.

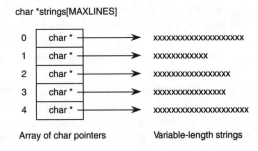

Figure 8.1. An array of *char* pointers (left) addresses a series of variable-length strings (right).

Any program that uses the qsort library function must implement a function named compare declared as

```
int compare(const void *a, const void *b)
{
    // return result of comparison
}
```

The compare function must return one of three integer values: –1 if the item addressed by parameter a is less than the item addressed by b; 0 if the two items are identical; or +1 if the first item is greater than the second. The nature of the items being compared, and the method you use to compare them, are entirely up to you.

Variations on compare's declaration are possible, and usually needed. For example, in SORTTXT, the standard declaration is changed to

```
int compare(const char **a, const char **b)
```

Because the program will rearrange the array of `char` pointers, but will need to do that by comparing the strings those pointers address, it's necessary to use the data type `const char **` (literally a pointer to a `char` pointer). The comparison itself is handled by calling the string library function `strcmp`, passing the dereferenced `char` pointers `*a` and `*b` as arguments. The result of `strcmp` is in the correct format for `qsort`'s required `compare` function, so line 29 merely passes that result back.

> **Note:** The `extern "C"` preface to the `compare` function (see line 27 in SORTTXT.CPP) is called a *linkage directive.* This directive tells C++ not to employ an internal scheme known as *name mangling,* by which the compiler generates unique identifiers for C++ function identifiers. Name mangling enables the linker to join modules containing conventional C-type programming and modules written using C++'s special features (such as classes). However, name mangling also prevents linking functions *compiled* with another C compiler, another language, or an assembler, none of which mangles identifiers as C++ does. The `qsort` library function was written in assembly language, and therefore `qsort` can't be linked directly to C++ functions with mangled names; that is why the `extern "C"` directive turns off name mangling.

SORTTXT's main function (lines 32-39) calls three functions: **readText** to read lines from a text file, **sortText** to sort those lines alphabetically, and **writeText** to write the sorted lines to a new file. Run the program by entering a command such as **sorttxt file.txt new.txt**. SORTTXT will read and sort lines from FILE.TXT, and then write the sorted text to NEW.TXT. (The program does not warn you about overwriting an existing target file, so type your file names carefully and keep backup copies of your original data.)

Function `readText` (lines 69-80) shows one way to read lines from a text file and store those lines as strings on the heap. The `while` loop at lines 76-78 calls `fgets` to read one line into a local `buffer` defined as a local variable at line 72. (This is similar to how READLN.CPP reads lines from text files.) The `while`-loop's conditional expression also prevents reading more than the number of lines specified by the `MAXLINES` constant.

Line 77 uses the `strdup` library function to duplicate the characters of each string loaded into `buffer`. If the result of `strdup` is `NULL`, then there wasn't enough memory to hold the new string, and line 78 aborts the program by calling `error`. If enough memory was available, `strdup` copies the characters from `buffer` to that space and returns a pointer to the first byte. The assignment saves this pointer in the `strings` array, advancing `index` by one for the next loop.

All of this preparatory work makes `sortText`'s job easy. Line 88 displays a message telling you how many lines are about to be sorted. Then, the next line calls `qsort`. Four arguments are passed to `qsort`:

- &strings—the address of the data to be sorted, here the array of char pointers. (Remember, the pointers will be rearranged, not the strings those pointers address.)

- index—representing the number of items to be sorted.

- sizeof(strings[0])—equal to the size of one item. All items to be sorted *must* be of the same size.

- compare—the address of the compare function explained earlier.

Note that compare is passed to qsort simply by stating the function's name. Functions have addresses, and therefore you can pass them to other functions that declare pointers to functions.

After sorting, function writeText at lines 94-104 writes the rearranged strings to disk. The for loop at lines 101-102 calls fputs to write each line via the char pointers in strings.

Data Files

Text files are only one of the many kinds of files C++ programs can process. Other *data files* are more general in nature. A data file is just a collection of bytes stored on disk. It's completely up to you to decide what those bytes represent.

The following sections describe techniques for reading and writing information in data files. One of the most common uses for these techniques is to process records in a database. You can also use data-file methods for reading and writing binary values. Just about anything you can represent in memory can be stored in a data file.

Basic Data-File Techniques

Open and close data files similar to the way you perform those operations on text files. First, you'll need a FILE pointer defined like the following:

```
FILE *fp;
```

Next, call fopen to open or create a data file. Use the same text-file options listed in Table 8.1, but add the lowercase letter b to indicate that the file consists of binary bytes. For example, to open a data file named STUFF.DAT for reading, use these statements:

```
fp = fopen("stuff.dat", "rb");
if (fp == NULL) error("Can't open file");
```

To create a fresh data file and prepare for writing new information to that file, use the option "wb". To append new data onto the end of an existing file, use "ab". To open a data file for reading and writing, use "rb+". Table 8.2 lists the complete set of data-file options available for fopen. These are the same options as listed for text files in Table 8.1, but include the letter b in the option argument.

Table 8.2. Data-File Options for fopen

Option	Description
"rb"	Open file for reading only
"wb"	Create new file for writing only
"ab"	Append file for writing only
"rb+"	Open file for reading and writing
"wb+"	Create new file for reading and writing
"ab+"	Append file for reading and writing

When done using a data file, always remember to call fclose(fp) where fp is your FILE pointer. As with text files, calling fclose updates the file's directory entry and transfers to disk any buffered data temporarily held in memory.

Readin' and Writin' Data Files

After opening a data file using one of the options from table 8.2, you can read and write data using one of three functions. To read bytes from a data file opened for reading, use fread. To write bytes to a disk file opened for writing or appending, use fwrite. To reposition the file to a specific record by number, use fseek. Sample listings in the next several sections show these three functions in action.

Writing Binary Values to Disk

Data files are useful for storing disk information in binary form. Binary representations often take less space than equivalent ASCII character forms of the same values. For example, the int value 12345 occupies two bytes, but the *string* "12345" requires six bytes including the NULL character at the end. Also, because binary data usually takes less disk space than text, binary file I/O tends to be faster than text I/O, although extra time may be required to translate binary information to and from ASCII for display and other purposes.

Listing 8.5, WDATA.CPP, demonstrates how to create a data file and write an array of floating-point values to disk. You can use similar techniques to write other kinds of variables.

Listing 8.5. WDATA.CPP

```
 1:  // wdata.cpp -- Write data file
 2:
 3:  #include <stream.hpp>
 4:  #include <stdlib.h>
 5:  #include <time.h>
 6:
 7:  #define MAX 100    // Number of values to write
 8:
 9:  void error(const char *s);
10:
11:  main()
12:  {
13:     double fpArray[MAX];
14:     int i, n;
15:     FILE *fp;
16:
17:     srand(time(NULL));    // Scramble random number generator
18:     cout << "Filling array with values\n";
19:     for (i = 0; i < MAX; i++) {
20:        fpArray[i] = 1.0 / rand();
21:        cout << form("%16.8f", fpArray[i]);
22:     }
23:     cout << "\nWriting array to TEST.DAT...\n";
24:     fp = fopen("TEST.DAT", "wb");
25:     if (fp == NULL) error("Can't create TEST.DAT");
26:     for (i = 0; i < MAX; i++) {
27:        n = fwrite(&fpArray[i], sizeof(double), 1, fp);
28:        if (n != 1) error("Writing data");
29:     }
30:     fclose(fp);
31:  }
32:
33:  void error(const char *s)
34:  {
35:     cout << "\nERROR: " << s;
36:     exit(1);
37:  }
```

After filling an array fpArray of double elements with random values (see lines 17-22), fopen creates a new file named TEST.DAT. The "wb" option in this statement (line 24) creates a fresh data file, erasing any existing file named TEST.DAT. Be aware of this side effect. You may want to warn people before they erase existing files.

With the newly created file open, a for loop at lines 26-29 writes individual values from fpArray to disk. Line 27 calls fwrite to transfer one value from memory to the file. Function fwrite requires four arguments:

- &fpArray[i]—A pointer to the value stored in memory. Either pass a pointer variable as this argument, or use the & operator to find the address of a variable as in Listing 8.5, line 27.

- sizeof(double)—The size in bytes of one element. Using sizeof is optional, but ensures that the program will work correctly if compiled with a different C++ compiler that uses a different number of bytes to represent a data type.

- 1—The number of elements to write to disk.

- fp—A pointer to a FILE struct opened by fopen for writing or appending.

Function fwrite returns an int value equal to the number of items transferred successfully to disk. Usually you should use this number to verify that the correct number of elements was written, as the sample listing does at line 28.

I purposely constructed the for loop at lines 26-29 the "long way" to show how to write individual values to disk. However, other variations are possible. For example, you can replace the entire loop with a single statement:

```
if (fwrite(&fpArray, sizeof(double), MAX, fp) != MAX)
    error("Writing data");
```

Simply altering the arguments passed to fwrite makes it possible to write all of fpArray to disk with one statement. As in the longer version, the first fwrite argument &fpArray addresses the first byte of the data to write. The second argument equals the size in bytes of one element. The third argument specifies the number of elements. And the fourth argument is the ever-present FILE pointer.

Usually the single-statement form is faster than writing individual elements, though the actual speed advantage may be minor for small files. Also, be aware that fwrite may write only *some* of the requested number of elements to disk. As written here, the single-statement solution would flag an error unless all data was written successfully. This approach might not be the best in all situations, and you may want to recode the single statement to this slightly longer form:

```
n = fwrite(&fpArray, sizeof(double), MAX, fp);
if (n == 0) error("Writing data");
cout << "\n" << n << " elements written to disk";
```

> **Note:** When writing single multibyte elements to disk with `fwrite`, the second and third arguments may be reversed. For example, to write a 4-byte `long` value v, you might use the statement `fwrite(&v, sizeof(long), 1, fp)`. Technically, that's the correct form—the second argument specifies the size in bytes of one element, and the third argument states how many of those elements to write. But the following alternate statement has the identical effect: `fwrite(&v, 1, sizeof(long), fp)`. If a `long` value takes four bytes, that statement writes to disk four single-byte elements starting at the address of v. Writing the statement in this alternate way reduces the *granularity* of the output to single-byte transfers; therefore, if an error occurs, the program can report exactly at which byte the problem developed. However, the first form (stating the size of the elements) ensures that only whole elements will be written. Be aware of this subtle difference in `fwrite` arguments—you'll see the alternate trick often in C and C++ listings.

Reading Binary Values from Disk

WDATA's counterpart is RDATA.CPP in Listing 8.6. Run the program to read the TEST.DAT file that you created when you ran WDATA.

Listing 8.6. RDATA.CPP

```
1:   // rdata.cpp -- Read data file
2:
3:   #include <stream.hpp>
4:   #include <stdio.h>
5:   #include <stdlib.h>
6:
7:   #define MAX 100    // Number of values to write
8:
9:   void error(const char *s);
10:
11:  main()
12:  {
13:      double fpArray[MAX];
14:      int i, n;
15:      FILE *fp;
16:
17:      fp = fopen("TEST.DAT", "rb");
```

```
18:         if (fp == NULL) error("Can't open TEST.DAT");
19:         cout << "Reading array from TEST.DAT...\n";
20:         for (i = 0; i < MAX; i++) {
21:             if feof(fp) error("Unexpected end of file");
22:             n = fread(&fpArray[i], sizeof(double), 1, fp);
23:             if (n != 1) error("Reading data");
24:         }
25:         fclose(fp);
26:         cout << "\nValues read from disk:\n";
27:         for (i = 0; i < MAX; i++)
28:             cout << form("%16.8f", fpArray[i]);
29:     }
30:
31:     void error(const char *s)
32:     {
33:
34:         cout << "\nERROR: " << s;
35:         exit(1);
36:     }
```

Here again, fopen opens TEST.DAT, but this time using the option "rb" to specify read-only status. The for loop at lines 20-24 reads values stored in the file. Because the file might not have as many values as expected, line 21 calls feof (*eof* stands for end of file). If this function returns true, then the program has reached the end of the file, and no statement should call fread to read any more elements. In this sample, reaching the end of the file too soon is considered to be an error. In another situation, you might simply continue the program with a message telling people how many items were read.

Note: To simulate the unexpected-end-of-file error, change MAX in a copy of WDATA (Listing 8.5) to 50. Recompile and run. Then, rerun RDATA. This time, the feof function will return true before 100 values are read, and the program will display an error message and halt.

Line 22 shows how to read a single element from a data file. As with fwrite, the statement requires four arguments. In fact, they are the *same* arguments (see line 27 in WDATA.CPP). Of course, the effect is different. The function stores data in memory at the address represented by the first argument, here &fpArray[i]. The second argument specifies the size in bytes of one element. The third argument is the number of those elements to read. The final element is the FILE pointer.

Function fread returns an int value equal to the number of elements read from disk. Usually, you should compare this value with the number of requested values, as done here at line 23. If the two values do not agree, then something went wrong during the transfer from disk to memory.

As with WDATA, the for loop at lines 20-24 is written the long way, showing how to read values from disk one-by-one. You can do away with the loop altogether by telling fread to load all values with a single statement:

```
if (fread(&fpArray, sizeof(double), MAX, fp) != MAX)
    error("Reading data");
```

Specifying the address of fpArray as the destination for fread, and requesting MAX values, reads the entire array from disk. (If you try this and receive an error message, run WDATA to make sure that there are 100 values stored in TEST.DAT.)

Creating Database Files

The data-file techniques described in the preceding sections can be used to save and retrieve records in database files. In general, the method is simple. First, design a struct data type containing the fields for your records. Then, read and write struct variables in binary form.

You'll usually want to store your struct declaration in a header file so that other programs can use the same data type. Listing 8.7, SAMPLE.H, shows an example of a struct that other programs in this section will use.

Listing 8.7. SAMPLE.H

```
 1:  // sample.h -- Sample database header file
 2:
 3:  #include <stdio.h>
 4:  #include <stdlib.h>
 5:  #include <string.h>
 6:
 7:  #define FALSE 0
 8:  #define TRUE 1
 9:  #define NAMELEN 30
10:  #define STATELEN 2
11:
12:  struct rec {
13:      long custnum;                  // Customer number
14:      char name[NAMELEN + 1];        // Name in string form
15:      char state[STATELEN + 1];      // State in string form
16:      double balance;                // Account balance
17:  };
```

The fields in the s t r u c t, and its name, are up to you. In SAMPLE.H, the r e c struct has four fields, c u s t o m e r, n a m e, s t a t e, and b a l a n c e. Note that the two string fields, n a m e and s t a t e, are declared as c h a r arrays, not as c h a r   * (pointers). There's nothing wrong with pointer fields in s t r u c t s, of course, but when designing records for disk storage, pointers complicate the works. Simple s t r u c t s like r e c exactly match the bytes that will be stored on disk. If the s t r u c t had pointer fields, however, it would make no sense to store those pointers on disk. Instead, you would have to write statements to read and write the data addressed by those pointers. The extra work involved to allocate space on the heap, assign addresses to pointer fields, and read and write data in files may be more trouble than it's worth.

After designing a record as a s t r u c t, the next step is to run a program that writes a few records to disk. Listing 8.8, MAKEDB.CPP, outlines the necessary steps.

Listing 8.8. MAKEDB.CPP

```
1:   // makedb.cpp -- Make sample database
2:
3:   #include <stream.hpp>
4:   #include "sample.h"
5:   #include "stdlib.h"
6:
7:   /* -- Function prototypes */
8:   int getNewRec(rec &oneRec);
9:   void error(const char *s);
10:
11:  main()
12:  {
13:      FILE *fp;
14:      rec oneRec;
15:
16:      cout << "\nCreating or updating sample database";
17:      fp = fopen("sample.dat", "ab");
18:      if (!fp) error("Opening file");
19:      for (;;) {
20:          cout << "\n\nEnter new record. (<Enter> quits).\n";
21:          if (!getNewRec(oneRec)) break;
22:          if (fwrite(&oneRec, sizeof(rec), 1, fp) < 1)
23:              error("Writing to file");
24:      }
25:      if (fclose(fp) != 0) error("Closing file");
26:      cout << "\nFile created or updated";
27:  }
28:
```

```
29:    /* -- Prompt for and let user enter one record. Return FALSE if user
30:    presses <Enter> for first field. Return TRUE otherwise. */
31:
32:    int getNewRec(rec &oneRec)
33:    {
34:        char buf[129];
35:
36:        memset(&oneRec, 0, sizeof(rec));      // Zero fill record
37:
38:        cout << "\nCustomer #  : ";
39:        gets(buf);
40:        if (strlen(buf) == 0) return FALSE;
41:        oneRec.custnum = atol(buf);
42:
43:        cout << "Name ...... : ";
44:        gets(buf);
45:        strncpy(oneRec.name, buf, NAMELEN);
46:
47:        cout << "State ..... : ";
48:        gets(buf);
49:        strncpy(oneRec.state, buf, STATELEN);
50:
51:        cout << "Balance ... : ";
52:        gets(buf);
53:        oneRec.balance = atof(buf);
54:
55:        return TRUE;
56:    }
57:
58:    void error(const char *s)
59:    {
60:
61:        cout << "\nERROR: " << s;
62:        exit(1);
63:    }
```

To keep the program short, MAKEDB doesn't include all the programming required to make record-entry easy. A more sophisticated database system would allow stepping from field to field, making corrections to fields entered earlier, and other operations. Run MAKEDB and enter a few test records. You can enter any characters for the customer "number"; for example, A10 or 99X. After typing a few sample records, press **<Enter>** at the "Customer #" prompt to end.

Line 17 shows a typical way to open a database file, using the "ab" option and fopen to prepare for appending new records. Line 22 writes a single record to disk with `fwrite`, similar to the way WDATA wrote floating-point values. In this case, however, the first argument to `fwrite` is the address of a `rec` variable, `oneRec`. The second argument, `sizeof(rec)`, specifies the size, in bytes, of one record. The third argument tells `fwrite` to write one of those records to disk. The final argument is, of course, the file pointer `fp`.

Reading Database Files

For a simple way to process records created by MAKEDB, open the sample database file with `fopen` and then use `fread`. Listing 8.9, ALLRECDB, plots the game plan.

Listing 8.9. ALLRECDB.CPP

```
 1:  // allrecdb.cpp -- Read all records in sample database
 2:
 3:  #include <stream.hpp>
 4:  #include "sample.h"
 5:  #include "stdlib.h"
 6:
 7:  void showRec(rec &oneRec, long recnum);
 8:  void error(const char *s);
 9:
10:  main()
11:  {
12:      FILE *fp;
13:      rec oneRec;
14:      long recnum = 0L;
15:
16:      fp = fopen("sample.dat", "rb");
17:      if (!fp) error("Opening file");
18:      while (fread(&oneRec, sizeof(rec), 1, fp) == 1)
19:          showRec(oneRec, recnum++);
20:      fclose(fp);
21:  }
22:
23:  void showRec(rec &oneRec, long recnum)
24:  {
25:      cout << form("\n%04ld: %-30s %-2s %+8.2f",
26:          recnum, oneRec.name, oneRec.state, oneRec.balance);
27:  }
28:
29:  void error(const char *s)
30:  {
```

```
31:        cout << "\nERROR: " << s;
32:        exit(1);
33:    }
```

After fopen successfully opens SAMPLE.DAT, a while loop calls fread to load successive records from disk. Each record is stored into oneRec. Function showRec displays the record's contents and record number on a single line.

The number of the first record in a file is always 0. By using that number as an index, another function, fseek, prepares a file for reading or writing a specific record. The fseek function makes it possible to write *random-access database programs*, as Listing 8.10, READDB.CPP, demonstrates.

Listing 8.10. READDB.CPP

```
 1:   // readdb.cpp -- Read records from sample database
 2:
 3:   #include <stream.hpp>
 4:   #include "sample.h"
 5:   #include "stdlib.h"
 6:   #define FATAL 1          // Pass to error to halt
 7:   #define NONFATAL 0       // Pass to error to continue
 8:
 9:   int getRec(FILE *fp, rec &oneRec, long recnum);
10:   void showRec(rec &oneRec, long recnum);
11:   void error(const char *s, int halt);
12:
13:   main()
14:   {
15:       FILE *fp;
16:       rec oneRec;
17:       long recnum = 0;
18:       char s[80];
19:
20:       fp = fopen("sample.dat", "rb");
21:       if (!fp) error("Opening file", FATAL);
22:       for (;;) {
23:           cout << "\nEnter record number (-1 to quit): ";
24:           cin >> s;
25:           recnum = atol(s);
26:           if (recnum < 0) break;
27:           if (getRec(fp, oneRec, recnum))
28:               showRec(oneRec, recnum);
29:           else
30:               error("Reading record", NONFATAL);
31:       }
```

```
32:        fclose(fp);
33:    }
34:
35:    /* -- Read one record from file fp at specified recnum. Return FALSE
36:    if any errors are detected; otherwise, return TRUE. If FALSE, then
37:    contents of oneRec are not defined. */
38:
39:    int getRec(FILE *fp, rec &oneRec, long recnum)
40:    {
41:        if (fseek(fp, recnum * sizeof(rec), SEEK_SET) != 0)
42:            return FALSE;
43:        if (fread(&oneRec, sizeof(rec), 1, fp) != 1)
44:            return FALSE;
45:        return TRUE;
46:    }
47:
48:    /* -- Display record number and contents of one record */
49:
50:    void showRec(rec &oneRec, long recnum)
51:    {
52:        cout << form("%04ld:%-30s %-2s %+8.2f",
53:            recnum, oneRec.name, oneRec.state, oneRec.balance);
54:    }
55:
56:    void error(const char *s, int halt)
57:    {
58:
59:        cout << "\nERROR: " << s;
60:        if (halt) exit(1);
61:    }
```

The m a i n function in READDB opens the database file, and prompts for record numbers (lines 22-31). Enter the number of a record to view, or enter –1 to quit.

Function getRec shows how to use fseek to find a specific record by its number. Lines 41-42 call fseek in an if statement, returning FALSE if the specified record number is out of range. (TRUE and FALSE are defined in SAMPLE.H.) Function fseek requires three arguments:

- fp—A FILE struct pointer returned by fopen.

- recnum * sizeof(rec)—A long integer offset representing the number of bytes relative to a fixed location where the record is located. Typically, you'll multiply the record number by the size of one record to determine the offset from the beginning of the file to that record.

- SEEK_SET—A predeclared constant that tells fseek to treat the offset value in the second argument relative to the beginning of the file. Use SEEK_CUR to position the file pointer relative to the *current* position. Use SEEK_END to position the file backwards relative to its end.

The fseek function returns 0 if the sought position is available in the file. The function returns an unspecified nonzero value if an error was detected, usually because an argument requested a record not stored in the file.

If you open a file for reading and writing, you can use fseek, fread, and fwrite to find records, display their values, and then write modified values back to disk. Before writing a numbered record this way, always call fseek before fwrite. Doing that positions the file to the correct record to be changed.

Working with Directories

Well-designed file programs should give people ways to view file names in disk directories. Amazingly, some commercial programs don't provide even the basic capability to list file names in the current directory—not to mention changing directories and listing files in other locations. Be kind to your users. Add directory commands to your programs as suggested in the following sections.

> **Note:** Programs that list file names in directories and perform other related operations are firmly tied to the operating system for which those programs were designed. The directory listings in the following sections require DOS 2.0 or a later version; they are unlikely to run correctly under other operating systems.

Determining Free Space on Disk

Before storing large amounts of data on disk, it may be a good idea to test how much free space is available. It's frustrating to start a lengthy operation—sorting a large database, for example—only to discover 20 minutes later that the operation has failed due to insufficient disk space.

Finding the amount of free space on disk is easy. Just call function dos_getdiskfreespace, prototyped in the DOS.H header. Pass an int argument representing the drive number to check. 0 represents the current drive.

1 represents drive A:, 2 stands for B:, 3 for C:, 4 for D:, and so on. Listing 8.11, FREE.CPP, shows how to use dos_getdiskfreespace. The program also makes a handy utility to keep around. (I use it to check the amount of free room available on floppy disks before I copy a large number of files from my hard drive to a backup diskette.)

Listing 8.11. FREE.CPP

```
1:   // free.cpp -- Report free space on drive
2:
3:   #include <stream.hpp>
4:   #include <dos.h>
5:   #include <ctype.h>
6:
7:   main(int argc, char *argv[])
8:   {
9:       int drive = 0;
10:      unsigned long freeSpace;
11:
12:      if (argc > 1)
13:          drive = toupper(*argv[1]) - ('A' - 1);
14:      freeSpace = dos_getdiskfreespace(drive);
15:      if (freeSpace == -1)
16:          cout << "Error reading drive";
17:      else
18:  cout << form("Free space on drive = %lu", freeSpace);
19:  }
```

To run FREE, enter **free** at the DOS prompt plus an optional drive letter. For example, to display the amount of free space on drive A:, enter **free a:**. (The colon is optional—**free a** is just as good.) Lines 12-13 detect the optional drive-letter argument and convert the letter into a value, 1 for A:, 2 for B:, 3 for C:, and so on. That value is assigned to drive, which is initialized to 0, the value that refers to the current drive.

Line 14 passes drive to dos_getdiskfreespace, which returns the number of bytes available. FREE saves that result in a variable called freeSpace, displayed at line 18. If freeSpace equals –1, then an error occurred (perhaps due to an open drive door).

Changing the Current Directory

Another simple command prototyped in DOS.H lets programs change the current directory. Adding this command to your programs makes them much easier to use, especially if the code reads and writes files that users might store in many different subdirectories.

Naturally, from DOS, you may as well use the CD command to change directories. But it's a useful exercise to duplicate that command as a demonstration of how to perform the same operation in a C++ program. Listing 8.12 demonstrates the basic idea. Compile the program, then run it by entering **cdir** and a path name to change the current directory.

Listing 8.12. CDIR.CPP

```
 1:   // cdir.cpp -- Change directories
 2:
 3:   #include <stream.hpp>
 4:   #include <direct.h>
 5:
 6:   main(int argc, char *argv[])
 7:   {
 8:       char *buf;
 9:
10:       if (argc == 1) {
11:           if ((buf = getcwd(NULL, 0)) != NULL)
12:               cout << buf;
13:       } else {
14:           if (chdir(argv[1]) != 0)
15:               cout << "Can't change to " << argv[1];
16:       }
17:   }
```

CDIR relies on two functions to duplicate DOS's CD command. The first is getcwd, which returns a string equal to the current working directory (hence the *cwd* in the function's name). This is the string that CDIR displays if you run the program with no arguments. Line 11 assigns the address of the current directory string to buf, a char pointer defined earlier at line 8. Normally, that's not a good idea—the strings to which various C++ functions return pointers are temporary, and future calls to the same (or, possibly, even to other) functions may cause the string's value to change. But CDIR is only a short program, and it calls getcwd only once, so it does no harm to use the temporary string directly. However, in your code you'll probably want to use a string function such as strdup to duplicate the temporary string to a more permanent location.

Line 14 shows how to call chdir, the function that switches to a new directory specified as an argument. If chdir returns 0, then the function successfully changed directories; otherwise, an error occurred (probably due to a nonexistent path name), and line 15 displays an error message.

Displaying a Directory

DOS includes two related subroutines that programs can use to retrieve file names in directories. The first of the two subroutines prepares various internal values and returns the first file name. The second subroutine returns the rest of the file names in the directory. You can also use the wild-card characters * and ? to find matching files. For example, *.CPP locates all file names that end in .CPP. (The wild-card string format is the same as that recognized by the DOS DIR command.) You can also specify attribute values to find hidden files, those with their archive bit set, directory names, and others.

DOS.H prototypes two C++ functions, findfirst and findnext, that call the two directory subroutines in DOS. Listing 8.13, SDIR.CPP, demonstrates how to use the functions.

Listing 8.13. SDIR.CPP

```
 1:   // sdir.cpp -- Show directory
 2:
 3:   #include <stream.hpp>
 4:   #include <string.h>
 5:   #include <dos.h>
 6:
 7:   main(int argc, char *argv[])
 8:   {
 9:       struct FIND *fp;
10:       char wildCard[13] = "*.*";
11:
12:       if (argc > 1)
13:           strncpy(wildCard, argv[1], 12);
14:       fp = findfirst(wildCard, FA_DIREC);
15:       while (fp) {
16:           cout << fp->name << '\n';
17:           fp = findnext();
18:       }
19:   }
```

The findfirst function returns a pointer to a struct named FIND and declared in DOS.H. The fields in FIND give access to a single file-name entry in a directory. Here's FIND's declaration:

```
struct FIND
{   char reserved[21];
    char attribute;
    unsigned time,date;
    unsigned long size;
```

```
    char name[13];
};
```

The `reserved` field is for DOS's private use. The `attribute` field specifies the file's attribute bits. The `time` and `date` are stored in a compressed format (I'll explain later how to decode that data). The `size` field holds the file's size in bytes, and `name` is the file's name minus any path information. Figure 8.2 shows how various elements are packed into bit-fields inside the `attribute`, `time`, and `date` fields in the `FIND` structure.

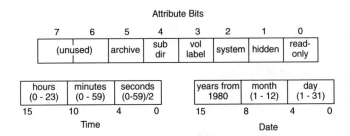

Figure 8.2.   Various bit-fields are packed inside the *attribute*, *time*, and *date* fields in the *FIND* structure.

SDIR uses the `name` field in `FIND` to display each file's name in a directory. Line 9 declares a pointer `fp` to `FIND`. Line 10 sets up a string to `"*.*"`, which matches all file names. If you add to SDIR an argument such as **sdir *.cpp** from the DOS prompt, an `if` statement at lines 12-13 copies the argument string `"*.cpp"` to `wildCard`, replacing the default wild-card assignment.

Line 14 starts the process of reading a directory by calling `findfirst`. The first argument to `findfirst` is the wild-card string to use for matching file names. The second argument is the attribute value. If `findfirst` returns `NULL`, then it could find no matching entries; otherwise, the function returns a pointer to a `FIND` structure. SDIR saves that value in `fp`, and uses the pointer in a `while` loop to display all matching file names and find any more matches.

After displaying the file's name—using the `name` field in the `FIND` structure—line 17 calls `findnext` with no arguments, again assigning the result to `fp`. No arguments are needed, because `findnext` must *always* follow a call to `findfirst`, which prepares internal values that `findnext` will use. (This implies also that there can be only one directory search in progress at a time.) When `findnext` returns `NULL`, there are no more matching file names in the directory.

Decoding Directory Information

A great way to become more familiar with DOS directories is to write a program that duplicates the DIR command's output. Listing 8.14, FSIZE.CPP, does that, with an added twist. The program also totals all listed file sizes, showing you how many bytes the files occupy on disk.

> **Note:** Because DOS stores files in clusters of fixed-size sectors, most files actually occupy more space than their file sizes indicate. Therefore, a set of files may not fit on a disk even though DIR reports that enough space is available.

Listing 8.14. FSIZE.CPP

```
 1:  // fsize.cpp -- Show file sizes, dates, times, and total size
 2:
 3:  #include <stream.hpp>
 4:  #include <string.h>
 5:  #include <dos.h>
 6:
 7:  /* -- Function prototypes */
 8:
 9:  void showFileInfo(FIND *fp);
10:  void adjustTime(FIND *fp, char &ampm);
11:
12:  /* -- Date and time bitfield structures */
13:
14:  struct dateStruct {
15:     unsigned day : 5;
16:     unsigned month : 4;
17:     unsigned year : 7;
18:  };
19:  typedef dateStruct *dsp;
20:
21:  struct timeStruct {
22:     unsigned seconds : 5;
23:     unsigned minutes : 6;
24:     unsigned hours : 5;
25:  };
26:  typedef timeStruct *tsp;
27:
28:  main(int argc, char *argv[])
29:  {
30:     struct FIND *fp;
31:     char wildCard[129] = "*.*";
32:     unsigned long total = 0L;
```

```
33:        int count = 0;
34:
35:        if (argc > 1)
36:           strcpy(wildCard, argv[1]);
37:        fp = findfirst(wildCard, 0);
38:        while (fp) {
39:           showFileInfo(fp);
40:           total += fp->size;
41:           count++;
42:           fp = findnext();
43:        }
44:        if (count == 0)
45:           cout << "no matching files";
46:        else {
47:           cout << dec(total, 21) << "  byte(s) in ";
48:           cout << count << " file(s)";
49:        }
50:     }
51:
52:     /* -- Display formatted file entry using information addressed by the
53:     FIND structure pointer fp. */
54:
55:     void showFileInfo(FIND *fp)
56:     {
57:        static char buf[65];
58:        static char dirStr[] = "<DIR>    ";
59:        char ampm;
60:
61:        adjustTime(fp, ampm);
62:        strcpy(buf, form("%-14s%7lu   %2d-%02d-%02d   %2d:%02d%c",
63:           fp->name,
64:           fp->size,
65:           dsp(&fp->date)->month,
66:           dsp(&fp->date)->day,
67:           dsp(&fp->date)->year + 80,
68:           tsp(&fp->time)->hours,
69:           tsp(&fp->time)->minutes,
70:           ampm));
71:        if ((fp->attribute & FA_DIREC) != 0)
72:           memcpy(buf+13, dirStr, 8);
73:        cout << buf << '\n';
74:     }
75:
```

```
76:    /* -- Adjust 24-hour time field in FIND structure addressed by fp
77:    to 12-hour format. Return AM or PM character in ampm. */
78:
79:    void adjustTime(FIND *fp, char &ampm)
80:    {
81:        unsigned theHour;
82:
83:        theHour = tsp(&fp->time)->hours;
84:        if (theHour >= 13) {
85:            ampm = 'p';
86:            theHour -= 12;
87:        } else {
88:            if (theHour == 0) theHour = 12;   // midnight
89:            ampm = 'a';
90:        }
91:        ((tsp)&fp->time)->hours = theHour;
92:    }
```

Two bit-mapped structs at lines 14-26 make it easy to decode date and time information in a FIND structure (see Figure 8.2). Note how at lines 19 and 26 typedef declares dsp and tsp as pointer types to their respective structs. This simplifies the type casting that's necessary to access the packed date and time information. For example, see lines 65-69. The statements there dereference the date and time fields in the FIND structure addressed by fp, and use the & symbol to locate the address of each field. The expression (&fp->date), for example, produces the address of the date field in the FIND structure addressed by fp. That field address is then cast to a dateStruct pointer (dsp). Finally, this result is dereferenced to extract a packed bit field such as month or day.

An example of a similar cast appears at line 91 inside function adjustTime. The function returns a char equal to 'a' or 'p', representing a.m. or p.m. In addition, the function adjusts the hours value in the FIND time field to keep that value within the range 1 to 12. Line 91 stores the adjusted value back into the time field, again using a cast and pointer dereferences to refer to the hours bit field packed in the time value.

Other fields such as size, name, and attribute are used directly (see lines 40, 63-64, and 71). Line 71 checks whether the directory bit (represented by the constant FA_DIREC) is set in the file's attribute field. If so, memcpy copies the string "<DIR>" plus a few extra blanks to the output buffer, buf. Function showFileInfo constructs and displays buf with an output statement at line 73.

Modifying Directory Entries

Functions findfirst and findnext are useful for reading file-name entries from directories. On occasion, you'll also want to modify some of the information in those entries. For instance, after backing up, it's helpful to update all file dates and times. That way, any new or modified files will be easy to spot in a directory listing. Listing 8.15, TOUCH.CPP, shows how to change a directory entry's date and time fields.

Listing 8.15. TOUCH.CPP

```
 1:  // touch.cpp -- Update file dates and times
 2:
 3:  #include <stream.hpp>
 4:  #include <stdlib.h>
 5:  #include <time.h>
 6:  #include <string.h>
 7:  #include <errno.h>
 8:  #include <dos.h>
 9:
10:  main(int argc, char *argv[])
11:  {
12:      struct FIND *fp;
13:      char wildCard[129] = "*.*";
14:
15:      if (argc > 1)
16:        strcpy(wildCard, argv[1]);
17:      fp = findfirst(wildCard, 0);
18:      cout << "\nUpdating " << wildCard;
19:      while (fp) {
20:        cout << form("\n%s", fp->name);
21:        if (utime(fp->name, NULL) == -1) {
22:            cout << "\nError setting time for file " << fp->name;
23:            cout << form("\nERROR #%d: %s\n", errno, strerror(errno));
24:            exit(errno);
25:        }
26:        cout << " updated";
27:        fp = findnext();
28:      }
29:  }
```

TOUCH is similar to the previous two programs, SDIR and FSIZE. As before, functions `findfirst` and `findnext` locate all matching file-name entries in a directory. For each match, line 21 calls `utime`, a function prototyped in the TIME.H header file. Calling `utime` updates the time and date of a file entry. If the function returns −1, an error occurred. Otherwise, you can assume that the change took hold.

The `utime` function requires two arguments. The first is the file's path name. The second is always `NULL`. That second argument is for compatibility with operating systems that can associate last-access and last-modified date and time values with files. DOS has no such capability, and for that reason, the second `utime` argument must be `NULL`.

A Class for Directories

The preceding examples outline the basic steps for reading directory information from disk. But they also demonstrate a serious flaw in the conventional methods. All the directory programs—FREE, CDIR, SDIR, FSIZE, and TOUCH—are likely to work correctly only on PCs running DOS. The same programs may not even compile with other C++ versions, and they probably won't give meaningful results under other operating systems even if the listings compile. When it comes to disk directories, there are no standards—except, perhaps, to use readable characters for file names.

For better portability, it makes good sense to relegate system-dependent details in classes. By hiding the specific file-entry details, a class can provide common directory services to programs. Of course, the class's programming will need revisions to work under other operating conditions. But programs that *use* the class will not require similar changes.

In the following sections, you'll develop a class module DIR, which you can use to access directory information. Then, after investigating how DIR's classes work, you'll build a disk-navigator program that uses those classes along with others from the LC++ class library from chapters 6 and 7.

The DIR.H Header

Like other classes in this book, the `fileItem` and `directory` classes are declared in a separate header file, Listing 8.16, DIR.H. Make sure to include that file in all programs that use the DIR module's classes.

Listing 8.16. DIR.H

```
1:  // dir.h -- Header for dir.cpp
2:
```

```
 3:   #ifndef __DIR_H      //
 4:   #define __DIR_H                  1    // Prevent multiple #includes
 5:
 6:   #include <dos.h>
 7:   #include "stritem.h"
 8:   #include "selector.h"
 9:
10:   class fileItem: public strItem {
11:       private:
12:           char ampm;                   // AM or PM indicator ('a' or 'p')
13:           char attribute;              // File entry's attribute
14:           unsigned time, date;         // Time and date of last update
15:           unsigned long size;          // Size of file in bytes
16:       public:
17:           fileItem(FIND *fp);
18:           virtual char *getString(void);
19:   };
20:
21:   class directory: public selector {
22:       public:
23:           directory(winStruct &ws, char *wildCard, int popup = 1);
24:           void resetDirectory(char *wildCard);
25:   };
26:
27:   #endif    // __DIR_H
```

The DIR module uses declarations from the STRITEM and SELECTOR modules listed in chapter 7 (see Listings 7.7 and 7.14). Any program that includes DIR.H gets a copy of STRITEM.H and SELECTOR.H free of charge.

Declared in DIR.H are two classes. The first is fileItem, which derives from strItem. A directory's file entry is, after all, mostly a string of characters plus other data; therefore, it makes sense to build fileItem with strItem as a base. Lines 12-15 add other fields to the fileItem class for storing details about each file item.

Class fileItem has only two functions. The first is a constructor at line 17, which initializes an instance of type fileItem. To this constructor you must pass a FIND pointer returned by findfirst or findnext.

The second function is a replacement for strItem's getString member function. The replacement will return a pointer to a string with all the details for this file entry spelled out. Because getString is virtual, existing code that calls getString can display and process directory entries.

The second class in DIR, directory, uses the virtual getString to good advantage. The directory class (see lines 21-25) derives from selector, which, as you'll see, is able to call the replacement getString function without requiring recompilation of the SELECTOR module. The directory class's constructor at line 23 initializes a directory-selection list, reading matching file names into memory. The second member function, `resetDirectory`, changes the current wild-card string and reloads matching file names. Remember, `selector` derives from `list`, and therefore, the mechanisms for storing and retrieving listed files are inherited. There is no need to duplicate those mechanisms in the new class.

Using the `Directory` Classes

The next three listings demonstrate how to write, compile and run programs that use the two classes in the DIR module. Before compiling the listings, make sure that your INCLUDE environment variable specifies paths to the C++ and LC++ class library subdirectories, as explained in the Introduction.

Compile the test program, TDIR, by running MTDIR.BAT (Make TDIR), Listing 8.17. To link TDIR and the various modules the program requires, the batch file uses a linker-response file TDIR.LNK, Listing 8.18. You can also compile and link TDIR manually by issuing the three commands **ztc -c dir**, **ztc -c tdir**, and **blink @tdir.lnk**.

The test program, TDIR.CPP, Listing 8.19, demonstrates how to use the `fileItem` and `directory` classes in the DIR module. After compiling, run TDIR. You should see a pop-up window listing the current directory's file names. Select a file by pressing **<Enter>**, or press **<Esc>** to quit to DOS and not make a selection. The program merely displays the selection you make—it doesn't write any data to disk, so feel free to experiment.

Listing 8.17. MTDIR.BAT

```
1:   echo off
2:   ztc -c dir
3:   if errorlevel==1 goto END
4:   ztc -c tdir
5:   if errorlevel==1 goto END
6:   blink @tdir.lnk
7:   :END
```

Listing 8.18. TDIR.LNK

```
1:   tdir.obj+
2:   \lcpp\lib\key.obj+
3:   \lcpp\lib\error.obj+
4:   \lcpp\lib\stritem.obj+
5:   \lcpp\lib\item.obj+
6:   \lcpp\lib\list.obj+
7:   \lcpp\lib\window.obj+
8:   \lcpp\lib\selector.obj+
```

```
 9:   dir.obj
10:   tdir.exe
11:   tdir.map
12:   /m/li/co/noi
```

Listing 8.19. TDIR.CPP

```
 1:  // tdir.cpp -- Test DIR module classes
 2:
 3:  #include <stream.hpp>
 4:  #include <string.h>
 5:  #include "dir.h"
 6:
 7:  void pause(void);
 8:  void runtest(void);
 9:
10:  char *selection;
11:
12:  main()
13:  {
14:     window::startup();
15:     runtest();
16:     window::shutDown();
17:     if (selection == NULL)
18:        cout << "\nNo file selected";
19:     else
20:        cout << "\nFile selected: " << selection;
21:     exit(0);
22:  }
23:
24:  /* -- Pause until user presses <Spacebar> */
25:
26:  void pause(void)
27:  {
28:     while (getch() != ' ') ;
29:  }
30:
31:  /* -- Execute the test. Assign a selected file name string to the
32:  global selection pointer, or, if no file is selected, assign NULL. */
33:
34:  void runtest(void)
35:  {
36:     winStruct ws = {
```

```
37:               4, 4, 41, 18,    // Row, column, width, height
38:               0x1f,            // Text attribute
39:               0x70,            // Border attribute
40:               0x70,            // Highlight attribute
41:               1                // Type
42:        };
43:        directory *dir = new directory(ws, "*.*");
44:        strItem *p;
45:
46:        p = dir->getSelection();
47:        if (p) selection = strdup(p->getString());
48:        delete dir;
49:     }
```

If you studied the listings in chapters 6 and 7, most of TDIR should be familiar. The main function initializes the window class and calls a local function runtest. That function (see lines 34-49) displays the directory window and lets you select a file name.

As with all windows, a winStruct variable at lines 36-42 specifies the position, size, and attributes for the directory window. Line 43 defines a pointer dir to class directory, calling new to initialize a variable of that type on the heap. To the directory object's constructor, the new statement passes the winStruct structure and a wild-card string. The next line defines a pointer to a strItem variable for saving the address of a selected item.

Most of the directory action is triggered at line 46. There, function getSelection is called for the directory variable addressed by dir. This is a good example of polymorphism at work. The getSelection function was written and compiled in the SELECTOR module. Still, because getString in fileItem is virtual, the precompiled code in the selector class is able to list directory information and let you choose file names.

After you press <Enter> or <Esc>, the pop-up window closes and getSelection returns NULL or the address of a selected item. Line 47 tests the value of p, and if it's not NULL, calls strdup to create and assign the selected item's string to the global selection pointer.

There's an important lesson to learn from line 47. Because the next line deletes the directory from the heap, the program *must* copy any information that it needs to use later on. It would be a serious mistake to assign getString directly to the global selection pointer. After deleting dir, the addressed information would no longer be valid, leading to a serious bug.

The DIR.CPP Module

Now that you've seen how to use the `fileItem` and `directory` classes, you'll be able to understand how the class functions work. Listing 8.20, DIR.CPP, implements the classes.

Listing 8.20. DIR.CPP

```
1:   // dir.cpp -- directory class
2:
3:   #include <stream.hpp>
4:   #include <direct.h>
5:   #include <dos.h>
6:   #include <string.h>
7:   #include "dir.h"
8:
9:   /* -- Date and time structures, plus pointer types to those
10:  structures. The module uses these structures to extract the packed
11:  fields in the unsigned date and time integer fields passed to a
12:  fileItem object during its construction. */
13:
14:  struct dateStruct {
15:     unsigned day : 5;
16:     unsigned month : 4;
17:     unsigned year : 7;
18:  };
19:  typedef dateStruct *dsp;
20:
21:  struct timeStruct {
22:     unsigned seconds : 5;
23:     unsigned minutes : 6;
24:     unsigned hours : 5;
25:  };
26:  typedef timeStruct *tsp;
27:
```

The DIR module declares the same `dateStruct` and `timeStruct` structures, plus the `dsp` and `tsp` pointer types, from FSIZE.CPP in Listing 8.14. The structures could go in the DIR.H header, but since you don't have to use them with the module's classes, they are probably best hidden inside the module's implementation file. If you need the `struct`s, copy their declarations to another file.

Listing 8.20. DIR.CPP (continued)

```
28:   /* -- Constructor for fileItem. Passes the directory file name to the
29:   base strItem constructor, and initializes its own fields. Also
30:   adjusts the time from 24- to 12-hour format. */
31:
32:   fileItem::fileItem(FIND *fp) : strItem(fp->name)
33:   {
34:       unsigned theHour;
35:
36:       attribute = fp->attribute;
37:       time = fp->time;
38:       date = fp->date;
39:       size = fp->size;
40:       theHour = tsp(&time)->hours;
41:       if (theHour >= 13) {
42:           ampm = 'p';
43:           theHour -= 12;
44:       } else {
45:           if (theHour == 0) theHour = 12;   // midnight
46:           ampm = 'a';
47:       }
48:       ((tsp)&time)->hours = theHour;
49:   }
50:
```

Class f i l e I t e m's constructor assigns values to the class instance's private data fields. Line 32 passes the file name to the base class s t r I t e m constructor, saving the file name, which can be retrieved later with a call to g e t S t r i n g. The other fields are simply copied from the F I N D structure addressed by the f p pointer argument. The constructor adjusts the time's hour value to 12-hour format.

```
51:   /* -- Return string stored by object plus the full size, date, and
52:   time of the most recent update to the file. This function is called
53:   by the selector class even though the fileItem class is declared
54:   after the selector module was compiled--a feature made possible by
55:   declaring the getString function virtual. */
56:
57:   char *fileItem::getString(void)
58:   {
59:       static char buf[65];
60:       static char dirStr[] = "<DIR>    ";
61:
62:   /* -- Insert file name, size, date, and time into the static buffer,
63:   using the form function to convert coded information into text. Note
64:   the call to the base class (strItem) getString function. This
```

```
65:   demonstrates how a derived class can access the base class's public
66:   members. */
67:
68:       strcpy(buf, form("%-14s%7lu   %2d-%02d-%02d   %2d:%02d%c",
69:           strItem::getString(),
70:           size,
71:           dsp(&date)->month,
72:           dsp(&date)->day,
73:           dsp(&date)->year + 80,
74:           tsp(&time)->hours,
75:           tsp(&time)->minutes,
76:           ampm));
77:
78:   /* -- Check whether a file is a directory. If so, replace the size
79:   of the file in the newly created string with "<DIR>". */
80:
81:       if ((attribute & FA_DIREC) != 0)
82:           memcpy(buf+13, dirStr, 8);
83:       return buf;
84:   }
85:
```

Function getString demonstrates a classic use for virtual functions—augmenting existing code with new capabilities. In this case, the basic getString function inherited from the strItem class is enhanced to include string representations of the directory information stored in the fileItem class variable.

Lines 59-60 define two static variables, buf and dirStr. The getString function will assemble the directory string in buf, adding the characters from dirStr for subdirectory names. The two variables are declared static because getString returns a pointer to buf. If buf were local to getString, returning buf's address would be a serious mistake. Remember, local variables exist only as long as their defining functions are active. After getString ends, a pointer to a local variable addresses stack space that is available for other functions to use.

The basic buf string is assembled by a call to strcpy at lines 68-76. Function form formats the string, which is copied to buf. Line 69 calls the strItem base class getString function to obtain the file name. The other fields are decoded as in FSIZE.CPP (see Listing 8.14).

Listing 8.20. DIR.CPP (continued)

```
86:   /* -- Constructor for directory. Passes the window struct variable,
87:   NULL for the window title (changed later by resetDirectory), and 1
88:   (true) for a pop-up style window to the base-class selector
89:   constructor. */
90:
91:   directory::directory(winStruct &ws, char *wildCard, int popup)
```

```
 92:        : selector(ws, NULL, popup)
 93:    {
 94:        resetDirectory(wildCard);
 95:    }
 96:
 97:    /* -- Dispose any current list of directory items, then read the
 98:    current directory into the list. Set the window's title to the
 99:    current working directory (cwd). */
100:
101:    void directory::resetDirectory(char *wildCard)
102:    {
103:        char *buf;              // Current working directory string
104:        struct FIND *fp;        // Pointer to DOS search-directory info
105:
106:    /* -- Read directory into a list of fileItems */
107:
108:        hideWindow();
109:        disposeList();
110:        fp = findfirst(wildCard, FA_NORMAL | FA_DIREC);
111:        while (fp) {
112:            insertItem(new fileItem(fp));
113:            fp = findnext();
114:        }
115:
116:    /* -- Set window title to current directory */
117:
118:        if ((buf = getcwd(NULL, 0)) != NULL) {
119:            setTitle(buf);
120:            free(buf);
121:        }
122:    }
```

The rest of the DIR module implements the constructor and function in the directory class. The constructor at lines 91-95 simply passes the ws and popup fields to the selector base class constructor. The NULL value for the second argument tells the selector not to assign a title string to the window. After constructing the base-class portion of the directory variable, the constructor calls resetDirectory with the current wildCard argument.

That function loads the directory names from disk into memory. Because a selector object is a descendent of list, it's a simple matter to insert new fileItem objects in the list (see line 112). Aside from this change, the while loop at lines 111-114 operates as in earlier directory programs, calling findfirst (line 110) and findnext to locate matching entries. Notice how new is called at line 112 to create new f i l e I t e m instances, passing the addresses of those instances directly to insertItem.

After creating the list of file items, g e t c w d gets the current directory name (see line 118). Function s e t T i t l e in the w i n d o w class changes the window's title to this string.

Directory Navigator

The d i r e c t o r y class makes a useful addition to any program that needs basic directory services. The next three listings demonstrate how to incorporate d i r e c t o r y into a finished product; in this case, a directory navigator nicknamed NAV.

Compile NAV by running MNAV.BAT (Make NAV), Listing 8.21. The instructions in the batch file assume that you have already compiled the DIR module. (If not, enter **ztc -c dir**, then rerun MNAV.) You can also compile NAV by entering the two commands **ztc -c nav** and **blink @nav.lnk**.

After compiling, run NAV and select a directory name. The program will switch to that directory. Select the double-dot entry, if listed, to move up one level in the directory hierarchy. Selecting file names has no effect.

Listing 8.21. MNAV.BAT

```
1:   echo off
2:   ztc -c nav
3:   if errorlevel==1 goto END
4:   blink @nav.lnk
5:   :END
```

Listing 8.22. NAV.LNK

```
 1:   nav.obj+
 2:   \lcpp\lib\key.obj+
 3:   \lcpp\lib\error.obj+
 4:   \lcpp\lib\stritem.obj+
 5:   \lcpp\lib\item.obj+
 6:   \lcpp\lib\list.obj+
 7:   \lcpp\lib\window.obj+
 8:   \lcpp\lib\selector.obj+
 9:   dir.obj
10:   nav.exe
11:   nav.map
12:   /m/li/co/noi
```

Listing 8.23. NAV.CPP

```
1:   // nav.cpp -- Directory navigator
2:
3:   #include <stream.hpp>
4:   #include <direct.h>
5:   #include <string.h>
6:   #include "dir.h"
7:
8:   /* -- Function prototype */
9:
10:  void navigate(void);
11:
12:  main()
13:  {
14:     window::startup();
15:     navigate();
16:     window::shutDown();
17:     exit(0);
18:  }
19:
20:  void navigate(void)
21:  {
22:     winStruct ws = {
23:        4, 4, 41, 18,    // Row, column, width, height
24:        0x0f,            // Text attribute
25:        0x70,            // Border attribute
26:        0x70,            // Highlight attribute
27:        1                // Type
28:     };
29:     directory *dir;     // Directory object
30:     strItem *p;         // Pointer to strItem returned by getSelection
31:     char buf[13];       // File name returned by getString
32:     char *t;            // Temporary pointer to char
33:
34:  /* -- Read directory. Then, while user makes a selection, change to
35:  that new directory. Ignore any errors (user may select a file instead
36:  of a directory). The 'if' statement truncates the directory name
37:  returned by getString at the first blank (if any). */
38:
39:     dir = new directory(ws, "*.*");
40:     while ((p = dir->getSelection()) != NULL) {
41:        strncpy(buf, p->getString(), 12);
42:        if ((t = strchr(buf, ' ')) != NULL) *t = 0;
```

```
43:           chdir(buf);
44:           dir->resetDirectory("*.*");
45:       }
46:     delete dir;
47:   }
```

For such a complex program, NAV's source code is relatively simple—a good sign that the classes used by NAV are doing their jobs. Most of the listing should be familiar. The only unique business appears at lines 39-45. After line 39 creates a new directory instance, a while loop calls getSelection to display the pop-up directory window and let you select a directory name. The call to strncpy at line 41 copies the selected string to a local buf character array. Line 42 inserts 0 at the location of the first blank space after the file name. That's necessary because chdir, called at line 43 to switch to a new directory, chokes when fed blanks. After the change, line 44 calls resetDirectory to load the file entries from the new location.

READ: An OOP Text-File Reader

The final listings in this chapter combine features from the LC++ class library in chapters 6 and 7 with the DIR module. The result is the READ program that you probably used to browse the README.TXT file on one of the disks packaged with this book. You can also use READ to browse any text file up to 500 lines long. The listings in the following sections describe how to compile and use READ.

Compiling and Using READ

The easiest way to compile READ is to run MREAD.BAT (Make READ), Listing 8.24. The batch file assumes that you have compiled DIR.CPP previously. If not, enter **ztc -c dir** before running MREAD. To compile READ manually, enter the commands **ztc -c read** and **blink @read.lnk**.

Listing 8.24. MREAD.BAT

```
1:  echo off
2:  ztc -c read
3:  if errorlevel==1 goto END
4:  blink @read.lnk
5:  :END
```

Listing 8.25. READ.LNK

```
 1:   read.obj+
 2:   \lcpp\lib\key.obj+
 3:   \lcpp\lib\error.obj+
 4:   \lcpp\lib\stritem.obj+
 5:   \lcpp\lib\item.obj+
 6:   \lcpp\lib\list.obj+
 7:   \lcpp\lib\window.obj+
 8:   \lcpp\lib\selector.obj+
 9:   dir.obj
10:   read.exe
11:   read.map
12:   /m/li/co/noi
```

After compiling, run READ by typing the program's name at the DOS prompt. You should see a directory window in the middle of the display. Select a file to read and press **<Enter>**. Or press **<Esc>** to quit. You can also select a directory name to switch to that directory and read text files there.

While reading a file, use the cursor, **<Page Up>**, and **<Page Down>** keys to browse. Press **<Esc>** or **<Enter>** to return to the directory window.

Another way to start READ is to specify a wild-card argument. For example, enter **read *.cpp** to list all the .CPP files in the current directory. You can then select and read one or more of the listed files. When using READ this way, you can't change directories (unless, that is, a directory name matches the wild-card argument).

Lastly, you can read an individual file by entering its name. For example, type **read readme.txt** to read a README.TXT file in the current directory. When you specify an individual file name, READ bypasses its directory display and shows you the file's contents. Press **<Esc>** or **<Enter>** to return to DOS.

The READ.CPP Program

You may be surprised by the shortness of READ.CPP's source code in Listing 8.26. You should *not* be surprised to discover that READ's streamlined appearance is due to the use of classes for just about every significant operation. Naturally, to display a directory of file names, READ uses the directory class from the DIR module you examined earlier in this chapter. But the program also uses the selector object from chapter 7 to list the text file's contents! After all, the selector class already knows how to scroll lines of text. Since those operations are just what READ needs to display text files, using the selector class in this new way eliminates the need to duplicate code that's already written and tested.

Listing 8.26. READ.CPP

```
 1:   // read.cpp -- Text file lister
 2:
 3:   #include <stream.hpp>
 4:   #include <direct.h>
 5:   #include <string.h>
 6:   #include "dir.h"
 7:
 8:   #define FALSE 0
 9:   #define TRUE 1
10:
11:   /* -- Function prototypes */
12:
13:   void listFiles(char *wildCard);
14:   int listOneFile(char *fname);
15:
16:   /* -- The main program calls listFiles with a wild-card argument such
17:   as *.cpp or ??.bak. Or, if only a single file is listed, it calls
18:   listOneFile, bypassing the directory display. If no arguments are
19:   entered on the command line, the program calls listFiles with the
20:   default *.* wild card string. */
21:
22:   main(int argc, char *argv[])
23:   {
24:       window::startup();
25:       if (argc == 2)
26:           if ( (strchr(argv[1], '*') != NULL) ||
27:                (strchr(argv[1], '?') != NULL) )
28:               listFiles(argv[1]);
29:           else
30:               listOneFile(argv[1]);
31:       else
32:           listFiles("*.*");
33:       window::shutDown();
34:       exit(0);
35:   }
36:
```

READ's main function initializes the window class in the usual way, and then calls listFiles or listOneFile depending on whether you enter a wild-card character, * or ?. The program calls strchr to search the argument string for one of those symbols. If you enter no arguments, line 32 displays a default directory of all file names.

Listing 8.26. READ.CPP (continued)

```
37:    void listFiles(char *wildCard)
38:    {
39:        winStruct dwin = {      // Directory window
40:            3, 19, 41, 18,      // Row, column, width, height
41:            0x1f,               // Text attribute
42:            0x70,               // Border attribute
43:            0x70,               // Highlight attribute
44:            0                   // Type
45:        };
46:        winStruct mwin = {      // Main window
47:            0, 0, 80, 24,       // Row, column, width, height
48:            0x4f,               // Text attribute
49:            0x0f,               // Border attribute
50:            0x70,               // Highlight attribute
51:            3                   // Type
52:        };
53:        directory *dir;         // Directory window object
54:        window *mainWin;        // Main display window
55:        strItem *p;             // Ptr to strItem returned by getSelection
56:        char buf[13];           // File name returned by getString
57:        char *t;                // Temporary pointer to char
58:
59:        buf[12] = 0;            // Make sure that strings are terminated
60:        mainWin = new window(mwin,
61:            " File Lister from \"Learning C++ by Tom Swan\" ");
62:        mainWin->showWindow();
63:        dir = new directory(dwin, wildCard, 0);  // 0 == no popup
64:        while ((p = dir->getSelection()) != NULL) {
65:            strncpy(buf, p->getString(), 12);
66:            if ((t = strchr(buf, ' ')) != NULL) *t = 0;
67:            if (!listOneFile(buf)) {
68:                chdir(buf);
69:                dir->resetDirectory(wildCard);
70:            }
71:        }
72:        delete dir;
73:        delete mainWin;
74:    }
75:
```

Function listFiles operates much like NAV (see Listing 8.23). Two windows are used to cover the entire screen and display a title at the top. A while loop at lines 64-71 calls getSelection to display the current directory, from which you can select a file to list. If you do that, the next lines copy the file name to buf, fix up the end of the string (see line 66), and call `ListOneFile`. If that function returns false, lines 68-69 assume that you selected a directory name. In that event, `chdir` switches to that directory, and `resetDirectory` loads and displays the file names from the new location.

Listing 8.26. READ.CPP (continued)

```
 76:   int ListOneFile(char *fname)
 77:   {
 78:       winStruct ws = {
 79:           0, 0, 80, 24,    // Row, column, width, height
 80:           0x1f,            // Text attribute
 81:           0x70,            // Border attribute
 82:           0x70,            // Highlight attribute
 83:           3                // Type
 84:       };
 85:       FILE *fp;
 86:       char buffer[256];
 87:       selector *listWindow = new selector(ws, fname, 1);
 88:       int n;
 89:
 90:       fp = fopen(fname, "r");
 91:       if (!fp) return FALSE;
 92:       while (fgets(buffer, 255, fp) != NULL) {
 93:           n = strlen(buffer);
 94:           if (n > 0) buffer[n - 1] = 0;    // Kill newline at end
 95:           listWindow->insertItem(new strItem(buffer));
 96:       }
 97:       fclose(fp);
 98:       listWindow->getSelection();
 99:       delete listWindow;
100:       return TRUE;
101:   }
```

Function `ListOneFile` handles the display of a text file's contents. Line 87 prepares a `selector` object in which the file's lines will appear. Then, lines 90-97 execute standard text-file commands to read the strings in the file. Lines 93-94 delete the new-line character appended to the end of each string. After that, for each string, `insertItem` inserts new `strItem` instances into the `selector` addressed by `listWindow`.

The `selector` class completely handles the display of lines in the text file. Line 98 simply calls `getSelection` to let you browse through the list of strings. When you are done, a single call to `delete` at line 99 erases the text from memory, along with the `selector` object. The program ignores `getSelection`'s result; therefore, pressing **<Enter>** or **<Esc>** ends the function.

Finding new uses for old classes like selector is one of the hallmarks of OOP. In this and preceding chapters, you've used the selector class to build simple selection lists, to write menu-driven programs, to display file names in a directory, and now, to list the contents of text files. What a remarkable array of jobs for a single class! But that's exactly what OOP is supposed to do—make reusing existing code as easy as bending a few classes to suit the job at hand.

Of course, every programmer eventually runs into at least one job that needs special handling. Not every programming problem can be solved neatly with the conventional and class techniques described in this and the preceding chapters. In the next chapter, you'll learn several advanced C++ tools that fall into the special-use category—tools that come in handy for those rare moments when standard approaches fail. You may not need these tools often, but when you do, you'll be glad you took the time at least to learn of their existence. Before continuing, however, make sure that you understand the concepts discussed in previous chapters, especially chapters 6, 7, and 8.

Questions and Exercises

8.1. Write a program that converts text in files to all lowercase letters.

8.2. On PCs, new lines are represented by carriage return and line feed control codes. On Unix systems, new lines are represented by line feeds alone. Write two programs that convert text files in each format to the other.

8.3. What are the main advantages and disadvantages of reading text files a character or a line at a time?

8.4. Write a program that can display text files containing embedded tab characters.

8.5. Store help text in a file and read that text into WINTOOL's helpCommand::performCommand function from chapter 6 (Listing 6.4, lines 124-143).

8.6. Give the commands needed to read and write an array named fparray that contains 100 double values.

8.7. Listing 8.10, READDB.CPP, lets you enter a record number to view that record's information. Using that program as a guide, write a new program that lets you modify records by number.

8.8. Write a program that prompts for a customer number and searches SAMPLE.DAT (created by MAKEDB.CPP, Listing 8.8) for a record with a matching customer number field.

8.9. Write a program that displays only the subdirectory names in the current directory.

Chapter 9

Advancing Your C++ Knowledge

In a famous study of chess masters, researchers were handed a surprise. During play, masters and lesser players were asked to explain how they selected their next moves. To everyone's amazement, the study showed that players of all levels examined about the same number of possibilities. From that evidence, researchers distilled what can only be classed as a pristine example of restating the obvious: master chess players, they said, become masters because they invariably select better moves.

There's more wisdom in that conclusion than you might suppose. The message is simple. You can memorize openings, closings, and situations till you turn blue. You can study past games, positions, and responses till the cows come home. But you'll become a better chess player only when you learn to apply your knowledge skillfully.

The same observation holds true for master programmers. The whiz kids in the programming shops don't necessarily know more about programming languages than their less capable colleagues; expert programmers are somehow able to *apply* in more creative ways the same commands that anyone can easily learn. How do expert programmers become experts? Perhaps those same researchers would say *"They select better programming commands."*

Developing that level of skill will take time, patience, and lots of practice. The previous eight chapters provide the raw material. The next step is yours. Write programs. Then write more programs. Use C++ to solve problems. Choose a game plan and implement your strategies. You'll fail plenty of times, but you'll also gain valuable experience from spending long hours at the computer terminal.

Along with that experience, you'll pick up numerous tidbits such as those in this chapter, which brings the C++ story to a close. (The next chapter is a reference to the C++ function library.) In the following sections, you'll learn how to use friends, how to customize C++'s memory management routines `new` and `delete`, how to overload functions and operators, and how to use other C++ advanced techniques. You won't use these special tools often, but when the need arises—when the King is in check—look here for hints. You may find just the method that will turn a losing situation to your advantage.

Good Friends and Neighbors

One of the main reasons for using OOP techniques is to isolate data inside classes. By doing that, only member functions can access critical values. Most of the time, hiding data in classes gives programs a good measure of control by preventing processes from modifying critical values indiscriminately.

You've seen many examples of the *data-hiding* concept in previous listings. For example, the window class described in chapter 7 hides many of the values that store a window's position, title, and text saved from "behind" a covered area. Other window fields are protected, providing access to those fields from derived classes, but not from the main program. Because window isolates its design details inside the class declaration, if you need to modify any of the class's private fields, you can do so without concern that you'll affect any statements outside the class.

Like many rules in life and programming, however, those of data hiding are made to be broken. In C++, you can break the rules for hiding data by using *friends*. Declaring a friend of a class is like giving a pal a copy of your house key. If you go away for the weekend, you shouldn't be surprised on returning to discover your buddy asleep on the couch and the 'fridge seriously depleted.

C++ classes can declare two kinds of friends. An entire class may be a friend of another class. Or, a single function may be declared a friend. The following sections describe both kinds.

> **Note:** If friends have a counterpart in C++, it's the goto statement. Like goto, a friend lets you break the very rules of C++ that help you to write reliable programs. You should learn about friends, if for no other reason, because the technique is available, and you'll undoubtedly see friends used in published listings. But don't take the following sections as an endorsement of friends. Top C++ programmers *avoid* using friends unless absolutely necessary.

Friend Classes

A class may declare another class as a friend. By doing that, the first class (the one doing the declaring) gives another class (the friend) permission to access all of the first class's private and protected fields. Public fields are, of course, always accessible, so they don't enter into the discussion. Any statement, including those in friend classes, may always access the public fields in class instances.

Typically, friend classes are used when two unrelated classes require access to one of the class's private or protected fields. A simple example explains the process. Suppose you declare a class like this:

```
class AClass {
   private:
      float value;
   public:
      AClass() { value = 3.14159; }
};
```

Class `AClass` contains a single private field, `value`, of type `float`. To that field, the class constructor assigns the value 3.14159. Except for that action, the class provides no means to change or even to inspect `value`. That field is as safe from harm as a bear cub by its mother's side.

Next, suppose you declare another class that stores an instance of `AClass` in a member field:

```
class BClass {
   private:
      AClass A;
   public:
      void showValue(void)
         { cout << A.value; }    // ???
};
```

Field `A` of type `AClass` is private to `BClass`. In addition to that field, function `showValue` displays `A`'s `value`. However, the declaration won't compile because `value` is private to `AClass`; therefore, *only* member functions in `AClass` may access `value`. Functions in `BClass` are prevented from using `value` directly as the inline statement here attempts to do.

Changing the status of `value` to `protected:` would not solve the problem. A protected field is available to its declaring class and to any derived class. `AClass` and `BClass` are unrelated, and for that reason, the two classes have no special access to each other's private and protected members. You could change the status of `value` to `public:`, but doing so would then make `value` available to *any* statement, an unhealthful remedy.

A better solution is to declare `BClass` to be a friend of `AClass`. Instances of `BClass` then can access `value`, but other statements outside the two classes are still prevented entry to `AClass`'s private section. To make this change, use the `friend` key word inside the class to which the *other* class needs access. In this example, `BClass` needs to access the private `value` field inside `AClass`. So to give `BClass` permission to use that private data, `AClass` can declare `BClass` to be a friend. Here's the new `AClass` declaration:

```
class AClass {
      friend class BClass;
   private:
      float value;
   public:
      AClass() { value = 3.14159; }
};
```

The only difference from before is the line friend class BClass. This tells the compiler that BClass should be granted access to AClass's private and protected members. Other statements in other classes and in the main program still can't use AClass's private and protected items; only BClass is given a backstage pass to AClass's private rooms. You may declare any number of classes to be friends this way. The only restriction is that the friend keyword must appear inside a class declaration. A few other facts are worth remembering:

- A class must name all of its friends in advance.

- The class that contains the private and protected data is the one that declares another class to be a friend, thus giving that friend special access to the declaring class's normally hidden members. A class can never declare *itself* to be a friend of another class.

- The friend class may be declared before or after the class that declares the friend. The order of the declarations is unimportant.

- Derived classes of the friend do *not* inherit special access to the original class's private and protected members. Only the specifically named friend has those permissions.

- A derived class may be a friend of its base class, although in such cases, using protected fields in the base will accomplish the same goal of giving the friend access to hidden fields in the base.

A second example, Listing 9.1, FRIEND.CPP demonstrates how friends can be used to access private data in class instances that are stored in another class or created as variables.

Listing 9.1. FRIEND.CPP

```
 1:   // friend.cpp -- Demonstrate friends
 2:
 3:   #include <stream.hpp>
 4:
 5:   class pal {
 6:        friend class buddy;      // buddy is a friend of pal
 7:     private:
 8:        int x;
 9:     protected:
10:        void doublex(void) { x *= x; }
11:     public:
12:        pal() { x = 100; }
13:        pal(int n) { x = n; }
14:   };
15:
```

```
16:    class buddy {
17:        private:
18:            pal palInstance;
19:        public:
20:            void showValues(void);
21:    };
22:
23:    main()
24:    {
25:        buddy abuddy;
26:
27:        abuddy.showValues();
28:    }
29:
30:    void buddy::showValues(void)
31:    {
32:        pal apal(1234);
33:
34:        cout << form("\nBefore, palInstance.x == %d", palInstance.x);
35:        palInstance.doublex();
36:        cout << form("\nAfter, palInstance.x  == %d", palInstance.x);
37:        cout << form("\napal.x == %d\n", apal.x);
38:    }
```

FRIEND begins by declaring a class named pal. Line 6 states that a second class buddy is a friend of pal. Because of this line, statements in buddy's member functions may access the private and protected members in pal. However, pal may *not* access any private or protected items in buddy.

At line 18, the buddy class declares an instance of type pal. As you can see when you run the code, even though buddy is unrelated to pal, the function showValues can directly access pal's private field x. The function also can call the protected member function doublex.

Those actions are demonstrated in the showValues implementation at lines 30-38. Because buddy is a friend of pal, the statements at lines 34-36 may directly refer to private and protected fields and functions in palInstance. Similarly, line 37 shows that inside a buddy function, a statement may refer to a local variable's private data. Normally, the compiler would reject the expression apal.x because x is private to the pal class. No error occurs because buddy is a friend of pal and therefore, statements inside buddy's lone function may use the normally hidden fields.

Keep in mind that outside of buddy, nothing has changed about the status of pal's private and protected fields. To demonstrate that fact, declare a variable of type pal in main and try to access the private x field. For example, you might revise main to this:

```
main()
{
   buddy abuddy;
   pal mypal(4321);
   abuddy.showValues();
   cout << mypal.x;      // ???
}
```

Compiling now gives the message *Syntax error: member 'x' of class 'pal' is private.* Class pal declares buddy as a friend; therefore, buddy may access pal's private and protected members. However, statements outside of pal and buddy, either in the main program or in another class, still may not access pal's hidden members.

Mutual Friend Classes

Two classes may declare each other as friends. Doing that gives each class access to the other's private and protected fields. Of course, this also destroys the barriers that prohibit unrestricted access to hidden fields. If you discover that you often need to make classes friends of each other, you probably need to redesign your program. Most classes are better off as strangers to one another.

Use a similar format as in the preceding examples to declare two classes to be friends of each other. Each class lists the other as a friend, giving both classes access to each other's private and protected members. For AClass and BClass to be friends of each other, their declarations could be written this way:

```
class AClass {
   friend class BClass;
   // ... other members
}
class BClass {
   friend class AClass;
   // ... other members;
}
```

Any member functions in either class may now access private and protected data in an instance of the other class. Typical uses for this design include array classes to which a member function in another class needs direct access. Another example is a list class that gives other classes direct access to its pointer fields.

If the first class refers to the second class by name—in a member function parameter, for example—you may declare the second class in a *forward class declaration*. The declaration tells the compiler the name of a class that you'll fill in later. To declare BClass forward, insert this line ahead of AClass.

```
class BClass;
```

The compiler then allows you to create member fields and function parameters of type B Class although that class has not yet been formally declared.

Friend Functions Part 1

A friend function is similar to but less onerous than a friend class. A friend function is given access to a class's private and protected members. If that function is a member of another class, as it usually will be, only that function and not any other members of the class have permission to access the declaring class's private members.

By declaring a specific function as a friend to two classes, you give that function access to private and protected fields in instances of *both* class data types. The friend function may be a global C++ function or a member of another class. In a typical design, the friend function declares parameters of the two classes to which the function owes its friendship. Inside the friend function, statements can then access normally hidden members in the parameters passed as arguments to the function.

Listing 9.2, FRIENDFN.CPP, demonstrates how to declare and use this kind of typical friend function.

Listing 9.2. FRIENDFN.CPP

```
1:   // friendfn.cpp -- Demonstrate global friend functions
2:
3:   #include <stream.hpp>
4:
5:   class two;
6:
7:   class one {
8:       friend void show(one &c1, two &c2);
9:     private:
10:       char *s1;
11:     public:
12:       one() { s1 = "Testing "; }
13:   };
14:
15:   class two {
16:       friend void show(one &c1, two &c2);
17:     private:
18:       char *s2;
19:     public:
20:       two() { s2 = "one, two, three"; }
21:   };
22:
23:   main()
```

```
24:   {
25:       one c1;
26:       two c2;
27:
28:       show(c1, c2);
29:   }
30:
31:   void show(one &c1, two &c2)
32:   {
33:       cout << c1.s1 << c2.s2 << '\n';
34:   }
```

FRIENDFN declares two classes one and two. Because each of those classes will refer to the other, and because C++ requires you to declare identifiers before using them, line 5 declares class two forward of one. Declaring a class forward tells the compiler to allow references to the class name before the class is formally declared.

Lines 8 and 16 list the prototype for a friend function named show. Because each class declares show to be a friend, statements in show are granted access to the private and protected members in classes one and two. (The classes have no protected sections, but if they did, the friend declaration would allow access to those members.)

Function show's declarations (see lines 8 and 16) list reference parameters c1 and c2 of the two class types. Because show is a friend of those two classes, statements inside show can access private and protected members in arguments passed to show. The reason for the forward declaration at line 5 should now be clear. Line 8 needs to declare a parameter of class two, which is formally declared later in the file. The forward reference allows the reference to the as yet undeclared two class.

The implementation for function show appears at lines 31-34. In this simple example, the code merely displays the value of the string pointers s1 and s2. Because show is a friend of the two classes, it may directly refer to the s1 and s2 fields, which are hidden in their respective classes. Other less friendly functions would not be allowed similar access to those fields.

It's important to realize that show is a common C++ function. The program can therefore call show in the usual way, as shown here at line 28. Because show is a common function and not a member of a class, it does not have a this pointer, and it is not called in conjunction with a variable of the class type. The next section explains how to create similar friend functions as class members.

Friend Functions Part 2

A friend function does not have to be a common C++ function as demonstrated in the preceding section. Friend functions can also be members of a class. In a typical case, one class will declare a function in another class as a friend. The friend function will then have access to the original class's private and protected members.

Listing 9.3, FRIENDMF.CPP (the MF stands for Member Function), outlines the basic strategy of friend member functions. The program is similar to FRIENDFN in the previous section. Comparing the two programs reveals several key differences between global friend functions and those that are members of a class.

Listing 9.3. FRIENDMF.CPP

```
 1:   // friendmf.cpp -- Demonstrate friend member functions
 2:
 3:   #include <stream.hpp>
 4:
 5:   class one;
 6:
 7:   class two {
 8:      private:
 9:         char *s2;
10:      public:
11:         two() { s2 = "one, two, three"; }
12:         void show(one &c1);
13:   };
14:
15:   class one {
16:         friend void two::show(one &c1);
17:      private:
18:         char *s1;
19:      public:
20:         one() { s1 = "Testing "; }
21:   };
22:
23:   main()
24:   {
25:      one c1;
26:      two c2;
27:
28:      c2.show(c1);
29:   }
30:
31:   void two::show(one &c1)
32:   {
33:      cout << c1.s1 << s2 << '\n';
34:   }
```

The first rule to remember about friend member functions concerns the order of the class declarations. The class that prototypes the member function must come *before* the class that declares that function as a friend. Using a forward declaration as at line 5 in Listing 9.2 is not enough. For example, this does not work:

```
class forward;
class aClass {
    friend int forward::fn(aClass &a);   // ???
    // ...
}
```

The goal here is to declare fn, a member function of class forward, as a friend of aClass. The purpose of the declaration is to give fn access to private and protected members in an argument of type aClass passed to fn's a reference parameter. But even though fn is declared to be a friend of aClass, inside fn's implementation (not shown here), the compiler rejects access to aClass's hidden items. Declaring the forward class ahead of aClass does not remove the conflict, even though it does allow the declaration to be compiled.

One solution to this sticky problem is to declare the entire class forward as a friend. This works:

```
class forward;
class aClass {
    friend class forward;
    // ...
}
```

Now function fn in forward may access aClass's private and protected members. However, declaring the entire class a friend of aClass also means that *every* member function in aClass can access the same private and protected items in the class. Such unrestricted access may be dangerous to your program's health, and an alternate solution may be less toxic. At such times, you should be able to rearrange the class declarations as in FRIENDMF to allow the program to compile.

To solve this problem for Listing 9.3, FRIENDMF.CPP, I reversed the two class declarations from Listing 9.2 so that two comes before one. That satisfies the rule that a friend member function must be declared before being listed as a friend. For example, see line 16. There, two::show is declared as a friend of class one. The compiler allows this because class two was declared previously. But if two came *after* one, as it did in Listing 9.2, even declaring two forward would not permit the program to compile. (Try this. Reverse the class declarations and change line 5 to class two;. You'll receive an error message at line 33 because the compiler rejected the illegal friend declaration.)

Another difference in Listing 9.3 is the way the show function refers to private data in the two classes. The function now has only one parameter, one &c1. Because the function is a member of class two, it doesn't need to list an argument of type two. In fact, doing so would be a mistake. The function is encapsulated in two; therefore, the statement at line 33 can refer to two's private s2 field directly. The reference to c1.s1 is allowed as in Listing 9.2 because show is a friend of class one.

Because function show is a member of two, it now has a this pointer that addresses the instance for which the function was called. Consequently, the program can no longer call the friend function directly. The program now has to define a variable of type two and call show for that variable (see line 28).

One final note: Friends are attractive for giving objects access to private data in other objects. Used carefully, friends can improve performance by eliminating the overhead associated with calling member functions. (Inline functions may give similar advantages, however.) But friends also break down the barriers that protect data in classes. Using friends reduces OOP's advantages of data hiding, encapsulation of functions and data, and isolation of statements that access critical values. By all means, use friends. But use them carefully. Don't let your best friends become your worst enemies!

Function Overloading

In most computer programming languages, when you declare identifiers like myValue or showResults, those symbols have one and only one meaning. But in C++, two or more functions may have the same name without causing a conflict. This unique feature, known as *function overloading,* is possible because C++ considers a function and its parameters to be inseparable. As long as multiple functions differ in at least one parameter, they may have the same name. For example, C++ allows you to write programs with functions declared like these:

```
void showResults(void);
void showResults(int count);
void showResults(int count, int max);
```

Each of these four functions has the same name but differs in at least one parameter. (The function return types must be identical.) A single difference in a parameter's data type or the number of parameters are all that C++ needs to distinguish between functions named the same. For the three sample functions here, if you write the statement showResults();, C++ correctly determines that it should call the first function. If you write showResults(k) where k is a variable of type int, C++ calls the function that lists a single int parameter.

Even though functions like showResults have the same name, they are still distinct functions and are not related in any way. Function overloading is merely a convenience that eliminates some of the need to invent new symbols for similar operations. In many languages, you would have to create functions named showResults1, showResults2, showResults3, and showResults4 so that the compiler can distinguish between them. In C++, if similar functions require a different number or type of parameters, they may have the same name. Usually, you'll want to make those functions perform similar jobs. But that's only a suggestion, not a requirement.

Name Mangling Revisited

Chapter 8 introduced the term *name mangling*, otherwise known as *type-safe linkage*. When C++ compiles a listing, it combines (mangles) function names and parameters using a complex scheme that pretty much guarantees every overloaded function will have a unique symbol for use internally during compilation and linking.

The mangled symbols make it possible for common linkers to join modules containing overloaded function names. Name mangling also allows common linkers to reject many sorts of illegal function calls, for example, a statement that passes a float argument to a char * parameter. This high degree of type checking across compiled modules (hence the term type-safe linkage) helps you avoid common mistakes caused by passing the wrong types of data to functions in precompiled modules.

Listings 9.4 (SUBBUG.CPP) and 9.5 (MAINBUG.CPP) demonstrate how type-safe linkage and name mangling can keep you out of trouble. The two modules illustrate a typical C and C++ trick: declaring in a source listing a prototype to a precompiled function in a library module. You'll have no problems compiling the modules separately with the two commands **ztc -c subbug** and **ztc -c mainbug.cpp**. But when you try to link the object-code files with the command **blink mainbug.obj subbug.obj**, you'll receive the error message Error: undefined symbols: _fn__Nc in mainbug.cpp (mainbug.obj). You'll receive a similar error from other linkers, too, even linkers that were not designed to work with C++.

Listing 9.4. SUBBUG.CPP

```
1:   // subbug.cpp -- Sub module for mainbug.cpp
2:
3:   #include <stream.hpp>
4:
5:   void fn(char *string)
6:   {
7:      cout << "\nstring = " << string;
8:   }
```

Listing 9.5. MAINBUG.CPP

```
1:   // mainbug.cpp -- Demonstrate type-safe linkage
2:
3:   #include <stream.hpp>
4:
5:   void fn(float f);      // ???
6:
7:   main()
8:   {
```

```
 9:        fn(3.14159);
10:   }
```

Examine the two listings carefully and you'll see why the linker refuses to join them. SUBBUG.CPP implements function `fn` with a `char *` parameter `string`. MAINBUG.CPP calls `fn`, but passes to the function the wrong type of data—a floating point value, not the expected pointer. Usually, this kind of mistake is easily avoided by including in MAINBUG a header file (not shown) that prototypes `fn`.

But whether such a header file exists, MAINBUG.CPP ignores it, choosing instead to prototype `fn` directly in the main program's source listing at line 5 in Listing 9.5. Avoiding an `#include` of a lengthy header file this way is a common method for reducing compilation times. Rather than include many long header files, a program can prototype only the functions and other declarations that it needs. However, the prototype at line 5 differs from the function declaration in SUBBUG.CPP, a serious mistake that the compiler misses. To allow separate compilation of related modules, the compiler assumes that all function prototypes are correct. That's why you can compile the modules with no errors.

If you compile similar programs with many C compilers, you'll be able to link the object-code files, though running the code may produce disastrous results when the program passes a floating point value to the expected character pointer. However, if you compile with C++, the linker will receive different mangled symbols for function `fn` in the two modules. The linker will therefore reject the function call in MAINBUG, not because of the mismatched parameter and argument, but because the linker will fail to find a mangled symbol for a `void` function named `fn` that requires a single floating point argument. You can't run the buggy program because the linker will refuse to create the final executable code file.

Unfortunately, the linker's "undefined symbols" error message is anything but clear. The message doesn't tell you the location or reason for the problem. But usually, when you receive this error, and when the error message refers to a strange word like `_fn__Nc`, you'll find a statement that passes the wrong type of data to a function in another module.

The `overload` *Key Word*

Early versions of C++ required the `overload` key word to specify multiple functions with the same names. To declare the `showResults` functions from the preceding section, you had to write

```
overload void showResults(void);
overload void showResults(int count);
overload void showResults(int count, int max);
```

In newer C++ versions (including the compiler supplied with this book), the `overload` key word is optional. Unnecessary key words in programming languages tend to disappear over time, so it's probably best not to use `overload` in your programs. This is one symbol that may not be around much longer.

Overloading Conventional Functions

Overloading conventional functions—those that are not members of a class—is often convenient for simulating inheritance without using OOP techniques. For instance, suppose that you are using a library function named `glitch` prototyped like this:

```
void glitch(float value);
```

You want to add a new statement to `glitch`, but you don't have the original source code. The solution is simple—just overload `glitch` with a new prototype that lists the same parameters as the original, but adds a new one:

```
void glitch(float value, int DEBUG);
```

Adding the `int DEBUG` parameter (the name and type are not important) overloads the `glitch` function. You can then implement the function, add the new statement, and call the original code this way:

```
void glitch(float value, int DEBUG)
{
    cout << "\nNew statement added to glitch";
    glitch(value);  // call original glitch function
}
```

In the main program, use a statement such as `glitch(10, 1)` to call the new overloaded function. Use a statement such as `glitch(10)` to call the original. Of course, you could achieve the same result simply by creating a function with a different name. But using the same name helps you remember that the two `glitch`es are related.

Overloading Class Member Functions

Starting with chapter 7, you've seen several class declarations that have more than one constructor. For example, Listing 7.7 (STRITEM.H) and Listing 7.11 (WINDOW.H) declare the `strItem` and `window` classes. In each of these classes, two constructors initialize class instances in different ways. Because constructors must have the same names as their classes, multiple constructors in a class are overloaded by default. It's not possible to name multiple constructors differently in the same class. Multiple constructors in the same class *must* have the same name.

In addition to constructors, classes may also overload member functions. As with common functions, overloaded members have the same names but must differ in at least one parameter.

Overloading member functions can improve a program's readability by using the same function name for similar operations. For example, in a graphics program, you might have separate classes for lines, circles, squares, and other shapes. In another class, you may want to create an object that knows how to draw instances of those shapes. Rather than invent separate function names for each shape class (drawLine, drawCircle, and so on), you can overload a draw function like this:

```
class overdrawn {
    public:
        void draw(line &q);
        void draw(circle &q);
        void draw(square &q);
}
```

Class overdrawn declares three member functions all named draw. Each function is separate and distinct, and the only reason for overloading the names is to improve the program's clarity. Because of the overloaded functions, you can write these kinds of statements for an overdrawn instance od:

```
od.draw(aLine);
od.draw(aCircle);
od.draw(aSquare);
```

where aLine, aCircle, and aSquare are instances of the line, circle, and square classes (not shown here). Derived classes can then add new draw functions for others kinds of shapes. In a program with dozens or more such functions, it's much easier to remember one function name like draw than it is to look up which kind of draw function goes with this or that shape.

Note: The only member function that may not be overloaded is a destructor. This restriction is a consequence of the rule that a class may have one and only one destructor, which may not declare a return type or any parameters. If you need multiple ways to destroy class instances, divide the code among other member functions, which the destructor can then call.

Operator Overloading

The topic of *operator overloading* in C++ has been needlessly smothered in mysterious explanations that require a graduate degree in mathematics to understand. Like most programming subjects, however, once you cut through the mustard, operator overloading is as simple as a ham sandwich.

Before devouring operator overloading, it will help for you to review what you know about operators in general. Of course, you know what an operator is. For example, the plus sign (+) is an operator that sums two values. The minus sign (−) is an operator that subtracts two values. These and other similar operators are called *binary operators* because they operate on two arguments. Some others, such as the *not* operator, (!) are *unary*—they require only one argument. The unary minus (−) is another good example of a unary operator. In the expression −count, the unary minus negates count's value.

> **Note:** A question mark (?) and associated colon (:) represent the only ternary (that is, "three-argument") operator in C and C++. The ternary operator doesn't enter into the discussion about operator overloading. See "Conditional Expressions" later in this chapter.

Most people have no trouble using common binary and unary operators. But consider an interesting fact about common operators like +, −, *, /, and others. In the expression 1234 + fp + count, if count is type long and fp is type float, the expression actually sums values of three *different* data types. Somehow, the plus operator can operate with arguments of different types. That observation may seem natural and intuitive, but mixing different types of data and operators is what operator overloading is all about.

Operator overloading is a mechanism that lets you add new data types to those that C++ operators are designed to handle. With operator overloading, you can create a class and write functions that implement a plus operation for two instances of the class type. After overloading the plus operator, you can write expressions using the familiar plus sign, and C++ calls your custom operator functions to sum the class instances.

Overloaded operators are C++ functions, which may or may not be members of a class. You write an overloaded operator function as you do other functions, although there are a few unique rules to memorize and follow. A hypothetical example will introduce those rules. Here's a partial declaration for a class named ZZ:

```
class ZZ {
    public:
        friend ZZ operator+(ZZ a, ZZ b);
```

```
          friend ZZ operator-(ZZ a, ZZ b);
          friend ZZ operator*(ZZ a, ZZ b);
          friend ZZ operator/(ZZ a, ZZ b);
     // ... other members
};
```

ZZ declares four overloaded operator functions. (Like all classes, in practice, ZZ would probably declare other public, private, and protected fields.) The overloaded function names are: operator+, operator-, operator*, and operator/. Normally, you can't use symbols like +, -, *, and / in identifiers, but for the special case of overloading an operator, C++ allows the function name to consist of the word operator and one of the symbols in the following list.

Operators That May Be Overloaded

+	-	*	/	%	^	&	|
~	!	,	=	<	>	<=	>=
++	--	<<	>>	==	!=	&&	||
+=	-=	/=	%=	^=	&=	|=	<<=
>>=	[]	()	->	new	delete		

The hypothetical class ZZ defines operator functions for the first four operators in the table. Each function has the general form

```
friend ZZ operator+(ZZ a, ZZ b);
```

The function is declared as a friend of the class, giving the function access to the class's private and protected members. The function returns type ZZ (it could return another type). Most important, the function's name is operator+, which identifies the function as the method by which expressions using + can process instances of the class. To the function, a statement must pass two parameters a and b, each of type ZZ.

The operator+ function name confuses some people. Remember, operator+ is simply the function's name. If you named the function feeblewitz rather than operator+, you could write a statement such as

```
feeblewitz(a, b);
```

where a and b are instances of type ZZ. If you change feeblewitz back to operator+, you can call the function with the statement

```
operator+(a, b);
```

There is no difference between those two function calls—only the function names were changed. The symbol operator+ is the function's name, and you can call the function in the same way you could if it were named feeblewitz.

However, as an overloaded operator, the function can also be called from an expression. For example, this statement is *exactly* equivalent to the preceding function call:

```
a + b;
```

The expression a + b and the statement operator+(a, b) do exactly the same jobs, and they generate exactly the same object code. The only reason for using one form over the other is clarity. Operator overloading adds nothing to C++ that you don't already know. It simply lets you write expressions rather than the equivalent function calls.

But don't discount operator overloading too quickly just because it's only new clothing on the same old wolf. It took centuries for mathematicians to develop an efficient symbology for representing complex formulas like ((a + b) * c) / q. That's a very concise way to state a potentially confusing combination of symbols. The equivalent function calls—let's name them add, multiply, and divide—are much less clear:

```
divide(multiply(add(a, b), c), q)
```

Even separating the expressions and assigning the function calls to a temporary variable isn't much better:

```
x = add(a, b);
x = multiply(x, c);
x = divide(x, q);
```

That's a bit easier to read, but now the relationship between the elements is lost. But that's exactly the sort of code that programmers have been writing since the first high-level languages appeared on the programming scene. Operator overloading lets you write familiar expressions that can operate with custom data types implemented as C++ classes.

A working example of a class that uses overloaded operators will help make these concepts clearer. Listing 9.6, STROPS.CPP, illustrates the beginnings of a class that can store integer values in string form. By using overloaded operators, the program can evaluate expressions that add strings without having to convert those strings to numeric values.

Listing 9.6. STROPS.CPP

```
1:  // strops.cpp -- Demonstrate operator overloading
2:
3:  #include <stream.hpp>
4:  #include <stdlib.h>
5:  #include <string.h>
6:
```

```
 7:  class strop {
 8:     private:
 9:        char value[12];
10:     public:
11:        strop() { value[0] = 0; }
12:        strop(const char *s);
13:
14:        friend long operator+(strop a, strop b);
15:        friend long operator-(strop a, strop b);
16:  };
17:
18:  main()
19:  {
20:     strop a = "1234";
21:     strop b = "4321";
22:
23:     cout << "\na + b +  6 == " << a + b + 6;
24:     cout << "\na - b + 10 == " << a - b + 10;
25:  }
26:
27:  strop::strop(const char *s)
28:  {
29:     strncpy(value, s, 11);
30:     value[11] = 0;
31:  }
32:
33:  long operator+(strop a, strop b)
34:  {
35:     return (atol(a.value) + atol(b.value));
36:  }
37:
38:  long operator-(strop a, strop b)
39:  {
40:     return (atol(a.value) - atol(b.value));
41:  }
```

STROPS is only a simple example of operator overloading, and the program would require extensive work to be practical. But the strop class at lines 7-16 demonstrates several important rules for overloaded operators that all such programs must obey.

The class stores characters in a small char array, which is large enough to hold 11 digits and a NULL terminator—room for the smallest possible long value, –2147483648, in string form. The largest possible long value is 2147483647, which takes ten digits. So with its 12-character array, strop can store any long value as a string.

Two constructors at lines 11-12 provide the means to initialize new instances of type `strop`. The first constructor takes care of a default variable definition. The second allows variables to be created with lines such as these:

```
strop v1 = "64";
strop v2 = "-1000";
```

The `strop` class does not specify member functions to retrieve and change the private `value` field. I left these out to keep the example short; in practice, you would need many more functions than those shown here.

The two `friend` functions at lines 14-15 overload the plus and minus operators for instances of the class type. The declarations are similar to those in the hypothetical `ZZ` class mentioned earlier. However, in this case, the functions return type `long`. Typically, overloaded operator functions return the same type as their class (or a reference to an instance of the class). But that's not a requirement. Overloaded operator functions, just like other functions, can return any data types.

Lines 20-24 in the `main` function show how useful overloaded operators can be. First, the program defines two instances a and bof the class type, assigning to those instances the strings `"1234"` and `"4321"`, respectively. The output stream statements at lines 23-24 use those instances in the expressions `a + b + 6` and `a - b + 10`.

Think about what those expressions are doing: They are adding and subtracting strings and integer values. Normally, the plus and minus operators can't do that; those operators were designed to operate only on numeric values. However, by overloading the two operators, the program teaches C++ how to evaluate expressions involving instances of the `strop` class type. As a consequence, C++ now knows how to add and subtract string representations of `long` values—a capability not built into the language.

Examine the implementations at lines 33-41 for the overloaded operator functions. Because the functions were declared as friends and not as member functions, their implementations are identical to other common C++ functions. The only differences are the special function names `operator+` and `operator-`, which permit the compiler to evaluate expressions with the plus and minus operators and instances of the `strop` class.

Because the operator functions are friends, they can access the private and protected parts of `strop` instances. That fact allows the functions to convert to a `long` the `value` string field in the two parameters a and b. Those conversions are handled by calling the standard `atol` (ASCII to `long`) function in the C++ library. The functions then return the addition or subtraction of the converted values.

Overloading Operator Member Functions

In Listing 9.6, the two overloaded operator functions `operator+` and `operator-` are declared as common friends. Another way to accomplish the same

goal of overloading the plus and minus operators (and others) is to list the functions
as members of the class.

Listing 9.7, STROPS2.CPP, is similar to the original STROPS, but shows how to
overload operators as member functions. Comparing the two programs will help you
decide which of the two methods is appropriate for your own code.

Listing 9.7. STROPS2.CPP

```
 1:   // strops2.cpp -- Demonstrate member operator overloading
 2:
 3:   #include <stream.hpp>
 4:   #include <stdlib.h>
 5:   #include <string.h>
 6:
 7:   class strop {
 8:       private:
 9:           char value[12];
10:       public:
11:           strop() { value[0] = 0; }
12:           strop(const char *s);
13:
14:           long operator+(strop b);
15:           long operator-(strop b);
16:   };
17:
18:   main()
19:   {
20:       strop a = "1234";
21:       strop b = "4321";
22:
23:       cout << "\na + b == " << a + b + 6;
24:       cout << "\na - b == " << a - b + 10;
25:   }
26:
27:   strop::strop(const char *s)
28:   {
29:       strncpy(value, s, 11);
30:       value[11] = 0;
31:   }
32:
33:   long strop::operator+(strop b)
34:   {
35:       return (atol(value) + atol(b.value));
36:   }
```

```
37:
38:   long strop::operator-(strop b)
39:   {
40:       return (atol(value) - atol(b.value));
41:   }
```

Compare the overloaded operator function prototypes at lines 14-15 with the equivalent friend functions in Listing 9.6, also at lines 14-15. Because the functions in STROPS2 are members, they already have access to the class's private and protected fields, so there's no need to specify them as friends of the class. In addition, because they are members of the class, they receive a `this` pointer to the instance that calls the functions. They therefore need only single parameters. To add two string `values`, the functions will combine `this->value` with `b.value`. There's no need to pass two parameters to the functions as there was in STROPS. In fact, doing so is an error because binary operators such as + and − *require* two and only two parameters. You could not write line 14 like this:

```
long operator+(strop a, strop b);   // ???
```

If that were possible (it's not), the prototype would define a ternary operation for the plus operator, involving three values of type `strop`: `*this`, a, and b. No such operation is possible. In the original STROPS.CPP, the two parameters are required because the friend functions are not members; therefore, they do not receive `this` pointers to instances of the class.

Getting back to Listing 9.7, notice that the `main` function at lines 18-25 is exactly the same as the `main` function in Listing 9.6. Whether the overloaded operator functions are declared as friends or as members of the class does not affect how those operators may be used in expressions.

The function implementations at lines 33-41 differ only slightly from those in the original STROPS. Because the new functions are members, they are tagged with the class name `strop::`. In addition to that change, the statements at lines 35 and 40 now refer directly to the `value` field in the instances for which the functions were called. The reference to the second argument, `b.value`, is the same as before.

Overloading Unary Operators

Unary operators, such as unary minus and ! operate on one argument. You can overload these and other unary operators with techniques similar to those illustrated in the preceding sections.

As with binary operators, you can declare an overloaded unary operator function as a friend or member of the class. To overload a unary operator as a friend function, you must list only one parameter of the class type. For example, add this declaration to STROPS.CPP (Listing 9.6) above line 14:

```
friend long operator-(strop a);
```

Even though line 15 already overloads the minus operator, because the new declaration specifies only one parameter, there is no conflict. This is not a special rule. It's just a consequence of function overloading, which allows multiple functions to share the same name as long as the function declarations differ in at least one parameter.

The overloaded function implementation returns the negation of the `value` field in parameter `a`. Add these lines above line 33 in STROPS.CPP:

```
long operator-(strop a)
{
    return -atol(a.value);
}
```

Because the unary `operator-` is a friend of the class, the `return` statement may directly access the private `value` field in parameter `a`. The function is now complete, and the compiler can evaluate unary expressions involving instances of the class type. For an example of how that works, add the following statement to `main` (after line 24 is a good place):

```
cout << "\n-a    == " << -a;
```

Compile the modified program and run. As you can see, the expression `-a` is replaced by the `long` negation of a's string field. You have taught C++ how to negate a `long` value that's represented in string form.

As with overloaded binary operators, you can also declare overloaded unary operators as member functions. Start with a copy of STROPS2.CPP and add the following declaration above line 14:

```
long operator-(void);
```

This is equivalent to the friend unary function you added to STROPS earlier. But in this case, the function is declared as a member of the `strop` class. Because all member functions receive a `this` pointer to the instance for which the functions are called, the `operator-` function can operate directly on the `value` field in a `strop` instance. For that reason, the function does not need any parameters. In fact, it must have *no* parameters, or C++ won't recognize the function as an overloaded unary operator.

To implement the function, add the following lines above line 33 in STROPS2.CPP:

```
long strop::operator-(void)
{
    return -atol(value);
}
```

The overloaded unary minus operator for `strop` is a member function, and therefore, it is tagged with the class name `strop::`, as are all member function implementations. The function simply returns the `long` negation of `value` after passing that string to the standard `atol` function in the C++ library.

To use the new unary member function, add the same statement you added to STROPS earlier. Insert this line after line 24 in STROPS2.CPP:

```
cout << "\n-a    == " << -a;
```

Whether you declare an overloaded unary operator function as a friend or as a class member, you can use that function in the same way. Because the class defines an operation for unary minus, C++ can evaluate the expression -a to give the negation of a long value represented as a character string.

Tips for Successful Operator Overloading

STROPS and STROPS2 demonstrate some of the fundamentals of operator overloading. The following sections in this chapter explain a few twists for special operators such as array index brackets, type conversion parentheses, the assignment operator, and memory management operators new and delete. Except for those special cases, the overloading of operators listed earlier (see *Operators That May Be Overloaded*) is demonstrated in STROPS and STROPS2.

The following tips will help you design classes with overloaded operators. (Assume that a and b are instances of appropriate class types.)

- C++ does not "understand" the meaning of an overloaded operator. It's your responsibility to provide meaningful overloaded functions. For example, if you change + to * at line 35 in STROPS2.CPP, the expression a + b will *multiply* the two instances. C++ makes no guarantee that an overloaded plus operator will actually add values. This means that operator overloading can be used to obscure meaning (a common criticism), but it also means that you are free to redefine the traditional meaning of an operator, which may be handy.

- C++ is not able to derive complex operators from simple ones. For instance, if you define overloaded operator functions operator* and operator=, you can't expect C++ to evaluate the expression a *= b correctly. For that and similar expressions to work, you must declare an overloaded operator function for the symbol *= as well as for * and =.

- You may never change the syntax of an overloaded operator. Operators that are binary must remain binary. Unary operators must remain unary. Because of this rule, it is not possible, for example, to create a unary division operator. The division operator / must be defined to operate on two arguments. The unary operator % must be defined to operate on only one value.

- You can't invent new operators for use in expressions. You may overload *only* the operators listed earlier under *Operators That May Be Overloaded*. However, you can always write functions for special cases. For example, it might be nice if you could redefine ! (or, perhaps, !! to avoid a conflict with the standard ! symbol) to mean "factorial of." Although that's not possible, you can just as easily write a function named `facto-rial`.

- You may overload the operators ++ and --. However, unlike with built-in C++ data types, the expressions ++a and a++ applied to class instances have identical effects. There is no way to specify a difference in prefix or postfix notation for the ++ and -- operators.

Overloading Array Indexing

When overloading the array-indexing operator `[ ]` (also known as the *subscript* operator), you are expected to provide a function that returns a reference to one of several values stored by a class. The index value may be any data type that can be passed to the `operator[ ]` function as a parameter. For example, this declaration overloads `[ ]` as a friend function that returns a reference to class `ZZ`:

```
friend ZZ &operator[](int i);
```

The index value for an array element is the parameter `int i`. If the declaration appears in a class `ZZ`, you could then use expressions such as `a[10]` and `a[i]` for an instance `a` of type `ZZ`.

Overloaded array indexing makes it possible to write expressions that appear to access arrays but that actually call a class function to perform the indexing. Because the array-indexing mechanism is neatly stowed inside the class, if you later change the way the class stores its data, you can simply update the overloaded `operator[ ]` function without having to modify programs that use the class.

A list class is a good example of where overloaded array indexing is useful. Programmers with limited experience find list functions confusing to use. In such cases, an array index function lets programmers write expressions like `array[i]` and `array[10]` rather than the equivalent function calls to step through a list and locate a specific element. The simpler array expressions may also help you convert array-based algorithms such as sorting routines to work with linked lists.

Listing 9.8, ARRAYLST.CPP, demonstrates how to add array-indexing to a derivative of the `list` class from chapter 7 (see Listings 7.4 and 7.6.) The program also shows how to create reference aliases to variables in C++—a topic I'll explain after the listing. You must link the program to the ITEM.OBJ, STRITEM.OBJ, LIST.OBJ, and ERROR.OBJ modules from the LC++ class library. To do that, compile ARRAYLST by entering the command **ztc arraylst ..\lib\item.obj ..\lib\stritem.obj ..\lib\list.obj ..\lib\error.obj**.

Listing 9.8. ARRAYLST.CPP

```
 1:  // arraylst.cpp -- List class with array-indexing operator
 2:
 3:  #include <stream.hpp>
 4:  #include "error.h"
 5:  #include "stritem.h"
 6:  #include "list.h"
 7:
 8:  class stringArray : public list {
 9:      public:
10:          const char *operator[](int i);
11:  };
12:
13:  void error(void);
14:
15:  main()
16:  {
17:      stringArray *a = new stringArray;
18:      stringArray &sa = *a;
19:
20:      a->insertItem(new strItem("First string"));
21:      a->insertItem(new strItem("Second string"));
22:      a->insertItem(new strItem("Third string"));
23:      a->insertItem(new strItem("Fourth string"));
24:
25:      for (int i = 1; i <= 4; i++)
26:          printf("\n%s", sa[i]);
27:
28:      cout << "\n\nString #2 == " << sa[2];
29:
30:      delete a;
31:  }
32:
33:  const char *stringArray::operator[](int i)
34:  {
35:      if (listEmpty() || (i <= 0)) error();
36:      resetList();
37:      for (int count = 1; count < i; count++) {
```

```
38:            nextItem();
39:            if (atHeadOfList()) error();
40:        }
41:        return ((strItem *)currentItem())->getString();
42:    }
43:
44:    void error(void)
45:    {
46:        error(99, "Index out of range");
47:    }
```

To the items inherited from list, the derived stringArray class adds an overloaded operator function for the [ ] subscript operator. The index value is type int, and the function returns a char pointer. To prevent the function from being used to alter private data in a class instance, the function is prefaced with the keyword const.

Lines 17-18 define a new stringArray object on the heap, assigning to pointer a the address returned by new. Immediately after that is the definition stringArray &sa = *a. That creates a reference variable named sa that refers to the object on the heap. By creating the reference sa variable—essentially an alias for *a—it will be possible to index the list using array-like expressions sa[i] and sa[2]. I'll explain the reason for creating the alias in a moment.

After inserting a few string items into the list addressed by a, two statements demonstrate how to use the overloaded subscript operator. Lines 25-26 execute a for loop that displays the four strings in the array. Line 28 displays the second string. Notice that in this example, the "arrays" are indexed starting with 1, not with 0 as is common in C and C++. I purposely wrote the program this way to demonstrate that C++ does not enforce its usual array-indexing rules for the overloaded subscript operator. If you want to begin array indexing at 0, 1, or 100, that's up to you.

Notice how much simpler the expressions sa[i] and sa[2] are when compared to the equivalent steps required to peruse the stringArray list. For example, to display the third string (pretending again that the first array index is 1), you would normally have to write all of this:

```
a->resetList();
for (int i = 1; i < 3; i++) {
    a->nextItem();
    if (a->atHeadOfList()) exit(1);  // Range error
}
cout << ((strItem *)a->currentItem())->getString();
```

With the overloaded subscript operator—and with the help of the sa alias—the equivalent statement is far simpler:

```
cout << sa[3];
```

The overloaded operator takes care of the messy list-processing details, thus clarifying the program's text. Of course, you could also hide the details inside a function. But the overloaded array operator is highly descriptive. There's no mistaking the purpose of the expression—to output the third element of the sa array. (With zero-based indexing, the expression would output the fourth element.)

The reason for using the sa alias is the list class's requirement that instances of type list or any derivations such as stringArray *must* be stored on the heap and addressed by pointers. Line 17 fulfills that requirement, creating a pointer a to a stringArray list allocated on the heap by new. However, it is *not* possible to use overloaded array subscripting directly with pointers. For example, this does not compile:

```
cout << a->[3];    // ???
```

That seems reasonable enough, but is not permitted. To use the pointer with the overloaded subscript operator function, you must instead write the equivalent function call in longhand:

```
cout << a->operator[](3);
```

Study that line carefully and you'll see how C++ implements an overloaded subscript. If you find the statement confusing, replace the function name with something else. For instance, just for illustration, suppose that the function is named lookup. The statement would then become

```
cout << a->lookup(3);
```

Looks more familiar, doesn't it? Remember, like operator+ from earlier, operator[] is simply a function name—the brackets have no special meaning except to identify the function as an overloaded operator. You can always call an overloaded operator function just as you can call any other function.

But the goal of creating an overloaded operator is to *avoid* making function calls. However, because a is a pointer, it's not possible to use the expression a->[3]. To take advantage of the overloaded subscript operator, you can define a reference alias like sa that means the same as *a, but meshes with C++'s syntax requirements. As line 18 in ARRAYLST.CPP demonstrates, you create a reference variable with the & symbol. For example, this line states that sa is a stringArray alias for *a:

```
stringArray &sa = *a;
```

You can now use sa as an alias for *a, and sa. as an alias for a->. C++ will accept the alias where it would reject a pointer. For example, with the alias, you can write array-like expressions such as sa[3], which is *exactly* equivalent to a->operator[](3). Both expressions call the operator[] function for the instance addressed by a.

The final step in overloading the subscript operator is to implement the overloaded function. Lines 33-42 in ARRAYLST take care of that remaining detail, using code that's similar to the lengthy list-processing steps outlined previously.

Lines 35 and 39 call **e r r o r** for out-of-range indexes. The other statements reset the list and step through items one by one to find the element at the requested index. Line 41 returns a pointer to the string item's characters.

As **s t r i n g A r r a y** illustrates, it takes some work to implement overloaded subscripts. But hiding messy list-processing statements inside a class member and being able to use simple array-like expressions such as **s a [3]** may make the extra programming more than worthwhile.

Overloading and User-Defined Type Conversions

The phrase *automatic type conversion* describes the internal steps that C++ takes when converting data types from one form to another. C++ compiler manuals (and the documentation for other languages) usually list a dozen or more rules that describe what happens, for example, when you pass a **c h a r** to an **i n t** parameter, or when you mix data types in expressions such as **a + b + c** where the three variables **a**, **b**, and **c** are of different, but compatible, numeric types. To handle such cases, C++ generally *promotes* values to a common form. C++ can't actually add integer and floating point values, though it may appear to do so. To evaluate that and similar multitype expressions, C++ converts the integer to an equivalent floating point value, then calls an internal routine that can add variables of type **f l o a t**. All these actions happen behind the scenes—you rarely even need to think about them.

But at times, it's necessary to add your own type-conversion rules to those built into the C++ language. For example, return to the **s t r o p** class in Listing 9.6 (STROPS.CPP). The **m a i n** function in that test program initialized **s t r o p** instances with the definitions:

```
strop a = "1234";
strop b = "4321";
```

Those commands work well enough, but what if you wanted to initialize a **s t r o p** instance with a binary value, not a string. For example, suppose that you want to write

```
strop c = 9876;    // ???
```

That will not compile because the **s t r o p** class does not provide a mechanism for converting an integer data type to a string. One way to solve that problem is to add a new constructor that takes a **l o n g** parameter. For example, add this inline function after line 12:

```
strop(long i) { strcpy(value, form("%d", i)); }
```

The new constructor takes a single **l o n g** parameter. The constructor's inline statement converts that parameter's value to a string, which is copied to the private `value` `char` array. As a result, you can now add the definition `strop c = 9876;` after line 21. The new constructor tells the compiler how to convert a `long` value to a `strop` data type—in other words, to a string. You have just added a new type-conversion rule to C++ for the `strop` class.

But there's a flaw in the solution because the reverse conversion is not possible. After initializing a `strop` instance, some way is needed to use the value stored in string form in the class instance. As written, `strop` does not provide a function that returns the value of its private `value` field. For that reason, statements like these fail:

```
strop c = 9876;
cout << c;         // ???
```

The first line compiles and runs just fine. Using the new constructor, C++ is able to convert 9876 to string form and store that string inside the `strop` instance `c`. But the output statement fails. (In fact, if you try this, you'll see that it brings the Zortech compiler to a screeching halt.) Output stream statements don't know how to handle values of type `strop`, and attempting to display such values doesn't compute.

There are several possible solutions to problems such as these. The standard approach is to provide a member function that returns the `value` character string converted to a `long` data type. For example, you could insert this inline function into `strop`:

```
long getValue(void) { return atol(value); }
```

You can then assign a value to `c` and display that value with statements such as these:

```
strop c = 9876;
cout << "\nc      == " << c.getValue();
```

There's nothing wrong with this method—it's a classic solution for accessing private data via member functions. However, there's another less obvious solution that uses an overloaded *conversion operator* to translate a class instance to another data type.

Conversion operators take the form *operator TYPE( )* where *TYPE* is the data type to which you want to convert instances of the class. For example, to provide a type conversion operation for translating `strop` instances to type `long`, insert this inline function inside the class's public section:

```
operator long() { return atol(value); }
```

This is a special use for the `operator` key word that C++ provides specifically for creating new type-conversion rules. In this example, the new rule lists the steps required to convert `strop`'s private `value` field from character format to `long`. (There's only one such step in this sample. In another setting, the type-conversion function might have many statements, and it doesn't have to be implemented inline.) Here, the actual conversion is handled by the standard `atol` library function. With the new type-conversion rule in place, it's now possible to write statements like these:

```
strop c = 9876;
cout << "\nc      == " << (long)c;
```

The type-cast expression (long)c converts the strop instance c to a long value. The expression calls the new type-conversion operator function in the strop class. You may also notice that by stating a type-conversion rule, it's now possible to access strop's value *without* explicitly calling a member function! In fact, other than the new type-conversion function, strop provides no means to get to its value field.

Another interesting benefit of the new type-conversion rule is the capability to pass variables of type strop to function parameters of type long. After all, the type-conversion rule tells C++ how to convert an instance of strop to a long value; therefore, it should be possible to use a strop instance wherever a long value is expected.

And that's exactly true. To see how the trick works, examine Listing 9.9, NEWOPS.CPP. The listing is similar to STROPS.CPP, but adds most of the modifications suggested previously in this section. To keep the listing short, I removed the friend overloaded operator functions from STROPS, but those functions could be reinserted without changing the way the new type-conversion function operates.

Listing 9.9. NEWOPS.CPP

```
 1:   // newops.cpp -- Demonstrate type-conversion rules
 2:
 3:   #include <stream.hpp>
 4:   #include <stdlib.h>
 5:   #include <string.h>
 6:
 7:   class strop {
 8:      private:
 9:          char value[12];
10:      public:
11:          strop() { value[0] = 0; }
12:          strop(const char *s);
13:          strop(long i) { strcpy(value, form("%d", i)); }
14:          operator long() { return atol(value); }
15:   };
16:
17:   void showValue(long v);
18:
19:   main()
20:   {
21:      strop c = 9876;
22:
```

```
23:        cout << "\nc == " << (long)c;
24:        showValue(c);
25:    }
26:
27:    void showValue(long v)
28:    {
29:        cout << "\nValue of v == " << v;
30:    }
```

Because of the type-conversion function at line 14, it's now possible to use type-cast expressions such as (long)c at line 23. It's also possible to pass strop instances directly to functions that declare long arguments. For example, the program calls function showValue to display c's value. When line 24 executes, C++ consults the rules it knows for converting data types to long. In this example, the compiler uses the inline statement for the operator long() function at line 14 to perform the conversion.

Line 14 in NEWOPS shows how to write a type-conversion function inline. As with other member functions, it's also possible to code type-conversions as callable functions. To do this for strop, change line 14 to

```
operator long();
```

Then insert the function implementation somewhere after function main

```
strop::operator long()
{
    return atol(value);
}
```

The result is the same, but now conversions of strop instances to long values will be handled by calling the type-conversion function. The inline code is probably best to reduce the number of such function calls, except when the conversion code is lengthy.

Overloading the Assignment Operator

Assigning one variable to another of a compatible type is an operation that most programmers perform without much thought. However, when the copied variables are class instances, you need to consider a few obscure consequences of assigning one instance to another. Although the compiler will allow you to write a = b; where a and b are class instances, the effects of that assignment may not be what you expect.

Before explaining why assignments of class instances can cause trouble—and describing how to deal sensibly with those situations—it will help to review how assignments work for variables of common C++ data types. For example, examine these lines:

```
float a, b;

a = 3.14159;
b = 100.0;
a = b;
```

After defining two float variables a and b, the program assigns 3.14159 to a and 100.0 to b. Upon assigning b to a, the two variables hold copies of the same value (see Figure 9.1). The variables, however, remain distinct. If one should go out of scope—perhaps because the function that defined the variable ends—the other variable will remain valid. Even though both variables hold the same value, they are stored separately in memory.

a   b

Figure 9.1. For simple data types, after the assignment *a = b;*, the variables
a and *b* hold copies of the same value.

However, consider a similar assignment that involves pointers. If p1 and p2 are *pointers* to variables of type float, the following assignments have a subtle and potentially dangerous effect that's not immediately obvious from reading the program's text:

```
float *p1 = new float;
float *p2 = new float;

*p1 = 3.14159;
*p2 = 100.0;
p1 = p2;          // ???
```

In this case, the variables p1 and p2 are pointers to the actual float variables allocated space on the heap. The two literal values are assigned to those variables by dereferencing the pointers. Copying the *pointer* p2 to the *pointer* p1 causes the two variables to address the same value in memory (see Figure 9.2). Usually it's best to avoid this situation. The space formerly addressed by p1 is disconnected from the pointer, and there is no way to recover that space. Worse, if the program deletes the space addressed by p2, the pointer p1 will address an invalid memory location.

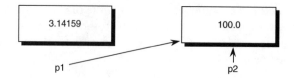

Figure 9.2. Assigning one pointer to another causes the two pointers to address the same location in memory.

The correct way to copy values addressed by pointers is to dereference the pointer variables. The correct assignment of p2's addressed value to the space addressed by p1 is

```
*p1 = *p2;
```

As Figure 9.3 shows, by dereferencing each pointer, C++ copies the value addressed by p2 to the space addressed by p1. Now, the two pointers continue to address unique locations in memory, and therefore, deleting the one will not cause the other to point to an invalid location.

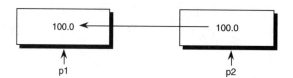

Figure 9.3. Dereferencing the pointers assigns the value addressed by one to the space addressed by the other.

Copying Class Instances

When copying one class instance to another instance of a compatible type, the results can be unexpected. C++ makes copies of instances not only in assignment expressions but at other times. So you must be aware of the consequences of copying class instances, even if you don't explicitly assign them with the = operator. There are four times when a copy of a class instance will be made:

- When one instance is used to initialize a newly defined instance of the same class.

- When an instance is passed to a function's value parameter of the class type.

- When a function returns a class instance (not a reference or pointer to the class).

- When a statement assigns one instance to another.

The first three of these cases initialize *new* copies of class instances using the value of an existing instance. The fourth case assigns the value of an existing instance to another instance that was previously defined. In all cases, the result is an object that contains copies of the data fields of another object.

After making such copies, all may seem well, but trouble brews when the class instances contain pointer fields that address variables allocated space on the heap. Problems can also arise when creating copies of instances that contain fields of other class types, which may contain their own pointer fields. As I explained in the previous section (see Figure 9.2), if two or more pointers happen to address the same location in memory, deleting one of those pointers will cause the others to address invalid data. Worse, deleting the same space more than once can corrupt the heap and cause a major bug. Because classes often inherit properties of many other classes, a simple assignment or function call might create dozens of duplicate pointers. And if those pointers address instances allocated by n e w, class destructors might deallocate the same memory spaces multiple times, which will almost always corrupt the heap.

C++ provides two mechanisms for ensuring that classes with pointer fields may be copied safely. Those two mechanisms are called *memberwise initialization* and *memberwise assignment*.

Memberwise Initialization

When an instance is used to initialize a new instance of a class, C++ copies each data field from the existing object to the new one. For example, here's a simple class with no pointer fields:

```
class simple {
   private:
      int i;
      float r;
   public:
      simple()
         { i = 0; r = 0; }
      simple(int ii, float rr)
         { i = ii; r = rr; }
};
```

In practice, s i mp l e would need other member functions to access its private data fields i and r, but the example will illustrate how instance copying works. The class declares two inline constructors. The default constructor (s i mp l e ( )) initializes fields i and r to 0. An alternate constructor allows a program to initialize a class instance with explicit values. The two constructors make these definitions possible:

```
simple v1;
simple v2(100, 3.14159);
```

The first line creates an instance v1 of type simple with fields i and r initialized to 0. The second line creates a second instance v2 with its fields initialized to 100 and 3.14159 respectively.

Suppose that you need to create another instance v3 somewhere else in the program. You want the new instance to have the same value as v2. To accomplish that, C++ allows you to use the existing instance (v2) to initialize the new instance v3 in its definition line like this:

```
simple v3 = v2;
```

That creates v3 as a copy of v2. For such definitions, C++ performs a memberwise initialization of v3's data fields by copying the field values one by one from v2 to v3. C++ does *not* call the class constructor for the instance v3! Always be aware of these facts when using an instance to initialize another. Although the definition appears to copy the bytes from v2 to the bytes of v3, C++ actually performs the equivalent of the two statements:

```
v3.i = v2.i;
v3.r = v2.r;
```

In other words, when one instance is used to initialize a new instance of the same class, C++ copies the existing instance's member fields to the new instance's same fields. (The statements are for illustration only. The class fields are private, and the statements would not compile.)

The identical memberwise initialization of a new class instance occurs also when you pass an instance to a function's value parameter. For example, suppose that the program contains this function prototype:

```
void doSomething(simple x);
```

Value parameters, as you learned in chapter 3, are passed as *copies* of arguments. When the arguments are class instances, C++ copies them to the function parameters using the identical memberwise initialization steps executed when initializing a new instance with another. For example, if the program calls a function like

```
doSomething(v2);
```

inside doSomething's implementation (not shown), parameter x will contain a copy of the data fields from the instance v2. In addition, the class constructor for x will not run—an important fact to consider when passing objects to functions.

Note: Class instances are *not* copied when passing them to reference parameters or when passing them by address to pointers. To prevent copies of instances from being made, declare the function parameter as simple &x (a reference) or simple *x (a pointer). However, in those cases, the function directly addresses the original instance passed as an argument. If the function changes the instance, the original will also change.

The third and final situation where C++ makes a memberwise initialization of a copied instance is when a function returns a class value. To see how this works, consider a function that's prototyped like this:

```
simple returnSomething(void);
```

The function returnSomething returns an instance of type simple. That instance will be a *copy* of the instance listed in the function's return statement. Suppose that the function is implemented as

```
simple returnSomething(void)
{
    simple q(1234, 43.21);
    return q;
}
```

Inside the function, a local simple variable is initialized with the values 1234 and 43.21. That variable is returned as the function result. However, and this is important, what's actually returned is a *copy* of q, not q itself. Returning q directly would be a serious error—that variable is local to the function, and after the function ends, q no longer exists. For that reason, C++ must copy the object to a new location (probably on the stack) and return that copy. To create the copy, C++ performs the identical memberwise initialization of the new instance, using the fields in q to make that copy. As in the previous two situations—initializing an instance with another and passing instances to value parameters—C++ does *not* call the class constructor for the copied object.

Memberwise initialization is automatic, and for uncomplicated classes like simple, you do not need to consider the effects on the instance copies that C++ makes. However, when classes declare pointer fields, memberwise initialization can cause serious problems. The next section demonstrates how a simple instance copy can lead to major bugs.

Copying Pointer Fields

When a class contains or inherits one or more pointer fields, you must carefully consider the consequences of memberwise initialization for the three situations outlined in the preceding sections. This is doubly important when the class also declares a destructor, as it probably will do in order to delete memory assigned to the pointer fields.

As an example of the problems that can arise, Listing 9.10 declares the same simple class you examined earlier. To that class, the program adds a destructor. Although the purpose of the demonstration is to illustrate why copying pointer fields is dangerous, the class does *not* declare such fields. (Doing so might corrupt the heap and though unlikely, could cause your computer to hang.) After the listing, I'll show you why the program is a potential troublemaker.

Listing 9.10. TROUBLE.CPP

```cpp
1:  // trouble.cpp -- Trouble with memberwise initialization
2:
3:  #include <stream.hpp>
4:
5:  class simple {
6:      private:
7:          int i;
8:          float r;
9:      public:
10:         simple()
11:             { i = 0; r = 0; }
12:         simple(int ii, float rr)
13:             { i = ii; r = rr; }
14:         ~simple();
15: };
16:
17: main()
18: {
19:     cout << "\nsimple v1;";
20:     simple v1;
21:
22:     cout << "\nsimple v2(100, 3.14159);";
23:     simple v2(100, 3.14159);
24:
25:     cout << "\nsimple v3 = v2;";
26:     simple v3 = v2;
27: }
28:
29: simple::~simple()
30: {
31:     cout << "\nInside simple's destructor";
32: }
```

When you run TROUBLE, you'll see that simple's destructor runs three times, once for each instance of the class. The program creates three such instances, v1, v2, and v3. The first two instances are defined normally at lines 20 and 23. The third instance v3 is initialized by making a copy of v2 (line 26).

So far, TROUBLE is trouble free. But suppose you declared the class to contain a pointer field:

```cpp
class simple {
    private:
        char *s;
    // ... other members
    }
```

In the constructors, you might then allocate space to the `char` pointer `s` using `new`. For example, the constructor could execute the statement

```
s = new char[129];
```

After that, `s` addresses a 129-byte space on the heap. So far so good. Of course, you'll also want to delete that space in the class destructor. Doing that will reclaim the allocated space for other uses—generally a wise move. The destructor will need a statement such as

```
delete s;
```

That seems harmless enough, but you have just introduced a nasty bug into the code! When the program initializes `v3` at line 26, C++ copies each data field from `v2` to `v3`, *including* the pointer field `s`. The `s` fields in `v2` and `v3` now address the same location in memory. When the destructor for `v2` runs, that space is deleted. But the destructor will also run for `v3`, causing the program to delete that *same* space twice. The memberwise initialization of `v3` caused the `s` pointer field to address the same location in the heap, a dangerous condition to be avoided at all costs.

The Copy Constructor

The solution to the duplicate pointer field problem is to prevent the condition from ever occurring. Doing that is possible by overriding C++'s default memberwise initialization of copied instances. As I mentioned earlier, when such copies are made, C++ does not call the class constructor. Rather, C++ copies each field from one instance to the new one. By providing a special *copy constructor* in a class, you can override that default action, thus preventing C++ from copying pointer fields.

To create a copy constructor, use the prototype form *CLASS(CLASS&)* where *CLASS* is the class in which the prototype appears. The prototyped function may be inline or declared as a callable function. It may not be virtual, and it is not inherited in a derived class, though a copy constructor in a derivation may call its base copy constructor (see "Copying Derived Class Instances" later in this chapter).

To add a copy constructor to the `simple` class from Listing 9.10, modify the class declaration to the following:

```
class simple {
    private:
        int i;
        float r;
        char *s;
    public:
        simple()
            { i = 0; r = 0; s = new char[129]; }
```

```
simple(int ii, float rr)
   { i = ii; r = rr; s = new char[129]; }
~simple();
simple(simple &copy);
};
```

The next-to-last line declares the copy constructor. Like all constructors, a copy constructor has the same name as its class (s imp l e). Because the constructor receives a reference to another class instance—the instance that's being copied to this one—the constructor must declare a single reference parameter of the class type. The parameter name copy can be anything you like. Later in the program, implement the copy constructor with code such as

```
simple::simple(simple &copy)
{
   cout << "\nInside simple's copy constructor";
   i = copy.i;
   r = copy.r;
   s = strdup(copy.s);
}
```

The output stream statement isn't necessary, but if you try these changes, the statement will show you when the copy constructor runs. The three assignments illustrate the correct way to override C++'s default memberwise initialization of copied class instances. The statements copy each field from the reference parameter copy to the new instance's data fields of the same names. But to handle the pointer field s, the final assignment allocates new space on the heap and copies the *value* addressed by the reference object. (In a real program, you'd also want to include error-handling checks to deal with out-of-memory conditions.) The pointer fields now address distinct locations that hold copies of the appropriate values. Bugs will no longer fly in when the class destructor deletes the space allocated to the pointer fields.

The copy constructor runs automatically for the three cases listed earlier: when an instance is used to initialize a newly defined instance of the same class, when a statement passes an instance to a function's value parameter of that class, and when a function returns an instance of the class data type. The other constructors still operate as before.

Unfortunately, the solution is not yet perfect. Although the copy constructor deals sensibly with the three situations when C++ makes a copy of a class instance, a possible hot spot remains. When a statement directly assigns one instance to another, you must again consider what will happen if those instances contain pointer fields. The next section explains how to handle these situations.

Memberwise Assignment

C++ always permits direct assignment of one variable to another of the same or a compatible type. Because one of the goals of OOP features and classes in C++ is to give programmers the means to invent new data types, it should be no surprise that C++ allows you to assign instances of the same classes to each other. But as explained in the previous sections, such assignments might cause pointers to address the same locations in memory, a dangerous situation to avoid at all costs.

Consider the simple case of defining a couple of instances of type `simple` (from Listing 9.10) and then copying one of those instances to the other. For example, you could write these lines:

```
simple v1;
simple v2(9876, 1.2345);

v1 = v2;
```

After defining `v1` with default values and defining `v2` with explicit values 9876 and 1.2345, an assignment statement copies `v2` to `v1`. As before, when making such copies, C++ transfers the individual fields from `v2` to `v1`. It does *not* call any class constructors for `v1`. If the class contains or inherits a pointer field, the copied pointers will now address the same location in memory, which almost certainly will lead to problems.

A copy constructor can't solve this problem because the instances involved have already been constructed. Remember that constructors run when new instances come into being. In the case of the assignment of `v2` to `v1`, no new instance is created. Rather, the one instance is copied to the other. Both instances already exist.

The cure is to overload the assignment operator. By doing that, any assignments of one instance to an instance of the same class will cause the overloaded function to run, replacing C++'s default memberwise assignment and giving you the opportunity to prevent pointer fields from addressing identical locations in the heap.

Overloading the assignment operator is no different from overloading other operators. (See *Operator Overloading* earlier in this chapter.) The overloaded function's prototype must be in the general form *void operator=(const CLASS&)*, where *CLASS* is the name of the class that declares the overloaded function.

To add an overloaded assignment operator function to the `simple` class, insert this line in the class's public section:

```
void operator=(const simple &copy);
```

That overloads the = operator and specifies a reference parameter named `copy` of type `simple`. The parameter is the one being copied to the instance that calls the `operator=` function. In the assignment `a = b`, `copy` would refer to `b`. The `const` key word tells the compiler to disallow any changes to the instance passed by reference to the overloaded function. You may change `copy` to a different name if you want.

Implement the overloaded assignment function using code that's similar to the statements you inserted earlier into the copy constructor:

```
void simple::operator=(const simple &copy)
{
    cout << "\nInside simple's operator= function";
    if (this == &copy) return;
    if (s != NULL) delete s;
    i = copy.i;
    r = copy.r;
    s = strdup(copy.s);
}
```

As before, the output statement is just for illustration. If you are making these changes, when you run the program, the statement will show you exactly when the overloaded function runs. The first if statement compares the this pointer to the address of the copy reference parameter. This catches the assignment of the *same* object to itself. For example, suppose that you execute

```
simple v1, v2;
v1 = v1;
```

That may be a mistake, but you certainly wouldn't want to have the code duplicate the same object on top of itself. Comparing this to the assignment operator function's reference parameter prevents executing wasteful code. (In a program that uses aliases to address objects, copying an object to itself might occur either by accident or by design, so this rule is an important one to remember for overloaded assignment functions.)

The second if statement in the assignment function deletes the space (if any) currently allocated to pointer s. Remember that the two instances have already been constructed; therefore, any pointer fields might have been allocated space on the heap. You'll probably want to delete that space in the object receiving the copy (the object to the left of =).

The other assignments in the overloaded function are the same as in the copy constructor. Each statement simply copies the field from the reference parameter to the instance that called the function. The result is a copy of the values, but not the pointers, of one object to another. Both object's destructors can now safely delete any space allocated to pointer fields in the class instances without worry that the same space will be deleted more than once.

With the overloaded operator= function in place, assignments of simple instances now call the function to perform the copy. When you write

```
a = b;
```

C++ actually executes the statement

```
a.operator=(b);
```

In other words, a reference to b is passed to instance a's o p e r a t o r = function, which is expected to copy the fields from b into a.

> **Note:** The preceding discussions about copying instances imply that only pointer fields can lead to trouble. That's the typical case; however, you should also consider *every* possible consequence that might arise when a copy of an object is made. For example, a constructor might perform some other critical action that will be skipped for a copied object. In that case, you might need to include a copy constructor and an overloaded assignment operator function to execute that same critical action for copies of the class instances.

Calling operator= *from a Copy Constructor*

Because a copy constructor and an overloaded assignment operator function o p e r a t o r = perform similar jobs, supplying both functions for a class is wasteful. Each of the functions copies the members of one object to another; the only significant difference is that the copy constructor creates a new instance. The assignment function copies values to an existing instance of the class.

Here's one way to combine the two functions to reduce duplication. First, declare the class as usual:

```
class simple {
   private:
      int i;
      float r;
      char *s;
   public:
      simple();
      ~simple();
      simple(simple &copy);
      void operator=(const simple &copy);
};
```

To keep s i m p l e even more simple, I've left out some of the details from earlier examples. The last two prototypes declare the copy constructor and overloaded o p e r a t o r = function.

The copy constructor will run when

- A definition initializes a new instance with a copy of another instance.

- A statement passes a class instance to a function's value parameter.

- A function returns an instance of type s i m p l e.

Those are the same three cases listed earlier. The overloaded `operator=` function runs when a statement assigns an existing instance of type `simple` to another instance of the same class.

To avoid duplicating the efforts of copying member fields in both functions, you can have the copy constructor call the overloaded `operator=` function. The implementations for both functions show one way to accomplish this:

```
simple::simple(simple &copy)
{
    s = NULL;
    *this = copy;
}

void simple::operator=(const simple &copy)
{
    if (this == &copy) return;
    if (s != NULL) delete s;
    i = copy.i;
    r = copy.r;
    s = strdup(copy.s);
}
```

The copy constructor (the first of the two functions) sets pointer field s to NULL and then assigns the reference parameter copy to *this. Because this addresses the instance that called the constructor, the assignment would normally kick C++'s default memberwise initialization code into action. But since the = operator has been overloaded by the operator= function, that function takes over C++'s default assignments to copy each field from the instance being copied to the new one's fields.

When pulling this trick, be sure to set all pointer fields to NULL in the copy constructor, as done here to field s. That way, when the operator= function carries out the assignment of *this = copy, it will be possible to test for a NULL pointer and avoid accidentally deleting a random address value. (In the sample functions, the if (s != NULL)... statement takes care of this important task.) Obviously, deleting unallocated space would be a serious error and would probably lead to a colossal crash.

Copying Derived Class Instances

A significant concern is the effect in a derived class of a copy constructor and overloaded operator= function in a base class declaration. The derived class inherits the copy constructor just as it inherits all other member functions from the base. And that constructor will be called automatically at the appropriate times. However, derived classes do *not* inherit overloaded operator functions, thus complicating assignments of derived class instances.

To handle those situations, when the derived class adds pointer fields, it too should have a copy constructor and an overloaded `operator=` function. The designs of those functions may be similar to those for `simple`. However, in the new `operator=` function, it's possible to call the base class function for copying values of inherited data fields. Assuming the derived class's function prototype is `void operator=(const complex &copy);`, to call the base class's similar function, use a statement such as `simple::operator=(copy);`.

Overloading and Memory Management

The C++ heap manager is capable enough to handle memory allocations for most programs. However, there are times when you'll want to exercise greater control over memory resources. For instance, you may want to provide for virtual memory, storing some objects in memory and others on disk until needed. Or you may want to allocate space from a fixed pool that the program reserves for specific class instances, a method that may reduce the potential for heap fragmentation.

To satisfy these and other special requirements, you can overload the `new` and `delete` operators. Doing that gives you the means to trap memory allocation requests for instances of a specific class. Other allocations continue to use the standard C++ heap management facilities. Overloading `new` and `delete` in a class declaration does not affect how those operators work for other data types.

Assignments to `this`

In early C++ versions, it was not possible to overload `new` and `delete`. To tap into the C++ heap manager, it was necessary to assign an address to the `this` pointer inside a class constructor. When the compiler detects such an assignment, it assumes that the class will handle all requests for memory in which to store instances of that class.

You may still use this method, although it's no longer recommended. One warning: Be sure to assign a value to `this` for every possible condition in the constructor. For example, examine this constructor:

```
theclass::theclass(void)
{
    if (condition == TRUE) {
```

```
        this = addressToAssign();
        // base class constructor called here only
    }
}
```

Function `addressToAssign` (not shown) handles the custom allocation of space and returns an address, assigned here to `this`. When the compiler detects such an assignment, it does *not* allocate any space for the object. Also, the compiler generates code to call a base class constructor *only* following the assignment to `this`. For these reasons, if you don't assign a value to `this` in this example when `condition` is false, no instance of the class will be created, which may cause a bug.

As a side effect of this technique, it is illegal to assign values to class data fields until `this` has been initialized. For example, if `theClass` declares an `int` field `x`, an assignment such as `x = 100` will cause serious problems if that or any similar statement comes before `this` is initialized. The reason for this rule is that class members are accessed through the `this` pointer. The assignment `x = 100` is actually carried out by executing `this->x = 100`; therefore, if `this` is not initialized, the value 100 in this sample will be copied to a random location in memory.

When an object is allocated space by `new`, if that object's constructor assigns a value to `this`, the `this` pointer will equal 0 at the start of the constructor. If such an object is not allocated space by `new`, `this` will be non-zero (it will equal the address of the space assigned to the object.)

This interesting fact lets an object detect whether it was allocated by `new`, which might be necessary to prevent a destructor from corrupting the heap by deleting other variables not stored there. Listing 9.11, THISIS.CPP, demonstrates the idea.

Listing 9.11. THISIS.CPP

```
 1:  // thisis.cpp -- Demonstrate assignment to this
 2:
 3:  #include <stream.hpp>
 4:
 5:  class aClass {
 6:      private:
 7:          int x;
 8:      public:
 9:          aClass();
10:  };
11:
12:  char buf[512];
13:
14:  main()
15:  {
16:      cout << "\nAllocating local instance";
```

```
17:        aClass c1;
18:
19:        cout << "\nAllocating dynamic instance";
20:        aClass *c2 = new aClass;
21:    }
22:
23:    aClass::aClass()
24:    {
25:        if (this == 0) {
26:            cout << "\n Object allocated by new";
27:            this = (aClass *)&buf;
28:        } else
29:            cout << "\n Object allocated without using new";
30:        x = 1234;
31:    }
```

In the constructor's implementation (lines 23-31), an if statement examines this. If that pointer equals 0, it must have been allocated by new. The reason that this equals 0 in that case is because the compiler has detected the assignment to this at line 27, which defeats the request for C++'s memory manager to reserve some space on the heap. The constructor takes advantage of that fact to store the object in a global buffer, defined at line 12.

If the this pointer is not 0, the object was allocated by other means (probably as a local or global variable).

Although this example shows how to override new's normal allocation of heap space, assigning an address to this is not the best way to take over memory management from C++. The next section explains the new and improved approach.

Overloading new

You may overload the new operator just as you can any other operator such as + or =. Overloading new in a class declaration tells the compiler that from now on you will take care of memory allocation requests for instances of the class.

To overload new, insert a function prototype of the form *void * operator new(size_t size);*. Future uses of new to allocate space for class instances will then be directed to the overloaded function. The function should return the address of space allocated for the instance. If no space is available, the function should return 0.

Listing 9.12, OVERNEW.CPP, is a simple though complete example showing how to trap uses of new to allocate space for instances. Instead of storing the instances on the heap in the usual way, the program stuffs them into a global buffer.

Listing 9.12. OVERNEW.CPP

```
 1:   // overnew.cpp -- Overload the new operator
 2:
 3:   #include <stream.hpp>
 4:
 5:   class brandNew {
 6:       private:
 7:           int x;
 8:       public:
 9:           brandNew();
10:           void * operator new(size_t size);
11:   };
12:
13:   char buf[512];
14:   int index;
15:
16:   main()
17:   {
18:       cout << "\nCreating local instance";
19:       brandNew b1;
20:
21:       cout << "\nAllocating space via new";
22:       brandNew *b2 = new brandNew;
23:       brandNew *b3 = new brandNew;
24:       brandNew *b4 = new brandNew;
25:       brandNew *b5 = new brandNew;
26:   }
27:
28:   brandNew::brandNew()
29:   {
30:       cout << "\nInside constructor";
31:       x = index;
32:   }
33:
34:   void *brandNew::operator new(size_t size)
35:   {
36:       cout << "\nInside overloaded new. Size == " << size;
37:       if (index >= 512 - sizeof(brandNew))
38:           return 0;
39:       else {
40:           int k = index;
41:           index += sizeof(brandNew);
42:           return &buf[k];
43:       }
44:   }
```

The overloaded n e w function at lines 34-44 checks whether space is available in the global buffer. If not, the function returns 0, causing n e w to return NULL. (The program doesn't check for this condition, but you should do that in a real setting.) If space is available, the global i n d e x is incremented by the size of the memory request, passed to the n e w function in the s i z e parameter. In that event, the function returns the address of the newly allocated space.

OVERNEW is a complete demonstration of an overloaded n e w operator, but the program lacks the sophistication of a finished product. In your own programs, you'll undoubtedly have to provide more extensive programming for keeping track of allocated space. Also, it probably makes little sense to store instances in a global buffer, used here only for illustration. Instead, you may want to allocate space for the buffer in another location, perhaps on the heap or in other available memory.

Overloading delete

Of course, the other side of the memory allocation coin is the d e l e t e operator. As with n e w, you can overload d e l e t e to trap deletions of objects addressed by pointers.

An overloaded d e l e t e function's prototype must be in the form *void operator delete(void *p)*, where *p* is the address of the object being deleted. Alternatively, you may declare the function using the form *void operator delete(void *p, size_t size)*. When using this second format, the compiler will pass in *size* the number of bytes to dispose.

To add an overloaded d e l e t e function to the b r a n d N e w class in Listing 9.12, add this prototype to the class's public section:

```
void operator delete(void *p);
```

Next, append the function's implementation to the end of the listing:

```
void brandNew::operator delete(void *p)
{
    cout << "\nInside overloaded delete.";
}
```

The overloaded function doesn't do anything except display a message. When you run the program, the message tells you exactly when the overloaded d e l e t e operator is called to action.

As this experiment shows, it's fairly simple to override d e l e t e. But it's another matter to manage the deletion of memory or other space allocated to class instances. Don't attempt this technique unless absolutely necessary. In most cases, the default n e w and d e l e t e operators will be adequate.

> **Note:** To use the C++ memory manager to allocate heap space for objects that override `new`, preface the operator with a double colon. For example, the line `brandNew *x = ::new brandNew` bypasses the overloaded `new` operator function. Similarly, `::delete x` calls the C++ deletion routine, not the overloaded `delete` function.

Overloading Streams

Sample listings throughout this book use input and output stream statements for reading and displaying values. You may be surprised to discover that streams are not part of the C++ language, but are implemented as classes in the C++ library. The declarations for those classes are stored in the header file STREAM.HPP, which nearly every program in this book includes during compilation.

The following sections explain how to tap into input and output stream statements for your own classes. As you'll see, by overloading the input and output stream operators, it's possible to teach C++ how to handle stream statements that include any type of class instance.

Overloading Output Streams

Normally, output streams can handle only simple data types, `int`, `long`, `float`, `char *`, and so on. However, by overloading the output stream operator `<<`, you can easily add your own classes to the data types that output stream statements are designed to use.

Listing 9.13 shows a typical example. The program declares a class named `point` that stores two `int` values x and y, representing the coordinate value of a location, perhaps on a graphics display. Usually, to display the values of private data fields like x and y, you would have to call member functions such as `getx` and `gety`. But by adding the `point` class to those that output streams can handle, it's possible to display point variables without going to all that trouble.

Listing 9.13. POINTOUT.CPP

```
1:  // pointout.cpp -- Demonstrate overloading output streams
2:
3:  #include <stream.hpp>
4:
```

```
5:  class point {
6:      private:
7:          int x, y;
8:      public:
9:          point() { x = y = 0; }
10:         point(int xx, int yy) { x = xx; y = yy; }
11:         void putx(int xx) { x = xx; }
12:         void puty(int yy) { y = yy; }
13:         int getx(void) { return x; }
14:         int gety(void) { return y; }
15:         friend ostream& operator<<(ostream& os, point &p);
16: };
17:
18: main()
19: {
20:     point p;
21:
22:     cout << p << '\n';
23:
24:     p.putx(100);
25:     p.puty(200);
26:
27:     cout << p << '\n';
28: }
29:
30: ostream& operator<<(ostream& os, point &p)
31: {
32:     os << "x == " << p.x << ", y == " << p.y;
33:     return os;
34: }
```

Line 15 overloads the output stream operator with a friend function named operator<<. The function returns a reference to ostream—one of the classes declared in STREAM.HPP. Two parameters are also listed for the overloaded function: os, a reference to ostream, and p, a reference to a point instance. In other classes, use this same format, but replace point with your own class name. The other elements remain the same.

The implementation of the friend function appears at lines 30-34. Because the function is a friend of class point, the statement at line 32 may directly access the x and y data fields in the parameter p. Notice that this line is itself an output stream statement, which writes the values of the two data fields plus two literal strings to the ostream reference os. Finally, the function returns os.

As a result of these steps, the statements at lines 22 and 27 may now pass instances of class point to the output stream cout. When those statements run, they display

```
x == 0, y == 0
x == 100, y == 200
```

Because the `operator<<` friend function returns an `ostream` reference, it's also possible to nest multiple uses of the output stream operator. For example, if p1, p2, and p3 are instances of type `point`, you can display their values with the single statement

```
cout << p1 << "; " << p2 << "; " << p3;
```

Technically, such statements are executed as multiple function calls to various overloaded output-stream operators. For example, the above line is executed as though it were written

```
((((cout << p1) << "; ") << p2) << "; ") << p3;
```

Luckily, there's no need to use all those confusing parentheses, although the statement will compile and run.

Note: Overloading output stream statements is a handy technique to remember for debugging. To display a series of member fields in a complex class, it may be easier to provide an output stream function rather than call member functions for every value you want to examine.

Overloading Input Streams

Overloading the input stream operator `>>` is similar to overloading output streams. Providing an overloaded stream function effectively teaches C++ how to read instances of a specific class type.

Listing 9.14 adds input stream capability to the POINTOUT.CPP sample program.

Listing 9.14. POINTIN.CPP

```
1:  // pointin.cpp -- Demonstrate overloading input streams
2:
3:  #include <stream.hpp>
4:
5:  class point {
6:      private:
7:          int x, y;
8:      public:
```

```
 9:              point() { x = y = 0; }
10:              point(int xx, int yy) { x = xx; y = yy; }
11:              void putx(int xx) { x = xx; }
12:              void puty(int yy) { y = yy; }
13:              int getx(void) { return x; }
14:              int gety(void) { return y; }
15:              friend ostream& operator<<(ostream& os, point &p);
16:              friend istream& operator>>(istream& is, point &p);
17:    };
18:
19:    main()
20:    {
21:        point p;
22:
23:        cout << p << '\n';
24:
25:        p.putx(100);
26:        p.puty(200);
27:
28:        cout << p << '\n';
29:
30:        cout << "\nEnter x and y values: ";
31:        cin >> p;
32:        cout << "\nYou entered: " << p;
33:    }
34:
35:    ostream& operator<<(ostream& os, point &p)
36:    {
37:        os << "x == " << p.x << ", y == " << p.y;
38:        return os;
39:    }
40:
41:    istream& operator>>(istream& is, point &p)
42:    {
43:        is >> p.x >> p.y;
44:        return is;
45:    }
```

Line 16 declares the input-stream friend function, overloading operator>> for the point class. Except for the reference to istream and the function result type, the input stream function is similar to the output function above.

The new function's implementation reads values for x and y via the istream reference parameter is. After that, a return statement returns the istream so that input statements may be nested.

When you run the program, you'll be prompted to enter x and y values. Type two integers separated by a space. As you'll see, the input stream statement at line 31 stores both values you enter in the class instance. Line 32 displays those values.

Miscellany

In any tool chest, there are always a few odds and ends that you'll rarely use, but that when the need arises, you'll be glad to have. The following C++ tips fall into this category.

Other I/O Streams

The STREAM.HPP header file declares one input stream instance of type `istream`, `cin`. As you've seen in earlier chapters, you can input values with input-stream statements such as

```
cin >> v;
```

The same header file also declares four output streams of type `ostream`: `cout`, `cerr`, `cprn`, and `caux`. You'll recognize the first; it's attached to the system's standard output device, usually the console. The statement

```
cout << v;
```

sends v's value in character form to `cout`. You can use the other three output streams in similar statements. To write an error message, use a statement like this:

```
cerr << "ERROR: Trouble in paradise!";
```

You can, of course, write error messages via `cout`. However, if someone redirects standard output, the messages will also be redirected. When you don't want that to happen, write the messages to `cerr`, which can't be redirected away from the console (at least not as easily as the system's standard output can).

To send output streams to the printer, use `cprn` in place of `cout`. For example, this prints a line of text:

```
cprn << "This appears on the printer\n";
```

To send output streams to the system's auxiliary output, often attached to a serial output port, use `caux`:

```
caux << "This line is directed to the auxiliary output\n";
```

> **Note:** Writing text to `caux` may not be a reliable method for communicating between two computers linked via a serial cable. It may be possible to use `caux` informally to display text on a terminal, but it probably is not possible to use output stream statements to communicate with remote systems via modems.

Conditional Expressions

C++ and C share a shorthand form of the common `if` statement. Both forms perform identical jobs, but the shorthand version can be useful at times, and it may even generate slightly smaller, though not necessarily more efficient, compiled code.

Suppose that you have defined a symbol `DEBUGGING`. If the symbol is true, you want a `char *` variable named `version` to address the string `"0.10b"`; otherwise, you want `version` to address the string `"1.00"`. You could initialize `version` with an `if` statement like this:

```
if (DEBUGGING)
    version = "0.10b";
else
    version = "1.00";
```

But that requires the compiler to create instructions that reference `version` twice. The equivalent shorthand conditional expression eliminates the duplicate reference. The expression uses the ternary operator composed of two symbols— `?` and `:`

```
version = DEBUGGING ? "0.10b" : "1.00";
```

The shorthand statement has the same effect as the longer `if` version. Actually, there are two statements: the conditional expression `DEBUGGING ? "0.10b" : "1.00"` and the assignment to `version`. Conditional expressions have values and therefore are typically assigned to a variable. In general, the conditional expression has the form

```
condition ? default : alternate
```

The *condition* may be any expression that evaluates to a true (nonzero) or false (0) result. The question mark is required. The *default* value will be the final value of the entire expression if *condition* is true. Otherwise, the *alternate* value will be the value of the expression. The two selection values, *default* and *alternate*, must be separated with a colon. A typical use for a conditional expression is to select the lesser of two values

```
result = (v1 < v2) ? v1 : v2;
```

That sets `result` to `v1` only if `v1` is less than `v2`. If `v1` is greater or equal to `v2`, `v2` will be assigned to `result`. The conditional expression has the identical effect as this `if` statement:

```
if (v1 < v2)
   result = v1;
else
   result = v2;
```

Shorthand conditional expressions are useful for assigning choices of values to arrays. For example, this expression sets the first character of a string to a British pound sign if an `int` variable `dollars` is false, otherwise the first character will be a dollar sign:

```
string[0] = (dollars == 0) ? '£' : '$';
```

The compiler may be able to generate smaller code because it has to create instructions to reference `string[0]` only once. The equivalent `if` statement requires two references to `string`:

```
if (dollars == 0)
   string[0] = '£';
else
   string[0] = '$';
```

Because only one of the references executes based on the value of `dollars`, both expressions take about the same amount of time to run. However, the conditional expression may occupy slightly less space in the finished program's code file.

It's also possible to nest conditional expressions, creating statements like this:

```
char c= (index > 100) ? 'c': (index <= 50) ? 'a': 'b';
```

When that statement executes, it will set `char c` to `'a'` if `index` is 50 or less, to `'b'` if `index` equals 51..100, or to `'c'` if `index` is greater than 100. The equivalent `if` statement is

```
char c;
if (index > 100)
   c = 'c';
else if (index <= 50)
   c = 'a';
else
   c = 'b';
```

Complex nested conditional expressions can be extremely difficult to read. For that reason, I usually prefer the longer `if` statements even though they may increase the size of the compiled code file.

Resolving Global Function Conflicts

Because classes encapsulate code and data, you are free to use any names you like for member functions and data fields. Those names are permanently associated with a class name, and therefore, the names can't conflict with others in the program.

However, if you use an existing identifier for a class member function or field, you may have to explain to the compiler which of the similar names you intend to use. For example, suppose you create this class:

```
class conflict {
   private:
      int x, y;
   public:
      conflict();
      int getx(void) { return x; }
      int gety(void) { return y; }
};
```

The class stores two private variables x and y. Because those identifiers are stowed inside the class, there's no possibility of a conflict with any other variables of the same name. But suppose that the program defines these two global values:

```
int x = 100;
int y = 200;
```

In the class constructor, you want to set a new conflict instance's x and y fields to the global default values. But you can't write the constructor this way:

```
conflict::conflict()
{
   x = x;   // ???
   y = y;   // ???
}
```

There's no way the compiler can know what those two statements are supposed to do. To tell the compiler to use the global x and y values, preface their names with the scope resolution operator : : as shown here:

```
conflict::conflict()
{
   x = ::x;
   y = ::y;
}
```

When an identifier is prefaced with ::, the compiler looks outside of the current scope for that symbol. In this example, the scope resolution operator tells the compiler to use the global symbols. Without the operator, the references to x and y are directed to those fields in the class instance.

You can use a double colon also to call functions. For example, if `int getx(void)` is a member function and if there is a global function of that same name, `::getx()` calls the global code; `getx()` inside another member of the class refers to the member function.

Default Status of Inherited Classes

It's best always to use the `private:`, `public:`, and `protected:` key words to mark the status of class members. In general, design your classes with this format:

```
class name {
   private:
      // private members
   protected:
      // protected members
   public:
      // public members
};
```

The order and number of sections in the class are not important. (Some C++ programmers prefer to list public members first, private ones last.) In the absence of an explicit status key word, members default to private status. In this class, the two data fields `count` and `value` are private:

```
class reference {
      int count;      // private field
      float value;    // private field
   public:
      reference();
      // other public members
};
```

It's also a good idea always to specify whether an inherited base class's members are to be `public` or `private`. Suppose, for example, that `newClass` inherits the `reference` class. You can write the new class declaration this way:

```
class newClass : public reference {
   // members for newClass
};
```

By stating that `reference` is `public`, all members inherited from `reference` retain their original public, private, or protected status. But changing the `public` key word to `private` in the derivation list causes the inherited members to become private to the new class:

```
class newClass : private reference {
    // members for newClass
};
```

The significance of this change becomes important only if *another* class inherits from newClass. Because the reference base class was converted to private status, a further derivation of newClass cannot access any of reference's members. The private key word says "inherit the members from the base, but prevent any future derivations from using any of those same members."

If you do not state public or private in a derivation list, the default status is private. If you write the derived newClass like this:

```
class newClass : reference {
    // members for newClass
};
```

future derivations of newClass will not be able to refer to any members of reference, regardless of those members' original private, protected, or public status. Because that consequence isn't obvious from reading the program's text, it's a good idea to state explicitly whether a base class is to be public or private.

Pointers to Member Functions

As you learned in chapter 4, it's possible to address conventional functions with pointers. To create a pointer to a function, use a definition such as this:

```
float (* myfnptr)(int k);
```

That defines a pointer named myfnptr to address any function that accepts one int parameter and returns a float value. If the program defines a function theFunction with that same type of parameter and return type, this statement assigns the address of that function to the pointer and then calls the function through the pointer:

```
myfnptr = &theFunction;
float fp = (* myfnptr)(100);
```

Calling functions via pointers provides a convenient method for programs to attach custom functions for critical operations. For instance, a graphics program might define a pointer to a putPixel function. By writing your own put-Pixel function and assigning that function's address to the function pointer, the compiled program can call your custom code.

The same techniques do not work for functions that are members of a class. The reason you can't create common function pointers to class members is that those members *must* be called in reference to an instance of the class. A pointer to a function may be called outside of the context of a class instance; therefore, common function pointers can't call member functions.

However, it is possible to create a member function pointer by binding the pointer to the class name. For example, for a class named firstClass, to design a pointer to a member function that requires no input and returns float, use the definition

```
float (firstClass::*myfnptr)(void);
```

To design myfnptr to address a member function that accepts two int parameters and returns void, use the line

```
void (firstClass::*myfnptr)(int, int);
```

Those two definitions do not specify *which* member function myfnptr addresses, only the *form* of the function that may be assigned to the pointer variable. It's still necessary to create an instance of the class and to assign to the pointer the address of a class member of the appropriate form.

Listing 9.15, MFNPTR.CPP, shows the basic steps that are required to define and use pointers to member functions.

Listing 9.15. MFNPTR.CPP

```
 1:  // mfnptr.cpp -- Member function pointers
 2:
 3:  #include <stream.hpp>
 4:
 5:  class firstClass {
 6:      private:
 7:          int count;
 8:      public:
 9:          firstClass() { count = 0; }
10:          int access(void);
11:  };
12:
13:  int (firstClass::*myfnptr)(void);
14:
15:  main()
16:  {
17:      int i;
18:      firstClass fc;
19:
20:      cout << "\nCall access the normal way:\n";
21:      for (i = 0; i < 9; i++)
22:          cout << dec(fc.access(), 8);
23:
24:      cout << "\n\nCall access via the member function pointer\n";
25:      myfnptr = firstClass::access;
26:      for (i = 0; i < 9; i++)
27:          cout << dec((fc.*myfnptr)(), 8);
```

```
28:
29:        cout << "\n\nMember function pointer and a dynamic instance\n";
30:        firstClass *fp = new firstClass;
31:        for (i = 0; i < 9; i++)
32:            cout << dec((fp->*myfnptr)(), 8);
33:    }
34:
35:    int firstClass::access(void)
36:    {
37:        return count++;
38:    }
```

Line 13 defines a pointer named my fnptr bound to a function that has no parameters and returns an int value. The pointer may address any function with that design in class firstClass. However, the pointer may *not* address a function even of an appropriate design that's not also a member of firstClass.

After defining a variable fc of type firstClass (line 18), the test program calls the class's access function in the usual way (see lines 20-22). The expression fc.access() calls the access function for the class instance fc. (The test function increments and returns a private variable, just to give the program something to do.)

Lines 24-27 perform the identical operation as the preceding for loop, but use the member function pointer myfnptr to call access. Line 25 assigns to myfnptr the address of the access member function in firstClass. The compiler accepts this statement because myfnptr is bound to firstClass and is designed to address any function with an appropriate prototype. You could also replace the pointer definition (line 13) and the address assignment (line 30) with the single line

```
int (firstClass::*myfnptr)(void) = firstClass::access;
```

That both defines myfnptr and assign's to the pointer the address of the access member function. When calling the member function, you must follow two rules: Refer to an instance of the class and surround the function call with parentheses. For example, if n is an int variable and fc is an instance of firstClass, this copies to n the result of function access called via the member function pointer:

```
n = (fc.*myfnptr)();
```

That's exactly equivalent to the more common statement

```
n = fc.access();
```

You can also call member functions via pointers when instances are addressed by other pointer variables. Lines 29-30 in MFNPTR show how to do that for a pointer fp, to which new allocates a dynamic instance of firstClass (line 30). The expression

```
(fp->*myfnptr)();
```

calls the access function for the instance addressed by fp. The statement is equivalent to

```
fp->access();
```

In addition to addressing member functions with pointers, it's also possible to address other public data fields. For example, if firstClass had a public float field named balance, you could define a pointer to that field by writing

```
float firstClass::*dataPtr;
```

That defines a pointer variable named dataPtr that can address any public float data field in class firstClass. The pointer may *not* address a float variable outside of the class. To assign the address of the hypothetical balance data field to dataPtr, execute this statement:

```
dataPtr = &firstClass::balance;
```

Or you could define the pointer and assign the address of the balance field with a single line. This replaces the previous two lines:

```
float firstClass::*dataPtr = &firstClass::balance;
```

Either way, dataPtr now addresses the balance field in firstClass. Actually, however, dataPtr does not hold the address of a memory location, but rather the offset to where the balance field will be stored in an instance of the class. As with member function pointers, it is still necessary to refer to the addressed data field through a class instance. These two statements assign a floating point value to the balance field and then use dataPtr to display that same value:

```
fc.balance = 3.14159;
cout << "\nBalance=" << fc.*dataPtr;
```

The notation fc.*dataPtr is similar to the notation used to call a member function. However, the extra parentheses are not required when referring to data field members.

Virtual Base Classes

When a derived class inherits from more than one base class—a situation commonly known as *multiple inheritance*—it's possible that somewhere along the line, more than one copy of a distant ancestor class's members will be brought along for the ride. For example, if classes X and Y each inherit the members of A, if a fourth class Z inherits both X and Y, the new class Z will have two copies of every member in A.

What's more, to refer to the correct copies of those members, the program will have to use a scope resolution operator for X::member and Y::member; otherwise, the compiler won't be able to resolve plain references to the multiple member fields.

That situation is not always undesirable, and there is nothing wrong with inheriting multiple copies of a distant class relative. However, when the multiple copies aren't needed, you can use *virtual base classes* to eliminate the duplications. A class that inherits a virtual base class will have only one copy of that base's members, regardless of how many derivations inherit that same base.

A few sample classes will illustrate the problem and show how to prevent inheriting multiple base class members. First, here's the granddaddy base class—the one that's about to cause all the trouble:

```
class base {
    protected:
        int basex;
    public:
        base();
};
```

The class stores a single protected field named basex. Next, you declare two derived classes that inherit base:

```
class derived1 : public base {
    public:
        void doNothing(void) { }
};
class derived2 : public base {
    public:
        void doNothing(void) { }
};
```

Each class inherits a copy of base's members. Both derived1 and derived2 have distinct copies of the basex field. So far so good. But now you create one more class that inherits both of the two derived classes above:

```
class derived3 : public derived1, public derived2 {
    public:
        void showValues(void);
};
```

Now there's a thorn in derived3's paw—the new class has just inherited two copies of the base class members. Because of that inheritance, the derived3 class has two basex fields, one that came from derived1 and one that came from derived2.

By using expressions such as derived1::basex and derived2::basex, you can easily resolve any ambiguous references to the multiple basex members. However, suppose you need only one copy of basex in derived3. To do away with the unused extra b a s e x copy, you can declare the derived bases to be virtual. To do that, change the declarations for d e r i v e d 1 and d e r i v e d 2 to

```
class derived1 : virtual public base {
    public:
        void doNothing(void) { }
};
class derived2 : virtual public base {
    public:
        void doNothing(void) { }
};
```

Now when d e r i v e d 3 inherits the derived classes, each of which inherits a virtual copy of b a s e, there will be only one instance of b a s e's member fields in the final derivation. Additionally, there's no longer any need to use a scope resolution operator and a class name to access the inherited b a s e x member.

Now That You've Learned C++...

You've come a long way from chapter 1, but your journey into learning C++ is just beginning. Learning a new language is a goal you will never completely achieve. There will always be new facts to learn, new tips to pick up, and new tools to acquire. As you write your own programs and learn more about C++, the following brief notes will answer a few questions that may arise.

Differences Between C and C++

C++ and C are cut from similar molds, so it's not surprising that C++ can compile most C programs. However, the reverse is not true. A C compiler will probably choke on a C++ listing. C++'s unique features, such as classes, stream operators, and function overloading (to name only a few), aren't part of the C language.

You can compile many C-style programs with the C++ compiler supplied with this book, and with other brands of C++. However, you will have to follow a few rules that C programmers sometimes break. When writing C-style programs, or when converting a C listing to C++, keep the following key differences between C and C++ in mind.

- All functions *must* have prototypes before being used. In C, prototyping is not enforced as strictly as in C++, although ANSI C compilers do encourage prototyping.

- C++ is much more strict about mixing data types in expressions. In assignment statements and when passing arguments to function parameters, try to use the same data types for variables.

- C++ also insists that calls to functions in other modules have the correct numbers and types of parameters. If all your modules compile with no errors, but the linker refuses to create the finished executable code file, you may have passed the wrong type of argument to a function.

- Don't use old-style function declarations where the parameters are listed by type, as in `void f(int, float)`, and then given names on separate lines below (`int x; float f;`). This format is ancient C history and should be avoided.

- Use `const void *` rather than `void *` as the type of a pointer that will address a constant value.

- Always list `void` in parentheses for functions that require no parameters. In other words, write `f(void);`, not `f()`, for the function prototype.

- Define variables only once. Use `extern` to refer to variables defined elsewhere, perhaps in another module.

- Use `new` and `delete` rather than `malloc` and `free` whenever possible. Remember, it's possible to overload the `new` and `delete` operators. The same trick is not possible with `malloc` and `free`, which are functions, not operators.

- All strings must end with `NULL` in C++. This means that definitions like `char network[3] = "ABC";` will be rejected by C++ because there isn't room in the variable for the `NULL` terminator.

Using Other C++ Compilers

If you want to convert the programs in this book for another C++ compiler, try these suggestions. Except for a few cases, most of the code should be easy to port to another environment:

- In Turbo C++, use `#include <iostream.h>` rather than `#include <stream.hpp>`.

- Programs that use Zortech's display package won't compile under other systems. To port these programs, you'll have to write your own DISP.H header and supply equivalent functions for display routines. All of these functions begin with `disp_`.

- It may be necessary under future C++ versions, even with those from Zortech, to declare `main(void)` instead of `main()`. Or you may have to use the forms `void main(void)` or `int main(void)`.

- To avoid a warning or error message, function `main` may have to include a `return 0` statement (the 0 can be another value you want to pass back to the program's caller, usually COMMAND.COM.) You can also satisfy this requirement with an `exit(0)` statement, but in that case, you'll also have to include the STDLIB.H header file.

Questions and Exercises

9.1. Suppose that you have two unrelated classes named `Engine` and `Fuel`. Using friends, how can you allow `Fuel` members to access the private and protected members in `Engine`?

9.2. List one or more disadvantages of friend classes and functions.

9.3. What does function overloading allow you to do?

9.4. What is the one kind of function that may not be overloaded?

9.5. Add times (`*`) and divide (`/`) overloaded operator functions to the `strop` class in STROPS.CPP, Listing 9.6.

9.6. Add `++` and `--` overloaded operators to the `strop` class in STROPS2.CPP, Listing 9.7. Implement the operators as member functions.

9.7. Given the declaration `strop *sp`, show how to create a reference alias named `spAlias` for an instance addressed by `sp`.

9.8. Declare and implement a `double` type-conversion operator for class `strop` in NEWOPS.CPP, Listing 9.9.

9.9. When are the four times that C++ makes a copy of a class instance? What is the primary danger of making such copies?

9.10. Given a class named `Fruit` and an instance of `Fruit` named `Orange`, write a definition that uses `Orange` to initialize a new instance named `Grapefruit`.

9.11. List the prototype for a copy constructor in the hypothetical `Fruit` class from exercise 9.10.

9.12. List an overloaded assignment operator for the `Fruit` class from exercise 9.10.

9.13. Describe the effect of assigning to `this` inside a class constructor. Why is this technique not recommended?

9.14. What is the default status of a member field in a class that does not use the `private:`, `protected:`, or `public:` key words?

9.15. What are the effects of the `public` and `private` key words when applied to a base class in a derived class's derivation list? What is the default status of the inherited class members if neither key word is used?

Chapter 10

The C++ Function Library

A rich function library is one of C++'s main attractions. This chapter documents a large subset (more than 150) of the hundreds of C++ library routines that are available and included on the disks packed with this book. For easy lookup, functions are arranged alphabetically by name, and most include a short example that shows how to use the functions in a program.

Note: Choosing a subset of commands that will suit every reader was difficult, but I tried to select those functions that: a) are practical for use with the compiler supplied with this book, b) are of general utility, and c) supplement the information in other chapters. Complete details on every library function are supplied with professional developer's compilers—including those products from Zortech, Borland, and other vendors. If you need more information than is listed in this chapter or if you need more sophisticated functions, you're probably ready to move up to a full developer's kit, which comes stocked with other tools you'll need to build complex applications.

How to Use the Reference

Each function in this reference is described in three sections.

- The *Syntax* shows the header file that you must include in your program before using the function. After that is the function's prototype. Use the prototype as a schematic of the function's design.

- The *Description* discusses how to use the function and explains what values (if any) the function returns.

- The *Example* shows the function in action. If you want to compile and run the sample statements, insert them into a `main` function in a small test program such as EXAMPLE.CPP, Listing 10.1. You don't have to include every header file as shown in EXAMPLE, but doing so ensures that every example in this chapter will compile correctly.

Listing 10.1. EXAMPLE.CPP

```
 1:  // example.cpp -- Shell for compiling examples
 2:
 3:  #include <conio.h>
 4:  #include <ctype.h>
 5:  #include <direct.h>
 6:  #include <dos.h>
 7:  #include <math.h>
 8:  #include <sound.h>
 9:  #include <stdio.h>
10:  #include <stdlib.h>
11:  #include <stream.hpp>
12:  #include <string.h>
13:  #include <time.h>
14:
15:  main()
16:  {
17:
18:  /* Insert example statements here */
19:
20:  }
```

Function names are sorted alphabetically ignoring case and underbars. The underbar is a significant character in an identifier, but sorting a list of names that include embedded underbars can produce confusing results. For example, if the underbar were significant for ordering function names in this reference, and assuming that symbols were converted to uppercase before sorting, `dos_set_crtl_break` would come between `dos_settime` and `dos_set_verify`. (The ASCII code for *T* in *TIME* is less than the ASCII code for an underbar.)

Ignoring the underbar for sorting causes `dos_set_ctrl_break` to come between `dos_get_verify` and `dos_setdate`. (The *c* in ctrl is compared to the *d* in date.) You should find this scheme easier to use than if underbars were included in the sort, as they are in some other references. When hunting for a function name, pretend any underbars don't exist.

In most cases, parameters are nameless in the function prototypes listed in .H and .HPP header files on disk. Nameless parameters are perfectly allowable in function prototypes, but they lend little clarity to the function designs. For example, in STDLIB.H, the `abs` function's prototype is

```
int    __CDECL abs(int);
```

Ignore the __C D E C L—that's one of several internal mechanisms that account for various memory models and in some cases, make possible linking C functions with C++ modules. Notice that the i n t parameter is nameless. In this chapter, that same prototype is listed like this:

```
int abs(int i);
```

The added parameter name i is arbitrary—it could be any legal identifier. In other references, you may find different parameter names for the same functions that are listed in this chapter. Traditionally, C and C++ references use such parameters as s t r i n g 1 and s t r i n g 2. In this reference, those parameters might be renamed s o u r c e and d e s t (destination), which better describe what the parameters do.

For functions that read and write disk files, the standard file names TEST.TXT and TEST.DAT are used. The examples do not check whether files of those names exist. For safety, run all file-related examples in a temporary subdirectory.

Function Reference

abs

Syntax

```
#include <stdlib.h>
int abs(int i);
```

Description

Returns an i n t's absolute value. If i equals –10, a b s (i) returns 10. The example sets j to 100.

Example

```
int i = -100;
int j = abs(i);
```

acos

Syntax

```
#include <math.h>
double acos(double x);
```

Description

Returns the arc cosine of x for $-1 <= x <= 1$.

Example

```
double f = acos(0.75);
```

asin

Syntax

```
#include <math.h>
double asin(double);
```

Description

Returns the arc sine of x for $-1 <= x <= 1$.

Example

```
double f = asin(0.75);
```

atan

Syntax

```
#include <math.h>
double atan(double);
```

Description

Returns the arc tangent of x.

Example

```
double f = atan(1);
```

atof

Syntax

```
#include <stdlib.h>
double atof(const char *s);
```

Description

Returns the double equivalent of the string addressed by s. If atof can't convert the string to a double value, the function returns 0.

Example

```
char *s = "1234.56";
double f = atof(s);
```

atoi

Syntax

```
#include <stdlib.h>
int atoi(const char *s);
```

Description

Returns the `int` equivalent of the string addressed by `s`. If `atoi` can't convert the string to an `int` value, the function returns 0.

Example

```
char *s = "1234";
int i = atoi(s);
```

atol

Syntax

```
#include <stdlib.h>
long atol(const char *s);
```

Description

Returns the `long` equivalent of the string addressed by `s`. If `atol` can't convert the string to a `long` value, the function returns 0.

Example

```
char *s = "123456789";
long l = atol(s);
```

calloc

Syntax

```
#include <stdlib.h>
void *calloc(size_t num_elems, size_t size_elem);
```

Description

Allocates and clears a memory block to all 0 bytes. Returns address of allocated memory or NULL if enough space is not available. Size of allocated memory block equals num_elems * size_elem bytes where num_elems equals the number of elements of size_elem bytes each to be stored in the block. Maximum block size is 64K bytes. Use free to dispose allocated memory. The example allocates a block of memory large enough to hold 100 values of type float. Each value is initialized to 0.

Example

```
float *fbuf;
fbuf = calloc(100, sizeof(float));
```

ceil

Syntax

```
#include <math.h>
double ceil(double x);
```

Description

Returns double value equal to the smallest integer greater or equal to x. The example sets f to 1235.

Example

```
double f = ceil(1234.56);
```

chdir

Syntax

```
#include <direct.h>
int chdir(char *path);
```

Description

Changes the current directory to the path name string addressed by p a t h. Returns 0 for success, nonzero if the path is invalid.

Example

```
char *path = "\zdemo";
if (chdir(path) != 0)
    cout << "Directory path not found";
```

chr

Syntax

```
#include <stream.hpp>
char *chr(int c, int columns = 0);
```

Description

Characters in C++ may be represented as type i n t, a typical method used in C programs. However, such characters will be displayed by output-stream statements as ASCII values, not as symbols. Use c h r to display integer values as equivalent ASCII characters. The function returns a character equal to the ASCII value c. The second parameter is optional. For this parameter, specify the positive number of columns in which to right justify the output.

Example

```
int c = 'A';
cout << "\nCharacter    == " << c;
cout << "\nASCII symbol == " << chr(c);
```

clearerr

Syntax

```
#include <stdio.h>
void clearerr(FILE *fp);
```

Description

Call clearerr after detecting and handling an error from a file function, for example, fwrite. Errors that occur during that and other file functions prevent future I/O until the program calls clearerr. Also clears the end-of-file flag for file fp.

Example

```
FILE *fp;
fp = fopen("myinfo.txt", "r");
fprintf(fp, "New information\n"); // ???
if (ferror(fp)) {
    cout << "\nFile error!";
    clearerr(fp);
    fclose(fp);
    exit(1);
}
```

cos

Syntax

```
#include <math.h>
double cos(double x);
```

Description

Returns the cosine of x radians.

Example

```
int angle = 45;
double c = cos((angle * 3.14159) / 180.0);
```

dec

Syntax

```
#include <stream.hpp>
char *dec(long n, int columns = 0);
```

Description

Returns a pointer to a string representation of long value n. The second parameter is optional. For this parameter, specify the positive number of columns in which to right justify n. Even if n is 0 or is too small to display all of n, the value will still be formatted correctly. Usually, you'll use dec output-stream statements to display integer values in decimal format.

Example

```
long number = 123456789;
cout << "Number == " << dec(number, 40);
cout << "\nNumber == " << dec(number);
```

disp_box

Syntax

```
#include <disp.h>
void disp_box(int type, int attr, unsigned trow,
    unsigned lcol, unsigned brow, unsigned rcol);
```

Description

Draws an outlined box on text screens. Parameter t y p e determines the border style—0 for double lines, 1 for single, 2 for solid, 3 for double horizontal and single vertical, 4 for double vertical and single horizontal. Parameter a t t r equals the attribute to use for the border color. The four u n s i g n e d parameters represent the top row (t r o w), left column (l c o l), bottom row (b r o w), and right column (r c o l) display coordinates for the border's upper left and lower right corners.

Example

```
disp_open();
disp_box(3, DISP_NORMAL, 10, 20, 18, 60);
disp_close();
```

disp_close

Syntax

```
#include <disp.h>
void disp_close(void);
```

Description

Call after you're done using other display-package routines, all of which begin with disp_. Restores cursor and video mode to their original settings before initializing the display package with disp_open.

Example

(See disp_box.)

disp_eeol

Syntax

```
#include <disp.h>
void disp_eeol(void);
```

Description

Erase display from the logical cursor to end of line, using the attribute set by disp_setattr. Use disp_move to position the logical cursor. Use disp_flush to make the logical and physical cursors match.

Example

```
disp_open();
disp_move(0, 0);
disp_puts("Your name? ");
disp_eeol();
//...
disp_close();
```

disp_eeop

Syntax

```
#include <disp.h>
void disp_eeop(void);
```

Description

Erase display from the logical cursor to the end of the page (that is, the screen), using the attribute set by disp_setattr. Use disp_move to position the logical cursor. The example clears the display.

Example

```
disp_open();
disp_move(0, 0);
disp_eeop();
disp_close();
```

disp_endstand

Syntax

```
#include <disp.h>
void disp_endstand(void);
```

Description

End stand-out (reverse video) display. Use only after calling disp_startstand.

Example

(See disp_startstand.)

disp_ fillbox

Syntax

```
#include <disp.h>
void disp_fillbox(unsigned attrchar, unsigned trow,
    unsigned lcol, unsigned brow, unsigned rcol);
```

Description

Fills a rectangular area on a text screen. Specify the top left corner of the rectangle in trow and lcol. Specify the bottom right corner in brow and rcol. The area is colored with the attribute and character in the unsigned attrchar value. The example shows how to assemble this value.

Example

```
unsigned char attribute = 0x1f;
char c = ' ';
unsigned attrchar = (attribute * 256) + c;
disp_open();
disp_fillbox(attrchar, 10, 20, 18, 60);
disp_close();
```

disp_ flush

Syntax

```
#include <disp.h>
void disp_flush(void);
```

Description

Positions the physical cursor to the logical display-package cursor's location. Use disp_move to position the logical cursor, then call disp_flush to show the physical cursor there.

Example

```
char buf[129];
disp_open();
disp_move(10, 20);
disp_eeol();
disp_puts("Your name? ");
disp_flush();
gets(buf);
disp_close();
```

disp_hidecursor

Syntax

```
#include <disp.h>
void disp_hidecursor(void);
```

Description

Call hidecursor to make the physical cursor invisible. Call showcursor to make the cursor visible again. If you call hidecursor more than once, you must call showcursor an equal number of times before the cursor will become visible.

Example

```
disp_open();
disp_hidecursor();
//...
disp_close();
```

disp_move

Syntax

```
#include <disp.h>
void disp_move(int row, int col);
```

Description

Moves the logical cursor to the specified row and column. All display-package output routines will begin at this new location. Coordinate (0, 0) is the upper left corner of the display. Call disp_flush after disp_move to show the physical cursor at the logical cursor's position.

Example

(See disp_flush.)

disp_open

Syntax

```
#include <disp.h>
void disp_open(void);
```

Description

Initializes the Zortech display package—a set of routines for displaying text on PCs and compatible systems. All routines in the package begin with disp_. The functions are optimized for speed and write directly to video RAM for quick displays. You must call disp_open before using most display-package functions (exceptions are noted in the descriptions for individual functions). Call disp_close() to restore the original display's mode and cursor.

Example

```
disp_open();
// other disp_ function calls
disp_close();
```

disp_peekbox

Syntax

```
#include <disp.h>
void disp_peekbox(unsigned *buffer, unsigned trow,
    unsigned lcol, unsigned brow, unsigned rcol);
```

Description

Transfers contents of a rectangular area on the text display to the address specified by buffer. The rectangle's top left corner is represented by trow and lcol. The lower right corner is represented by brow and rcol. The buffer must be large enough to hold the characters *and* attributes from the display. See the example for details on how to allocate adequate buffer space on the heap. Use disp_pokebox to redisplay a saved area, for example, when a window is closed.

Example

```
#define TROW 10
#define LCOL 20
#define BROW 18
#define RCOL 60
#define SIZE ((BROW - TROW + 1) * (RCOL - LCOL + 1)) * sizeof(unsigned)
unsigned *buffer = new unsigned[BUFSIZE];
if (buffer == NULL) exit(1);
disp_open();
disp_peekbox(buffer, TROW, LCOL, BROW, RCOL);
disp_move(0, 0);
disp_eeop();
disp_pokebox(buffer, TROW, LCOL, BROW, RCOL);
disp_close();
```

disp_pokebox

Syntax

```
#include <disp.h>
void disp_pokebox(unsigned *buffer, unsigned trow,
    unsigned lcol, unsigned brow, unsigned rcol);
```

Description

Redisplays a rectangular area of text and attributes previously saved by
disp_peekbox. The parameters have the same meanings in both functions.

Example

(See disp_peekbox.)

disp_printf

Syntax

```
#include <disp.h>
void disp_printf(char *format, ...);
```

Description

Displays a formatted string at the logical cursor position. Use disp_move to move
the logical cursor. Function disp_printf is one of several similar formatting
functions available in the library. See form and printf for more information.

Example

```
disp_open();
disp_move(0, 0);
```

```
disp_eeop();
int v = 123;
float f = 3.14159;
disp_move(10, 0);
disp_printf("v==%d, f==%f", v, f);
disp_move(24, 0);
disp_close();
```

disp_putc

Syntax

```
#include <disp.h>
void disp_putc(int c);
```

Description

Displays at the logical cursor's location a character represented by the ASCII value of c. After disp_putc, the logical cursor is positioned to the right of the displayed character.

Example

```
disp_open();
disp_move(0, 0);
disp_eeop();
disp_move(10, 0);
for (int c = 'A'; c <= 'Z'; c++) {
    disp_putc(c);
    disp_putc(' ');
}
disp_move(24, 0);
disp_close();
```

disp_puts

Syntax

```
#include <disp.h>
void disp_puts(const char *s);
```

Description

Displays at the logical cursor's location a string addressed by s. After disp_puts, the logical cursor is positioned to the right of the last character in the string.

Example

```
disp_open();
disp_move(0, 0);
disp_eeop();
disp_move(10, 0);
disp_puts("  ==  Learning C++  ==");
disp_move(24, 0);
disp_close();
```

disp_reset43

Syntax

```
#include <disp.h>
void disp_reset43(void);
```

Description

After calling disp_set43 to enable 43- or 50-line mode for EGA and VGA displays, call disp_reset43 to restore the original screen to 25 lines.

Example

(See disp_set43.)

disp_scroll

Syntax

```
#include <disp.h>
void disp_scroll(int lines, unsigned trow, unsigned lcol,
    unsigned brow, unsigned rcol, unsigned attr);
```

Description

Scrolls a rectangular area on the text screen. Parameter lines represents the number of lines to scroll. If lines is positive, text scrolls up. If lines is negative, text scrolls down. The rectangle's top left corner is represented by trow and lcol. The lower right corner is represented by brow and rcol. The attr is the attribute to use for blanking lines at the top or bottom of the scrolled-away area. The example slowly scrolls the entire display, painting blanked lines blue (visible only on color displays, of course). Note: Some early PC BIOS chips have a bug that causes display problems when scrolling one-row-high areas. For that reason, it's best never to call disp_scroll when trow == brow.

Example

```
disp_open();
for (int i = 0; i <= 24; i++) {
    msleep(100);
    disp_scroll(1, 0, 0, 24, 79, 0x1f);
}
disp_close();
```

disp_set43

Syntax

```
#include <disp.h>
void disp_set43(void);
```

Description

Call `disp_set43` on EGA and VGA displays to enable 43- or 50-line modes. Call `disp_reset43` to restore the original 25-line display. Unlike most display-package routines, never call `disp_set43` after initializing the display with `disp_open`. Always call `disp_set43` before calling `disp_open`.

Example

```
disp_set43();
disp_open();
for (int j = 0; j < 8; j++) {
   disp_move(j * 2, 0);
   for (int c = '0'; c <= ']'; c++)
      disp_putc(c);
}
disp_move(40, 0);
disp_puts("Press a key to continue");
while (!kbhit()) ;
disp_reset43();
disp_close();
```

disp_setattr

Syntax

```
#include <disp.h>
void disp_setattr(int attr);
```

Description

Changes the display attribute used by display-package output routines `disp_putc`, `disp_puts`, `disp_eeop`, and `disp_eeol`. The integer `attr` holds the background color in the upper four bits and the foreground color in the lower four bits. Table 10.1 lists background and foreground colors for PCs and compatibles.

Table 10.1. Background and Foreground Colors

Color	Value	Color	Value
Black	0	Red	4
Blue	1	Magenta	5
Green	2	Brown	6
Cyan	3	White	7

You may also pass to disp_setattr these constants defined in DISP.H: `DISP_REVERSEVIDEO`, `DISP_NORMAL`, `DISP_UNDERLINE`, `DISP_NONDISPLAY`. Experiment with these values—they may have varying effects on different types of displays. To any value passed to disp_setattr, you may also combine the constants `DISP_INTENSITY` and `DISP_BLINK` with a logical OR. For example, insert this line after the first in the example: `color |= DISP_INTENSITY;`.

Example

```
int color = 0x10;      // black on blue
disp_open();
disp_move(0, 0);
disp_eeop();
disp_move(10, 0);
for (int c = 'A'; c <= 'P'; c++) {
   disp_setattr(color++);
   disp_putc(c);
}
disp_move(24, 0);
disp_close();
```

disp_showcursor

Syntax

```
#include <disp.h>
void disp_showcursor(void);
```

Description

After hiding the cursor with disp_hidecursor, call disp_showcursor to make the cursor visible. If you call disp_hidecursor more than once, you must call disp_showcursor an equal number of times before the cursor will become visible.

Example

(See disp_hidecursor.)

disp_startstand

Syntax

```
#include <display.h>
void disp_startstand(void);
```

Description

Enable stand-out (reversed) video for display-package output routines disp_putc and disp_puts. To return to normal display mode, call disp_endstand.

Example

```
disp_open();
disp_move(0, 0);
```

```
disp_eeop();
disp_move(8, 0);
disp_startstand();
disp_puts("Reversed video");
disp_move(12, 0);
disp_endstand();
disp_puts("Normal video");
disp_move(24, 0);
disp_close();
```

dos_get_ctrl_break

Syntax

```
#include <dos.h>
int dos_get_ctrl_break(void);
```

Description

Returns 0 if <Ctrl>-<Break> checking is off during DOS I/O. Returns nonzero if <Ctrl>-<Break> checking is on. Use dos_set_ctrl_break to change the state of the flag. When <Ctrl>-<Break> checking is on, pressing those keys during I/O will halt the current program.

Example

```
cout << "\n<Ctrl>-<Break> checking is ";
if (dos_get_ctrl_break())
    cout << "ON\n";
else
    cout << "OFF\n";
```

dos_getdate

Syntax

```
#include <dos.h>
int dos_getdate(struct dos_date_t *date);
```

Description

Stores the current date in `date`. (Note: Though prototyped to return `int`, `dos_getdate` returns no useful function value. Probably, the `int` should be `void`, a minor mistake that does no harm because you can simply ignore the function result.) The `dos_date_t` structure is documented in DOS.H and repeated here for reference:

```
struct dos_date_t
{
    char day;        // 1-31
    char month;      // 1 (Jan) to 12 (Dec)
    int  year;       // 1980-2099
    char dayofweek;  // 0 (Sun) to 6 (Sat)
};
```

Example

```
dos_date_t today;
dos_getdate(&today);
printf("Today is %02d-%02d-%d", today.month,
today.day, today.year);
```

dos_getdiskfreespace

Syntax

```
#include <dos.h>
long dos_getdiskfreespace(int drive);
```

Description

Returns amount of free space on a disk drive. Set parameter `drive` to 0 for the current drive; 1 for A:, 2 for B:, and so on. Note: The function does not work correctly with large DOS partitions greater than about 32 megabytes.

Example

```
long free = dos_getdiskfreespace(0);
cout << "Free space == " << free << " bytes";
```

dos_getdrive

Syntax

```
#include <dos.h>
void dos_getdrive(unsigned *driveP);
```

Description

Sets an `unsigned` variable addressed by pointer `driveP` to a value that represents the current drive letter where 1 stands for drive A:, 2 for B:, 3 for hC:, and so on. A common mistake is to pass a variable directly to `dos_getdrive`. That will not work. You must pass the address of an `unsigned` variable, as in the example.

Example

```
unsigned drive;
dos_getdrive(&drive);
printf("Logged onto drive %c:", 'A' + drive - 1);
```

dos_getfileattr

Syntax

```
#include <dos.h>
int dos_getfileattr(char *path, unsigned *attr);
```

Description

Stores attributes in an unsigned value addressed by attr for a file located by the path name string addressed by path. Use logical operators and DOS.H constants FA_RDONLY, FA_HIDDEN, FA_SYSTEM, and FA_ARCH to extract bits from the attribute value. Function returns an error code if the requested file can't be found or 0 for no errors.

Example

```
char path[129];
unsigned attributes;
cout << "Enter file name: ";
gets(path);
if (dos_getfileattr(path, &attributes) == 0) {
   cout << "Attribute bit is ";
   if (!(attributes & FA_ARCH)) cout << "NOT ";
   cout << "set for that file";
} else
   cout << "File not found";
```

dos_gettime

Syntax

```
#include <DOS.h>
int dos_gettime(struct dos_time_t *time);
```

Description

Stores the current time in `time`. (Note: Though prototyped to return `int`, `dos_gettime` returns no useful function value. Probably, the `int` should be `void`, a minor mistake that does no harm because you can simply ignore the function result.) The `dos_time_t` structure is documented in DOS.H and repeated here for reference:

```
struct dos_time_t
{
    char hour;      // 0-23
    char minute;    // 0-59
    char second;    // 0-59
    char hsecond;   // 0-99
};
```

Example

```
dos_time_t now;
dos_gettime(&now);
printf("The time is now %2d:%02d:%02d:%02d",
    now.hour, now.minute, now.second, now.hsecond);
```

dos_get_verify

Syntax

```
#include <dos.h>
int dos_get_verify(void);
```

Description

Returns 0 if the DOS VERIFY switch is off for disk writes. Returns nonzero if the switch is on. Use `dos_set_verify` to change the state of the flag. When VERIFY is on, disk writes are followed by automatic disk reads to ensure that no errors occurred. However, bytes read from disk are *not* compared with bytes written; therefore, the usefulness of the VERIFY switch is limited.

Example

```
cout << "\nDisk verification is ";
if (dos_get_verify())
    cout << "ON\n";
else
    cout << "OFF\n";
```

dos_set_ctrl_break

Syntax

```
#include <dos.h>
void dos_set_ctrl_break(int flag);
```

Description

Sets DOS's <Ctrl>-<Break> switch to on if f l a g is 1 (or any nonzero value) or to off if f l a g is 0. The example toggles the current setting on or off. Use the DOS BREAK command to view the setting. (See also dos_get_ctrl_break.)

Example

```
dos_set_ctrl_break(!dos_get_ctrl_break());
```

dos_setdate

Syntax

```
#include <dos.h>
int dos_setdate(struct dos_date_t *date);
```

Description

Changes the current date to the values in a `dos_date_t` structure addressed by parameter `date`. See `dos_get_date` and the DOS.H header file for the format of this structure. The example sets the date to the first of the same month in next year. If you run the code, be sure to reset the current date with the DATE command.

Example

```
dos_date_t today;
dos_getdate(&today);
today.day = 1;
today.year++;
dos_setdate(&today);
```

dos_setdrive

Syntax

```
#include <dos.h>
void dos_setdrive(unsigned drive, unsigned *num_drives);
```

Description

Changes the current drive. Set `drive` to 1 for A:, 2 for B:, 3 for C:, and so on. To keep the same current drive, set `drive` to 0. The second parameter, which must be passed by address, is filled with a value representing the last possible drive letter for this system. On systems with a single floppy, `num_drives` will equal 2 because DOS treats single-floppy systems as having two logical drives A: and B:. The value returned by `num_drives` may not match the actual number of disk drives available, but rather the value assigned to LASTDRIVE in CONFIG.SYS.

Example

```
unsigned num_drives;
dos_setdrive(0, &num_drives);
```

```
cout << "\nLast possible drive letter is ";
cout << chr('A' + num_drives - 1) << ":\n";
```

dos_setfileattr

Syntax

```
#include <dos.h>
int dos_setfileattr(char *path, unsigned attr);
```

Description

Changes a file's attributes to the bits in a t t r. The p a t h parameter should address a string in the form " \ \ d i r e c t o r y \ \ f i l e ". The function returns an error code if the requested file can't be found or 0 for no errors. The example resets the archive bit for a specified file. On DOS systems with the ATTRIB command, this is equivalent to the command *ATTRIB -a filename*.

Example

```
char path[129];
unsigned attributes;
cout << "Enter file name: ";
gets(path);
if (dos_getfileattr(path, &attributes) != 0) {
    cout << "File not found";
    exit(1);
}
attributes &= ~FA_ARCH;
if (dos_setfileattr(path, attributes) == 0)
    cout << "File attribute bit reset";
else
    cout << "Error resetting attribute bit";
```

dos_settime

Syntax

```
#include <dos.h>
int dos_settime(struct dos_time_t *time);
```

Description

Changes the current time to the values in a `dos_time_t` structure addressed by parameter `time`. See `dos_get_time` and the DOS.H header file for the format of this structure. The example sets the time back one hour. You might run the code in the Spring if daylight savings is in effect in your area.

Example

```
dos_time_t time;
dos_gettime(&time);
time.hour--;
dos_settime(&time);
```

dos_set_verify

Syntax

```
#include <dos.h>
void dos_set_verify(int flag);
```

Description

Sets DOS's VERIFY switch to on if `flag` is 1 (or any nonzero value) or to off if `flag` is 0. The example toggles the current setting on or off. Use the DOS VERIFY command to view the setting. (See also `dos_get_verify`.)

Example

```
dos_set_verify(!dos_get_verify());
```

exit

Syntax

```
#include <stdlib.h>
void exit(int exitstatus);
```

Description

Exits the current program immediately, flushing output buffers, and closing all open files. Passes exitstatus to DOS. Detect this value in a batch file with the ERRORLEVEL command. Pass 0 for no errors; nonzero to indicate a problem. The interpretation of exitstatus is up to you. Note: It's a good idea to end main with exit(0). Otherwise, an unpredictable value will be passed back to DOS.

Example

```
int errorCode;
// ...
errorCode = 12; // Simulate error condition
if (errorCode != 0) {
    cout << "\nERROR: #" << errorCode;
    exit(errorCode);
}
// ...
exit(0);   // no error
```

exp

Syntax

```
#include <math.h>
double exp(double x);
```

Description

Returns the natural exponent of x. Note: The example uses the P I constant defined in MATH.H.

Example

```
double f = exp(PI);
cout << f;
```

fabs

Syntax

```
#include <math.h>
double fabs(double x);
```

Description

Returns the absolute value of x. The example sets f to 1234.56.

Example

```
double f = -1234.56;
f = fabs(f);
cout << f;
```

fclose

Syntax

```
#include <stdio.h>
int fclose(FILE *fp);
```

Description

Close file addressed by fp. The file should have been opened by calling fopen. Closing a file opened for writing or appending flushes any buffered data from memory to disk. If the function is successful, it returns 0. If unsuccessful, it returns –1.

Example

(See fopen.)

fcloseall

Syntax

```
#include <stdio.h>
int fcloseall(void);
```

Description

Closes all open files. Returns the number of files successfully closed.

Example

```
int numOpenFiles = 0;  // Increment for each file opened
//...
if (condition) {
```

```
        cout << "\nClosing all files...";
        if (fcloseall() != numOpenFiles)
            error();
        else
            exit(0);
}
```

feof

Syntax

```
#include <stdio.h>
int feof(FILE *fp);
```

Description

Returns true (nonzero) if the open file addressed by f p is positioned at the end of the file's contents. Returns false (0) if the file is not at the end. Reading information from a file when f e o f returns true is an error. The example reads and displays an ASCII text file named TEST.TXT.

Example

```
FILE *fp;
fp = fopen("test.txt", "r");
if (fp != NULL)
    while (!feof(fp)) putchar(fgetc(fp));
fclose(fp);
```

ferror

Syntax

```
#include <stdio.h>
int ferror(FILE *fp);
```

Description

Call ferror following any file operation to check the status of that operation. The function returns false (0) if the file operation failed or true (nonzero) if the operation succeeded. The example uses ferror to detect whether fopen successfully opened a file named XYZ.$$$. If that file does not exist, the program displays "Can't open file."

Example

```
FILE *fp;
fp = fopen("xyz.$$$", "r");
if (ferror(fp))
    cout << "Can't open file";
```

fflush

Syntax

```
#include <stdio.h>
int fflush(FILE *fp);
```

Description

Flushes the buffer for a file addressed by fp. Clears the buffer for files opened for reading. Writes buffered data to disk for files opened for writing or appending. In a program that writes information to disk, it's a good idea to call fflush for all open files at times when the program will pause, perhaps before entering a loop that waits for a user command. That way, any information held temporarily in memory will be transferred to disk, minimizing data loss if the power should fail.

Example

```
FILE *fp;
fp = fopen("test.txt","a");
//...
```

```
fflush(fp);  // Flush fp's data to disk
//...
fclose(fp);
```

fgetc

Syntax

```
#include <stdio.h>
int fgetc(FILE *fp);
```

Description

Returns the next character from a file addressed by f p. The file must have been opened in text mode (see f o p e n). It is an error to call f g e t c if f e o f returns true for the file. The f g e t c function returns a value from 0 to 255 and can therefore read extended ASCII characters and control codes stored in a text file.

Example

(See f e o f.)

fgets

Syntax

```
#include <stdio.h>
char *fgets(char *string, int n, FILE *fp);
```

Description

Use f g e t s to read strings from a text file. The strings should be delimited with new-line characters (carriage return and line feed control codes for MS-DOS systems). The first parameter should address a buffer large enough to hold at least n characters, as specified by the second parameter. No more than n characters will be transferred from the file to the buffer. Any control codes, including carriage returns and line feeds, are also copied to the string buffer, which will be terminated with a null (ASCII 0). The file f p must have been opened for reading in text mode (see f open).

Check the function result after calling f g e t s. If the function returns NULL, either no characters were transferred to the string buffer or a disk error occurred. (Use ferror to differentiate between these conditions.) In the event of trouble, the string buffer may have no characters or it may contain invalid information. The example program uses f g e t s to display line numbers for the lines in a text file named TEST.TXT.

Example

```
#define LINELEN 132
FILE *fp;
char line[LINELEN];
char *errorFlag;
int lineNumber = 0;
fp = fopen("test.txt", "r");
if (fp != NULL) {
   while (!feof(fp)) {
      errorFlag = fgets(line, LINELEN, fp);
      if ((errorFlag == NULL) && (ferror(fp))) {
         cout << "\nError reading file";
         exit(1);
      }
      cout << dec(lineNumber++, 4) << ": " << line;
   }
}
```

filesize

Syntax

```
#include <stdio.h>
long filesize(char *path);
```

Description

Returns the size in bytes of a file identified by the path name string addressed by path. The file should not be open.

Example

```
char path[129];
unsigned attributes;
cout << "Enter file name: ";
gets(path);
long size = filesize(path);
if (size < 0)
   cout << "File not found";
else
   cout << "File size = " << size << " bytes";
```

findfirst

Syntax

```
#include <dos.h>
struct FIND *findfirst(char *path, int attribute);
```

Description

Call findfirst to begin a search for file names in a directory. The path parameter should address a path name string, which may contain wild cards. The attribute lists the types of files to locate. Table 10.2 lists the attribute values you can insert into an attribute argument with logical OR expressions. Set attribute equal to FA_DIREC to locate all files *and* directory names. Set the argument equal to FA_NORMAL to find files but *not* directories.

Table 10.2. Attributes for findfirst

Symbol	Value
FA_NORMAL	0x00
FA_RDONLY	0x01
FA_HIDDEN	0x02
FA_SYSTEM	0x04
FA_LABEL	0x08
FA_DIREC	0x10
FA_ARCH	0x20

If findfirst returns NULL, no matching files were found; otherwise the function returns the address of a FIND structure. (See the DOS.H header file for the structure's format.) If findfirst does not return NULL, you may call findnext to locate additional matches. The example displays the names of read-only, hidden, and system files in the current directory.

Example

```
struct FIND *fp;
char wildCard[13] = "*.*";
char attribute = FA_RDONLY | FA_HIDDEN | FA_SYSTEM;
fp = findfirst(wildCard, attribute);
while (fp) {
   if ((fp->attribute & attribute) != 0)
      cout << fp->name << '\n';
   fp = findnext();
}
```

findnext

Syntax

```
#include <dos.h>
struct FIND *findnext(void);
```

Description

Call `findnext` to continue a directory search started with `findfirst`. If subsequent matching file entries are found, `findnext` returns a pointer to a filled-in `FIND` structure. (See DOS.H for the format of that structure.) If no additional matching files are found, `findnext` returns `NULL`.

Example

(See `findfirst`.)

floor

Syntax

```
#include <math.h>
double floor(double x);
```

Description

Returns `double` value equal to the largest integer less than or equal to x. The example sets f to 1234.

Example

```
double f = floor(1234.56);
```

flushall

Syntax

```
#include <stdio.h>
int flushall(void);
```

Description

Flushes all file buffers. Clears buffers for files opened for reading. Transfers buffered data to disk for files opened for writing or appending. Returns the number of buffers flushed. You can use `flushall` to determine how many files are currently open, including the five standard files (`stdin`, `stdout`, `stderr`, `stdaux`, `stdprn`) defined in STDIO.H and opened for all programs.

Example

```
int n = flushall();
cout << n << " file buffers flushed";
```

fmod

Syntax

```
#include <math.h>
double fmod(double x, double y);
```

Description

Returns a `double` value equal to x modulo y for nonzero values of y. The result f satisfies the formula `x == (k * y) + f` where k is an integer value equal to the ceiling of (`x / y`) if the result of that division is negative or to the floor of (`x / y`) if the result of the division is positive or zero. The sample code lets you enter test values for x and y. For example, enter –5 3. The program displays `fmod (x, y)` then recalculates x, which for very large or small quantities of x and y, may only approximate the original x value.

Example

```
double d, k, x, y, f;
cout << "x y? ";
cin >> x >> y;
if (y == 0) exit(1);
f = fmod(x, y);
```

```
cout << "fmod(x, y) == " << f;
d = (x / y);
if (d < 0)
    k = ceil(d);
else
    k = floor(d);
cout << "\noriginal value of x == " << (k * y) + f;
```

fopen

Syntax

```
#include <stdio.h>
FILE *fopen(const char *path, const char *mode);
```

Description

Opens or creates a file for reading, writing, or appending. The first parameter should address a path name string, which may not contain any wild card characters. The second parameter should address a one-, two-, or three-character string that specifies the file's access mode if successfully opened. Table 10.3 lists all possible mode values. After opening a file for a text mode, use functions fgetc, fgets, fputc, and fputs to read and write characters in the file. After opening a file for a binary mode, use fread and fwrite. Use fseek to position the file for a subsequent read or write operation. Always close files by calling fclose when you're done reading and writing.

Table 10.3. File-Access Modes for fopen

Mode	Function
"r"	Open existing text file for reading
"w"	Create or overwrite new text file for writing
"a"	Create or append to text file for writing
"r+"	Open existing text file for reading and writing
"w+"	Create or overwrite new text file for reading and writing
"a+"	Create or append to text file for reading and writing
"rb"	Open existing binary file for reading
"wb"	Create or overwrite new binary file for writing
"ab"	Create or append to binary file for writing

continued

Table 10.3. Continued

Mode	Function
`"rb+"`	Open existing binary file for reading and writing
`"wb+"`	Create or overwrite new binary file for reading and writing
`"ab+"`	Create or append to binary file for reading and writing

The `fopen` function returns a pointer to a `FILE` structure. Be sure to save this pointer—you'll need it for other file operations. If `fopen` returns `NULL`, the function could not open the file as requested.

Example

```
FILE *fp;
fp = fopen("test.txt", "r");
if (fp != NULL)
    while (!feof(fp)) putchar(fgetc(fp));
fclose(fp);
```

form

Syntax

```
#include <stream.hpp>
char *form(const char *format, ...);
```

Description

Returns a pointer to a formatted string. The string addressed by `format` (usually it's a literal string) may contain formatting commands prefaced with a percent sign (%) for inserting various values listed after the `format` parameter. Usually, you'll use `form` in output-stream statements as demonstrated in the example, but you can use the function for other purposes, too. Be aware that the string addressed by the function result is temporary. *Never* write any characters to this string, and don't expect it to retain its value. If you need to keep the string that `form` creates, use `strdup` or another string function to copy the string's characters to a more permanent buffer.

The f o r m function is one of several similar formatting functions available in the library. See p r i n t f for more information.

Example

```
double r = 3.14159;
long n = 987654321;
cout << form("r == %f, and n == %ld", r, n);
```

fprintf

Syntax

```
#include <stdio.h>
int fprintf(FILE *fp, const char *format, ...);
```

Description

Writes a formatted string to the text file addressed by f p. That file should have been opened by f o p e n for writing or appending. The f o r m a t parameter should address a string with embedded formatting commands prefaced with percent signs (%). Usually the string is literal. The f p r i n t f function returns the number of characters written to the file, or –1 if an error is detected. Function f p r i n t f is one of several similar formatting functions available in the library. See f o r m and p r i n t f for more information.

Example

```
double r = 3.14159;
long n = 987654321;
int numOut;
FILE *fp;
fp = fopen("test.txt", "a");
if (fp != NULL) {
    numOut = fprintf(fp, "\nr == %f, and n == %ld\n", r, n);
    cout << numOut << " characters written to TEST.TXT";
    fclose(fp);
}
```

fputc

Syntax

```
#include <stdio.h>
int fputc(int c, FILE *fp);
```

Description

Writes a character to a file addressed by f p. The file should have been opened by calling f o p e n for writing or appending in text mode. The function returns the same character written to disk, or if an error occurs, the function returns E O F. The example appends the alphabet to a text file named TEST.TXT.

Example

```
FILE *fp;
fp = fopen("test.txt", "a");
for (int c = 'A'; c <= 'Z'; c++)
   if (fputc(c, fp) != c) {
      cout << "ERROR writing to file";
      exit(1);
}
fputc('\n', fp);
fclose(fp);
```

fputs

Syntax

```
#include <stdio.h>
int fputs(const char *string, FILE *fp);
```

Description

Writes the string addressed by s t r i n g to the file addressed by f p. The file should have been opened by calling f o p e n for writing or appending in text mode. The function returns a nonzero value if no errors were detected; otherwise the function returns E O F.

Example

```
FILE *fp;
fp = fopen("test.txt", "a");
int result = fputs("0123456789\n", fp);
if (result == EOF)
    cout << "ERROR writing to file";
else
    cout << "String written to file";
fclose(fp);
```

fread

Syntax

```
#include <stdio.h>
size_t fread(void *p, size_t size_elem, size_t n, FILE *fp);
```

Description

Call f r e a d to read n elements of s i z e _ e l e m bytes each from a file addressed by f p. The file should have been opened by calling f o p e n for reading in binary mode. Information read from disk is transferred to memory at the address specified by pointer p, which may address a buffer of any data type, a variable, an array, or other structure.

It's your responsibility to ensure that the buffer addressed by p can hold at least s i z e _ e l e m * n bytes. The function returns the number of *elements* (not bytes) that it read from disk. If this number is less than n, the file at the current position either did not contain the requested number of elements or a disk read error occurred.

The example creates a file TEST.DAT with integers from 0 to 9 stored in an array named source, calls fseek to position the file to its beginning, then uses fread to read the integer values from disk into an array named copy. The values are then displayed.

Example

```
int source[10];
int copy[10];
FILE *fp;
for (int i = 0; i < 10; i++)
    source[i] = i;
fp = fopen("test.dat", "w+");
i = fwrite(&source, sizeof(int), 10, fp);
cout << i << " elements written to disk\n";
fseek(fp, 0, SEEK_SET);
i = fread(&copy, sizeof(int), 10, fp);
cout << i << " elements read from disk\n";
for (i = 0; i < 10; i++)
    cout << dec(copy[i], 2);
fclose(fp);
```

free

Syntax

```
#include <stdlib.h>
void free(void *p);
```

Description

After allocating space with calloc or malloc, you can return that space to the heap by calling free. Pass the pointer returned by a memory-allocation function to free. The memory addressed by the pointer will then be available for new allocations. *Never* use memory disposed by free. And *never* dispose of the same memory more than once. Such errors are almost always serious and may corrupt the heap. If free detects this condition, it will halt the program.

Note: For allocating heap space, you may want to use the C++ operators new and delete described elsewhere in this book. See the index for page numbers.

Example

```
char *buffer;
buffer = malloc(1024);
if (buffer != NULL)
    cout << "1024 bytes allocated";
// .. use buffer here
if (buffer) free(buffer);
```

fscanf

Syntax

```
#include <stdio.h>
int fscanf(FILE *fp, const char *format, ...);
```

Description

Call f s c a n f to read formatted information from a file addressed by f p into variables formatted according to commands embedded in the string addressed by f o r m a t. Usually, this string is literal. The file should have been opened by f o p e n for reading in text mode. The function returns the number of elements (not bytes) transferred from disk to memory. If f s c a n f returns E O F, either the end of file was reached unexpectedly or a disk read error occurred. Function f s c a n f is one of two similar routines in the library. See s c a n f for more information.

Example

```
FILE *fp;
float f;
char s[80];
int d;
cout << "\nCreating TEST.DAT";
fp = fopen("test.dat", "w");
if (fp != NULL) {
    fputs("12345.678 This-is-a-string -100\n", fp);
    fclose(fp);
}
```

```
   cout << "\nReading TEST.DAT\n";
   fp = fopen("test.dat", "r");
   if (fp != NULL) {
      int n = fscanf(fp, "%f %s %d", &f, s, &d);
      cout << n << " items read\n";
    cout << form("f == %f, s == %s, d == %d\n", f, s, d);
   }
```

fseek

Syntax

```
#include <stdio.h>
int fseek(FILE *fp, long offset, int origin);
```

Description

A file's position is the location in the file where the next read or write operation will take place. That position is marked by an internal value called the *file pointer*. Call fseek to change the file pointer to a new location in the file. Pass a FILE fp returned by fopen. Specify an offset equal to the number of bytes relative to origin to move the file pointer. The origin may be one of three values defined in STDIO.H and listed in Table 10.4.

Table 10.4. Values for fseek

Symbol	Value	Offset Relative To
SEEK_SET	0	Beginning of the file
SEEK_CUR	1	The current file pointer
SEEK_END	2	The end of the file

For example, to reset the file to its beginning, execute fseek(fp, 0L, SEEK_SET). To move a file back 10 bytes from the current position, execute fseek(fp, -10L, SEEK_CUR). To position a file to the last record in a file, if that record is of type rec, execute fseek(fp, -sizeof(rec), SEEK_END).

You'll normally use fseek to locate a specific record's location. The function returns 0 for success or nonzero if an error was detected. After fseek, you may read or write data to the file at the new position—that is, if the file was opened with an appropriate access mode.

You may use f s e e k on text files, but in that case, a nonzero o f f s e t value *must* come from function f t e l l and o r i g i n *must* be SEEK_SET. However, you may specify an o f f s e t of 0 and any of the three o r i g i n values in Table 10.4.

Example

(See f r e a d.)

ftell

Syntax

```
#include <stdio.h>
long ftell(FILE *fp);
```

Description

Returns the current file pointer position in a file addressed by f p as returned by f o p e n. For files opened in binary modes, you may use f t e l l as the byte offset to the current position. For files opened in text mode, use f t e l l only in conjunction with f s e e k to reposition the file pointer. For text files, f t e l l's result does not necessarily equal the byte offset to the file pointer and using the function result that way may corrupt the file. The example reads and displays every line in a text file twice. (There are, of course, easier ways to do this! But the example demonstrates how to use f t e l l to back up to a string that was just read by f g e t s.)

Example

```
#define MAX 256
FILE *fp;
char buffer[MAX];
fp = fopen("test.txt", "r");
if (fp == NULL) exit(1);
while (!feof(fp)) {
    if (fgets(buffer, MAX, fp) == NULL) exit(0);   // EOF
    cout << buffer;
    fseek(fp, ftell(fp) - (1 + strlen(buffer)), SEEK_SET);
```

```
            fgets(buffer, MAX, fp);
            cout << buffer;
    }
```

fwrite

Syntax

```
#include <stdio.h>
size_t fwrite(const void *p, size_t size_elem, size_t n, FILE *fp);
```

Description

Call f w r i t e to write n elements of s i z e_e l em bytes each from a buffer addressed by p to a file addressed by f p. The file should have been opened by calling f o p e n for writing or appending in binary mode. The buffer pointer p may address any variable, array, or other structure in memory.

The function returns the number of *elements* (not bytes) written to disk. If this number is less than n, an error occurred during writing.

Example

(See f r e a d.)

getc

Syntax

```
#include <stdio.h>
int getc(FILE *fp);
```

Description

Returns next character from file f p. Requires a carriage return to be entered *after* the character that g e t c will return. Echoes the character to s t d o u t and gives users the opportunity to press <Backspace> to erase typing. You'll normally use `getc` with `stdin`, one of five standard files defined in STDIO.H. Though you may use `getc` with a disk text file opened with `fopen`, you'll probably have better luck with `fgetc`. For reading characters from the console, see also `getch`.

Normally, `getc` returns the character read from the file identified by `fp`. Attempting to read past the end of the file causes `getc` to return `EOF`, a symbol defined in STDIO.H. The example demonstrates how to detect this condition. Run the program, press a key followed by <Enter>, and type <Ctrl>-Z to simulate an end-of-file error.

Example

```
int c;
cout << "\nAre you ready? (Type Y or N and press <Enter>):";
if ((c = getc(stdin)) == EOF)
    cout << "End of file was detected!";
else if (toupper(c) == 'Y')
    cout << "Then, here we go...";
else
    cout << "Spoil sport";
```

getch

Syntax

```
#include <conio.h>
int getch(void);
```

Description

Reads one character from `stdin`. Does not require user to press <Enter> after the character. Does not echo the returned character to `stdout`. Unlike `getc`, `getch` does not detect an end-of-file condition. Compare the example here with the one for `getc`, which is similar. Run both programs and type **Y**, **N**, and **<Ctrl>-Z**.

Example

```
int c;
cout << "\nAre you ready? (Type Y or N): ";
c = getch();
if (toupper(c) == 'Y')
    cout << "Then, here we go...";
else
    cout << "Spoil sport";
```

getchar

Syntax

```
#include <stdio.h>
int getchar(void);
```

Description

Identical to `getc(stdin)` but doesn't require you to specify the file parameter. For a full example showing how to use `getchar`, replace the third line in the example for `getc` with the line here.

Example

```
if ((c = getchar()) == EOF)
```

getche

Syntax

```
#include <conio.h>
int getche(void);
```

Description

Identical to get ch except that the character returned by get ch e is echoed to st d out. For a full example showing how to use get ch e, replace the third line in the example for get c h with the line here.

Example

```
c = getche();
```

getcwd

Syntax

```
#include <direct.h>
char *getcwd(char *path, size_t length);
```

Description

Call get c w d for a path name string representing the current working directory. The p a t h pointer may address a buffer large enough to hold the result. Usually, however, you'll set p a t h to NULL. In that case, get c w d calls m a l l o c to allocate heap space of at least l e n g t h bytes and then copies the directory path string to that space. Set l e n g t h to 0 to have get c w d allocate only the minimum amount of space required to hold the string. Set l e n g t h to another value if you intend to use the string to hold other paths.

Unlike many c h a r * functions, the string created by get c w d is *not* temporary. Each call to get c w d may allocate fresh heap space; therefore, when you are done with the string, call f r e e to dispose of it. The example echoes the current directory path name.

Example

```
char *path;
path = getcwd(NULL, 0);
cout << path;
```

getenv

Syntax

```
#include <stdlib.h>
char *getenv(const char *name);
```

Description

Returns a char pointer to an environment string identified by name. Use the DOS SET command to enter strings in the environment. You can then use getenv to inspect those strings. The function is also useful for inspecting preset environment values—PATH and COMSPEC, for example. If getenv returns NULL, the function could not find the environment variable specified by name.

Example

```
char *s;
s = getenv("PATH");
if (s != NULL) cout << "\nPATH == " << s;
s = getenv("COMSPEC");
if (s != NULL) cout << "\nCOMSPEC == " << s;
```

gets

Syntax

```
#include <stdio.h>
char *gets(char *string);
```

Description

Use gets to read lines of text from stdin. The function stores characters in the buffer addressed by string. For safety, it's a good idea to make this buffer at least 129 characters long. That will hold the maximum number of characters that DOS allows on a single input line plus one byte for a NULL byte at the end. The function returns the value of string if no errors are detected. If an error occurs or if gets reads past an end-of-file condition, the function returns NULL.

The example prompts for a file name. Function gets deposits your response in path, a 129-byte char buffer. The program calls fopen and reports whether the file exists.

Example

```
FILE *fp;
char path[129];
cout << "Enter a file name: ";
gets(path);
fp = fopen(path, "rb");
if (fp != NULL) {
    cout << "The file exists!";
    fclose(fp);
} else
    cout << "File not found";
```

hex

Syntax

```
#include <stream.hpp>
char *hex(long n, int columns = 0);
```

Description

Returns a pointer to a string representation of long value n in hexadecimal. The second parameter is optional. For this parameter, specify the positive number of columns in which to right justify n. Even if n is 0 or is too small to display all of n, the value will still be formatted correctly. Usually, you'll use hex in output-stream statements to display integer values in hexadecimal format.

Example

```
long x = 0xface;
cout << "\nx in decimal == " << dec(x);
cout << "\nx in hex       == " << hex(x);
cout << "\njustified x   == " << hex(x, 10);
```

*is******

Syntax

```
#include <ctype.h>
int is*****(int c);
```

Description

Use these 12 macros to determine the character of a character, so to speak. Replace
is***** with one of the macro identifiers listed in Table 10.5. Each macro returns
true (nonzero) or false (0) depending on whether parameter c matches a certain set
of ASCII characters. For example, iscntrl(c) is true only if the character represented by c is a control code.

Table 10.5. Results of the is***** Macros

Macro	True if c Is...
isalnum	a letter or digit
isalpha	a letter
isascii	an ASCII value from 0 to 127
iscntrl	a control code (0 to 0x1f) or 0x7f
isdigit	a digit from 0 to 9
isgraph	a printable nonspace character
islower	lowercase
isprint	printable or a space
ispunct	a punctuation mark
isspace	a white-space character*
isupper	uppercase
isxdigit	a hex digit 0 to 9, a to f, or A to F

*tab, line feed, vertical tab, form feed, carriage return, or space.

Except for isascii, the macros use symbol tables in the library to determine their results. Because of this design, the macros are very fast and are especially well suited for use inside tight loops that must run quickly. The value of parameter c must be from –1 to 255, though the macros return false for values from 128 to 255. Macro isascii is different from the others; it determines whether c's value is 0 to 127. Therefore, isascii can handle any value for c and does not look up its results from a table.

Example

```
int c;
char *s;
cout << "Enter ASCII value: ";
cin >> c;
if ((c < -1) || (c > 255)) {
    cout << "Must be from -1 to 255";
    exit(1);
}
cout << "ASCII " << c << "...\n";
if (isalnum(c))  puts("is alphanumeric");
if (isalpha(c))  puts("is alpha");
if (isascii(c))  puts("is ascii");
if (iscntrl(c))  puts("is ctrl");
if (isdigit(c))  puts("is digit");
if (isgraph(c))  puts("is graph");
if (islower(c))  puts("is lower");
if (isprint(c))  puts("is print");
if (ispunct(c))  puts("is punctuation");
if (isspace(c))  puts("is space");
if (isupper(c))  puts("is upper");
if (isxdigit(c)) puts("is hex digit");
```

kbhit

Syntax

```
#include <conio.h>
int kbhit(void);
```

Description

Returns true (nonzero) if a key was pressed and not yet read by an input routine. Returns false (0) if no key was pressed. The example uses a while loop to wait for a keypress, then calls getch to read that key's value.

Example

```
int c;
cout << "Press any key to end program...\n";
while (!kbhit()) ;
c = getch();
if (isprint(c))
    cout << "You pressed key: " << chr(c);
else
    cout << "You pressed an unprintable key";
```

ldexp

Syntax

```
#include <math.h>
double ldexp(double x, int exp);
```

Description

Returns a double value equal to x times 2 to the exp power.

Example

```
float x;
int y;
cout << "Enter values for x and y: ";
cin >> x >> y;
cout << "ldexp(x, y) == " << ldexp(x, y);
```

log

Syntax

```
#include <math.h>
double log(double x);
```

Description

Returns natural logarithm of x for x > 0.

Example

```
float x;
cout << "Enter value for x: ";
cin >> x;
if (x <= 0)
    cout << "x must be greater than 0";
else
    cout << "log(x) == " << log(x);
```

log10

Syntax

```
#include <math.h>
double log10(double x);
```

Description

Returns base ten logarithm of x for x > 0.

Example

```
float x;
cout << "Enter value for x: ";
cin >> x;
if (x <= 0)
    cout << "x must be greater than 0";
else
    cout << "log10(x) == " << log10(x);
```

malloc

Syntax

```
#include <stdlib.h>
void *malloc(size_t n);
```

Description

Allocates a memory block of n bytes on the heap. Returns address of allocated memory or NULL if enough space is not available. (NULL is returned also if n == 0.) Use free to dispose allocated memory. The example allocates a block of memory large enough to hold 100 values of type float. The values in that block are uninitialized.

Example

```
float *fbuf;
fbuf = malloc(100 * sizeof(float));
if (fbuf == NULL) {
    cout << "Insufficient space!";
    exit(1);
}
//...
free(fbuf);
```

mkdir

Syntax

```
#include <direct.h>
int mkdir(char *path);
```

Description

Call mkdir to create a new directory specified by the path string addressed by path. Returns –1 for errors, 0 for success. The path string may contain nested subdirectories, but all but the final directory in the string must exist. In other words, mkdir("c:\temp\stuff\games"); will create the games subdirectory only if C:\TEMP and C:\TEMP\STUFF exist.

Example

```
char path[129];
int result;
cout << "Make what directory? ";
gets(path);
result = mkdir(path);
if (result == 0)
    cout << "\nDirectory created";
else
    cout << "\nError creating directory";
```

modf

Syntax

```
#include <math.h>
double modf(double x, double *ptr);
```

Description

Returns d o u b l e value equal to the signed fractional value of x. Transfers the signed integer portion of x to the d o u b l e variable addressed by p t r. Remember to pass this second parameter by address!

The example sets x to 3.14159, then calls m o d f to assign 0.14159 to f p a r t and 3.0 to i p a r t.

Example

```
double x, ipart, fpart;
x = 3.14159;
fpart = modf(x, &ipart);
cout << "x == " << x;
cout << "\nipart == " << ipart << ", fpart == " <<
fpart;
```

msleep

Syntax

```
#include <time.h>
void msleep(unsigned long milliseconds);
```

Description

Pause for the specified number of milliseconds. (A millisecond is one thousandth of a second.) The amount of pause is approximate. Depending on the system's hardware, the minimum length of a pause may be as high as 0.055 seconds.

Example

```
cout << "Pausing for 4.5 seconds (more or less)...\n";
msleep(4500);
cout << "Resume normal operation.";
```

oct

Syntax

```
#include <stream.hpp>
char *oct(long n, int columns = 0);
```

Description

Returns a pointer to a string representation of long value n in octal. The second parameter is optional. For this parameter, specify the positive number of columns in which to right justify n. Even if n is 0 or is too small to display all of n, the value will still be formatted correctly. Usually, you'll use oct in output-stream statements to display integer values in octal format.

Example

```
long x = 0xface;
cout << "\nx in decimal == " << dec(x);
cout << "\nx in octal   == " << oct(x);
cout << "\njustified x  == " << oct(x, 10);
```

pow

Syntax

```
#include <math.h>
double pow(double x, double y);
```

Description

Returns x raised to the power y.

Example

```
double x = 2;
double y = 6;
cout << "2 to the 6th power == " << pow(x, y);
```

printf

Syntax

```
#include <stdio.h>
int printf(const char *format, ...);
```

Description

One of several similar functions in the library, `printf` sends a formatted string to `stdout`. The string addressed by `format` may contain commands that mark the locations where various values will be inserted in the final result. The function returns the number of characters written to `stdout`, although this value is typically ignored. A typical `printf` statement looks like this:

```
printf("Your balance is $%8.2f\n", balance);
```

The statement displays the value of a `double` variable `balance` formatted in eight columns with two decimal places. The embedded command `%8.2f` tells `printf` to insert `balance`'s value at this location in the output and in the specified format. The other characters in the string are printed literally. If `balance` equals 159.72, the statement displays

```
Your balance is $  159.72
```

All formatting commands begin with a percent sign (%) followed by various digits and symbols that select among a smorgasbord of output formats for values of all C++ data types. There may be zero, one, or more formatting commands embedded in the `format` string. For each such command, you *must* supply a value (usually a variable name) of the appropriate type or the results are unpredictable. Each value after the `format` string replaces an embedded command from left to right. The formatting commands follow this recipe:

```
'%'{flag}[width]['.'precision['l']]conversion
```

The order of the elements in this schematic is critical; all symbols must be placed as shown. Single-quoted characters are literal and you must type them as printed here. The braces around f l a g indicate that zero, one, or more flag symbols may appear at this location. (Don't type the braces!) Similarly, the brackets around the following three items indicate that these items are optional but if included, may be inserted only once. The c o n v e r s i o n character at the end is required and always comes last. This character tells p r i n t f what type of value to insert in the formatted output.

The next several sections describe each of the items listed in the p r i n t f schematic.

'%'

All embedded formatting commands must begin with a percent sign. To insert a percent-sign character into the output string, type the symbol twice % %.

{*flag*}

The flag is optional. If specified, it may consist of one or more of these characters:

- **–**   Left justify the result

- **+**   Display + or – in front of numeric values

- **' '**   Display a blank or – in front of numeric values. Don't type the quotes. (This is the default action. Don't use ' ' and + together.)

- **#**   If c o n v e r s i o n is x or X and the value is not 0, prefaces value with 0 x or 0 X, respectively. If c o n v e r s i o n is o, # prefaces the result with 0.

If an i n t value n equals 31, the following p r i n t f statement displays 0 x 0 0 1 f. The # flag in the format string prefaces the result with 0 x. The 0 6 is the field width. The x stands for an i n t value in hex:

```
printf("%#06x", n);
```

[*width*]

This is a positive integer value that specifies the minimum column width for the result. Normally, any extra space is filled with blanks. But if the width value begins with the digit 0, any extra space will be filled with 0 characters.

The field width may also be the character *, which tells p r i n t f to take the next i n t value as the column width. With this command, you specify two values: the one to insert and an integer that represents the width to use. In this event, if the width variable is negative, the effect is the same as if you used a − flag and the absolute value of that same width.

Specifying a 0 width is legal and is necessary to pad values with leading 0s within a variable column width. Specifying fewer columns than needed to display a value is also legal. In that case, p r i n t f enlarges the column to the minimum size in which the entire value can be displayed.

['.'precision['l']]

If a period appears at this location, the next value represents the precision to use for the formatted value. The meaning of the precision value depends on the type of item being formatted.

Normally, an integer value follows the period. The default value is 0. If the c o n v e r s i o n character is g or G, the precision represents the maximum number of significant digits for the formatted result. If c o n v e r s i o n is e, E, or f, the precision equals the number of decimal places to use. If c o n v e r s i o n is s, the precision stands for the maximum characters to use from the string. Begin the precision value with 0 to pad blanks with 0s.

After the precision value (which may be blank, in which case the value is taken to be 0), you may insert a lowercase l. In that case, for c o n v e r s i o n characters o, u, x, X, i, d, and b, the value will be treated as a l o n g type. If c o n v e r s i o n is p, the value will be treated as a far pointer. Adding l for other conversions has no effect.

Some versions of p r i n t f may allow an uppercase L in place of the lowercase l. Zortech C++ ignores L here.

These lines display the address of a pointer p in the form segment:offset:

```
char *p = new char[129];
printf("Address of p == %9.0lp", p);
```

conversion

The conversion character, which is not optional, may be one of the following symbols. This character tells p r i n t f the data type of the item to be formatted. Note: Case is significant.

%   A percent sign. The command %% inserts a single % into the formatted string.

b   Unsigned binary.

c A character. Only the least significant byte of a multibyte value will be used.

d Signed decimal.

e A double value to be formatted using scientific notation. The default precision is 6 digits. If you specify a precision value of 0, a decimal point will not be inserted. The result will look something like this: 1.0765e+10.

E Same as e, but inserts an uppercase E into the result.

f A double value to be formatted in decimal format. Use the precision value to specify how many decimal places to include in the formatted result. No decimal places will be used for an explicit precision of 0. The result will look something like this: 12.345678.

g A double value to be formatted in either scientific or decimal notation. If the value's exponent is less than –3 or greater than the specified precision, the result will be formatted as for conversion e; otherwise, the result will be formatted according to the rules for f. Use the precision value to specify a maximum number of significant digits in the result. The default precision is 6 digits.

G Same as g, but if scientific notation is used, the uppercase letter E appears in the result rather than a lowercase e.

i Same as d, signed decimal.

n Treats the argument value as a pointer to an int variable. The printf function will set that variable to the number of characters output up to this point. The n conversion doesn't insert any characters into the formatted string.

o Unsigned octal.

p A pointer. Use the l precision character for far pointers to be formatted into segment:offset notation in hexadecimal. Near pointers are formatted as the offset value only.

s A string. Up to 32,767 characters, or the value specified by a precision, will be inserted into the result.

u Unsigned decimal.

x Unsigned hexadecimal.

X Same as x, unsigned hexadecimal.

Example

```
int n = 127;
printf("My %s has %d fleas.\n", "dog", n);
printf("In hex, that's %#04x", n);
```

putc

Syntax

```
#include <stdio.h>
int putc(int c, FILE *fp);
```

Description

Use this simple function to write one character, represented as an ASCII int value c, to the file addressed by fp. The file can be one that you open by calling fopen or a standard output file, as in the example, which prompts for a string and then displays your typing in uppercase.

The putc function returns c if no errors occur; otherwise, the function returns EOF.

Example

```
char string[129];
cout << "Enter a string: ";
gets(string);
for (int i = 0; i < strlen(string); i++)
   putc(toupper(string[i]), stdout);
```

putchar

Syntax

```
#include <stdio.h>
int putchar(int c);
```

Description

Same as `putc(c, stdout)`. Use this function to avoid having to specify the `stdout` output file. Returns c for no errors; otherwise, returns E 0 F. For a full example, replace the final line in the example for `putc` with the line here.

Example

```
putchar(toupper(string[i]));
```

puts

Syntax

```
#include <stdio.h>
int puts(const char *string);
```

Description

Writes the string addressed by `string` to `stdout`. Also writes a new line (carriage return and line feed in MS-DOS) after the last character.

Example

```
char string[] = "ABCDEFGHIJKLMNOPQRSTUVWXYZ";
for (int i = 0; i < 20; i++)
   puts(string + i);
```

rand

Syntax

```
#include <stdlib.h>
int rand(void);
```

Description

Returns a number from 0 to 32767 selected from a random sequence. Will generate the same sequence for every program run unless srand is used to "seed" a new sequence. The example displays a suggested lottery number of seven double-digit numbers selected at random.

Example

```
cout << "\Pick a lottery number:";
srand(time(NULL));
for (int i = 0; i < 7; i++)
   cout << dec(rand() % 100, 4);
```

remove

Syntax

```
#include <stdio.h>
int remove(const char *path);
```

Description

Deletes a file identified by the path name string addressed by path. The function returns 0 if the file was found and removed or –1 if an error occurred. Create a temporary file TEST.DAT in the current directory before running the example.

Example

```
if (remove("test.dat") == 0)
    cout << "TEST.DAT removed";
else
    cout << "File not found";
```

rename

Syntax

```
#include <stdio.h>
int rename(char *oldname, char *newname);
```

Description

Renames a file identified by the path name string addressed by oldname to the name addressed by newname. You may specify drive letters and subdirectories in each argument, although you can't rename a file to place it on a different drive.

The example shows a typical use for rename: changing the name of a file to name.BAK before creating a new file of the same name. Copy any text file to TEST.TXT before running the program.

Example

```
FILE *fp;
remove("test.bak");
rename("test.txt", "test.bak");
fp = fopen("test.txt", "w");
if (fp != NULL) {
    fputs("New text in the file", fp);
    fclose(fp);
}
```

rewind

Syntax

```
#include <stdio.h>
void rewind(FILE *fp);
```

Description

Repositions an open file identified by fp to its beginning. Exactly equivalent to fseek(fp, 0L, SEEK_SET).

Example

```
FILE *fp;
fp = fopen("test.dat", "r");
// ... process data from file
rewind(fp);
// ... reprocess file from beginning
fclose(fp);
```

rmdir

Syntax

```
#include <direct.h>
int rmdir(char *path);
```

Description

Removes directory identified by the path name string addressed by path. You can't remove directories that contain files, other subdirectories, or are at the root level. The function returns 0 for success, –1 for failure.

The example shows how to create a temporary directory, switch to it, perform some work there, and then step out of the directory and remove it.

Example

```
int result;
result = mkdir("temp");
if (result == 0) {
    cout << "\nTemporary directory created";
    chdir("temp");
    // .. perform work in temporary directory
    chdir("..");
    result = rmdir("temp");
    if (result == 0)
        cout << "\nTEMP removed.";
}
```

scanf

Syntax

```
#include <stdio.h>
int scanf(const char *format, ...);
```

Description

Function s c a n f is one of several in the library that perform formatted input of data in character form, storing binary representations of that data in program variables. The f o r m a t string parameter is a common C++ string that contains embedded commands prefaced with a percent sign (%) and followed by various symbols that tell s c a n f how to read upcoming characters. The f o r m a t string may contain zero, one, or more such commands. For each command, a suitable variable must follow the string in the same order the commands appear in the f o r m a t string.

The function returns the number of characters that it read. Typically, however, this value is ignored.

The commands % l d and % l f tell s c a n f to read a l o n g decimal value and a d o u b l e in character form from s t d i n and store the result in the variables. Notice that the variables are passed by address. This is important. *All* input variables after the f o r m a t string must be passed by address. Because these parameters are untyped, the compiler does not warn you of errors. A common mistake is to write n rather than & n, which causes s c a n f to deposit its input at a random location. However, remember that strings in C++ are addressed by pointers; therefore, a string variable is already in the correct form. For instance, to input a string to a variable defined as char string[80], the correct symbol to use is string, *not* &string.

In general, scanf's format string follows this scheme. Refer to the schematic for the following discussions on commands that you can embed in the string:

```
'%'['*'][width][precision]conversion
```

The items in the format string are similar to those used by the printf family. Characters in single quotes must be typed as shown, but without the quote marks. Items in brackets are optional. Items outside of brackets are required. The order of items is critical and can't be changed. The items in scanf's format string are described next.

'%'

All formatting commands must begin with a percent sign. Use %% to input a percent sign character.

['*']

Use an asterisk when you don't want to save the results of an embedded command, usually while debugging a complex scanf statement. The command is still performed, but no corresponding variable is required and no information is stored in memory.

[width]

Specify an integer value equal to the maximum number of characters to be processed for this value.

[precision]

The precision may be one of the following characters. The meaning of the character depends on the conversion character being used.

l   When the conversion character is b, d, i, o, u, or x, a lowercase l indicates that the argument addresses a long value. If you don't specify l, scanf assumes the addressed argument is an int value.

When the conversion character is e, E, f, g, or G, a lowercase l precision tells s c a n f to expect a pointer to a d o u b l e rather than the default f l o a t argument.

L   Same as l, but only for conversions e, E, f, g, or G.

h   Tells s c a n f to expect a pointer to a s h o r t value.

conversion

A conversion character ends a s c a n f formatting command and is required. Only the following characters are allowed:

%   Input a percent sign.

[ ]   Input characters from a specified set. The set is expressed as a string. All other characters not in that string are ignored. For example, the statement s c a n f (" %9[' 0123456789 '] " , string); inputs up to nine characters to a variable defined as c h a r s t r i n g [1 0] ; . Only digit characters 0 to 9 are accepted. To express a set of characters to ignore, follow [with ^. For example, [^ ' 0123456789 '] tells s c a n f to allow all characters *except* digits.

b   Input binary digit characters to an i n t or l o n g variable.

c   Input a character to a c h a r variable. To input an array of characters, specify the size of the array with the precision value and address an array of c h a r big enough to hold at least that many characters. The result is *not* N U L L terminated.

d   Input decimal digit characters to an i n t or l o n g variable.

e   Input floating point value to a f l o a t or d o u b l e variable.

E   Same as e.

f   Same as e.

g   Same as e.

G   Same as e.

i   Input integer value to an i n t or l o n g variable. If the first character is the capital letter O, the value is assumed to be in octal. If the first two characters are 0x or 0X, the value is assumed to be in hexadecimal.

n   No conversion input performed. At the address of the corresponding argument, in i n t stores value equal to the number of characters read up to this point.

o   Input octal characters to an `int` or `long` variable.

p   Input an integer address value to a pointer. The argument corresponding to this command should be a pointer that addresses a pointer. The address value is assumed to be in hexadecimal. It is not possible to enter far pointers in segment:offset format with a single command.

s   Input a string. Result is `NULL` terminated. It is not possible to input white space (blanks, tabs, etc.) with this command.

u   Input an unsigned integer to an `unsigned int` or an `unsigned long` variable. If the first character is the capital letter O, the value is assumed to be in octal. However, it is not possible to input hexadecimal values (see conversion x).

x   Input an unsigned integer to an `unsigned int` or an `unsigned long` variable. The format is expected to be in hexadecimal, but may not be preceded with 0x or 0X.

If n is type `long` and f is type `double`, the example `scanf` statement lets you type values for both variables. For example, enter **34 3.14159**. Insert a comma in the `format` string to read values separated by commas in the input. For example, if you change the format string to `"%ld, %lf"`, you can then enter **34, 3.14159**.

Example

```
long n;
double f;
cout << "\nEnter an integer and a floating point
value\n";
cout << "separated with a blank on one line:\n";
scanf("%ld %lf", &n, &f);
printf("You entered: n == %ld, f == %f", n, f);
```

sin

Syntax

```
#include <math.h>
double sin(double x);
```

Description

Returns the sine of x radians.

Example

```
int angle = 45;
double c = sin((angle * 3.14159) / 180.0);
```

sleep

Syntax

```
#include <time.h>
void sleep(time_t seconds);
```

Description

Pause the program for the specified number of seconds, which must be an unsigned integer value. The amount of pause is approximate. Depending on the system's hardware, the minimum length of a pause may be as high as 0.055 seconds.

Example

```
cout << "\nBegin countdown\n\n";
sleep(1);
for (int i = 10; i > 0; i--) {
   cout << dec(i, 4) << '\n';
   sleep(1);
}
cout << "\n\nBlast off!\n";
```

sound_beep

Syntax

```
#include <sound.h>
void sound_beep(int frequency);
```

Description

Sounds a tone of the specified frequency. To approximate a specific frequency, use the formula (1193180.0 / hertz) as the frequency argument. The example sounds a short tone of about 440 Hertz (A above middle C in music).

Example

```
sound_beep(1193180.0 / 440);
```

sound_click

Syntax

```
#include <sound.h>
void sound_click(void);
```

Description

Clicks the speaker. Try this one before using. On some systems, the power supply fan may drown out the click.

Example

```
for (int i = 0; i < 6; i++) {
    msleep(250);
```

```
        sound_click();
}
```

sound_tone

Syntax

```
#include <sound.h>
void sound_tone(int cycles, int uptime, int dntime);
```

Description

This function doesn't work correctly on all hardware. The `cycles` parameter represents the number of cycles (not in Hertz), `uptime` is the amount of time the speaker is toggled on, and `dntime` is the amount of time the speaker is off. The result should be a square wave that approximates a particular frequency. But unfortunately, on some hardware and in some operating conditions, the tone is about as musical as a sick cricket.

Example

```
sound_tone(5000, 50, 50);
```

sprintf

Syntax

```
#include <stdio.h>
int sprintf(char *buffer, const char *format, ...);
```

Description

Identical in every way to `printf` but stores the formatted result at the address pointed to by `buffer`. Be sure to allocate a buffer that's large enough to hold the expected result from `sprintf`. The function returns the number of characters written to the buffer. The string in the buffer is `NULL` terminated.

Example

```
char buffer[256];
int result;
double f = 3.14159;
int i = 1234;
sprintf(buffer, "i == %d, f == %f", i, f);
cout << "Buffer contains: " << buffer;
```

sqrt

Syntax

```
#include <math.h>
double sqrt(double x);
```

Description

Returns the square root of x for x >= 0.

Example

```
double x;
cout << "Enter x: ";
cin >> x;
cout << "Square root of x == " << sqrt(x);
```

srand

Syntax

```
#include <stdlib.h>
void srand(unsigned seed);
```

Description

Call s r a n d to begin a new random sequence of numbers returned by r a n d. If a program doesn't call s r a n d, r a n d returns the same sequence of values as though s r a n d (1) was executed. You can use any unsigned value as the s e e d, but the time, date, or another continually changing value will make the random sequence virtually unpredictable. The example passes the value of the t i m e function to s r a n d as the seed. (See r a n d for a more complete example.)

Example

```
srand(time(NULL));
```

sscanf

Syntax

```
#include <stdio.h>
int sscanf(char *buffer, const char *format, ...);
```

Description

Identical to s c a n f but takes its input from the buffer addressed by b u f f e r. The function returns the number of items converted from character to a specified form. As the example shows, s s c a n f is particularly handy for converting values in character form to their equivalent binary representations.

As with s c a n f and f s c a n f, be sure always to pass target variables by address. For instance, examine how the example passes the address of f as & f. Because these arguments are untyped, the compiler does not check for mistakes here. If you pass f by value to sscanf, the function will use that value as an address and may overwrite data or code in memory.

Example

```
char *buffer = "3.14159";
double f;
sscanf(buffer, "%lf", &f);
cout << "After conversion, f == " << f;
```

str

Syntax

```
#include <stream.hpp>
char *str(const char *string, int columns = 0);
```

Description

Use str to right justify a string within a certain number of columns. The columns parameter is optional. Usually, you'll use str to display strings in output-stream statements. The example displays a string with the last character against the right display border.

Example

```
char *string = "The means to justify the ends: str";
cout << str(string, 80);
```

strcat

Syntax

```
#include <string.h>
char *strcat(char *dest, const char *source);
```

Description

Concatenates (joins) two strings. The first string is addressed by dest, the second by source. The string at source is appended to the string at dest, which must be large enough to hold both strings and a NULL terminator. The function returns dest.

Example

```
char dest[256] = "Copyright 1991 by ";
char *name = "Your Name";
cout << strcat(dest, name);
cout << "\nDestination string == " << dest;
```

strchr

Syntax

```
#include <string.h>
char *strchr(const char *string, int c);
```

Description

Searches for the first occurrence of character c in a string addressed by string. If c is found in the string, strchr returns a pointer to that character; otherwise the function returns NULL.

Example

```
char *filename = "TEST.DAT";
char *extension = strchr(filename, '.');
if (extension != NULL)
    cout << "Extension = " << extension;
```

strcmp

Syntax

```
#include <string.h>
int strcmp(const char *string1, const char *string2);
```

Description

Compares the strings addressed by the two parameters. Returns an integer value that represents the result of the comparison. Table 10.6 lists the meanings of strcmp's value. Case is significant. The function reports that "BANANA" is alphabetically less than "Banana".

Table 10.6. String Comparison Results for strcmp.

Function Result n	Meaning
n < 0	string1 < string2
n == 0	string1 == string2
n > 0	string1 > string2

Example

```
char *string1 = "BANANA";
char *string2 = "Banana";
int result = strcmp(string1, string2);
cout << "Result == " << result;
```

strcmpl

Syntax

```
#include <string.h>
int strcmpl(const char *string1, const char *string2);
```

Description

Identical to `strcmp`, except that case is insignificant. The function reports that "BANANA" equals "Banana". For a full example, replace the third line in `strcmp`'s example with the line here.

Example

```
int result = strcmpl(string1, string2);
```

strcpy

Syntax

```
#include <string.h>
char *strcpy(char *dest, const char *source);
```

Description

Copies the string addressed by `source` to the location addressed by `dest`. The destination must be large enough to hold all the source string's characters plus a `NULL` terminator. The function returns `dest`.

Example

```
char buffer1[129];
char buffer2[129];
```

```
cout << "Enter a string: ";
gets(buffer1);
strcpy(buffer2, buffer1);
cout << "\nBuffer 1 == " << buffer1;
cout << "\nBuffer 2 == " << buffer2;
```

strdup

Syntax

```
#include <string.h>
char *strdup(const char *source);
```

Description

Calls malloc to allocate heap space for a new string. If enough space is available, strdup copies into the new string's memory the string addressed by source. If the new string can't be created—usually because the heap doesn't have enough free space—strdup returns NULL. When you're done with the copy, call free as in the example to recover space occupied by the duplicate string.

Example

```
char source[129];
cout << "Enter your name: ";
gets(source);
char *copy = strdup(source);
if (copy != NULL) {
   cout << "The copy is " << copy;
   free(copy);
} else
   cout << "Out of memory";
```

strlen

Syntax

```
#include <string.h>
size_t strlen(const char *source);
```

Description

Returns an integer value equal to the length of the string addressed by source. The length does not include the NULL terminator; therefore, the length of a null string (one that contains *only* a NULL terminator byte) is zero.

Example

```
char source[129];
cout << "Enter your name: ";
gets(source);
cout << "Your name is: ";
for (int i = 0; i < strlen(source); i++)
    cout << '\n' << chr(source[i], i + 1);
```

strlwr

Syntax

```
#include <string.h>
char *strlwr(char *source);
```

Description

Changes to lowercase all uppercase letters in the string addressed by source. Ignores nonalphabetic characters. Returns source.

Example

```
char *alphabet = "ABCDEFGHIJKLMNOPQRSTUVWXYZ";
cout << "Before : " << alphabet;
strlwr(alphabet);
cout << "\nAfter  : " << alphabet;
```

strncat

Syntax

```
#include <string.h>
char *strncat(char *dest, const char *source, size_t n);
```

Description

Identical to strcat but appends to the string addressed by dest only up to n characters from the string addressed by source. Parameter n is limited to strlen(source). No matter how many characters are copied from source, a NULL terminator is added to the final result at dest. As with strcat, you must be sure that dest addresses space large enough to hold at least strlen(dest) + n + 1 characters.

Example

```
char result[80];
char *alphabet = "ABCDEFGHIJKLMNOPQRSTUVWXYZ";
char *digits = "0123456789";
strcpy(result, digits);
strcat(result, " -- ");
strncat(result, alphabet, 10);
cout << result;
```

strncmp

Syntax

```
#include <string.h>
int strncmp(const char *string1, const char *string2, size_t n);
```

Description

Compares at most n characters addressed by string2 with that many characters addressed by string1. Regardless of n's value, comparisons are limited to characters in the two strings. The function result is the same as for strcmp.

The example compares the results of strcmp and strncmp. In the first case, strcmp reports that "TEST.DAT" is greater than "TEST". In the second case, strncmp reports that the first four characters of the two strings are equal.

Example

```
char *filename = "TEST.DAT";
char *name = "TEST";
int result;
result = strcmp(filename, name);
cout << "\nstrcmp result  == " << result;
result = strncmp(filename, name, strlen(name));
cout << "\nstrncmp result == " << result;
```

strncpy

Syntax

```
#include <string.h>
char *strncpy(char *dest, const char *source, size_t n);
```

Description

Copies at most n characters from the string addressed by `source` to the location addressed by `dest`. If n is greater than the length of the source string, k bytes equal to 0 will be added to the end of the destination where k equals `strlen(source)` − n. However, when n is less or equal to the length of `source`, you must be sure the result is terminated properly as the example demonstrates.

Example

```
char name[9];
char *filename = "TEST.DAT";
char *extension = strchr(filename, '.');
int n = strlen(filename);
if (extension != NULL)
    n -= strlen(extension);
strncpy(name, filename, n);
name[n + 1] = 0;
cout << "\nExtension == " << extension;
cout << "\nName      == " << name;
```

strnset

Syntax

```
#include <string.h>
char *strnset(char *dest, int c, size_t n);
```

Description

Changes to c at most n characters starting with the first character addressed by `dest`. Only characters up to but not including the `NULL` terminator are changed, even if n is greater than `strlen(dest)`.

Example

```
char *string = "This is a string";
cout << "\nBefore : " << string;
strnset(string, '*', 4);
cout << "\nAfter  : " << string;
```

strrchr

Syntax

```
#include <string.h>
char *strrchr(const char *source, int c);
```

Description

Returns a pointer to the *last* occurrence of character c in the string addressed by source. If c is not found in the source string, strrchr returns NULL. The example uses strchr to separate dash and letter pairs from a string.

Example

```
char *string = "a-b-c-d-e-f-g";
cout << "String at start == " << string;
char *last = strrchr(string, '-');
while (last != NULL) {
    cout << '\n' << last;
    last[0] = 0;
    last = strrchr(string, '-');
}
cout << "\nFinal string == " << string;
```

strset

Syntax

```
#include <string.h>
char *strset(char *dest, int c);
```

Description

Call strset to change to c all characters in the string addressed by dest. Equivalent to strnset(dest, c, strlen(dest));.

Example

```
char *password = "XYZ-Secret";
cout << "\nBefore : " << password;
strset(password, '-');
cout << "\nAfter  : " << password;
```

strstr

Syntax

```
#include <string.h>
char *strstr(const char *target, const char *pattern);
```

Description

Searches for the first occurrence of the string addressed by pattern in the string addressed by target. If the pattern string is found in the target, the function returns the address of the matching pattern in target. If the pattern is not found, the function returns NULL.

A zero-length pattern string is considered to match everything; therefore, the statement strstr(s, ""); returns the address of s, not NULL.

Example

```
char *filename = "TEST.TXT";
char *extension = strstr(filename, ".TXT");
if (extension != NULL)
    cout << "Extension == " << extension;
else
    cout << "Extension .TXT not found";
```

strtod

Syntax

```
#include <string.h>
double strtod(const char *source, char **endptr);
```

Description

Converts and returns a `double` value represented by the string addressed by `source`. Skips leading white space. Use the function to convert floating-point values from string to binary form. If you pass the address of a pointer defined as `char *` as the `endptr` argument, `strtod` will set the pointer to the first character in the source string that could not be interpreted as belonging to a floating-point value. If you set `endptr` to `NULL`, `strtod` ignores the parameter. The example converts a string to a floating point value and sets pointer `endp` to the X in the original string.

Example

```
double f;
char *source = "3.14159XQP";
char *endp;
f = strtod(source, &endp);
cout << "\nf == " << f;
cout << "\nendp == " << endp;
```

strtol

Syntax

```
#include <string.h>
long strtol(const char *source, char **endptr, int base);
```

Description

Similar to s t r t o d, but returns the signed l o n g equivalent of the string addressed by s o u r c e. Skips leading white space.

Pass a b a s e argument of 0 to have s t r t o l interpret the source string in normal C and C++ styles. If the string begins with the digits 1 to 9, the source is treated as a decimal value. If the string begins with 0x or 0X, the source is considered to be in hex. If the source begins with a capital letter O, the characters are treated as octal representations.

If b a s e is not zero, it represents a numeric base, for example, 2 for binary or 16 for hexadecimal. The example shows how this works. Run the statements and enter values such as **1234, 1011, 0xFA9C** and others to see the results of converting those values in string form to binary using different values for b a s e.

Example

```
char string[129];
cout << "Enter a signed long integer: ";
gets(string);
cout << "\nbase 0  : " << strtol(string, NULL, 0);
cout << "\nbase 2  : " << strtol(string, NULL, 2);
cout << "\nbase 8  : " << strtol(string, NULL, 8);
cout << "\nbase 16 : " << strtol(string, NULL, 16);
```

strtoul

Syntax

```
#include <string.h>
unsigned long strtoul(const char *source,
char **endptr, int base);
```

Description

Identical to `strtol`, but returns the unsigned `long` equivalent of the string addressed by `source`. Skips leading white space.

Example

```
char string[129];
cout << "Enter an unsigned long integer: ";
gets(string);
cout << "\nbase 0  : " << strtoul(string, NULL, 0);
cout << "\nbase 2  : " << strtoul(string, NULL, 2);
cout << "\nbase 8  : " << strtoul(string, NULL, 8);
cout << "\nbase 16 : " << strtoul(string, NULL, 16);
```

strupr

Syntax

```
#include <.h>
char *strupr(char *source);
```

Description

Changes to uppercase all lowercase letters in the string addressed by `source`. Ignores nonalphabetic characters. Returns `source`.

Example

```
char *alphabet = "abcdefghijklmnopqrstuvwxyz";
cout << "Before : " << alphabet;
strupr(alphabet);
cout << "\nAfter  : " << alphabet;
```

system

Syntax

```
#include <string.h>
int system(const char *command);
```

Description

Executes a DOS command. After the command finishes, the program continues at the next statement. Some commands may not produce expected results. For example, you can't use s y s t e m to set environment variables. Although the SET command will be accepted, the results will be stored in a copy of the master environment. That environment copy will then be discarded with the program continues. The example issues a DOS DIR command to display a directory.

Example

```
cout << "\nWide-body directory:\n";
system("DIR /w");
cout << "\nBack inside program.\n";
```

tan

Syntax

```
#include <math.h>
double tan(double x);
```

Description

Returns the tangent of x radians.

Example

```
int angle = 45;
double c = tan((angle * 3.14159) / 180.0);
```

time

Syntax

```
#include <time.h>
time_t time(time_t *timeptr);
```

Description

Call t i me to find the number of seconds elapsed from the first second of January 1, 1970, to the present. The function returns and stores this value at the address specified by t i mept r. To prevent storing the value at any address, pass NULL as the function's argument. The example shows both uses for t i me, pausing for about four seconds between function calls so that the two times will be different.

The t i me function also provides a useful random-number seed. See s r a nd.

Example

```
time_t *timeptr;
cout << "\nElapsed seconds #1 == " << time(NULL);
cout << "\n wait...\n";
sleep(4);
time(timeptr);
cout << "Elapsed seconds #2 == " << *timeptr;
```

toascii

Syntax

```
#include <ctype.h>
int toascii(int c);
```

Description

Standard ASCII values range from 0 to 127. When representing characters in ASCII, use toascii to force int values to that range.

Example

```
int a, c;
for (a = 0; a < 256; a++) {
    c = toascii(a);
    if isprint(c) cout << chr(c);
}
```

tolower

Syntax

```
#include <ctype.h>
int tolower(int c);
```

Description

Returns lowercase equivalent of character c. Changes only characters from A to Z. Other characters are returned unchanged.

Example

```
for (int c = 'A'; c <= 'Z'; c++)
    cout << ' ' << chr(c) << chr(tolower(c));
```

toupper

Syntax

```
#include <ctype.h>
int toupper(int c);
```

Description

Returns uppercase equivalent of character c. Changes only characters from a to z. Other characters are returned unchanged.

Example

```
for (int c = 'a'; c <= 'z'; c++)
    cout << ' ' << chr(c) << chr(toupper(c));
```

ungetc

Syntax

```
#include <stdio.h>
int ungetc(int c, FILE *fp);
```

Description

Returns ("ungets") character c to the character file identified by fp. The file may be one you opened with fopen in text mode or stdin. If successful, the function result equals c. If an error occurs, the function returns NULL, in which case c was not returned.

Returned characters will be read by the next character input routine except for getch and getche. Those two functions take their input directly from DOS and therefore, can't be used along with ungetc.

Example

```
cout << "Type a character: ";
int c = getchar();
if (c != EOF) {
   if (ungetc(c, stdin) == c) {
      cout << "Getting character again: ";
      cout << chr(getchar());
   } else
      cout << "Error ungetting char";
} else
   cout << "End of file detected";
```

usleep

Syntax

```
#include <time.h>
void usleep(unsigned long microseconds);
```

Description

Pause for the specified number of microseconds. (A microsecond is one millionth of a second.) The amount of pause is approximate. Depending on the system's hardware, the minimum length of a pause may be as high as 0.055 seconds.

Example

```
unsigned long pause = 4500000;
cout << "Pausing for 4.5 seconds (more or less)...\n";
usleep(pause);
cout << "Resume normal operation.";
```

utime

Syntax

```
#include <time.h>
int utime(char *path, time_t times[2]);
```

Description

Call utime to change the date and time of a file identified by the path name string addressed by path. Set the second argument to NULL to update the file to the present date and time.

The times parameter is included for compatibility with other operating systems. On those systems, the first value in the array stands for the time the file was last accessed. The second value represents the time the file was last modified. Under DOS, the first value is ignored.

If the file is successfully updated, utime returns 0. If an error occurs, the function returns –1.

Example

```
char *filename = "TEST.DAT";
int result = utime(filename, NULL);
if (result == 0)
    cout << filename << " updated";
else
    cout << "ERROR updating " << filename;
```

Reserved Key Words

Do not use the following key words for your own identifiers. These reserved words are treated specially by the C++ compiler and they may not be redefined:

```
asm, auto, break, case, catch, cdecl, char, class, const,
continue, default, delete, do, double, else, entry, enum,
extern, far, float, for, friend, goto, if, inline, int,
long, near, new, operator, overload, pascal, private,
protected, public, register, return, short, signed,
sizeof, static, struct, switch, template, this, typedef,
union, unsigned, virtual, void, volatile, while
```

Operator Precedence

In expressions, operators with lower precedence-level numbers in the following table are given priority over operators with higher levels. For example, in the expression a + (b + c), because parentheses have a higher precedence (level 1) than + (level 4), the subexpression (b + c) is evaluated before the addition to a.

Level	Operators
1	( ) . [] -> :: ->* this &
2	* & new delete ! ~ ++ -- - sizeof
3	* / %
4	+ -
5	<< >>
6	< <= > >=
7	== !=
8	&
9	^
10	|

continued

Level	Operators
11	&&
12	||
13	? :
14	= += -= *= /= %= <<= >= &= ^= |=
15	,

Note: The symbol * at level 2 is the pointer dereference operator. The same symbol * at level 3 is the multiplication operator.

Bibliography

Eckel, Bruce, *Using C++*, Osborne McGraw-Hill, 1989.

Kernighan, Brian W. and Ritchie, Dennis M., *The C Programming Language, 2nd Ed.*, Prentice Hall, 1988.

Knuth, Donald E., *The Art of Computer Programming, Volume 1/Fundamental Algorithms*, Addison-Wesley Publishing Company, 1973.

Lafore, Robert, *Turbo C Programming for the PC, Rev. Ed.*, Howard W. Sams & Company, 1989.

Paulos, John Allen, *Innumeracy*, Vintage Books, 1988.

Plauger, P. J. and Brodie, Jim, *Standard C*, Microsoft Press, 1989.

Stroustrup, Bjarne, *The C++ Programming Language*, Addison-Wesley Publishing Company, 1986.

Swan, Tom, *Mastering Turbo Pascal 5.5, 3rd Ed.*, Hayden Books, 1989.

Wiener, Richard S. and Pinson, Lewis J., *An Introduction to Object-Oriented Programming and C++*, Addison-Wesley Publishing Company, 1988.

Zortech C++ Compiler Reference, Zortech Incorporated, 1165 Massachusetts Avenue, Arlington, MA 02174; and Zortech Limited, 106-108 Powis Street, London SE18 6LU, England.

Answers to Questions and Exercises

This section lists answers to the exercises at the end of chapters 1 through 9. In some cases, only one answer is given, though others may be correct for a given problem.

For most problems, when you are asked to write a program, you'll find a sample listing here. On disk, you can locate the programs in the ANSWERS subdirectory by the file name noted in the first line of the listing. For example, ASK.CPP is the disk file for the answer to exercise 1.1. When an answer includes only a few statements or a function or two, not a full program, that text is listed here but is not stored on disk. If you want to run these fragments, insert them into a small test program. Be sure to #include the necessary header files.

You've probably heard (or read) this advice before, but I'll give it anyway: Try the exercises on your own before looking up the answers. If you don't have time to work out the solutions, at least spend a few minutes thinking about how you would solve each problem. Then check here to see whether you're on the right track. Use the exercises and answers as self tests of what you learned in a chapter. If you find the exercises difficult, you need to review the material in that chapter. If you find the problems relatively easy to solve, you're ready to go on to the next chapter.

> **Note:** Unlike the numbered listings in this book, the listings in this section do not have line numbers.

Chapter 1

1.1.

```
// ask.cpp -- Prompt for and display a name

#include <stream.hpp>

main()
{
    char name[128];

    cout << "What's your first name? ";
    cin >> name;
    cout << "\nYou entered: " << name;
}
```

1.2. The first line is a C-style comment bracketed by /* and */. The compiler igores all text between these symbols. The second and third lines end with C++ comments. The compiler ignores all text after // to the end of the line.

1.3.

```
main(){}
```

1.4. myMoney, _max, max_Value, A_L_P_H_A_B_E_T_. Insert the identifiers into a program. The compiler will reject the ill-formed ones.

1.5.

```
// puncs.cpp -- Display C++ punctuators

#include <stream.hpp>

main()
{
    cout << "#  ()  []  {}  ,  :  ;  ...";
}
```

1.6. White space separates elements of C++. The compiler ignores white space, which includes blanks, tabs, carriage returns, and line feeds.

1.7. The program is missing #include directives that read the declarations in STREAM.HPP for output-stream statements, or STDIO.H for printf-style output, commonly used in C programs. Because STREAM.HPP references STDIO.H, you don't need to include both files, but doing so does no harm. To fix the program, add these two lines at the top:

```
#include <stream.hpp>
#include <stdio.h>
```

1.8. 145540—long, unsigned long, float, double, long double; 145.543—float, double, long double; 10—all numeric types. The smallest type that can store the value 10 is char, which takes one byte.

1.9.

```
char alpha = 'A';
```

1.10. Local variables are stored on the stack; global variables are stored in the data segment. Local variables exist only while their defining blocks are active; global variables exist for the duration of the program.

1.11.

```
cout << dec(134, 12);
```

1.12. The following line is correct, but doesn't give ideal results. For information about how to format digits, inserting leading 0s for days and limiting floating point values to a certain number of decimal places, see the form function in chapter 10.

```
cout << form("Age = %d, Birth Date = %d/%d/%d, Balance = $%f",
    age, month, day, year, balance);
```

1.13. The first program (RAIN1.CPP) uses an input-stream statement to read a value directly into rainFall. The second program (RAIN2.CPP) reads your response into a string and then calls atof to convert the string to a floating point value. This is safer because it prevents errors from affecting future input statements. To demonstrate the difference, run RAIN1 and enter a bad value—for example, type **XYZ**. Run RAIN2 and enter that same value. The first program displays a random result for bad input; the second displays 0:

```
// rain1.cpp -- Use input stream to read a floating point value
#include <stream.hpp>

main()
{
    float rainFall;
```

```
      cout << "Enter rain fall in inches: ";
      cin >> rainFall;
      cout << "You entered : " << rainFall;
}


// rain2.cpp -- Use string to read a floating point value

#include <stream.hpp>
#include <stdlib.h>

main()
{
   float rainFall;
   char response[128];

   cout << "Enter rain fall in inches: ";
   cin >> response;
   rainFall = atof(response);
   cout << "You entered : " << rainFall;
}
```

1.14. The trick is to precede the quotes with a backslash escape symbol, which is required because double quotes normally begin and end strings. The apostrophe requires no special treatment:

```
// dogcat.cpp -- Display a string with embedded quotes

#include <stream.hpp>

main()
{
   cout << "\"It's raining \"dogs and cats\" in here!\"";
}
```

1.15. Because a single quote mark delimits literal characters, you must use the escape sequence \ ' to specify a single quote. You could also use a single quote's ASCII value:

```
// aquote.cpp -- Assign single quote to a char variable

#include <stream.hpp>

main()
{
```

```
        char c = '\'';
        cout << "c = " << c;
    }
```

1.16. You can use #define control lines as in the listing printed here, or you could declare const values. Either answer is correct, but #define is probably more common for simple numeric constants like **MIN** and **MAX**:

```
// minmax.cpp -- Demonstrate #defined constants

#include <stream.hpp>

#define MIN 1
#define MAX 999

main()
{
    cout << "\nMinimum value = " << MIN;
    cout << "\nMaximum value = " << MAX;
}
```

1.17. You can use upper- or lowercase for the element names, but uppercase is more common:

```
enum flowers {ROSE, CARNATION, ORCHID, GARDENIA};
```

1.18. The final value of count in 98. Compile and run COUNTS.CPP for the results of the other expressions:

```
// counts.cpp -- Test effects of ++ and --

#include <stream.hpp>

main()
{
    int count = 98;
    cout << "At start, count = " << count;
    cout << "\ncount++ = " << count++ << "; count = " << count;
    cout << "\n++count = " << ++count << "; count = " << count;
    cout << "\ncount-- = " << count-- << "; count = " << count;
    cout << "\n--count = " << --count << "; count = " << count;
    cout << "\nfinal count = " << count;
}
```

1.19.

```cpp
// circum.cpp -- Calculate circumference of a circle

#include <stream.hpp>
#include <stdlib.h>

#define PI 3.14159

main()
{
    char response[129];       // Holds response to prompt

    cout << "Calculate circumference of a circle.";
    cout << "\nDiameter? ";
    cin >> response;
    cout << "Circumference = " << (PI * atof(response));
}
```

Chapter 2

2.1. C++ represents true as 1; false as 0.

2.2. == is C++'s relational equality operator. = is the assignment operator. The expression (a == b) evaluates to true if a equals b; the expression (a = b) *assigns* b to a.

2.3. There are many solutions to this problem, but a good one uses a *flag* such as goodResponse to check for a response within a defined range. The flag is initialized to 0 (false)C and then set to true or false based on whether response is within the range 1 to 100. Using a flag to store the result of the relational expression avoids having to repeat that expression in the loop:

```cpp
// prmpt.cpp -- Prompt for value between 1 and 100

#include <stream.hpp>

main()
{
    int goodResponse = 0;
    int response;
```

```
   while (!goodResponse) {
      cout << "Enter value from 1 to 100: ";
      cin >> response;
goodResponse = ((1 <= response) && (response <= 100));
      if (!goodResponse)
         cout << "ERROR: Try again!\n";
   }
   cout << "Final value == " << response;
}
```

2.4.

```
counter = 0;
while (counter > -8) {
   cout << "\nValue of counter = " << counter;
   cout << "\n---";
   counter--;
}
```

2.5. The statement `value &= 0x1f` applies to `value` the bit mask `0x1f`, equal to 00011111 in binary or 31 in decimal. This forces all bits except the lower five to 0, thus limiting the result to the range of values that can be expressed in five bits, 0 to 31:

```
// limit.cpp -- Limit integers to the range 0 ... 31

#include <stream.hpp>

main()
{
   int value;

   cout << "Enter value: ";
   cin >> value;
   value &= 0x1f;    // value = value & 0x1f
   cout << "Limited value == " << value;
}
```

2.6. The listing uses only elements that were introduced in chapters 1 and 2. There are other, and perhaps better, ways to solve this problem. The solution listed here uses two `for` loops. The first combines successive characters in the `password` string with characters in `anyString`. A second `for` loop repeats this operation to recover the original string. This works because the exclusive OR operator (^) applied twice to the same value recovers that value. Notice how the first `for` loop finds the end of anyString by looking for its terminating NULL (0). The second for loop can't do this because one of the encrypted characters might equal 0; therefore, another variable count is used to store the number of loops from the first time around. The second loop then uses count to cycle that same number of times. Run the program and enter moon for the password and starlight for the string (other values may cause strange but harmless effects on screen if characters are encrypted to ASCII control codes):

```cpp
// encrypt.cpp -- Demonstrate encryption with XOR

#include <stream.hpp>

main()
{
    char password[129];
    char anyString[129];
    int i, j, count;

    cout << "Enter your password: ";
    cin >> password;
    cout << "Enter a string (no blanks): ";
    cin >> anyString;
    cout << "Before encryption: " << anyString;

    for (i = 0, j = 0; anyString[i] != 0; i++, j++) {
        if (password[j] == 0)
            j = 0;
        anyString[i] ^= password[j];
    }
    count = i - 1;
    cout << "\nAfter encryption: " << anyString;
    for (i = 0, j = 0; i <= count; i++, j++) {
        if (password[j] == 0)
            j = 0;
        anyString[i] ^= password[j];
    }
    cout << "\nAfter reencryption: " << anyString;

}
```

2.7. There are two listings here. The first is a C++ program that prompts for an unsigned integer value and then passes that value via exit back to DOS. The second is a batch file that retrieves the passed value by examining errorlevel. The batch file checks whether `errorlevel` is greater or equal to 10. Type `GETVALUE` at the DOS prompt to run the batch file and enter test values such as 1, 8, 10, and 25. Here's the C++ program:

```
// pass2dos.cpp -- Pass integer values to DOS

#include <stream.hpp>
#include <stdlib.h>

main()
{
    unsigned value;

    cout << "\nEnter value: ";
    cin >> value;
    exit(value);
}
```

Here's the GETVALUE.BAT batch file:

```
echo off
rem
rem Get value from PASS2DOS.EXE
rem
echo Calling PASS2DOS
pass2dos
echo Back from PASS2DOS
if errorlevel == 10 goto CONTINUE
echo Value entered was less than 10
goto END
:CONTINUE
echo Value entered was greater than or equal to 10

:END
```

2.8. Compile WORDS2.CPP and run it with a command such as `words2 < words2.cpp`:

```
// words2.cpp -- Count words in standard input

#include <stream.hpp>
#include <ctype.h>

main()
{
    char c;
    int words, chars, lines, insideWord;
```

```
      words = chars = lines = insideWord = 0;

      while ((c = getchar()) != EOF) {
         chars++;
         if (c == '\n') {
            lines++;
            chars++;
         }
         if (!isspace(c)) {
            if (!insideWord) {
               insideWord = 1;    // True
               words++;
            }
         } else
            insideWord = 0;       // False
      }

      cout << chars << " total character(s)\n";
      cout << words << " word(s)\n";
      cout << lines << " line(s)\n";
   }
```

2.9. Compile HEAD2 and run with a command such as `head2 < head2.cpp`:

```
// head2.cpp -- Use while instead of do/while

#include <stream.hpp>
#include <stdlib.h>

#define MAXLINE 10
#define NEWLINE '\n'

main()
{
   char c;
   int linenum = 1;

   while ((((c = getchar()) != EOF) && (linenum <= MAXLINE)) {
      if (c == NEWLINE) {
         linenum++;
         cout << NEWLINE;
      } else
         putchar(c);
```

```
      }
  }

      2.10. Compile TOUPPER and run with a command such as
      toupper < toupper.cpp:

      // toupper.cpp -- Convert standard input to uppercase

      #include <stream.hpp>
      #include <ctype.h>

      main()
      {
          char c;

          while ((c = getchar()) != EOF)
              putchar(toupper(c));
      }


      2.11.

      // odd.cpp -- Determine if an integer is odd or even

      #include <stream.hpp>

      main()
      {
          int value;

          cout << "\nEnter value: ";
          cin >> value;
          if (!(value & 1))
              cout << "Value is even";
          else
              cout << "Value is odd";
      }


      2.12.

      // alphabet.cpp -- switch-statement demonstration

      #include <stream.hpp>
      #include <ctype.h>

      main()
```

```
{
    char c;

    cout << "Alphabet demonstration\n";
    cout << "\nD-do/while, F-for, W-while? ";
    cin >> c;

    switch (toupper(c)) {
        case 'D' :
            cout << "do/while-loop demonstration\n";
            c = 'a';
            do {
                cout << c++;
            } while (c <= 'z');
            break;
        case 'F' :
            cout << "for-loop demonstration\n";
            for (c = 'a'; c <= 'z'; c++)
                cout << c;
            break;
        case 'W' :
            cout << "while-loop demonstration\n";
            c = 'a';
            while (c <= 'z')
                cout << c++;
            break;
        default :
        cout << "Run program again and enter D, F, or W";
    }
}
```

2.13. Using a goto is not *wrong*, but it's probably unnecessary. A goto statement jumps to a labeled location, and many such jumps make the logic of a program difficult to follow. Experts frown on using gotos because other C++ features are easier to use and are less prone to cause bugs. Avoid gotos if you can. Use for, while, and do/while loops and make decisions with if/else. Be aware of how gotos work, but try to find alternative solutions that don't require jumping to labels.

2.14. Using single-byte char fields to store small values avoids waste:

```
struct dnt {
    char month, day;
    int year;
    char hour, minute, second;
```

```
};
```

2.15. You can use any legal identifier in place of dateArray:

```
dnt dateArray[50];
```

2.16. The trick is to treat the input string as an array of char, indexing each character to display it plus a blank:

```
// cblanks.cpp -- Insert blanks into character strings

#include <stream.hpp>

main()
{
    char original[129];

    cout << "Enter a string (no blanks): ";
    cin >> original;

    cout << "Original string : " << original;
    cout << "\nWith blanks    : ";
    for (int i = 0; original[i] != 0; i++)
        cout << original[i] << ' ';
}
```

2.17. By eliminating the second field and limiting years to an offset of 0 to 59 from a base of 1980, it's possible to pack the date and time into 4 bytes, exactly half the size of the dnt structure. Adding the second field increases the bit-field's size to 6 bytes. The comments to the right of packdnt show the range of legal values each field can store, plus the maximum value that the specified number of bits can represent:

```
// bitdate.cpp -- Pack date and time in a bit-field struct

#include <stream.hpp>

struct dnt {
    char month, day;
    int year;
    char hour, minute, second;
};

struct packdnt {
    unsigned month  : 4;      // 0 .. 11 (max == 15)
```

```
    unsigned day     : 5;      // 1 .. 31 (max == 31)
    unsigned year    : 6;      // 0 .. 59 (assume base = 1980)
    unsigned hour    : 5;      // 0 .. 23 (max = 31)
    unsigned minute  : 6;      // 0 .. 59 (max = 63)
//    unsigned second : 6;     // 0 .. 59 (max = 63)
};

main()
{
    dnt regular;
    packdnt compressed;
    cout << "Size of regular dnt = " << sizeof(regular);
    cout << "\nSize of packed dnt = " << sizeof(compressed);
}
```

Chapter 3

3.1. Functions divide large programs into manageable pieces. Functions can be compiled separately in modules that are linked to produce the final program. Simple functions simplify complex processes into easy-to-understand steps.

3.2. A function prototype lists the name, return type, and any parameters. The function implementation contains the statements that run when the program calls the function. Usually, prototypes are listed before `main`. Implementations are listed after `main`.

3.3. Use the function's name in an expression or statement.

3.4. `void`.

3.5. Another function.

3.6. The program sizes may be the same, even though register variables don't take up any memory space. Inside a function, local variables are created at runtime on the stack. Local variables are not stored in the code file.

3.7. Use a `static` variable in the function. The variable will retain its value between function calls.

```
// fncount.cpp -- Count function calls
```

```
#include <stream.hpp>

void test(void);

main()
{
    for (int i = 0; i < 10; i++)
        test();
}

void test(void)
{
    static int count = 0;
    count++;
    cout << "\nFunction call # " << count;
}
```

3.8. The function uses the `factorial` function from COCO.CPP.

```
double coco(int selections, int elements)
{
    double answer = elements;
    for (int i = 1; i < selections; i++)
        answer *= --elements;
    answer /= factorial(selections);
    return answer;

}
```

3.9. Notice how the functions are designed to return values in reference paramters (`&low` and `&high`, for example). Other parameters such as `min` and `max` are passed by value.

```
// getvals.cpp -- Get values in ranges

#include <stream.hpp>

void getValues(int &low, int &high, int min, int max);
void getOneValue(const char *prompt, int &v, int min, int max);

main()

{
```

```
    int low, high;
    getValues(low, high, 10, 50);
    cout << "\nlow == " << low << " high == " << high;
}

void getValues(int &low, int &high, int min, int max)
{
    int result;

    cout << "\nEnter two values between " << min << " and " << max;
    cout << "\nThe first value must be less or equal to the second.";
    do {
        getOneValue("\nLow value?  ", low, min, max);
        getOneValue("\nHigh value? ", high, min, max);
        result = (low <= high);
        if (result == 0)
            cout << "\nERROR: Low value must be <= high.";
    } while (result == 0);
}

void getOneValue(const char *prompt, int &v, int min, int max)
{
    int result;
    do {
        cout << prompt;
        cin >> v;
        result = (min <= v) && (v <= max);
        if (result == 0)
            cout << "\nERROR: value out of range";
    } while (result == 0);
}
```

3.10. The default parameter z lets the program pass to a r e a two arguments for a square or three for a cube.

```
// cube.cpp -- Find area of cubes and squares

#include <stream.hpp>

double area(double x, double y, double z = 0);

main()
{
```

```
    double x, y, z;
    cout << "\nEnter three values to find the area of a cube.";
    cout << "\nType 0 for the third value for a square.";
    cout << "\nFor example, type 2 4 8, or 2 4 0.\n";
    cin >> x >> y >> z;
    if (z == 0)
        cout << "Area of square == " << area(x, y);
    else
        cout << "Area of cube   == " << area(x, y, z);
}

double area(double x, double y, double z)
{
    double result = x * y;
    if (z != 0)
        result *= z;
    return result;
}
```

3.11. Writing a recursive factorial function is an interesting exercise, but the function in COCO.CPP runs faster because only one function call is required. A recursive function calls itself over and over until done. That takes time and wastes stack space.

```
long factorial(int number)
{
    if (number > 1)
        return number * factorial(number - 1);
    return 1;
}
```

3.12. To convert factorial to an inline function, add the inline keyword to the left of long in the function's declaration. If the function is called only once or twice, the inline version may save space in the compiled result. (Functions have some associated overhead instructions that don't exist in inline code.) However, the usual effect of inline functions is to expand the compiled code file because, rather than call functions, statements are replaced with all of an inline function's contents.

3.13. Variables may be declared extern as often as necessary. External declarations are typically stored in header files, which other modules can include to gain access to the variables. Only one module may define space for an extern variable.

3.14. The expression limits c1 and c2 from 0 to 255, shifts c1 left 8 bits, and logically ORs the values into 16 bits.

```
unsigned int pack(int c1, int c2)
{
    return ((c1 & 0xff) << 8) | (c2 & 0xff);
}
```

3.15.

```
void unpack(int &c1, int &c2, unsigned int source)
{
    c1 = source >> 8;
    c2 = source & 0xff;
}
```

Chapter 4

4.1. Either of the last two lines is correct.

```
float *pfloat;
char *string;
customer *prec;
struct customer *prec;
```

4.2. An address.

4.3. Did you remember to dereference the pointer with an asterisk?

```
cout << "Value == " << *fp;
```

4.4. Dereferencing a pointer uses the value stored at the location addressed by the pointer.

4.5.

```
double bigValue;
double *aliasPtr = &bigValue;

bigValue = 3.14159;
cout << "Value == " << *aliasPtr;
```

4.6. NULL is a constant *value*, void is a data type. A pointer that equals NULL addresses no particular location. A pointer with a type of void * addresses no particular information.

4.7. You must use a type cast expression such as *(int *)p to tell the compiler what type of data p addresses.

```
int value = 12345;
void *p = &value;
cout << "Value == " << *(int *)p;
```

4.8.

```
double *counter;
cout << "\nSize of pointer == " << sizeof(counter);
cout << "\nSize of addressed value == " <<
sizeof(*counter);
```

4.9.

```
// ticks.cpp -- Display system clock ticker

#include <stream.hpp>
#include <conio.h>
#include <dos.h>

main()
{
   unsigned long far *ticks = MK_FP(0x0040, 0x006C);

   cout << "System ticker. Press any key to quit.\n";
   while (!kbhit())
      cout << *ticks << chr(13);
}
```

4.10.
```
// strheap.cpp -- Create string on heap

#include <stream.hpp>

main()
{
   char *string = new char[129];

   cout << "Enter string: ";
   gets(string);
   cout << "You entered : " << string;
}
```

4.11.

```
// fptable.cpp -- Create & display float array

#include <stream.hpp>

main()
{
    int i;
    float *fpa = new float[100];

    for (i = 0; i < 100; i++)
        fpa[i] = i * i;
    for (i = 0; i < 100; i++)
        cout << form("%10.2f", fpa[i]);
}
```

4.12.

```
record *rp = new record;

rp->count = 1234;
rp->balance = 450.95;
rp->title = "My Report";
```

4.13.

```
rp->title = new char[80];
```

4.14. Be sure to delete the space assigned to title *before* deleting the space assigned to the variable in which the title field is stored.

```
delete rp->title;
delete rp;
```

4.15. NULL.

4.16. Fragmentation can occur after deleting selected variables from the heap, creating spaces between other variables still in use.

4.17. Study how the function returns NULL if it can't allocate space to a new lstring structure or to the char* field in that structure.

```
struct lstring {
    int length;
    char *s;
```

```
};

lstring *makelstr(const char *s)
{
    lstring *t = new lstring;
    if (t != NULL) {
        t->length = strlen(s);
        t->s = strdup(s);
        if (t->s == NULL) {
            delete t;
            t = NULL;
        }
    }
    return t;
}
```

4.18.

```
int *array1 = new int[100];
delete array1;

int *array2 = malloc(100 * sizeof(int));
free(array2);

int *array3 = calloc(100, sizeof(int));
free(array3);
```

4.19. There are many correct answers to this problem. The solution shown here simply sets all trailing blanks in a string to NULL bytes equal to 0.

```
void detail(char *s)
{
    if (s != NULL)
        for (int i = strlen(s) - 1; i >= 0; i--)
            if (s[i] == ' ')
                s[i] = 0;
            else
                return;
}
```

4.20.

```
double (* fp)(int i, float f);
// ...
double result = (* fp)(100, 3.14159);
```

4.21.

```
// fpmul.cpp -- Multiply two values from DOS command line

#include <stream.hpp>
#include <stdlib.h>

main(int argc, char *argv[])
{
    if (argc != 3) {
        cout << "Enter two floating point values.\n";
        cout << "ex. fpmul 3.14159 2.5\n";
        exit(0);
    } else
        cout << atof(argv[1]) * atof(argv[2]);
}
```

Chapter 5

5.1. A class encapsulates data and code. Functions declared in a class typically are the only functions permitted to access the class's data fields. Encapsulating code and data this way in classes helps so prevent many common bugs caused by statements in wide-spread locations that change and depend on global variables.

5.2. Only functions declared as members of a class may access private fields in the class.

5.3. Constructors are member functions that initialize class instances—variables of the class. Constructors run automatically when a class instance comes into scope or is created.

5.4.

```
// rect.cpp -- Rectangle class

#include <stream.hpp>
#include <disp.h>

class rectangle {
    private:
        int top, left, bottom, right;
```

```
   public:
      rectangle(int x1, int y1, int x2, int y2);
      void showRect(void);
};

main()
{
   disp_open();
   disp_move(0, 0);
   disp_eeop();
   rectangle rect(10, 4, 70, 16);
   rect.showRect();
   disp_move(24, 0);
   disp_close();
}

void twoChar(int x1, int y1, int x2, int y2)
{
   disp_move(y1, x1);
   disp_putc('#');
   disp_move(y2, x2);
   disp_putc('#');
}

rectangle::rectangle(int x1, int y1, int x2, int y2)
{
   top = y1;
   left = x1;
   bottom = y2;
   right = x2;
}

void rectangle::showRect(void)
{
   int i;
   for (i = left; i <= right; i++)
      twoChar(i, top, i, bottom);
   for (i = top; i <= bottom; i++)
      twoChar(left, i, right, i);
}
```

5.5. The answer here defines a square as a rectangle with a fixed x and y coordinate at upper left and an equal size for the rectangle's width and height. Create a square with a statement such as `square sq(8, 15, 6);` and display the square with `sq.showRect();`, the function inherited from `rectangle`. Because characters on screen are not perfectly square, the shape's boundaries may not appear equal. However, they will have the same number of characters.

```
class square : public rectangle {
    public:
        square(int size, int x, int y) :
        rectangle (x, y, x + size, y + size) { }
};
```

5.6. Only one function, the constructor, is a logical candidate for conversion to an inline member function. Function `showRect` may be too complex for inline expansion. (If you wrote your own `rectangle` class, however, other functions may be suitable for inline conversion.)

```
class rectangle {
    private:
        int top, left, bottom, right;
    public:
        rectangle(int x1, int y1, int x2, int y2);
        { top = y1; left = x1; bottom = y2; right = x2; }
        void showRect(void);
};
```

5.7.

```
class buttonCollection {
    private:
        button ba[NUMBUTTONS];
    public:
        buttonCollecton();
        void push(int buttonNumber, int upDown);
        int stateOfButton(int buttonNumber);
};
```

5.8. Only two changes are required to ELEVSIM.H. Set `MAXELEVS` to 2 and `MAXFLOORS` to 5. The point of this exercise is to demonstrate the importance of using constants for items like these. Simple changes to a few well-chosen constants can drastically affect the program's actions.

5.9. If you tried the modifications suggested in exercise 5.8, you'll notice that this is a *very* busy building. It's probably unrealistic to have about 200 people a minute lining up for two elevators in a 5-story structure. Changing the frequency to about 15 or 20 people per minute seems more reasonable—at least the two elevators are able to handle that load. To make this change, modify the formula for WANTS_TO_ENTER to the following (the exact value isn't important; if you lowered the original setting of 200, you solved the problem correctly):

```
#define WANTS_TO_ENTER  rand() < 25
```

5.10. Increase constant TRAVELTIME in ELEVSIM.H from 5 to 10. Notice that when you run the new program, a few more people take the stairs than before, but the elevators still handle the traffic flow fairly well.

Chapter 6

6.1. Class libraries tend to be easier to use because new classes can inherit properties of classes in the library. Inheritance lets you build new classes on the foundations in the library, even if you don't have the source text to the original programming.

6.2. The steps are marked in ROW.CPP with comments. Steps a), b), and c) can be shortened to the single line: canoe *cp = new canoe;:

```
// row.cpp -- Answer to exercise 6.2

#include <stream.hpp>

class canoe {
   public:
       void row(void);
};

main()
{
   canoe *cp;          // a)
   cp = new canoe;     // b), c)
   cp->row();          // d)
}

void canoe::row(void)
{
   cout << "Row, row, row your boat...";
}
```

6.3. To make a function virtual, preface its prototype with the key word `virtual`. The sample shows the `canoe` class with `row` converted to a virtual function. Virtual functions let pointers to instances of related objects call the correct function in a derived class.

```
class canoe {
   public:
      virtual void row(void);
};
```

6.4. Polymorphism refers to the capability of instances to change form at runtime. A pointer to a base class that declares a virtual function may actually address an instance of a class derived from that base class. In that case, calling the virtual function through the pointer can execute a virtual function in the derivation, even though the pointer's declared type was to the base. Polymorphism lets you design statements that can call member functions added later, without also requiring the original statements to be recompiled.

6.5. Early binding is what C++ (and other compilers) do to *bind* a call to a function's address during compilation. Late binding is what C++ (and other OOP languages) do to look up a virtual function's address at runtime.

6.6. The main disadvantage of virtual functions is that calls to the functions require an additional lookup at runtime. C++ can bind calls to normal functions at compile time, but it has to generate code that looks up a virtual function's address when the program runs. That lookup operation takes a small amount of time, which normally won't affect performance. However, the lookup does take *some* time and might have a negative effect on critical code that has to execute as fast as possible.

6.7. Did you remember to initialize the `window` class by calling the static member function `startup` and to deinitialize the class with `shutDown`?

```
// smallwin.cpp -- Use window class to display a window

#include <stream.hpp>
#include "window.h"
#include "key.h"

main()
{
   winStruct ws = {
      6, 20, 40, 12, // row, column, width, height
      0x07,          // text attribute
```

```
            0x0f,            // border attribute
            0x70,            // highlight attribute
            1                // border type
        };

        window *wp;          // Define pointer to window

        window::startup();
        wp = new window(ws, " Small Window ");
        wp->showWindow();
        wp->gotorc(2, 4);
        wp->puts("Press <Esc> to quit...");
        while (getKey() != 27) ;
        delete wp;
        window::shutDown();
    }
```

6.8. If you tried your hand at this exercise, you probably came up with several statements like those that follow. The statements work, but having to position the cursor before each call to puts is tedious, a problem you'll address in the next chapter. To complete WINTOOL's Help command (unless you already finished the job on your own), replace lines 136-138 with the following statements. Run the ZZ.BAT batch file to recompile and link WINTOOL.

```
helpWindow->gotorc(5, 12);
helpWindow->puts("Use the cursor keys to move the highlight");
helpWindow->gotorc(6, 12);
helpWindow->puts("bar and press <Enter> to select a command.");
helpWindow->gotorc(7, 12);
helpWindow->puts("Note the effect on the sample window. When");
helpWindow->gotorc(8, 12);
helpWindow->puts("the colors or attributes are as you want them,");
helpWindow->gotorc(9, 12);
helpWindow->puts("jot down the attribute values near the bottom");
helpWindow->gotorc(10, 12);
helpWindow->puts("left of the screen for your own windows.");
helpWindow->gotorc(15, 12);
```

6.9. Advantages include the capability of letting future programs inherit properties of keyboard and error classes and to isolate internal data structures in those classes. These are the same advantages that classes can give any programs. The disadvantages include the extra work involved with creating and using classes where conventional techniques will suit. The answer is a toss-up. It's not always easy to choose between conventional and OOP approaches.

6.10. To compile ONEKEY, enter the command **ztc onekey d:\path\key.obj** where *d:\path* is the path to KEY.OBJ.

```
// onekey.cpp -- Function to get a specific key

#include <stream.hpp>
#include "key.h"
#include "key.doc"

int oneKey(int keyToGet);

main()
{
    cout << "Press <F1>...";
    while (!oneKey(KEY_F1)) ;
    cout << "\nOkay, thanks!";
}

int oneKey(int keyToGet)
{
    int c;

    while ((c = getKey()) != keyToGet) ;
    return c;
}
```

6.11. <F7> equals –191; <Ctrl>-Q equals 17; <Alt>-<F9> equals –144. Use the TKEY program to determine `getkey` values for these and other keypresses.

6.12. Declare `errorignore` external and set that variable to true (1). After doing that, `error` will no longer halt the program, and you can use `getError` to retrieve error codes. The following two lines show how to turn on the `errorignore` switch. The first line should appear above `main`; the second may be in any function (including `main`):

```
extern int errorignore;
errorignore = 1;
```

6.13. To compile REDALERT, enter the command **ztc redalert d:\path\error.obj** where *d:\path* is the path to ERROR.OBJ. Any value (preferably negative) is allowed for the error code.

```
// redalert.cpp -- Demonstrate how to call error function

#include <stream.hpp>
```

```
#include "error.h"

main()
{
    error(-999, "Red alert");
}
```

6.14. A side effect occurs when a function changes a global value. It's called a side effect because, when a function is called in an expression, the effect on the global value may not be obvious by examining the function call.

6.15. One design for a saveCommand class follows. Other designs are also possible (see Listing 6.2, WINTOOL.H, lines 43-53).

```
class saveCommand : public command {
    public:
        helpCommand() : command(" Save") { }
        virtual void performCommand(void);

};
```

Chapter 7

7.1. Class strItem derives from item. Class selector derives from list, window, and item.

7.2. The term *multiple inheritance* refers to a class that derives from two or more base classes. The term *single inheritance* describes a class that derives from only one base class.

7.3. The fourFloats class here is probably the minimum design. A parameterless constructor initializes new fourFloats variables. Two member functions let you store and retrieve floating point values, specifying the value's number as int n. Because the class derives from item, you *must* allocate space for fourFloats instances on the heap.

```
class fourFloats : public item {
    private:
        double da[3];       // Array of 4 double values
    public:
        fourFloats();
```

```
        int setFloat(int n, double x);
        double getFloat(int n);
   };
```

7.4. A sample program puts the `fourFloats` class to the test. Notice how the common C++ function `showFloats` accepts a reference to a `fourFloats` instance, allowing the main program to pass *f4 as an argument to the function. To compile FOURFPS.CPP, enter `ztc  fourfps.cpp  d:\path\item.obj` where *d:\path* is the path to ITEM.OBJ.

```
// fourfps.cpp -- Class with four floating point values

#include <stream.hpp>
#include <item.h>

class fourFloats : public item {
   private:
      double da[3];       // Array of 4 double values
   public:
      fourFloats();
      int setFloat(int n, double x);
      double getFloat(int n);
};

void showFloats(fourFloats &ff, const char *s);

main()
{
   fourFloats *f4 = new fourFloats;

   showFloats(*f4, "\nBefore assignments:\n");
   for (int i = 0; i <= 5; i++)  // Use bad index for test
      f4->setFloat(i, 3.14159 * (i + 1));
   showFloats(*f4, "\nAfter assignments:\n");
}

void showFloats(fourFloats &ff, const char *s)
{
   cout << s;
   for (int i = 0; i <= 5; i++)  // Use bad index for test
      cout << form("value %d: %f\n", i, ff.getFloat(i));
}

fourFloats::fourFloats()
```

```
{
    for (int i = 0; i <= 3; i++)
        da[i] = 0;
}

int fourFloats::setFloat(int n, double x)
{
    if ((0 <= n) && (n <= 3)) {
        da[n] = x;
        return 0;    // no error
    } else
        return -1;   // error: n out of range
}

double fourFloats::getFloat(int n)
{
    if ((0 <= n) && (n <= 3))
        return da[n];
    else
        return 0;    // bad n values return 0
}
```

7.5. Member functions in a class derived from room may use numBooks, putInfo, and getInfo. Derived instances have direct access to items in their base class's protected and public sections. Derived class member functions may not access any private items in the base class.

Member functions putInfo and getInto in room may access all members of the class, including items in the private section. Member functions of a class may *always* access every member declared in that class.

Statements outside of the class or any derivatives may access room's public items, in this case, putInfo and getInfo. Statements outside of a class may never access any private or protected members.

7.6. The solution here is almost a complete program, but lacks a main function. With the info structure, putInfo and getInfo now require only single arguments, not three as in the original design. In general, passing structs to functions conserves memory during compilation by reducing the number of symbols the compiler needs to track. At runtime, passing the address of a struct may also improve performance over code that passes many small argument values to functions.

```
struct info {
    int chairs;
    int tables;
    int books;
};
```

```
class room {
   private:
      int numChairs;
      int numTables;
   protected:
      int numBooks;
   public:
      void putInfo(const info &x);
      void getInfo(info &x);
};

// Member function implementations ...

void room::putInfo(const info &x)
{
   numChairs = x.chairs;
   numTables = x.tables;
   numBooks = x.books;
}

void room::getInfo(info &x)
{
   x.chairs = numChairs;
   x.tables = numTables;
   x.books = numBooks;
}
```

7.7. A constructor runs when a variable of a class is created or comes into scope, for example, when a function that declares a local variable of a class type runs. A destructor runs when a variable is deleted or goes out of scope. In general, constructors initialize instances of their class. Destructors clean up class instances before those instances are deleted.

7.8. Constructors run from the ground up; that is, base constructors run before constructors in derived classes. Destructors run from the top down; derived constructors always run before any destructors in base classes. In this example, because A is the base class, A's constructor runs first. However, B's destructor runs before A's.

7.9. Inside an active member function, the this pointer addresses the instance of the class that called the function. You can use this *only* inside a member function; the pointer doesn't exist at any other locations. If name is the class's name, the this pointer's data type is name *. Inside exercise 7.5's getInfo member function, this's data type is equivalent to room *.

7.10. At a minimum, the derived ListCount class needs to provide replacement functions for insertItem and removeItem. The other functions do not require updating. Examine the implementations for the replacement functions. Each time an item is inserted, insertItem increments the private itemCount field. Each time an item is deleted, removeItem decrements itemCount. The actual insertions and deletions are handled by the base class functions, called by prefacing the function names with List::.

In addition to the replacement functions, ListCount defines an inline constructor that sets itemCount to 0. The class also includes a new inline member function getCount that returns the current itemCount value.

To compile the sample program, enter **ztc lstcount.cpp d:\path\item.obj d:\path\list.obj** where *d:\path* is the path to ITEM.OBJ and LIST.OBJ.

```
// lstcount.cpp -- A list class that counts listed items

#include <stream.hpp>
#include <item.h>
#include <list.h>

class ListCount : public List {
   private:
      unsigned int itemCount;
   public:
      ListCount()
         { itemCount = 0; }
      item *insertItem(item *ip);
      item *removeItem(item *ip);
      unsigned int getCount(void)
         { return itemCount; }
};

main()
{
   ListCount *lcp = new ListCount;
   cout << "\nBefore insertions count == " << lcp->getCount();
   lcp->insertItem(new item);
   lcp->insertItem(new item);
   lcp->insertItem(new item);
   cout << "\nAfter 3 insertions count == " << lcp->getCount();
   lcp->removeItem(lcp->currentItem());
   cout << "\nAfter 1 deletion count == " << lcp->getCount();
}


item * ListCount::insertItem(item *ip)
{
```

```
    list::insertItem(ip);
    itemCount++;
}

item * listCount::removeItem(item *ip)
{
    list::removeItem(ip);
    itemCount--;
}
```

7.11. Because the strItem class stores its sp pointer privately, the derived class can't modify the string directly. The only good alternative is to create new constructors that convert stored strings to uppercase after the base-class constructors are finished initializing the strItem instances. As shown here, upperStr adds two constructors similar in design to those in strItem. The constructors call strdup to create a temporary copy of the string passed to the constructors. Errors here halt the program with a call to the error function in ERROR.CPP. Member function putString, inherited from strItem, replaces the string converted to uppercase with strupr, a function prototyped in STRING.H. Finally, the temporary string copy is deleted.

To compile UPPERSTR.CPP, enter the command **ztc upperstr d:\path\error.obj d:\path\item.obj d:\path\stritem.obj** where *d:\path* is the path to ERROR.OBJ, ITEM.OBJ, and STRITEM.OBJ.

```
// upperstr.cpp -- An uppercase-string class

#include <stream.hpp>
#include <string.h>
#include <error.h>
#include <item.h>
#include <stritem.h>

class upperStr : public strItem {
    public:
        upperStr(const char *s);
        upperStr(const char *s, int maxLen);
};

main()
{
    upperStr *usp = new upperStr("An upper class string");
    cout << "String == " << usp->getString();
}
```

```
upperStr::upperStr(const char *s) : strItem(s)
{
    char *sp = strdup(s);
    if (sp == NULL) error(ERRMEM);
    putString(strupr(sp));
    delete sp;
}

upperStr::upperStr(const char *s, int maxLen) :
  strItem(s, maxLen)
{
    char *sp = strdup(s);
    if (sp == NULL) error(ERRMEM);
    putString(strupr(sp), maxLen);
    delete sp;
}
```

7.12. What's needed is a put l n function that performs a carriage return and line feed after writing a string to a window. The new function needs to scroll the window up one line after writing text to the bottom line. The derived class needs to keep track of the current cursor's line, which requires replacing the gotorc function.

PUTLN.CPP shows one approach to solving this problem. Compile the program with the command **ztc putln ..\lib\error.obj ..\lib\item.obj ..\lib\stritem.obj ..\lib\window.obj** where *d:\path* is the path to ERROR.OBJ, ITEM.OBJ, STRITEM.OBJ, and WINDOW.OBJ. When you run the program, you'll see a sample window with random text lines scrolling upward. Press any key to end the demonstration. So you can see the scrolling action, a call to ms l eep slows the program's wh i l e loop. Take out this line and recompile to see the window scroll at the fastest possible rate.

```
// putln.cpp -- Add putln function to window class

#include <stream.hpp>
#include <conio.h>
#include <time.h>
#include <stdlib.h>
#include <window.h>

class window2 : public window {
    private:
        int yline;
    public:
        window2() : window()
            { yline = 0; }
```

```
window2(winStruct &ws, const char *title): window(ws, title)
        { yline = 0; }
      void putln(char *s);
      void gotorc(int row, int col);
};

void fillBuffer(char *buf);

main()
{
    winStruct ws = { 4, 44, 31, 18, 0x07, 0x1f, 0x70, 3 };
    window2 *theWindow;
    char buffer[80];
    window::startup();
    theWindow = new window2(ws, " Scrolling Window ");
    theWindow->showWindow();
    while (!kbhit()) {
        fillBuffer(buffer);
        theWindow->putln(buffer);
        msleep(125);         // Remove this line for top speed
    }
    window::shutDown();
}

/* Write string and perform carriage return, line feed */
void window2::putln(char *s)
{
    winStruct ws;
    puts(s);
    ws = getInfo();
    int n = ws.height - 2;
    if (yline > n) yline = n;
    if (yline == n) {
        scrollUp(1);
        gotorc(yline, 0);
        eeol();
    } else
        gotorc(++yline, 0);
}

/* -- Replacement gotorc function */
void window2::gotorc(int row, int col)
{
```

```
        yline = row;
        window::gotorc(row, col);
    }

    /* -- Fill character buffer with random letters */
    void fillBuffer(char *buf)
    {
        for (int i = 0; i <= 20; i++)
            buf[i] = 'a' + (rand() % 26);
        buf[i] = 0;
    }
```

7.13. Static member fields resemble global variables in several ways. Static fields are stored in a fixed location and retain their values for the life of the program. However, by declaring static members privately inside a class, you limit the scope of those members to the class. Statements outside the class's member functions can't use the static variables.

7.14. Returning pointers to a class's private member fields gives programs a sneaky way to peek into a class instance's normally hidden sections. The compiler allows this, but generally, it's best to avoid this situation by returning a reference (&) to private data rather than a pointer that addresses that data directly.

7.15. A simple answer is listed here. More sophisticated programs would operate like WINTOOL and let you select border styles. Compile BORDER.CPP with the command **ztc border d:\path\error.obj d:\path\item.obj d:\path\stritem.obj d:\path\window.obj** where *d:\path* is the path to ERROR.OBJ, ITEM.OBJ, STRITEM.OBJ, and WINDOW.OBJ. Run the program by typing **border n** where *n* is a number from 0 to 4. Values outside this range will produce some unusual (and probably useless) "special effects."

```
// border.cpp -- Test window border styles

#include <stream.hpp>
#include <conio.h>
#include <window.h>

main(int argc, char *argv[])
{
    window *theWindow;
    int windowType;

    if (argc < 2)
        windowType = 3;
    else
```

```
     windowType = atoi(argv[1]);
  winStruct ws = { 4, 44, 31, 18, 0x07, 0x1f, 0x70, windowType };
  window::startup();
  theWindow = new window(ws, " Border Test ");
  theWindow->showWindow();
  theWindow->gotorc(4, 3);
  theWindow->puts(form("Type == %d", windowType));
  while (!kbhit()) /* wait */ ;
  theWindow->hideWindow();
  window::shutDown();
}
```

Chapter 8

8.1. After compiling, run UPFILE by entering **upfile file** where *file* is the name of any text file. To save the result, enter a command such as **upfile file >save** where *save* is the name of a new file you want to create. Note: UPFILE does not warn you before overwriting an existing file.

```
// upfile.cpp -- Convert text file to uppercase

#include <stream.hpp>
#include <ctype.h>
#include <stdlib.h>

main(int argc, char *argv[])
{
   FILE *fp;
   char c;
   if (argc == 1) {
      cout << "ERROR: No file name";
      exit(1);
   }
   fp = fopen(argv[1], "r");
   if (!fp) {
      cout << "ERROR: File not found";
      exit(2);
   }
   while ((c = fgetc(fp)) != EOF)
      cout << chr(toupper(c));
```

```
      fclose(fp);
      exit(0);
}
```

8.2. Compile and run CR2LF.CPP to convert carriage returns to line feeds. For example, enter a command such as **cr2lf cr2lf test.txt** to transfate CR2LF.CPP to TEST.TXT. Then enter **type test.txt** to see the effect the program had on the text. (The results will be virtually unreadable under DOS because of the lack of carriage returns in the output.) The second half of the answer—a program to convert line feeds back to carriage return and line feed pairs—is not shown. Use CR2LF as a guide for completing this program.

```cpp
// cr2lf.cpp -- Convert carriage returns to line feeds

#include <stream.hpp>
#include <ctype.h>
#include <stdlib.h>

#define CR 13   // ASCII carriage return
#define LF 10   // ASCII line feed

main(int argc, char *argv[])
{
    FILE *fpin, *fpout;
    unsigned char c, lf = LF;
    int nout;

    if (argc < 3) {
        cout << "ERROR: No file names";
        exit(1);
    }
    fpin = fopen(argv[1], "rb");
    if (!fpin) {
        cout << "ERROR: File not found";
        exit(2);
    }
    fpout = fopen(argv[2], "wb");
    if (!fpout) {
        cout << "ERROR: Can't create output file";
        exit(3);
    }
    while (fread(&c, 1, 1, fpin) > 0) {
        if (c == CR)
            nout = fwrite(&lf, 1, 1, fpout);
```

```
         else if (c != LF)
            nout = fwrite(&c, 1, 1, fpout);
         if (nout != 1) {
            cout << "ERROR: Writing to disk";
            exit(4);
         }
      }
      fclose(fpin);
      fclose(fpout);
      exit(0);
}
```

8.3. Reading a text file one character at a time imposes no maximum line length. Reading text a line at a time requires you to allocate space for the largest line in a file. However, reading text a line at a time is usually faster than the single character approach.

8.4. Many C and C++ listings are formatted with embedded tab characters to align text at columns n + 4, where the first column equals 1. Because DOS expands tabs to 8-column widths, displaying 4-column-tab files with the DOS TYPE command overexpands the lines. TAB4.CPP shows one way to display files with 4-column tabs to all blanks. Compile the program and enter a command such as **tab4 source.txt**. Or to convert tabs to blanks, enter **tab4 source.txt >new.txt** where NEW.TXT is the new file you want to create. (TAB4 does not warn you before overwriting an existing file.)

```
// tab4.cpp -- Display text with 4-column tabs

#include <stream.hpp>
#include <stdio.h>
#include <stdlib.h>

#define TABSTOP 5         // 5 == 4-column tabs

main(int argc, char *argv[])
{
   FILE *fp;
   char c;
   int count;

   if (argc == 1) {
      cout << "ERROR: No file name";
      exit(1);
   }
   fp = fopen(argv[1], "r");
```

```
    if (!fp) {
        cout << "ERROR: File not found";
        exit(2);
    }
    count = 1;
    while ((c = fgetc(fp)) != EOF) {
        if (c == '\t')
            while ((++count % 5) != 1) cout << ' ';
        else {
            if (c == '\n')
                count = 1;
            else
                count++;
            cout << c;
        }
    }
    fclose(fp);
}
```

8.5. Add the first two lines here to the beginning of WINTOOL.CPP. Then replace function `helpCommand::performCommand` with the new function listed below. You'll also need to create a file named WINHELP.TXT containing the help text to display in the window.

```
#include <dos.h>
#include <string.h>

void helpCommand::performCommand(void)
{
    winStruct ws = {
        2, 2, 76, 21,    // row, column, width, height
        0x1f,            // text attribute
        0x70,            // border attribute
        0x70,            // highlight attribute
        0                // border type
    };
window *helpWindow = new window(ws, " WinTool Help ");
    int row = 0;
    FILE *fp;
    char buffer[80];
    int len;

    helpWindow->showWindow();
    fp = fopen("winhelp.txt", "r");
    if (fp) {
```

```
        while (!feof(fp)) {
            helpWindow->gotorc(row++, 0);
            if (fgets(buffer, 75, fp) != NULL) {
                len = strlen(buffer);
                if (len > 0) buffer[len - 1] = 0;
                helpWindow->puts(buffer);
            }
        }
    }
    fclose(fp);
    while (!keyWaiting()) ;
    getKey();
    delete helpWindow;
}
```

8.6. Assume the array is defined as `double fparray[100];`.

```
fwrite(fparray, sizeof(double), 100, fp);
fread(fparray, sizeof(double), 100, fp);
```

8.7. To solve this problem, you need to make a few changes to READDB. First, to allow reading and writing SAMPLE.DAT, change `"rb"` in the `fopen` command to `"rb+"`. Add the following `putRec` function and call it to write a modified record to disk. The new function is nearly identical to `getRec`, but calls `fwrite` rather than `fread`. You'll also need to create a function (not shown here) that lets people edit records.

```
int putRec(FILE *fp, rec &oneRec, long recnum)
{
    if (fseek(fp, recnum * sizeof(rec), SEEK_SET) != 0)
        return FALSE;
    if (fwrite(&oneRec, sizeof(rec), 1, fp) != 1)
        return FALSE;
    return TRUE;

}
```

8.8. The key to this exercise is a function that can search for records with specific values in a field. Following is a sample that should help you to finish the program. The `searchRec` function returns true if it can locate at least one record with the specified `custnum` value. The `rewind` statement resets the file to its beginning. Then a `while` loop reads each record and compares the `custnum` field with the customer number passed to the function. A more sophisticated solution would prepare an index of customer and record numbers and use some other method to search for matches. The sequential search demonstrated here works, but only for relatively small database files.

```
int searchRec(FILE *fp, rec &oneRec, long &recnum, long custnum)
{
    rewind(fp);
    recnum = 0;
    while (!feof(fp)) {
        if (fread(&oneRec, sizeof(rec), 1, fp) != 1)
            return FALSE;
        if (oneRec.custnum == custnum)
            return TRUE;
        recnum++;
    }
    return FALSE;
}
```

8.9. The solution to this problem requires two changes to the basic directory reading program SDIR.CPP. First, you need to specify the FA_DIREC attribute in the call to findfirst. That locates all directory names, but it also locates all files in the current directory. There's no easy way to prevent DOS from matching file names; therefore, to list only directories, you also have to check for the directory attribute bit in the filename's attribute field. The example shows how to do this with an if statement and a logical AND operator (&).

```
// subdirs.cpp -- List subdirectory names

#include <stream.hpp>
#include <dos.h>

main()
{
    struct FIND *fp;
    char *wildCard = "*.*";

    cout << "Directories in current path:\n";
    fp = findfirst(wildCard, FA_DIREC);
    while (fp) {
        if ((fp->attribute & FA_DIREC) != 0)
            cout << fp->name << '\n';
        fp = findnext();
    }
}
```

Chapter 9

9.1. To allow unrelated classes to access each other's private and protected members, declare the classes as friends. In the sample classes here, function `engine_fn` will be permitted to access `fuel` parameter f's private `fuelLevel` field. Likewise, function `fuel_fn` will be allowed direct access to the `engine` parameter e's private `powerLevel`. If the classes were not declared as friends, they would not be permitted to access hidden data in each other. Notice how `fuel` is declared forward on the first line, allowing the reference to `fuel` in the parameter list for `engine_fn` before the `fuel` class is formally declared.

```
class fuel;

class engine {
     friend class fuel;
  private:
     int powerLevel;
  public:
     engine() { powerLevel = 0; }
     void engine_fn(fuel &f);
};

class fuel {
     friend class engine;
  private:
     int fuelLevel;
  public:
     fuel() { fuelLevel = 0; }
     void fuel_fn(engine &e);
};
```

9.2. Friends allow unrelated classes to fiddle with normally hidden variables. Later changes to those variables may cause problems, especially in programs that declare many friend classes. Friends are like `gotos`—they break the very rules that, when used sensibly, can help you write reliable programs.

9.3. Function overloading lets you name two or more functions the same as long as at least one parameter differs.

9.4. A class destructor.

9.5. The full class plus the two additional operator functions are listed here. Add these to STROPS.CPP for a complete demonstration.

```
class strop {
   private:
      char value[12];
   public:
      strop() { value[0] = 0; }
      strop(const char *s);

      friend long operator+(strop a, strop b);
      friend long operator-(strop a, strop b);
      friend long operator*(strop a, strop b);
      friend long operator/(strop a, strop b);
};

// ...

long operator*(strop a, strop b)
{
   return (atol(a.value) * atol(b.value));
}
long operator/(strop a, strop b)
{
   return (atol(a.value) / atol(b.value));
}
```

9.6. Add the first two lines here to strop's pubic section and also insert the two operator functions in STROPS.CPP. You can then write statements like cout << "\na++   == " << a++; and cout << "\nb--   == " << b--;.

```
// Add to strops:
long operator++(void);
long operator--(void);

// Add to STROPS.CPP:
long strop::operator++(void)
{
   return atol(value) + 1;
}

long strop::operator--(void)
{
   return atol(value) - 1;
}
```

9.7. strop &spAlias = *sp;

9.8. Add the following line to `strop`'s public section:

```
operator double() { return atof(value); }
```

After making that change, you can then insert statements like this one into `main`:

```
cout << "\nc == " << form("%8.3f", (double)c);
```

9.9. When one instance initializes a newly defined instance of the same class, when an instance is passed to a function's value parameter of the class type, when a function returns a class instance, and when a statement assigns one instance to another.

The danger of copying class instances is that fields in those instances might be pointers to data stored on the heap or elsewhere. The instance copies must not copy the pointer fields, but rather should copy the addressed information. Having two pointers address the same data is dangerous because the program might delete the same locations in the heap more than once.

9.10.

```
Fruit Orange;
Fruit Grapefruit = Orange;
```

9.11.

```
Fruit(Fruit &copy);
```

9.12.

```
void operator=(const Fruit &copy);
```

9.13. When a class constructor assigns an address to `this`, the compiler assumes that the class will handle allocation of memory for instances of the class. The technique, a hold-over from early C++ versions, is no longer recommended. A better approach for customizing memory allocations for a class is to overload the `new` and `delete` operators.

A primary danger of assigning an address to `this` is that the constructor *must* account for all situations. If the constructor returns without initializing `this`, the program may continue unaware that a memory allocation request failed.

9.14. The member field defaults to private status.

9.15. Using the `public` key word in a derivation list causes inherited members from a base class to retain their original private, protected, and public status. Using the `private` key word in a derivation list causes all inherited members to become private to the derived class. As a result, future derivations may not access the base class members. If neither key word is used, the default status is private.

Index

~ destructor, 385
$gb, inserting into string, 35
-> operator, 196, 202

A

A class, 347-349
abs function, 575
abstract class, 351-352
abstract function, 443
access function, 565-566
aClass class, 344-346, 382-383, 507-508, 510
aClass function, 514
acos function, 576
action class, 256-267, 269, 273
action data type, 256

action function, 267-269, 272, 286, 288, 291, 293, 309, 313
ACTION program, 269, 271-274, 276
    listing, 270-271
ACTION.H header file, 256, 266-269, 271-272, 274, 276, 324
    conditional directives, 266-267
ACTION.OBJ file, 272, 274
additem function, 212
addition (+) operator, 45, 520
address buffers, void pointers, 187
addressToAssign function, 550
adjustTime function, 486
advanced operators, 54-56
afunction function, 228-229
algorithms, 167
    elevator movement, 309-311
alias, 184
ALIAS program, 183-184
    listing, 183
ALLRECDB program, 476-477
    listing, 476-477

alphabet, displaying, 183-184
ALPHABET.CPP listing, 695-696
`animal` class, 317-318, 320-321, 323
ANIMAL.CPP listing, 317-322
AQUOTE.CPP listing, 688-689
`argc` command-line argument, 242-244, 246, 248-249
arguments, 134
`argv` command-line argument, 242-244, 246, 249
`array` function, 529
ARRAY program, 106-108
   listing, 106
ARRAYLST program, 529-533
   listing, 530-531
ARRAYPTR program, 229-231
   listing, 230
arrays, 39, 105-115
   character, 115
   defining size, 105
   dynamic, 213-214
   elements
      addressing directly with pointers, 231-232
      assigning values, 111
   flat, 111
   global, 110
   indexes, 105, 107-108, 115
      overloading, 529-533
   initializing, 110-111
   multiple-dimension, 111-115
   multiple `struct` variables, 108
   pointers and, 106, 117-118, 229-234
   reserving space on heap, 199
   size, 123, 213-214
   storing information, 108-110
   two-dimensional, 111
   values
      listing constant, 111
      sorting, 168-170
ASC program, 174, 176-179
   listing, 174-176

ASCII
   characters, 33, 88
   hexadecimal ('\x00') escape code, 35
   octal ('\000') escape code, 35
   text displaying 256 characters, 174-179
   text files, 452-467
ASCII.CPP listing, 88-89
`asctime` function, 235-236
`asin` function, 576
ASK.CPP listing, 686
assignment operator, overloading, 536-549
assignment statements, 16
asterisk (*) wild-card character, 482
`atan` function, 577
`atHeadOfList` function, 396
`atof` function, 30-31, 577
`atoi` function, 249, 578
`atol` function, 30, 524, 527-578
ATONUMS program, 29-31
   listing, 30
`attrCommand` class, 341-342, 359, 363-364
attribute values, 177-178
automatic type conversion, 533-536

B

B class, 347-349
backslash
   ('\\') escape code, 35
   (\), joining characters in string, 5
backspace ('\b') escape code, 34
base class, 316-327, 567
   constructor and virtual member functions, 405
   public and private, 318-319
   virtual, 566-568

bClass class, 383, 507-510
bell ('\a') escape code, 34
binary
    %b formatting instruction, 26
    files, 467-479
    operators, 520, 526
    values
        displaying, 26
        read from disk, 471-473
        written to disk, 468-471
_bios_disk function, 452
_bios_equiplist function, 120, 122,
 127
BIOS.H header file, 120-122
bird class, 319-323
bit fields, 119-122
BITDATE.CPP listing, 697-698
bits, 118-122
    moving left and right, 68-69
bitwise AND (&) operator, 63-64, 67
bitwise exclusive OR (^) operator, 63, 66-68
bitwise inclusive OR (|) operator, 63-65, 67
bitwise operators, 62-69
    .AND (&), 63-64, 67
    exclusive OR (^), 63, 66-68
    inclusive OR (|), 63-65, 67
    complement (~), 63, 69
    shift bits left (<<), 63, 68-69
    shift bits right (>>), 63, 68-69
BLINK program, 275, 277
BLINK.EXE file, 274
blocks, 3, 57
    nested, 17-18
Boolean data type, 43
BORDER.CPP listing, 721-22
BOX program, 159-160
    listing, 158-159
boxes, drawing on-screen, 158-159
BP program, 135, 137-138
    listing, 135-137
braces ({})
    checking for mismatched, 132-135
    delimiter in compound statement, 57

brandNew class, 553
break statements, 81-83, 91-93
BREAKER program, 91
    listing, 91
buddy class, 509-510
buffer array, 188
buffers, allocating, 215
BUILDER.H header file, 329
building class, 324-329
BUILDING program, 276
    listing, 325-328
BUILDING.H header file, 276, 324
    listing, 323-324
button class, 257-261
BUTTON program, 258-260, 264
    listing, 257-258
BUTTON2 program, 261-263
    listing, 262
buttonDown function, 306
buttons, simulating, 257-258
buttonUp function, 306
bytes, combining into words, 178

C

C programming language
    C-style comments, 7
    differences from C++, 568-569
    output, 22-23
    old-style input, 28
C++ programming language
    comment, 7
    differences from C, 568-569
    hardware and software requirements, iii
    program parts, 1-12
calloc function, 214-215, 579
carriage return ('\r') escape code, 35

cases, 81-83
   sensitivity, 9-10
categorized lists, 41
CBLANKS.CPP listing, 697
CD (DOS) command, 481
CDIR program, 481
   listing, 481
ceil function, 579-580
center function, 166
CENTER program, 166
   listing, 164-165
centerText function, 147
char constant, 33-35
char data type, 13, 22-23
character arrays, 115
   initializing, 116-117
characters, 24
   command-line arguments, 245-247
   converting to lowercase, 72
   escape codes, 34-35
   getting from file, 133
   lowercase to uppercase, 72
chdir function, 481, 580
chr function, 23-24, 580-581
circle class, 351-352, 519
CIRCUM.CPP listing, 690
class instances, 540
   copying, 538-539
class library (LC++), 335-448
class - functions, 259-260, 273
   naming, 259
   overloading, 518-519
class variables, 343-346
classes, 253-333, 506-515, 554
   as data type, 264-267
   base, 316-325, 327, 567
   constructors, 267-269
   copying pointer fields, 541-543
   creating, 257-261
   declaring fields and functions, 258
   derived, 316-325, 327, 386-387

duties, 269, 271-273
extinct, 320
forward class declaration, 510
functions
   defining, 259
   encapsulating, 255
   friend, 511-515
friends, 506-515
   mutual, 510
header files, 274
hierarchy in LC++ class library, 380-381
inheritance, 316-328
initializing global aspect, 413
members, 258-259
modules and, 273-276
multiple inheritance, 380, 566-567
pointers to variables, 342-346
private section, 294
public section, 294
selector, 432-441, 443, 446, 500, 503-504
shape, 350-353
tactics, 269, 271-273
clearerr function, 581
closeCommand class, 446
closeTopWindow function, 220
CMDLINE program, 243-244
   listing, 243
cmpkeys function, 195, 197
COCO program, 149
   listing, 149
colasc function, 177
colors data type, 41
COLUMN program, 247-249
   listing, 248
combinatorial coefficient, 148-151
combined assignment operator, 70, 110
command class, 339, 341, 358, 441-447
command-line arguments, 242-249
   argc, 242-244, 246, 248-249
   argv, 242-244, 246, 249
   character, 245-247
   numeric, 247-249

COMMAND.H header file, 337, 339, 441-443
  listing, 441-442
commands, 440-441, 446-447
  menus, 341
COMMENT program, 7-8
  listing, 7-8
comments, 6-9
  #define control line, 38
  /* */ symbols, 6-7
  // symbols, 7
  C++, 7
  C-style, 7
  nested, 7
commonInits function, 412
COMP1 program, 99-101
  listing, 99-100
COMP2.CPP listing, 101-102
compare function, 465-467
COMPDB.H header file, 99-101, 103, 108,
  117, 123
  listing, 99
compilers
  converting programs for, 569-570
  minimum overhead, 9
complement (~) operator, 63, 69
compound statements, 57-58
computers, equipment attached, 120-121
conditional
  directives, 266-267
  expressions, 559-560
  statements, nesting, 560
cone, volume, 172-173
cone function, 173
CONE program, 172-173
  listing, 172-173
conflict class, 561-562
CONIO.H header file, 366
const key word, 39-40, 545
CONST program, 39
  listing, 39

constants, 31-45
  declared, 32, 39-40
  defined, 32, 37-38
  enumerated, 32, 40-45
  floating point, 37
  literal, 32-37
  named, 32, 37
  pointers, 569
  signed char, 33
  signed int, 34
  string, 35-36
  types, 32
  unsigned char, 33
  whole number, 36
constructors, 518
  base classes vs. derived classes, 388
  chaining, 322
  multiple in strItem class, 402
  overloading, 402, 414-415
container class, 381
CONTINUE program, 92-93
  listing, 92-93
continue statement, 92-93
continues function, 256, 269, 324, 326
control
  codes, escape codes as, 34
  lines, 37
  structures, 71
conversion operators, 534
CONVERT.CPP listing, 31
copy constructor, 543-548
  calling operator= function, 547-548
  memberwise assignment, 545-547
cos function, 582
countchars function, 134-135
countdown function, 129
COUNTS.CPP listing, 689
countup function, 129-130
cout object, 3-4
CPP file extension, 101

CR2LF.CPP listing, 723-724
`createMainWindow` function, 356
createSampWindow function, 357
CRSTAT program, 192-193
    listing, 192
CTYPE.H header file, 72, 79
CUBE.CPP listing, 700-701

D

`dashes` function, 161-162
data encapsulation, 303
data fields, returning values, 260
data files, 467-479
    basic techniques, 467-468
    binary values
        read from disk, 471-473
        written to disk, 468-471
    person, 284
    reading and writing, 468
data segment, global variables, 19
data structures, 95-124
    arrays, 105-118
    bit fields, 118-122
    nested, 102-103
    recursive, 210
    strings, 95, 115-117
    struct, 96-03
    unions, 103-115, 121
data types
    action, 256
    assignments, 537-538
    automatic type conversion, 533-536
    `Boolean`, 43
    `char`, 13, 22-23
    class as, 264-267

`colors`, 41
declared constants, 39
`double`, 13
expressions, 569
`float`, 13
`int`, 13, 22
LANGUAGE, 42
literal constants, 33-37
`long`, 13
`long double`, 13
member, 96
number of 8-bit bytes occupied, 122-124
`pfptr`, 228
pointers and, 185
reserving space on heap, 199-200
scale, 42
`short`, 13
signed and unsigned values, 33-34
`struct`, 96-103, 201-202
unnamed enumerated, 42-43
user-defined, overloading, 533-536
variables, 13-15
void pointers, 187-190
data-hiding concept, 506
database files, 473-479
    computer system, 99-102
    fields, 96-98
    reading, 476-479
    saving and retrieving, 473-476
date
    converting to ASCII string, 235
    displaying, 21
`dec` function, 23-24, 26, 163, 582-583
decimal
    10 significant digits, `%.10f` formatting
        instruction, 26
    displaying integers as, 25
    converting to hex and octal, 31
    or scientific notation values, `%g` format-
        ting instruction, 26
    values, 10 character columns `%10d`
        formatting instruction, 26

standard, %f formatting instruction, 26
declarations, 2-3
declared constants, 32, 39-40
   data types, 39
   evaluating values, 40
declared void far pointer, 197
decrement — operator, 46-49
default function arguments, 161-166
   library functions, 163
default: selector, 83
#define conditional directive, 266
#define control line, 37, 40, 84
   comments, 38
DEFINE program, 37-38
   listing, 38
defined constants, 32, 37-38
definitions, 2-3
deinitializing variables, 385
delete operator, 199-200, 237, 549-550, 554, 569
   overloading, 553
delitem function, 212
dereferencing pointer, 182-185
derived class, 316-323, 387
   copying instances, 548-549
   multiple inheritance, 432-433
   pointers, 346, 387
   public and private, 318-319
   single inheritance, 431
derivedItem class, 386-387
destination address, strings, 238-239
destructors, 385, 390, 519
   base classes vs. derived classes, 388
difference symbol (~), 385
DIR (DOS) command, 483-484
DIR.CPP listing, 493-497
DIR.H header file, 488-490
   listing, 488-489
directives
   #ifdef, 266
   #include, 12
   linkage, 466

directories, 451, 479-499
   changing, 480-481
   decoding information, 483-486
   DIR module, 488-492
   DIR.CPP module, 493-497
   displaying, 482-483
   include, 12
   modifying entries, 487-488
   navigating, 497-499
directory class, 488-500
discharge function, 291, 294
disks, checking free space, 479-480
DISP.H header file, 159, 356, 569
display function, 256, 324, 328
displayArray function, 170
disposeList function, 394, 398
disp_box function, 160, 220, 339, 583
disp_close function, 583-584
disp_eeol function, 213, 584
disp_eeop function, 585
disp_endstand function, 585
disp_fillbox function, 220, 586
disp_flush function, 586-587
disp_hidecursor function, 587
disp_move function, 588
disp_open function, 159, 588-589
disp_peekbox function, 220, 589
disp_pointer function, 189-190
disp_pokebox function, 220, 423, 590
disp_pokew function, 177
disp_printf function, 195, 213, 590-591
disp_putc function, 591
disp_puts function, 592
disp_reset43 function, 592-593
disp_scroll function, 593
disp_setattr function, 594-595
disp_set43 function, 594
disp_showcursor function, 596
disp_startstand function, 596-597
division (/) operator, 45
dnwaiting functions, 288-289, 294

do key word, 85
do-forever loops, 90
do/while loop, 85-87
    interrupting, 91-92
DOGCAT.CPP listing, 688
DOS
    functions, 452
    passing unsigned integer to, 71, 73
dos_getfileattr function, 600
DOS.H header file, 21, 192, 479-480, 482
doSomething function, 397, 540
dos_abs_disk_read function, 452
dos_abs_disk_write function, 452
dos_getdate function, 598
dos_getdiskfreespace function,
    479-480, 598-599
dos_getdrive function, 599
dos_gettime function, 127, 600-601
dos_get_ctrl_break function, 597
dos_get_verify function, 601-602
dos_setdate function, 602-603
dos_setdrive function, 603-604
dos_setfileattr function, 604
dos_settime function, 605
dos_set_ctrl_break function, 602
dos_set_verify function, 605-606
dot notation, 98, 101
double data type, 13
double quote ('\"') escape code, 35
draw function, 350-352, 519
drawbox function, 160
DSTRUCT program, 201-203
    listing, 201-202
DT program, 21-22
    listing, 21
dynamic
    arrays, 213-214
    lists, 205-213
    variables, 198-205

E

early binding, 354
eeol function, 420, 438
eeow function, 362, 420
elevator class, 305-315
elevator movement algorithm, 309-311
ELEVATOR program, 276
    listing, 307-309, 311-315
elevator simulation program, 276, 278-332
    compiling, 277
    general header file, 279-281
    linker response file, 277
    running, 278
ELEVATOR.H header file, 276, 306
    listing, 305-306
elevCollection class, 306, 314-315
ELEVSIM program, 276-315, 326, 329-332,
    348
    listing, 329-332
ELEVSIM.EXE file, 277
ELEVSIM.H header file, 276, 281, 288, 330
    listing, 279-280
ELEVSIM.LNK file, 276
    listing, 277
elevStopping function, 309, 313
ENCRYPT.CPP listing, 692
#endif directives, 374
enum key word, 41
ENUM program, 41-43
    listing, 42
enumerated constants, 32, 40-45
    assigning element values, 43-45
EOF (end of file), 76
equal (==) relational operator, 55
equal sign (=)
    assigning values to variables, 16
    operator, 45
EQUIP program, 120-122
    listing, 120-121
error function, 372-376

error-handling, 370-376
ERROR module, 337, 371-376, 417
   listing, 372-375
   testing, 375-376
ERROR.H header file, 337, 372-374, 404
   listing, 371
escape character, 25
escape codes
   as control codes, 34
   ASCII hexadecimal('\x00'), 35
   ASCII octal ('\000'), 35
   backslash ('\\'), 35
   backspace ('\b'), 34
   bell ('\a'), 34
   carriage return ('\r'), 35
   character, 34, 35
   double quote ('\$dq'), 35
   form feed ('\f'), 34
   horizontal tab ('\t'), 35
   new line ('\n'), 35
   question mark ('\?'), 35
   single quote('\''), 35
   vertical tab ('\v'), 35
EXAMPLE program, 574
   listing, 574
EXE file, 9
exercises, answers, 685-730
exit function, 61, 71-74, 606
exp function, 607
exponents, 37
expressions, 2, 49-50
   conditional, 559-560
   data types, 569
   fully qualified, 98
   short-circuit evaluation, 59
extern key word, 142
EXTERN1 program, 141-142
   listing, 141-142
EXTERN1.EXE file, 141
EXTERN2.CPP listing, 142
external variables, 141-142
extinct class, 320

F

f function, 162, 347-349
fabs function, 607
factorial function, 148-153
_farptr_norm function, 233
far pointers, 190-192
   keyboard, 193-197
   normalized, 233
fclose function, 133, 456, 460, 468, 608
fcloseall function, 608-609
feof function, 472, 609
ferror function, 609-610
fflush function, 610-611
fgetc function, 133, 460-462, 611
fgets function, 462, 611-612
fields, 96-98, 118-122
   bit, 119-121
   class declaration, 258
   overlaying at same location, 103-105
   separating from next field, 98
   static member, 414, 423
FIFO (first-in first-out), 206
file extensions
   .CPP, 101
   .H, 12, 101
   .HPP, 12, 101
FILE variable, 137
file-handling techniques, 452
FILE.TXT file, 466
fileItem class, 488-490, 492-493
files, 451-479
   ACTION.OBJ, 272, 274
   BLINK.EXE, 274
   closing, 133
   data, 467-479
   database, 473-479
   ELEVSIM.EXE, 277
   ELEVSIM.LNK, 276
   EXE, 9
   EXTERN1.EXE, 141

FILE.TXT, 466
getting character from, 133
handles, 133
ITEM.OBJ, 394
linker response, 274, 277
LIST.OBJ, 394
MAIN.LNK, 275
MAP, 275
MTESTS.BAT, 380
NEW.TXT, 466
object-code, 274-275
output, 275
README.TXT, 451, 499-500
SAMPLE.DAT, 477
SIMULATE.EXE, 269, 274
STUFF.DAT, 467
TEST.DAT, 470, 472, 575
TEST.TXT, 453, 575
TESTYN.BAT, 74
text, 452-467
WELCOME.CPP, 1
WELCOME.EXE, 1
WINTOOL.EXE, 336
YESNO.EXE, 73-74
YESNO2.EXE, 74
ZZ.BAT, 274, 276, 336-337, 380
filesize function, 612-613
fillArray function, 170
FILO (first-in last-out), 206
FILTER program, 76-77
listing, 76
filters, 74-80
connecting, 75
findfirst function, 482-483, 487-488,
496, 613-614
findnext function, 482-483, 487-488,
496, 614-615
firstClass constructor, 299
flags, 80
flat arrays, 111
float data type, 13

floating-point constants, 37
floating-point values
formatting instruction, 27
displaying, 26
floor class, 296-304
floor constructor, 298
floor function, 615
FLOOR program, 276
listing, 297-298, 300-304
FLOOR.H header file, 276, 297
listing, 296-297
floorCollection class, 297
flushall function, 615-616
fmod function, 616-617
fn function, 514, 517
FNCOUNT program, 128-130
listing, 128-129, 699
fopen function, 137-138, 455, 460,
467-468, 470, 472, 475-476, 617-618
for loop, 87-90
form feed ('\f') escape code, 34
form function, 24-28, 361, 495, 618-619
FORMAT program, 24-26
listing, 24-25
formatted
input, 28-31
output, 23-27
text files, 456-458
formatting instructions 25-27
forward class, 510, 514
FOURFPS.CPP listing, 714-715
FPMUL.CPP listing, 706
fprintf function, 456, 619
FPTABLE.CPP listing, 704
fputc function, 455-456, 458, 620
fputs function, 455-456, 458, 620-621
FP_OFF function, 189
FP_SEG function, 189
fread function, 468, 472-473, 476-477,
479, 621-622

`free` function, 622-623
`free` operator, 237, 569
FREE program, 480
  listing, 480
`friend` classes, 506-515
friend functions, 506-515, 524
  global, 513-515
  operator<<, 555-556
  operator>>, 557
`friend` key word, 507
FRIEND program, 508-510
  listing, 508-509
FRIENDFN program, 511-512
  listing, 511-512
FRIENDMF program, 513-515
  listing, 513
`fscanf` function, 623-624
`fseek` function, 468, 477-479, 624-625
FSIZE program, 483-484, 486
  listing, 484-486
`ftell` function, 625-626
fully qualified expressions, 98
function library, 127-128, 573-677
  descriptions, 573
  syntax, 573
functions, 2, 124, 127-179, 568-569
  see also function library
  arguments, 30, 134, 152
    default, 161-164, 166
    passed by value, 153-157
  array index, 529
  body, 2
  calling, 129, 171-173, 353-354, 569
  cascading inside functions, 236
  class
    declaration, 258
    member, 259-260, 273
    defining, 259
    encapsulated by, 255
  constructors, 267-269
  declarations, 130, 569

early binding, 354
factorial, 148-153
friend, 511-515
global, 561-562
implementation, 130
impure virtual, 443
inline, 171-173, 261-264, 297-304
keypresses, 366
mathematical, 2
  plotting graph, 227-229
  values, 148-151
name mangling, 516-517
naming, 128
output-formatting, 23
overloaded operators as, 520-522, 531-532
overloading, 515-519
parameters, 2, 129, 134-135
  adding new, 163-164
  by reference, 155-157
  passing, 152-164, 166
pointers
  as arguments, 220-225
  string, 234-236
  to functions, 225-229
prototypes, 129-130, 133-134, 152, 161, 259
pure virtual, 442-443
recursive, 168-171
reference, 415-416
  parameter, 157-160
replacement, 351
sorting, 166
statements performing actions, 130
static member, 355-356, 424
string, 236-242
tasks, 128
top-down programming and, 131-135
values, 129, 147-151
  parameters, 156-160
variables, 138-146

virtual, 347-354
void, 147
writing your own, 128-130
`fwrite` function, 468, 470-471, 476, 479, 626

G

`g` function, 162-163
garbage collector, 205
GAS program, 60-61
    listing, 60-61
`getc` function, 626-627
`getch` function, 366-367, 627-628
`getchar` function, 75-76, 78, 628
`getche` function, 628-629
`getcoords` function, 160
`getcwd` function, 481, 497, 629
`getenv` function, 630
`geterror` function, 372, 375-376
`getfloat` function, 142
`getInfo` function, 416, 420
`getKey` function, 363, 366-368
`getName` function, 319-321
`getRec` function, 478
`gets` function, 137, 630-631
`getSelection` function, 436, 446, 492, 502-503
`getString` function, 402, 408, 489, 492, 494-495
`getTime` function, 269, 327
GETVALS.CPP listing, 699-700
`getValue` function, 344
GETVALUE.BAT listing, 693
`getx` function, 554
`gety` function, 554
`glitch` function, 518
global

arrays, 110
friend functions, 513-515
functions, conflicts, 561-562
pointers, 186
scope, 17
GLOBAL program, 19-20
    listing, 19-20
global variables, 17, 110, 135, 141, 198, 278-279, 281
    data segment, 19
    initializing, 19-20
    modifying, 375
    side effect, 375
    uninitialized, 20
`goto` statements, 93-95
`gotorc` function, 361, 420, 438
GRADE program, 108-110
    listing, 108-109
`grades` array, 109
graphics, bitwise exclusive OR operator, 68
greater than (>) relational operator, 55
greater than or equal (>=) relational operator, 55

H

H file extension, 12, 101
hard drive installation of Zortech compiler, iv
hardware requirements, ii
HEAD.CPP listing, 86-87
HEAD2.CPP listing, 694-695
header files, 11-12, 101, 278-281, 574
    ACTION.H, 256, 266-269, 271-272, 274, 276, 324
    BIOS.H, 120, 122
    BUILDER.H, 329
    BUILDING.H, 276, 324

classes, 274
COMMAND.H, 337, 339, 441-443
COMPDB.H, 99-101, 103, 108, 117, 123
CONIO.H, 366
CTYPE.H, 72, 79
DIR.H, 488-490
DISP.H, 159, 356, 569
DOS.H, 21, 192, 479-480, 482
ELEVATOR.H, 276, 306
ELEVSIM.H, 276, 281, 288, 330
ERROR.H, 337, 372-374, 404
FLOOR.H, 276, 297
ITEM.H, 337, 381-385, 409
KEY.H, 337, 339, 364, 366
LIST.H, 337, 359, 392-394, 408
PERSON.H, 276, 283-285
SAMPLE.H, 473-474, 478
SELECTOR.H, 337, 339, 432-433
STDDEF.H, 35, 185
STDIO.H, 12, 35, 75-76, 133, 137, 185, 454-455, 459
STDLIB.H, 30, 35, 71, 185, 372, 409, 570
STREAM.H, 123
STREAM.HPP, 11, 21, 30, 100, 123, 186, 256, 355, 361, 372, 554-555, 558
STRING.H, 35, 185, 236
STRITEM.H, 337, 401-403, 408-409
TIME.H, 235, 488
WINDOW.H, 337, 339, 355, 409-417
WINTOOL.H, 337, 339, 341-342, 355-356, 358-359
heap, 198
    not enough space left, 203
    reserving space for dynamic variables, 198-200
helpCommand class, 341-363
hex function, 23-24, 163, 361, 631-632
hexadecimal
    converting decimal numbers to, 31
    displaying values in, 23, 26
    standard, %#x formatting instruction, 26
    unornamented, %x formatting
        instruction, 26
    uppercase standard, %#X formatting
        instruction, 26
hideWindow function, 420
horizontal tab ('\t') escape code, 35
HPP file extension, 12, 101

I

I/O streams, 558, 559
identifiers, 9-10
if statements, 21, 57-58, 61, 94, 559-560
    goto statement, 94
if/else statements, 56-59, 77-78, 80-81, 135
#ifdef directives, 266, 374
#ifndef conditional directive, 266
impure virtual functions, 443
INCDEC program, 48-49
    listing, 48
#include directives, 11-12, 339
increment (++) operator, 46-49
indexes of arrays, 105, 107-108, 115
inherited classes, 316-328
    default status, 562-563
initDisplay function, 330
initializing
    arrays, 110-111, 116-117
    class global aspect, 413
    global variables, 19-20
    local variables, 19-20
    member functions, 539-541
    pointers, 182
    static variables, 145
    strings, 116-117
    struct data type, 98
    variables, 14-16

`inline` key word, 171
inline member functions, 171-173, 261-264, 297-304
   -C option, 264
input, 20-31
   formatted, 28-31
Input and Output (I/O) statements, 20
input streams
   errors, 29
   overloading, 556-558
   reading numeric values, 28-29
input values, converting strings to other data types, 29-31
`insertItem` function, 359-360, 394, 396, 408
INSTALL program, i, iii
instances, 343-346
`instruct` function, 455
instructions, 3
`int` constants, 33
`int` data type, 13, 22
`int` values, 36
integers, 24
   displaying, 25-26
   output-formatting functions, 23
`is*****` functions, 632-633
`isspace` function, 79
`item` class, 359, 381-392, 396, 401, 433
   ~ item destructor, 385
ITEM program, 337, 388-392
   listing, 388-391
ITEM.H header file, 337, 381-385, 409
   listing, 381-382
ITEM.OBJ file, 394

J

JUSTIFY program, 23-24
   listing, 23-24

K

`kbhit` function, 326, 368, 633-634
KEY module, 337, 364-370
   defining KEY values, 369
   listing, 365-366
   testing, 369-370
KEY.DOC listing, 369
KEY.H header file, 337, 339, 364, 366
   listing, 365
keyboard
   far pointers, 193, 195-197
   flag byte, 195-196
   handling routines, 339
   stream input, 27-28
keypresses, functions, 366
KEYSTAT program, 193, 195-197
   listing, 193-195
`keyWaiting` function, 368

L

LANGUAGE data type, 42
late binding, 354
LC++ class library, 335-448
   class hierarchies, 380-381
   ERROR module, 371-376
   ITEM.CPP module, 388-389
   KEY module, 364-370
   LIST.CPP module, 397-400
   SELECTOR.CPP module, 436-441
   STRITEM.CPP module, 404-407
   WINDOW.CPP module, 427-431
`ldexp` function, 634
less than (<) relational operator, 54-55
less than or equal (<=) relational operator, 55
library functions, 127-128

default arguments, 163
LIFO (last-in first-out), 206
LIMIT.CPP listing, 691
`Line` class, 351-352, 519
LINENUM program, 77-78
    listing, 77-78
`Link` function, 382-387, 391-392
linkage directive, 466
linker response files, 274, 277
    -c option, 275
    /noi option, 275
`List` class, 359, 392-401, 529, 531-532
    implementing, 397-400
    list head, 396
    root, 396
list heads, 210, 396
LIST program, 337-398
    listing, 398-400
LIST.H header file, 337, 359, 392-394, 408
    listing, 392-393
LIST.OBJ file, 394
`ListFiles` function, 501-502
listings *see* program listings
`ListOneFile` function, 501, 503
lists, 381
    dynamic, 205-206, 209-213
    strings, 407-408
literal constants, 32-37
    char, 33-35
    data types, 33-37
    string, 35-36
    whole number, 36
`LoadAny` function, 294
`LoadIfGoing` function, 290-291
`LoadIfWaiting` function, 289-290
`LoadOne` function, 294
LOCAL program, 139-140
    listing, 139-140
local variables, 17, 19, 138-142, 198
    initializing, 19-20
    pointers as, 186

popping, 19
pushing, 19
sharing memory, 139
stack, 19
uninitialized, 20
`log` function, 635
`log10` function, 635-636
logical operators, 59-62, 178-179
    AND (&&), 59-61
    changing program operation, 61-62
    OR (||), 60
long data type, 13
long double data type, 13
long integers, displaying
    signed, `%Lb` formatting instruction, 26
    unsigned, `%lb` formatting instruction, 26
long values, 36
    loops
    do-forever, 90
    do/while, 91-92
    for, 87-93
    goto, 94
    starting next iteration from top, 92-93
    while, 75-77, 84-88, 91-92, 133, 195
LSTCOUNT.CPP listing, 717-718

M

macros, 37-38
`main` function, 2, 9, 124, 127, 129, 134, 242-244, 256, 260, 262, 352, 354-356, 408, 445, 454, 466, 478, 492, 501, 509-510, 524, 526, 570
MAIN.LNK file, 275
MAINBUG program, 516-517
    listing, 516-517

MAKE program, 276
MAKEDB program, 474-476
    listing, 474-475
MAKETXT program, 453-458
    listing, 453-454
`malloc` function, 214-215, 220, 236, 569, 636
`mammal` class, 318-319, 321, 323
MAP files, 275
mask, 64
mathematical functions, 2
    plotting graph, 227-229
mathematical values returned from functions, 148-151
MAXGRADES constant, 109
MEETING program, 113-115
    listing, 113-114
member data type, 96
member functions, 258-259
    see also functions
    calling other member functions, 391
    initializing, 539-541
    pointers, 389, 563-566
memory
    fragmentation, 204-205
    management
        overloading and, 549-554
        pointers, 198-220
    reserving, 214-220
    values stored, 144
    variables
        defining, 264-265
        sharing local, 139
        storing, 101
MENU program, 84-85
    listing, 84
message passing, 257
MFNPTR program, 564-566
    listing, 564-565
miles, converting to kilometers, 55-56
MILES program, 55-56, 58

listing, 55-56
MINMAX.CPP listing, 689
minus – operator, 520
`mkdir` function, 637
MK_FP macro, 192
MNAV.BAT listing, 497
`modf` function, 637-638
modules
    classes and, 273-276
    compiling with −c option, 274
MREAD program, 499
    listing, 499
MS-DOS (version 2.0 and later) file and directory techniques, 451
`msleep` function, 331, 638
MTDIR program, 490
    listing, 490
MTEST.BAT file, 380
multiple
    dimension arrays, 111-115
    inheritance, 380, 566-567
multiplication (*) operator, 45
multiword identifiers, 10
mutual friend classes, 510
myfnptr function, 225-226, 564

N

name mangling, 466, 516-517
NAV program, 451, 497-499
    listing, 498-499
NAV.LNK listing, 497
near pointers, 190-191
NEARFAR program, 190-191
    listing, 190-191
nested

blocks, variables, 17-18
comments, 7
conditional statements, 560
`struct` data type, 102-103
new line ('\n') escape code, 35
`new` operator, 199-200, 203, 206, 212-213, 549-554, 569
  overloading, 551, 553
NEW.TXT file, 466
`newClass` class, 562-563
newline character (\n), 3-5, 27, 34
NEWOPS program, 535-536
  listing, 535-536
next pointer, 209
`next1` function, 145-146
`next2` function, 145-146
`nextItem` function, 394
nonOOP code mixing with object-oriented programming, 364
`normalVideo` function, 420
NOT (!) relational operators, 62
not equal (!=) relational operator, 55
NOTHING program, 9
  listing, 9
NULL constant, 35-36
NULL pointers, 185-187
null statement, 90, 137
NULL terminator, 116
number bases, 31
numbers
  aligning columns, 23
  commas and punctuation, 36
  factorial, 148
numeric command-line arguments, 247-249
NUMIN program, 28-29
  listing, 29
`numOffspring` function, 319
`numWaiting` function, 293, 300

O

object-code files, 274-275
object-oriented programming (OOP), 132, 254-504
  mixing with nonOOP code, 364
objects, 3, 342
`oct` function, 23-24, 639
octal
  converting decimal numbers to, 31
  displaying values in, 23
ODD.CPP listing, 695
offset address, 189
`one` class, 512
ONEKEY.CPP listing, 712
OOP *see* object-oriented programming
`openCommand` class, 444, 446
`openfile` function, 133-134, 137
`openFiles` function, 148
`openWindow` function, 220
operator member functions, overloading, 524-526
`operator*` function, 521, 528
`operator+` function, 521, 524
`operator-` function, 521, 524, 527
`operator/` function, 521
`operator<<` function, 555-556
`operator=` function, 528, 545-546, 549
  calling from copy constructor, 547-548
`operator>>` function, 557
operators, 45-49
  ->, 196, 202
  adding to or subtracting one from argument, 46-49
  addition (+), 45, 520
  advanced, 54-56
  binary, 520, 526
  bitwise, 62-69
  combined, 70, 110
  decrement —, 46-49
  `delete`, 199-200, 237, 549-550, 554,

569
    division (/), 45
    equal sign (=), 45
    free, 237, 569
    increment (++), 46-49
    logical, 59-62, 178-179
        AND (&&), 59-61
        OR (||), 60
    multiplication (*), 45
    new, 199-200, 203, 206, 212-213,
        549-554, 569
    overloading, 415, 520-529, 534
        tips, 528-529
    precedence, 45-46, 681-682
    relational, 54-56
    scope-resolution, 272
    sizeof, 97, 122-124
    subscript ([]), 529
    subtraction –, 45, 520
    ternary, 520, 559
    unary, 520
operator[] function, 532
OPTIONS program, 246-247
    listing, 245-246
ostream class, 555
output, 20-27
    files, 275
    formatted, 23-27, 456-457
    old-style (C programs), 22-23
    reducing granularity, 471
output streams, 3-5, 21-22
    objects, 3
    output symbol (<<), 3
    overloading, 554-556
output symbol (<<), 3
output-formatting functions, 23
output-stream statements, 3, 21-22
overdrawn class, 519
overlayTest subfunction, 420-421
overload key word, 517-518
overloaded conversion operator, 534
overloaded operator function, 520-522,

531-532
overloading, 164
    array indexing, 529-533
    assignment operator, 536-549
    delete operator, 553
    functions, 515-519
    memory management and, 549-554
    new operator, 551, 553
    operator member functions, 524-526
    operators, 520-529
    streams, 554-558
        input, 556-558
        output, 554-556
    unary operators, 526-529
    user-defined data types, 533-536
OVERNEW program, 551, 553
    listing, 552

P

pal class, 509-510
paragraphs, 189, 460
parameters, 152-160
    functions, 2
    pointer, 221-222
    reference, 221-222
parentheses (), checking for mismatched,
    132-135
parsing, 240
PASS2DOS.CPP listing, 693
pause function, 139
pc pointer variable, 183-184
percent sign (%) as escape character, 25
perform function, 256, 269, 324, 327
performCommand function, 342, 363-364,
    442, 444-447

`performCommands` function, 358-359
`perscollection` class, 282, 284-285, 292-294, 303
`person` class, 282-293
`person` function, 284-285
PERSON program, 276
   listing, 285-293, 295
person constructor, 285-286, 293
PERSON.H header file, 276, 283, 285
   listing, 282-283
   person data fields, 284
`pfptr` data type, 228
`PI` constant, 32
pipes (|), 75
`playCheckers` function, 131
PLOT program, 228-229
   listing, 227-228
`point` class, 555, 557
pointer fields
   copying, 541-543
   preventing copying, 543-544
pointers, 24, 100, 116, 181-249
   addressing array elements directly, 231-232
   arithmetic, 232
   arrays, 106, 117-118, 229-234
   as function arguments, 220-225
   as local variables, 186
   class variables, 342-346
   constants, 569
   data types and, 185
   declaring, 181-182
   dereferencing, 182-185
   derived class, 346, 387
   displaying values and addresses, 188
   far, 190-197
   functions, 225-229
   global, 186
   initializing, 182
   list heads, 210
   member functions, 389, 563-566
   memory management, 198-220

near, 190-191
normalized, 233
NULL, 185-187
parameters, 221-222
root, 210
segment and offset address, 189
sorting text files, 465-467
strings, 236-242
   returned from functions, 234-236
`struct` variables, 195
structures, 201-203
system locations, 191-193
`this`, 549-551
type casts, 187-190
type checking, 185
uninitialized, 186
variables, 182
   addressable, 198
   displaying, 554
   swapping, 222-225
void, 185-190
POINTIN program, 556-558
   listing, 556-557
POINTOUT program, 554-556
   listing, 554-555
POLY.CPP listing, 350-353
polymorphism, 346, 350-364, 492
   virtual functions and, 347-351
`pop` function, 210-212
popping local variables, 19
POPUP program, 219-220
   listing, 216-219
POPUP.H header file, 215-216
`pow` function, 148, 639-640
power, 148
`prevItem` function, 394
`printf` function, 22-23, 27, 195, 640-644
`private:` key word, 258, 562-563
`private:` 384, 412
PRMPT.CPP listing, 690, 691
procedures, 127

program flow statements, 71-95
program listings
ACTION.CPP, 270-271
ACTION.H, 265-266
ALIAS.CPP, 183
ALLRECDB.CPP, 476-477
ALPHABET.CPP, 695-696
ANIMAL.CPP, 317-322
AQUOTE.CPP, 688-689
ARRAY.CPP, 106
ARRAYLST.CPP, 530-531
ARRAYPTR.CPP, 230
ASC.CPP, 174-176
ASCII.CPP, 88-89
ASK.CPP, 686
ATONUMS.CPP, 30
BITDATE.CPP, 697-698
BORDER.CPP, 721-722
BOX.CPP, 158-159
BP.CPP, 135-137
BREAKER.CPP, 91
BUILDING.CPP, 325-328
BUILDING.H, 323-324
BUTTON.CPP, 257-258
BUTTON2.CPP, 262
CBLANKS.CPP, 697
CDIR.CPP, 481
CENTER.CPP, 164-165
CIRCUM.CPP, 690
CMDLINE.CPP, 243
COCO.CPP, 149
COLUMN.CPP, 248
COMMAND.H, 441-442
COMMENT.CPP, 7-8
COMP1.CPP, 99-100
COMP2.CPP, 101-102
COMPDB.H, 99
CONE.CPP, 172-173
CONST.CPP, 39
CONTINUE.CPP, 92-93
CONVERT.CPP, 31
COUNTS.CPP, 689

CR2LF.CPP, 723-724
CRTSTAT.CPP, 192
CUBE.CPP, 700-701
DEFINE.CPP, 38
DIR.CPP, 493-497
DIR.H, 488-489
DOGCAT.CPP, 688
DSTRUCT.CPP, 201-202
DT.CPP, 21
ELEVATOR.CPP, 307-309, 311-315
ELEVATOR.H, 305-306
ELEVSIM.CPP, 329-332
ELEVSIM.H, 279-280
ELEVSIM.LNK, 277
ENCRYPT.CPP, 692
ENUM.CPP, 42
EQUIP.CPP, 120-121
ERROR.CPP, 372-375
ERROR.H, 371
EXAMPLE.CPP, 574
EXTERN1.CPP, 141-142
EXTERN2.CPP, 142
FILTER.CPP, 76
FLOOR.CPP, 297-298, 300-304
FLOOR.H, 296-297
FNCOUNT.CPP, 128-129, 699
FORMAT.CPP, 24-25
FOURFPS.CPP, 714-715
FPMUL.CPP, 706
FPTABLE.CPP, 704
FREE.CPP, 480
FRIEND.CPP, 508-509
FRIENDFN.CPP, 511-512
FRIENDMF.CPP, 513
FSIZE.CPP, 484-486
GAS.CPP, 60-61
GETVALS.CPP, 699-700
GETVALUE.BAT, 693
GLOBAL.CPP, 19-20
GRADE.CPP, 108-109
HEAD.CPP, 86-87
HEAD2.CPP, 694-695

INCDEC.CPP, 48
ITEM.CPP, 388-391
ITEM.H, 381-382
JUSTIFY.CPP, 23-24
KEY.CPP, 365-366
KEY.DOC, 369
KEY.H, 365
KEYSTAT.CPP, 193-195
LIMIT.CPP, 691
LINENUM.CPP, 77-78
LIST.CPP, 398-400
LIST.H, 392-393
LOCAL.CPP, 139-140
LSTCOUNT.CPP, 717-718
MAINBUG.CPP, 516-517
MAKEDB.CPP, 474-475
MAKETXT.CPP, 453-454
MEETING.CPP, 113-114
MENU.CPP, 84
MFNPTR.CPP, 564-565
MILES.CPP, 55-56
MINMAX.CPP, 689
MNAV.BAT, 497
MREAD.BAT, 499
MTDIR.BAT, 490
NAV.CPP, 498-499
NAV.LNK, 497
NEARFAR.CPP, 190-191
NEWOPS.CPP, 535-536
NOTHING.CPP, 9
NUMIN.CPP, 29
ODD.CPP, 695
ONEKEY.CPP, 712
OPTIONS.CPP, 245-246
OVERNEW.CPP, 552
PASS2DOS.CPP, 693
PERSON.CPP, 285-293, 295
PERSON.H, 282-283
PLOT.CPP, 227-228
POINTIN.CPP, 556-557
POINTOUT.CPP, 554-555
POLY.CPP, 350-353

POPUP.CPP, 216-219
POPUP.H, 215-216
PRMPT.CPP, 690-691
PTRARRAY.CPP, 231
PUNCS.CPP, 686
PUTLN.CPP, 719-721
RAIN1.CPP, 687-688
RAIN2.CPP, 688
RDATA.CPP, 471-472
READ.CPP, 501-503
READ.LNK, 500
READDB.CPP, 477-478
READLN.CPP, 461-462
READSTR.CPP, 233-234
READTXT.CPP, 458-459
RECOUNT.CPP, 167
RECT.CPP, 706-707
REDALERT.CPP, 712-713
REF.CPP, 156
REG.CPP, 144
ROW.CPP, 709
SAMPLE.H, 473
SCOPE.CPP, 18
SDIR.CPP, 482
SELECTOR.CPP, 436-441
SELECTOR.H, 432
SIMULATE.CPP, 255-256
SIZEOF.CPP, 123
SMALLWIN.CPP, 710-711
SORTER.CPP, 168-170
SORTTEXT.CPP, 462-465
STACK.CPP, 207-209
STATIC.CPP, 145-146
STRHEAP.CPP, 703
STRITEM.CPP, 404-406
STRITEM.H, 401-402
STROPS.CPP, 522-523
STROPS2.CPP, 525-526
SUBBUG.CPP, 516
SUBDIRS.CPP, 727
SWAP.CPP, 222-224
TAB4.CPP, 724-725

TAND.CPP, 63-64
TAX.CPP, 49-50
TCOMMAND.CPP, 443-447
TCOMP.CPP, 69
TDIR.CPP, 491-492
TDIR.LNK, 490-491
TERROR.CPP, 375-376
TESTYN.BAT, 73
THEDATE.CPP, 235
THISIS.CPP, 550-551
TICKS.CPP, 703
TITEM.CPP, 386
TKEY.CPP, 370
TLIST.CPP, 394-396
TOR.CPP, 64-65
TOUCH.CPP, 487
TOUPPER.CPP, 695
TROUBLE.CPP, 542
TSELECT.CPP, 434-436
TSTRITEM.CPP, 403
TSTRLIST.CPP, 407-408
TWINDOW.CPP, 416-420
TXOR.CPP, 66
UNION.CPP, 104-105
UPFILE.CPP, 722-723
UPPERSTR.CPP, 718-719
VARIABLE.CPP, 15
VOID.CPP, 188
WDATA.CPP, 469
WELCOME.CPP, 2
WINDOW.CPP, 421-431
WINDOW.H, 409-412
WINTOOL.CPP, 354-364
WINTOOL.H, 338-341
WORDS.CPP, 79
WORDS2.CPP, 693-694
YESNO.CPP, 71-72
YESNO2.CPP, 74
ZZ.BAT, 277, 338
programming
    object-oriented, 132
    state machine, 288
    top-down, 131-135
programs
    blocks, 3
    calling functions vs. virtual functions,
        353-354
    case sensitivity, 9-10
    changing variable value, 16
    checking for keypresses, 193, 195-197
    comments, 6-9
    compiling, viii-ix
    continuing at marked location, 93-95
    converting for other compilers, 569-570
    counting from 1 to 20, 167
    data encapsulation, 303
    describing design, 132
    elevator simulation, 276-315, 329-332
    functions, 2
    halting, 61, 71-74
    header files, 11-12
    identifiers, 9
    logical operators changing operation,
        61-62
    organizing, 273-276
    parts of, 1-12
    passing switches to, 245-247
    performing several actions until true,
        85-86
    punctuators, 10
    random-access database, 477-479
    relational expressions changing opera-
        tion, 61-62
    revision history, 8
    selecting one of several actions, 80-85
    separators, 11
    statements, 2
    streams, 3
    strings, 3
    system-independent, 123
    writing first 10 lines of input as standard
        output, 86-87
prompt function, 153-155
prompt1 function, 156-157

`prompt2` function, 156-157
`protected:` key word, 562
`protected:` 382-384, 412
prototype functions, 259
pseudo code, 132
    replacing descriptions with function
        names, 132-133
PTRARRAY program, 231-232
    listing, 231
`public:` key word, 258, 562-563
`public:` 384, 412
PUNC.CPP listing, 686
punctuators, 10
pure virtual function, 351, 442-443
`push` function, 210-212, 259-260, 356
`putc` function, 644
`putchar` function, 75-78, 645
PUTLN.CPP listing, 719-721
`putPixel` function, 563
`puts` function, 361, 420, 438, 645
`putsat` function, 423-424
`putString` function, 402-403, 405-407

Q

`qsort` function, 229, 465-467
question mark
    ('\?') escape code, 35
    (?) wild-card character, 482
questions, answers, 685-730
Quicksort algorithm, 167
`quicksort` function, 170
`quitCommand` class, 446

R

radixes, 31
RAIN1.CPP listing, 687-688
RAIN2.CPP listing, 688
`rand` function, 170, 281, 646
random-access database programs, 477-479
RDATA program, 471-473
    listing, 471-472
READ program, 335, 451, 499-504
    listing, 501-503
READ.EXE file, iii
READ.LNK listing, 500
READDB program, 477-479
    listing, 477-478
READLN program, 460, 462
    listing, 461-462
README.TXT file, iii, 451, 499-500
READSTR.CPP listing, 233-234
`readstring` function, 234
`readText` function, 466
READTXT program, 458-460
    listing, 458-459
`recordtemp` function, 221-222
`recount` function, 167-168
RECOUNT program, 167-168
    listing, 167
RECT.CPP listing, 706-707
recursion, 166-171
    data structures, 210
REDALERT.CPP listing, 712-713
redirection symbols
    < (take input from), 74
    > (send output to), 74
`reduceTime` function, 269, 327
REF program, 156-157
    listing, 156
`reference` class, 562-563
`reference` function, 415-416
reference parameters, 221-222
REG program, 144

listing, 144
`register` key word, 143, 145
register variables, 143-145
relational expressions, changing program
  operation, 61-62
relational operators, 54-56
  equal (==), 55
  greater than (>), 55
  greater than or equal (>=), 55
  less than (<), 54-55
  less than or equal (<=), 55
  NOT (!), 62
  not equal (!=), 55
`remove` function, 646-647
`removeItem` function, 394
`rename` function, 647
replacement functions, 324-328, 351
reserved key words, 679
`resetDirectory` function, 490
`results` function, 256
`return` statement, 147-148
`returnSomething` function, 541
`reverseVideo` function, 362, 420
`rewind` function, 648
`rmdir` function, 648-649
root, 396
  pointers, 210
ROW.CPP listing, 709
`rowasc` function, 177
`runtest` function, 417, 419-420, 435, 446,
  492

S

SAMPLE.DAT file, 477
SAMPLE.H header file, 473-474, 478
  listing, 473

`saveCommands` class, 444, 446
`scale` data type, 42
`scanf` function, 28, 649-652
scientific notation, 37
  %e formatting instruction, 26
  exponents, 37
scope of variables, 17-19
SCOPE program, 18-19
  listing, 18
scope-resolution operator, 272
screens
  centering text, 164-166
  writing text to, 159
`scrollDown` function, 420
`scrollUp` function, 420
SDIR program, 482-483
  listing, 482
segment address, 189
`selector` class, 339, 359, 380, 432-441,
  443, 446, 500, 503-504
SELECTOR program, 337, 436-438
  listing, 436-441
SELECTOR.H header file, 337, 339, 432-433
  listing, 432
selectors, 81-83, 431-441
semicolon (;) as statement terminator, 4-6,
  10
send output to (>) redirection symbol, 74
separators, 11
`setDirection` function, 309, 313
`setDownButton` function, 302
`setFloorNumber` function, 299, 302
`setInfo` function, 362
`setTime` function, 269, 326
`setTitle` function, 420, 497
`setUpButton` function, 302
`setVolume` function, 164
`shape` class, 350-353
shift bits left (<<) operator, 63, 68-69
shift bits right (>>) operator, 63, 68-69
`short` data type, 13
short-circuit expression evaluation, 59

show function, 512, 514
showASCII function, 177
showBird function, 321
showColors function, 361
showElevator function, 309
showElevators function, 314-315
showFileInfo function, 486
showFloor member function, 299-303
showItem function, 438
showList function, 213
showMammal function, 321
showRec function, 477
showResults function, 134, 515, 517
showSample function, 362
showValue function, 507, 536
showValues function, 509
showWindow function, 420
shutDown function, 355-356, 413, 417, 425
signed
    char constants, 33
    int constants, 34
    values, 33-34
        %+d formatting instruction, 26
        displaying integers as, 26
simple class, 539-548
SIMULATE program, 256, 269, 323
    listing, 255-256
SIMULATE.EXE file, 269, 274
sin function, 148, 652-653
single quote ('\'') escape code, 35
sizeof operator, 97, 122-124, 224
SIZEOF program, 122-123
    listing, 123
sleep function, 331, 653
SMALLWIN.CPP listing, 710-711
software requirements, ii
SORTER program, 168, 170-171
    listing, 168-170
sorting function, 166
sortText function, 466
SORTTEXT program, 462, 465-467

    listing, 462-465
sound_beep function, 654
sound_click function, 654-655
sound_tone function, 655
source address, strings, 238-239
sphere class, 353
sprintf function, 655-656
sqrt function, 656
square class, 351-352, 519
srand function, 657
sscanf function, 657-658
STACK program, 206, 209-213
    listing, 207-209
stacks, 19
    custom, 206, 209-213
    popping, 206
    pushing, 206
    storing variables, 139
startup function, 355-356, 413-414, 417, 425
state function, 259-260
state machine, 288
statements, 2, 53-54
    assignment, 16
    break, 81-83, 91-93
    comments in, 6-7
    compound, 57-58
    continue, 92-93
    do/while, 85-87
    exit, 71-74
    goto, 93-95
    if, 57-58, 61, 94, 559-560
    if/else, 56-59, 80-81, 135
    Input and Output (I/O), 20
    input-stream, 27-28
    null, 90, 137
    output-stream, 3
    program flow, 71-95
    repeating while true, 75-77
    switch, 81-85
    terminator (;), 4-6, 10
    while, 74-80

`static` functions, 355-356, 412, 413, 424

`static` key word, 146, 413

`static` member fields, 414, 423

STATIC program, 145-146

    listing, 145-146

static variables, 145-146

    initializing, 145

STDDEF.H header file, 35, 185

STDIO.H header file, 12, 35, 75-76, 133, 137, 185, 454-455, 459

STDLIB.H header file, 30, 35, 71, 185, 372, 409, 570

`str` function, 23-24, 658

`strcat` function, 239, 659

`strchr` function, 241, 501, 659-660

`strcmp` function, 240, 466, 660

`strcmpl` function, 240, 661

`strcpy` function, 234, 237-238, 242, 495, 661-662

`strdup` function, 236, 238-239, 242, 466, 481, 662

STREAM.H header file, 123

STREAM.HPP header file, 11, 21, 30, 100, 123, 186, 256, 355, 361, 372, 554-555, 558

streams, 3-5

    input, 27-28

    objects, 28

    overloading, 554-558

STRHEAP.CPP listing, 703

string constants, 35-36

    NULL constant, 35-36

STRING.H header file, 35, 185, 236

`stringArray` class, 531

strings, 3, 5, 23-24, 95, 115-117, 234, 400-408, 569

    allocating space while copying, 238-239

    assigning address of first character, 116

    case comparison, 240

    comparing, 240

    converting input to other data types, 29-30

    copying, 237-238

    destination address, 238-239

    functions, 236-242

    initializing, 116-117

    inserting, %s formatting instruction, 27

    joining, 239-240

    backslash (\), 5

    length, 238

    lists of, 407-408

    locating, 241

    pointers, 236

        returned from functions, 234-236

    searching, 240-242

    source address, 238-239

`strItem` class, 401-408, 427, 489, 495, 518

    multiple constructors, 402

STRITEM program, 337, 404-407, 518

    listing, 404-406

STRITEM.H header file, 337, 401-403, 408-409

    listing, 401-402

`strlen` function, 234, 236, 238, 663

`strlwr` function, 241-242, 663-664

`strncat` function, 239-240, 664

`strncmp` function, 665

`strncpy` function, 238, 322, 665-666

`strnset` function, 666-667

`strop` class, 523-524, 533-536

STROPS program, 522-524, 526-527, 533

    listing, 522-523

STROPS2 program, 525-526, 528

    listing, 525-526

`strrchr` function, 241, 667

`strset` function, 668

`strstr` function, 241, 668-669

`strtod` function, 669

`strtol` function, 670

`strtoul` function, 670-671

`struct` data type, 96-103, 201-202

    defining and initializing, 98

    nested, 102-103

    storing multiple variables in arrays, 108

    variables, 98, 101

struct key word, 96-103, 119
struct variables, 21
    pointers, 195
structures
    building, 53-54
    control, 71
    pointers, 201-203
    size, 123
strupr function, 671
STUFF.DAT file, 467
SUBBUG program, 516-517
    listing, 516
SUBDIRS.CPP listing, 727
subroutines, 127
subscript ([]) operator, 529
subtraction – operator, 45, 520
SWAP program, 224-225
    listing, 222-224
swapbytes function, 224-225
switch key word, 81
switch statements, 81-85, 440
    cases and selectors, 81-83
    goto statement, 94-95
switches, 245-247
system function, 672
system location pointers, 191-193
system-independent programs, 123

T

TAB4.CPP listing, 724-725
take input from (<) redirection symbol, 74
tan function, 672-673
TAND.CPP listing, 63-64
TAX.CPP listing, 49-50
TCOMMAND program, 443-447

listing, 443-447
TCOMP.CPP listing, 69
TDIR program, 490, 492
    listing, 491-492
TDIR.LNK listing, 490-491
ternary operators, 520, 559
TERROR.CPP listing, 375-376
test function, 376
TEST.DAT file, 470, 472, 575
TEST.TXT file, 453, 575
TESTYN.BAT file, 74
    listing, 73
text
    centering on-screen, 164-166
    displaying inside window, 361
    storing behind windows, 215-220
    writing to screen, 159
text files, 452-467
    closing, 453, 456
    copying, 76
    counting words, characters, and lines,
        78-80
    defining lines, 460
    formatted output, 456-457
    numbering lines, 77-78
    opening, 453, 455
    paragraphs, 460
    reader, 499-504
    reading, 455, 458-462
        one character at a time, 458-460
        one line at a time, 460-462
    sorting, 462-467
    writing, 453, 455
THEDATE program, 235-236
    listing, 235
theFunction function, 563
this key word, 388-391
this pointer, 549-551
THISIS program, 550-551
    listing, 550-551
threesum function, 147

TICKS.CPP listing, 703
time
    converting to ASCII string, 235
    displaying, 21
time function, 235, 673
TIME.H header file, 235, 488
TITEM program, 385-388
    listing, 386
TKEY program, 370
    listing, 370
TLIST program, 394, 396-397
    listing, 394-396
toascii function, 673-674
tolower function, 674
tolower macro, 72
top-down programming, 131-135
    functions and, 131-135
TOR.CPP listing, 64-65
TOUCH program, 487-488
    listing, 487
toupper function, 247, 675
toupper macro, 72
TOUPPER.CPP listing, 695
trigraphs, 34
TROUBLE program, 542-543
    listing, 542
TSELECT program, 433, 435-436
    listing, 434-436
TSHL program, 68
TSHR program, 68
TSTRITEM program, 403
    listing, 403
TSTRLIST program, 407-408
    listing, 407-408
TWINDOW program, 416-421
    listing, 416-420
two class, 512
two-dimensional arrays, 111
TXOR.CPP listing, 66

type mismatch compiler error, 185
type-cast expression, 22, 535-536
type-safe linkage, 516-517

U

unary operator, 520
    overloading, 526-529
#undef control command, 40
underlines and identifiers, 9
ungetc function, 366, 675-676
ungetKey function, 368
uninitialized
    global variables, 20
    local variables, 20
    pointers, 186
union key word, 103-105
UNION program, 104-105
    listing, 104-105
unions, 103-105, 121
unitialized variables, 16
unlink function, 382, 387-388, 390-392
unnamed enumerated data type, 42-43
unsigned
    char constants, 33
    integer passing to DOS, 71, 73
    values, 33-34, 36
UPFILE.CPP listing, 722-723
UPPERSTR.CPP listing, 718-719
upwaiting functions, 288-289, 294
useregister function, 144
usevolatile function, 144
usleep function, 676
utime function, 488, 677

V

values
  assigning
    enumerated elements, 43-45
    same to series of variables, 80
    to array elements, 111
    to variables, 16
  comparing, 54-56
  CPU direct access to program's, 143
  displaying
    arrays, 107
    binary, 26
    hexadecimal, 26
    hexadecimal or octal, 23
  forcing type, 36
  inserting bits, 65
  int, 36
  listing constant in arrays, 111
  long, 36
  masking portion, 64
  returned
    functions, 147-151
    data fields, 260
  short, 36
  signed, 33-34
  sorting in array, 168, 170
  stored in memory, 144
  unsigned, 33-34, 36
VARIABLE program, 15
  listing, 15
variables, 12-20, 23, 569
  assigning
    new roles to, 22
    same value to series, 80
    values to, 16
  changing values in program, 16
  data types, 13-15
  defining, 14, 264-265
  deinitializing, 385

displaying values and addresses, 188
  dynamic, 198, 200-205
  external, 141-142
  functions, 138-146
  global, 17, 110, 135, 141, 198, 278-279, 281
  initializing, 14-16
  levels, 17-19
  local, 19, 138-142, 198
  naming, 12
  nested blocks, 17-18
  number of 8-bit bytes occupied, 122-124
  pointers, 182
    addressable, 198
    swapping, 222-225
  register, 143-145
  scope, 17-19
  static, 145-146
  storing, 101, 105-115, 139
  struct data type, 98, 101
  type casting, 22
  uninitialized, 16
VDE editor, iv, vii
vertical tab ('\v') escape code, 35
virtual base classes, 566-568
virtual functions, 347-351, 353-354
  calling, 353-354
  late binding, 354
  polymorphism and, 347-351
  pure, 351
`virtual` key word, 349, 354
virtual member functions, constructor of `base` class, 405
`void` key word, 134, 186
void pointers, 185-190
  address buffers, 187
  data types, 187-190
VOID program, 188-190
  listing, 188
`volatile` key word, 143-144

W

WDATA program, 468
   listing, 469
`welcome` function, 133-134
WELCOME program, 1
   listing, 2
WELCOME.EXE file, 1
`while` key word, 85
`while` loop, 74-80, 84-88, 133, 195
   interrupting, 91-92
   register variables, 145
white space, 11, 79
whole number constants, 36
wild-card characters
   asterisk (*), 482
   question mark (?), 482
`window` class, 339, 355-357, 362, 409-431,
   501, 518
WINDOW program, 337, 421-427, 518
   listing, 421-427
WINDOW.H header file, 337, 339, 355,
   409-417
   listing, 409-412
windows, 409-431
   attributes, 336-364
   displaying in color, 362
   pop-up, 339
WINTOOL program, 336-364, 435
   compiling, 336
   listing, 354-364
   polymorphism, 354-364
WINTOOL.EXE file, 336
WINTOOL.H header file, 337, 339, 341-342,
   355-356, 358-359
   listing, 338-341
words, combining bytes into, 178
WORDS program, 78-80
   listing, 79
WORDS2.CPP listing, 693-694
`writeText` function, 466-467

X

XOR operator *see* bitwise exclusive OR

Y

YESNO program, 71-73
   listing, 71-72
YESNO.EXE file, 73-74
YESNO2.CPP listing, 74
YESNO2.EXE file, 74

Z

Zortech C++ compiler
   display package, 159-160
   installing, iii
      360k floppy drive system, v-vi
      hard drive system, iv
      large-capacity floopy system, iv-v
      testing installation, vi
register variables, 143
ZZ.BAT file, 274, 276, 336-337, 380
   listing, 277, 338

Sams—Covering The Latest In Computer And Technical Topics!

Audio

Audio Production Techniques for Video $29.95
Audio Systems Design and Installation $59.95
Audio Technology Fundamentals $24.95
Compact Disc Troubleshooting and Repair . . .$24.95
Handbook for Sound Engineers:
  The New Audio Cyclopedia $79.95
Introduction to Professional Recording Techniques $29.95
Modern Recording Techniques, 3rd Ed. $29.95
Principles of Digital Audio, 2nd Ed. $29.95
Sound Recording Handbook $49.95
Sound System Engineering, 2nd Ed. $49.95

Electricity/Electronics

Basic AC Circuits $29.95
Electricity 1, Revised 2nd Ed. $14.95
Electricity 1-7, Revised 2nd Ed. $49.95
Electricity 2, Revised 2nd Ed. $14.95
Electricity 3, Revised 2nd Ed. $14.95
Electricity 4, Revised 2nd Ed. $14.95
Electricity 5, Revised 2nd Ed. $14.95
Electricity 6, Revised 2nd Ed. $14.95
Electricity 7, Revised 2nd Ed. $14.95
Electronics 1-7, Revised 2nd Ed. $49.95

Electronics Technical

Active-Filter Cookbook $19.95
Camcorder Survival Guide . . . .$ 9.95
CMOS Cookbook, 2nd Ed. $24.95
Design of OP-AMP Circuits with Experiments . .$19.95
Design of Phase-Locked Loop Circuits
  with Experiments $19.95
Electrical Test Equipment $19.95
Electrical Wiring $19.95
How to Read Schematics, 4th Ed. $19.95
IC Op-Amp Cookbook, 3rd Ed. $24.95
IC Timer Cookbook, 2nd Ed. $19.95
IC User's Casebook $19.95
Radio Handbook, 23rd Ed. $39.95
Radio Operator's License Q&A Manual, 11th Ed. $24.95
RF Circuit Design $24.95
Transformers and Motors $24.95
TTL Cookbook $19.95
Undergrounding Electric Lines $14.95
Understanding Telephone Electronics, 2nd Ed. . .$19.95
VCR Troubleshooting & Repair Guide $19.95
Video Scrambling & Descrambling
  for Satellite & Cable TV $19.95

Games

Beyond the Nintendo Masters . . . .$ 9.95
Mastering Nintendo Video Games II . . . .$ 9.95
Tricks of the Nintendo Masters . . . .$ 9.95
VideoGames & Computer Entertainment
  Complete Guide to Nintendo Video Games . .$ 9.50
Winner's Guide to Nintendo Game Boy . . . . .$ 9.95
Winner's Guide to Sega Genesis . . . .$ 9.95

Hardware/Technical

Hard Disk Power with the Jamsa Disk Utilities . .$39.95
IBM PC Advanced Troubleshooting & Repair . .$24.95
IBM Personal Computer
  Troubleshooting & Repair $24.95
IBM Personal Computer Upgrade Guide $24.95
Microcomputer Troubleshooting & Repair $24.95
Understanding Communications Systems, 2nd Ed. $19.95
Understanding Data Communications, 2nd Ed. . .$19.95
Understanding FAX and Electronic Mail $19.95
Understanding Fiber Optics $19.95

IBM: Business

Best Book of Microsoft Works for the PC, 2nd Ed. $24.95
Best Book of PFS: First Choice $24.95
Best Book of Professional Write and File $22.95
First Book of Fastback Plus $16.95
First Book of Norton Utilities $16.95
First Book of Personal Computing $16.95
First Book of PROCOMM PLUS $16.95

IBM: Database

Best Book of Paradox 3 . . . .$27.95
dBASE III Plus Programmer's Reference Guide $24.95
dBASE IV Programmer's Reference Guide $24.95
First Book of Paradox 3 . . . .$16.95
Mastering ORACLE
  Featuring ORACLE's SQL Standard $24.95

IBM: Graphics/Desktop Publishing

Best Book of Autodesk Animator $29.95
Best Book of Harvard Graphics $24.95
First Book of DrawPerfect $16.95
First Book of Harvard Graphics $16.95
First Book of PC Paintbrush $16.95
First Book of PFS: First Publisher $16.95

IBM: Spreadsheets/Financial

Best Book of Lotus 1-2-3 Release 3.1 . . . . . .$27.95
Best Book of Lotus 1-2-3, Release 2.2, 3rd Ed. . $26.95
Best Book of Peachtree Complete III $24.95
First Book of Lotus 1-2-3, Release 2.2 . . . . . .$16.95
First Book of Lotus 1-2-3/G $16.95
First Book of Microsoft Excel for the PC $16.95
Lotus 1-2-3: Step-by-Step $24.95

IBM: Word Processing

Best Book of Microsoft Word 5 . . . .$24.95
Best Book of Microsoft Word for Windows . . .$24.95
Best Book of WordPerfect 5.1 . . . .$26.95
Best Book of WordPerfect Version 5.0 . . . . . .$24.95
First Book of PC Write $16.95
First Book of WordPerfect 5.1 . . . .$16.95
WordPerfect 5.1: Step-by-Step $24.95

Macintosh/Apple

Best Book of AppleWorks $24.95
Best Book of MacWrite II $24.95
Best Book of Microsoft Word for the Macintosh $24.95
Macintosh Printer Secrets $34.95
Macintosh Repair & Upgrade Secrets $34.95
Macintosh Revealed, Expanding the Toolbox,
  Vol. 4 . . . .$29.95
Macintosh Revealed, Mastering the Toolbox,
  Vol. 3 . . . .$29.95
Macintosh Revealed, Programming with the Toolbox,
  Vol. 2, 2nd Ed. $29.95
Macintosh Revealed, Unlocking the Toolbox,
  Vol. 1, 2nd Ed. $29.95
Using ORACLE with HyperCard $24.95

Operating Systems/Networking

Best Book of DESQview $24.95
Best Book of DOS $24.95
Best Book of Microsoft Windows 3 . . . .$24.95
Business Guide to Local Area Networks $24.95
Exploring the UNIX System, 2nd Ed. $29.95
First Book of DeskMate $16.95
First Book of Microsoft QuickPascal $16.95
First Book of MS-DOS $16.95
First Book of UNIX $16.95
Interfacing to the IBM Personal Computer,
  2nd Ed. $24.95
Mastering NetWare $29.95
The Waite Group's Discovering MS-DOS $19.95
The Waite Group's Inside XENIX $29.95
The Waite Group's MS-DOS Bible, 3rd Ed. . . .$24.95
The Waite Group's MS-DOS Developer's Guide,
  2nd Ed. $29.95
The Waite Group's Tricks of the MS-DOS Masters,
  2nd Ed. $29.95
The Waite Group's Tricks of the UNIX Masters $29.95
The Waite Group's Understanding MS-DOS,
  2nd Ed. $19.95
The Waite Group's UNIX Primer Plus, 2nd Ed. . $29.95
The Waite Group's UNIX System V Bible $29.95
The Waite Group's UNIX System V Primer,
  Revised Ed. $29.95
Understanding Local Area Networks, 2nd Ed. . .$24.95

Understanding NetWare $24.95
UNIX Applications Programming:
  Mastering the Shell $29.95
UNIX Networking $29.95
UNIX Shell Programming, Revised Ed. $29.95
UNIX System Administration $29.95
UNIX System Security $34.95
UNIX Text Processing $29.95
UNIX: Step-by-Step $29.95

Professional/Reference

Data Communications, Networks, and Systems . .$39.95
Gallium Arsenide Technology, Volume II $69.95
Handbook of Computer-Communications Standards,
  Vol. 1, 2nd Ed. $39.95
Handbook of Computer-Communications Standards,
  Vol. 2, 2nd Ed. $39.95
Handbook of Computer-Communications Standards,
  Vol. 3, 2nd Ed. $39.95
Handbook of Electronics Tables and Formulas,
  6th Ed. $24.95
ISDN, DECnet, and SNA Communications $44.95
Modern Dictionary of Electronics, 6th Ed. $39.95
Programmable Logic Designer's Guide $29.95
Reference Data for Engineers: Radio, Electronics,
  Computer, and Communications, 7th Ed. . . .$99.95
Surface-Mount Technology for PC Board Design $49.95
World Satellite Almanac, 2nd Ed. $39.95

Programming

Advanced C: Tips and Techniques $29.95
C Programmer's Guide to NetBIOS $29.95
C Programmer's Guide to Serial Communications $29.95
Commodore 64 Programmer's Reference Guide .$19.95
DOS Batch File Power $39.95
First Book of GW-BASIC $16.95
How to Write Macintosh Software, 2nd Ed. . . .$29.95
Mastering Turbo Assembler $29.95
Mastering Turbo Debugger $29.95
Mastering Turbo Pascal 5.5, 3rd Ed. $29.95
Microsoft QuickBASIC Programmer's Reference $29.95
Programming in ANSI C $29.95
Programming in C, Revised Ed. $29.95
QuickC Programming $29.95
The Waite Group's BASIC Programming
  Primer, 2nd Ed. $24.95
The Waite Group's C Programming
  Using Turbo C++ $29.95
The Waite Group's C++ Programming $24.95
The Waite Group's C: Step-by-Step $29.95
The Waite Group's GW-BASIC Primer Plus . . .$24.95
The Waite Group's Microsoft C Bible, 2nd Ed. . .$29.95
The Waite Group's Microsoft C Programming
  for the PC, 2nd Ed. $29.95
The Waite Group's Microsoft Macro
  Assembler Bible $29.95
The Waite Group's New C Primer Plus $29.95
The Waite Group's QuickC Bible $29.95
The Waite Group's Turbo Assembler Bible $29.95
The Waite Group's Turbo C Bible $29.95
The Waite Group's Turbo C Programming
  for the PC, Revised Ed. $29.95
The Waite Group's TWG Turbo C++Bible $29.95
X Window System Programming $29.95

For More Information,
Call Toll Free

1-800-257-5755

All prices are subject to change without notice.
Non-U.S. prices may be higher. Printed in the U.S.A.

Programming Is Easy
With Books From The Waite Group!

The Waite Group's C Programming Using Tubo C++
Robert Lafore

This book has been updated for the latest version of Borland's Turbo C Compiler and provides tips, hints, tricks, and strategies to help professional and experienced programmers master Turbo C.

700 pages, 73/8 x 91/4, $29.95 USA
0-672-22737-1

The Waite Group's Turbo C++ Bible
Naba Barkakati

A user-friendly guide to the Turbo C library, this book contains debugged real-world examples for each routine that will suit both novice programmers and software developers.

1,000 pages, 73/8 x 91/4, $29.95 USA
0-672-22742-8

Find The Latest Technology
And Most Up-To-Date Information
In Hayden Books

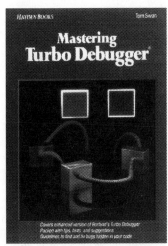
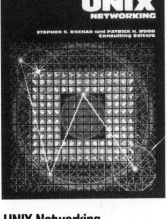

If your computer uses
3 1/2-inch disks . . .

While most personal computers use 5 1/4-inch disks to store information, some newer computers are switching to 3 1/2-inch disks for information storage. If your computer uses 3 1/2-inch disks, you can return this form to SAMS to obtain a 3 1/2-inch disk to use with this book. Simply fill out the remainder of this form, and mail to:

Learning C++
Disk Exchange
SAMS
11711 N. College Ave., Suite 140
Carmel, IN 46032

We will then send you, free of charge, the 3 1/2-inch version of the book software.

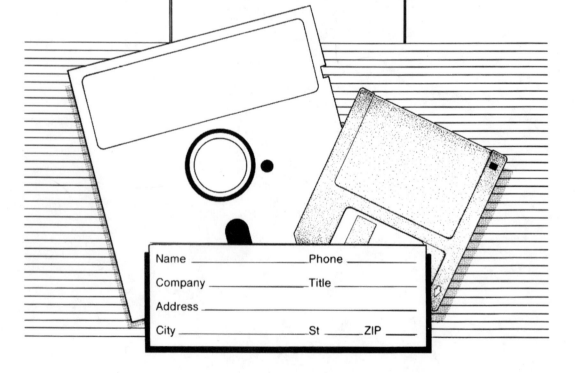

Name _____ Phone _____

Company _____ Title _____

Address _____

City _____ St ____ ZIP ____